This belongs to:

_____

_____

_____

_____

This is the first version of The Zettelkasten Notebook ©.

It's designed to let you record quick notes in context e.g. during a lecture, webinar, meeting, whilst travelling, etc.
Then later, you create a zettel note, which will help to clarify and reinforce your thinking.
After that, when and if it's required, it can be transcribed to your software system of choice (which will help to clarify and reinforce your thinking even further, if you do the transcription yourself).

If you have any requests for different formats, please post a question or comment.

Wishing you great success with your future learning and writing.

uid: parent uid:

ettel:

gs:

efs:

uid: parent uid:

zettel:

tags:

refs:

id: parent uid:

ettel:

gs:

efs:

uid: parent uid:

zettel:

tags:

refs:

uid: parent uid:

ettel:

gs:

efs:

uid: parent uid:

zettel:

tags:

refs:

d: parent uid:

ttel:

gs:

fs:

uid: parent uid:

zettel:

tags:

refs:

id: parent uid:

ettel:

gs:

efs:

uid: parent uid:

zettel:

tags:

refs:

uid: parent uid:

zettel:

tags:

refs:

id: parent uid:

ettel:

gs:

fs:

uid: parent uid:

zettel:

tags:

refs:

uid: parent uid:
ettel:

ags:
efs:

uid: parent uid:

zettel:

tags:

refs:

uid: parent uid:

zettel:

uid: parent uid:

zettel:

tags:

refs:

uid: parent uid:

zettel:

tags:

refs:

uid: parent uid:

zettel:

tags:

refs:

uid:

parent uid:

zettel:

tags:

refs:

uid: parent uid:

zettel:

tags:

refs:

uid: parent uid:

zettel:

tags:

refs:

uid: parent uid:

zettel:

tags:

refs:

uid: parent uid:

zettel:

tags:

refs:

uid: parent uid:

zettel:

tags:

refs:

uid: parent uid:
zettel:

uid: parent uid:

zettel:

tags:

refs:

uid: parent uid:

zettel:

tags:

refs:

uid: parent uid:

zettel:

tags:

refs:

uid: parent uid:

zettel:

tags:

refs:

uid: parent uid:

zettel:

tags:

refs:

uid: parent uid:

zettel:

tags:

refs:

uid: parent uid:

zettel:

tags:

refs:

uid: parent uid:

zettel:

tags:

refs:

uid: parent uid:

zettel:

tags:
refs:

uid: parent uid:

zettel:

tags:

refs:

uid: parent uid:

zettel:

tags:

refs:

uid: parent uid:
zettel:

tags:
refs:

uid: parent uid:

zettel:

tags:

refs:

uid: parent uid:
zettel:

tags:

refs:

uid: parent uid:

zettel:

tags:

refs:

uid: parent uid:
zettel:

tags:
refs:

uid: parent uid:

zettel:

tags:

refs:

uid: parent uid:

zettel:

tags:

refs:

uid: parent uid:

zettel:

tags:

refs:

uid: parent uid:

zettel:

tags:

refs:

uid: parent uid:

zettel:

tags:

refs:

uid: parent uid:
zettel:

tags:
refs:

uid: parent uid:

zettel:

tags:

refs:

uid: parent uid:

zettel:

tags:

refs:

uid: parent uid:

zettel:

tags:

refs:

uid: parent uid:

zettel:

tags:

refs:

uid: parent uid:

zettel:

tags:

refs:

uid: parent uid:

zettel:

tags:

refs:

uid: parent uid:

zettel:

tags:

refs:

uid: parent uid:

zettel:

ags:

efs:

uid: parent uid:

zettel:

tags:

refs:

uid: parent uid:

zettel:

tags:

refs:

uid: parent uid:

zettel:

tags:

refs:

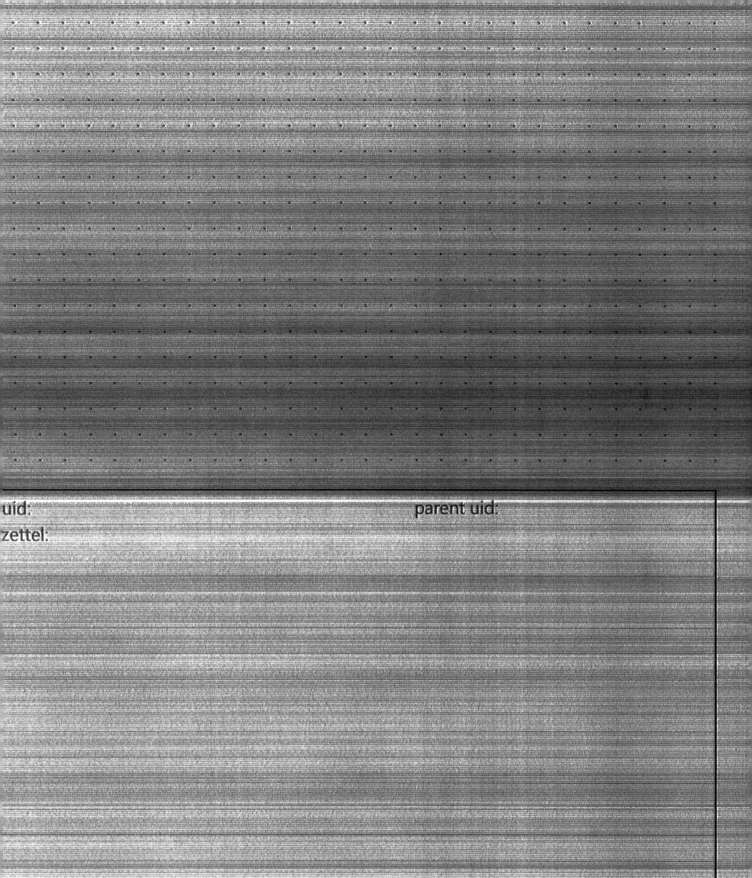

uid: parent uid:

zettel:

tags:

refs:

uid: parent uid:

zettel:

uid: parent uid:
zettel:

tags:

refs:

uid: parent uid:

zettel:

tags:

refs:

uid: parent uid:

zettel:

tags:

refs:

uid: parent uid:

zettel:

tags:

refs:

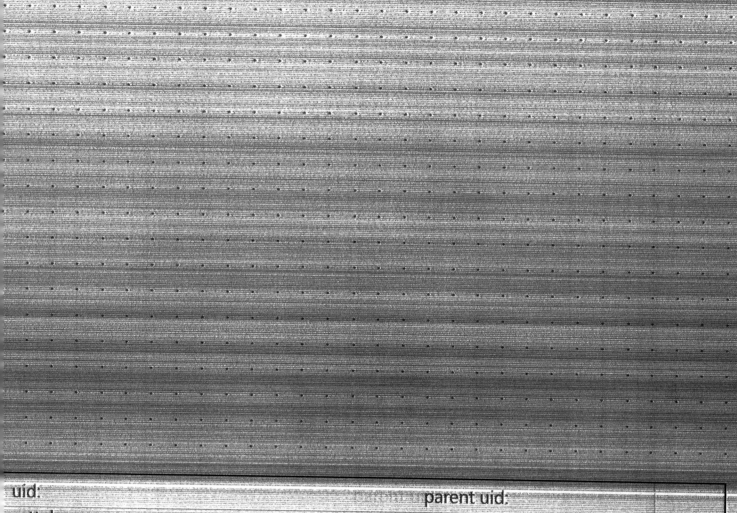

uid: parent uid:

zettel:

tags:

refs:

uid: parent uid:

zettel:

tags:

refs:

uid: parent uid:

zettel:

tags:

refs:

uid: parent uid:

zettel:

tags:

refs:

uid: parent uid:

zettel:

tags:

refs:

uid: parent uid:

zettel:

tags:

refs:

uid: parent uid:

zettel:

tags:

refs:

uid: parent uid:

zettel:

tags:

refs:

uid: parent uid:
zettel:

tags:

refs:

uid: parent uid:

zettel:

tags:

refs:

uid: parent uid:

zettel:

tags:

refs:

uid: parent uid:

zettel:

tags:

refs:

uid: parent uid:

zettel:

tags:

refs:

uid: parent uid:

zettel:

tags:

refs:

uid: parent uid:

zettel:

tags:

refs:

uid: parent uid:

zettel:

tags:

refs:

uid: parent uid:

zettel:

tags:

refs:

uid: parent uid:

zettel:

tags:

refs:

uid: parent uid:

zettel:

tags:

refs:

uid: parent uid:

zettel:

tags:

refs:

uid: parent uid:

zettel:

tags:

refs:

uid: parent uid:

zettel:

tags:

refs:

uid: parent uid:

zettel:

tags:

refs:

uid: parent uid:

zettel:

tags:

refs:

uid: parent uid:

zettel:

tags:

refs:

uid: parent uid:

zettel:

tags:

refs:

uid: parent uid:

zettel:

tags:

refs:

uid: parent uid:

zettel:

tags:

refs:

uid: parent uid:

zettel:

uid: parent uid:

zettel:

tags:

refs:

uid: parent uid:
zettel:

tags:
refs:

uid: parent uid:

zettel:

tags:

refs:

uid: parent uid:

zettel:

tags:

refs:

uid: parent uid:

zettel:

tags:

refs:

uid: parent uid:

zettel:

uid: parent uid:

zettel:

tags:

refs:

uid: parent uid:

zettel:

tags:

refs:

uid: parent uid:

zettel:

tags:

refs:

uid: parent uid:

zettel:

uid: parent uid:

zettel:

tags:

refs:

uid: parent uid:

zettel:

tags:

refs:

uid: parent uid:

zettel:

tags:

refs:

uid: parent uid:

zettel:

tags:

refs:

uid: parent uid:

zettel:

tags:

refs:

uid: parent uid:

zettel:

tags:

refs:

uid: parent uid:

zettel:

tags:

refs:

uid: parent uid:

zettel:

tags:

refs:

uid: parent uid:

zettel:

tags:

refs:

uid: parent uid:

zettel:

tags:

refs:

uid: parent uid:

zettel:

tags:

refs:

uid: parent uid:

zettel:

tags:

refs:

uid: parent uid:

zettel:

tags:

refs:

uid: parent uid:

zettel:

tags:

refs:

uid: parent uid:

zettel:

tags:

refs:

uid: parent uid:

zettel:

tags:

refs:

uid: parent uid:

zettel:

tags:

refs:

uid: parent uid:

zettel:

tags:

refs:

uid: parent uid:

zettel:

tags:

refs:

uid: parent uid:

zettel:

tags:

refs:

uid: parent uid:

zettel:

tags:

refs:

uid: parent uid:

zettel:

tags:

refs:

uid: parent uid:
zettel:

tags:
refs:

uid: parent uid:

zettel:

tags:

refs:

uid: parent uid:
zettel:

tags:
refs:

uid: parent uid:

zettel:

tags:

refs:

uid: parent uid:
zettel:

tags:
refs:

uid: parent uid:

zettel:

tags:

refs:

uid: parent uid:
zettel:

tags:
refs:

uid: parent uid:

zettel:

tags:

refs:

uid: parent uid:

zettel:

tags:

refs:

uid: parent uid:

zettel:

tags:

refs:

uid: parent uid:

zettel:

tags:

refs:

uid: parent uid:

zettel:

tags:

refs:

uid: parent uid:

zettel:

tags:

refs:

uid: parent uid:

zettel:

tags:

refs:

uid: parent uid:

zettel:

tags:

refs:

uid: parent uid:

zettel:

tags:

refs:

uid: parent uid:
zettel:

tags:
refs:

uid: parent uid:

zettel:

tags:

refs:

uid: parent uid:

zettel:

tags:

refs:

uid: parent uid:

zettel:

tags:

refs:

uid: parent uid:

zettel:

tags:

refs:

uid: parent uid:

zettel:

tags:

refs:

uid: parent uid:

zettel:

tags:

refs:

uid: parent uid:

zettel:

tags:

refs:

uid: parent uid:

zettel:

tags:

refs:

uid: parent uid:
zettel:

tags:
refs:

uid: parent uid:

zettel:

tags:

refs:

uid: parent uid:

zettel:

tags:

refs:

uid: parent uid:

zettel:

tags:

refs:

uid: parent uid:

zettel:

tags:

refs:

uid: parent uid:

zettel:

tags:

refs:

uid: parent uid:

zettel:

tags:

refs:

uid: parent uid:

zettel:

tags:

refs:

uid: parent uid:

zettel:

tags:

refs:

uid: parent uid:

zettel:

tags:

refs:

uid: parent uid:

zettel:

tags:

refs:

uid: parent uid:

zettel:

tags:

refs:

uid: parent uid:

zettel:

tags:

refs:

uid: parent uid:

zettel:

tags:

refs:

uid: parent uid:

zettel:

tags:

refs:

uid: parent uid:

zettel:

tags:

refs:

uid: parent uid:

zettel:

tags:

refs:

uid: parent uid:

zettel:

tags:

refs:

uid: parent uid:

zettel:

tags:

refs:

uid: parent uid:

zettel:

tags:

refs:

uid: parent uid:

zettel:

tags:

refs:

uid: parent uid:

zettel:

tags:

refs:

uid: parent uid:

zettel:

uid: parent uid:

zettel:

tags:

refs:

uid: parent uid:

zettel:

tags:

refs:

uid: parent uid:

zettel:

tags:

refs:

uid: parent uid:

zettel:

tags:
refs:

uid: parent uid:

zettel:

tags:

refs:

uid: parent uid:

zettel:

tags:

refs:

uid: parent uid:

zettel:

tags:

refs:

uid: parent uid:

zettel:

tags:

refs:

uid: parent uid:

zettel:

tags:

refs:

uid: parent uid:

zettel:

tags:

refs:

uid: parent uid:

zettel:

tags:

refs:

uid: parent uid:

zettel:

tags:

refs:

uid: parent uid:

zettel:

tags:

refs:

uid: parent uid:

zettel:

tags:

refs:

uid: parent uid:

zettel:

tags:

refs:

uid: parent uid:

zettel:

tags:

refs:

uid: parent uid:

zettel:

tags:

refs:

uid: parent uid:

zettel:

tags:

refs:

uid: parent uid:

zettel:

tags:

refs:

uid:	parent uid:

zettel:

tags:

refs:

uid: parent uid:

zettel:

tags:

refs:

uid: parent uid:

zettel:

tags:

refs:

uid: parent uid:

zettel:

tags:

refs:

uid: parent uid:

zettel:

tags:

refs:

uid: parent uid:

zettel:

tags:

refs:

tag list

tag list

Made in the USA
Middletown, DE
12 August 2024

58974402R00123

GB GRAND BANKS YACH

FLAGSHIP OF THE GREAT PACIFIC NORTHWEST:
THE ALEUTIAN SERIES BY GRAND BANKS YACHTS

ARROWCAT

Giving your story
a new ending

You have put the trip on your calendar. Everyone is counting on a week in the islands.

The day before the trip, you check the weather again to find it's turning for the worse...now what?

You remain confident. You'll go as far as you want.

An Arrowcat is designed to slice through the tallest chop while maintaining cruising speeds in great comfort

making seasickness a thing of the past. You will find more stability and economy than you can imagine.

ArrowCats have been engineered for this type of boating, exactly for our Pacific Northwest's constantly changing environment.

All in a rugged sexy package that says, **You are in control of your trip.** A happy ending at last!

Get an ArrowCat today, and stop letting conditions dictate how much

you can do on the water!

30   32   42

WAGGONER CRUISING GUIDE 2014

Cover photo by Mark Bunzel: We were pleased to find several classic wooden boats in Glenthorne Passage in the Gulf Islands in August 2013.

WAGGONER CRUISING GUIDE eNews

Sign up to receive Waggoner eNews! Receive updates on the most current cruising information in the Pacific Northwest (bi-weekly during the summer and monthly during the winter).

www.WaggonerGuide.com
e-mail: waggtalk@WaggonerGuide.com

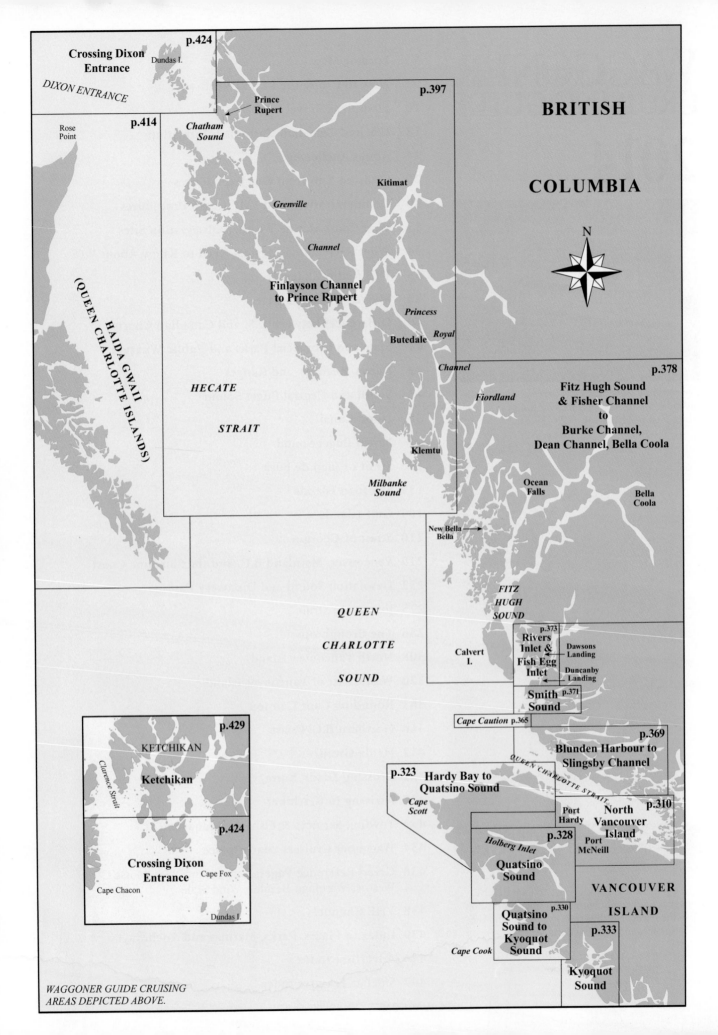

p.424

Crossing Dixon Entrance

Dundas I.

DIXON ENTRANCE

p.397

BRITISH

Prince Rupert

Chatham Sound

Kitimat

COLUMBIA

Grenville

N

Channel

Finlayson Channel to Prince Rupert

Princess

Royal

Butedale

Channel

p.378

p.414

Rose Point

Fiordland

Fitz Hugh Sound & Fisher Channel to Burke Channel, Dean Channel, Bella Coola

HAIDA GWAII (QUEEN CHARLOTTE ISLANDS)

HECATE

STRAIT

Klemtu

Ocean Falls

Bella Coola

Milbanke Sound

New Bella Bella

FITZ HUGH SOUND

QUEEN

CHARLOTTE

Calvert I.

p.373

Rivers Inlet & Fish Egg Inlet

Dawsons Landing

Duncanby Landing

SOUND

Smith Sound **p.371**

Cape Caution p.365

p.369

p.429

KETCHIKAN

Clarence Strait

Ketchikan

Blunden Harbour to Slingsby Channel

QUEEN CHARLOTTE STRAIT

p.323 Hardy Bay to Quatsino Sound

Cape Scott

Port Hardy

North Vancouver Island **p.310**

p.424

Crossing Dixon Entrance

Cape Fox

Port McNeill

p.328

Holberg Inlet

Quatsino Sound

Cape Chacon

Dundas I.

VANCOUVER

ISLAND

Quatsino Sound to Kyoquot Sound **p.330**

Cape Cook

p.333

Kyoquot Sound

WAGGONER GUIDE CRUISING AREAS DEPICTED ABOVE.

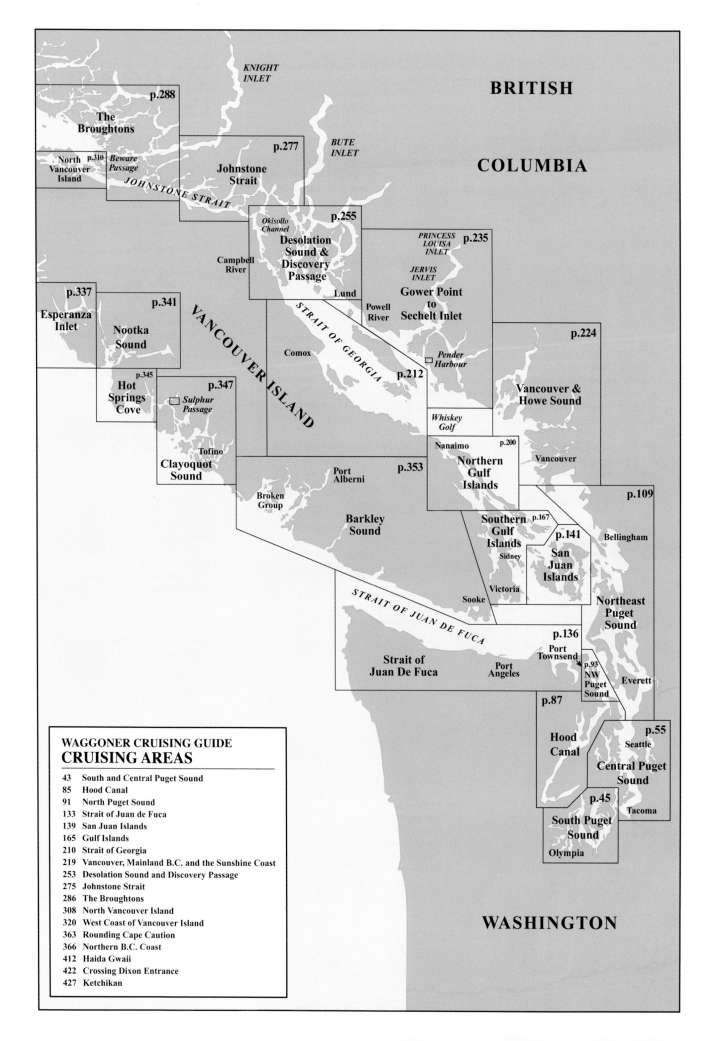

BRITISH

COLUMBIA

KNIGHT INLET

p.288
The Broughtons

North Vancouver Island p.310 *Beware Passage*

JOHNSTONE STRAIT

p.277
Johnstone Strait

BUTE INLET

Okisollo Channel

p.255
Desolation Sound & Discovery Passage

Campbell River

Lund

PRINCESS LOUISA INLET

p.235

JERVIS INLET

Gower Point to Sechelt Inlet

Powell River

p.337
Esperanza Inlet

p.341
Nootka Sound

VANCOUVER ISLAND

STRAIT OF GEORGIA

Comox

Pender Harbour

p.224

Vancouver & Howe Sound

p.212

p.345
Hot Springs Cove

p.347
Sulphur Passage

Tofino

Clayoquot Sound

Port Alberni

Whiskey Golf

Nanaimo

p.200

Northern Gulf Islands

Vancouver

p.353

Broken Group

Barkley Sound

Southern Gulf Islands

p.167

p.141
San Juan Islands

p.109

Bellingham

Sidney

Victoria

Sooke

STRAIT OF JUAN DE FUCA

Strait of Juan De Fuca

Port Angeles

p.136

Port Townsend

Northeast Puget Sound

Everett

p.93
NW Puget Sound

p.87

Hood Canal

p.55
Seattle

Central Puget Sound

Tacoma

p.45
South Puget Sound

Olympia

WASHINGTON

We want to hear from you!

Your comments, suggestions and corrections are invited. We appreciate hearing from anyone who finds errors in this publication.

We are interested in ideas about what you would like in future editions of the Waggoner Cruising Guide. There are a number of members of the Waggoner community who contribute to our website. Our readers are interested in your experiences and tips. We post cruising reports, pictures, video, updates about changes in specified areas, and tips that range from anchoring to restaurants to technical issues.

Contact us through our website www.WaggonerGuide.com, or by telephone, mail, or e-mail at waggtalk@WaggonerGuide.com.

CAUTION

This book was designed to provide experienced skippers with cruising information about the waters covered. While great effort has been taken to make the Waggoner Cruising Guide complete and accurate, it is possible that oversights, differences of interpretation, and factual errors will be found. Thus none of the information contained in the book is warranted to be accurate or appropriate for any specific need. Furthermore, variations in weather and sea conditions, a mariner's skills and experience, and the presence of luck (good or bad) can dictate a mariner's proper course of action.

The Waggoner Cruising Guide should be viewed as a reference only and not a substitute for official government charts, tide and current tables, coast pilots, sailing directions, and local notices to mariners. The Waggoner Cruising Guide assumes the user to be law-abiding and of good will. The suggestions offered are not all-inclusive, but are meant to help avoid unpleasantness or needless delay.

The publisher, editors, and authors assume no liability for errors or omissions, or for any loss or damages incurred from using this publication.

Printed in the United States of America
ISBN-13: 978-0-9882877-2-3

Library of Congress information available upon request.

Published by:
Burrows Bay Associates

| | |

WAGGONER CRUISING GUIDE

Founding Editor
Robert Hale
Editor/Publisher
Mark Bunzel
Managing Editor
Sam Landsman
Art Director & Production
Sheila Powell
Advertising Sales
Lisa Selfridge
Advertising Production
Sara White
Contributing Editor
Tom Kincaid
Contributors
Jim Bathurst, Ted Gage, Chuck Gould, Rich Hazelton, Deane Hislop, David Hoar, Steve & Elsie Hulsizer, John Lund, Lydia McKenzie, Kevin Monahan, Noreen Rudd, Duart Snow, Kay Spence (dec'd.)
Correspondents
Bruce & Margaret Evertz, Gil & Karen Flanagan, Carol-Ann Giroday & Rick LeBlanc, Tom Green, Mike Guns, Jennifer & James Hamilton, David Helland, Linda Lewis & Dave Parker, John & Lorraine Littlewood, John Mifflin, Pat Shera, Al & Becca Szymanski, Fred Triggs, Gary Wyngarden
Proofreading
Lara Dunning, Carrie Engels
Reference Maps
Sue Athmann, Melanie Haage
Photography
Jim Bathurst, Monica Bennett, Sheri Berkman, Mark Bunzel, M.J. Bunzel, Susan Churchhill, John Forde, Stacia A.M. Green, Marilynn Hale, Robert Hale, Dave Helland, Deane Hislop, David Hoar, Sam Landsman, Rick LeBlanc, John Lund, Lydia McKenzie, Don Odegard, Noreen Rudd, Lisa Selfridge, Sandy Swartos, Ivar Weierholt

Direct advertising inquiries to:
Waggoner Cruising Guide
Burrows Bay Associates
14004 Biz Point Lane
Anacortes, WA 98221 USA
Phone (425) 780-5015
Fax (360) 299-0535
Email: waggtalk@WaggonerGuide.com
www.WaggonerGuide.com

Book Sales U.S.
Fine Edge Nautical Publishing
14004 Biz Point Lane
Anacortes, WA 98221 USA
Phone (360) 299-8500
Fax (360) 299-0535
Email: orders@FineEdge.com
www.FineEdge.com

Book Sales Canada
Chyna Sea Ventures, Ltd.
Suite 10, 327 Prideaux St.,
Nanaimo, BC V9R 2N4
Phone: (250) 740-1184
Fax: (250) 740-1185
Toll Free: 866-627-8324
Email: orders@ChynaSea.com
www.ChynaSea.com

Heritage Group Distribution
Suite 8, 19272 - 96th Avenue,
Surrey, BC V4N 4C1
Phone: (604) 881-7067 or (800) 665-3302
Fax: (604) 881-7068 or (800) 566-3336
orders@hgdistribution.com

Like us on Facebook
Waggoner Cruising Guide
WaggonerGuide.com

PUBLISHER'S COLUMN

Last summer was one of the sunniest, fairest weather cruising seasons in memory. The weather, combined with growing confidence in the economy, helped coastal businesses prosper. We noticed more boats, including a few superyachts not previously seen in this area.

At the Waggoner Cruising Guide, we put in a lot of miles. I cruised more than 2,300 nautical miles in my 30' Tollycraft, from Anacortes to Ketchikan and back. Managing Editor Sam Landsman circumnavigated Vancouver Island in his 22' C-Dory, adding 1,250 nautical miles to our tally. (In 2012 he took his C-Dory to Glacier Bay and back). Founding Editor Bob Hale and his wife, Marilynn, cruised to the top of Vancouver Island, visiting old friends and favorite anchorages. Each of us has cruised extensively aboard boats in the 22- to 30-foot range, and we're here to tell you that you don't need a big boat to enjoy cruising in the northwest.

This summer, I spent time in some wonderful places. In Alaska, I recommend Misty Fjords. When southbound from Southeast Alaska, Misty Fjords is a short side trip away. It's a visually stunning exit from Alaska. I discovered there is a lot to do in Prince Rupert. Take the bus to the Northern Pacific Cannery museum, or rent a car and go the Khutzeymateen Sanctuary, also known as the "Valley of the Grizzly." Prince Rupert is a destination, not just a crossroads. Again and again, the many waterfalls along the channels in northern B.C. took my breath away. One Sunday morning, I declared my visit to the "Church of Ursula" a religious experience. The many waterfalls, sheer rock walls, and snowcapped mountains were breathtaking as I cruised down the channel (see page 404). The food choices continue to amaze, with farmers markets, artisan food purveyors, wineries, cideries, and waterfront restaurants. As always, the plentiful prawns, crab, and salmon, direct from Mother Nature, are terrific. If good food is a part of your cruising agenda, the northwest and B.C. have much to offer.

Like other cruisers, we made many new friends last summer. We met them on docks, at potlucks, and at the next table in the pub. Our love of boating unites us all, big boat or small.

Throughout the summer we posted cruise reports and updates to www.WaggonerGuide.com and Waggoner eNews. Many more updates are included in this edition of the Waggoner Cruising Guide.

Last spring we launched Waggoner eNews. If you haven't already signed up, I urge you to (on the right column of our homepage). When we learn of changes on the coast, interesting new products, cruising tips, or restaurants, we share them with our eNews readers. We send eNews out bi-monthly in summer and monthly in winter, and we don't share our email list with anyone.

Enjoy planning your next trip and cruising in 2014. After putting this 21st edition of the Waggoner Cruising Guide together, I am looking forward to getting out on the water soon to explore many places I was not able to visit last season. After reading the Waggoner, you probably will too.

– Mark Bunzel

What's New in the 2014 WAGGONER CRUISING GUIDE

For 21 years, the Waggoner Cruising Guide has been presenting boaters with all that is new and different along the Inside Passage. Our staff is thrilled to work on a publication that has such a sterling reputation after all these years.

When Bob and Marilynn Hale started the Waggoner they had strong feelings about what the cruising boater wanted. Their formula was to provide accurate, concise, and timely information about boating destinations and marinas. When in doubt, Bob asked a simple question: does this change serve the reader?

Bob's *Serve the Reader* mantra lives on. Readers seem to appreciate this, since they purchase about 7,000 Waggoners each year and have dubbed it "the bible" for Northwest cruising. Look into the windows of boats as you walk down the dock and you'll find a Waggoner Cruising Guide aboard almost every boat.

Bob and Marilynn retired three years ago, but they are still cruising and contributing to the Waggoner. Bob helps with editing, and he regularly writes cruising reports for Waggoner eNews and our website. Bob enjoys working the boat show, too.

For this edition, we invited Bob to write an article on the history of the Waggoner, featured on page 36. Longtime readers may enjoy reminiscing with Bob. Newer readers may wonder how the book got started. We are happy to continue the journey Bob started over 20 years ago.

The 2014 Waggoner is our team's third book. This year we worked to make information clearer and easier to understand. Docks in marina diagrams are now labeled so it's easier to find your slip when you're given a slip assignment over the radio. We've added additional overview maps, clarifying areas like Campbell River and Tsehum Harbour. New listings describe places we think you might find interesting, like Weewanie Hot Springs (page 405). We added new sidebars telling stories of the coast, its special characters, and its must-see destinations.

We cruised to Alaska and around Vancouver Island, discovering countless updates along the way, but we didn't ignore areas closer to home. We focused on changes in the San Juan and Gulf Islands. In the 2014 Waggoner, we share new information on shoreside activities, dining, and recreation. New tips for making safe, comfortable passages are included. And, we took thousands of new pictures to capture the visual side of waterways, marinas, and anchorages.

Every word in this book has been reviewed, every listing and chartlet checked. We work hard to make the Waggoner Cruising Guide the most accurate on-the-water resource available.

We're proud of this 21st edition and we look forward to using it in 2014.

COASTAL CRAFT
65' Concord Performance

Performance, luxury and advanced technology are combined to engender an entirely new yacht class.

The 65 Concord designed by Greg Marshall, exemplifies the latest in high performance alloy luxury yachts. Powered by twin Volvo IPS1200s, the Concord offers cruising speeds of 26 knots with a top speed of over 30 knots! Her impressive range is 500 nm at 25 knots and 1000 nm at 10 knots. Four Volvo joystick docking stations provide precise ease of handling - even for a couple.

She also features a spacious, full-height walk in engine room with swim platform and interior entry doors. An impressively spacious full-beam master en suite with granite walls, floors & ceiling and in- floor radiant heat. Call for more details on this amazing high performance luxury yacht.

COASTAL CRAFT

Semi-custom welded aluminum yachts hand built in North America

Phone: 604.886.3004   Website: *www.coastalcraft.com*

Design by Gregory C. Marshall Naval Architect, Ltd.

The Inside Passage is one of the best cruising grounds in the world. From Olympia, Washington to Ketchikan, Alaska is a distance of 600 nautical miles as the crow flies. On a boat, meandering through fjords and between islands, the distance multiplies. Most of these waters are protected, open water passages are relatively short, and anchorages are plentiful.

Wildlife is outstanding. Whales—orcas, humpbacks, grays, and more—are regularly spotted. Bald eagles are *everywhere*. Bears snatch salmon from seaside rivers. Porpoises, seals, sea lions, sea otters, and myriad other life call the Inside Passage home.

Natural beauty overwhelms. The great volcanoes of the Cascade mountains are visible throughout Puget Sound and the San Juan Islands. Sandstone in the Gulf Islands, eroded by wind and water, forms impossible patterns and shapes. Magnificent, glacier-carved fjords run deep into British Columbia's interior. Waterfalls plunge thousands of feet, from snow-covered peaks all the way to waters' edge.

We have world class cities, too. Seattle, Victoria, and Vancouver are easily visited by boat and have every amenity imaginable. Smaller cities like Tacoma, La Conner,

Bell Harbor Marina makes visiting downtown Seattle by boat convenient.

Anacortes, Sidney, Cowichan Bay—even Port McNeill, Port Hardy, Prince Rupert, and Ketchikan farther north— roll out the red carpet for visiting boats. They have restaurants, shops, and museums.

Small resorts and marinas, many family run, dot the coast. Some are as simple as local logs felled, milled, and lashed together to form a dock. Others have spas and high-end

restaurants. Potluck dinners and happy hours are common at these smaller marinas.

You won't go hungry cruising this area. Bigger towns have grocery stores. Many marinas stock the essentials. Farmers markets, local bakers, artisan cheese makers, and craft wineries and breweries operate along the Inside Passage. Seafood, of course, is plentiful. Cruisers catch salmon, halibut,

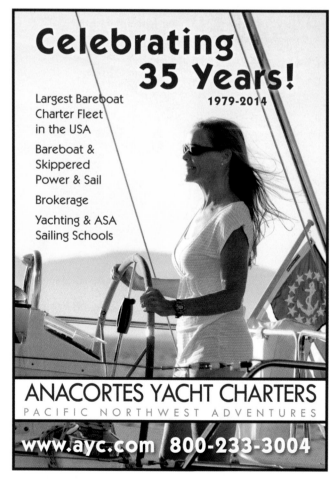

lingcod, prawns, and crab. They pick oysters and harvest sea asparagus.

History is rich along the Inside Passage. Yuculta and Alert Bay have superb museums detailing the history of Native cultures. In Ketchikan, Totem Bight State Park has a remarkable collection of totems. Cruisers can follow in the footsteps of Capt. George Vancouver's 1790s expedition, during which many of the waterways and land masses in this area were named.

The diversity of experiences, the majesty of the vistas, and the splendor of the wildlife keep us cruising.

"Gates" and their effect. The Pacific Northwest is a series of cruising areas separated by "gates"— significant bodies of water that must be crossed. Although gates define our experience and abilities, they also serve as natural stopping points. Some cruisers stay in Puget Sound because the Strait of Juan de Fuca is a gate. Some stay in the Gulf Islands because the Strait of Georgia and Dodd Narrows is a gate. Some go no farther than Desolation Sound because Johnstone Strait and the reversing tidal rapids north of Desolation Sound are gates. And some stay south of Cape Caution because the ocean swells of Queen Charlotte Sound can be looked at as a gate. Gates exist all the way up the coast, all the way to Alaska.

Once beyond a gate and in a given cruising area, the waters are protected. Fortunately, summer weather usually is agreeable. With a study of the tide and current books, a close eye on the winds, and a properly-equipped boat, the gates can be negotiated in safety, and often in comfort. The farther one decides to explore, the more time is needed. For the dedicated summertime Northwest cruiser, time is the principal element limiting cruising choices.

Chartering. The most popular charter boat waters run from the San Juan Islands to Desolation Sound, a distance of approximately 160 miles. These waters include the San Juan Islands, the Canadian Gulf Islands, the cities of Victoria and Vancouver, Howe Sound, Princess Louisa Inlet, and, of course, Desolation Sound. Most charters are for a week or two. It would take years of careful planning and repeat visits for a regular charter cruiser to see all there is to see.

Trailering a Boat. Trailering is faster and more affordable than running a boat on its own bottom, and it avoids difficult passages across open water—the "gates" described earlier. Trailer boats can be towed to all the cruising grounds from Puget Sound to the far end of Vancouver Island. Even the sounds and inlets of the west coast of Vancouver Island can be seen easily and safely. Some people trailer all the way up Vancouver Island, launch

Wildlife is abundant. Bears, whales, seals, sea lions, otters, eagles, and more.

at Port Hardy, and—watching the weather carefully—cruise north past Cape Caution to Rivers Inlet and beyond.

Many boats are trailered from the B.C. Interior to launch at Bella Coola or Prince Rupert. It's a long drive, but the waters they get to are some of the finest in the world. From Prince Rupert, you can cruise north and into Southeast Alaska, which is not accessible by road. Another option is to tow the boat and trailer on the ferry. Although expensive, both the BC Ferries and the Alaska Marine Highway ferries allow trailered boats.

Anchoring vs. marinas. Compared with the waters farther north, Puget Sound has relatively few good anchorages. Most Puget Sound cruising is from marina to marina, or hanging off state park buoys. The San Juan Islands and Canadian Gulf Islands have many marinas and many anchorages. Desolation Sound is mostly anchorages with a few marinas. State and provincial marine parks dot the waterways from Puget Sound to Desolation Sound, many but not all with mooring buoys. The Broughtons have a wide variety of marinas and many, many anchorages. The west coast of Vancouver Island and the waters north of Cape Caution have a few marinas but mostly anchorages.

About the boat. Northwest cruising is coastal cruising in generally protected waters, so bluewater ocean voyaging vessels are not required. But the waters can get rough. Whether power or sail, good Northwest cruising boats are strongly built and seaworthy. Lightweight pontoon boats or open ski boats that are so popular on inland lakes are not well suited to these waters.

The weather can be cool and often wet. Northwest cruising powerboats tend to have large cabins and ample window area. Northwest cruising sailboats tend to have dodgers across the fronts of the cockpits or even full cockpit enclosures. Winds often are light and on the nose—"noserlies"—so sailboats should have good power.

Most Northwest cruising boats are equipped with cabin heat. It could be heat generated while the engine is running, a

diesel heater or diesel furnace, or electric space heaters on the dock's shore power. Heat can add comfort when it is raining, on a cool night, or when cruising in the off-season.

GPS has become so affordable that no Northwest cruising boat should be without a GPS system. A chartplotter, whether a dedicated marine unit or computer software, makes it easy to always know your position.

AIS (Automatic Identification System) is increasingly popular. AIS receivers display vessel name, course, speed, and closest point of approach for nearby boats equipped with an AIS transponder, which broadcasts the vessel's boat information, course, and speed. Large commercial craft, such as ferries, cruise ships, and freighters, all broadcast AIS signals.

Radar has grown better and prices are trending down. Since fog and rainclouds can lower visibility to near-zero any time of the year, cruising boats in the Northwest often end up with radar. Autopilots take the uncertainty out of steering in fog, and make long passages less tiring. They too are quickly added.

Dinghies and tenders and convenient dinghy-launching/recovery systems are important. When anchored or tied to a mooring buoy, the dinghy will be used to travel to shore. Some cruisers use their dinghies extensively for exploring and fishing.

Cruising in the northwest can be wet. A high quality canvas enclosure greatly increases comfort while cruising.

Substantial anchoring systems are important. See page 24 for more information about anchoring.

The minimum size for a cruising boat probably is in the 18- to 20-foot range, and that's pretty minimum. Most mom-and-pop cruising boats fall into the 25- to 50-foot size range, with the majority in the 32- to 50-foot range—large enough to be comfortable, small enough to be handled by two people.

Best months. The prime cruising months begin in April and end by October, with July-August the most popular. Boats are used year-round in Puget Sound. On winter weekends Puget Sound's popular ports are surprisingly busy. Cabin heat is a must in the winter. As mentioned above, cabin heat is almost a must the rest of the year.

North of Puget Sound, pleasure boating is best done between early May and late

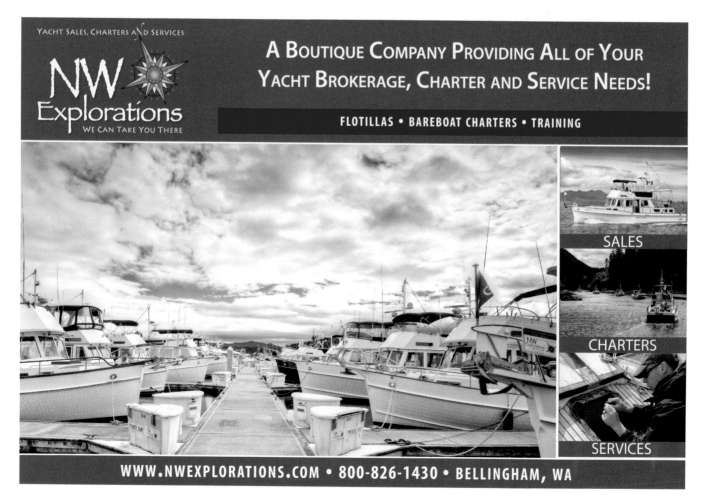

Cruising boats in the northwest tend to prioritize strength and efficiency over speed.

unyielding advocates of chartplotters, charts, and navigation publications. Properly used, charts not only keep a boat out of trouble, they also let it enter places you wouldn't want to try without the chart.

With advancements in electronic charting in recent years, more mariners are asking whether carrying paper charts is still worthwhile. For years, we would not leave the dock without a set of paper charts. Even with computer navigation and a complete selection of electronic charts, it seemed wise to have paper charts as a backup.

But times are changing. Tablets and smartphones, with built-in GPS receiver systems and robust batteries, provide excellent redundancy. Low-cost, highly effective chartplotting software is available for most tablet platforms. Many of these "apps" make updating charts easy. If relying on a tablet or smartphone as a backup, consider carrying an extra battery pack. They're inexpensive and greatly extend battery life.

Whatever form of charts you decide to carry, keep them updated. While rocks haven't changed location, navigation aids do change. Recently, significant buoyage changes were made in Swinomish Channel. New charts reflect the change.

Many cruising guides cover the Inside Passage and each offers a different point of view. We carry as many as we can fit, and keep several open at the helm. The U.S. Coast Pilot

September. Really dependable summer weather (little rain, long days of glorious sunshine) normally doesn't arrive in the Northwest until July. September can be an outstanding cruising month. The crowds are gone, and the weather can be perfect.

Use caution with winter cruising north of Puget Sound. (Be careful in Puget Sound, too.) Storms lash the British Columbia coast. A Northwest boat with a warm and

dry pilothouse is the way to enjoy winter cruising. Some, with flexible schedules, cruise year-round. It takes a good weather eye, and a warm, dry boat.

About GPS chartplotters, charts and other publications. To keep this book informative and up-to-date, we have stuck our nose into many ports, bays, and coves along the coast. In the process we have become

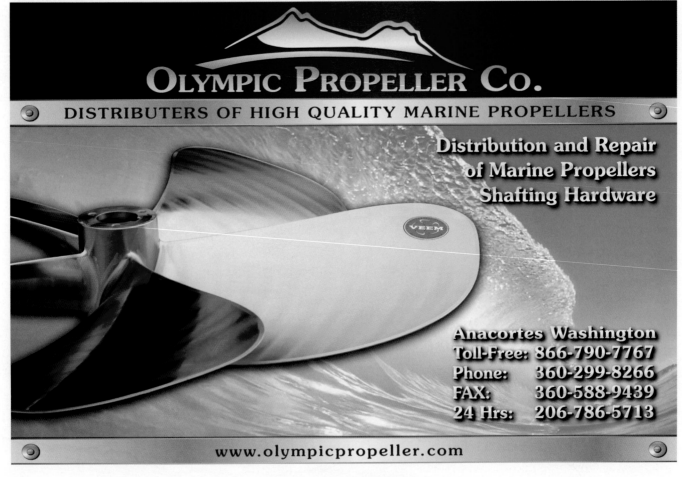

Potlucks, like this one at Kwatsi Bay, are a common social activity at marinas in the northwest.

Humpback whales are often encountered on the West Coast of Vancouver Island and north of Vancouver Island.

and Canadian Sailing Directions are good resources to have aboard, but they are focused on large commercial craft navigation.

Accurate tide and current tables are essential. Most electronic charting packages include tide and current data. However, we've found these are often inaccurate. *Note:* Canadian government tide tables are not corrected for Daylight Saving Time, so you'll have to make the corrections manually. *Capt'n Jacks*, covering Puget Sound, and *Ports and Passes*, covering Olympia to Prince Rupert, are both excellent and inexpensive, and times are corrected for Daylight Saving Time.

U.S. Coast Guard Local Notices to Mariners, Canadian Notices to Shipping, and Canadian Notices to Mariners provide updated information on navaids and regulatory changes. U.S. and Canadian light lists are useful, too. The links to these sites are available in the "cruise planning" section of the Waggoner website.

We do not understand the mentality of the owner that will make a major investment in a boat and fuel, then hold back on charts and other navigation information. At the other extreme is the person who has very little invested, and won't buy navigation information because it costs too much compared to the value of the vessel.

Remember: the rocks, tides and weather are indifferent to how much the boat cost. They treat all boats equally.

Clothing. Except for some areas of Desolation Sound in the summer, most of the waters of the Northwest are cold. Even during warm weather you may welcome a sweatshirt or jacket. Layering clothing works well. Rain gear is essential on sailboats. On an enclosed powerboat, rain gear makes exploring shoreside attractions more pleasant when it is raining. Rubber boots are useful. Shoreside attire can be as nice as you want; most people do fine with comfortable sports clothes.

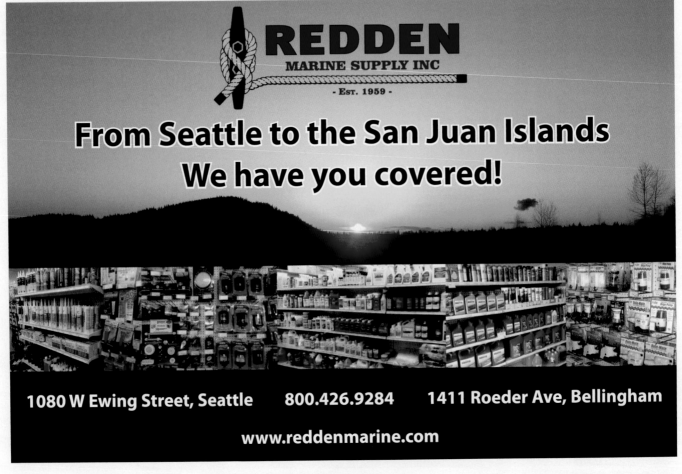

For cruisers who need to travel home during a cruise, need parts shipped to them, or want to have guests join them in remote areas, floatplane travel can be a good option.

Floatplane flying provides a new perspective for boaters. If you can, sit in a window seat, or even the co-pilot seat up front. Take a small map, or this book, and pick out the islands as you fly by. The view is unforgettable—especially on a sunny day, the islands unfold dramatically. Currents are visible. Sometimes whales are spotted, and the pilot may even spend a few moments circling for a better view. On cloudy days you'll fly low—300 to 500 feet above the water.

Be prepared for a flight to have several stops along the route. If transiting from one country to the other, there will be a stop for customs clearance.

Many marinas offer boat watching service, perfect for when owners fly home. Some can even clean, fuel, and provision boats. For time-strapped cruisers, these services can be useful.

Floatplane operators are accommodating. They can deliver parts or crew just about anywhere, even if it's not on a normal route.

The cost to use a floatplane service may initially appear high, but the time savings and convenience are huge. Consider that from Port McNeill you can be in Seattle or Vancouver in about 3 hours.

THE BEAVER

For airplane buffs, a floatplane ride can be particularly thrilling. The venerable de Havilland DHC-2 Beaver is among the most widely used floatplanes in the northwest. De Havilland began producing the Beaver in 1948, and built nearly 1700 of them during a 19-year production run. Although the last Beaver was produced in 1967, operators and enthusiasts alike still appreciate its unparalleled combination of short field performance, durability, and versatility. Kenmore Air, Pacific Coastal, NW Seaplanes, Seair, Inland Air, and Tofino Air all operate Beavers. Pilots rave about flying them.

Equipped with a powerful engine (450hp for piston Beavers) and a large wing optimized for short take off and landing distances, Beavers can reach places other planes can't. They can carry things other planes can't, too.

De Havilland engineers designed the Beaver with doors wide enough to accommodate a 45-gallon drum and the ability to carry 2100 pounds of payload. Piston Beavers cruise at about 100 knots burning about 23 gallons of fuel per hour—enviable economy compared to many powerboats. Some operators have upgraded the original piston power plant to a newer turbine engine, increasing speed, payload capacity, and range.

The Beaver is so popular that well maintained examples have actually appreciated in value. When new, Beavers sold for about $50,000. Today, they can fetch $500,000.

Customs must be cleared whenever the U.S.-Canada border is crossed, in either direction. Generally the process is quick and straightforward, but if the skipper isn't prepared with the proper information it can be time consuming. It is extremely important to follow all the rules and be polite. While customs officers are trained in courtesy and usually are cordial, they have at their disposal regulations that can ruin your day.

You do not clear out of the U.S. or Canada, as other countries often require. You do need to clear Customs when arriving at either the U.S. or Canada from a foreign port.

Important: Customs hours, rules and requirements can and do change with short notice throughout the year. We stay in regular contact with U.S. and Canadian offices, and report changes on the www.WaggonerGuide.com website. We urge readers to check the website for updates.

CANADA BORDER SERVICES AGENCY

All vessels arriving in Canada from a foreign country must clear Border Services

Clearing Canadian Customs is sometimes done by phone, like this one in Victoria.

immediately after the vessel comes to rest. The master, or the master's designated representative, must report to Border Services in person, or by telephone from a Border Services direct land line phone, or by calling (888) 226-7277. No one else may leave the vessel, and no baggage or merchandise may be removed from the vessel.

Passports. If you don't have passports, get

them. Lacking a passport, carry proof of citizenship such as birth certificate, certificate of citizenship or naturalization, and photo ID. Citizens of other countries need passports, and some need visas. Carry birth certificates for all minors aboard—you may be asked for them. If you are bringing a child other than your own into Canada, carry a notarized statement authorizing you to take the child into Canada, and proof that the person signing the statement has custody of the child. The letter should include parents' or guardians' addresses and phone numbers.

You must report at a designated port of entry unless you have Canpass or Nexus. At some locations Border Services officers will be present; at others you will report by telephone. Even if you report by telephone, your boat may be subject to inspection.

To avoid delays, have the following ready when you report:
- Vessel documentation or registration number
- Vessel name and length
- Names, addresses, citizenship, and birth dates of all passengers
- Destination and purpose of trip with length of stay for each passenger
- Estimated return date (U.S. boats)
- Declare all goods being imported, including firearms

Once cleared, either by phone or by an officer, you will be given a clearance number. Post your clearance number in a side window. Log this number, with the date, time, and place of clearance. Vessels are subject to reinspection while in Canadian waters, usually by RCMP officers when their patrol boat reaches a marina. The officers are well trained and polite, but be sure you don't have anything on board you shouldn't have. *Note:* Unlike the U.S., where the U.S. Coast Guard handles inspections and enforcement, in Canada the RCMP and the police in Victoria and Vancouver handle enforcement.

B.C. POINTS OF ENTRY

DESIGNATED B.C. POINTS OF ENTRY FOR PLEASURE CRAFT REPORTING ALL LOCATIONS CONTACT CANADA BORDER SERVICES AGENCY
TOLL-FREE (888) 226-7277
(7 DAYS A WEEK, 24 HOURS A DAY)

Bedwell Harbour:	May 1–Friday before Victoria Day 9:00 a.m. to 5:00 p.m.
	Friday before Victoria Day–Labour Day 8:00 a.m. to 8:00 p.m.
	Labour Day–Sept. 30 9:00 a.m. to 5:00 p.m.
	Oct. 1–Apr. 30 (Canpass/Nexus only)
Cabbage Island:	(Canpass/Nexus only)
Campbell River:	Coast Marina; Discovery Harbour Marina
Galiano Island:	Montague Harbour Marina (Canpass/Nexus only)
Mayne Island:	Horton Bay (Canpass/Nexus only)
	Miners Bay (Canpass/Nexus only)
Nanaimo:	Nanaimo Port Authority Basin–E Dock Summer 8:00 a.m. to 5:00 p.m. Winter 8:00 a.m. to 4:30 p.m.
	Townsite Marina (Canpass/Nexus only)
North Pender Is.:	Port Browning Marina (Canpass/Nexus only)
Prince Rupert:	Lightering Dock
	Prince Rupert–Fairview Govt. Dock
	Prince Rupert Rowing and Yacht Club
	Rushbrooke Government Dock
Saltspring Is.:	Ganges Harbour Seaplane Dock– First floating breakwater (Canpass/Nexus only)
Sidney:	Canoe Cove Marina
	Port Sidney Marina
	Royal Victoria YC Outstation
	Tsehum Marina
	Van Isle Marina
Ucluelet:	52 Steps Dock June 1–Sept 30 only 8:00 a.m. to 10:00 p.m.
	Oct. 1–May 31 (Canpass/Nexus only)
Vancouver:	False Creek Public Dock
	Delta Marina
	Steveston Harbour Authority Dock
	Burrard Inlet/Coal Harbour
	All marinas until further notice
Victoria:	Oak Bay Marina
	Royal Victoria YC (Cadboro Bay)
	Inner Harbour Border Services Dock
White Rock:	White Rock Public Dock
	Crescent Beach Marina

NO DISCHARGE ZONES IN B.C.

Approved holding tanks are required in these areas. Macerator treatment systems, even if approved in the U.S., do not qualify.

"Gray water" is not included in the regulations. It's okay to take a shower and wash dishes.

- Carrington Bay
- Cortes Bay
- Gorge Harbour
- Mansons Landing
- Montague Harbour
- Pilot Bay
- Prideaux Haven
- Roscoe Bay
- Smuggler Cove
- Squirrel Cove
- Victoria Harbour

Nexus vessels may not clear at those stations.

All persons on board must be approved for Canpass or the vessel must clear Border Services in the same way as non-Canpass vessels.

The Canpass application comes with four pages of instructions. Briefly, the program is limited to citizens or permanent residents of Canada or the U.S. with no criminal records and no customs or immigration violations. The approval process takes several weeks. Each person must complete and sign an application. The cost for Canpass is $40 (Cdn.) and is good for five years (no charge for dependents under 18). Visa and Mastercard accepted.

For more information and an application call 604-538-3689 or 1-866-496-3987. Applications can be downloaded from their website at www.cbsa-asfc.gc.ca/prog/canpass/canpassprivateboat-eng.html

Nexus. If you have Nexus, you don't need Canpass. Reporting requirements are the same as Canpass, above. See Nexus instructions in the U.S. Customs section.

Firearms restrictions. You may not bring switchblades, most handguns, automatic weapons, anti-personnel pepper spray or mace into Canada. Under certain circumstances some long guns are allowed. Bear spray, if labeled as such, is permitted if declared. A Non-Resident Firearm Declaration Form is needed to bring firearms into Canada. Call the Canadian Firearms Centre at (800) 731-4000 for a copy of the form, or download one from www.cfc-cafc.gc.ca. The cost is $25 (Cdn.) and it is good for 60 days. All weapons and firearms must be declared to CBSA. See www.WaggonerGuide.com for links for more information and the application form.

Liquor & tobacco restrictions. Not more than 1.14 liters (38.5 oz.) of hard liquor, or 1.5 liters of wine, or a total of 1.14 liters of wine and liquor, or 24 12-ounce bottles of beer or ale per person of legal drinking age (19 years old in B.C.). Not more than 1 carton of cigarettes and 2 cans (200 grams) of tobacco and 50 cigars or cigarillos, and 200 tobacco sticks per person 19 or older without paying duty and taxes on the excess amount.

Food restrictions. Other than restricted foods, you can carry quantities of food appropriate to your stay. However, no apples, no pitted fruit (such as apricots, plums, quince, peaches, nectarines). Cherries are sometimes okay. No potatoes, no fresh corn. Because of possible restrictions don't bring houseplants. If in doubt, call (204) 983-3500 for inspection.

Pets. Owners of dogs and cats must bring a certificate issued by a licensed U.S. or Canadian veterinarian clearly identifying the pet and certifying that it has been vaccinated against rabies during the previous 36 months.

Currency. Not more than $10,000 Cdn. or equivalent in cash or other monetary instruments.

For current rules and regulations check out the Canada Border Services Agency website www.cbsaasfc.gc.ca.

Canpass-Private Boats. With a Canpass permit, a vessel clears Canada Border Services Agency by calling, toll-free, (888) 226-7277 at least 30 minutes and up to 4 hours before departing U.S. waters. If the 888 number is not available, call (250) 363-0222. The vessel still must physically check in at a designated CBSA or Canpass reporting station.

At the time of Canpass call-in, the Border Services officer will ask for the vessel's intended reporting station and the estimated time of arrival. If no officer is present at the reporting station at that time, the vessel may continue on its way without further action. In the accompanying list of designated reporting stations, *note that some are for Canpass/Nexus vessels only* (see below). Non-Canpass/

The Customs dock at Friday Harbor has a phone and video camera for reporting in from the dock area.

U.S. CUSTOMS AND BORDER PROTECTION (CBP)

Effective June 1, 2009 the Western Hemisphere Travel Initiative (WHTI) requires approved identification, such as U.S. or Canadian passport, U.S. Passport card, Trusted Traveler Program cards (Nexus, FAST and Sentri), I-68, State or Provincial issued enhanced driver's license, and others, for entry to the U.S. We recommend that everyone in the crew have a passport.

Duty-free limits. U.S. residents out of the U.S. less than 48 hours can import merchandise up to $200 in value per person without duty. If more than 48 hours the limit is $800 per person. For ease and simplicity, try to restrict what you bring back home to products made or grown in Canada (see below: sometimes even that isn't sufficient). For the latest customs information, go to the U.S. Customs and Border Protection website pages for pleasure boats at www.cbp.gov/xp/cgov/travel/pleasure_boats/.

Clearing by telephone. Boaters with nothing to declare normally can clear U.S.

Customs by telephone, but only if all on board have I-68s or Nexus. Otherwise, the vessel must report at a designated port of entry for physical inspection.

With I-68 or Nexus, after entering U.S. waters you can call the Small Boat Reporting Office at (800) 562-5943 and be cleared. If you call by cell phone while underway, call from an area with good reception. While you report, slow to idle speed to reduce background noise and remain in the good reception area. The Small Boat Reporting Office operates from 8:00 a.m. to 10:00 p.m. from the second week in May through September, and from 8:00 a.m. to 5:00 p.m. the balance of the year. If you enter the U.S. outside these hours you must remain aboard your boat until you can clear.

I-68. The I-68 Permit is valid for 1 year from the date of issue. U.S. citizens, Lawful Permanent Residents, Canadian citizens and Landed Immigrants of Canada who are nationals of Visa Waiver Program countries are eligible to apply. The cost is $16 per person, $32 for families. Apply at CBP offices within the Puget Sound area. Bring proof of citizenship, such as a passport, certified copy of your birth certificate, and photo ID. Vessel

information also helps. Each person applying must appear. Children under 14 can be listed on parents' I-68.

Nexus. With Nexus, each person applies online, then is contacted to set an appointment for interview by both Canadian and U.S. customs agents at the Vancouver, B.C., Blaine, or Seattle CBP offices. The card is good for 5 years, and the cost is $50 U.S. or Cdn. per person (Cdn. funds fee may change due to exchange rates). From start to finish, the entire process takes several months. If you travel by car to Canada, once you have your card you'll have the additional benefit of using the Nexus lanes both ways at the border, which are like an express lane. For general information or to begin the application process, go to www.cbp.gov/xp/cgov/travel/trusted_traveler/. For Canadians, go to www.cbsa-asfc.gc.ca/prog/nexus/menu-eng.html.

Small Vessel Reporting System (SVRS). The Small Vessel Reporting System is a web-based, automated, online reporting program. Once enrolled in the system, an SVRS float plan can be filed online well in advance of a scheduled trip. It is then activated within no more than 24 hours of departure from the U.S., or from Canada. Activation is online only. The program allows for expedited arrival back in the U.S. Upon phoning U.S. Customs, you will be asked a series of questions. Based on your responses, you may be given a clearance number or asked to present your vessel to an agent at a port of entry. You can learn more at https://svrs.cpb.dhs.gov/.

Food restrictions. Food restrictions are subject to change without notice. See our website for changes.

As a general guideline, any food you bring into the U.S. must be made or grown in Canada or the U.S., and labeled as such. Don't bring fresh tropical fruits or vegetables in, even if you bought them in Seattle. Subject to change without notice, use the following list to minimize problems:

No beef, lamb or goat, whether fresh or cooked, canned or frozen, or part of another dish (lamb stew, for example). Regardless of where you bought it, you can't bring it into the U.S. This restriction is due to mad cow disease concerns.

- No pet food made in Canada with lamb or goat in any form. Pet food must be in original package.
- No fresh citrus, regardless of where you bought it.
- No fresh produce (vegetables or fruit) grown outside the U.S. or Canada. Canned fruits and vegetables, however, are unrestricted regardless of origin. Leave labels/stickers on produce.
- No corn on the cob, regardless of origin.
- No cut flowers or potted plants (they are subject to so many restrictions that it's better to leave them in Canada and avoid the hassle).

LARGE SCALE, LARGE DETAIL

*L*arge scale, large detail, that's the easy way to remember the difference between small scale and large scale charts. A small scale chart shows a large part of the earth's surface, but in small detail. Conversely, a large scale chart shows a small part of the earth's surface, but of course in great detail. Yes, it's counter-intuitive and confusing, but that's how it is. In the Northwest, large scale harbor charts typically have scales of 1:6,000, 1:12,000, 1:24,000. Medium scale charts have a scale of 1:40,000. Small scale charts have scales of 1:73,000 or 1:80,000.

At a scale of 1:12,000, 1 inch on the chart equals 12,000 inches (1,000 feet) on the earth. At a scale of 1:80,000, 1 inch on the chart equals 80,000 inches (6,667 feet) on the earth. When you are looking for the rock or picking your way through a narrow channel, the larger the scale of your chart, the easier your task will be.

If the Waggoner Cruising Guide is obsessed with anything, it is with safe navigation and the tools needed to accomplish safe navigation. *Large scale, large detail.* It works.

— Robert Hale

- Swine (pork, ham, bacon, pork sausage) is okay.
- Seafood is okay.
- Dairy products are okay.

Processing fee. Pleasure vessels 30 feet in length or more must pay an annual processing (user) fee of $27.50 to enter or re-enter the United States. This applies to U.S. and non-U.S. vessels alike. Vessels less than 30 feet are not subject to the fee, provided they have nothing to declare. Payment is required at or before the vessel's first arrival each calendar year. If you report by telephone, they charge your credit card. A non-transferable decal will be issued upon payment. Renewal notices for the next year's decal are mailed in the autumn.

Order your sticker before you need to enter the U.S. Even if you have Nexus or I-68 pre-clearance, lack of a current-year sticker may direct you to a designated port of entry for inspection.

User Fee stickers are not sold at CBP offices, but can be ordered online or by phone. The online website address is https://dtops.cbp.dhs.gov. The help desk telephone number is (317) 298-1245, or email decals@dhs.gov. Unfortunately, we found the website too difficult to understand, and called the help desk. Forms were faxed to us. We filled them in and sent them back with a check.

Reporting to U.S. Customs. You must clear CBP at a designated point of entry or, if you are a participant in the I-68 or Nexus program, clearance may be conducted by calling (800) 562-5943. Whether in person or by phone, to avoid delays have the following information available when you report your arrival:

- Name, date of birth and citizenship of all persons on board (including passport numbers)
- Name of the boat and/or BR number, vessel registration or documentation number
- Vessel name, builder and length
- CBP (Customs and Border Protection) user fee decal number (if over 30 feet in length)
- Date vessel entered Canada (U.S. boats)
- Canadian clearance number. Required for U.S. moored boats.
- Estimated date of return. Required for Canadian moored vessels.

Designated U.S. Ports of Entry. Arrivals requiring an in-person report may be made at any of the following ports of entry: Friday Harbor, Roche Harbor, Port Angeles, Point Roberts, Anacortes. Regular hours are 8:00 a.m. to 5:00 p.m. September 26 to May 13; and 8:00 a.m. to 8:00 p.m. May 14 to September 25. Roche Harbor hours 9:00 a.m. to 5:00 p.m. All other ports will require appointments to be made in advance for face-to-face inspections (during regular business hours only). Don't assume that if you call for an appointment you will get one. To save time and aggravation, clear U.S. Customs at one of the five designated ports of entry. If you arrive after a port's normal business hours, call (800) 562-5943 for further instructions.

Local customs office numbers are listed below. I-68s are available at all locations listed.

DESIGNATED PORTS OF ENTRY:
Anacortes (360) 293-2331
Friday Harbor (360) 378-2080
Point Roberts (360) 945-2314
Port Angeles (360) 457-4311
Roche Harbor (360) 378-2080

OTHER CUSTOMS OFFICES
(call ahead for availability and instructions):
Aberdeen (360) 532-2030 or
  (360) 310-0109
Bellingham (360) 734-5463
Blaine (360) 332-6318
Everett (425) 259-0246
Oroville (509) 476-3132
Port Townsend (360) 385-3777
Seattle (Boeing Field) (206) 553-0667
Spokane (509) 353-2833
Tacoma/Olympia (253) 593-6338

Bold indicates designated small boat port of entry, hours shown on this page. Advance appointments required for clearance at all other ports of entry.

AMERICAN TUGS SPOTTERS GUIDE

Now sold factory direct!
Built in La Conner, WA

Made in USA

AMERICAN TUGS AND TRAWLERS
360-466-2961   www.americantugsandtrawlers.com

THE AMERICAN TUG 485

LOA: 49'   LWL: 46'   Beam: 16'
Displacement: 34,000 Lbs   Draft: 4'10"
Diesel: 640 g   Water: 210 g   Waste: 60 g
Cummins QSC-550 or Cummins QSL9-405 your choice.
The latest model from American Tug. Spacious salon and galley. Commanding pilothouse. Two-cabins and two-heads. Expedition and long-term cruise capable.

THE AMERICAN TUG 435

LOA: 43'7"   LWL: 38'6"   Beam: 15'10"
Displacement: 29,200 Lbs   Draft: 4'10"
Diesel: 640 g   Water: 210 g   Waste: 60 g
Cummins QSC-500 or Cummins QSC-550 available
Built since 2004 with over 50 boats delivered. Two-cabins and two-heads. Semi-displacement hull. Ideally suited for comfortable family cruising.

THE AMERICAN TUG 395

LOA: 41'6"   LWL: 37'   Beam: 13'5"
Displacement: 25,000 Lbs   Draft: 3'5"
Diesel: 400 g   Water: 150 g   Waste: 45 g
Cummins QSB-380 electronic fuel injected engine
Introduced in 2010 and considered the best 40-footer! Two-cabins and one-head. Fast semi-displacement performance, economical 8-knot cruise at near 2-gph.

THE AMERICAN TUG 365

LOA: 36'6"   LWL: 32'6"   Beam: 13'3"
Displacement: 18,700 Lbs   Draft: 3'5"
Diesel: 400 g   Water: 150 g   Waste: 45 g
Cummins QSB-330 or Cummins QSB-380 available
Launched the Company! Over 150 boats delivered sinc 2000. Perfect for the couple that wants full-size ameniti and enjoys occasional guests. Master cabin & one-hea

AMERICAN TUGS AND TRAWLERS

Factory Direct sales of new American Tugs — Call for a factory tour, come and see the quality build.

800 South Pearle Jensen Way
La Conner, WA 98257
www.americantugsandtrawlers.com
360-466-2961

Quality Brokerage:
Specializing in Tugs &
trawlers. See us at:
www.trawlerrow.com

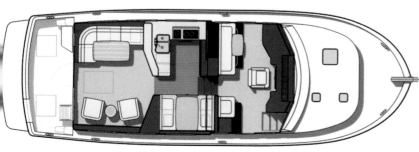

Custom design your salon & galley on the AT-485. Very large upper boat deck allows up to 15-foot dinghy. Fits in a 50-foot slip.

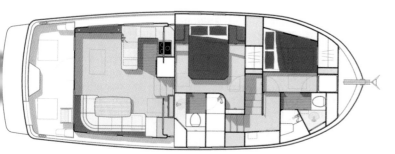

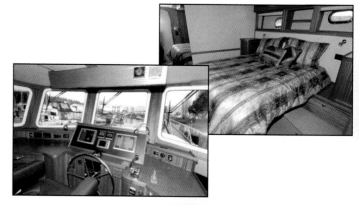

The full width master is below the pilothouse on the 435 & 485. Two staterooms, big pilothouse. Flybridge available on all boats.

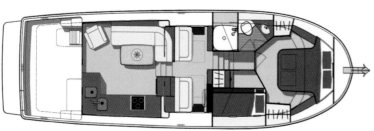

Second stateroom is forward, large salon with room for lounging chair. The pilothouse has great sightlines. Full size shower.

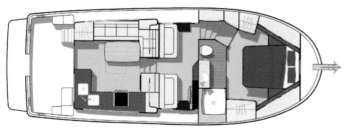

Excellent build quality. Large accommodations with abundant storage. 1600nm range for Inside Passage.

In addition to being the founding editor of the Waggoner, for more than 15 years I was the Pacific Northwest sales representative for Bruce anchors. I have specified anchors, compared anchors, argued anchors, studied anchors, taught anchors, and written about anchors. Most importantly, I have gone out and used anchors. Gathering information for the Waggoner has meant that more time is spent at docks, but given the choice, the little ship *Surprise* prefers to anchor.

Many people do not share this enthusiasm for anchoring. Watching how some of them go about it, their fears are understandable. But there are a few general principles that will help even a novice anchor successfully.

Use good gear. Big, strong anchors work; small, cheap anchors don't. The most experienced cruisers seem to carry the biggest anchors. For obvious reasons I like Bruce anchors. But the other popular designs are good, too. Well-equipped, wide-ranging boats are found carrying all of the common designs: Bruce, CQR (plow), Danforth, Delta, Northhill, Rocna, and Manson Supreme.

Make sure your anchor is made of high-quality steel. If it's wedged in a rock, you don't want it to bend. While Danforth style anchors are easiest to bend, within the limits of their design they can be made strong and expensive, or weak and cheap. There are no strong, cheap Danforth style anchors.

Read the sizing charts carefully, and size your anchor for storm conditions. Some sizing charts are written for 20-knot winds. Others are written for 30 knots. The Bruce chart is written for 42 knots. When the wind comes on to blow *hard* at 3:00 a.m., you don't want a 20-knot anchor out there.

Pick your spot. Unless you're setting out a stern anchor or running a stern-tie ashore, plan on your boat swinging through an entire 360-degree circle. You don't want to bump up against a rock, a dock or another boat. We've seen anchored boats aground at low tide because they didn't allow for drying flats or a sand bar in their swing circle. Other anchored boats will tend to swing as your boat swings, but not always. One night at Jones Island in the San Juans, swirling tidal currents had anchored boats swooping toward one another in a "dance of death."

Carry ample rode. For an anchor to bury and hold properly, you should pay out anchor rode at least five times the water depth. In 20 feet of water you would want 100 feet of rode out. In 60 feet of water you would want 300 feet out. Often, especially in crowded anchorages during high summer season, it will not be possible to anchor on 5:1 scope (five times the depth of the water). That is understood. In fact, the norm for most Northwest anchorages seems to be 3:1. But I've watched people put out 30 feet of rode

Learning good anchoring techniques opens up cruising possibilities.

in 20 feet of water, and wonder why the anchor wouldn't bite. For the deep waters of the Pacific Northwest, carry at least 300 feet of anchor rode, whether all-chain or combination chain and rope. Opinions vary about how much chain a combination rode should include, but no one would criticize you for having about a foot of chain for every foot of boat length.

Rope or chain? For years we used a combination anchor rode—a length of chain backed up with 300 feet of top-quality nylon rope—and we anchored successfully. On the smaller boat with no anchor windlass, a combination rode is the way to go. When we moved to the 37-footer, we found a new religion: all-chain. With all-chain, if we let out 100 feet of chain in 30 feet of water, 70 feet of chain will be lying on the bottom after the anchor is set. At a pound a foot, that's 70 pounds of chain that must be lifted off the bottom before we get to the anchor. During settled conditions we now get by with less scope, and our swinging circle is smaller. In storm conditions, of course, we're back to 5:1, or as close to 5:1 as we can manage.

Read the tide tables. If the overnight low tide isn't very low, a shallow anchorage can be just right. On the other hand, if the moon is either new or full (the two times during the month when the tidal range is the greatest) the shallow anchorage might go dry at low tide. You also want to know the maximum height of the tide during your stay. Set your scope for five times the water depth at high tide, or if you can't get five times, as much as you can get away with.

Set the anchor well. To get the best bury in the bottom, you want the angle between the anchor and the boat to be as flat as possible. After lowering the anchor, back well down before you set the hook. As you set, the rode should seem to stretch almost straight out from the bow. If the rode angles downward very much, you don't have enough scope out. When the anchor is set, you can shorten up to avoid swinging into other boats or onto a sand bar.

You'll know, by the way, when the anchor is set. The anchor rode pulls straight. The boat stops. If you have any doubt as to whether the anchor is set, then it probably isn't. Weed can foul an anchor, especially a Danforth style anchor, and many bottoms have weed. I've heard of anchors grabbing a sunken tire and dragging it across the bottom. Contributing Editor Tom Kincaid recalls an anchor caught in a mess of old electrical wire.

Once the anchor is set, you don't have to pour on all 600 horsepower to prove your point. Anchors gain holding power through pulling and relaxing over time, a process called *soaking*. An anchor put down for lunch might be recovered with little effort. Left overnight it might feel as if it had headed for China.

Look at your chart. For happy anchoring you want a good holding bottom, appropriate depths, and protection. The nautical chart can help with all these needs. If the chart says *Foul*, don't anchor there. If the chart shows submerged pilings at the head of the bay, avoid the head of the bay. If the chart shows 200-foot depths right up to the shoreline, that's a bad spot. If the chart shows the bay open to the full sweep of the prevailing wind and seas, find another bay or you'll be in for a rough night.

I find the easiest anchorages to be in 20 to 50 feet of water, with a decided preference

Being comfortable anchoring makes visiting off the beaten path destinations possible.

for the 20 to 30 foot depths. Approach slowly, take a turn around the entire area to check the depths, and decide where you want the boat to lie after the anchor is set. Then go out to a spot that will give you sufficient scope and lower the anchor. Back way down, set the hook, and shorten up to the desired location.

Carry a stern-tie. In some locations you will set the anchor offshore, back in toward shore to set, and take the dinghy in with a line from a stern cleat to tie around a rock or tree. Boats line Tod Inlet tied this way. In many deep bays it's the only way you can anchor. And sometimes you'll find a little niche that will hold just your boat—if the stern is tied to shore. We carry 600 feet of inexpensive polypropylene rope for stern ties. Often we can pass the line around a tree and bring it back to the boat. When we depart, we can recover the shore tie without leaving the boat. We

use a dead tree if we can. It's better to not scar the bark of a live tree.

Secure the anchor rode to the boat. I talked with a man with a 32-foot boat, a brand-new Bruce anchor, and several hundred feet of expensive chain anchor rode, which he had not made fast to the boat. He laid the anchor down in deep water and backed away. The anchor rode snaked out faster and faster, until to his horror the man saw the chain's end shoot across the foredeck and vanish overboard.

Cruising from dock to dock is fun, and no one can fault the conveniences. But a world of possibilities open to those who have good anchoring gear and know how to use it. These guidelines cover most anchoring situations. Practice in good anchorages, where it's safe. Watch how other boats anchor. The skills are easy to learn. [*Hale*]

STERN-TIES AND HOW TO CARRY THEM

Stern-ties are desirable and often necessary when a boat anchors in the Northwest. In crowded anchorages, stern-ties keep boats from swinging into one another. Often they are essential if a boat is to remain safely at anchor between two rocks, rather than swing onto them. We have seen stern-tie tackle of varying lengths and appropriateness, from sailboat spinnaker sheets tied together, to reels of rope cleverly mounted, ready for use. While rope of any kind will serve in a pinch, we think the best choice is polypropylene. It's strong, it floats, and it's cheap. We also think it's better to have too much line, not too little. A 600-foot reel of ½-inch polypropylene rope will meet almost any need, yet stow nicely on nearly any size boat. With 600 feet available, a stern-tie can be run around a tree and back to the boat. A dead tree is best, to prevent damage to the bark. When it's time to depart the tie can be recovered without rowing ashore. The trick is to mount the reel of rope so it can pay out and be recovered quickly, easily, and without tangling. The pictures here show some alternatives.

A beautiful Pro-Tech Yacht Services reel mounted on rails.

This custom-built stainless steel reel probably cost a fortune, but it fits perfectly and holds a lot of line.

An elegant semi-custom assembly by Clear Marine sends a messenger line with the stern-tie line. Photo courtesy of Clear Marine.

Rough and ready, but this reel on the back of a converted fishing boat is just right.

An off-the-shelf plastic hose reel serves well on the back of a powerboat.

CRUISING TIPS
FROM OUR EXPERIENCES

Every year when we cruise, we think about all the little things that make a difference when we are out on the boat. Some of these points are mentioned elsewhere in the Waggoner, but listing them again does no harm.

Kill the wake. Sailboats don't make much wake, but most powerboats do. Even when a powerboat slows down, its following wake will chase it to the dock. We don't understand why this works, but we've found that if the boat is brought to a full stop and then shifted to reverse for a moment, it seems to kill the following wake.

Slow down when passing, either direction. Shortly after selling the sailboat and going over to the dark side (power), I came to understand what I call the First Rule of

Watch your wake when around other boats.

Powerboating: *Never look back*. Because if we powerboat skippers would look back, we would be appalled at what our wakes do to other boats.

Slow down when being passed, same direction. If a faster boat wants to pass, slow down for a moment and wave it by. If the slow boat is going 6 knots, the faster boat will have to speed up to 8 or 9 knots minimum, which will put out a sizeable wake. Better to idle back, let the big fuel-burner pass at a moderate speed, and then resume cruise speed.

Leave ample room around other boats. The water is not Interstate 5, and boats do not pass without a trace. We're not driving a car, we're pushing water out of the way. When we pass other boats too close we throw them a sizeable wake. It's ridiculous, not to mention dangerous, to have two boats, each weighing 10,000 to 100,000 pounds, anywhere near each other.

Be courteous. The more experienced we become, the more patient and courteous we are with other boat traffic. We think nothing of slowing down or stopping while another boat figures out what it's going to do next. We give kayakers a break by slowing down to reduce our wake. We follow the rules of the road, but we see no need to demand them.

Dinghies make wakes, too. When the bow of an outboard powered dinghy goes up the stern goes down, and digs a hole in the water. Motor slowly around other boats.

Show some side. When two boats approach each other bow-on, both should turn to starboard to avoid collision. A little tweak isn't enough. The change of course should be clear and deliberate. Turn enough to show the oncoming boat some of the side of your boat.

Have flexible expectations. Marina facilities run the range from elegant to, shall we say, rustic. Managements span the same range. A person who expects 5-star facilities and service at every stop will be disappointed. Especially in the remote areas, the docks and other facilities can be rather on the rough side. Service at the Native villages up the coast, for example, is provided on their terms, in their way, and that's different from the city approach most Waggoner readers are accustomed to. When we're out cruising we have found it helpful to relax and take things as they come. We appreciate the places that do things our way, but we get along with the places that don't.

The one area we have less patience with is cleanliness. We think public washrooms, showers and laundry areas should be clean and in good condition, always. If we could have one message for marina operators, it would be, *keep those areas sparkling.*

Be self-reliant. Don't venture out with the idea that if things go wrong, you can always call the Coast Guard. An important part of good seamanship is being able to handle

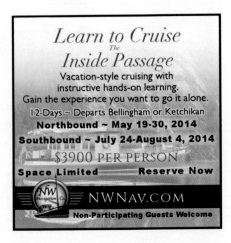

NAVIGATION TIP

Tom and Barbara Wilson, on their boat *Toba*, have a good system to keep them out of trouble. "We agree where we are or we stop the boat until we do," they told us one day. Marilynn Hale and I have followed that practice somewhat over the years, but since meeting the Wilsons we have tried to follow it religiously.

Some years ago the Wilson's system paid off handsomely. At high tide, we were entering Montague Harbour from the northwest. We would leave Wise Island to port and Sphinx Island to starboard. As the chart shows, it's important to favor the Sphinx Island side of the passage, because a reef lies off the south end of Wise Island. A dot islet is on the reef in the middle of the passage.

At high tide I mistook the dot islet for Sphinx Island and prepared to pass between the islet and Wise Island. Marilynn, bless her, was not so sure. She didn't like the look of things and insisted that we confirm our location. Grudgingly, I complied, remembering the Wilson's requirement that they stopped the boat until they agreed where they were.

Careful observation confirmed that Marilynn was correct. Chagrined, I went through the proper passage instead of over the top of the reef. Thank you Tom and Barbara.

– Robert Hale

whatever's thrown at you. Calling the Coast Guard is for true emergencies.

Update credit cards. Before traveling out of the country call your credit card companies to tell them where you will be and the dates of your trip. Otherwise they might (will) refuse a charge, usually at the most awkward moment. Getting it straightened out is exasperating. We speak from experience.

Turn everything off. When you leave the boat or turn in for the night, be sure that appliances, stoves and heaters are turned off.

Take your own paper to public toilets. Especially outhouses at parks and campgrounds.

Keep pets on leash, and clean up after them. Marina owners would prefer that pets didn't exist, but since so many people do cruise with pets the marinas accommodate them. Use the designated pet-walking areas. Don't let the dog lift his leg against the water faucet or power box. Carry plastic bags and clean up if the pet doesn't make it to the potty area.

Help arriving boats land. Even if dinner must be interrupted.

When helping arriving boats, follow the skipper's instructions. When we take a line we hold it loosely, awaiting instructions. Most skippers have a plan that will stop the boat and lay it alongside the dock. A bow line pulled tight at the wrong time can ruin the plan: the bow swings toward the dock and the stern swings away. Obviously, if the landing plan has failed and the boat is being swept off, the dock crew goes into action. Even then it's a good idea to confirm with the skipper rather than acting on one's own.

Pick up mooring buoys from the stern, not the bow. If the bow of the boat is very high off the water it may be impossible to loop a line through a mooring buoy ring. Carry a line aft to a low point of the hull (it may be the swim step), loop it through the ring on the buoy, then carry the line back to the bow. You may want to cleat or tie off one end of the line amidships to keep control of it throughout the process.

Carry and use all appropriate publications. Charts! Tide and current tables. Local cruising guides. Good information adds to the enjoyment of the trip.

Use FRS radios. Inexpensive, handy, no license required. Excellent for replacing shouts or if you get separated at the county fair or at Costco. If cruising with other boats, they keep needless chatter off VHF channels.

Carry tools and spares. Our tool box is in the main cabin, available for immediate access. It seems like we are in that box at least once

a day, usually for something minor, but it has to be fixed. Carry all owner's manuals, extra engine oil, transmission fluid, hydraulic fluid, coolant, and distilled water (for the batteries), spare V-belts, ignition parts, impellers and filters. Carry a spare raw water pump. The list of tools and spares has no end. You can't prepare for everything, but you can prepare for likely problems.

Carry self-amalgamating tape. This is stretchy tape that sticks to itself but not to what it's wrapped around. Usually it is available in black or white. The black is stronger. We have used self-amalgamating tape to repair a leaking high pressure fuel line, and to repair a broken oven door handle. The stuff is magic. We wouldn't cruise without it.

Carry shore power adapters for every electrical combination. If your boat has 30 amp shore power, you will need adapters for 15 amp, 20 amp and 50 amp outlets.

Carry a second shore power cord. It hasn't happened often, but there have been times when the nearest power receptacle was more than 50 feet away. We carry a second 50-foot shore power cord.

Turn off shore power before plugging in or unplugging. Since not all docks have breakers to turn off individual outlets, we turn the boat's 110-volt switch to OFF before we hook up or unplug shore power. If the dock

Many Canadian lightstations are manned. Lightkeepers provide regular weather updates, available on the continuous marine broadcast and online.

power has its own breaker, we turn it to OFF, too. When everything is hooked up, we turn the dock switch to ON, and then the boat switch.

De-squeak fenders with dishwashing soap. Joy, Ivory Liquid, whatever is handy seems to work. Slather it on. One application lasts for hours.

Try smaller paper towels. We began using the ½-sheet paper towels and found the rolls last much longer. It's not so much the money saved as the storage space liberated.

First aid is important. Nobody knows when an accident might occur (that's what makes it an accident). In many areas you will need to be self-reliant. It could be hours or even the next day before medical aid might be available at your location. Carry a comprehensive medical kit and know how to use it. Carry spare medication for many of the common ailments. Call the Coast Guard if you do have a medical emergency. The U.S. Coast Guard has a medical professional on duty somewhere (it might be Kodiak, AK); they can be patched through for medical advice if needed. If you have guests onboard, ask if there are any medical issues or allergies. While your cruising may be recreational boating, the skipper has responsibility for crew and guests.

Use Scoot-gard. This is the bumpy, rubbery material carried on big rolls at the marine store. It keeps things from sliding around. We use it for drawer and shelf liners. The microwave oven and the laptop computer with our charting and navigation program sits on it. Whenever we want something to stay where we put it but don't want to bolt or tie it into place, we use Scoot-gard. It's inexpensive and it works.

Consider making a boat card. One of the joys of cruising is the people you meet along the way. Boat cards are like business cards for your boat, and make it easy to stay in touch with people you meet.

Pack finger food for happy hour gatherings, potlucks, and entertaining on board. Impromptu gatherings are common.

Don't be cheap. It's bad form to use a private marina's facilities and not pay for the privilege. Even if a direct charge is not made, usually something can be purchased. When we overnight at a marina, we pay the moorage, just as our readers do. We're glad the marina is there, and we want it to be there for the future. We are pleased to do our part.

The VHF radio is an important piece of safety equipment, and should be monitored when the boat is underway. While monitoring, you will hear weather and safety warnings, and be aware of much that is happening around you. A boat close by, for example, may be having problems and call for help. By monitoring your radio you can respond.

Station licenses, U.S. Vessels. Until 1996, U.S. pleasure craft were required to have station licenses for their marine VHF radios. In 1996, however, the requirement was dropped for pleasure craft under 20 meters (65 feet), operating inside the U.S. only.

SCOLDING ON THE RADIO

Correspondent Gil Flanagan notes that while some people do stupid and dangerous things such as passing too close at high speed, proper radio protocol does not allow the injured party to start yelling at "the boat that just went by" without identifying itself—especially on high power. If it's necessary to talk to the other boat try to call it by name, then switch the conversation to a working channel.

Most people don't realize they're doing something stupid, so this sounds like a good idea. At least it would get it off channel 16. I recall, however, listening as one angry skipper was told by the U.S. Coast Guard that channel 16 was for calling and distress only. "I'm calling, and you can be darn sure I'm distressed!" came the reply. He'd taken some very deep rolls off a passing boat's wake.

Normally on our boat, we just let things go. But if we get slammed hard by the wake from a boat that passes us as if we were cars on the freeway, I'm going to try Gil Flanagan's advice. I'm going to call the s.o.b.—er, other boat—switch to a working channel, and try to explain what had just happened. I'll try to avoid lecturing or scolding, and see if my reporting of what happened to us has more effect than telling him what I think of him. I think it might work.

— Robert Hale

All U.S. vessels operating in foreign waters, including Canada, still need a U.S. station license. With the 1999 dropping of station licenses in Canada (see below), it was hoped that pleasure craft exempted from station licenses in the U.S. no longer would need a station license to travel in Canadian waters. It now appears that it would require an act of Congress—literally!—to exempt U.S. pleasure craft from needing a station license for Canadian travel, and that's not likely.

As a practical matter, Canadian authorities do not enforce U.S. radio license laws, and U.S. authorities are not going to follow a boat into Canada. In other words, there's no enforcement. We have our station license, however, and would not be without it, enforcement or no enforcement. We recommend that our readers do the same.

Apply for your station license at the same time you register for your Maritime Mobile Service Identity (MMSI) number. You will need this number to use the Digital Selective Calling (DSC) and emergency calling features of newer VHF radios.

You can register online at www.fcc.gov using the Universal Licensing System (ULS). The online process is cumbersome but the processing time is short. The forms are also available from the FCC at (888) 225-5322 (Monday through Friday) if you apply by mail. If you call, choose menu option 2, Licensing. The woman who took our call was well-informed and helpful.

A station license serves the entire vessel, regardless of the number of VHF radios the vessel has. The station license also covers the use of a tender's VHF radio (such as a handheld model) as long as the radio is used in tender service, and as long as it is not used on land. It's all right for two or more radios from the same vessel with the same call sign to talk to each other.

U.S. pleasure craft longer than 20 meters, and all U.S. commercial vessels, are required to have an FCC station licenses.

Station licenses, Canadian Vessels. Beginning in March 1999, station licenses no longer were issued to Canadian vessels so long as 1) the vessel is not operated in the sovereign waters of a country other than Canada or the U.S.; 2) the radio equipment on board the vessel is capable of operating only on frequencies that are allocated for maritime mobile communications or marine radio navigation. Canadian vessels not meeting those two requirements must have station licenses.

Operator's Permit, U.S. The U.S. does not require operator's permits for VHF radio use within the U.S. For foreign travel, however, a Restricted Radio Operator's permit is required. The U.S. individual permit is issued for life, and costs $60. If you are from the U.S. and take a boat to Canada, you will need a Restricted Radio Operator permit. Use Schedule E of FCC Form 605 to apply, and Form 159 to remit payment. If you are applying for both a station license and a Restricted Radio Operator permit you will need a separate Form 159 for each application. The forms can be downloaded from www.fcc.gov, or you can apply electronically on the FCC website.

Operator's Permit, Canada. Canada requires each person operating a VHF radio to have a Restricted Operator's Certificate. For Canadian residents a test must be passed, but the certificate is free and issued for life. Training for the test and the issuing of certificates is handled by the Canadian Power and Sail Squadrons.

How to use the VHF radio. The easiest way to get a general sense of radio use is to monitor VHF 16, the hailing and distress channel; VHF 22A, the U.S. Coast Guard channel; VHF 83A, the Canadian Coast Guard channel, and the working channels. The VTS channels are good, too, because you'll be listening to professional mariners at work. VTS transmissions are brief and often informal, but you'll be listening to experienced people in action. On VHF 16 and the ship-to-ship working channels you'll also hear inexperienced people. The difference will be obvious.

To use the radio, call on the *calling channel*, VHF 16. When communication is established, switch to a *working channel* for your conversation. Except instances of distress, you may not have a conversation on VHF 16. VHF 09 may be used for conversations, but because it is an alternate calling channel in the U.S., the conversations should be brief.

The low power switch. VHF radios can transmit at 25 watts, their highest power rating, or at 1 watt, the low power mode. Handheld VHF radios usually have a maximum power of 5 watts and low power of 1 watt. *Whenever practical, use the low-power mode.* Other vessels a few miles away then can use the same channel without interference from you. The difference between high power and low power affects transmission distance only. Reception ability is unaffected.

Handheld radios should use low power whenever possible. The battery lasts longer.

When not to call on channel 16. Large vessels in the VTS traffic lanes usually do not monitor VHF 16. They monitor the VTS channel for their area. In Puget Sound waters covered by Seattle VTS Traffic, large vessels also must monitor VHF 13, the bridge-to-bridge communications channel. Seattle

You can use your VHF radio to call another ship bridge to bridge or on the local area VTS frequency. Photo courtesy of BoatU.S.

Traffic covers all U.S. waters and the entire Strait of Juan de Fuca, including the Canadian side. If you are disabled in a traffic lane and a large vessel is bearing down on you, call the vessel on the appropriate VTS channel (see VTS channel chart on page 34). If you are still unsure about what to do, call the Coast Guard on VHF 16 and ask them to contact the vessel for you, or to provide you with the correct channel.

Wireless internet. Wi-Fi is just about everywhere now. Even remote marinas in British Columbia that do not have telephone service often have a dish aimed at a satellite, and have Wi-Fi. The problem now is capacity. It's easy to overwhelm a broadband "hotspot." Don't download large files or pictures, or watch movies. No one else will be able to use the system. In a busy marina, evenings can be the worst time, with several boats sending and receiving emails or surfing the web, and service will be slow. We sometimes find it better to write emails in the evening but send them early the next morning. Although Wi-Fi systems allow the use of internet telephone programs (VoIP) such as Skype, these programs use a lot of bandwidth. Use an internet cafe.

Many of the popular ports and marinas in Puget Sound and southern B.C. have Beacon Wi-Fi, formerly Broadband Xpress, or another pay Wi-Fi service. Service plans, ranging from daily to yearly, can be purchased. Marinas with their own wireless equipment sometimes charge for use.

DSC & GMDSS. DSC stands for Digital Selective Calling, and is part of the Global Maritime Distress and Safety System (GMDSS). Basically, if you have a DSC radio and push the covered red button, the radio can send out an automatic digital distress message on VHF 70, with your vessel's MMSI (Maritime Mobile Service Identity) number. This number is then linked to a database which includes your name, vessel information, contacts, and other information. If the vessel's GPS system is wired to your VHF, the radio also transmits your location. For this to work, the vessel must have a MMSI number. BOAT U.S. is authorized to issue MMSI numbers for use within the U.S. For more information see

www.boatus.com.

Important for U.S. vessels traveling to Canada: A BoatU.S. MMSI number will not be recognized outside the U.S. For DSC and GMDSS to work in Canada, U.S. vessels must carry an FCC Ship Station license, described above. The MMSI will be assigned by the FCC, and will work both within the U.S. and internationally. Register for both at the FCC website www.fcc.gov.

Canadian boaters can register by filling out a form accessible through the Transport Canada (www.tc.gc.ca) or Industry Canada (www.ic.gc.ca) websites.

Mayday hoaxes. Each year, hoax Mayday calls cost the U.S. and Canadian Coast Guards millions of dollars ($2 million in Seattle alone) and in some cases put lives at risk. Sometimes the hoax is Junior playing with Grandpa's radio, sometimes it the result of things getting too festive, sometimes the caller has a mental problem. Now that direction-finding equipment can locate the sources of radio calls, arrests can be made and penalties assessed. Radios are not toys, and hoax Mayday calls are not jokes. Large fines and even jail terms are the penalties.

Cellular telephones. Cellular telephone coverage is excellent throughout Puget Sound, much of the San Juan Islands, and the entire Strait of Georgia area. Coverage is spotty from Desolation Sound north. In some places coverage is excellent; in other places it is non-existent. The west coast of Vancouver Island, at least from in Quatsino Sound and from Tofino south, has coverage. Verizon calls go through Telus in Canada and vice versa. AT&T Wireless calls go through the Rogers system but sometimes roam on Telus and other systems. For U.S. residents cruising in B.C., determine if your wireless carrier has a plan for unlimited or reduced rate coverage in Canada. Without the plan, you're apt to be shocked at your cell phone bill for roaming in Canada.

Important: For emergency, distress, and rescue operations, *cellular telephones are not substitutes for VHF radios*. If you have a problem and need help, get on channel 16 and start calling. The Coast Guard and neighboring vessels will hear you. You will be impressed with the Coast Guard's efficiency and professionalism.

RESOURCES FOR CRUISING HAMS

*L*ydia and Patrick McKenzie, longtime northwest cruisers and active ham radio users sent us the following information on using a ham radio while cruising.

Ham radio enthusiasts have some excellent resources available in the Pacific Northwest. Dedicated individuals run morning and evening networks where boaters can check in and stay in touch with each other and learn about what is happening on the coast. Cruisers can report where they are, where they are headed, weather conditions and other information. We have met new friends and learned about everything from interesting new anchorages to up-to-the-minute weather conditions in a particular area.

The *Great Northern Boaters Network* meets each morning with a northern and a southern section. Tune your single sideband radio to frequency 3870 KiloHertz at 7:30 a.m. Pacific Daylight Time to hear the cheerful voice of Darlene (KL0YC) in Dora Bay, AK, greeting the day. From April through early September, she runs the northern half of the network until 8:00 a.m. when Barbara (VE7KLU) in Sidney, B.C. takes over and runs the southern portion of the net. The southern portion of the net runs year-round.

The *West Coast Boaters Network*, run by Bill (VE7WSM) in Tofino, meets each evening from late spring or early summer until the last boater checks in safely in the fall. It covers from San Francisco to northern Alaska. Starting at 6:00 p.m. PDT, tune to frequency 3860 KHz.

The Great Northern and West Coast Networks pass traffic (messages) between them, a great help to boaters who are trying to get in touch with each other or even receive important messages from home. These cruising nets can be both fun and helpful to cruisers.

Text, or SMS messages, are an efficient means of communicating. Messages will squeak through in areas of limited or spotty reception.

Smartphones. Most smartphones have a data roaming function that can be turned off or on. Data roaming charges are often applied once you cross the border and can easily accumulate to hundreds of dollars or more. This is not just for your data when checking information on the web, but also for sending and receiving email and updating apps. A day's worth of email, with pictures and spam mail, can add to the data roaming charges. Check your data roaming plan to understand coverage and charges. Many cruisers turn data roaming off when over or near the border and use only the Wi-Fi capabilities of their smartphone for email, or looking up information on the internet. Wi-Fi service is available in many marinas.

Satellite telephones. Satellite telephones are now a practical reality for many cruising boats. While providers have come and gone, the costs for equipment and airtime are dropping. Sat phones provide complete telephone and data service without concern about coverage area. Boats cruising Puget Sound and the Strait of Georgia up to Desolation Sound can use cellular telephones quite reliably. But from Desolation Sound north, cellular service is spotty. For special situations or short terms, sat phone rental programs are available.

Satellite messengers. Satellite messengers like those from SPOT and DeLorme offer an inexpensive way for cruisers to check in. Depending on the device and service plan selected, satellite messengers can send automated position reports, link to smartphones to send and receive text messages via satellite, or send a distress signal.

Satellite messengers rely on private satellite constellations, not the internationally organized Cospas-Sarsat network that EPIRBs and PLBs use. Satellite messengers are not EPIRBs and should not take the place of an EPIRB.

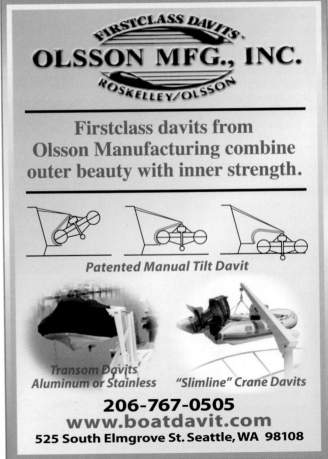

WEST COAST MARINE WEATHER
Observation Sites

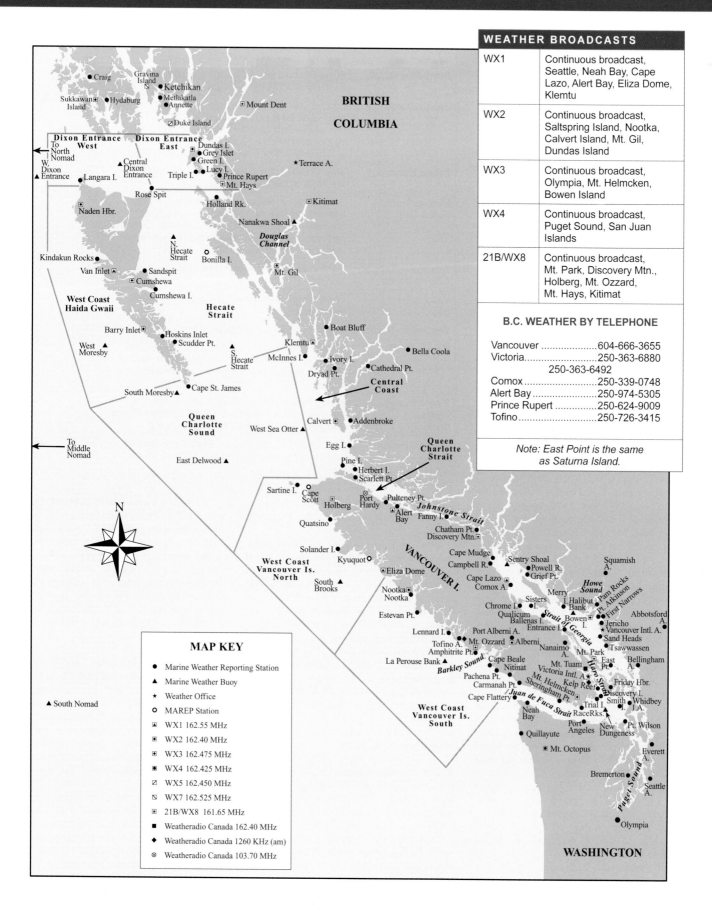

WEATHER BROADCASTS

WX1	Continuous broadcast, Seattle, Neah Bay, Cape Lazo, Alert Bay, Eliza Dome, Klemtu
WX2	Continuous broadcast, Saltspring Island, Nootka, Calvert Island, Mt. Gil, Dundas Island
WX3	Continuous broadcast, Olympia, Mt. Helmcken, Bowen Island
WX4	Continuous broadcast, Puget Sound, San Juan Islands
21B/WX8	Continuous broadcast, Mt. Park, Discovery Mtn., Holberg, Mt. Ozzard, Mt. Hays, Kitimat

B.C. WEATHER BY TELEPHONE

Vancouver 604-666-3655
Victoria.........................250-363-6880
250-363-6492
Comox 250-339-0748
Alert Bay 250-974-5305
Prince Rupert 250-624-9009
Tofino 250-726-3415

Note: East Point is the same as Saturna Island.

MAP KEY

- ● Marine Weather Reporting Station
- ▲ Marine Weather Buoy
- ★ Weather Office
- ○ MAREP Station
- ◩ WX1 162.55 MHz
- ◪ WX2 162.40 MHz
- ⊡ WX3 162.475 MHz
- ◩ WX4 162.425 MHz
- ☑ WX5 162.450 MHz
- ◖ WX7 162.525 MHz
- ⊡ 21B/WX8 161.65 MHz
- ■ Weatheradio Canada 162.40 MHz
- ◆ Weatheradio Canada 1260 KHz (am)
- ⊗ Weatheradio Canada 103.70 MHz

▲ South Nomad

Much of the information below is general in nature. It is intended to give recreational boaters a broad understanding of the Vessel Traffic Service (VTS) and how VTS can improve safety for all boats.

VTS is primarily for commercial vessels, although all power driven vessels 40 meters (131 feet) or longer, commercial or recreational, must be active participants. Active VTS participants are required to maintain radio watch on the assigned VTS channel for the waters they are in, and to call in at designated points with their location, course, speed, and estimated time of arrival (ETA) at the next call-in point. The VTS centers keep track of all active participant vessels and advise of any traffic that might interfere.

All power driven vessels between 20 meters (66 feet) and 40 meters (131 feet) must be passive participants, meaning they must keep a radio watch on the appropriate VTS radio channels.

Pleasure craft should monitor VTS. Although recreational vessels shorter than 20 meters are exempt from being active or passive participants in VTS, they must know how to keep out of the way of large, slow-maneuvering vessels.

Turn Point Special Operating Area. Turn Point is the northwest corner of the San Juan Islands' Stuart Island, where Haro Strait joins Boundary Pass. Turn Point is a blind corner. A recreational vessel could be completely unaware of a fast approaching ship on the other side. Monitor channel 11. We had a near-miss in fog a few years ago. It was scary.

Separation Zones. The VTS lanes in Puget Sound, the Strait of Juan de Fuca, and the approaches to Haro Strait and Rosario Strait are divided into inbound and outbound lanes, with a separation zone between the two. The separation zones vary in width, and are shown in magenta on the charts.

With the following precautions, pleasure craft are free to operate in the Puget Sound VTS lanes:

Pleasure craft, even vessels under sail, do not have right-of-way over VTS participant vessels, and must not impede them in any way.

Wherever practical, pleasure craft should stay out of the VTS lanes, or at least minimize the length of time spent in the lanes. Large commercial vessels are required to remain in the VTS lanes unless cleared to do otherwise. It makes no sense to compete for that space.

If inbound in the VTS lanes, run in the inbound lane; if outbound, run in the outbound lane.

If crossing the VTS lane(s), try to cross at right angles to minimize the time spent in the traffic lanes. This is not always possible or

VTS RADIO CHANNELS		
TRAFFIC AREA	**AREA DESCRIPTION**	**VHF CHANNEL**
Seattle Traffic	Puget Sound west of Whidbey Island and south of Bush Point.	14
Seattle Traffic	Strait of Juan de Fuca (including Canadian waters), and Puget Sound north of Bush Point on the west side of Whidbey Island, including the San Juan Islands and Rosario Strait. Also the entire east side of Whidbey Island.	05A
Tofino Traffic	West Coast of Vancouver Island & approaches to the Strait of Juan de Fuca.	74
Victoria Traffic – Sector One	Southern Area, Race Rocks (Victoria) to Ballenas Island/ Merry Island. This includes Haro Strait, Boundary Pass, the Gulf Islands, and the southern part of the Strait of Georgia, except for Vancouver Harbour and the Fraser River.	11
Turn Point Special Operating Area	Haro Strait/Boundary Pass. See map and text.	11
Victoria Traffic – Sector Two	Fraser River, Sand Heads to Shoal Point, New Westminster.	74
Vancouver Traffic	Vancouver Harbour and approaches.	12
Comox Traffic	Ballenas Island/Merry Island north to Cape Caution. This includes the northern part of the Strait of Georgia and Inside Passage waters north to Cape Caution.	71
Prince Rupert Traffic – Sector One	Prince Rupert Harbour & approaches, including the north end of Grenville Channel, Chatham Sound, and all of Dixon Entrance to Langara Island.	71
Prince Rupert Traffic – Sector Two	Remainder of Zone. Hecate Strait, Cape Caution north to Alaska on the west side of Haida Gwaii.	11

practical, but it should be the objective.

Do not loiter or fish in the separation zones.

Be aware of what is going on—ahead, astern, and to the sides. In the jargon this is called "situational awareness." Give large vessels lots of room. Make early and substantial course adjustments. Show them some side, meaning the side of your boat. (This is good practice whenever two vessels meet, regardless of size.)

If there's any doubt at all, cross behind a large vessel, not in front of it. A container ship traveling at only 11 knots needs more than a mile to come to a complete stop. Many container ships travel at 20 knots or more, which lengthens their stopping distance.

If you see a tug, look for a tow. Never, ever, pass between a tug and its tow. Leave ample room when crossing behind a tow.

Radio communication. While active VTS participants (large vessels and tugs with tows) are required to maintain radio watch on the appropriate VTS radio channel, such as VHF 14 in Puget Sound south of Bush Point, they are not required to monitor VHF 16, and many do not. Participants in Seattle Traffic waters also are required to monitor VHF 13, the U.S. bridge-to-bridge channel. Canada does not use VHF 13.

To contact a large vessel, in Seattle Traffic waters call on VHF 13. In Canada VTS waters call on the appropriate VTS channel, such as VHF 11 in southern Strait of Georgia waters.

We have made such calls a few times with excellent results. Twice in narrow channels, the large vessel voluntarily reduced speed to lower its wake. One time it was a cruise ship in northern B.C.; the other time it was a deadly-looking U.S. warship at the mouth of Admiralty Inlet.

Monitor VTS channels. This is called being a passive VTS participant. Many of the transmissions are extremely brief: a vessel calls in and is off the air almost before you realize it. But by monitoring you'll learn that a ferry is departing the dock, or that a large vessel is about to emerge from a channel just around the next point, or that a container ship is calling in from 5 miles behind you, traveling at 22 knots.

These are good things to know, even in clear weather. In thick weather, or at night, or in fog, the information is invaluable. We have even called the VTS center ourselves, such as prior to a fog-bound crossing of Puget Sound. We kept our transmission brief, and made sure we weren't a pest. Their response always was helpful, polite, and professional.

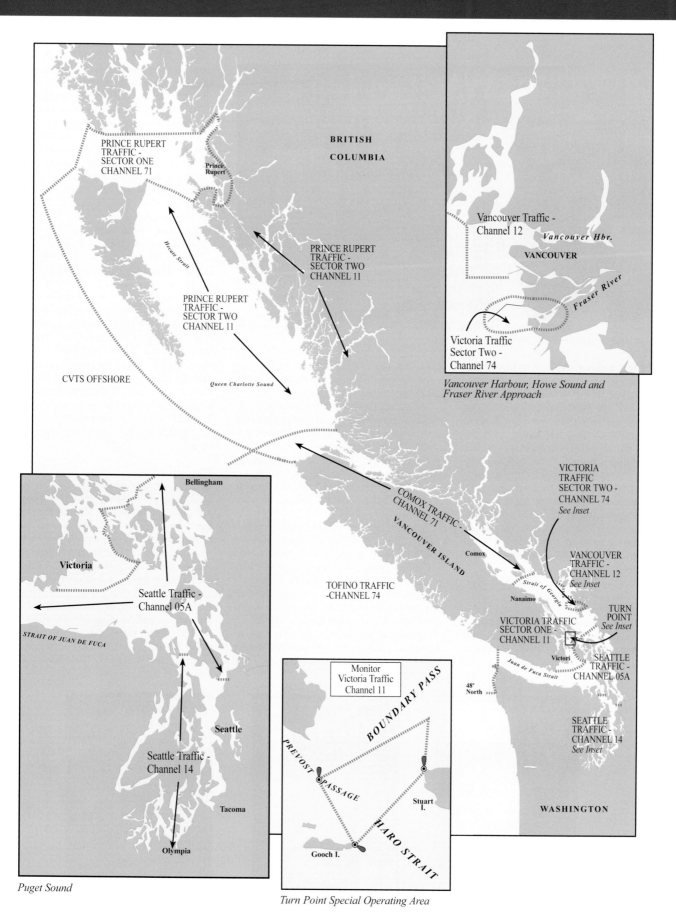

PRINCE RUPERT TRAFFIC - SECTOR ONE CHANNEL 71

Prince Rupert

BRITISH COLUMBIA

PRINCE RUPERT TRAFFIC - SECTOR TWO CHANNEL 11

PRINCE RUPERT TRAFFIC - SECTOR TWO CHANNEL 11

Hecate Strait

CVTS OFFSHORE

Queen Charlotte Sound

Vancouver Traffic - Channel 12
Vancouver Hbr.
VANCOUVER

Fraser River

Victoria Traffic Sector Two - Channel 74

Vancouver Harbour, Howe Sound and Fraser River Approach

Bellingham

COMOX TRAFFIC - CHANNEL 71

VANCOUVER ISLAND

VICTORIA TRAFFIC SECTOR TWO - CHANNEL 74 *See Inset*

Victoria

Seattle Traffic - Channel 05A

Comox

VANCOUVER TRAFFIC - CHANNEL 12 *See Inset*

TOFINO TRAFFIC -CHANNEL 74

Strait of Georgia

Nanaimo

TURN POINT *See Inset*

STRAIT OF JUAN DE FUCA

Seattle Traffic - Channel 14

Seattle

VICTORIA TRAFFIC SECTOR ONE - CHANNEL 11

Victori

SEATTLE TRAFFIC - CHANNEL 05A

Juan de Fuca Strait

48° North

SEATTLE TRAFFIC - CHANNEL 14 *See Inset*

Tacoma

Monitor Victoria Traffic Channel 11

BOUNDARY PASS

Stuart I.

WASHINGTON

Olympia

PREVOST PASSAGE

HARO STRAIT

Gooch I.

Puget Sound

Turn Point Special Operating Area

MY YEARS WITH WAGGONER

By Robert Hale, Founding Editor/Publisher

Bob and Marilynn Hale at the 2010 Seattle Boat Show.

The Waggoner was born in June, 1994 but it was conceived almost a year earlier, aboard our boat in B.C.'s Gulf Islands. My wife Marilynn and I were on our Tollycraft 26 powerboat (wonderful small cruiser, the Tolly 26), researching a second volume of preplotted waypoint coordinates for what then was Loran-C navigation. Every day, we plotted waypoints and entered them in our Micrologic Loran. Then we ran to each of the waypoints to confirm their accuracy and appropriateness. It was tedious work. By suppertime we were worn out. We needed a place to tie up or to anchor, and we were in unfamiliar waters. Fortunately, we had a guidebook.

At least we thought we did. Although it was the most popular book on the market, the more we used that book the less we thought of it. The text was full of typos, the layout was unfriendly and hard to follow, and the information was too wordy. Marilynn is intelligent but she's also dyslexic, which

makes her a slow and uncertain reader. "Just get to the point!" she would demand, as she was trying to find a place for the night.

Worse, the facility information was in the pocket of the advertisers, who were presented as the reward at the end of the rainbow. Non-advertisers, no matter how important they might be, got the barest of listings in the plainest of type. The leading guidebook was poorly written, poorly edited, and poorly designed—and we couldn't trust it. We were astonished.

Someone, I was certain, would publish a better guide. When that someone did, we would be there to help sell it. Robert Hale & Co. had grown to be the largest specialty wholesaler of nautical books. We had about 3000 titles on our shelves and sold them all over the world. We'd be pleased to add a good, annual, Northwest guide to the list.

Then I wondered, why shouldn't we be the one to publish such a book? The Robert Hale & Co. distribution was in place and I had

the skills. Prior to starting the company I had supported our family as a freelance writer/photographer. For nearly two years in the late 1970s I had been the editor of *Nor'westing*, at that time the most popular boating magazine in the Puget Sound region. In the late 1960s I spent a year as an ad salesman for a small-market radio station. And we were already publishing the annual *Washburne's Tables* and *Weatherly Waypoint Guide Vol. 1, Puget Sound and the San Juan Islands*, with Vol. 2, Gulf of Georgia, in the works.

But there were negatives. The project would take much time and a certain amount of capital. Henceforth our boating would be for work, not pleasure. Our privacy would be lost—we would belong to the public. Producing an annual cruising guide might seem exciting at first, but when the excitement wore off would it be a burden?

Cautiously, I floated the idea past Marilynn. She wasn't surprised and she wasn't against it, but we needed to talk. For days we talked. By the end of the trip we'd made the decision. If the staff at the office would get behind the project, we would do it. The staff said yes. We knew our lives would be changed. We were giddy and scared all at once.

The first edition. It was a bigger job than we expected. For one thing, I didn't know nearly enough. Banging around the buoys in a sailboat taught me a lot about some things, but it didn't tell about all the marinas, parks, communities and waterways. We needed someone who had that knowledge. That someone was my old boss, Tom Kincaid, the founding editor/publisher of *Nor'westing* magazine.

Tom wrote much of what appeared in the early editions of the Waggoner. He also wrote several sidebar pieces that set the tone for future sidebars. Tom Kincaid's sidebars still appear in the Waggoner. They never go out

Waggoner Guide, 1994

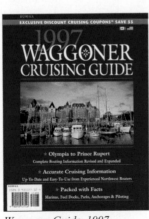

Waggoner Guide, 1997

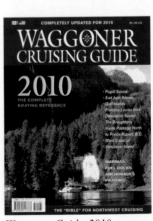

Waggoner Guide, 2010

Surprise *anchored in Prideaux Haven, Mt. Denman in the background.*

of date.

I owe Tom Kincaid everything. Back in the early 1970s he published my first paid-for writing, a monthly column called "The Weather Leg." In the late 1970s Tom hired me as editor of his beloved *Nor'westing*, and taught me about publishing. He was a mentor, a standard to live up to, and a friend.

It takes more than writing to make an annual guidebook. It takes careful research and painstaking checking of spellings, contact information, and other relevant detail. Every element of the finished product—from the physical size of the book, to the placement of page numbers, to the paper it's printed

on—has to be decided.

Then there was the advertising. What kinds of ads should the book carry and how much did we dare charge? How did we promote the idea of buying an ad in a brand-new publication?

In the end we ran out of time. We reduced the coverage area to include Puget Sound, the San Juan Islands and the Gulf Islands, ending at Nanaimo. The first edition had nothing about Vancouver, Princess Louisa Inlet, Desolation Sound, or any of the other prime cruising grounds in the Northwest. The 1994 *Pacific Northwest Waggoner* (its first name) had only 128 pages. We printed it on

thick paper to make it seem more substantial. Eighteen brave businesses were advertisers. Today the number exceeds 200.

In early June we pulled an all-nighter to get the 1994 edition ready for the printer—a heroic effort for everyone. Even so, the first edition was far from perfect. But it didn't need to be perfect, it just needed to be published. I expected to take five years to get the Waggoner out of the nursery and up and walking. Essential Rule: *You can't get to year five without beginning at year one.* The 1994 edition was year one.

With the book at the printer, Marilynn and I departed for the long research and ad sales cruise to Port Hardy, at the top of Vancouver Island. We were well away when the shipment came in. We didn't see the first copy until later.

Serve the Reader. Although many tourism guides tie editorial content to advertising support, that approach didn't seem right for a boating guide. From the beginning, the Waggoner's motto has been *Serve the Reader.* If you're out there and need a fuel dock or place to tie up, you don't care if the place advertises. You need the information. The Waggoner would provide that information, along with whatever else the reader might need to know. Advertisers would not get special favors; non-advertisers wouldn't be penalized. I figured that if we really served the reader our

PAST & PRESENT: A HISTORY *of* THE WAGGONER

About 1584 the Dutch pilot Lucas Janzoon Waghenaer published a volume of navigational principles, tables, charts, and sailing directions, which served as a guide for other such books for the next 200 years.

These *"Waggoners,"* as they came to be known, met with great success, and in 1588 an English translation of the original book was made. During the next 30 years, 24 editions of the book were published in Dutch, German, Latin, and English. Other authors followed the profitable example set by Waghenaer. Soon, American, British, and French navigators had *Waggoners* for most of the waters they sailed.

The success of these books and the resulting competition led to their eventual demise. Each writer attempted to make his work more inclusive than any other; the result was a tremendous book difficult to handle. In 1795 the British Hydrographic Department was established, and charts and sailing directions were issued separately. Within a few years the *Waggoners* disappeared.

We hope you find this new Waggoner to be as useful as the *Waggoners* of old, but without their excess bulk or needless detail. *Waggoner* is an ancient name with a proud history. Use and enjoy!

---

audience would grow, and advertisers would want to reach that audience.

Many of my "Great Ideas" turn out to be duds. Happily, Serve the Reader worked. Our audience grew, we got rave reviews in boating publications, and our list of advertisers increased. The book needed those advertisers. The low cover price encouraged sales, but copy sales produced only enough to pay the print bill and little more. Copy sale revenue didn't pay for the boat, the sales trips, the research, or (ahem) something for my wife to buy groceries.

A second reason was the overall editorial product. Advertising improved the book. The text told readers what to expect; the ads invited readers to visit. In the case of products or services, ads provided education. The relationship was symbiotic.

Serve the Reader also guided the layout of each edition. We made sure the ad for a facility in the Gulf Islands got placed in the Gulf Islands. Serve the Reader might as well have been tattooed on the inside of our eyelids. We never forgot it.

Coverage expands. The early years were a high-stress time of expansion and advancing deadlines. The 1994 edition came out in June. The 1995 edition came out the following April, to get a jump on the cruising season. By the fifth edition in 1998 the print deadline had advanced to early January, in time for the Seattle Boat Show, and the name had

changed to Waggoner Cruising Guide, where it has remained. The book included Puget Sound and the San Juan Islands, the Gulf Islands, Sunshine Coast, Desolation Sound, the west coast of Vancouver Island, and B.C.'s central and north coast to Prince Rupert. We had fleshed out our intended coverage area and were over the hump financially. The page count was 256. We had 100 advertisers.

Art project. All along, I followed my instincts about what to put in the book. My instincts told me to run drawings from the kids at Kwatsi Bay Marina, beginning with "Fish Jumping," by 5-year-old Marieke. Instinct told me what might make a good sidebar. "We Almost Died from Shellfish Poisoning" was one result. I still shiver when I read it. I turned down good writers who asked to send in sidebars, because I couldn't tell them what I wanted—I would know it when I saw it. A reader said to me, "Bob, the Waggoner is your art project." The Waggoner was a business, too—it had to be. But the book came from somewhere inside me. The reader was right. The Waggoner truly was my "art project."

Technological advances. Beginning in the late 1990s the digital era produced rapid changes in the publication and printing industries. We went from setting type on paper, which we cut and pasted down on flats, to all-digital, which we edited and laid out

  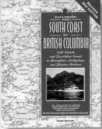 

Bob and Marilynn Hale in front of the waterfall in Nimmo Bay.

on desktop computers and copied to CDs (thank you, Photoshop), to sending files to the printer via the Internet. Printing advances made color printing sufficiently affordable that beginning in 2005 the Waggoner was printed in full color. We were dazzled.

My most difficult year. That would be the 2006 edition. The page count had grown to 352 and the Advertisers' Index filled an entire page. The Waggoner was clearly the leading guide in the Northwest. The cruising community, the charter boat agencies, new boaters—all of them depended on the book.

And I had a problem. We were losing our son, Dan, to cancer. In late May, 2005, as Marilynn and I were preparing to depart for the research and sales cruise north, chemo treatment had destroyed Dan's resistance to infection. A case of the sniffles one evening exploded into fast-progressing pneumonia by the next morning. The magicians at Virginia Mason Hospital somehow brought Dan back from the very edge, but it took time and left the family exhausted. Dan and his wife Alison also were in the midst of closing on a home in Tacoma, near Alison's work. It was a terrible few weeks.

With Dan at last recovering from pneumonia I felt the urgency of research and sales for the 2006 Waggoner. People were depending on me. With very mixed feelings, we decided it would be best for Marilynn to stay home and for me to shorten the boat trip to include the Broughtons and the north end of Vancouver Island and no more. Wendell Hedges, my longtime friend and former boss (I have many former bosses) agreed to

put his own business on hold and be my crew north. I would single-hand home. It all worked out. Dan's situation improved to the point where a few weeks later Marilynn could fly up to Montague Harbour in the Gulf Islands and accompany me back to Seattle.

The question was how much longer we would have Dan. The Waggoner's print deadline now was the first part of November, to have books for Christmas shopping. By early fall it was clear that Dan's health was worsening. He was in constant pain and growing steadily weaker. We raced to finish the book. I didn't know if we would make it, but we did. In early November the files went off to the printer. *We'd served our readers.*

We lost Daniel Hale late in the afternoon, November 13, 2005. I'm still crying. I hope I never stop.

Correspondents. Moving on: From the beginning, comment and input from readers have been one of the strengths of the book. Those whose material we used were listed as Correspondents (still are). In most cases I was able to give them credit for their information (still do).

Staff. I had a great staff to help with the Waggoner project. Our son Dan and daughter Sheri made huge contributions in the early years. Dan did the computer work that got the book ready for the printer. He had an innate sense of typography and design. Sheri helped gather and confirm the facilities information the book carried. She took over the graphics role after Dan moved on to another job, and stayed until just a few days before her first

daughter was born. Book sales were the province of 20-plus-year employee Oscar Lind, who got Waggoners on the dealers' shelves and kept them there. Stacia Green was the book's managing editor. Stacia kept track of the paperwork and advertiser details. And she pretty much ran the whole Robert Hale & Co. operation. Blanca Garcia was the bookkeeper. Blanca kept the bills paid on time and was on top of collections like a blanket. The rest of the staff members were vital as well, but over the years Oscar, Stacia and Blanca were the core. With them in place Marilynn and I could be away on the boat for nearly two months researching the next year's edition, and come home to a smoothly running operation.

Another core person: Bob Smith, Book Printers Network, in Portland, Oregon. First as a print salesman then as a print broker, Bob oversaw every edition. He saved our bacon repeatedly.

Finally, the one person who made it possible for me to create and build a book that has affected so many lives—my enduring wife, Marilynn. Without Marilynn it

wouldn't have happened.

Retirement. By the end of 2010 it was time for the Waggoner to move to new hands—in this case Mark Bunzel. Mark had been a customer and a supplier for 10 years with never a bad moment. For some time he had said he would like to be the Waggoner's next owner. We flew proposals back and forth, we spent sums on lawyers, and finally worked out an arrangement that suited both parties—although it took more than two months after agreement to get the contracts right.

I had always hoped to retire when I was 70. Four days before my 71st birthday, Mark Bunzel and his wife Leslie sat with Marilynn and me at our kitchen table and we signed papers. When all was completed and we were shaking hands I told Mark I had something to say. Then I choked and couldn't speak. The Waggoner had consumed me for nearly 20 years and now it wouldn't be mine. I recovered, looked Mark in the eye and managed to get it out:

"Captain Bunzel, the helm is yours."

DIFFERENCES BETWEEN U.S. & CANADIAN CHARTS

Canada and the United States are two separate nations, and their charts, while similar in many ways, have important differences.

U.S. charts are in fathoms and feet; most Canadian charts are metric. *With all charts, read the chart title and margin information to see if the chart is metric, fathoms and feet, or feet.* Metric charts show soundings and heights in meters. A meter (spelled metre in Canada) equals 39.37 inches, or 3.28 feet. Two meters equals 6 feet 7 inches, or just over one fathom. The difference is significant. Don't confuse fathoms with meters.

Waters appear to be deeper on U.S. charts of Pacific Northwest waters. This difference is important wherever the water is shallow, and is the result of the two countries using different *chart datums.*

Depths on a chart are measured from the chart datum, also called the reference plane or **tidal datum.** On Canadian charts, the chart datum is either Lowest Normal Tides, or Lower Low Water, Large Tide. For that reason, you don't find many "minus tides" in Canadian tide tables.

On U.S. charts of Pacific Northwest waters, however, the chart datum is Mean Lower Low Water. Mean Lower Low Water is the mean, or average, level of the lower of the two low tides each day. Since the U.S. chart datum has half the lower waters above it and half below it, U.S. tide books show minus tides.

It's not a question of whether the tide drops lower in Canada or the U.S. It's a question of where the depth is measured from. U.S. charts start their measurements from a point higher than Canadian charts. The difference can be as much as 1.5 meters, or almost 5 feet.

Example: Assume that you are in the U.S., skippering a sailboat. The sailboat's keel draws 5 feet, and you want to anchor overnight in a bay with a charted depth of one fathom (6 feet). According to the tide table, low tide will be minus 1.5 feet at 0700. Knowing that your boat, with its 5 feet of draft, would be aground in 4.5 feet of water, you would look for a more suitable anchorage.

If this bay were in Canada, the chart would show a depth of perhaps just 1 meter (assuming a Lowest Normal Tide lower than the tide at 0700). The tide table would show a low tide at 0700 of perhaps .4 meters. You would add the 1 meter depth from the chart to the .4 meter low tide from the tide table, and get 1.4 meters of water at 0700. Since you draw more than 1.4 meters (55 inches), you would not anchor in the bay that night.

Important exception: Both Canadian and U.S. charts show soundings in the other country's system when the charts cover both sides of the border. The U.S. chart would convert Canadian meters to U.S. fathoms, but would adopt the Canadian chart datum in Canadian waters. The Canadian metric chart would convert U.S. fathoms to meters, but would adopt the U.S. chart datum in U.S. waters. This is explained in the chart legends.

Clearances appear to be greater on U.S. charts. U.S. charts for Northwest waters measure clearances from Mean High Water. One-half the high waters are above the mean. Canadian charts measure clearances from Higher High Water, Large Tides. The same bridge, over the same waterway, would show less vertical clearance on a Canadian chart than on a U.S. chart. Metric Canadian charts show heights and depths in meters; Canadian charts in fathoms and feet show heights in feet and depths in fathoms. A Canadian metric chart might show a bridge clearance as "3," meaning 3 meters above Higher High Water, Large Tides. A U.S. chart would show a bridge clearance as "12" or more, meaning 12 feet or more above Mean High Water.

Canadian charts use more symbols to show buoys and tide rips. Canadian charts use symbols that approximate the shapes of buoys, with letters to indicate the buoy's characteristics. U.S. charts use a single diamond-shaped symbol for nearly all navigation buoys, with descriptive letters to indicate the buoy's characteristics.

On U.S. Chart 18421, Strait of Juan de Fuca to Strait of Georgia (1:80,000), for example, the bell buoy marking Buckeye Shoal, north of Cypress Island, is shown as:

But on Canadian Chart 3462, Juan de Fuca Strait to Strait of Georgia (1:80,000), the buoy is shown as:

Canadian charts may use arrows to show the location of the buoy or beacon. If other detail on the chart makes precise location difficult, the Canadian chart will offset the symbol slightly, in the direction of the preferred navigable water. The offset is indicated by an arrow pointing to the actual location of the buoy or beacon. Sometimes the arrow is easy to overlook.

Chart No. 1 cracks the code. Nautical charts are filled with important navigation information. Unfortunately, so much of the information is in the form of symbols, abbreviations, and undefined terms that it can be confusing. Each country has published a book that shows each symbol and defines each term used on its charts. The U.S. book is titled *Chart No. 1*, and the Canadian book is titled *Chart 1*. The Canadian book is available from Canadian Hydrographic chart agencies. The U.S. book is produced by several private publishers. Copies are available at marine supply outlets.

The Canadian Coast Guard publication *The Canadian Aids to Navigation System* explains the Canadian buoyage and light system, and is highly recommended. A PDF version is available on the Canadian Coast Guard website. The cost for the print version is $7.50 (Cdn) from Canadian Hydrographic chart agents, nautical bookstores and chandleries.

The introduction pages of both these books are filled with essential information. Don't overlook them.

THE END OF PAPER CHARTS?

At press time, NOAA announced that U.S. government lithographic charts will not be printed after April 13, 2014. Charts will be updated and released on a daily basis for download and by Print on Demand (POD) map vendors.

This does not mean U.S. paper charts will not be available. POD charts from private vendors have been available for almost 10 years. They'll continue to be available, and will always have the most up-to-date information.

The waters from Puget Sound north into B.C. are dotted with more than 200 state, provincial, and national parks, and in B.C., more than 220 public wharves.

Washington Parks. At the state level, parks are administered by the Washington State Parks and Recreation Commission and by the Department of Natural Resources (DNR). Usually, DNR sites are on the primitive side. State parks, which tend to be more developed, charge for moorage at buoys and docks. For docks and floats, expect to pay $.60 per foot, $12 minimum. Mooring buoys are $12. The dock or buoy fee applies after 1:00 p.m., payable for even a stop-and-go visit, such as walking the dog. *Unless otherwise marked, buoys are for boats 45 feet and less; boats longer than 45 feet are not allowed.* Rafting is allowed for boats 36 feet and less. Each rafted boat must pay a moorage fee.

State parks charge moorage fees year-round. Annual moorage permits are available and valid from January 1 to December 31, $4 per foot, $60 minimum. Contact Washington State Parks Information, (360) 902-8844 (Monday through Friday), or infocent@parks.wa.gov. Or check their informative website at www. parks.wa.gov/boating/moorage.

Campsite fees are paid in addition to dock or mooring buoy fees. Self-register ashore for moorage or campsites.

Boat launch sites. State parks with boat launches charge fees of $7. The launch fee includes the daily parking fee. Annual launch permits cost $80 and are valid for a year from date of purchase. Contact Washington State Parks, (360) 902-8844, or from www. parks.wa.gov/boating/launch/.

Reservations. Moorage is unreserved. Leaving a dinghy or other personal property at a buoy or dock does not reserve moorage. Rafting is permitted but not mandatory. Rafting is allowed on buoys, within specified limits. Reservations (for campsites only) in all state parks are accepted. Call toll-free (888) 226-7688.

Department of Natural Re-sources parks generally are primitive or have few facilities, and most do not charge fees.

Washington Boater Education Card. The mandatory Washington Boater Education Card is being phased in gradually. In 2013, all operators ages 12 to 50 of boats with motors of 15 horsepower or more are required to have their card. Washington State Parks administers this program. See their website at www.parks. wa.gov/boating/boatered/ or (360) 902-8555.

If you are boating in Canadian waters, if for a period of longer than 44 days, a Canadian Operator Card or the equivalent issued by a state in the U.S. is required. The Washington Boater Education Card qualifies for cruising more than 44 days, as do U.S. Coast Guard licenses such as Captain's or Mate's license.

Canadian Boater Pleasure Craft Operator Card (PCOC). Canada has a similar program for its boaters, requiring boater education and certification. In B.C., several firms offer classes and testing services to prove competency. A special program called "Rental Boating Safety Checklist" is for power-driven rental boats and bareboat charter boats. Consult your Canadian charter company for more information and requirements.

B.C. Parks including Gulf Islands National Park Reserve Parks. Most B.C. marine parks have floats or mooring buoys, and safe, all-weather anchorages. Marine parks are open year-round. Some have no on-shore facilities, others have day-use facilities, picnic areas, developed campsites. Most parks have drinking water. Overnight moorage fees ($12 for a buoy; $2/meter for dock moorage) are charged at a number of the more developed parks. No rafting is permitted on mooring buoys. No charge for anchoring, even with a stern-tie to shore. Tent sites are extra. Contact B.C. Parks General Information at www.env.gov.bc.ca/bcparks. For more information on the Gulf Islands National Park Reserve, contact (866) 944-1744 or see

Public docks provide access to parks and islands.

their website at www.pc.gc.ca. On the home page select "Find a National Park" and select "Gulf Islands National Park Reserve."

Public Wharves. In British Columbia, public wharves provide moorage for commercial vessels (primarily the fishing fleet) and pleasure craft. Especially in the off-season, public wharves are filled with fish boats, leaving little or no moorage for pleasure craft. Facilities vary, from a dock only, to fully-serviced marinas. Most of the public wharves now are operated by local harbor authorities or their equivalents. Locally-run public wharves charge market rates, and may reserve space for pleasure craft. Moorage fees vary. Public wharves are easily identified by their red-painted railings.

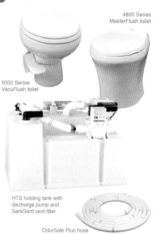

BUOYS, BEACONS AND RANGES

Red, Right, Returning means leave **Red** navigation aids off your **Right** hand when you're **Returning** from seaward. If the navigation mark is not red, leave it off your left hand when you're returning from seaward.

This is the general rule in U.S. and Canadian waters, with three subtle refinements:

- Safe water mark A buoy with red and white vertical stripes that marks an approach or mid-channel (an example would be the Shilshole Bay Approach Lighted Bell Buoy, commonly called the Ballard Blinker). Unobstructed water surrounds this mark. Both inbound and outbound, it is good practice to leave this buoy to port.
- Preferred channel mark. A buoy or a beacon with red and green horizontal bands. This aid marks a channel junction or an obstruction. While the aid can be passed on either side, the color of the top band indicates the preferred or main channel.
- Isolated danger mark. An aid—either a buoy or a beacon—with black and red horizontal bands that marks an isolated danger (an example would be the Blakely Island Shoal Isolated Danger Buoy DS, west of Blakely Island in the San Juan Islands). These marks have navigable water all around, but should not be approached closely without caution.

Nuns

All red buoys marking channels are shaped as cones, and are called nuns. Most nun buoys are painted solid red. If the nun buoy has a green horizontal band painted on it, the buoy marks the meeting of two channels, with the left channel being the preferred, or main, channel. (If you leave the buoy to starboard, you will be in the left channel.) If lighted, the light will be red.

Cans

All green buoys marking channels are called cans. They are shaped like, well, *cans*. Most can buoys are painted solid green. If the can buoy has a horizontal red band painted on it, the buoy marks the meeting of two channels, with the right channel the preferred, or main, channel. If lighted, the light will be green.

Beacons

Buoys float, and are held in place by heavy anchoring systems, but beacons are permanent navigation aids attached to the earth. Beacons can be located on land, installed on docks or breakwaters, or mounted on pilings. A lighthouse is a beacon. A beacon not on land will be placed in shallow water outside a channel. *Do not pass a beacon close aboard.* Give it considerable room.

An unlighted beacon is called a **daybeacon.** A lighted beacon is called a **minor light.** A minor light marking the right side of a channel will carry a red light (Red, Right, Returning). A minor light marking the left side of a channel will carry a green light. If a minor light marks the meeting of two channels, it will be red if the left channel is preferred; green if the right channel is preferred.

Daymarks are the colored panels mounted on beacons. Red panels are triangle shaped; green panels are square. A triangle shaped red panel with a green horizontal stripe indicates the meeting of two channels, with the left channel the preferred, or main, channel. A square panel painted green with a red horizontal stripe indicates the meeting of two channels, with the right channel the preferred channel.

Whenever a navigation aid is marked with a horizontal stripe of contrasting color, the color at the top of the aid indicates the preferred, or main, channel.

Approaching a channel from seaward, buoys and beacons are numbered, beginning with the marks to seaward. Red buoys, daybeacons, and minor lights carry even numbers, such as 2, 4, 6, and so on. Green buoys, daybeacons, and minor lights carry odd numbers, such as 1, 3, 5, and so on. Depending on the channel, it might be appropriate to skip some numbers, so that buoy 6 is roughly opposite buoy 5, even if no buoy 4 exists.

Ranges

Ranges are used to help a boat stay in the middle of a narrow channel.

Ranges are rectangular panels stood vertically, each with a wide stripe running from top to bottom down the middle of the panel. Ranges are attached to the earth and arranged in pairs, one behind the other. The rear range board stands taller than the front range board. To use a range, steer until the rear range board appears to be on top of the front board. You can steer toward a range, looking ahead (leading range), or away from a range, sighting astern (back range).

Buoys and beacons are not selected and placed at random. They follow a plan, although to a newcomer the plan may at times seem obscure.

Despite the complexity of the buoyage and light system, you will find that as you understand it better your enjoyment afloat will increase. At some point you will want a thorough explanation of the entire system. For U.S. waters it will be found in the introduction to the Coast Guard Light List. For Canadian waters it will be found partly in the introduction to the Canadian Coast Guard List of Lights, Buoys and Fog Signals, and completely in the Canadian Coast Guard publication, The Canadian Aids to Navigation System. Latest editions of these publications should be aboard every boat. They are available at chart agencies and chandleries.

RED, RIGHT RETURNING

Nun Buoy

RED, RIGHT RETURNING from the sea means the conical red nun buoy marks the right side of the channel. Vessels returning from the sea upstream will leave red navigation aids to starboard. Red aids are assigned even numbers, beginning with No. 2 at the seaward end of the channel.

Can Buoy

A GREEN CAN BUOY marks the left side of the channel. Vessels returning from the sea or upstream will leave green navigation aids to port. Green aids are assigned odd numbers, beginning with No. 1 at the seaward end of the channel. Buoys and beacons can be lighted or unlighted.

Lighted Beacon

A BEACON, such as this light at Webster Point in Lake Washington, is attached to the earth, and should be given a good offing. Port-hand beacons carry square green dayboards; starboard-hand beacons carry red triangular dayboards.

Restricted Operation Buoy

CYLINDRICAL WHITE RESTRICTED OPERATIONS BUOYS, such as this one, mark speed zones, restricted anchoring areas, fish habitats and other important information.

SOUTH & CENTRAL PUGET SOUND

SOUTH PUGET SOUND
Olympia • Case Inlet • Carr Inlet • Tacoma Narrows

CENTRAL PUGET SOUND
Gig Harbor • Tacoma • Vashon Island • Seattle • Bremerton • Poulsbo • Bainbridge Island

South Puget Sound begins at Olympia and ends at Tacoma Narrows. For scenic quality, relatively calm seas and solitude, it is an excellent region to explore. For some reason, Seattle boats that voyage hundreds of miles north often do not consider venturing just a few miles south. Yet South Sound is dotted with marine parks and served by enough marinas to meet most needs. We like South Sound and recommend it.

The waters are generally flatter in South Sound. The channels are relatively narrow and have enough bends to minimize fetch and prevent wind from creating large seas. Tide-rips, of course, still form where channels meet, and skippers must be aware of them.

Olympia is South Sound's only significant city. Getting away from civilization is easy, yet it is always close by. First-time visitors usually are surprised at the beauty of this area. Mt. Rainier, an inactive volcano 14,410 feet high, dominates many vistas. The islands and peninsulas tend to be either tree-covered or pastoral, with pockets of homes or commercial enterprise. Most marine parks have docks, buoys, and anchoring. The marinas are friendly and well-kept.

BUDD, ELD, TOTTEN INLETS

Budd Inlet. The mile-wide entrance to Budd Inlet is between Dofflemyer Point and Cooper Point. Approaching from the north, simply round Dofflemyer Point, where a white-painted light blinks every 4 seconds, and head for the Capitol dome (unless the political fog rising from a convening Legislature obscures it).

Anchorage in Budd Inlet is along both shores in 10 to 20 feet, mud bottom, with Butler Cove and Tykle Cove preferred. Private mooring buoys line the shores, so consider your swinging room when anchoring.

Launch Ramps: Swantown Marina has a 2-lane launch ramp. Another launch ramp is at the Thurston County park just south of Boston Harbor, near Dofflemyer Point. Boston Harbor also has a launch ramp and parking for tow vehicles and trailers.

The City of Olympia's Priest Point Park, on the east side of Budd Inlet, has one of the finest sand beaches in southern Puget Sound.

CHARTS

18445 sc folio small-craft Puget Sound	Possession Sound to Olympia including Hood Canal (1:80,000)
18448	Puget Sound, Southern Part (1:80,000)
18456	Olympia Harbor and Budd Inlet (1:20,000)
18457	Puget Sound – Hammersly Inlet to Shelton (1:10,000)
18474	Puget Sound – Shilshole Bay to Commencement Bay (1:40,000)

LOCAL KNOWLEDGE

MILITARY SECURITY ZONE: When military vessels are loading or unloading at the Port of Olympia docks, you will be directed to the far west side of the channel. Patrol boats with .50 cal. machine guns mounted on deck will explain.

Olympia. Olympia is one of the most charming stops in Puget Sound, the more so because so few boats from central and northern Puget Sound ever visit. Northern boats should change their ways. Olympia is an undiscovered treat.

Moorage in Olympia is at five marinas: NorthPoint Landing, Port Plaza Dock, Percival Landing Park, West Bay Marina, and Swantown Marina.

To get to the marinas, continue past Olympia Shoal, marked by lighted beacons on the shoal's east and west sides. From Olympia Shoal pick up the 28-foot-deep dredged and buoyed channel leading to the harbor. A spoils bank from channel dredging is east of the channel. The spoils area is quite shoal and parts of it dry. Stay in the channel.

The channel branches at a piling intersection marker south of the privately owned West Bay Marina. The dayboard on the marker is green on top, red on the bottom. The green top-color marks the main channel. Leave it to port and you'll proceed down the western leg past the Port of Olympia large ship docks to the new docks at Percival Landing, and to the Olympia Yacht Club at the head of the inlet. If you leave the marker to starboard, you'll take the eastern leg to the Port of Olympia's Swantown Marina and Boatworks. On both sides of each channel

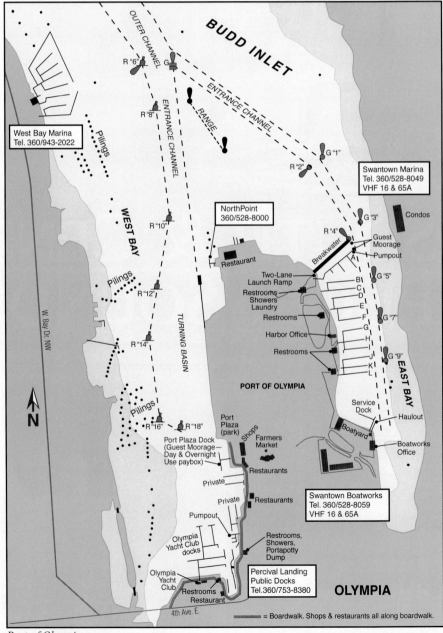

Port of Olympia

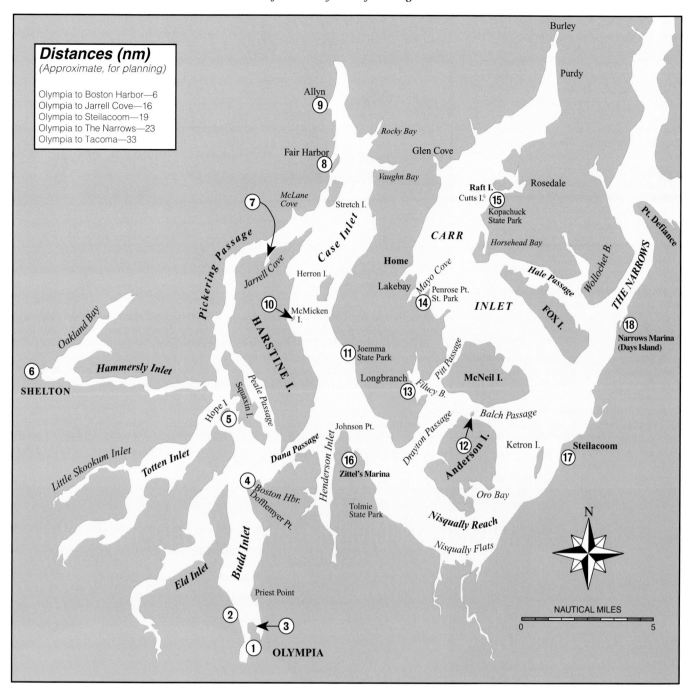

Distances (nm)
(Approximate, for planning)

Olympia to Boston Harbor—6
Olympia to Jarrell Cove—16
Olympia to Steilacoom—19
Olympia to The Narrows—23
Olympia to Tacoma—33

the water shoals rapidly to drying flats. The Olympia harbor has a no-wake rule.

West Bay Marina has a few guest slips and a restaurant, but no fuel dock. The Olympia Yacht Club has guest moorage for members of reciprocal clubs only. Percival Landing at the head of the western channel, and Swantown Marina in the eastern channel, have moorage for all.

A newly landscaped walkway surrounds the Percival Landing area. It's a popular place for strolling, with an excellent view of harbor activities. Good restaurants and a fish market are nearby. Some boaters find the number of people walking just above their boats disconcerting, although we have found nights to be quiet. Swantown Marina, in East Bay, does not have the crowds looking at the boats.

Deschutes Basin, the southernmost tip of

Puget Sound, and Capitol Lake are blocked by a dam and crossed by city streets. They are used by small boats launched from the city park just across the road from Percival Landing and the yacht club.

Olympia is the state capital, and we urge a tour of the Capitol Campus and its buildings. The grounds are beautiful and the buildings are magnificent. (If the lawmaking were as impressive as the buildings, we would have quite a government.) Informative tours are conducted on the hour, 10:00 a.m. to 3:00 p.m. on weekdays, 11:00 a.m. to 3:00 p.m. on weekends. No charge for these tours. The free Dash shuttle bus runs regularly from the farmers market to the campus and back.

Downtown Olympia has its own charm. Parts of it got stuck in the '50s. If you've seen the film "Pleasantville," you'll recognize the

storefronts. The State Theater's tall art deco sign is not a bit out of place in Olympia's downtown. The Eastside Club Tavern was the inspiration for Moe's Tavern on "The Simpsons" TV show. Some of the restaurants have employees who have been there 20 to 40 years, and they're open every day of the year so regular customers have somewhere to go, even at Christmas.

Take the self-guided Historical District Walking Tour to learn local history: www.olympiawa.gov/city-services/history-preservation/walking-tours-of-historic-olympia.

About 20 antiques stores are located in the downtown area and out past Percival Landing. Art galleries are springing up. If you need a jolt of caffeine, coffee roaster Batdorf & Bronson is just east of the farmers market. They have a tasting room, just like a winery, only with coffee. Samples are free, but we always buy at least a couple bags of coffee. We enjoy it. Free Wi-Fi.

Olympia Farmers Market. The farmers market, between Percival Landing and Port of Olympia's Swantown Marina, is open 10:00 a.m. to 3:00 p.m. Thursday through Sunday from April through October, weekends in November and December, closed January and February. Everything sold is grown or made locally, except for a few fruits that come from Yakima. Musicians perform on a covered stage and take-out food is available from several outlets. No pets allowed. The market's roof is topped by a weathervane in the shape of a traditional flying pig.

THINGS TO DO

The docks at Percival Landing Park.

1. **Washington State Capitol**. Take a short walk from the marinas for a free 60-minute tour of the architecturally magnificent legislative building.

2. **Washington State Capital Museum**. Good exhibits on the history of Washington State. Seven blocks from the Capitol.

3. **Hands on Children's Museum**. This new children's museum has exhibits and an outdoor discovery center. A must-see for kids. Adjacent to Swantown Marina.

4. **Olympia Farmers Market**. One of the largest farmers markets in all of Puget Sound. It is open Thursday through Sunday, April to October. Also open weekends before the holidays in November and December. Located between Swantown Marina and Percival Landing.

5. **Percival Landing Park**. See classic boats, sculptures, and views of the Capitol on this landscaped walkway around the harbor.

6. **Antique and specialty shops**. More than 20 in the downtown area, a short walk from the waterfront.

7. **Batdorf & Bronson Coffee Roasters**. Taste the difference.

① **Percival Landing Park**. 217 Thurston Ave., Olympia, WA 98501; (360) 753-8380; www.olympiawa.gov. Newly renovated Per-

The marinas in Olympia are in the shadow of the Capitol building.

cival Landing Park has improved showers and restrooms. The park, with moorage, is adjacent to downtown Olympia, near shopping, restaurants, and other facilities. Four hours day moorage no charge. No water or shore power. Guest moorage is along the float on the east side of the waterway. D dock, below the Olympia Oyster House restaurant on the west side, has limited space. Register at The Olympia Center. Group reservations available from October 1 to March 31. F Dock is scheduled to be replaced with new floats, pumpout, water and power by summer 2014.

The floats have access to toilets, showers, pumpout, and portapotty dump. After-hours or weekends, self-register at kiosks at each restroom building. Cash or checks only at the kiosks, no credit cards. First-come, first-served. Maximum 7 days in a 30-day period. No manager is on site, so you may have to search for everything, including the registration kiosks. Good grocery shopping at Bayview Thriftway, west of the yacht club. The Harbor House meeting center was built as part of the Percival Landing renovation, and is available for group gatherings to 30 people. Call (360) 753-8380.

Limited guest moorage during the Wood-en Boat Show in May, and Harbor Days, with its tugboat races, early September.

① **Port Plaza Dock.** 915 Washington St. NE, Olympia, WA 98501; (360) 528-8049; marina@portofolympia.com; www.swantownmarina.com. Monitors VHF 65A. This is a modern, all-concrete set of floats on the east side of the waterway leading to Percival Landing and Olympia Yacht Club. The docks are intended for day use and are convenient to dining and shopping, 4 hours no charge. Potable water, no power. Self-register at kiosk at the head of the ramp. Reservations accepted for $5 non-refundable fee.

The Port Plaza itself is a work of art. The sculpted concrete work suggests waves. It's completely flat but very effective. Bronze shells, golf balls, drafting tools—all sorts of things are set into the cement. The more you look, the more you see.

ANTHONY'S
HOMEPORT RESTAURANT
704 Columbia St. NW
(360) 357-9700

① **NorthPoint Landing.** 915 Washington St. NE, Olympia, WA 98501; (360) 528-8000; www.portolympia.com. Small dock operated by the Port of Olympia at the north end of the waterway leading to Percival Landing and Olympia Yacht Club. Day use only. Not much depth at low tide. Anthony's Hearthfire Grill is adjacent to the dock.

1675 Marine Drive NE
(360) 705-3473

② **West Bay Marina.** 2100 Westbay Drive NW, Olympia, WA 98502; (360) 943-2022; westbaymarina@hotmail.com; www.westbaymarina.com. On the west side of Budd Inlet. Mostly permanent moorage but a few guest slips are sometimes available; call ahead for guest moorage. Restrooms, showers, coin operated laundry, and pumpout. Tugboat Annie's restaurant and pub, a longtime favorite, is there.

③ **Swantown Marina.** 1022 Marine Drive NE, Olympia, WA 98501; (360) 528-8049; marina@portolympia.com; www.swantown-marina.com. Certified Clean Marina. Monitors VHF 65A. This is the Port of Olympia small boat moorage. Open all year, 70+ guest moorage slips for vessels to 100 feet. Outstanding restrooms, showers, and laundry. Pumpout, porta-potty dump, 30 & 50 amp power, garbage drop, waste oil dump, security patrols, well-tended grounds, free Wi-Fi. Reservations accepted. Dry boat storage, 2-lane launch ramp. Block and crushed ice at Harbor Office. Groceries are a 20-minute walk away. The Olympia Farmers Market and a seafood market are in the marina area. Downtown Olympia attractions and a children's museum are within walking distance.

The channel leading from the intersection beacon with its green and red dayboard can be confusing. If the weather is clear, you'll see a long, low 2-story condominium block on the eastern shore. Aim for those condominiums. At the entry to Swantown Marina, Beacon 1 will be at the north end of the condominiums; Beacon 2 will be at the south end.

Guest moorage is on A-dock a short distance inside the entry, next to the launch ramp. Register and pay moorage at the kiosk at the head of the ramp, or in the office at the head of I-Dock. Swantown Marina is parklike: clean, quiet, spacious and well-maintained.

Swantown Boatworks, with 77-ton Travelift, is at the south end of the marina. Other boating related services are available. Call (360) 528-8059.

Burfoot County Park. 6927 Boston Harbor Rd. NE, Olympia, WA 98506. Located a half-mile south of Dofflemyer Point. This is a 60-acre county park, open all year, day use only. Restrooms, picnic tables, trails, and play area. Anchoring or beaching only. Buoys mark an artificial diving reef.

The busy Farmers Market is a popular attraction in Olympia.

The large deck adjacent to the Boston Harbor Store is popular.

Boston Harbor, with its sandy beach.

④ **Boston Harbor.** Boston Harbor is a halfmoon-shaped bay between Dofflemyer Point and Dover Point. Anchorage is limited but possible. Much of the bay is taken up by the Boston Harbor Marina.

④ **Boston Harbor Marina.** 312 - 73rd Ave. NE, Olympia, WA 98506; (360) 357-5670; bhm@bostonharbormarina.com; www.bostonharbormarina.com. Monitors VHF 16, switch to 68. Open all year with guest moorage, gasoline and diesel, CNG, 20 amp power, picnic area, beach access, Wi-Fi, restrooms but no showers, launch ramp (dries on minus tide). Easily seen from the mouth of Boston Harbor. The store has groceries, ice, beer and wine, fresh seafood, and some marine supplies. Sandwiches, soup, salad, and ice cream served at the store. Rental boats available.

This is a real neighborhood place, a throwback to when small marinas up and down Puget Sound serviced surrounding communities. The old, quaint store is built on pilings, and there's not a level floor to be found. The store is packed with merchandise, though, including gifts and clothing, a good book selection, and unexpected local art. The store and docks are gathering places for locals, and a cheery bunch they are. On Fridays during the season you might find a barbecue

on the dock in the early evening. Breakfast is served on the dock Sunday mornings from 9:00 a.m. to 11:00 a.m. May to September. Wine tastings are held on some Fridays from 5:00 p.m. to 7:00 p.m., call for details. If you relax and just let it happen, you'll think Boston Harbor is a delight.

No-wake zone: Several white warning buoys off the mouth of Boston Harbor mark a no-wake zone. Slow down. Wakes from passing craft play havoc with the moored boats.

Eld Inlet. Eld Inlet is immediately west of Budd Inlet, and extends about 5 miles south from Cooper Point before it becomes Mud Bay (aptly named). Hold to a mid-channel course past Cooper Point, which has an extensive drying shoal northward from the point.

Eld Inlet has no marinas, but anchorage is good, mud bottom, along both shores. Directly across the inlet is the waterfront activities center for The Evergreen State College. The center has a float and buildings to store canoes and other small craft used by students.

Frye Cove County Park. 4000 NW 61st Ave., Olympia, WA 98502. Just north of Flapjack Point in Eld Inlet. Open all year, day use only. Toilets, no other services. Anchoring

or beaching only. Picnic shelters, barbecues, hiking trails.

⑤ **Hope Island Marine State Park.** (360) 902-8844. Junction of Totten Inlet and Pickering Passage. Undeveloped Hope Island is one of the newest parks in the state system. Boat access only. Trails crisscrossing the island lead through forest, meadows, and old orchards. Interpretive signs explain the island's history and ecology. Visitors rave about this park. A resident caretaker lives on the island. The park has 5 mooring buoys, and decent anchorage is in 30 feet or less on the east side. Other than trails through primeval woods, there are no facilities ashore. No fires, no dogs. Pack out all garbage.

Totten Inlet. Enter Totten Inlet past Steamboat Island, connected to the the mainland by a causeway from Carlyon Beach. Homes and a private marina are on the island and mainland beach. The beach is marked by a quick flashing light. All of Totten Inlet is less than 60 feet deep. The inlet shoals to drying mud flats toward its south end, called Oyster Bay. Use Chart 18448.

About 3 miles southwest of Steamboat Island on the west side of Totten Inlet is the entrance to **Skookum Inlet**, called by the

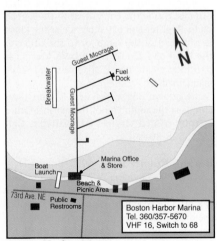

Boston Harbor Marina

Hope Island Marine State Park has mooring buoys on the south shore. The windmill pumps water, and interpretive displays recall the island's history. The caretaker's cabin is the middle of the photo.

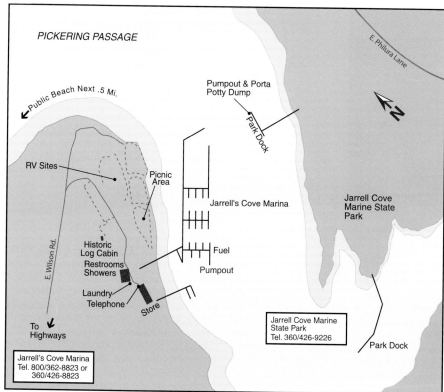

PICKERING PASSAGE

Public Beach Next .5 Mi.

RV Sites

Picnic Area

E. Wilson Rd.

Historic Log Cabin
Restrooms
Showers

Laundry
Telephone

Store

To Highways

Pumpout & Porta Potty Dump

Park Dock

Jarrell's Cove Marina

Fuel

Pumpout

E. Philura Lane

Jarrell Cove Marine State Park

Jarrell Cove Marine State Park
Tel. 360/426-9226

Park Dock

Jarrell's Cove Marina
Tel. 800/362-8823 or 360/426-8823

Jarrell's Cove

com. Open all year, 120 feet of guest moorage, 30 amp power. No fuel. Least depth 10 feet. Portable toilet on the dock, pumpout. Home to Shelton Yacht Club. Groceries, restaurants, and services are a mile away. The Port continues making improvements to the pier and uplands. Visitors welcome.

PEALE AND PICKERING PASSAGES AND CASE INLET

Pickering Passage extends northward from Totten Inlet past the west sides of Squaxin Island and Harstine Island. Mid-channel courses encounter no obstructions.

Peale Passage extends along the east side of Squaxin Island, through shallow but passable depths.

Harstine Island is connected to the mainland at Graham Point by a bridge with a mean high water vertical clearance of 31 feet.

The small marina between Jarrell Cove and Dougall Point is private and serves Harstine Island residents.

LOCAL KNOWLEDGE

SHALLOW AREA: A shallow spit at Jarrell Cove State Park extends from the point that protects the second park dock, the dock deeper in the cove. Boats sometimes cut the point too closely on low tides and go aground.

⑦ **Jarrell Cove.** Jarrell Cove is off Pickering Passage near the northwest corner of Harstine Island. Jarrell's Cove Marina and 43-acre Jarrell Cove State Marine Park occupy this pleasant, sheltered cove.

⑦ **Jarrell's Cove Marina.** 220 E. Wilson Rd., Shelton, WA 98584; (360) 426-8823. Open 7 days a week Memorial Day to Labor Day. The fuel dock has diesel and gasoline. In the winter the store is closed and fuel is by appointment. Facilities include 3 RV sites, 30 amp power, restrooms, showers, laundry,

locals "Little Skookum," to differentiate it from Hammersley Inlet, which they call "Big Skookum." Little Skookum is a pleasant exploration, but is not navigable beyond Wildcat Harbor except by dinghy. Little Skookum is one of south Puget Sound's major oyster growing areas.

HAMMERSLEY INLET AND SHELTON

Hammersley Inlet extends westward about 6 miles to **Oakland Bay** and the city of **Shelton**. A shoal blocks the entire south side of the entrance to Hammersley Inlet. The shoal has geoducks—Contributing Editor Tom Kincaid admits that he dug some one day while he was aground. Enter Hammersley Inlet on the north shore past Point Hunger-

ford, marked by a beacon with a flashing red light. As Chart 18457 shows, depths in Hammersley Inlet range from 10 to 30 feet. Currents flood in and ebb out. The strongest currents occur around Cape Horn, a sharp, constricted bend just inside the entrance. Moorage is at the Port of Shelton's Oakland Bay Marina, about a mile from Shelton.

Shelton. Shelton is the site of a major lumber mill, with rafted logs in storage in front of the town. Oakland Bay grows shallow north of Shelton, but is navigable at other than extreme low tide, and could offer anchorage on mud bottom.

⑥ **Oakland Bay Marina (Port of Shelton).** 21 W. Sanderson Way, Shelton, WA 98584; (360) 426-1425; www.portofshelton.

Jarrell Cove Marine State Park gets crowded on holiday weekends.

Jarrell's Cove Marina is a popular stop. The store has excellent snow cones.

pumpout, very limited guest moorage. Get a slip assignment from the fuel dock before landing, even for a short stay. This is a large, well-maintained marina. The store has groceries, beer, ice, some marine hardware, books, propane. The piña colada shaved ice sno-cones are popular with adults who add a little something when they get back to the boat. Lots of other flavors available, too. Gary and Lorna Hink are the owners.

⑦ Jarrell Cove Marine State Park. 391 E. Wingert Road, Shelton, WA 98584; (360) 426-9226.

Northwest end of Harstine Island. Open all year. This is a large, attractive park with 650 feet of dock space, 14 mooring buoys, clean and well-maintained restrooms and showers, pumpout, portapotty dump, picnic shelters, RV sites and standard campsites. Except for the single buoy between the inner dock and shore, mooring buoys have minimum 10 feet of water at all tides. The inner end of the outer dock can rest on mud bottom on minus tides. The outer end has sufficient depths for most drafts on all tides. Fishing, clamming, hiking, and bird watching.

Harstine Island State Park. This park is across the bay from McMicken Island. Open all year, day use only. No power, water, or toilets. At low tide you can cross to McMicken Island State Park. Anchoring only. Clamming, beachcombing.

McLane Cove. Across Pickering Passage from Jarrell Cove. Protected, quiet, lined with forest. Anchorage in 10 to 20 feet.

Stretch Island has good anchorage in the bay south of the bridge to the mainland. The bridge has a mean high water clearance of 14 feet. The channel under the bridge dries at low tide.

Stretch Point Marine State Park. On Stretch Island. Open all year, accessible only by boat. No power, water, restrooms or showers. Day use only, with 5 buoys for overnight mooring. Buoys are close to shore because of a steep dropoff. Swimming and diving, oysters and mussels, and a smooth sand beach.

The rustic shelters built behind the beach are on private land and not part of the park.

Reach Island. The southern end of Reach Island is **Fair Harbor**, location of Fair Harbor Marina. The bay has limited anchorage. The channel north of the marina, under a bridge with a mean high water clearance of 16 feet, dries on a minus tide.

⑧ Fair Harbor Marina. 5050 E. Grapeview Loop Rd., P.O. Box 160, Grapeview, WA 98546; (360) 426-4028; info@fairharbormarina.com; www.fairharbormarina.com.

Open 7 days a week in the summer, call for hours in the winter. Gasoline only at the fuel dock, 350 feet of guest moorage, 20 & 30 amp power. This is a comfortable, well-maintained marina in a lovely setting, owned and operated by Susan and Vern Nelson. Best to call ahead for moorage. Haulout, minor repairs, kerosene, alcohol, propane, snacks, charts, hardware, tackle and bait, gift shop, restroom and showers (cleanest in the area), picnic areas. Golfing at nearby Lakeland Village Golf Course can be arranged, call ahead.

⑨ Allyn Waterfront Park (Port of Allyn). P.O. Box 1, Allyn, WA 98524; (360) 275-2430; portofallyn@aol.com; www.portofallyn.com.

Open all year, launch ramp, 250 feet of moorage on a "T" shaped float at the end of a 600-foot pier, seasonal pumpout. No fuel. The float is a bit primitive. Services, shopping, restaurants, and a 24-hour paramedic station are nearby. Allyn is surrounded by shoal water, but can be approached by holding a mid-channel course until opposite the wharf, then turning in. The depth at the mooring float is 5.25 feet at zero tide. A 120-foot-long boat launch ramp eases access at low tide.

A waterfront park, grocery and liquor store, post office, restaurants, wine tasting room, and the George Kenny School of Chainsaw Carving are a short walk inland.

If you're experiencing a craving for a manly, heart-stopping burger and shake, visit Big Bubba's Burgers, an Allyn landmark.

Rocky Bay. The best anchorage is behind a small sandspit extending from Windy Bluff. Enter with caution and round the little rocky islet off the end of the spit before circling in to anchor.

Vaughn Bay. Vaughn Bay can be entered at half tide or higher. Take a mid-channel course past the end of the spit, then turn to parallel the spit until safe anchoring depths are found near the head of the bay. Jet skis and water skiers sometimes roar around during the day, but they quit at sundown and leave the bay peaceful at night. A launch ramp is on the north shore of the bay.

Herron Island. Privately owned.

⑩ McMicken Island Marine State Park. (360) 426-9226.

On Case Inlet, off the east side of Harstine Island. Open all year, day use only, no overnight camping. Toilets and 5 mooring buoys. No power, water, or showers. Mooring buoys are on the north and south sides of 11½-acre McMicken Island. The buoys on the north side are a little close to shore on minus tides. Anchorage is on either side of the island, good holding bottom.

A trail on McMicken Island leads to a nice view of the beach and surrounding waters. A sign says to watch for poison oak. An artificial reef is north of the island. Fishing, good clamming and oyster gathering, swimming. McMicken Island is accessible only by boat except on low tides, when it and Harstine Island are connected by a drying spit. The spit comes up quickly, and you could find yourself aground if you try to pass between the two islands.

⑪ Joemma State Park.

Formerly Robert F. Kennedy Recreational Area, southeast Case Inlet, just north of Whiteman Cove. Cascadia Marine Trail campsite, 500 feet of dock space in place from mid-May through mid-October, 5 mooring buoys, boat launch, good restrooms. No power, no showers. The docks are excellent. Good camping and picnic sites (including a covered shelter) on shore. Dungeness crabbing has occasionally been reported as excellent, right at the dock. The docks are exposed to southeast storms.

DRAYTON PASSAGE, PITT PASSAGE, BALCH PASSAGE

Taylor Bay. Taylor Bay, on Anderson Island, offers limited anchorage near the entrance, but is exposed to southerlies.

Oro Bay has a shallow entrance, but good anchorage is inside. Oro Bay has a tranquil, rural feeling about it. Entering, the first dock you come to is a Tacoma Yacht Club outstation. Burwell's Landing is a Bremerton Yacht Club outstation. The Oro Bay Marina is home to Oro Bay Yacht Club with some reciprocal moorage.

McMicken Island Marine State Park has mooring buoys and good anchorage.

Amsterdam Bay indents Anderson Island and is very shallow. Safe anchoring depths are right in the middle, when that spot is not already occupied by local residents' boats. The shores are rural and picturesque. If low tide isn't too low, it's a good place to spend the night. Observe a 5 mph or lower no-wake speed to prevent damage along the shoreline.

⑫ **Eagle Island Marine State Park.** (360) 426-9226. Ten-acre island on Balch Passage, off north side of Anderson Island. Open all year, day use only, 1 mooring buoy on the east side, 2 mooring buoys on the west side. No toilets, power, or water. Boat access only. Avoid the reef, marked by a buoy, off the west side of the island. Fishing and clamming. Watch for poison oak. No fires, no garbage drop, no camping.

Eagle Island is a lovely spot. Except for the current, which can roar through, this is an excellent South Sound layover location. Lots of seals, a fine view of Mt. Rainier, and good anchoring on the east side. The island is covered with dense forest, but well-maintained trails lead through the trees. Correspondents James and Jennifer Hamilton call Eagle Island "a gem." Don't be oversold, but do expect a good place to spend some time.

Filucy Bay. Filucy Bay is a popular destination and a fine anchorage. Anchor inside the spit to the south of the entrance, or in the north section, farther in. The north section

is wooded, quiet, and protected, with good holding bottom. The view of Mt. Rainier from the entrance of Filucy Bay is stunning. Longbranch Improvement Club Marina welcomes visiting boaters.

⑬ **Longbranch Improvement Club Marina.** 5213 Key Penninsula Hwy. S. Longbranch, WA 98351; (253) 884-5137; dockmaster@licweb.org; www.longbranchimprovementclub.org. Longbranch is a good South Sound stopover, and especially popular as a destination for boating club cruises. Open all year, but hours vary in winter. The marina has 760 feet of side-tie dock space for guest moorage, 30 amp power, ice, Wi-Fi, garbage drop, water, portable toilets. No showers. Cash or check only, no credit cards. No charge for 2-hour day moorage. First-come, first-served, although advance notification for groups is requested. Group cruises stack the boats in tightly, and raft several deep. The guest moorage bull rails are painted yellow. The docks have a large covered area with roll-down canvas sides, tables, chairs, barbecues, book exchange. This marina has a warm, friendly atmosphere.

If you've anchored out, the dinghy dock is on the west side of the main dock, next to the ramp. Mechanic and divers are on call. Dances are held Memorial Day and Labor Day at the historic Longbranch Improvement Club Hall, located about a half-mile away. The dances are popular and usually sell out.

Pitt Passage is a winding, shallow passage between McNeil Island and the mainland. Because the passage is shoal, many skippers avoid it. Safe transit, however, can be made by following the navigation aids between tiny Pitt Island and McNeil Island. The waters west of Pitt Island are shoal.

Red, Right, Returning assumes you are returning from the north. This means that from the north, run an S-shaped course to leave the green can Wyckoff Shoal Buoys 1 and 3 to port, then turn east across the north side of Pitt Island to leave the red Daybeacon 4 to starboard. Continue between Pitt Island and McNeil Island, to leave the red nun Buoy 6 to starboard. Study the chart carefully before

making your first run through Pitt Passage. Note how Wyckoff Shoal extends westward from McNeill Island almost across the mouth of the passage.

McNeil Island was a major state prison. It closed in 2011.

CARR INLET

⑭ **Mayo Cove.** Mayo Cove is pretty. The bay is shallow, however, and drying shoals are on either side. For exploring, take the dinghy part way up the inlet leading to Bay Lake.

⑭ **Lakebay Marina.** 15 Lorenz Road, Lakebay, WA 98349; (253) 884-3350; www.lakebaymarina.com. Located across Mayo Cove from Penrose Point Marine State Park. Open all year with 30 guest slips, 30 amp power, water, restrooms, boat launch, and a small store. Gas at the fuel dock, no diesel. Campsites and one cabin for rent. The Shipwreck Cafe is on site and has good meals. A tandem bicycle is available for overnight guests. Kayak and stand-up paddleboards can be rented.

⑭ **Penrose Point Marine State Park.** (253) 884-2514. West shore of Carr Inlet at Mayo Cove. Open for mooring and camping 7 days a week in summers; day use only in winters, except overnight mooring weekends and holidays. Dock has 304 feet of side-tie space, 8 mooring buoys, and a mooring float. The float grounds on lower tides. Facilities include Cascadia Marine Trail campsite, picnic sites, restrooms, showers, pumpout, portapotty dump, and showers. No power. Standard and primitive campsites, 2.5 miles of hiking and 2.5 miles of biking trails, clamming, oyster picking, swimming, fishing. At low tide enter the cove with care.

Von Geldern Cove. Von Geldern Cove is a shallow bay, but anchorage, exposed to northerly winds, is possible near the entrance. Most of the shoreline is residential. The town of Home, with a launch ramp, has some supplies. Take the dinghy under the bridge at the head of the bay and explore the creek until it's too shallow.

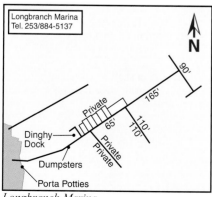

Longbranch Marina

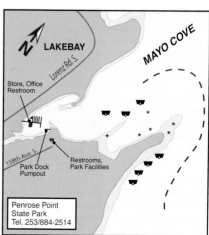

Penrose Point State Park

The shore of Wollochet Bay is lined with homes, many with docks and mooring buoys, but good anchorage is available.

Glen Cove is protected by a spit, but is very shallow and not recommended for overnight anchorage.

Rosedale. Rosedale is a small community tucked in behind **Raft Island**. Good anchorage. Enter the bay to the north of Raft Island, since a causeway connects the island to the mainland across the very shoal south side.

Cutts Island Marine State Park. (206) 265-3606. Open all year, day use only, overnight on 8 mooring buoys. Accessible by boat only. Toilets, no power or water. No camping or fires allowed. Easy row to Kopachuck Marine State Park. Cutts Island is connected to Raft Island by a drying shoal. Watch your depths if you try to cross between Cutts Island and Raft Island. We are told that in bygone days Cutts Island was an Indian burial ground, and its local name is Dead Man's Island.

⑮ **Kopachuck Marine State Park.** (253) 265-3606. Three miles north of Fox Island, just north of Horsehead Bay. Open all year for day use and overnight camping and mooring. Restrooms, showers, 3 mooring buoys. Good bottom for anchoring, but unprotected. Underwater park with artificial reef for scuba diving. Kitchen shelters, picnic sites. Standard and primitive campsites, one of which is a Cascadia Marine Trail campsite. Playground, trail, clamming, fishing. Swimming in shallow water off the beach area.

Horsehead Bay. Horsehead Bay is an excellent anchorage, surrounded by fine homes. A launch ramp is near the harbor entrance. Good holding ground is a short distance inside the bay.

Hale Passage separates Fox Island from the Olympic Peninsula, and is crossed by a bridge with a mean high water clearance of 31 feet. A short distance east of the bridge a green can buoy marks a drying, boulder-studded shoal. Pass to the north of the buoy. Currents run strongly through Hale Passage, with 1 to 2.5 knots common, flooding west and ebbing east. The ebb current is stronger than the flood.

Fox Island is connected to the mainland by a bridge with a mean high water clearance of 31 feet. Good anchorage can be found behind **Tanglewood Island**, which has a pavilion used by yacht clubs and other groups for special occasions. Residents of Fox Island are protective of their privacy, so it is a good idea to stay aboard unless invited ashore.

Wollochet Bay. Wollochet Bay winds a couple of miles into the mainland off Hale Passage. The shores of the bay are lined with homes, many with mooring buoys, but good anchorage can be found. The mouth of the bay is open to southerly winds. Inside, the waters are protected. Tacoma Yacht Club has an outstation near the head of the bay.

We've had good luck catching crab at the mouth of the bay.

A favorite pastime while visiting Wollochet Bay is launching the dinghy and exploring the saltwater marsh and estuary area at Wollochet Bay Estuary Park. The park, at the very head of the bay, has 854 linear feet of shoreline including the confluence of Artondale Creek.

Ketron Island. Privately owned.

HENDERSON INLET, NISQUALLY, STEILACOOM, TACOMA NARROWS

Henderson Inlet extends about 5 miles south from Itsami Ledge. The inlet has been the site of major logging operations over the years, and log rafts are still stored along the west side. Anchorage is good along about half of the inlet before it becomes too shallow, near the entrance to Woodward Creek.

⑯ **Zittel's Marina Inc.** 9144 Gallea St. NE, Olympia, WA 98516; (360) 459-1950;

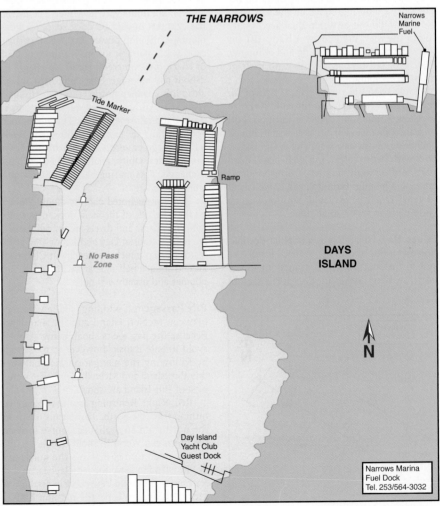

Days Island

The Gig Harbor Maritime Museum is modern and informative.

Arabella's Landing has good moorage in Gig Harbor.

www.zittelsmarina.com. Open all year, hours may vary in the winter. Gasoline and diesel at the fuel dock. Guest moorage in unoccupied slips when available (don't count on availability), 30 amp power, launch ramp, restrooms, pumpout, portapotty dump. No showers. Haulout and repairs, limited marine supplies, boat rentals, groceries, stove alcohol, bait and tackle. Owned and operated by Mike and Kathi Zittel.

Johnson Point is a popular salmon fishing area. Two launch ramps are at Johnson Point, but no facilities for visiting boaters.

Tolmie Marine State Park. (360) 753-1519. Eight miles northeast of Olympia. This 105-acre park open all year for day use and overnight moorage, except closed for day use Mondays and Tuesdays in winter. Restrooms, showers, 5 mooring buoys, no power. Buoys are well offshore; beach and shallows extend out some distance. The underwater park for scuba diving includes sunken wooden barges. Hiking trails, picnic sites with kitchens. Nice sandy beach. The park includes a small saltwater lagoon marsh area good for watching wildlife. No camping.

Nisqually Reach is the body of water south of Anderson Island, between the island and the mainland. The channel is marked by buoys along the extensive mudflats of the Nisqually River delta. The delta is a wildlife refuge, and is accessible by boat at half tide or better, by way of the Luhrs Beach launch ramp near Nisqually Head. Contributing Editor Tom Kincaid has entered the river itself by dinghy, but from the water side the entrance is hard to spot.

⑰ **Steilacoom.** Picnic area on a small pebble beach, launch ramp, float, and fishing pier. Steilacoom, incorporated in 1854, is the oldest incorporated town in Washington. A museum, restaurant, and other services are nearby.

Tacoma Narrows. All of the water in southern Puget Sound flows through Tacoma Narrows, with 4- to 6-knot currents common. Day Island Yacht Club, Narrows Marina, and Day Island Marina are on the east side of the south end of the Narrows. The Tacoma Narrows bridges, more than a mile long and 180 feet above the water, are two of the world's longest suspension bridges.

Back eddies form along the sides of the narrows, useful when transiting with an opposing current.

⑱ **Narrows Marina (Days Island).** 9007 S. 19th St. Suite 100, Tacoma, WA 98466; (253) 564-3032; nmbt@narrowsmarina.com; www.narrowsmarina.com. Open all year, with gasoline and diesel fuel. Limited guest moorage in unoccupied slips, call ahead. Restrooms, concrete launch ramp, long term parking, convenience store, charts, hardware, tackle and bait. Full service repairs. This is a large fishing and marine-oriented facility.

The fuel dock is on the east shore at the mouth of the lagoon between Days Island and Tacoma. The fuel dock is not obvious if you haven't been there before. Approaching, turn to port and run along the wooden breakwater that protects covered moorage. This route and the fuel dock have adequate depths at all tides.

If your destination is the Day Island Yacht Club at the back of the lagoon, run down the west side, close to Days Island and its boathouses. At lower tides this will be obvious, because a big drying shoal blocks the middle. Time your passage for mid-tide or higher. Least depth at zero tide is said to be 4 feet.

In 2012 the dockside Boathouse 19 restaurant opened. The top of the bar is made from the old Day Island Bridge and the table tops are from Nalley Valley pickle barrels.

Titlow Park. Tacoma Narrows Waterway. Located on the Tacoma side, about 1 mile south of the Tacoma Narrows Bridge. Open all year, mooring buoys, park with swimming pool, volleyball and tennis courts. Restaurants a short walk away. Titlow Park is a marine preserve with excellent diving.

CENTRAL PUGET SOUND

LOCAL KNOWLEDGE

SPEED LIMIT: A no-wake speed of 5 mph or less is enforced within Gig Harbor and 200 feet outside the entrance.

⑲ **Gig Harbor.** www.gigharborguide.com. Gig Harbor is one of the most perfectly protected harbors in Puget Sound, and one of the most charming towns. The south shore is lined with moorages for the substantial commercial fish boat and pleasure boat fleets. The entrance to Gig Harbor is narrow, especially at low tide. Maintain a mid-channel course around the end of the spit.

Gig Harbor has overnight moorage, marine supplies, major repairs, and haulout. Beacon/BBX Wi-Fi covers much of the bay. Anchorage is in 20 to 42 feet with good holding, although the bay shoals close to both shores and toward the head. In some areas, weed on the bottom can foul anchors.

CHARTS	
18441	Puget Sound – Northern Part (1:80,000)
18445 sc folio small-craft	Puget Sound-Possession Sound to Olympia including Hood Canal
18446	Puget Sound – Apple Cove Pt. to Keyport (1:25,000) & Agate Passage (1:10,000)
18447 sc folio small-craft	Lake Washington Ship Canal (1:10,000) & Lake Washington (1:25,000)
18448	Puget Sound – Southern Portion (1:80,000)
18449	Puget Sound – Seattle to Bremerton (1:25,000)
18453	Tacoma Harbor (1:15,000)
18474	Puget Sound – Shilshole Bay to Commencement Bay (1:40,000)

The City of Gig Harbor maintains Jerisich Park with its dinghy dock, long moorage float, and holding tank pumpout.

We enjoy walking up and down Gig Harbor's village-like commercial streets. The shops, galleries, and antiquing are excellent, and the architecture turn-of-the-20th-century. At least two shops serve enormous ice cream cones and have chairs out front where you can enjoy your treat in the shade. Several good restaurants, from casual to elegant. On the casual side, Tides Tavern, a short distance inside the mouth of the bay, is a longtime favorite. If you are lucky, you'll find room to tie the boat at their private dock. More likely, you'll take the dinghy or approach by land.

For a great view of Gig Harbor and Mt. Rainier, the local Lions Club built an observation area called the Finholm View Climb. The stairway is at the head of the bay, across the street from Anthony's Restaurant.

The recently renovated Gig Harbor History Museum (www.harborhistorymuseum.org) is superb. Located at the west end of Harborview Drive, the main road along the waterfront. Pleasant walk from Jerisich Park.

⑲ **Arabella's Landing.** 3323 Harborview Drive, Gig Harbor, WA 98335; (253) 851-1793; arabellas@harbornet.com; arabellaslanding.com. Open all year, guest moorage along 220 feet of dock, six 50-foot slips and two 60-foot slips, 30 & limited 50 amp power, Beacon/BBX Wi-Fi, restrooms, showers, laundry, secured gate, pumpout. Stan and Judy Stearns developed this classy marina, located a short distance past the city dock, close to shopping, restaurants, services, groceries. They have a well-trained crew to help with landings and make life pleasant. New on-site store, Ship to Shore Marine, carries marine supplies, groceries, ice.

The marina can accommodate boats larger than 100 feet. It has excellent concrete docks, impeccable lawns, lush flower gardens, brick walkways, complete wheelchair access, and a clubhouse and lounge for group gatherings. The moorage fee includes power and showers. Reservations recommended.

Bayview Marina, just east of Arabella's

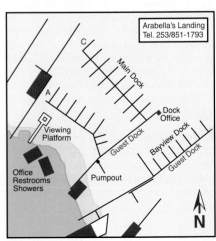

Arabella's Landing

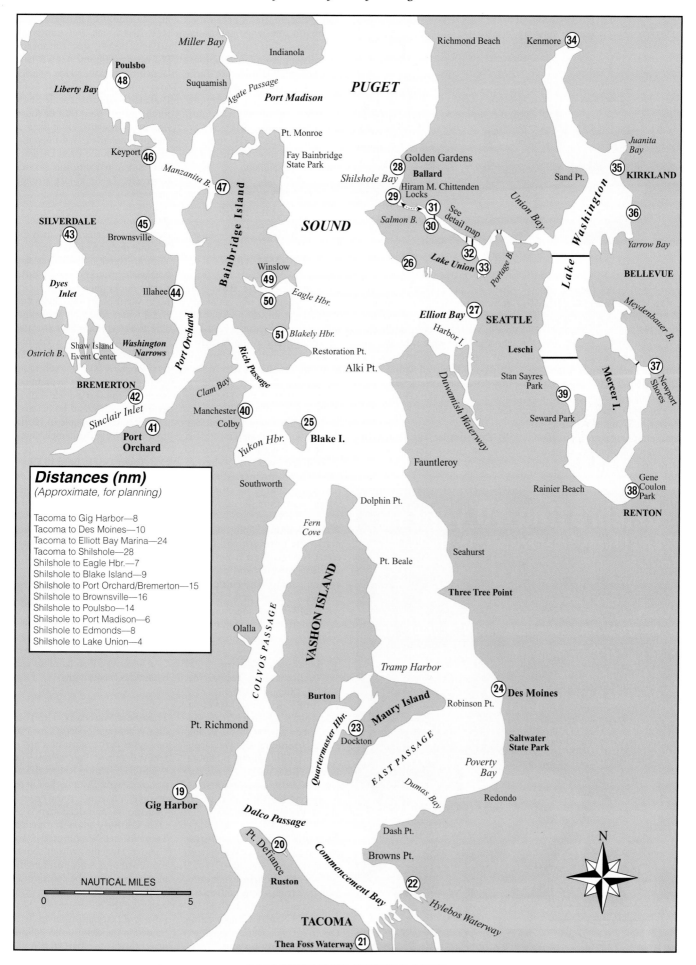

Miller Bay

Indianola

Poulsbo 48

Liberty Bay

Suquamish

Agate Passage

Port Madison

Richmond Beach

Kenmore 34

PUGET

Pt. Monroe

Fay Bainbridge
State Park

Keyport 46

Manzanita B.

47

Golden Gardens

Ballard

28 *Shilshole Bay*

Hiram M. Chittenden
Locks

29

31 See
detail map

30 *Salmon B.*

Juanita
Bay

35 **KIRKLAND**

Sand Pt.

Union Bay

36

Yarrow Bay

SILVERDALE

43

45

Brownsville

Bainbridge Island

SOUND

26

Lake Union 33

32

Portage B.

Lake Washington

BELLEVUE

*Dyes
Inlet*

Illahee 44

Winslow
49

50

Eagle Hbr.

Port Orchard

51 *Blakely Hbr.*

Elliott Bay 27

Harbor I.

SEATTLE

Meydenbauer B.

37 *Newport
Shores*

*Washington
Narrows*

Ostrich B. Shaw Island
Event Center

Restoration Pt.

Alki Pt.

Leschi

Stan Sayres
Park

Mercer I.

Rich Passage

Duwamish Waterway

39

Seward Park

BREMERTON

42

Clam Bay

Manchester 40

Colby

25

Blake I.

Fauntleroy

Rainier Beach

Gene
Coulon
Park

38

Sinclair Inlet

41

**Port
Orchard**

Yukon Hbr.

Southworth

Dolphin Pt.

Seahurst

RENTON

Distances (nm)
(Approximate, for planning)

Tacoma to Gig Harbor—8
Tacoma to Des Moines—10
Tacoma to Elliott Bay Marina—24
Tacoma to Shilshole—28
Shilshole to Eagle Hbr.—7
Shilshole to Blake Island—9
Shilshole to Port Orchard/Bremerton—15
Shilshole to Brownsville—16
Shilshole to Poulsbo—14
Shilshole to Port Madison—6
Shilshole to Edmonds—8
Shilshole to Lake Union—4

*Fern
Cove*

Pt. Beale

Three Tree Point

VASHON ISLAND

COLVOS PASSAGE

Tramp Harbor

24 **Des Moines**

Olalla

Robinson Pt.

**Saltwater
State Park**

Pt. Richmond

Burton

Quartermaster Hbr.

23

Dockton

Maury Island

EAST PASSAGE

*Poverty
Bay*

Dumas Bay

Redondo

19

Gig Harbor

Dalco Passage

Pt. Defiance

20

Ruston

Dash Pt.

Browns Pt.

Commencement Bay

22

Hylebos Waterway

NAUTICAL MILES

0   5

N

TACOMA

Thea Foss Waterway 21

Tides Tavern has moorage for diners, 4 hours no charge.

Landing, is under the same ownership, with 300 feet of dock, 30 & 50 amp power and water on the dock.

⑲ **Jerisich Park.** 3211 Harborview Drive, Gig Harbor, WA; (253) 851-6170; www.cityofgigharbor.net. Open all year, 420 feet of dock space, no water or power, maximum 48-hour no-charge moorage, no reservations, free seasonal pumpout. This is an attractive and well-used public

dock and park, located just west of Tides Tavern on the downtown side of Gig Harbor. Excellent dock, with a dinghy dock near shore on the west side. Restaurants, groceries, restrooms, and portapotty dump all within walking distance. Check your tide table; close to shore you could touch at low tide.

⑲ **Peninsula Yacht Basin.** 8913 N. Harborview Drive, Gig Harbor, WA 98332; (253) 858-

2250; dockmaster@peninsula-yachtbasin.com; www.peninsula-yachtbasin.com. Open all year, no transient moorage, reciprocal privileges with Gig Harbor Yacht Club only. Maximum boat length 85 feet, 6-foot depth at zero tide, 20 & 30 amp power, restrooms, showers, Beacon/BBX Wi-Fi. Located on the north shore of Gig Harbor, next to Anthony's Shoreline Restaurant.

TACOMA AREA

Commencement Bay. The southern shoreline of Commencement Bay is mostly parks, interspersed with buildings, housing, restaurants, and other facilities. At least two restaurants provide moorage for their patrons. Following this shoreline southeastward leads into the Thea Foss Waterway.

Tacoma's Commencement Bay is busy with commercial traffic. Most visiting boats choose to moor in the Thea Foss Waterway, with several marinas. Museums, restaurants, and other attractions a short walk from the docks.

Point Defiance. Point Defiance marks the northern end of Tacoma Narrows and is noted for swirling currents and excellent salmon fishing. The entire point is a major Tacoma park, complete with trails, a zoo, aquarium, gardens, sports facilities, and picnic areas.

⑳ **Breakwater Marina.** 5603 N. Waterfront Drive, Tacoma, WA 98407; (253) 752-6663; (253) 752-6685; www.breakwatermarina.com. Certified Clean Marina. Open all year, 15 & 30 amp power, restrooms, showers, laundry, portapotty dump, pumpout, Beacon/BBX Wi-Fi. *The fuel dock closed in 2013.* Guest moorage is in unoccupied slips only, so call ahead. Repairs available.

⑳ **Point Defiance Boathouse Marina.** 5912 N. Waterfront Drive, Tacoma, WA 98407; (253) 591-5325; boathouse@tacomaparks.com; www.metroparkstacoma.org. Certified Clean Marina and 5-Star EnviroStar rating. Open 7 days a week all year except Thanksgiving and Christ-

mas. Ethanol-free gasoline available. Restrooms, free pumpout, 30 amp power, guest moorage (72 hour maximum stay), 8-lane launch ramp. Bait, tackle, snacks, souvenirs and gift items at Point Defiance Boathouse Tackle Shop. Public fishing pier. Harbor tours. Anthony's Restaurant is at the east end of the marina. Within walking distance of the Point Defiance Zoo and Aquarium. Bus service to greater Tacoma. Dry storage available.

Ruston. Ruston is about 2 miles east of Point Defiance. This is the Tacoma terminus of the ferry to Vashon Island. The smelter slag breakwater protects Tacoma Yacht Club's docks (members of reciprocal yacht clubs welcome) and Breakwater Marina's moorage. The Point Defiance Boathouse Marina and Anthony's Harbor Lights restaurant are west of the ferry dock. A large launch ramp operated by the Parks Department is east of the ferry dock. Long-term tow vehicle and trailer storage is available a couple of blocks up the hill from the launch ramp.

Old Town Dock. Next to Commencement Park. The docks are usable, but don't appear to get much traffic. Smaller boats only. Johnnie's Ocean Fish Co. fish market and deli is at the head of the dock and The Lobster Shop is at the west end of the park.

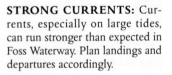

LOCAL KNOWLEDGE

STRONG CURRENTS: Currents, especially on large tides, can run stronger than expected in Foss Waterway. Plan landings and departures accordingly.

Thea Foss Waterway. The Thea Foss Waterway (formerly City Waterway) is in the midst of a major renewal and revitalization. The magnificent Union Railroad Station on Pacific Avenue has been restored and rebuilt as the Federal Courthouse, and decorated with Dale Chihuly glass sculpture. The must-see Washington State History Museum, which shares the courthouse's beautiful architecture, is next to the courthouse.

Just inside the mouth of the waterway the Foss Waterway Seaport is a fascinating stop. It is housed in the century-old Balfour warehouse, once part of a mile-

long row of wheat warehouses. The 300-foot-long by 150-foot-wide building itself is a museum exhibit. Displays inside include a lab, a working boatbuilding shop, Willits canoe exhibit, marine biology exhibit, and an extensive display detailing Puget Sound's maritime history. Some 1200 feet of public floats make boat access easy.

At the head of the waterway, the Museum of Glass fronts on the waterway, immediately east of the courthouse and the Washington State History Museum.

The Washington State History Museum is excellent. Allow at least two hours to see it; three or four hours is better. Adult or child, it's a knockout.

The Tacoma Art Museum features regularly rotating exhibits, and the building itself is a work of architectural art.

The Chihuly Bridge of Glass connects the courthouse and history museum complex with the Museum of Glass. You can spend several hours there. The hot shop furnaces roar, and the crew may create a bowl, a vase, or candlestick holders before your eyes. Exhibits in the galleries rotate. The works on display are exciting.

LeMay-America's Car Museum, across the

road from the Tacoma Dome, opened in 2012 and has been drawing large crowds from the beginning. More than 350 cars, trucks and motorcycles are on display, dating from the beginning of motorized transport. Founding Editor Bob Hale and his wife spent more than four hours at the museum and could have stayed longer. Hale warns that men in their 60s and 70s are apt to be lost in memories of the post-WWII car craze—their first adventures and their missed opportunities. Open 7 days a week, 10:00 a.m. to 5:00 p.m. Highly recommended.

Downtown Tacoma is very different from other Puget Sound cities. Many of the old buildings are beautiful, and some are historic. One building has a plaque commemorating Russell G. O'Brien, who, on October 18, 1893, originated the custom of standing during the playing of the Star Spangled Banner. We learn the most interesting things when we walk around.

Guest moorage: Modern, 30-slip Dock Street Marina, with guest moorage, is in front of the Museum of Glass. Guest moorage is also available at Foss Harbor Marina. Train lovers will enjoy passing freight trains during the night.

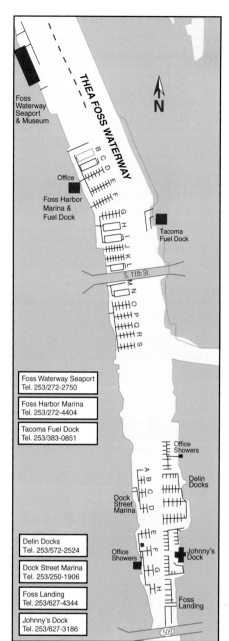

Thea Foss Waterway

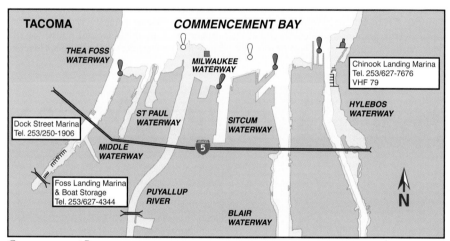

Commencement Bay

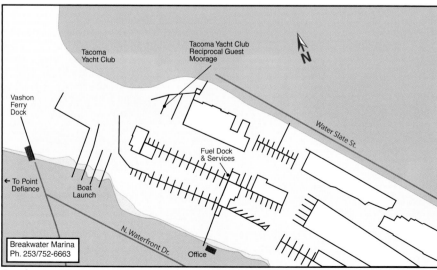

Breakwater Marina

Another alternative is to anchor off Old Town or Ruston, and take the dinghy down the waterway.

Supermarket: The well-stocked IGA City Grocer market, with deli, wine and liquor, is on Pacific Avenue at the corner of 13th Street. Ride light rail to the Commerce Street stop, walk down the hill on 15th Street to Pacific Avenue, and turn right. Open 7:00 a.m. to 10:00 p.m.

Farmers market: On Broadway between 9th and 11th Streets, a farmers market with 70 to 90 vendors sets up Thursday mornings during the summer months.

Light rail: Free light rail runs from the theater district at the north end of downtown Tacoma to a last stop, 2½ blocks from the Tacoma Dome and LeMay-America's Car Museum. At the museum district, the tracks are in the middle of Pacific Avenue, fronting the Washington State History Museum. The trains are clean and safe. They run every few minutes from morning to evening.

THINGS TO DO

1. LeMay-America's Car Museum. This museum is housed in a dramatic building, just up from the waterfront. See over 350 cars, trucks and motorcycles on display in the world's largest auto museum.

2. Museum of Glass. With its iconic architecture near the waterfront and beautiful glasswork, this has become a key part of the Tacoma art scene.

3. Tacoma Art Museum. Art in Tacoma continues with photography, paintings, Chihuly glass.

4. Tacoma Glassblowing Studio. See how glass art is made.

5. Point Defiance Zoo & Aquarium. See an Asian Forest Sanctuary, elephants and tigers. The large aquarium has octopi, sharks, and a beluga whale.

㉑ Foss Waterway Seaport. 705 Dock St, Tacoma, WA 98402; (253) 272-2750 ext. 106; earla.harding@fosswaterwayseaport.

LeMay-America's Car Museum is located close to the Thea Foss Waterway in this distinctive building.

org; www.fosswaterwayseaport.org. Located at the mouth of Foss Waterway. Visitor moorage along 1200 feet of floating dock, 30 & 50 amp power, water. Reservations only for groups. Payment is made at the Seaport office, or drop box after hours, 4-hour free stay. No public restrooms or garbage drop. Pumpout available.

㉑ Foss Harbor Marina. 821 Dock Street, Tacoma, WA 98402; (253) 272-4404; info@fossharbor.com; www.fossharbormarina.com. Certified Clean Marina. Monitors VHF 71. Open all year, gasoline and diesel at end of D dock. Visitor moorage to 95 feet in unoccu-

pied slips. Restrooms, showers, laundry, water, pumpout, portapotty dump, 30 & 50 amp power, free Wi-Fi. The restrooms have been redone and two showers have been added. The docks have been redecked and improved, and are excellent. Store has expanded beer and wine selection, deli sandwiches, bait, tackle, marine supplies, propane, in office store. Walk to downtown.

㉑ Dock Street Marina. 1817 Dock St., Tacoma, WA 98402; (253) 250-1906; info@dockstreetmarina.com; www.dockstreetmarina.com. Call ahead by cell phone for slip assignment. Certified Clean Marina. Concrete

docks, security gates, 30, 50 & 100 amp power, water, pumpout, garbage, recycling drop, laundry, restrooms, free showers, free cable TV, some wheelchair access, kayak rentals. This is the new marina in front of the Museum of Glass. It is made up of two sets of docks—the southern, guest moorage docks in front of the Albers Mill building, and the permanent moorage 17th St. docks immediately north.

The office, showers, and laundry are at the Albers Mill guest moorage docks, 30 slips 36-60 feet, with 127-foot pier ends. Concierge service. Pet-friendly. Reservations recommended. Moorage in the north docks is by assignment in unoccupied slips only. A 320-foot dock is in the north moorage.

㉑ **Dock Street North Pier.** This is the long, ill-maintained wooden float north of Dock Street Marina. No power or water, day use only. Watch your depths at zero tide or lower.

㉑ **Delin Docks.** 1616 East D St., Tacoma, WA 98421; (253) 572-2524; info@delindocksmarina.com; www.delindocksmarina.com. Open all year, 30 & 50 amp power, water, restrooms, free showers, laundry, pumpout, portapotty dump. Certified Clean Marina. These are new docks with 30- to 60-foot slips, located immediately north of Johnny's Dock on the east side of Foss Waterway. They're primarily permanent moorage, although unoccupied slips might be used for guest moorage.

Note: Dock Street Marina and the Delin Docks are under the same management.

㉑ **Johnny's Dock.** 1900 East D St., Tacoma, WA 98421; (253) 627-3186; www.johnnysdock.com. Open all year with moorage to 55 feet, power, and water. Transient moorage primarily serves Johnny's Dock restaurant.

㉑ **Tacoma Fuel Dock.** 820 East D St., Tacoma, WA 98421; (253) 383-0851; (800) 868-3681, www.cbmsi.com. Fuel dock open all year except Thanksgiving, Christmas, and New Year's Day. Summer hours 8:00 a.m. to dusk, winter hours 8:00 a.m. to 4:30 p.m. Monitors VHF 69, summer only. Gasoline, diesel, ice, frozen herring, soft drinks, snacks. Located on the east side of Thea Foss Waterway; look for the large Tacoma Fuel Dock sign. The uplands house Commencement Bay Marine Services and the Tacoma Youth Marine Center, training young people in the skills needed for work on boats and along the waterfront.

Hylebos Waterway. The Hylebos Waterway follows the north shore of Commencement Bay and includes a number of moorages, boat builders, and boat service businesses. The shores are lined with heavy industry of many kinds, not all of it scenic. Still, an interesting exploration.

Guest moorage is at Chinook Landing Marina, a short distance up the waterway.

You can walk to the Tacoma Museum of Glass from the Dock Street Marina.

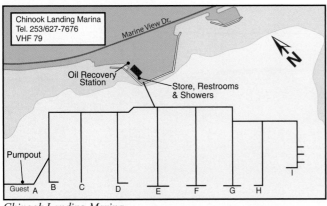

Chinook Landing Marina

Des Moines Marina is protected by a rock breakwater.

㉒ **Chinook Landing Marina.** 3702 Marine View Drive Suite 100, Tacoma, WA 98422; (253) 627-7676. Monitors VHF 79. Certified Clean Marina. Open all year, guest moorage available. This is an excellent facility, 30 & 50 amp power, restrooms, showers, laundry, pumpout, portapotty dump, 24-hour security. Larger boats should call ahead for availability.

Browns Point Park. Open all year, day use only and overnight mooring. Has 3 mooring buoys, picnic tables, and a swimming beach. The lighthouse is the focal point.

VASHON ISLAND, COLVOS PASSAGE, EAST PASSAGE, DES MOINES, BLAKE ISLAND

Colvos Passage. The current always flows north in Colvos Passage, so heading north on a flood tide is a good choice. Colvos Passage offers little to entice a boater to stop, although Contributing Editor Tom Kincaid has anchored off Olalla and dinghied to the little store for a snack.

Harper State Park. Located 1.5 miles west of the ferry landing at Southworth. Open all year, day use only. Anchoring only. The gravel launch ramp is usable at high tide only, but is the closest launch to Blake Island, 1 mile away.

Quartermaster Harbor. Quartermaster Harbor indents the south end of Vashon Island about 4 miles. It is protected on the east side by Maury Island, which connects to Vashon Island by a narrow spit of land. Dockton Park is a popular destination.

Anchorage is good throughout most of Quartermaster Harbor, including the village of Burton, beyond Burton Peninsula. Anchorage at Burton is well-protected with excellent holding on a sticky mud bottom. Be prepared to spend extra time cleaning the anchor and chain. The Quartermaster Yacht Club (members of reciprocal clubs welcomed) is at Burton, as is the Quartermaster Marina, but it discourages visitor boats. The village of Burton has a well-stocked convenience store and several small shops. Taxi service is available on Vashon Island, and buses run to Tacoma and Seattle.

㉓ **Dockton Park.** 9500 SW Dock Road, Dockton, WA 98070; (206) 463-9602; www.vashonparkdistrict.org. Open all year, concrete launch ramp, 58 guest slips, rafting okay, restrooms, showers, pumpout and portapotty dump (March through October only), no power, no garbage pickup, no services

within walking distance. Dockton is a popular 23-acre park on the west side of Maury Island in Quartermaster Harbor. The park has play equipment, trails, bandstand, fire pits, picnic tables, barbecue areas. Group reservations call (206) 296-4287.

About two blocks down 260th street, which runs eastward just above the dock, trailheads lead southward into DNR property with one of the largest madrona forests in the area.

Anchoring note: Holding can be fair to poor in the area north of the Dockton Park docks. If anchoring, be sure of your set.

East Passage is between Vashon Island and the mainland. Large ships bound to or from Tacoma or Olympia use this route. Tidal currents flood south and ebb north, and normally are a little stronger in East Passage than in Colvos Passage on the west side of Vashon Island.

Dash Point State Park. 5700 SW Dash Point Rd., Federal Way, WA 98023; (253) 661-4955. Open all year, 398 acres, restrooms, showers, no power. Sandy beach, swimming, and primitive, partial utility, and full utility campsites.

Redondo. A new launch ramp, with 2 floats and a floating breakwater, is operated by the city of Des Moines.

Saltwater Marine State Park. 25205 8th Place South #1, Des Moines, WA 98198; (253) 661-4956. Two miles south of Des Moines. Open all year, 2 mooring buoys, overnight camping. Restrooms, showers, no power. Artificial reef for scuba diving, and outside shower for scuba rinse-off. Great sand bottom swimming beach. The mooring buoys are exposed to southerly winds. Vault toilets, primitive campsites, picnic tables and shelters, kitchen shelter, children's play equipment. Seasonal concession stand.

Maury Island Marine Park. 5405 SE 244th Street, Dockton, WA . This is a relatively new 300-acre park at the site of what once was a sand and gravel operation, 1.5 miles south of Point Robinson. Trails lead through the park. The anchorage, with fair holding, is well protected in a northerly breeze. Popular with locals. On sunny days

Des Moines Marina has been upgraded in recent years. It's a good stop, with restaurants and shopping up the hill.

the winds are warmed as they cross Maury Island, making for good sunbathing. Operated by King County Parks.

Point Robinson. Point Robinson is surrounded by a 10-acre county park that can be approached by dinghy. The lighthouse is beautiful and the park has a nice beach, but no facilities for boaters.

Tramp Harbor, where Vashon Island joins Maury Island, has convenient anchoring depths, but only minimal protection from winds, particularly from the north. It is seldom used for overnight anchorage.

㉔ **Des Moines.** The City of Des Moines, between Tacoma and Seattle, is a good destination for clubs and groups. The City of Des Moines Marina has recently been renovated.

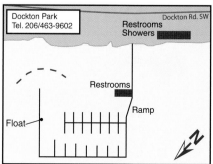

Dockton Park

Des Moines Marina fuel dock

The Blake Island State Park marina. The tour boat, far right, brings guests from Seattle to Tillicum Village on Blake Island.

Full services are available.

Des Moines Beach Park is next to the marina and provides boater beach access.

㉔ City of Des Moines Marina. 22307 Dock Ave. S., Des Moines, WA 98188; (206) 824-5700; info@desmoinesmarina.com; www.desmoinesmarina.com. Monitors VHF 16, switch to 68. Certified Clean Marina. Open all year. Gasoline, diesel, propane, 30 amp power, Wi-Fi. This 840-slip marina and public pier has 1500 feet of guest moorage, much of it side-tie for boats to 100 feet. Maximum boat length in permanent slips is 54 feet. Channel depth is 10 feet at zero tide. Stop at the fuel dock for directions to an empty berth. Restrooms, free showers, 1 free pumpout. Reservations accepted for boats 32 feet and larger, or groups of 5 or more boats, 1 to 7 days in advance.

The marina can assist yacht club or rendezvous with planning and special needs, including free shuttle service.

The marina has undergone a major renovation. The permanent docks were unchanged, but the guest moorage area now has a 25×100-foot concrete activity float with shelter, and all new concrete floats. An 80-foot-long ADA-compliant ramp has been installed. The boatlift was removed. The grounds have been landscaped. Des Moines, already a popular destination for clubs and groups, is now even more attractive.

All services, including laundry, groceries, and several restaurants, are within walking distance. Shuttle service by request. The 670-foot public fishing pier runs east-west. To enter the marina leave the fishing pier to port and turn to starboard at the north end of the breakwater. At low tide the entrance is tight, especially with opposing traffic. At the south end of the marina Des Moines Yacht Club has guest moorage for visiting members of reciprocal clubs.

Farmers market on Saturdays, June through October. July 4th "Fireworks over Des Moines."

CSR Marine, a highly regarded boatyard on Seattle's Lake Washington Ship Canal, operates the repair yard at the Des Moines Marina. Travelift haulout to 25 tons.

Yukon Harbor offers good anchorage, well protected from the south but open to the northeast.

㉕ Blake Island Marine State Park. (360) 371-8330. Open all year, 475 acres with 1500 feet of dock space in the breakwater-protected marina, and 24 mooring buoys around the island. Pumpout, water, 30 amp power. No garbage drop. Moorage is limited to 7 consecutive days. Mooring buoys on the south side of the island are restricted to boats less than 37 feet, limits posted on buoys. Blake Island is just a short hop from Elliott Bay Marina or Shilshole Bay Marina. The park is accessible only by boat, and is one of the most popular stops on Puget Sound. Trails

crisscross the island. Wildlife is abundant.

Blake Island has primitive campsites, including a Cascadia Marine Trail campsite. An underwater reef is good for scuba diving. The park has picnic shelters, volleyball courts, nature trail, approximately 16 miles of hiking trails through dense forest, and 5 miles of shoreline to explore. The Tillicum Village restaurant is a replica of an Indian longhouse. It is open only when tours are scheduled, and features dinner of salmon cooked on sticks facing an open fire. Tours include dinner and a show with dancing and masks, and compares favorably with the show at Alert Bay. Call Argosy Tours (888) 623-1445; (206) 623-1445, www.tillicumvillage.com.

The marina is on the northeast shore of the island. To enter, follow the dredged channel marked by red and green beacons. The water is shoal on both sides of the beacons; stay in the marked channel. Immediately inside the breakwater, one float is for the boat that brings guests to Tillicum Village, and another is for the State Parks boat. The rest of the floats are available on a first-come, first-served basis. Expect to find them full during high season and on weekends any time of the year.

A gem of a park.

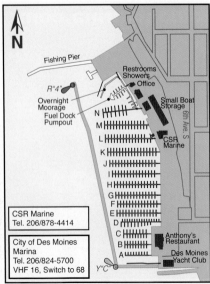

City of Des Moines Marina

Blake Island Marine State Park

Mount Rainier is a prominent landmark throughout south and central Puget Sound. This is the Seattle waterfront from Bell Harbor Marina.

SEATTLE

Elliott Bay, the center of Seattle's shipping industry, is a busy ocean port. Keep a sharp watch for ferries coming and going from Colman Dock, for tugs with tows, and for commercial vessels of all kinds. Large vessels are slow to maneuver, and should always be given a wide berth. When there's any doubt at all, *any* doubt, cross *behind* commercial vessels, not in front of them.

Piers 89, 90, and 91 in Smith Cove are heavily used by commercial ships. The Port of Seattle's grain terminal occupies part of the shoreline north of the regular commercial piers. Myrtle Edwards Park, including a fishing pier, stretches along about a mile of the Elliott Bay waterfront. The piers on the central waterfront, too small for modern maritime commerce, have been converted to other uses, including a hotel, shops, museums, an aquarium, and places to sit and watch the harbor activity.

At Pier 36, south of the Colman ferry dock, the U.S. Coast Guard has its Seattle headquarters, including the Coast Guard Museum and Vessel Traffic Service.

Downtown Seattle is served by two excellent marinas: Elliott Bay Marina on the north shore below Magnolia Bluff, and Port of Seattle's Bell Harbor Marina at Pier 66. These two marinas make downtown Seattle easy and safe to visit.

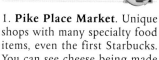

THINGS TO DO

1. **Pike Place Market**. Unique shops with many specialty food items, even the first Starbucks. You can see cheese being made at Beechers. Watch out for flying salmon in the market. Don't miss the nearby Olympic Sculpture Park.

2. **Seattle Aquarium.** See a coral reef, giant Pacific octopus, pinecone fish, and potbellied seahorses. Located at Pier 59, a few blocks south of Bell Harbor Marina.

3. **Seattle Art Museum (SAM)**. Locally curated exhibits and rotating exhibitions from the best art collections of the world.

4. **Fremont Farmers Market**. Year round on Sundays in this funky neighborhood. You never know what you might find.

5. **Burke-Gilman Trail**. Rent a bike and see Seattle from Shilshole to Kenmore, mostly along the city's lakefront. Some detours on streets through Ballard.

6. **Seattle Center**. Tour the Space Needle, EMP—the Experience Music Project—and the new Chihuly Garden and Glass museum.

7. **Pacific Science Center** at **Seattle Center**. Enjoy the IMAX Theater, the Planetarium or unique exhibits. Great for kids and adults.

8. **Tillicum Village, Blake Island**. Take your boat to Blake Island State Park and make a reservation for a tribal salmon buffet dinner and show. Experience the Coast Salish people through storytelling and dance.

9. **Center for Wooden Boats**. Walk around the antique restored boats on South Lake Union. With membership and checkout you can even rent a classic sailboat or powerboat for a cruise on lake.

10. **Museum of History and Industry (MOHAI)**. Newly relocated to South Lake Union. Many exhibits on the heritage of Seattle.

11. **Kenmore Air Tour**. What better way to learn the islands and waterways of this spectacular cruising area than from the air? Stay local or take an extended flight from Lake Union to the San Juan Islands and back.

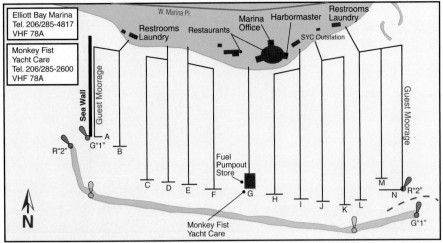

Elliott Bay Marina

12. **Museum of Flight**. A short taxi ride away is one of the nation's best flight museums. The Concorde, WWII aircraft, a Space Shuttle Simulator, and more.

13. **Seattle Zoo**. An outstanding zoo for the day or an afternoon, just a cab ride away.

㉖ **Elliott Bay Marina.** 2601 W. Marina Place, Seattle, WA 98199; (206) 285-4817; info@elliottbaymarina.net; www.elliottbaymarina.net. Monitors VHF 78A. Certified Clean Marina. This is a beautiful marina, immaculately maintained, open all year. The fuel dock has gasoline, diesel, free pumpout, and a store with light groceries. Forty guest slips and unoccupied slips, first-come, first-served. Reservations can be made for vessels 50 feet and longer. The marina has Beacon/BBX Wi-Fi, free cable TV, 30 & 50 amp power, up to 150 amp on outside moorage, restrooms, free showers, laundry, pumpout, free use of kayaks and bikes, and excellent 24-hour security.

Enter through either end of the breakwater. The marina office is on the ground level of the main building, near Maggie Bluffs café. A concierge service can book reservations at other marinas, get float plane tickets, help with routes, set up repairs, and more. Elegant dining at Palisade Waterfront Restaurant and casual dining at Maggie Bluffs. The fuel dock has a mini-mart. It's 5 minutes by car to downtown Seattle.

The marina is headquarters for the Downtown Sailing Series, 10 informal races Thursday nights during the summer, with barbecue and awards afterward.

A bike and walking path runs from the marina along scenic Myrtle Edwards waterfront park to the downtown waterfront. We took about an hour each way to walk between the marina and Pier 70. Seattle Yacht Club has an outstation (no reciprocal moorage) at the marina. Views of downtown, Mt. Rainier, Olympic Mountains.

㉗ **Bell Harbor Marina.** Pier 66, 2203 Alaskan Way, Seattle, WA 98121; (206) 787-3952; (800) 426-7817; bhm@portseattle.org; www.portseattle.org. Monitors VHF 66A. Certified Clean Marina. Open all year, 30 & 50 amp power, water, restrooms, free showers, garbage/recycling drop, pumpout, 24-hour security, free Wi-Fi. Entrance at 47°36.55'N/122°20.85'W—look for the distinctive spire as a landmark. Moorage reservations can be made by telephone or email. Checkout time is noon; check-in is 1:00 p.m.

The Port of Seattle's Bell Harbor Marina is part of Seattle's Central Waterfront Development, and has made downtown Seattle an easy cruising destination. Depending on the mix, the docks will hold as many as 70 visitor boats, 30 to 150 feet. The waterfront, with the Seattle Aquarium, a variety of shops, and the new Seattle Great Wheel, is just outside the marina. It's a safe, 2-block walk to the excitement of Pike Place Market.

Visitors can leave their boat at Bell Harbor and take in a ballgame at Safeco Field or CenturyLink Field. Three restaurants and a convenience store are just above the marina with many more restaurants within walking distance.

Bell Harbor's facilities are top-notch, with excellent wheelchair access. The staff is professional and alert.

Because of rough water in Elliott Bay, the breakwater entry is narrow. Boats larger than 70 feet will find the entry and turning basin a little tight. Approximately 1900 feet of outside pier apron is devoted to large vessels, including superyachts and cruise ships.

East Waterway. Both sides of East Waterway are lined with docks for commercial vessels, most of them loading or unloading containers. The waterway is navigable to Spokane Street, where a fixed bridge and foul ground block further navigation.

West Waterway. West Waterway and the connecting Duwamish River make a splendid sightseeing voyage. Use large-scale Chart 18450.

Enter past busy Vigor Industrial shipyard (formerly Todd Shipyard) and the now-closed Lockheed Shipyard at the mouth, and motor along a fascinating variety of docks, ships, barges, small pleasure boats, mega-yachts, and abandoned hulks. Commercial buildings and the modest homes of South Park are on both sides.

You will go under the 1st Ave. S. Bridge, vertical clearance 39 feet, and past the former site of the Boeing Company's Plant 2, to the 16th Ave. S. Bridge (renamed the South Park Bridge), removed in 2010. New construction could restrict access in 2014. The 1st Ave. S. Bridge will open on signal, except during rush hour traffic. The famed Delta Marine facility, builder of commercial fish boats and megayachts, is a short distance beyond the 16th Ave. S. (South Park) Bridge.

Not far past Delta Marine, a low bridge blocks progress to all but small, open boats. Contributing Editor Tom Kincaid has followed the river upstream as far as Kent in an outboard-powered dinghy.

Don Armeni Park and Seacrest Park are located between Harbor Island and Duwamish Head. Don Armeni Park has a 4-lane launch ramp with floats. Seacrest Park has a fishing pier.

Harbor Island Marina. 1001 Klickitat Way S.W., Seattle, WA 98134; (206) 787-3006; him@portofseattle.org; www.portofseattle.org. This Port of Seattle marina is located on the south end of Harbor Island and caters to long term tenants. No transient moorage.

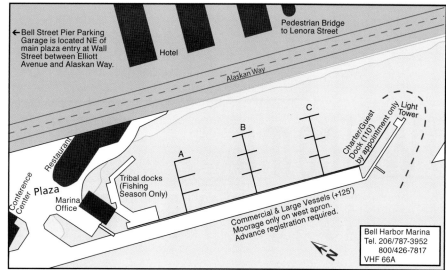

Bell Harbor Marina

LOCAL KNOWLEDGE

SHALLOW AREA: Do not stray south of the buoyed channel in Shilshole Bay. The water between the channel and Magnolia Bluff shoals rapidly.

Shilshole Bay indents the shoreline of Puget Sound north of West Point, and leads via a dredged channel to the Hiram M. Chittenden Locks (Ballard Locks) and the Lake Washington Ship Canal. Shilshole Bay Marina is north of the dredged channel, with entrances around a long rock breakwater from both north and south.

Lacking local knowledge, boats bound for the locks should pick up the Shilshole Bay Lighted Approach Buoy (locally called the Ballard Blinker) and follow the marked channel to the locks.

(28) **Shilshole Bay Marina.** 7001 Seaview Ave. NW, Suite 100, Seattle, WA 98117; (206) 787-3006; (800) 426-7817; sbm@portseattle.org; www.portseattle.org. Certified Clean Marina. Monitors VHF 17. Open all year, office hours 8:00 a.m. to 4:30 p.m., Monday through Saturday. Monitors VHF 17 24 hours. This is a large, busy, well-equipped marina operated by Port of Seattle. The marina has guest moorage for more than 100 boats to 250 feet, 30, 50, & 100 amp power, restrooms, showers, laundry, free cable TV on the guest docks, pumpout, bicycle racks, portapotty dump, Beacon/BBX and Cascade Link Wi-Fi. Least depth is 15 feet at zero tide. Waste oil disposal stations, recycling and garbage drop. Check-out time is 1:00 p.m.

A complete boatyard (Seaview West) with 55-ton Travelift haulout is at the south end of the marina. The boatyard has repair-yard supplies and propane. A wide launch ramp is at the north end of the marina. Walking distance to restaurants, a fast-food stand, and a West Marine. Golden Gardens Park, with beach and picnic areas, is a short walk north of the marina. The marina provides guests a free shuttle to the Ballard shopping area.

Shilsole Bay Marina has undergone a

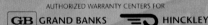

The well-known statue of Leif Eiriksson at Shilshole Bay Marina.

complete rebuild, with new docks and power, and a new marina office building. The large Central Plaza, in front of the office building and adjacent to the guest docks, is good for gatherings and events.

ANTHONY'S
HOMEPORT RESTAURANT
6135 Seaview Ave. NW
(206) 783-0780

㉘ **Shilshole Bay Fuel Dock.** 7029 Seaview Ave. NW, Seattle, WA 98117; (206) 783-7555. Open 7 days a week all year. Gasoline, diesel, bio-diesel, CNG, kerosene. At the end of H dock. The Port of Seattle operates a pumpout and portapotty dump at the outer end of the dock. Convenience store carries ice, beverages, snacks, local guidebooks. Friendly people, clean and efficient operation.

㉙ **Hiram M. Chittenden Locks.** The dredged, well-marked channel leading to the Hiram Chittenden Locks passes under the Burlington Northern bascule bridge. *Caution: Although Chart 18447 shows vertical clearance of this bridge to be 43 feet from mean high water, Local Notice to Mariners reports that the actual clearance may be closer to 41 feet. Clearance gauges have been installed at the draw.* The bridge is kept open unless a train is due. The opening signal is one long and one short blast, the same signal as for the Ballard, Fremont, University, and Montlake Bridges. Remember, though, if a train is due you will be ignored.

Your wait at the locks, in either direction, can be as short as zero or as long as several hours depending on the flow of commercial traffic.

Approaching from Puget Sound: If you are approaching from Puget Sound, you'll starboard-side tie to the wall on the south side of the channel under the railroad bridge. If traffic is heavy, as it often is at the end of fair weather summer weekends, you may end up port-side tying to the wall west of the railroad bridge. Normally, only large commercial craft tie to that wall, but if the waiting area is crowded, you may be there, too. The current always flows from the lake into the sound.

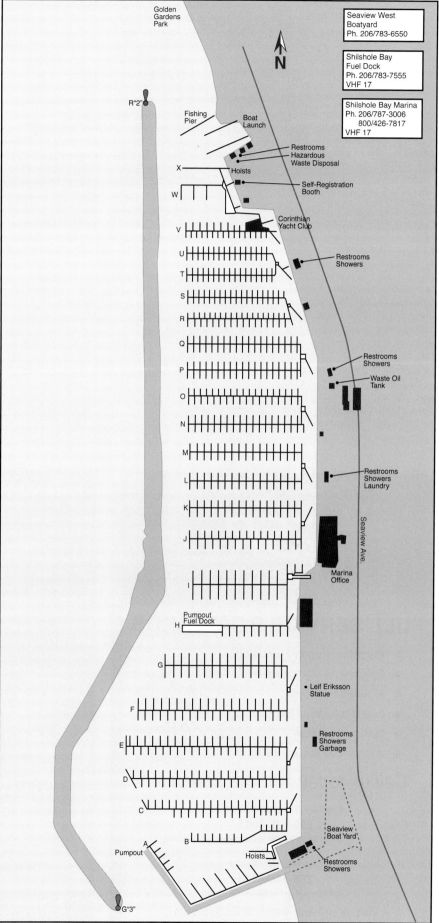

Shilshole Bay Marina

The fuel dock at Shilshole is conveniently located for boats transiting the locks.

The Lake Washington Ship Canal is lined with moorages and marine service providers.

Approach carefully and be ready with extra fenders. Wait your turn and do not crowd ahead. Government vessels and commercial vessels have priority over pleasure craft, and will be directed into the locks ahead of pleasure craft.

Red and green lights on the large and small locks signal when you can enter. Red light means no; green light means yes. A loud hailer system also announces directions to the traffic waiting to transit.

Lock attendants do not respond to most radio calls from pleasure craft, but if you must communicate with them, call on VHF 13, using the 1-watt low-power mode. If you need help, they will answer. If you're calling to complain, forget it.

There are two locks: a large lock 825 feet long and 80 feet wide, and a small lock 150 feet long and 30 feet wide. On a busy summer weekend, the large lock can take a half-hour or more to fill with vessels. Lock attendants will direct entering vessels to one lock or the other by light signals and the loud hailer. Each vessel should have bow and stern mooring lines at least 50 feet long with a 12-inch eye in one end. Fenders should be set out on both sides of the boat. You may be placed against the lock wall or rafted to another boat.

The lock attendants are conscientious, experienced, and helpful. They make eye contact with the helmsman of each vessel as it enters, and signal their intentions clearly. They are polite, but they give direct orders. Do exactly what they tell you to do. They have seen everything and know

how to deal with problems.

If directed into the large lock, larger vessels will be brought in first and tied along the walls. Smaller vessels will raft off. Large vessel or small, be sure you have 50-foot mooring lines bow and stern in case you are put along the wall. The lock attendants will throw messenger lines to you. Tie your mooring lines to the messenger lines and they will take them to bollards on top of the lock wall.

There is usually some current in the locks, flowing from the lakes toward the Sound. Enter slowly but with enough speed for steerage. Once your lines are made fast, prepare to assist boats that lie alongside you. When the lock is closed and the water begins to rise, the vessels along the wall must keep a half-turn on their cleats and continuously take in slack. When the water has stopped rising, make all lines fast until you are told to leave.

If directed into the small lock, you will lie alongside a floating wall equipped with yellow-painted "buttons." Loop your bow and stern lines around the buttons, bring the lines back, and make

On a busy day the large lock will hold more boats than you think possible.

Marilynn Hale watches the fenders in the small lock.

them fast to cleats. The floating walls rise or fall with the water level, so you don't need to tend your lines during the transit. *Caution:* It is always possible that a floating wall could jam in its tracks. Stand by to slack your lines quickly if that happens.

When directed to do so, loosen your lines and move out of the locks slowly but with good steerage.

Approaching from the lake: If you are westbound from the lake to the Sound, you still need 50-foot mooring lines bow and stern in case you lie along the wall of the large lock. However, you will be able to hand your lines to the attendant instead of tying them to messenger lines. Boats along the large lock wall will slack their lines as the water drops.

LAKE WASHINGTON SHIP CANAL

The Lake Washington Ship Canal connects the Hiram Chittenden Locks with Lake Washington, a distance of approximately 5.5 miles. Except for a marked course in the middle of Lake Union, a 7-knot speed limit is enforced all the way to Webster Point, at the entrance to Lake Washington.

Most boats travel about 6 knots. If no bridge openings are needed, allow about 30 minutes between Lake Union and the locks, and about an hour between Lake Washington and the locks. The Lake Washington Ship Canal has fuel docks, ship repair yards, boatyards, and moorages. Keep an alert lookout for vessels pulling out or turning. This can be an active area.

LOCAL KNOWLEDGE

SOUND SIGNALS: For all of the bridges, the sound signal to request an opening is 1 long blast and 1 short. The bridge tender will answer with 1 long and 1 short blast if the bridge can be opened or 5 short blasts if it cannot.

Ship Canal Bridge Information. From west to east, the Lake Washington Ship Canal is crossed by the Ballard Bridge, vertical clearance 44 feet at the center; Fremont Bridge, vertical clearance 30 feet at the center; University Bridge, vertical clearance 42 feet at the center; and the Montlake Bridge, vertical clearance 46 feet at the center.

During weekdays, these bridges remain closed from 7:00 a.m. to 9:00 a.m. and from 4:00 p.m. to 6:00 p.m., except the Montlake Bridge. Its closures are from 3:30 p.m. to 6:30 p.m. May through August, and 7:00 a.m. to 10:00 a.m and 3:30 p.m. to 7:00 p.m. October through April. From 12:30 p.m. to 3:30 p.m. the Montlake Bridge opens only on the hour and half-hour, Monday through Friday, year-round.

Nighttime bridge openings: The Ballard, Fremont and University Bridges are untended at night between 11:00 p.m. and 7:00 a.m. One crew, based at the Fremont Bridge, stands by to open bridges for vessel traffic. For openings call one hour ahead on VHF 13, or by telephone (206) 386-4251.

The Montlake Bridge is tended 24 hours a day, but between 11:00 p.m. and 7:00 a.m. vessels needing an opening must call ahead on VHF 13 or by telephone, (206) 720-3048. This telephone number is displayed at both ends of the Montlake Cut.

㉚ **24th Avenue Landing.** At the foot of 24th Ave. NW on the north side of the Ship Canal, east of locks. Open 7:00 a.m. to 2:00 a.m. all year, no overnights. Dock has 300 feet of space, 40-foot maximum boat length. No power, water or showers. The Ballard business district is within walking distance.

㉚ **Ballard Oil Co.** 5300 26th Ave. NW, Seattle, WA 98107; (206) 783-0241; info@ballardoil.com; www.ballardoil.com. Open Monday through Saturday. Just east of the locks, on the north side of the Ship Canal. Diesel only. Set up to handle larger and commercial vessels.

Salmon Bay. The Port of Seattle's Fishermen's Terminal is located on the south side of the Lake Washington Ship Canal at Salmon Bay, a half-mile east of the locks. Although Fishermen's Terminal caters primarily to the large Seattle-based fishing fleet, guest and permanent moorage is available for pleasure craft. A short term guest float is located along the inner bulkhead at the head of the west wall. Major repair facilities are nearby, as are stores offering a variety of marine services and supplies.

㉛ **Salmon Bay Marina.** 2100 W. Commodore Way, Seattle, WA 98199; (206) 282-5555; sales@salmonbaymarina.com; www.salmonbaymarina.com. Open 8:00 a.m. to 5:00 p.m. Monday through Saturday, Sunday 1:00 p.m. to 5:00 p.m. Closed Sunday and Monday December through March, and holidays. Restrooms, showers, and laundry facilities, 30 & 50 amp power. This marina is primarily full time leased moorage, but they do rent slips for temporary moorage with prior reservations. Seattle Marine & Fishing Supply, a large chandlery, is across the street. Walking distance to restaurants and Fishermen's Terminal.

㉛ **Salmon Bay Marine Center.** 2284 W. Commodore Way #100, Seattle, WA 98199;

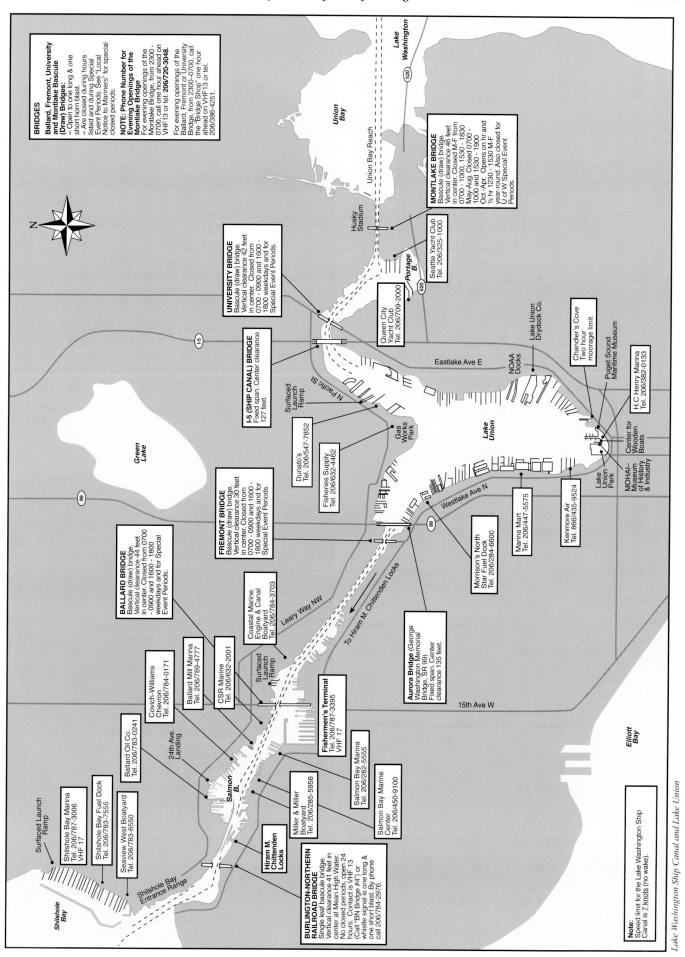

BRIDGES
Ballard, Fremont, University and Montlake Bascule (Draw) Bridges:
– Open to one long & one short horn blast.
– Are closed during hours listed and during Special Event Periods. See "Local Notice to Mariners" for special closed periods.
NOTE: Phone Number for Evening Openings of the Montlake Bridge
For evening openings of the Montlake Bridge, from 2300 - 0700, call one hour ahead on VHF13 or tel. **206/720-3048.**
For evening openings of the Ballard, Fremont or University Bridge, from 2300-0700, call the "Bridge Shop" one hour ahead on VHF13 or tel. 206/386-4251.

MONTLAKE BRIDGE
Bascule (draw) bridge. Vertical clearance 46 feet in center. Closed M-F from 0700 - 1000, 1530 - 1830 May-Aug. Closed 0700 - 1000 and 1530 - 1900 Oct.-Apr. Opens on hr and ½ hr 1230 - 1530 M-F year-round. Also closed for U of W Special Event Periods.

Seattle Yacht Club Tel. 206/325-1000

UNIVERSITY BRIDGE
Bascule (draw) bridge. Vertical clearance 42 feet in center. Closed from 0700 - 0900 and 1600 - 1800 weekdays and for Special Event Periods.

Queen City Yacht Club Tel. 206/709-2000

I-5 (SHIP CANAL) BRIDGE
Fixed span. Center clearance 127 feet.

Lake Union Drydock Co.

Chandler's Cove Two hour moorage limit

Puget Sound Maritime Museum

H.C. Henry Marina Tel. 206/382-0133

NOAA Docks

Eastlake Ave E

Center for Wooden Boats

Lake Union Park

MOHAI– Museum of History & Industry

Surfaced Launch Ramp

Gas Works Park

Dunato's Tel. 206/547-7852

Fisheries Supply Tel. 206/632-4462

FREMONT BRIDGE
Bascule (draw) bridge. Vertical clearance 30 feet in center. Closed from 0700 - 0900 and 1600 - 1800 weekdays and for Special Event Periods.

Westlake Ave N

Kenmore Air Tel. 866/435-9524

Marina Mart Tel. 206/447-5575

Morrison's North Star Fuel Dock Tel. 206/284-6600

BALLARD BRIDGE
Bascule (draw) bridge. Vertical clearance 44 feet in center. Closed from 0700 - 0900 and 1600 - 1800 weekdays and for Special Event Periods.

Coastal Marine Engine & Canal Boatyard Tel. 206/784-3703

Leary Way NW

Aurora Bridge (George Washington Memorial Bridge, SR 99) Fixed span. Center clearance 135 feet.

To Hiram M. Chittenden Locks

15th Ave W

Covich-Williams Chevron Tel. 206/784-0171

Ballard Mill Marina Tel. 206/789-4777

CSR Marine Tel. 206/632-2001

Surfaced Launch Ramp

Ballard Oil Co. Tel. 206/783-0241

24th Ave. Landing

Fishermen's Terminal Tel. 206/787-3395 VHF 17

Salmon B.

Surfaced Launch Ramp

Shilshole Bay Marina Tel. 206/787-3006 VHF 17

Shilshole Bay Fuel Dock Tel. 206/783-7555

Seaview West Boatyard Tel. 206/783-6550

Miller & Miller Boatyard Tel. 206/285-5958

Salmon Bay Marina Tel. 206/282-5555

Salmon Bay Marine Center Tel. 206/450-9100

Hiram M. Chittenden Locks

BURLINGTON-NORTHERN RAIL ROAD BRIDGE
Single leaf bascule bridge. Vertical clearance 41 feet in center at Mean High Water. No closed periods, open 24 hours. Contact is VHF 13 (Call "BN Bridge #4") or whistle signals is one long & one short blast. By phone call 206/784-2976.

Shilshole Bay

Shilshole Bay Entrance Range

Note:
Speed limit for the Lake Washington Ship Canal is 7 knots (no wake).

Lake Washington Ship Canal and Lake Union

Green Lake

Union Bay

Union Bay Reach

Lake Washington

Husky Stadium

Portage B.

Lake Union

Elliott Bay

N Pacific St

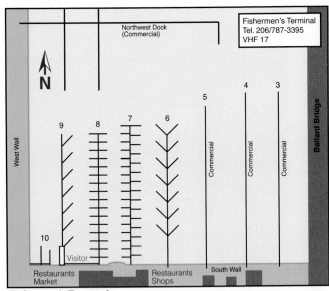

Fishermen's Terminal

You never know what boats you might encounter in Fishermen's Terminal. Here is a boat from the TV show "Deadliest Catch."

(206) 450-9100; www.sbmc.com. On the south side of the Ship Canal, this new facility has 18 slips to accommodate vessels from 100 to 240 feet. Most slips are sold or on long term lease. Short term moorage for large vessels may be available by reservation. Slips are 30 feet to 45 feet wide with a minimum depth of 12 feet. Power is single and 3-phase 240/480 volt–200 amp. A 50-cycle transformer is available. Black water connection at each slip with gray water pumpout. Wi-Fi, parking, and 4 electric utility cars for dock use. The offices of several large yacht brokerages and dealers are in the shoreside building.

㉚ Covich-Williams Chevron. Dock Office, 5219 Shilshole Ave. NW, Seattle, WA 98107; (206) 784-0171; www.covichwilliams. com. On the north side of the Ship Canal, next to Salmon Bay Sand & Gravel. Open weekdays 8:00 a.m. to 5:00 p.m., Satur-

days until noon; closed Sundays. Gasoline, diesel, kerosene. Carries filters, absorbent products, antifreeze, environmental products, fuel additives.

㉚ Ballard Mill Marina. 4733 Shilshole Ave. NW, Seattle, WA 98107; (206) 789-4777; ballardmillmarina@gmail.com; www. ballardmillmarina.com. Open all year, limited guest moorage in unoccupied slips, 18 to 150 feet. Restrooms, pumpout, 20 & 30 amp power, showers. East of Covich-Williams Chevron fuel dock on the north side of the Ship Canal. Free pumpout on the east dock. Stores, restaurants, marine supplies, haulout and repairs nearby.

㉛ Fishermen's Terminal. 3919 18th Ave. W., Seattle, WA 98119; (206) 787-3395; (800) 426-7817; ft@portseattle.org; www.portseattle.org. Monitors VHF 17, 24 hours a day, 30, 50

& 100 amp power, water, restrooms & showers, security cameras, free pumpout (sewage and bilge), recycling, waste oil dump, flare recycling. Major repair and supply facilities nearby. Restaurants, shops, postal service on site. A small grocery store and chandlery are within walking distance. The marina is on the

south side of the Ship Canal, immediately west of the Ballard Bridge. Guest moorage welcomed, first-come, first-served, call for slip assignment.

Major upgrade: The marina has completed a $22 million upgrade to the inner harbor docks. The old wooden docks have been replaced with new concrete docks, the

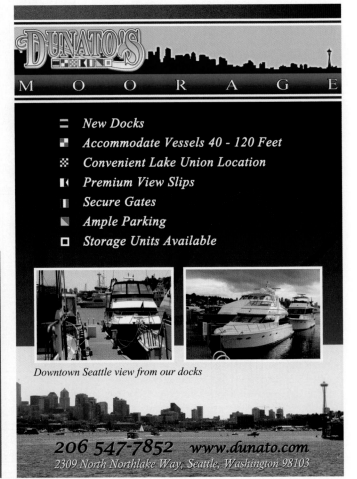

power upgraded, and the docks reconfigured for easy landing.

Dining: Chinook's at Salmon Bay is good for sit-down dining. A takeout seafood window is on the east side of the building. Tables and chairs are on the deck or in a covered area. An excellent fish market is in the front of the building. The Highliner Pub and the Bay Café also offer dining. The side-tie guest mooring float is in front of the restaurant building, 4 hours moorage complimentary.

CHINOOK'S
AT · SALMON · BAY
1900 W. Nickerson St.
(206) 283-4665

Lake Union is lined with ship and boat moorages, houseboat moorages, and boating related businesses. It's the center of Seattle's boat sales industry. In the middle of the lake a speed range, marked by 4 buoys, is for sea trials. Other than the speed range, a 7-knot speed limit is enforced. A launch ramp is on the north shore, east of Gas Works Park. Gas Works Park is easily identifiable by the painted remnants of an industrial coal gas plant. Tyee Yacht Club and Puget Sound Yacht Club have moorages on Lake Union. The large Fisheries Supply marine store is located near Gas Works Park. Transient moorage is limited on Lake Union.

The south end of Lake Union is the home of Northwest Seaport. Next door is the Center for Wooden Boats and the new Lake Union Park with the Museum of History and Industry (MOHAI). Kenmore Air's seaplane base is on the southwest shore, just across from the park. A large West Marine store is within walking distance on Westlake Ave. N. A major ship repair yard, Lake Union Drydock, is on the eastern shore near the south end of the lake. Ivar's Salmon House, a popular waterfront restaurant, is at the north end of the lake under the I-5 freeway bridge, with temporary moorage for tenders and small boats while dining.

㉜ Morrison's North Star Marine. 2732 Westlake Ave. N., Seattle, WA 98109; (206) 284-6600. Open all year, 7 days a week. Fuel dock with gasoline and diesel, no guest moorage. Restrooms, pumpout. Handles oil changes; call for appointment. Limited marine hardware, local charts, groceries, ice. Friendly and well-run.

㉜ Nautical Landing Marina. 2500 Westlake Ave. N., Seattle, WA 98109; (206) 464-4614; info@nautical-landing.com; www.nautical-landing.com. Open all year for permanent and transient use with 1900 feet of moorage, 30, 50 & 100 amp power, security, Wi-Fi, garbage and recycling drop. This facility is popular with superyachts and has services to match.

㉝ Chandler's Cove. 901 Fairview Ave. N., Seattle, WA 98109. Two-hour day moorage limit, no overnight moorage. Several restau-

rants, snacks, ice. Easy walk to the Center for Wooden Boats, Northwest Seaport, and the Museum of History and Industry (MOHAI).

㉝ H.C. Henry Marina. 809 Fairview Place N., Seattle, WA 98109. Located at the south end of Lake Union. Two-hour limit, no overnight moorage. Pumpout, but no restrooms or showers.

㉝ Marina Mart. 1500 Westlake Ave. N., Seattle, WA 98109; (206) 268-3322; www.marinamart.com. No guest moorage, free pumpout only.

Portage Bay. East of the University Bridge, vertical clearance 42 feet at the center, Portage Bay is the home of Seattle Yacht Club and Queen City Yacht Club. The University of Washington has several facilities along the north shore. The University Bridge opens to 1 long blast and 1 short.

Montlake Cut. East of Portage Bay, the Montlake Cut connects to Union Bay and Lake Washington. The cut is narrow. When boat traffic is heavy, boat wakes can be turbulent as they bounce off the concrete side walls. Slow, steady speeds are called for. The Montlake Bridge, which crosses the cut, has a vertical clearance of 46 feet at the center. The bridge opens to 1 long blast and 1 short.

Montlake Bridge has a clearance of 46 feet. On sunny summer days boat traffic ranges from heavy to very heavy.

Union Bay. Union Bay is just east of the Montlake Cut and connects with Lake Washington. The dredged channel is well buoyed. The University of Washington's waterfront activities center is on the north shore, and the arboretum is on the south shore. Except for the dredged channel, the bay is shoal.

The annual Seafair festivities draw thousands of people to Lake Washington for air shows, hydroplane races, and parties.

LAKE WASHINGTON

Lake Washington, 16 miles long, defines the eastern border of Seattle, and washes the edges of Kenmore, Bothell, Kirkland, Medina, Bellevue, Mercer Island and Renton. The SR-520 floating bridge has a vertical clearance of 45 feet at its west end and 57 feet at its east end. The I-90 floating bridge has maximum vertical clearance of 34 feet at the west end and 37 feet at the east end. Least clearance at each end is 28 feet.

Summer weekends can be busy. Seafair weekend borders on madness.

Sand Point. North from Webster Point, the first notable place for visiting boats is the former Naval Aviation base of Sand Point. Sand Point now includes Magnuson Park, which has a 2-lane launch ramp with floats. It is also the Northwest District headquarters for the National Oceanic and Atmospheric Administration (NOAA), which has a long piling pier along its north shore. The small marina west of the NOAA pier belongs to the Navy.

Kenmore. North Lake Marina in Kenmore provides access to a restaurant, and anchorage is possible anywhere in the area. Kenmore is home to Kenmore Air, a major seaplane operation. Stay well clear of seaplane operating areas. Kenmore is also the mouth of the Sammamish River. Shoal water abounds. Find the buoys and stay in the dredged channel. The river is navigable by small, low, shallow-draft boats all the way to Lake Sammamish.

(34) North Lake Marina. 6201 NE 175th St., Kenmore, WA 98028; (425) 482-9465; lorij@northlakemarina.com; www.northlake-marina.com. Open all year, closed weekends November through March. Gasoline at the fuel dock, no diesel. No guest moorage. Restrooms, pumpout. Parts, accessories, ice. Complete repairs available. Haulout to 20 tons.

Logboom Park. North shore of Lake Washington, Kenmore. Open all year, day use only, moorage available. Restrooms, no power, no showers. Trails, fishing pier, children's play equipment, picnic areas, and outdoor cooking facilities. The park is on the Burke-Gilman Trail, a walking and cycling trail that runs from Lake Union to the Sammamish River Trail.

Saint Edward State Park. 14445 Juanita Drive NW, Kenmore, WA 98028; (425) 823-2992. Northeast shore of Lake Washington. Open all year, day use only. Restrooms, showers, no power. Anchoring or beaching only. Picnicking, trails, fishing, indoor swimming pool. Tennis courts, gymnasium. An approximately 300-acre park is at the top of a bluff; trails lead down to a sandy beach.

Juanita. Anchorage is possible in Juanita Bay, which shoals gradually toward all shores.

Kirkland. Kirkland is an outstanding cruising destination. The City of Kirkland's Marina Park visitor docks are well maintained, and connect directly with downtown. A good launch ramp is immediately north of the docks. If you enjoy tree-lined streets, superb dining, interesting boutiques and upscale galleries, you will not be disappointed. Kirkland is prosperous and it shows.

Next to Marina Park is the fairly new **Kirkland Homeport Marina**, which is primarily full-time, leased moorage: www.kirklandhomeportmarina.com.

A mile south of Marina Park is privately-owned Carillon Point Marina, with some guest moorage and access to restaurants and other businesses. Several restaurants in the area have their own docks for patrons.

(35) Marina Park. 25 Lakeshore Plaza Drive, Kirkland, WA 98033; (425) 587-3300; www.kirklandwa.gov. Launch ramp adjacent, fee required. Open all year, 90 guest slips, restrooms, 30 amp power in some slips, Wi-Fi. No showers. This is a large and popular Lake Washington destination. Moorage is paid through electronic public pay stations located on the dock. First 3 hours free. Excellent access to downtown Kirkland. Nearby groceries, ice, and post office.

Launch ramp access is by a special key card, available only at City Hall, Suite A, 8:00 a.m. to 5:00 p.m., Monday through Friday. You can get a one-day card or a season card. No card needed November through March. It's more complicated than we can describe here, but you can call direct (425) 587-3300 and they will answer all your questions.

They manage 150 feet of the Anthony's Restaurant dock and accept reservations.

ANTHONY'S
HOMEPORT RESTAURANT
135 Lake Street South
(425) 822-0225

(36) Carillon Point Marina. 4100 Carillon Point, Kirkland, WA 98033; (425) 822-1700; www.carillon-point.com. Certified Clean Marina. Open all year, guest moorage when available, 30 & 50 amp power, Beacon/BBX Wi-Fi, restrooms, showers, pumpout, porta-potty dump. This is a nice marina adjacent to a high-quality hotel, with restaurants, spa, shopping, and 400-foot fishing pier. They offer 2-hour free moorage while dining or shopping. Downtown Kirkland is 1.5 miles away by road.

(36) Yarrow Bay Marina. 5207 Lake Washington Blvd. NE, Kirkland, WA 98033; (425) 822-6066; service@yarrowbaymarina.com; www.yarrowbaymarina.com. Open all year with gasoline and diesel, no guest moorage. Marine parts, restrooms, seasonal pumpout, haulout and repairs.

Cozy Cove and Fairweather Bay. Cozy Cove and Fairweather Bay are entirely residential, but anchorage is possible.

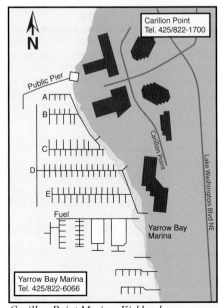

Carillon Point Marina, Kirkland

Meydenbauer Bay. Meydenbauer Bay is the home of a marina that does not normally offer overnight moorage, and the Meydenbauer Bay Yacht Club, which has some moorage for members of reciprocal clubs. Downtown Bellevue, with outstanding shopping, is nearby. Anchorage is possible in Meydenbauer Bay, although the water is deeper than most pleasure craft prefer. The marina off **Beaux Arts Village**, a short distance south of Meydenbauer Bay, is reserved for Beaux Arts residents.

Luther Burbank Park. 2040 84th Avenue SE, Mercer Island, WA 98040; www.mercergov.org. Open all year, day use only, dock space for 30 or more boats. Restrooms, no power, no showers. No anchoring. Park has picnic areas, swimming areas, tennis courts, amphitheater.

East Channel Bridge. Vertical clearance is 65 feet.

㊲ **Newport Shores.** Newport Shores has a large marina with launch ramp and fuel dock.

㊲ **Seattle Boat - Newport.** 3911 Lake Washington Blvd. SE, Bellevue, WA 98006; (425) 641-2090; www.seattleboat.com. Open all year, call or visit website for hours. Fuel dock with gasoline and diesel. No guest moorage. Located at Newport Yacht Basin. Complete repairs available. Marine supplies and parts, new and used boats, self-serve storage. Haulout to 35 tons.

㊳ **Gene Coulon Memorial Beach Park.** 1201 Lake Washington Blvd., Renton, WA 98055; (425) 430-6700; www.rentonwa.gov. Open all year, day use only. Restrooms, showers, no power. Pay at the automated pay box. Showers in summer only, at the swim center. Ivar's and Kidd Valley restaurants in the park. Eight lanes for boat launching, very well organized, credit and debit cards only. No overnight parking in winter. This is a big, attractive, and much-used park, with picnic shelters, playground equipment, tennis courts, horseshoe pits, volleyball courts, grassy areas and beaches. It has a fishing pier and a paved

Kirkland's Marina Park has good moorage.

walkway along the water. Popular with everyone, especially families. Located on the southeast shore of Lake Washington, next to Boeing's Renton 737 complex.

Rainier Beach. Has a launch ramp and a private marina. It is the home of the Rainier Yacht Club, www.raineryachtclub.com. Limited guest moorage for visiting members of reciprocal clubs.

Andrews Bay. 5895 Lake Washington Blvd. S., Seattle, WA 98118; (206) 684-4396; www.seattle.gov. Andrews Bay is a popular anchoring spot, with room for many boats. Nestled in between **Seward Park** on Bailey Peninsula and the mainland, it is the only authorized pleasure boat anchorage in Seattle. Signs on the Seward Park shoreline mark the anchorage area. Put the hook down in 25 to 50 feet, excellent mud bottom, 72-hour maximum stay in 7-day period. A Seattle Parks swim area with bathhouse and lifeguards is at the head of the bay. A large grassy playfield is adjacent. Miles of trails lead through dense forest. Excellent stop, especially for families.

㊴ **Lakewood Moorage.** 4400 Lake Washington Blvd. S., Seattle, WA 98118; (206) 722-3887; www.seattle.gov. Open all year. Very limited guest moorage. Water, 20 and 30 amp power, restrooms, no showers.

Stan Sayers Memorial Park. www.seattle.gov. Open all year. Temporary, day use moorage only, not enough depth for larger boats. Restrooms, no power, no showers. Launch ramp with boarding floats. Tie up to the floats. This is the pit area for hydroplanes during annual Seafair races.

RICH PASSAGE, PORT ORCHARD, BREMERTON, SILVERDALE

LOCAL KNOWLEDGE

HEAVY TRAFFIC: Rich Passage is the ferry route between Seattle and Bremerton. Keep a sharp lookout ahead and astern and stay well clear of the ferries. Naval vessels also use Rich Passage to and from the Bremerton Naval Shipyard.

Rich Passage is winding but well-buoyed. From the west entrance the city of Bremerton and the Naval Shipyard are clearly visible. For security reasons, stay well off the Naval facilities.

Currents run to 2 knots at the eastern entrance and 5.5 knots at the west entrance, flooding west and ebbing east.

Gene Coulon Park moorage, with the busy launch ramp behind.

Port Orchard Marina guest dock.

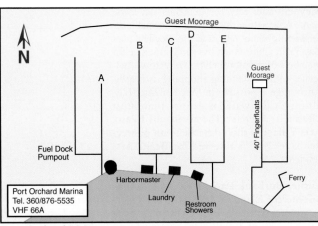

Port Orchard Marina

Manchester State Park. 7767 E. Hilldale, Port Orchard, WA 98366; (360) 902-8844; www.stateparks.com. Open 7 days a week in the summer, 111 acres, day use and overnight camping. Open weekends and holidays in winter. Restrooms, showers, no power. Anchoring only; a bit rough because of boat traffic in Rich Passage. Park is in a shallow cove, good for wading in summer and scuba diving offshore. Picnic tables and shelters with fireplaces, campsites, nature and hiking trails. Old gun battery and emplacements are fun to explore.

⑷ Port of Manchester. P.O. Box 304, Manchester, WA 98353; (360) 871-0500; www.portofmanchester.com. Open all year, 400 feet of guest dock space, day use only, restroom. Dock can be dry on zero or minus tide. A launch ramp is adjacent to the dock. No power or other facilities at the dock, but services are nearby.

Fort Ward Marine State Park. 2241 Pleasant Beach, Bainbridge Island, WA 98110; (206) 842-2306; www.biparks.org. Open all year. Anchorage is exposed to wind and wakes from passing boat traffic. Toilets, launch ramp and hiking trails. Because of strong currents in Rich Passage, the underwater park is for expert scuba divers only. Bird watching from 2 bird blinds. Remains of historic fort emplacements to explore. No camping.

⑷ Port Orchard. The city of Port Orchard has long been a popular destination for Puget Sound boaters. It has a number of marinas that welcome visiting boats, including one, Port Orchard Marina, that is operated by the Port of Bremerton. Port Orchard Yacht Club, which welcomes visiting reciprocal yachts, is west of the Port Orchard Marina. Several other marinas have permanent moorage. Anchorage is in 50 to 60 feet, mud bottom. A passenger ferry runs between Port Orchard and Bremerton.

⑷ Port Orchard Marina. 707 Sidney Pkwy., 8850 SW State Hwy. 3, Port Orchard, WA 98366; (360) 876-5535; www.portof-bremerton.org. Monitors VHF 66A. Open 7 days a week all year, except closed Thanksgiving, Veteran's Day, Christmas and New Year's Eve day. Gasoline and diesel at the fuel dock, guest moorage in 44 slips (40-foot), and side-tied along 1500 feet of inside dock space. Another 1500 feet is on the outside of the long dock. The marina is well-managed and well-maintained, with beautiful landscaping and clean restrooms.

The marina has 30 amp power, water, restrooms, laundry, free showers, free pumpout, portapotty dump, Wi-Fi. Internet and email hookup also available in the office. An excellent children's play area is at the north end of the marina grounds. This is one of Puget Sound's popular destinations. Reservations accepted, 4 hours of day use free. It's one block to downtown Port Orchard, where you will find several antique and collectibles shops, restaurants, and the other usual services: library, post office, doctor. Repairs are nearby. Close to Marina Park, where concerts are held during the summer, and Water Street boat launch. Extended long term parking for tow vehicles and trailers. Seasonal farmers market, 9:00 a.m. to 3:00 p.m. on Saturdays, April through October. Enter the marina around the west end of the breakwater. The entrance

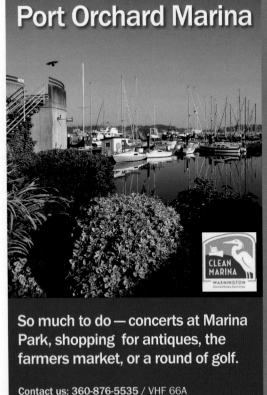

is marked with navigation lights.

Golf: McCormick Woods (800) 323-0130; Trophy Lakes (360) 874-8337; and Gold Mountain (360) 415-5432 are nearby. The courses have transportation available.

㊷ **Bremerton.** The Bremerton waterfront has been redeveloped recently. The new Bremerton Harborside Kitsap Conference Center, with a Starbucks, Anthony's Restaurant, and Cold Stone Creamery, overlooks the marina. A new Hampton Suites Hotel is next door. Bremerton is doing its best to shed a dowdy image and make a name for itself.

Points of interest include the Naval Museum, the historic destroyer USS *Turner Joy*, and the attractive city boardwalk. Many boaters take the passenger ferry for the 10- to 12-minute ride to Port Orchard, where the dining, seasonal farmers market, antiques shopping, and boutiques are popular. Bremerton Marina is secured by a locked gate. Kitsap County buses in the adjacent transporation center can take you anywhere you wish to go, or take the ferry to downtown Seattle.

The Blackberry Festival is held Labor Day weekend, with booths ashore selling wonderful blackberry treats and more. We just happened to be there, and the festival was a hoot.

LOCAL KNOWLEDGE

STRONG CURRENTS: Tidal currents can make boat handling tricky in Bremerton Marina. It is best to time arrival and departure to coincide with slack water.

㊷ **Bremerton Marina.** 120 Washington Beach, Bremerton, WA 98367; (360) 373-1035; kathyg@portofbremerton.org. www.

portofbremerton.org. Monitors VHF 66A. Certified Clean Marina. Open all year, except closed Thanksgiving, Veteran's Day, Christmas, and New Year's Eve. Guest moorage in 80 to 100 slips and 990 feet of side-tie dock space, 30, 50 and one 100 amp power, water, garbage and recycling drop, restrooms, free showers, laundry, Beacon/BBX and free Wi-Fi, free dockside pumpouts, 2 portapo-

tty dumps. Located next to the ferry dock. Shuttle service.

No fuel is available. The nearest fuel dock is at Port Orchard.

This is an all-new marina, with excellent docks and a new breakwater to protect against ferry wakes. Fountain Park, a short walk to the other side of the ferry dock, is lovely. The dramatic fin-like sculptures are meant to

Bremerton harborside boardwalk leads to the USS Turner Joy.

Harborside sculpture dedicated to the ship builders of the Bremerton shipyard.

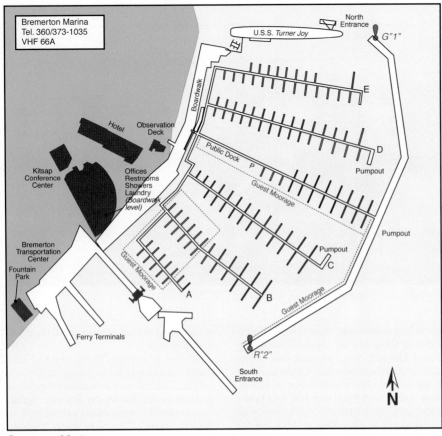

Bremerton Marina Tel. 360/373-1035 VHF 66A

Bremerton Marina

resemble the superstructure (called the sail) of a modern submarine.

Washington Narrows connects **Sinclair Inlet** with **Dyes Inlet**. The narrows are crossed by 2 bridges with a minimum vertical clearance of 80 feet. Tidal currents, averaging over 2 knots, flood west and ebb east. Signs ask boaters to maintain minimum speed to reduce wake damage to the shore and to boats moored at the marina. A launch ramp with float and fishing pier are on the north side of the narrows about halfway along, part of the Lebo Street Recreation Area.

Port Washington Marina. Port Washington Marina has a free pumpout on the outer end of the east dock.

Phinney Bay. Phinney Bay is the home of the Bremerton Yacht Club, with guest moorage for visiting reciprocal boats. Anchorage is good throughout the bay, which shoals toward each shore.

Shaw Island Event Center. Contact@ shawislandeventcenter.com; www.shawisland-eventcenter.com. Slated to open in 2014, the

Shaw Island Event Center docks serve a new high-end residential community and offer transient moorage for boats to 75 feet. Power, water, garbage drop.

Ostrich Bay. Ostrich Bay offers good anchorage, mud bottom. The most popular anchorage is along the west side of the bay, facing dense forest. We have spent several pleasant nights at this spot. For some reason this entire area is overlooked. Even when the docks at Port Orchard and Bremerton are full on summer holiday weekends, Ostrich Bay has been almost empty.

Caution: Unexploded ordnance from years ago, when the Navy pier was used for loading munitions, has been found in the bay, especially in the vicinity of the pier.

Oyster Bay. A narrow but easily-run channel leads off Ostrich Bay into Oyster Bay, where perfectly protected anchorage is available toward the center of the bay. To enter, keep between the lines of mooring buoys and mooring floats on both sides of the channel. The channel shoals to about 6 feet at zero tide. Oyster Bay is surrounded by homes.

Dyes Inlet indents the Kitsap Peninsula northwest of Bremerton. Silverdale is on the north shore of Dyes Inlet and has a marina, waterfront park, boat ramp, and boardwalk. Dyes Inlet is connected to Sinclair Inlet via Port Washington Narrows.

㊸ Silverdale Marina (Port of Silverdale). P.O. Box 310, Silverdale, WA 98383; (360) 698-4918; www.portofsilverdale.com. Open all year. Guest moorage along 1300 feet of wide, side-tie dock with a least depth of 10 feet at zero tide. Moorage is on the honor system, confirmed by security patrols that record the moored boats. Three-night maximum stay. Reservations accepted online for a $75 fee. Restrooms, 30 amp power, seasonal potable water, pumpout, showers, laundry, 2-lane concrete launch ramp. No long-term parking. The pumpout operates 8:00 a.m. to 10:00 p.m., weekends, April to October.

The marina is adjacent to county-run Silverdale Waterfront Park. The park has picnic tables, fire pits, children's play area and a pavilion. Restrooms are at the park. A farmers market is open 10:00 a.m. to 4:00 p.m. on Tuesdays, April through October. Interesting shops and dining are in adjacent Old Town Silverdale. Complete shopping is at the Kitsap Mall about a mile away. The nearby Clear Creek Trail & Interpretive Center and Veteran's Memorial is a good walk.

Whaling Days: Whaling Days, a 3-day celebration the last weekend of July, always draws big crowds, both from land and the water. Plan to anchor out. No rafting. If you're on the dock, expect to be included in the carnival atmosphere. It's a big fair, with live bands all weekend, activities for the kids, outrigger canoe races, a fun run and more. See their website at www.whalingdays.com.

Port of Brownsville docks.

BROWNSVILLE, POULSBO, NORTHERN PORT ORCHARD

Northern Port Orchard separates Bainbridge Island from the Kitsap Peninsula. Rich Passage and Sinclair Inlet are at the south end; Agate Passage is at the north. Brownsville and Poulsbo are the major marina destinations. Agate Passage has a vertical clearance of 75 feet. Currents in Agate Passage run to 6 knots on spring tides, flooding south and ebbing north.

LOCAL KNOWLEDGE

ROCK: A nasty rock, almost awash at zero tide, is inshore from the mooring buoys at Illahee Park, approximately between the buoy nearest the dock and shore. Thanks to Correspondents Al & Becca Szymanski, S/V *Halona*, for the report.

㊹ Illahee Marine State Park. 3540 NE Bahia Vista Drive, Bremerton, WA 98310; (360) 478-6460. Located 3 miles northeast of Bremerton. Open all year, mooring and overnight camping. Guest moorage with 356 feet of side-tie dock space, 5 mooring buoys. Restrooms and showers, no power. The dock is protected by a floating concrete breakwater. Park has 3 kitchen shelters, picnic tables, campsites, horseshoe pits, ball field, hiking trails, and portable toilet. Popular for fishing and sunbathing. Most services are in the upland area, reached by a steep trail.

㊺ Port of Brownsville. 9790 Ogle Rd. NE, Bremerton, WA 98311; (360) 692-5498; jerry@portofbrownsville.org; www.portofbrownsville.org. Certified Clean Marina. Monitors VHF 16, switch to 66A. Open all year, 7 days a week. Fuel dock has gasoline, diesel, and propane. Guest moorage in 25 24-foot slips, 20 40-foot slips, and 550 feet of side-tie moorage along the breakwater, 30 amp power, Beacon/BBX and free Wi-Fi,

restrooms, showers, laundry, free pumpout, portapotty dump. Paved 2-lane launch ramp with ample parking.

Up on the wharf, a covered picnic/gathering pavilion, with tables, is inviting. Additional picnic tables are on the docks and in Burke Bay Overlook Park above the wharf, with barbecue. This is a popular destination for club cruises. Reservations invited.

A breakwater marks the entrance to the marina. The area around the fuel dock has been dredged, so you don't have to hug the south side of the dock. The Deli has groceries, beer, an excellent wine selection, and limited marine supplies. They make take-out food, and can cater a gathering. The Keyport Naval Museum of Undersea Warfare (excellent) is nearby. This is a pleasant, friendly marina.

In summer 2012 the Port began a multiyear project to replace the docks in the permanent moorage area of the marina.

Brownsville Appreciation Day: Fourth Saturday of September. Folksy and fun, small community at its best. Classic boats and cars,

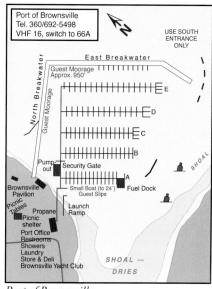

Port of Brownsville

treasure hunt, unicycles, hot dogs and hamburgers. All proceeds (not just profits) divided among the local elementary schools.

Tasty treat: A short walk up the road from the marina, Sweeney's Country Meats has mouth-watering specialty meats. We tried a marinade, jerky, and some of the bacon. All were delicious.

㊻ Port of Keyport Marina. P.O. Box 195, Keyport, WA 98345; (360) 779-4259; www.keyport98345.com. New docks with 250 feet (five 50-foot slips) of guest moorage, first-come, first-served. Water, 30 amp power, 6 hours free. No restrooms. Upland is the Keyport Mercantile, deli, Whiskey Creek Steakhouse, Naval Base Kitsap-Keyport, and the Naval Undersea Museum.

A pedestrian gate, open 10:00 a.m. to 4:00 p.m., is about a quarter of a mile straight up Washington Street from the dock. The gate leads onto the Naval Base and the Naval Undersea Museum. You can view a simulation of a nuclear fast attack submarine, torpedoes and torpedo tubes, a Confederate mine from the Civil War, and learn the history of naval diving. The museum is open daily. Admission is free.

Fletcher Bay. Fletcher Bay is shallow and not a good anchorage.

Poulsbo is a vibrant community easily accessed from Poulsbo Marina.

㊼ Manzanita Bay. Manzanita Bay is a good overnight sheltered anchorage for Seattle-area boats. The bay is all residential and has no public facilities, but the holding ground is excellent. Observe the 5-knot no-wake speed limit beginning halfway down the bay. Although the bay is lined with lovely homes, the surrounding hills give a feeling of seclusion.

On the north end of the bay, Manzanita Landing, a former Mosquito Fleet landing, provides access to the trail system of Manzanita Park. From the landing take Manzanita Road NE to NE Day Road West. Walk east to the park, which is on the left (north) side of the street.

Liberty Bay. The entrance to Liberty Bay is past the Keyport Naval torpedo research and testing facility and around Lemolo Point. The Navy requests boats travel at no-wake speed past its facility. A power cable crosses overhead with a 90-foot clearance. A sign on the beacon off Lemolo Point asks boaters to slow down in all of Liberty Bay; buoys post the speed limit. Much of Liberty Bay is covered by Beacon/BBX Wi-Fi. Three major marinas are along the north shore of Liberty Bay: a

Left: Who can resist stopping in for fresh bakery treats?

Right: Parts of downtown Poulsbo feel like a Norwegian hamlet.

private marina; the Poulsbo Yacht Club; and the Port of Poulsbo Marina.

The private marina has no guest moorage. At the Poulsbo Yacht Club, reciprocal moorage is along the northwest perimeter of the floating breakwater. Some reciprocal moorage is still available on the inside of the older breakwater.

⑱ Poulsbo. Poulsbo, on Liberty Bay, is one of the most popular destinations on Puget Sound, partly because it is close to the major population centers, and partly because it is such a delightful place to visit. Settled originally by Scandinavians, the downtown business district still loudly (to say the least) maintains its Norwegian heritage. Everything most visitors need is available either near the water or at the malls located on the highway about a mile away.

The waterfront portions of Poulsbo make for a lovely walk. Victorian homes and gardens have been restored and preserved to perfection. The highway above may have the malls, but the town below has the charm.

⑱ Poulsbo Marina/Port of Poulsbo. 18809 Front St., P.O. Box 732, Poulsbo, WA 98370; (360) 779-3505; (360) 779-9905; office@portofpoulsbo.com; www.portofpoulsbo.com. Monitors VHF 66A. Open 7 days a week, all year. Call ahead to be sure the marina isn't completely taken by a rendezvous. Register by 8:00 p.m. to get the combination for the showers and restrooms. The fuel dock has gasoline and diesel. The marina has 130 guest slips, 12-foot depths at low tide, and 30 amp power on all docks. Good restrooms and showers, laundry, free pumpout and portapotty dump, launch ramp, Beacon/BBX and free Wi-Fi, picnic area. Reservations accepted for groups of 8 or more boats. Single boat reser-

Poulsbo fuel dock

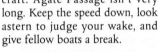

The cold water didn't deter these swimmers at Indianola.

vations limited to 10 at any one time. A meeting room is available. Groceries, tackle and bait nearby.

If anchored out, dinghy tie-up is on the shore side of the dock closest to shore.

Restaurants, bakeries and many shops that specialize in gifts, collectibles, and home accessories are a few steps away in downtown Poulsbo. Dining and shopping are popular. The marina is close to doctors and a post office. The nearby Poulsbo Marine Science Center is excellent, especially for families. Shopping

centers, with supermarkets and the usual stores, are a few blocks away.

Agate Passage connects Port Orchard with Port Madison, and is crossed by a highway bridge with a vertical clearance of 75 feet. Currents in the pass run as high as 6 knots at spring tides, flooding south and ebbing north. The channel through the pass is well marked, but in general, a mid-channel course will serve.

For some reason, many craft go through Agate Passage too

fast, creating havoc for slower craft. Agate Passage isn't very long. Keep the speed down, look astern to judge your wake, and give fellow boats a break.

PORT MADISON AND BAINBRIDGE ISLAND

Miller Bay. Miller Bay indents the Northwest corner of Port Madison. It is very shallow and should be entered only at half tide or better, or with local knowledge. Like many bays on Puget Sound, Miller Bay has a drying shoal in the middle, so navigable water can be found only around the perimeter.

Island View Marine. 20622 Miller Bay Rd. NE, Poulsbo, WA 98392; (360) 598-4900; www.islandviewmarine.net. Open Tuesday through Saturday all year. Haulout to 30 feet, parts and complete repairs. Launch ramp, dry storage.

Suquamish. Suquamish is best known as the winter home of Chief Seattle and the former site of his longhouse, the Old Man House. With its restaurants and other cultural attractions it makes a good day trip from Seattle.

The Suquamish community dock and float, just north of Agate Pass, provides short-term moorage for visiting boats. The east side of the float is exposed to chop from boat traffic and weather in outer Port Madison. If the protected space on the west side is not available, boaters can anchor and take the dinghy to the float. Good anchorage is northeast of the float. A boat ramp is south of the float; it's not usable at low tide.

Today, the town of Suquamish is the center the Suquamish Indian Reservation. A new community center across the street from the dock, the House of Awakened Culture, is patterned after the Old Man House, as is the new Suquamish Museum up the hill.

Visible above the community center is an impressive veteran's

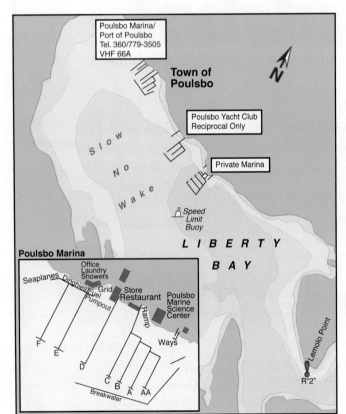

Poulsbo

memorial, with carved figures honoring Chief Kitsap, Chief Seattle, and Suquamish veterans.

From the veteran's memorial, follow signs to Chief Seattle's grave in the Suquamish Tribal Cemetery behind the white church of St. Peter's Catholic Mission. The original gravestone placed by Seattle pioneers is still there, along with more recent Native carvings and inscriptions of his words.

From Chief Seattle's grave, continue walking uphill to the new Suquamish Museum. The museum is open daily, 10:00 a.m. to 5:00 p.m.

Since 1911, the Suquamish Tribe has been celebrating Chief Seattle Days on the third weekend of August. Activities include a traditional salmon bake, canoe races, baseball, drumming and dancing, and a memorial service honoring Chief Seattle.

Readers have reported that the Agate Pass Cafe and Bella Luna Pizzeria, both within easy walking distance of the dock, are excellent.

Indianola. Indianola is distinguished by the long pier that served passengers and freight during Mosquito Fleet days. A float is installed during the summer to give access to the town, which has some supplies. The float grounds on low and minus tides. Overnight moorage is not allowed.

View looking across Puget Sound at the Seattle skyline from Bainbridge Island.

Inner Port Madison. The inner, residential bay extends for about 1.5 miles into the north end of Bainbridge Island. This is where Port Madison Yacht Club and a large Seattle Yacht Club outstation (no reciprocals) are located. Anchorage is good throughout, with a wide bight about 0.75 mile inside the entrance. We are told that shore access is possible from a dinghy dock at a newly-acquired park just west of the SYC outstation. Farther in, **Hidden Cove** is a lovely spot. For Seattle area boats, this is an often-overlooked area to have a picnic lunch or a quiet night at anchor. The shores are private but the setting is idyllic.

Fay Bainbridge State Park. www.biparks. org. South of Point Monroe on Bainbridge Island. Open all year; exposed. Restrooms, showers, no power. The park has 3 kitchen shelters, fireplaces, fire rings, a beach area, launch ramp, and utility and primitive campsites. Also, children's play equipment, horseshoe pits, fishing, clamming, concession stand in summer.

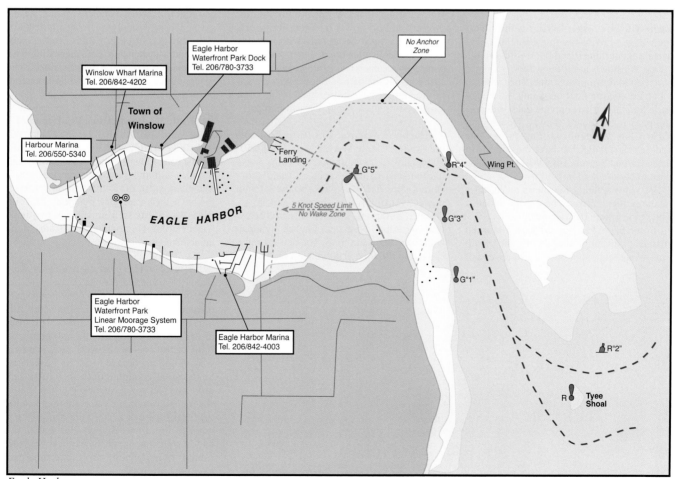

Eagle Harbor

Eagle Harbor Waterfront Park dock

Enjoying the summer sun at Winslow Wharf Marina.

Murden Cove. Murden Cove has convenient anchoring depths, but little protection from winds. It's a long row to shore, partly over drying flats. The residential community of Rolling Bay is at the head of the bay.

Local Knowledge

NO ANCHOR ZONE: The bottom around the south entrance to Eagle Harbor has been capped to prevent the spread of pollutants from a former creosote facility. Do not anchor in this area.

Eagle Harbor. Eagle Harbor is the site of the village of Winslow (old name; the new name is Bainbridge Island but we still call the village Winslow), and is the western terminus of a ferry to downtown Seattle. The town has a lighted visitors float off a fine waterfront park. Several marinas provide guest moorage if a permanent tenant is away. Queen City Yacht Club, Meydenbauer Bay Yacht Club, and Seattle Yacht Club have outstations in Eagle Harbor. Beacon/BBX Wi-Fi is available throughout the harbor.

We enjoy walking the streets of Winslow. Its shops offer art, crafts, books, and antiques. The grocery store has *everything*.

Enter Eagle Harbor through a marked channel past foul ground that extends south from Wing Point. Nun Buoy 2 is at the end of this foul ground, and the Tyee Shoal Beacon is a short distance south of Buoy 2. The ferries round Tyee Shoal Beacon, but other craft can use Buoy 2 safely, following the rule of Red, Right, Returning. Follow the markers all the way in. Shoal water extends out to the channel on both sides. Observe the 5-knot speed limit from Buoy 5.

㊾ **Eagle Harbor Waterfront Park.** 280 Madison Ave. N., Bainbridge Island, WA 98110; (206) 780-3733; www.ci.bainbridge-isl.wa.us. Open all year, overnight moorage on 200 feet of dock, use both sides except at pumpout, 400 feet of offshore guest moorage. Watch the depth at low tide. Restrooms, free showers, but no power or water. Restrooms are open daylight hours only with portable toilets available after hours. Pumpout, portapotty dump, launch ramp, dinghy dock. Good anchorage in the harbor, but it's very crowded. You might have better luck at the linear moorage system. A popular year-round park.

㊾ **Harbour Marina.** 233 Parfitt Way SW, Bainbridge Island, WA 98110; (206) 550-5340; info@harbour-marina.com; www.harbour-marina.com. Open all year. Unoccupied slips used for guest boats, 30 amp power, restrooms, free showers and Wi-Fi, laundry, pumpout. Located directly below Harbour Public House, an English-style pub with beer, wine, and food. The pub is bright, clean, and the food is good. No kids allowed in the pub. Moorage for visiting the pub and Pegasus Coffee House is clearly marked. Short walk to downtown Winslow.

㊾ **Winslow Wharf Marina.** P.O. Box 10297, 141 Parfitt Way SW, Winslow, WA 98110; (206) 842-4202; mike@winslowwharfmarina.com; www.winslowwharfmarina.com. Open 7 days a week, 9:00 a.m. to 5:00 p.m. Guest moorage in unoccupied slips. Maximum boat length 50 feet, 20 & 30 amp power, restrooms, free showers and Wi-Fi, laundry, pumpout, portapotty dump. Look for the sign at the end of the registration dock. A deposit is required for the locked security gate and restroom card. Chandlery Marine, a well-stocked marine supply store, has a little bit of everything, (206) 842-7245. Seattle Yacht Club and Meydenbauer Bay Yacht Club have dock space reserved for their members. The spaces are clearly marked, and non-member boats may not use them.

㊿ **Eagle Harbor Marina.** P.O. Box 11217, 5834 Ward Ave. NE, Bainbridge Island, WA 98110; (206) 842-4003; www.eagleharbormarina.com. Open all year, closed Sunday and Monday. Limited guest moorage, call ahead. Marina has 20, 30 & 50 amp power, restrooms, showers, laundry, pumpout, Beacon/BBX Wi-Fi. Located on the south side of Eagle Harbor. No restaurants or stores in the immediate area.

(51) **Blakely Harbor.** In the early days Blakely Harbor was the site of major lumber and shipbuilding activities. Now it is a quiet residential neighborhood. Some stub pilings remain from the old docks. The head of the bay, including the old mill pond and ruins of the concrete powerhouse, is now a park. Good anchorage in 35 to 50 feet can be found far enough into the bay to be well protected, yet still have a view of the Seattle skyline. Sunset on a clear evening is beautiful. Blakely Rock is 0.5 mile off; give it a good offing. Enter Blakely Harbour in the middle of the mouth of the bay. A drying reef extends from the north shore, and shoals are along the south side.

Evening sailing on Puget Sound.

HOOD CANAL

HOOD CANAL
Dabob Bay • Pleasant Harbor • Alderbrook

Hood Canal is a 65-mile-long glacier-carved fjord. Because the shorelines are fairly straight with few protected anchorages, Hood Canal is less used by pleasure craft than many other waterways. Most boaters don't realize that shrimping, oyster gathering, clamming and fishing can be outstanding. The shrimping season is short: 3 weeks in May, just 2 days each week. But on those days, the boats are thick. In clear weather the views of the Olympic Mountains from Hood Canal are outstanding. Other than shrimpers and knowing fishermen, however, Hood Canal is largely undiscovered.

Several rivers flow from the Olympic Mountains into Hood Canal, and each has formed a mudflat off its mouth. Although the shoal off the Dosewallips River, a couple of miles south of Pulali Point, is marked, the shoals off the Duckabush, Fulton Creek, Hama Hama, and Lilliwaup rivers are not marked, nor is the extensive shoal off the Skokomish River at the Great Bend. Care must be taken to avoid running aground.

Pleasant Harbor and the Alderbrook Inn Resort can take larger boats, but many of the other marinas and parks on Hood Canal are aimed at trailerable boats. This has disappointed some people in larger boats, who had hoped for more facilities for boats their size.

Hood Head. Anchorage can be found behind Hood Head on the western shore of Hood Canal, but the water shoals rapidly to drying flats near the head of the bay.

Shine Tidelands State Park. Stretches 1 mile north of the Hood Canal Bridge into Bywater Bay on the west shore of Hood Canal. Day use only, toilets, no power, water or showers. Anchoring only, well offshore. Launch ramp, crabbing and clamming, hiking trails.

Bywater Bay. Anchor in 6 to 12 feet, good holding on a soft bottom with room to swing. The spit provides wave protection from north winds. A shallow draft boat can easily enter

Crossing under the Frances Rose Bridge.

the lagoon in the undeveloped Wolfe Property State Park at the northwest corner of the bay. [*Hamilton*]

Port Gamble. Port Gamble is a fine anchorage, protected from wave action by a sandspit at the entrance. Anchorage in 18 to 30 feet is possible everywhere. Many people prefer the area just inside the spit. A range outside Port Gamble will keep you to a mid-channel course when entering or departing. Sight astern to keep the range lined up while entering. Your course will lead you close to the ends of the old Pope & Talbot sawmill docks. A section of the old I-90 floating bridge from Lake Washington is moored in the bay, with some Indian-owned fishboats tied to it. Mooring to this bridge is discouraged.

LOCAL KNOWLEDGE

DANGEROUS ROCKS: Sisters, two substantial rocks about 200 yards apart, lie 0.4 mile south of the Hood Canal bridge on the west side. The rocks dry at half tide. The southern rock is marked by a large lighted beacon, yet from time to time an unwary boat manages to go up on these rocks. For safety, if you have passed under the western end of the bridge, turn eastward at once and run parallel to the bridge to the middle before turning south into Hood Canal.

Hood Canal Floating Bridge. The east end of the Hood Canal Floating Bridge has 55 feet of vertical clearance. Clearance on the west end is 35 feet. The bridge can be opened for larger vessels, but it is not manned. To arrange an opening you must call (360) 779-3233, which connects to a State Department of Transportation office in Tacoma. They will take your name, telephone number, name of your vessel, date and time of desired opening, and whether you are inbound or outbound.

They also will ask what width opening you need (300 feet or 600 feet). One hour's notice is needed to get a crew to the bridge and prepare it for opening.

Salsbury Point County Park. Just off the northeast end of the Hood Canal Bridge. Day use only, restrooms, no power. Anchoring only, 2 launch ramps. Picnic tables, fireplaces, children's play area. Nature trail. Sandy beach for experienced divers only because of strong currents.

Kitsap Memorial Marine State Park. Four miles south of Hood Canal Bridge. Open all year, day use and overnight camping, 2 mooring buoys. Restrooms, showers, no power. Picnic sites, kitchen shelters, fireplaces. Standard campsites, swimming beach, playground, horseshoe pits, volleyball courts, baseball field. Buoys are exposed to tidal currents and wind.

Squamish Harbor. Squamish Harbor has convenient anchoring depths, but the harbor is quite open and has numerous rocks and reefs that must be avoided. It is seldom used for overnight anchorage.

Thorndyke Bay. Thorndyke Bay is too open to provide a snug anchorage.

LOCAL KNOWLEDGE

RESTRICTED AREA: For about 4 miles south from Vinland, the eastern shore of Hood Canal is a Naval Restricted Area, and is patrolled constantly to keep passing vessels well away. The patrol craft are fitted with guns, and are authorized to blow intruders out of the water. Best practice is to stay west of mid channel when transiting this area.

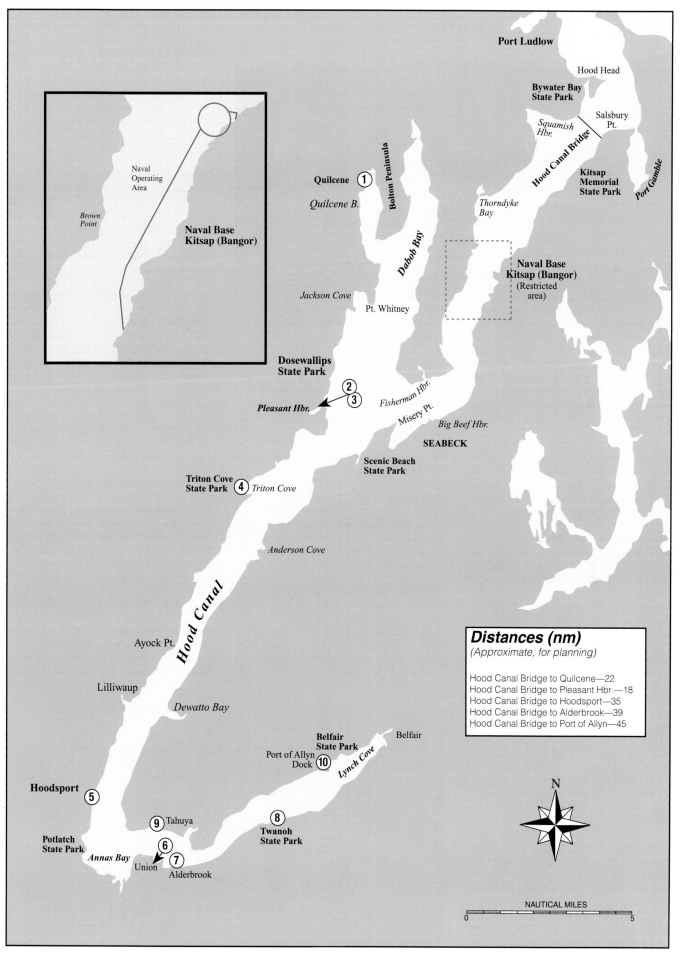

Port Ludlow

Hood Head

Bywater Bay State Park

Squamish Hbr.

Salsbury Pt.

Hood Canal Bridge

Kitsap Memorial State Park

Port Gamble

Quilcene ①

Quilcene B.

Bolton Peninsula

Thorndyke Bay

Dabob Bay

Naval Base Kitsap (Bangor) (Restricted area)

Jackson Cove

Pt. Whitney

Dosewallips State Park

②
③

Pleasant Hbr.

Fisherman Hbr.

Misery Pt.

Big Beef Hbr.

SEABECK

Scenic Beach State Park

Triton Cove State Park ④ *Triton Cove*

Anderson Cove

Hood Canal

Ayock Pt.

Lilliwaup

Dewatto Bay

Belfair

Belfair State Park

Port of Allyn Dock ⑩

Lynch Cove

Hoodsport

⑤

⑨ Tahuya

⑧

Twanoh State Park

Potlatch State Park

⑥
⑦

Annas Bay

Union

Alderbrook

Inset map
Naval Operating Area

Brown Point

Naval Base Kitsap (Bangor)

Distances box

Distances (nm)
(Approximate, for planning)

Hood Canal Bridge to Quilcene—22
Hood Canal Bridge to Pleasant Hbr.—18
Hood Canal Bridge to Hoodsport—35
Hood Canal Bridge to Alderbrook—39
Hood Canal Bridge to Port of Allyn—45

N

NAUTICAL MILES
0   5

The Naval Base Kitsap (Bangor) is a well-marked restricted area. The Navy is authorized to use "deadly force" to protect it. Pass well clear and out of the restricted area.

Naval Base Kitsap (Bangor). This is the location of Bangor Naval Station, home port for a fleet of nuclear submarines. Several of these awesome machines often are visible to passing craft. Stay outside of the marked restricted area.

Seabeck Bay. Anchorage is possible behind Misery Point, with good protection from the south and west. A 200-slip marina has been proposed. See updates on www.Waggoner-Guide.com and Waggoner eNews.

Scenic Beach State Park. South of Seabeck. Open for day use all year and overnight camping in summer only. Restrooms, showers, no power. Anchoring only. Kitchen shelter, fireplaces, fire rings, horseshoe pits, volleyball areas. Standard and primitive campsites. Scuba diving, swimming, hiking, shellfishing.

Fisherman Harbor. Fisherman Harbor can be entered only at high water, but once inside offers protected anchorage in 5 to 15 feet. Follow the natural channel into the bay, then turn south and follow the spit until anchoring depths are found. All the land around the bay is privately owned. Years ago, we tiptoed into Fisherman Harbor in a sailboat at something less than high tide. It was careful going, with a close watch from the bow and a bit of luck, but the boat got in without touching. Less foolish souls should wait for higher water. [*Hale*]

Dabob Bay. Most of Dabob Bay is a Naval Restricted Area, with lights on Point Syloplash, Point Whitney, and Point Zelatched that warn when caution must be used (flashing green) or when the area is closed (flashing red). South of Pulali Point, the western shore of Dabob Bay is not within this restricted area, and includes Jackson Cove, where good anchorage can be found.

A State Department of Fish and Wildlife oyster research laboratory is at Whitney Point, with a good launch ramp alongside. A breakwater-protected marina is at the village of Quilcene. Caution should be exercised when transiting Dabob Bay and Quilcene Bay to avoid the large number of shrimp pots during the season.

Broad Spit Park. On the east shore of Bolton Peninsula in Dabob Bay. Anchor on either side of the spit, depending on wind direction. Easy beach access, trails ashore. Lagoon that fills at high tide. [*Thanks to readers David and Sharon von Wolffersdorff.*]

Quilcene Bay. Anchor in 12 feet, good holding in mud, along the east shore opposite the marina, with protection from moderate southerly winds. On a 10-foot tide, a shallow draft vessel can travel at least a quarter mile up Donovan Creek through winding grasslands at the head of the bay. [*Hamilton*]

① **Herb Beck Marina.** 1731 Linger Longer Rd., Quilcene, WA 98376; (360) 765-3131; www.portofpt.com/quilcene_marina.htm. Formerly Quilcene Boathaven, now managed by the Port of Port Townsend. Monitors VHF 09 & 16. Open 7 days a week in summer, as needed in winter. Gasoline and diesel at fuel dock. Guest moorage to 40 feet, 20 & 30 amp power, water, showers, restrooms, pumpout, repairs, supplies, ice. Reservations accepted. This is a small, rustic marina.

Dosewallips State Park. South of Brinnon. Park open all year for day use and overnight camping. Accessible by kayak or canoe. Restrooms, showers. Hiking trails, picnic areas, standard, utility, and primitive campsites.

Pleasant Harbor. Pleasant Harbor is a major stopping point on Hood Canal, with a good destination resort marina and a state park dock. Enter through a narrow channel with least depth of 8.5 feet at zero tide. Inside, there's room to anchor, 18 to 42 feet, mud bottom. Pleasant Harbor Marina has excellent facilities for visiting boats. Home Port Marina of Pleasant Harbor (formerly, Pleasant Harbor "Old" Marina) has no guest moorage.

Pleasant Harbor is full of boats in May, when the annual 3-week-long shrimping season is under way. Shrimping is allowed only on Wednesdays and Saturdays, and during those three weeks it can be crazy.

② **Pleasant Harbor Marina.** 308913 Hwy 101, Brinnon, WA 98320; (360) 796-4611; (800) 547-3479; info@pleasantharbormarina.com; www.pleasantharbormarina.com. Monitors VHF 9 & 16. Open all year. Closed Thanksgiving and Christmas. Café open Friday through Sunday from October through February. Gasoline and diesel at the fuel dock. The marina has approximately 60 guest slips and unoccupied slips as available, 30 & 50 amp power. Side-tie moorage can accommodate large boats. Facilities include sparkling clean restrooms and showers, laundry, Wi-Fi, on-site security. Pumpout at the fuel dock. A barge they call "The Caboose,"

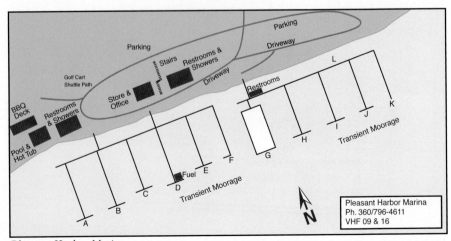

Pleasant Harbor Marina

The well-protected moorage at Pleasant Harbor Marina has approximately 60 guest slips.

Pleasant Harbor Marina's docks are well maintained.

with clean showers and toilets, is moored at the north docks.

For exercise, a shuttle van can take you to four local hikes. They range in length from a 0.2 mile trail to 130-foot-high Dose Falls, to a 3.5-mile loop of Dosewallips State Park.

This is a popular destination. Reservations strongly recommended, especially on weekends and holidays. Many of the permanent tenants spend considerable time at the marina, and life on the docks is quite friendly. Upland, you'll find groceries (well-stocked convenience store but not a supermarket),

espresso, ice, bait, tackle, marine hardware, beer and wine, gift shop, barbecue and picnic area. The new restaurant offers steak, seafood, pizza, and burgers. Swimming pool, hot tub, kayak rentals, live music and scavenger hunts April through September. Diane Coleman is the very capable manager.

Planned for 2014: The last of the wood docks (E & F docks) and the old marina store building are being replaced. The new building will offer a full restaurant and marina office with store. Upstairs will be a lounge and outdoor seating. At press time the old build-

ing had been demolished and plans call for everything to be completed by the summer 2014 season. See www.WaggonerGuide.com and Waggoner eNews for updates.

③ **Pleasant Harbor Marine State Park.** (360) 796-4415. Open all year for day use and overnight mooring. No camping. Dock has 218 feet of space. Boaters may stay up to 3 consecutive nights. Vault toilet, porta-potty dump, pumpout, no power. This is the first dock on the right as you enter Pleasant Harbor.

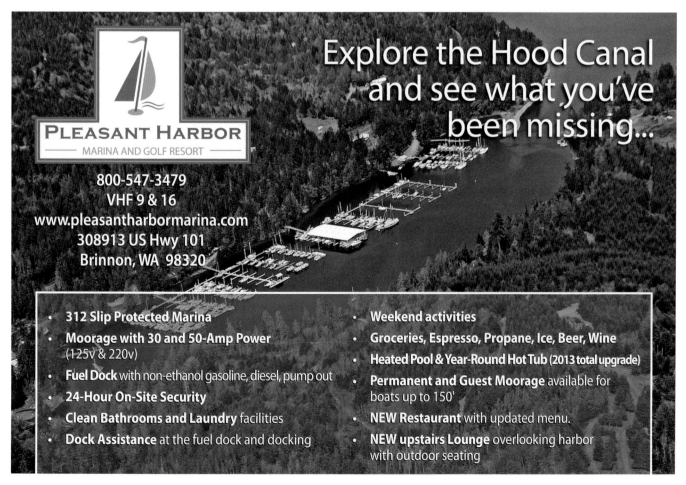

Triton Head. A state park launch ramp is at Triton Head, and anchorage is possible off this little bight.

④ **Triton Cove State Park.** West side of Hood Canal, south of the Dosewallips River. Open all year, day use only, small dock with float. Restrooms, no power, no showers. Improved concrete launch ramp, picnic area.

⑤ **Hoodsport.** Hoodsport is popular with scuba divers as a place to view the giant Pacific octopus. Local marine preserves such as Octopus Hole and Sund Rock offer divers the chance to see octopus, wolf eels, rockfish, anemones and other marine life.

The town has a grocery store, hardware store, restaurants, an espresso shop, a dentist, a beauty salon and gift shops. The Washington Department of Fish and Wildlife operates a fish hatchery in town.

⑤ **Port of Hoodsport.** P.O. Box 429, Hoodsport, WA 98548; (360) 877-9350; portmail@hctc.com; www.portofhoodsport. us. New docks with guest moorage. Self-register at head of dock, $10/night. Grocery store, park nearby.

Sunrise Motel & Resort. 24520 Hwy 101, Hoodsport, WA 98548; (360) 877-5301; sunrise@hctc.com; myweb.hcc.net/sunrise. Open all year, no power. Restrooms and showers in motel rooms. Stay on your boat or rent rooms. Maximum length 20 feet. Underwater park, dive shop, scuba air station, propane, barbecue.

Potlatch Marine State Park. South of Hoodsport. Open all year, day use and overnight camping and mooring. Restrooms, showers, no power. Four mooring buoys are offshore in deep water, except the second buoy as you approach from the north. We are told this buoy swings into 5-foot depths at zero tide. The park has a picnic area, an underwater park for scuba diving, short hiking trails, standard, utility and primitive campsites. Good wildlife-watching.

Alderbrook Resort, at the south end of Hood Canal, is elegant yet relaxed.

⑥ **Hood Canal Marina.** P.O. Box 305, 5101 E. Hwy 106, Union, WA 98592; (360) 898-2252; hoodcanalmarina@hctc. com; www.hood-canal-marina.com. Certified Clean Marina. Open all year. Fuel dock with gasoline & diesel, open daily 8:00 a.m. to 5:00 p.m. Limited guest moorage, 30 amp power, restrooms, pumpout. Call ahead for moorage. New docks and pilings. A Boat US/Vessel Assist marina, mechanic on call. Grocery store nearby, launch ramp adjacent. Union Paddle and Row offers kayak, paddleboard, and rowing rentals.

⑦ **Alderbrook Resort & Spa.** 10 E. Alderbrook Drive, Union, WA 98592; (360) 898-2200; (360) 898-2252; hoodcanalmarina@hctc.com; www.alderbrookresort.com. Monitors VHF 66A. Open all year, 1500 feet of guest moorage. Restrooms, showers, 30 & 50 amp power, pumpout, free Wi-Fi, water, telephone hook-up, swimming pool and whirlpool spa. Seaplane dock and kayak, paddleboard, and rowing rentals.

If you're looking for a quality development, you'll find it here. After a long decline, Alderbrook was taken over by a new owner who closed the facility for nearly two years and completely rebuilt it to luxury resort standards. The rooms are beautifully appointed, the grounds are immaculate, and the din-

ing room is superb.

They have an indoor pool, with a spa adjacent. Everything you're looking for in a luxury resort is here, including golf. Best to call ahead for reservations and prices.

Golf: Alderbrook Golf & Yacht Club, 18 holes, par 72; (360) 898-2560.

⑧ **Twanoh Marine State Park.** (360) 275-2222. Eight miles west of Belfair. Open all year, day use and overnight camping and mooring, except no camping in winter. Has 200 feet of overnight moorage and an additional 100 feet of day-use only dock, 7 mooring buoys. Restrooms, showers, pumpout, portapotty dump, no power. This is a large and popular park, with launch ramp, wading pool and playground, picnic areas, kitchen shelters, and fireplaces. Standard, utility and primitive campsites, tennis courts, hiking trails, seasonal concession stand.

⑨ **Summertide Resort & Marina.** P.O. Box 450, 15781 NE Northshore Rd, Tahuya, WA 98588; (360) 275-9313; www. summertideresort.com. Guest moorage, 50-foot maximum boat length. Restrooms, showers, no power. Launch ramp, RV spaces with hook-ups. Rental cottages available. Store carries groceries, beer and wine, snacks, ice, bait, tackle. Reservations necessary.

Belfair State Park. (800) 452-5687. Three miles southwest of Belfair on the north shore of Hood Canal. Open all year for day use and overnight camping. Restrooms, showers, no power. Anchor far offshore if at all. Drying mudflats restrict approach to small, shallow-draft boats only. Popular park, camping reservations required in summer.

⑩ **Port of Allyn.** P.O. Box 1, Allyn, WA 98524; (360) 275-2430; www.portofallyn. com. Open all year, 10 slips. Newly renovated pier and floats. Has 20 amp power, portable toilets, pumpout and portapotty dump ($2, quarters only). No water, no showers. Launch ramp. Very limited space for visiting boats. Call ahead to hook up to power.

The docks at Alderbrook are right in front of the main hotel.

NORTH PUGET SOUND

NORTHWEST PUGET SOUND
Kingston • Admiralty Inlet • Port Ludlow
• Port Townsend

NORTHEAST PUGET SOUND
Edmonds • Everett • Langley • Saratoga Passage
• Coupeville • Oak Harbor • La Conner •
Deception Pass • Anacortes • Bellingham
• Semiahmoo Bay • Blaine • Point Roberts

Kingston.

Kingston. Kingston, in Appletree Cove on the west side of Puget Sound, is the western terminus of the ferry run to Edmonds. A Port-owned marina, with park, is behind a breakwater in Appletree Cove. The park's meticulously maintained lawn and gardens are inviting. Kingston's main street is lined with cafés, many with outdoor seating. Farther uptown are a grocery store and hardware store. On the north side of the ferry holding area a deck overlooks Puget Sound. A path leads to a Port-owned broad sandy beach filled with driftwood. It's a pleasant walk and great for families. On the the park grounds next to the marina a farmers market, quite popular, is open 9:00 a.m. to 2:00 p.m. Saturdays, May to mid-October. Concerts in the Park, with a beer garden, are held Saturday evenings during July and August.

A pavilion on the park grounds, just up from the marina, is used for music concerts, gatherings, and weddings. The pavilion is dedicated to the memory of Michael Bookey, the farsighted and imaginative port manager from 2007 to 2009.

Anchoring is good south of the marina breakwater. Watch your depths. It gets shallow close to shore.

① **Port of Kingston.** P.O. Box 559, Kingston, WA 98346; (360) 297-3545; info@portofkingston.org; www.portofkingston.org. Monitors VHF 65A but prefers telephone calls. Open all year, 49 guest slips to 50 feet, water and 30 amp power. At the outer end of the guest dock an 86-foot-long float, with water and 30 & 50 amp power, accommodates larger boats. The marina has restrooms, laundry, portapotty dump, free showers, free pumpout, free Wi-Fi. The fuel dock has gasoline, diesel and Delo lubricants. A dual-lane concrete launch ramp, with a float between the two lanes, is available. A kayak center is located on A Dock; key cards issued by Port office required for access. Parking (fee charged) for tow vehicles and trailers. An electric courtesy car is available for local trips to shopping several blocks away. The car is popular; one hour usage recommended; we suggest reserving it well in advance.

Kingston moorage on an overcast day. Fuel dock is in the foreground; visitor moorage parallels the breakwater.

Four mooring buoys for boats to 35 feet are outside the breakwater, north of the ferry dock. They are exposed to winds and the wakes of passing boat traffic.

Moorage reservations are accepted with one day advance notice. Kingston has become quite popular—during the summer months reservations are important. Reserved slips are marked and are not available, even for temporary use.

Enter the marina around the end of the rock breakwater. Leave two pilings that mark the edge of the dredged channel to port. Leave the red buoy marking the end of the breakwater to starboard. Guest moorage is in slips extending from the dock that runs parallel to the breakwater, plus the side-tie float for larger boats at the outer end. The fuel float is at the shore end of the guest dock. Working from the shore end of the guest dock: the first five are 20-foot slips; then two 50-foot Kingston Cove Yacht Club reciprocal slips; then the 50-foot slips; then the 40-foot slips; and then the 30-foot slips. Moor in any unreserved guest dock slip and register at the Port office.

On the guest dock, two gazebos with picnic tables and power are popular with visiting boaters. One is located adjacent to the 40-foot slips and the other in the area of the 30-foot slips. First-come, first-served. See the website for a schedule of music events.

Golf. Nearby, the new White Horse Golf Club has been getting excellent reviews. They have a free shuttle to the ferry dock and marina. Call (360) 297-4468. The Point No Point Casino (360) 297-0070 and the Clearwater Casino (360)598-8700, also offer shuttle service.

ADMIRALTY INLET

Admiralty Inlet begins at Point No Point in the south and ends at Point Wilson in the north. Admiralty Inlet is wide, deep, and straight, with no hazardous reefs or shoals. It makes up for this good design by often being the only patch of rough water for miles. Flood current or ebb, Admiralty Inlet waters swirl and lump up. If the wind is light, you'll see the swirls. If the wind is blowing, you'll be in the lump. Use the Bush Point current tables to predict the times of slack water, and the time and strength of maximum current.

If Admiralty Inlet is rough and you have to be there anyway, try to favor the eastern or western shores. The western shore is preferred. A suggested route is along Marrowstone Island, far enough off to avoid the rocks shown on the chart. Approach around Marrowstone Point inside the rough water just outside, and into Port Townsend Bay.

If you are northbound past Point No Point and you can see that Admiralty Inlet is rough (you can see it), head west across the south tip of Marrowstone Island, and go through Port Townsend Canal into Port Townsend Bay. Port Townsend Canal currents are based on the Deception Pass current tables.

CHARTS	
18441	Puget Sound – Northern Part (1:80,000)
18445 sc folio small-craft	Puget Sound-Possession Sound to Olympia including Hood Canal
18446	Puget Sound – Apple Cove Pt. to Keyport (1:25,000)
18464	Port Townsend (1:20,000)
18471	Dungeness to Oak Bay (1:40,000)
18473	Puget Sound – Oak Bay to Shilshole Bay (1:40,000)
18477	Puget Sound – Entrance to Hood Canal (1:25,000)

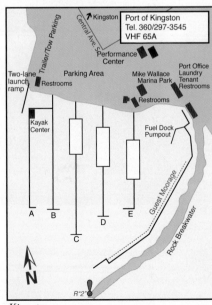

Kingston

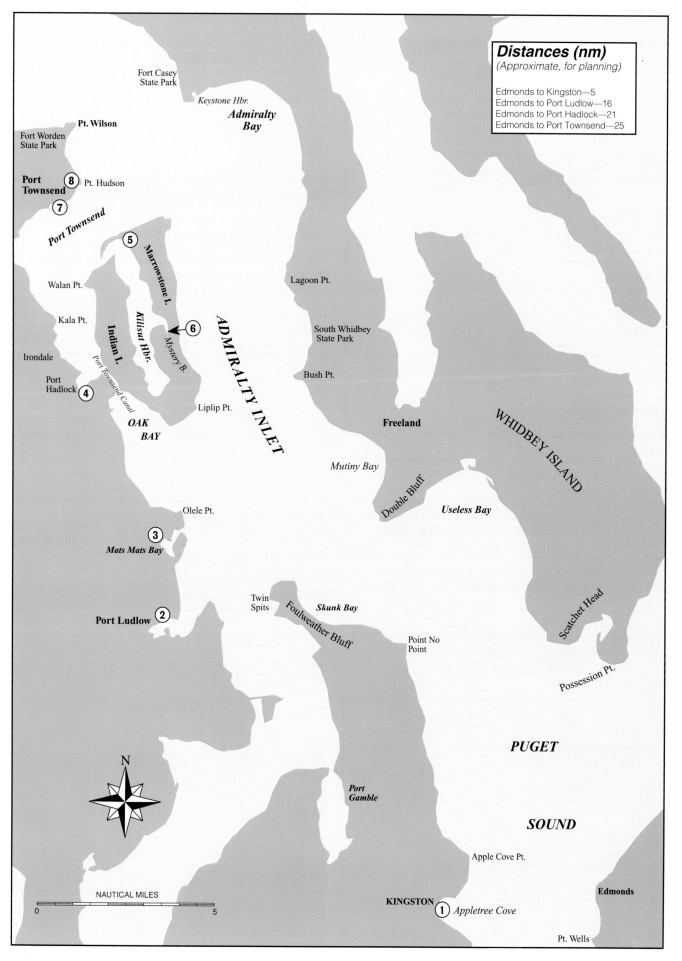

Fort Casey
State Park

Keystone Hbr.

*Admiralty
Bay*

Distances (nm)
(Approximate, for planning)

Edmonds to Kingston—5
Edmonds to Port Ludlow—16
Edmonds to Port Hadlock—21
Edmonds to Port Townsend—25

Pt. Wilson

Fort Worden
State Park

**Port
Townsend** ⑧ Pt. Hudson

⑦

Port Townsend

⑤

Marrowstone I.

Lagoon Pt.

Walan Pt.

Kilisut Hbr.

South Whidbey
State Park

Kala Pt.

Indian I. ⑥ *Mystery B.*

ADMIRALTY INLET

Irondale

Port Townsend Canal

Bush Pt.

Port
Hadlock ④

Liplip Pt.

Freeland

WHIDBEY ISLAND

*OAK
BAY*

Mutiny Bay

Olele Pt.

Double Bluff

Useless Bay

③

Mats Mats Bay

Scatchet Head

Twin
Spits *Skunk Bay*

Port Ludlow ②

Foulweather Bluff

Point No
Point

Possession Pt.

PUGET

N

*Port
Gamble*

SOUND

Apple Cove Pt.

NAUTICAL MILES

Edmonds

0   5

KINGSTON ① *Appletree Cove*

Pt. Wells

POINT NO POINT AT ITS WORST

Bob and Marilynn Hale had an experience on Labor Day in 1999 when they saw a Sea Ray, about 27 feet long, drying out in Kingston. The day before, a strong wind blowing against the current had set up high, steep seas off Point No Point, and the Sea Ray went through. It came off one wave and buried its nose in the next. The foredeck hatch was torn open and about 50 gallons (400 pounds) of green water poured below. When the Hales met the owner the following day he still was visibly shaken. He'd had an uncomfortably close call.

About the time the Sea Ray had its adventure, a 40-footer had it worse. It too buried its bow in a wave and tore open the foredeck hatch, putting much water below. The next wave blew out the windshield. Water came aboard, and that boat went down. Fast. Other boats were in the area and everybody was saved, but they had to be pulled from the water.

These conditions are rare at Point No Point. Most round it all the time without a problem. But in a way, that makes Point No Point more dangerous. In Vancouver, for instance, locals know that Point Atkinson often is very rough, and always treat the waters off Point Atkinson with respect. Since Point No Point usually is fairly easy to get by, there's a tendency to assume it always will be easy, and that's when you can get in trouble.

Point No Point. Point No Point, on the west side of Puget Sound, is a popular salmon-fishing spot and a place where boats heading up-sound and down-sound tend to converge. Boat traffic can get heavy, especially when the salmon are running and the waters are literally covered with small sport fishing boats working along the tide-rip.

Watch out for this tide-rip. When a strong wind opposes a big tide, the waters off Point No Point can turn dangerous.

LOCAL KNOWLEDGE

NAVIGATION NOTE: Check your chart before entering the landlocked Port Ludlow inner harbor and be sure you pass between the two islets. Passing outside of either islet could put you aground.

SPEED LIMIT: A 5-mph "no wake" speed limit is in effect throughout Port Ludlow and applies to all vessels, including dinghies.

② **Port Ludlow.** Well-protected Port Ludlow indents the western shore of Puget Sound. It was once the site of a major Pope & Talbot sawmill, and now is a nice residential area, a destination resort, and a marina. Anchorage is good south of the marina, and in the landlocked inner harbor, reached by passing between two little islands near the head of the bay. Deeper draft boats should watch the depth sounder closely when entering the inner harbor at low tide. The passage is shallower than the bays it connects. Good anchorage, mud bottom, is in about 15 feet. An 8-foot shoal area a short distance northeast of the entrance is noted on large scale Chart 18477.

The inner harbor is a favorite destination in Puget Sound, protected from all winds. Until a few years ago it was surrounded by dense forest. Development has removed much of the forest and replaced it with upscale private homes. The homes are set well back and often screened by trees, so the bay retains at least some of its old charm. Meydenbauer Bay Yacht Club has an outstation on the peninsula that forms the inner harbor.

② **Port Ludlow Resort and Marina.** 1 Gull Drive, Port Ludlow, WA 98365; (360) 437-0513; (877) 344-6725; marina@portludlowresort.com; www.portludlowresort.com. Monitors VHF 68. Certified Clean Marina. Open 7 days a week, all year. Gasoline, diesel, and propane at the fuel dock. Excellent concrete docks. Guest moorage in 50 slips and along 460 feet of dock plus unoccupied slips as available, 30 & 50 amp power, water, restrooms, laundry, Wi-Fi, gazebo with barbecue, pumpout, porta-potty dump, free showers. Reciprocal moorage is on A dock. Pavilion tent for groups. Kayak and fishing boat rentals. Reservations recommended.

A resort restaurant and lounge are within walking distance. Locals speak highly of the restaurant. Free shuttle for marina guests to the resort's 18-hole golf course. The marina store carries convenience groceries, sandwiches, ice cream, beer, wine, ice, books, and limited marine hardware and supplies. Nearby doctor, camping, post office. Marine mechanics are on call from Port Townsend. With its large grounds, pavilion tent, dining and golf, this a popular destination for groups and rendezvous.

The resort often runs cruise-in specials that include moorage, golf, and restaurant credit. Check website.

③ **Mats Mats Bay.** A course between Port Ludlow and Mats Mats Bay should avoid Snake Rock, close to shore, and Colvos Rocks and Klas Rocks, farther offshore. Colvos Rocks are marked by flashing lights at the north and south ends, and Klas Rocks by a bell buoy. Snake Rock is not marked.

Mats Mats Bay has a dogleg entrance with a least depth of 5 feet. A lighted range shows the center of the narrow channel. A rock once almost blocked the entrance to the bay. It was blasted out years ago, and buoys now mark the channel. Pay attention to all buoys, and do not stray from the marked channel, especially at low water. You'll find anchorage in 18 feet in the middle

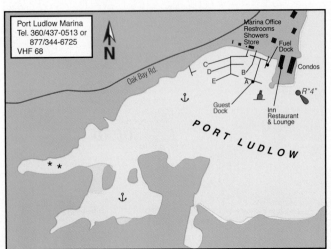

Port Ludlow

The Port Ludlow Marina has excellent docks and is well managed.

The Ajax Café is just a short row from Port Hadlock Marina.

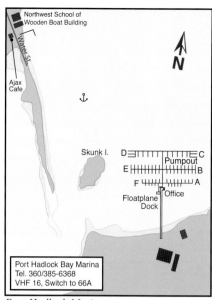

Port Hadlock Marina

and south parts of the bay. The large number of boats on permanent moorings restrict anchoring options. Mats Mats Bay is well protected from almost any wind. A launch ramp is at the south end of the bay.

Oak Bay. Oak Bay, with convenient anchoring depths, is at the southern approach to Port Townsend Canal. Oak Bay County Park is on the west side of the channel, approximately one mile south of the entrance to the canal.

Oak Bay County Park. Northwest shore of Oak Bay. Open all year, restrooms, launch ramp, campsites, picnic tables, no power, no water. Anchoring or beaching only. Marked by a rock jetty. Swimming, scuba diving, clamming, crabbing.

Port Townsend Canal. Port Townsend Canal (also known as Hadlock Canal) runs from Oak Bay to Port Townsend Bay through a relatively narrow dredged channel. The canal is well marked, easy to transit, and spanned by a bridge with 58-foot vertical clearance. Currents run to 3 knots. Port Townsend Canal is a secondary station under the Deception Pass reference station in the current tables.

Port Hadlock and Irondale. The towns of Irondale and Port Hadlock are west of the northern entrance to Port Townsend Canal. The hotel and restaurant at Port Hadlock are closed, but the marina is fully operational. Anchorage is good, sand bottom. Stay north of Skunk Island, due west from the marina.

④ **Port Hadlock Marina.** 173 Hadlock Bay Rd., Port Hadlock, WA 98339; (360) 385-6368; harbormaster@porthadlock-marina.com; www.porthadlockmarina.com. Monitors VHF 16, switch to 66A. Open all year, 30 & 50 amp power, call two days ahead for availability of transient moorage. Managed by enthusiastic Ted and Diane Hornick. Restrooms, showers, laundry, garbage, pumpout, free Wi-Fi. Rental kayaks. Mostly permanent moorage. The marina has 600 feet of nice beach and 3 picnic areas with tables,

power, barbecues, and a 6-foot fire pits. The marina hosts a customer appreciation barbecue the second Saturday of each month, year-round, weather permitting. No groceries, repairs, or marine supplies at marina, but a general store and laundromat are about a mile away. The highly regarded Ajax Café, (360) 385-3450 (closed Mondays and reservations recommended) is a short dinghy ride to the west, across the street from the dinghy dock and the Northwest School of Wooden Boat Building.

Kilisut Harbor. Kilisut Harbor is entered

through a channel between Walan Point and the spit protecting the harbor. When approaching the entrance stay clear of the Navy restricted area off Walan Point. The channel is well marked though shallow, averaging about 11 feet. The channel swings past Fort Flagler State Park on the north shore, with launch ramp and dock. Picnicking and camping facilities are ashore.

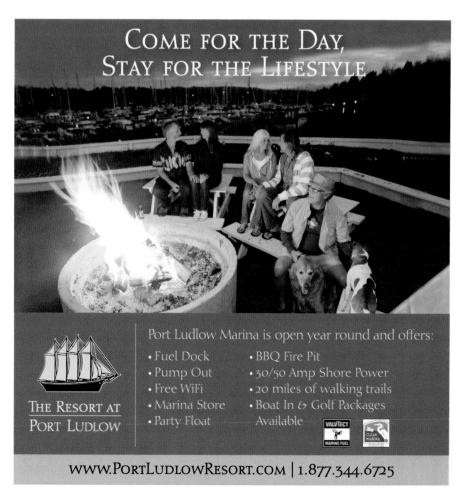

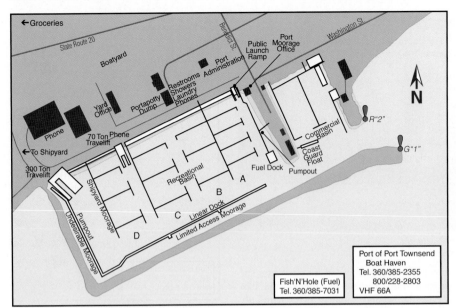

Port Townsend Boat Haven

The channel leads through Kilisut Harbor to Mystery Bay, where the village of Nordland has a float and a great old general store. **Mystery Bay Marine State Park** has a long mooring float parallel to the shore. Small boats can be launched over the beach. Anchorage is good, mud bottom, throughout the bay.

⑤ **Fort Flagler Marine State Park.** (360) 385-1259. On Marrowstone Island. Open all year, 784 acres, day use, overnight mooring and camping. Has 256 feet of dock space with 6-foot depths at zero tide (docks removed in winter), 7 mooring buoys, and launch ramp. The current can run strongly through this area; allow for it while mooring. Restrooms, showers, laundry, portapotty dump, no power. Easy trails lead to old fortifications along the north shore of Marrowstone Island. Underwater park for divers. Snack and grocery concession. Boat rentals, fishing supplies. Standard, utility, and primitive campsites. Campsite reservations are a good idea in summer, call (800) 452-5687.

⑥ **Mystery Bay Marine State Park.** (360) 385-1259. In Kilisut Harbor on Marrowstone Island. Open all year, 10 acres, 683 feet dock space with 4.5-foot depth at zero tide, 7 mooring buoys. Pumpout, portapotty dump, toilets, launch ramp, no power, no showers. This park is open for day use only, but overnight mooring is permitted at the dock. The dock runs parallel to shore. Call Fort Flagler office for more information (360) 388-1259. The charming Nordland General Store is at the shallow end of the bay with a dock in front. Dinghy landing only.

Port Townsend. Port Townsend has two Port-owned marinas, Point Hudson Marina and the Port of Port Townsend's Boat Haven Marina. Boat Haven is closer to a supermarket, but Point Hudson is closer to downtown.

Port Townsend is a major boatbuilding and repair center, with craftsmen skilled in every nautical discipline. It is the home of the annual Wooden Boat Festival at Point Hudson Marina, held the weekend after Labor Day. Next to the Port Hudson Marina is the Northwest Maritime Center and the Wooden Boat Chandlery. Northwest Maritime Center welcomes visitors. Wooden Boat Chandlery carries an array of nautical items.

Port Townsend is a favorite destination. The commercial district is lined with imposing stone and brick buildings from before 1900. At that time, residents hoped Port Townsend would become the western terminus of the transcontinental railroad and the principal city on Puget Sound. Victorian homes, many of them beautifully restored and cared for, are on the hill above the business district. Port Townsend's upper business district is at the top of a long flight of stairs from the lower district on Water Street. The town of Port Townsend is a haven for writers, craftspeople and artists of all kinds. Tourists overwhelm the town during the summer, but

PORT TOWNSEND MARKETPLACE

RESTAURANTS & SHOPS

THE WINE SELLER

The Small Town Wine Shop With a Big City Selection, since 1982. Amazing Selection of Fine Wines, Champagne, Beer & Ale, Ciders, Gourmet Foods, Cheese, Coffee Chocolate & CIGARS. Surprisingly Competitve Prices! Generous Mixed-Whole and 1/2 Case Discounts. Knowledgeable Friendly Wine Specialists!! OPEN 7 DAYS a WEEK. Marina Delivery Available!
360-385-7673 • 1010 Water St. • www.PTwineSeller.com

ELEVATED ICE CREAM & CANDY SHOP

We use the freshest local Ingredients in our flavorful ice creams, ices and sherbets, and handcraft our own chocolates and truffles. See our assortment of dark chocolate bars, candies and gifts. We're open late during boating season! Just two blocks west of Point Hudson. Find us on Facebook.
360-385-1156 • 627 Water St. • www.elevatedicecream.com

THE WOODEN BOAT CHANDLERY

For boatbuilders we supply bronze hardware, copper nails, oakum, varnish and rope. For boat owners and maritime lovers, we offer navigational instruments, ship's bells, Gill jackets & gloves, hats & scarves, unbreakable dinnerware, NOAA charts & cruising guides, maritime books, prisms, portholes, lighting, Shipmate stoves and nautical gifts.
431 Water St. • Inside Northwest Maritime Center
360-385-3628 x101 • www.woodenboatchandlery.com

DON'S PHARMACY

Port Townsend's Locally Owned/Operated Community Pharmacy and Old Fashioned Soda Fountain. We offer a large selection of merchandise, amazing banana splits, malts/milkshakes, and burgers with good old hometown customer service! Located right along the waterfront next to the ferry – within walking distance to Downtown.
1151 Water Street • 360-385-2622
www.donspharmacy-pt.com

SIRENS — A PUB OF DISTINCTION

Above the waterfront, with a fun and eclectic decor, featuring an extensive food and drink menu and a casual, welcoming atmosphere, Sirens is a favorite for visitors and locals alike. In the summer, enjoy a table on one of our two decks overlooking the historic Port Townsend waterfront. In the winter, cozy up to the fireplace. Live music Fri. and Sat. nights. Open at noon. Happy Hour from 4:00 - 6:00 p.m. 21 and over please.
360-379-1100 • 823 Water St. • www.sirenspub.com

NIFTY FIFTYS SODA FOUNTAIN

Step back in time and relive the past. Burgers, fries, hot dogs, chicken strips, shakes, ice cream sodas and more. Even Italian cream sodas, beer and wine. Finish with an ice cream sundae or our fried ice cream. All served to the beat and swing of the 50s on the waterfront.
360-385-1931 • 817 Water Street
www.niftyfiftyspt.com

GETABLES

Boaters, campers, and those on the go will discover a wide variety of local beer, wine, cider, cheese, snacks, soda, and gifts to enhance your visit to this historic Victorian seaport. Family-owned and operated. Open daily: 10-6 • 10% discount for mentioning the Waggoner Cruising Guide.
810 Water Street #1 • 360-385-5560
www.getablespt.com

ALCHEMY BISTRO & WINE BAR

Romantic dinners • Get-togethers for lunch • Sunday brunch
Explore our menu with dishes from Italy, Spain and France. Favorites include our farmers market risotto, fresh ravioli, cioppino, or seafood and chorizo paella. Finish with Kahlua cake, or four port wines with cheese. Featuring over 150 wine selections and "Bar & Bites," our small plate menu. Lunch at 11, dinner at 5, Bar & Bites at 4. Sunday Brunch 9-3.
360-385-5225 • 842 Washington St. • alchemybistroandwinebar.com

ADDIE MAES - DOWN-HOME SOUTHERN COOKING

The flavors of the south evoke words like "mouthwatering" and "comfort food." Our classic southern fried chicken is done just right, crisp and juicy. Our other favorites such as jambalaya, gumbo, and crawfish ettouffee will delight. Or, choose one of our traditional specialties such as mac 'n cheese, shrimp and grits, St. Louis spare ribs or BBQ beef brisket. Arrive hungry and bring your friends or family for our delicious southern cooking. Voted best new restaurant in Port Townsend. Open daily for lunch or dinner, breakfast on Saturday and Sunday.
360-385-1236 • 634 Water St. • addiemaesouthernkitchen.com

PORT TOWNSEND COMMUNITY EVENTS

Gallery Walk	First Saturday of each month 5:30-8PM
Farmer's Market	Saturdays from April-December
Concerts on the Dock	Thursday during July and August
January 24-26	Strangebrew Festival
March 21-23	4th Annual Spring Boating Symposium
March 22	Victorian Heritage Day
May 10-17	Port Townsend Rhododendron Festival
June 6-8	3rd Annual Steampunk Hootenanny
June 12	Taste of Port Townsend
June 13-15	31st Annual Classic Mariners' Regatta
June 28	Raker's Car show
July 25-26	Centrum's Jazz Festival
September 5-7	38th Annual Wooden Boat Festival
September 6-7	41st Annual Crafts by the Dock Fair
September 19-21	Port Townsend Film Festival
October 3-5	PT Kinetic Skulpture Weekend

There's always something interesting being built at the Northwest School of Wooden Boat Building.

Point Hudson Marina

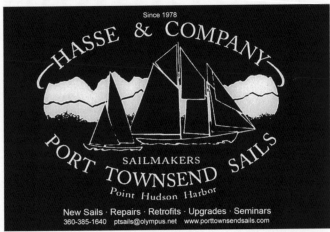
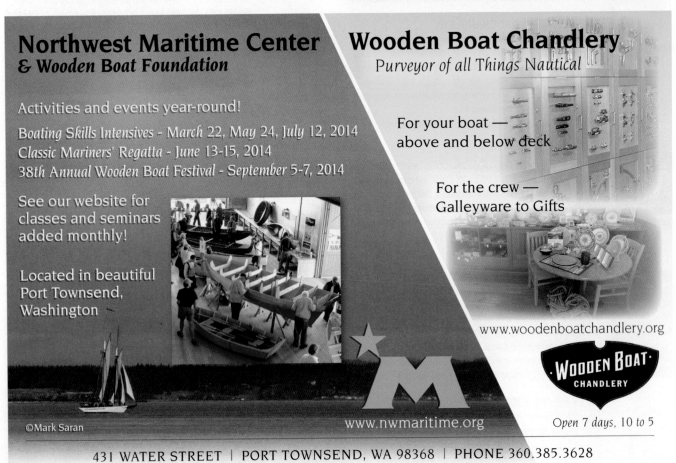

that shouldn't keep anybody away.

Golf: The Port Townsend Golf Club, 9 holes with separate tee boxes for a second 9, is within walking distance of the Boat Haven marina (if you like to walk and have a pull cart). Call (360) 385-4547.

⑦ **Port of Port Townsend Boat Haven.** P.O. Box 1180, 2601 Washington Street, Port Townsend, WA 98368; (360) 385-2355; (800) 228-2803; info@portofpt.com; www.portofpt.com. Monitors VHF 66A. Open all year. Gasoline and diesel fuel at The Fish'n' Hole. Guest moorage along 900 feet of dock space and unoccupied slips as available, 30 & 50 amp power, restrooms, showers, laundry, pumpout, portapotty dump, Beacon/BBX Wi-Fi, launch ramp. Customs clearance is available by appointment only during normal business hours (360) 385-3777.

The marina is west of the ferry dock, and entered between a rock breakwater and a piling wavebreak. The first section is reserved for Coast Guard vessels and commercial fish boats. The fuel dock is to starboard after passing the Coast Guard pier. Moorage arrangements should be made at the marina office.

Call ahead to check slip availability. After hours, empty slips are marked on a map board at the top of the launch ramp and fuel dock. Temporary tie-up is just past the fuel dock, towards the launch ramps, for use while checking for an empty slip.

A hardware store and a large Safeway supermarket are across the highway. The local co-op market is a few blocks closer to town. Key City Fish, an excellent fish market, is in the repair yard area. The Chamber of Commerce Visitor Information Center is just beyond Safeway. Several good restaurants are nearby with a few local favorites and a brew pub in the Boat Haven.

A 330-ton Travelift and a smaller Travelift are available for haulout. Major boatbuilding and repair facilities and a chandlery (Admiral Ship Supply) are at the Boat Haven, and a West Marine is nearby.

⑦ **The Fish'n' Hole.** (360) 385-7031. Gasoline and diesel fuel, open all year. Located inside the Boat Haven breakwater. Floating store carries soda, snacks, ice, bait, tackle.

⑧ **Point Hudson Marina & RV Park.** P.O. Box 1180, Port Townsend, WA 98368; (360) 385-2828; (800) 228-2803; pthudson@portofpt.com; www.portofpt.com. Monitors VHF 09. Open 7 days a week all year, moorage slips to 70 feet, 800 feet of side-tie dock space, plus a mix of 30, 40, 50 and 70-foot slips on the east side. Launch ramp, 30 & 50 amp power, restrooms, showers, water, pumpout, laundry, Beacon/BBX Wi-Fi and free Wi-Fi. Reservations recommended. Customs clearance by appointment, call (360) 385-3777. Ice, event facility, RV park and restaurants are on the property or nearby. The marina is adjacent to downtown.

Enter the marina between two piling

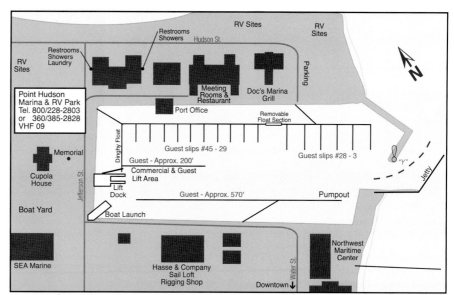

Point Hudson Marina

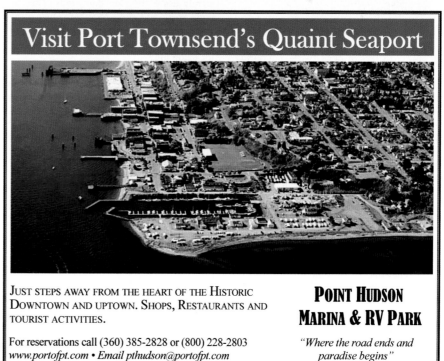

The Northwest Maritime Center in Port Townsend.

The well-maintained Port of Edmonds marina.

breakwaters that force the channel into a distinct bend, directly into the prevailing northwesterly summer winds. This discourages sailing into the marina in anything larger than a dinghy. The marina office is in a white building on the east side. The Sea Marine haulout and boatyard facility is at the north end of the basin. There's no grocery store nearby, so Sea Marine also has milk, bread, ice, propane, beer, wine, and cheeses. Other marine businesses in the area include Port Townsend Sails, Hasse & Co., Brian Toss Rigging, several wooden boat shops, and the Wooden Boat Chandlery.

Fort Townsend Marine State Park. (360) 385-3595. Open summers only, 367 acres, 4 mooring buoys, restrooms, showers, no power. The park has campsites, swimming, playgrounds, hiking trails, picnic tables, fire rings, kitchen shelters, play equipment. Self-guided nature trail, clamming, fishing and scuba diving.

Fort Worden Marine State Park. (360) 344-4400. North of Port Townsend. Open all year, 128 feet of dock space, 7 mooring buoys. Restrooms, showers and laundry, no power. The dock is protected by a wharf. Use the dock or a buoy—this is not a good anchorage, although a friend found good sand bottom in about 18 feet. He also reported that the wakes from passing ship traffic rolled him out of his bunk all night, and he won't overnight there again. Others say they've had no trouble at all. Underwater park for scuba diving. Boat launch with two ramps. Tennis courts, picnic areas, snack bar concession near moorage area. Hiking trails, swimming, fishing. Utility and primitive campsites. Campsite reservations taken year-round. Call (800) 452-5687.

Upland, the old officers' quarters can be rented overnight. Fort buildings house the Marine Science Center and the Centrum Foundation, which conduct workshops and seminars on the arts each summer.

LOCAL KNOWLEDGE

TIDE-RIP: The tide rip at Point Wilson can be dangerous to cruising boats. The bigger the ebb, the greater the chance for a tide-rip. A small ebb can produce no rip at all, particularly if the wind is light. Use the Bush Point current tables to predict the time of slack water and strength of maximum current. Those who think that a fast boat makes current tables unnecessary are wrong and Point Wilson will prove them so.

Point Wilson. Point Wilson is the corner where Admiralty Inlet turns into the Strait of Juan de Fuca. On an ebb, a nasty tide-rip can build immediately north of Point Wilson, and stretch well across the mouth of Admiralty Inlet. If it's a big ebb and opposed by strong westerly winds, the seas in this area are not merely nasty, they are dangerous. They are high, steep and close together. They break. They are not long rollers; they are pyramid-shaped, and have no consistent pattern except for being ugly.

Since boats bound for the San Juan Islands or out the Strait of Juan de Fuca often schedule their passages to take advantage of the ebb, skippers must be aware of what can happen at Point Wilson, especially if a westerly is blowing. In such conditions, the wise approach is to favor the Whidbey Island side.

The even wiser choice is to wait until slack water or the beginning of the flood. Better yet, wait for the wind to drop and then go at slack water.

For information on crossing the Strait of Juan de Fuca, go to page 137.

NORTHEAST PUGET SOUND

⑨ **Edmonds.** Edmonds, a prosperous community with a small-town feel to it, is about 8 miles north of Shilshole Bay on the east side of Puget Sound. It has a major rock breakwater-protected marina (the Port of Edmonds Marina) with excellent facilities for visiting boats. At the marina and in the town a

CHARTS	
18423 sc folio small-craft	Bellingham to Everett including San Juan Islands (1:80,000) Blaine (1:30,000)
18441	Puget Sound – Northern Part (1:80,000)
18443	Approaches to Everett (1:40,000)
18444	Everett Harbor (1:10,000)
18445 sc folio small-craft	Puget Sound – Possession Sound to Olympia including Hood Canal

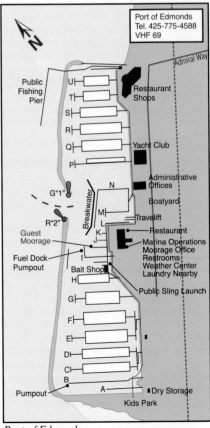

Port of Edmonds

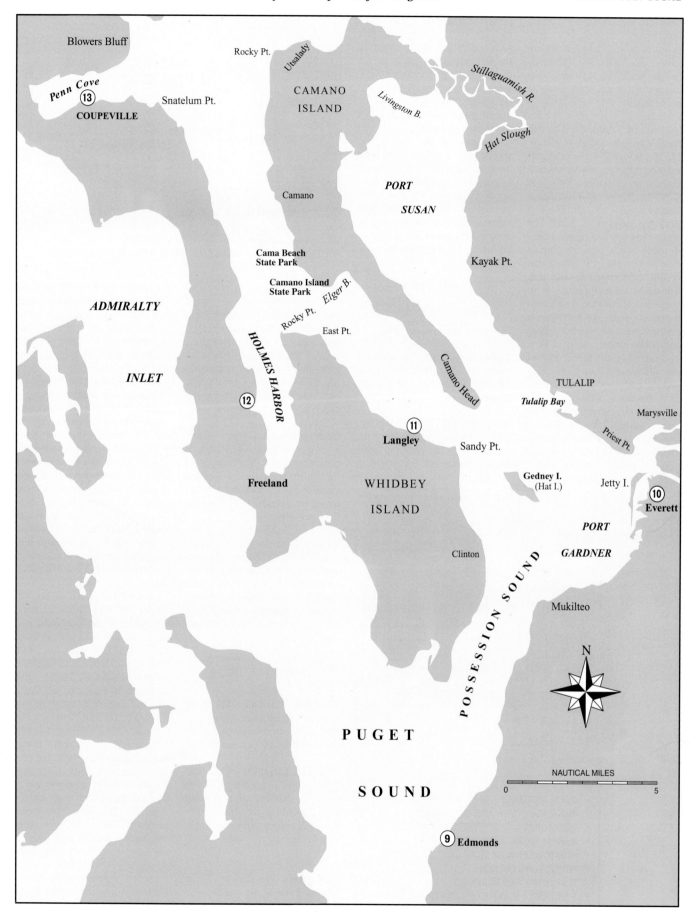

short distance away, you'll find a number of very good restaurants, antiques stores, and interesting shops and galleries. Edmonds "walks" well. This is an ideal destination for a weekend runaway, year-round.

⑨ Port of Edmonds. 336 Admiral Way, Edmonds, WA 98020; (425) 775-4588; info@portofedmonds.org; www.portofedmonds.org. Monitors VHF 69. Certified Clean Marina. Open 7 days a week all year. The fuel dock has gasoline & diesel. The marina has 500 feet of guest side-tie dock space, plus unoccupied slips when available. They can accommodate boats to 100 feet. The docks are served by 30 & 50 amp power, Frontier Wi-Fi, restrooms, showers, two pumpouts, a covered outdoor weather center, and public plaza.

Enter through the middle of the breakwater. Guest moorage and the fuel dock are immediately to the south. The marina has a large do-it-yourself work yard, and a 50-ton Travelift. Limited groceries, laundry nearby. Tackle and bait available. Close to two popular public beaches and a

public fishing pier. An artificial reef for scuba diving (the first such site in the state) is next to the ferry dock just north of the marina. Fishing charters are available. It's a short walk to several restaurants. Post office, laundry, doctor, groceries and shops are in town, about 9 blocks away. When you register at the marina you will be given a welcome bag with discount coupons for Edmonds businesses. On Saturdays a market is set up near the downtown business district. The marina provides a courtesy van service to downtown Edmonds. The marina personnel are friendly and helpful.

Possession Sound is on the southeast side of Whidbey Island between Possession Point and Mukilteo.

Mukilteo. (425) 263-8000 ext. 225. Mukilteo Lighthouse Park has a 4-lane launch ramp with floats in summer. It is exposed to

The Port of Everett Marina is excellent, with attractions nearby.

ferry wakes and waves generated by winds on Possession Sound and Port Gardner. A launch fee is charged. Call for more information. Adjacent to the ferry dock a small float, part of the state park, gives access to restaurants and other businesses ashore. The Mukilteo Lighthouse can be visited.

Gedney Island. Gedney Island, known locally as Hat Island, is privately owned. The marina on the north shore is for Gedney Island property owners, who are served by a private ferry from the Everett Marina.

Tulalip Bay. Anchorage is possible, but Tulalip Bay is very shallow, with a reef guarding the entrance and drying shoals inside. Several private floats and mooring buoys owned by members of the Tulalip Indian Tribe often occupy the bay.

LOCAL KNOWLEDGE

STRONG CURRENTS: River currents can be quite strong, particularly on an ebb tide. Allow for the current as you maneuver.

NIGHT LIGHTS: At night, lights ashore in the Navy facilities make the entrance channel buoys very difficult to see and identify. A vessel approaching at night should be extremely cautious.

⑩ Everett. The Port of Everett Marina is home to a substantial fishing fleet as well as private pleasure craft. Entry is about a mile upstream from the marked mouth of the Snohomish River.

Information about moorage can be obtained from the fuel dock just inside the piling breakwater.

When you are in the river and approaching the marina entrance, watch for debris in the water and pay close attention to your navigation. Several aids to navigation, including one buoy marking a sunken ship, can be confusing. Although the channel can be entered between Lighted Buoy 3 and Light 5 off the south end of Jetty Island, the water between them is somewhat shoal. For complete safety we recommend entering by leaving Lighted Buoy 3 to port. The channel leads past the U.S. Navy homeport facilities.

The marina is a long hike from the central business district, but bus and taxi service are available.

Everett has much to do. The Everett Marina hosts a farmers market at the disabled-access dock on Sundays, June through October, 11:00 a.m. to 4:00 p.m. It also hosts a summertime waterfront concert series from 6:30 p.m. to 8:30 p.m. on Thursday and Saturday, and 2:00 p.m. to 4:00 p.m. on Sunday. The Comcast Arena at Everett (www.comcastarenaeverett.com) brings big-name entertainment. For professional sports with an intimate feeling, take in a minor league baseball game and cheer on the Aquasox. The July 4 fireworks show is Puget Sound's largest outside Seattle and right in the laps of the Everett moorage. A courtesy shuttle bus, 4 guest minimum, connects to the Tulalip Casino with return service to the marina as late as 2:00 a.m. Call (888) 272-1111 to arrange.

Across the river from the marina is a Port-owned float at Jetty

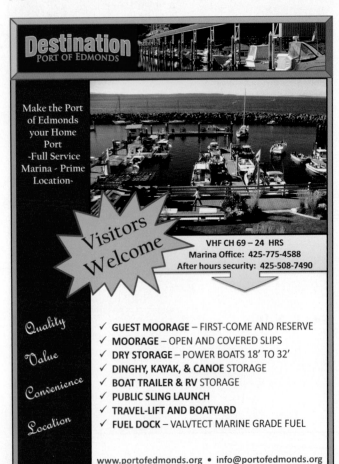

RESTAURANTS, SHOPS & SERVICES

ANTHONY'S HOMEPORT EVERETT

Located on Port Gardner Bay, the restaurant offers fresh northwest seafood with majestic views of Puget Sound islands and the Olympic Mountains. Lunch served Monday-Saturday, Sunday brunch and dinner served daily. Located at Everett Marina Village. Visitor moorage along the dock in front of the restaurant.

1726 West Marine View Drive, Everett Marina Village
425-252-3333 • www.anthonys.com

BAYSIDE MARINE AND DRYSTACK

Offering consignment brokerage, used boat sales, parts and service for most major brands of pleasure boats and inside boat drystack. Keep your boat inside with secure rack storage with private dock and launching.

425-252-3088 • 1111 Craftsman Way
www.baysidemarine.com

BLUEWATER ORGANIC DISTILLING

Bluewater's responsibly-crafted artisan spirits are copper distilled, certified organic and bottled in American glass. Inspired by Pacific Northwest coastal cruising, our sail-in distillery at the Port of Everett offers award-winning spirits for your boat bar.

At the Port of Everett Marina • 1205 Craftsman Way, Ste. 116
www.bluewaterdistilling.com • info@bluewaterdistilling.com

HARBOR MARINE & FISHERMAN'S GRILL

Established in 1979. We offer a wide range of boating supplies, along with a transmission sales and repair shop. Full service boat repair & installation available. Retail sales and Fisherman's Market and Grill open 7 days a week.

A block North of the Everett Marina • 1032 West Marine View Dr.
425 259 3285 • www.harbormarine.net

INN AT PORT GARDNER

Boutique style inn located at the Everett Marina. Enjoy our signature breakfast in a basket delivered to your guest room each morning. Walking distance to 7 marina restaurants.

1700 West Marine View Drive
425.252.6779 • www.innatportgardner.com

PORT GARDNER YACHT BROKERAGE-POWER & SAIL

"Boats are our life, not just our business." Our sales professionals own, live on and have cruised or raced boats as a lifelong passion. Bob, Martin and Kim would be happy to assist you in buying or selling.

New North Everett Marina • 607 11th Street
800-781-9917 • www.portgardneryachts.net

SCUTTLEBUTT BREWING COMPANY

Brewing handcrafted beer from the Northwest's finest ingredients since 1995. Come visit our family friendly brewery and pub. Offering a variety of handcrafted ales and root beer and a full menu, we have something for everyone. Just steps from the dock, on the water at the north end of the Everett Marina.

1205 Craftsman Way
425-257-9316 • www.scuttlebuttbrewing.com

SEA'S THE DAY CAFE

Located next to the marina office in Waterfront Center we offer rich and flavorful Caffe Vita espresso and coffee, smoothies and frappe's, shakes, pastries, pies, pasta salads and made to order sandwiches. Check out our t-shirts and sweatshirts too!

1205 Craftsman Way
425-212-9752 • seasthedaycafe@comcast.net

ANTHONY'S WOODFIRE GRILL

Featuring specialties from its custom-built rotisserie, applewood-burning oven and applewood grill. Serving signature fresh northwest seafood selections, as well as northwest beef selections at lunch and dinner daily. Located at Everett Marina Village. Visitor moorage along the dock in front of Anthony's HomePort.

1722 West Marine View Drive, Everett Marina Village
425-258-4000 • www.anthonys.com

Everett Community Calendar

All Summer Long:
Everett Farmer's Market
Music at the Marina
Jetty Island Days
Harbor Tours

April:
Heroes Half Marathon

May:
Cruzin' to Colby Classic Car Show

June:
Sorticulture, Everett's Garden Arts Festival

July:
Colors of Freedom, Fourth of July Celebration

August:
Fresh Paint Festival of Artist at Work

September:
Wheels on the Waterfront Classic Car Show
Everett Coho Salmon Derby

December:
Holiday on the Bay

For more information contact:
Port of Everett www.portofeverett.com or 800-729-7678

Island, which has what is probably the largest pure sand beach on Puget Sound. The Langus Waterfront Park, with good launching facility, is on the north shore of the main river channel, a short distance up the river from the Port of Everett Marina.

Farther up the Snohomish River, Dagmar's Landing is a large dry-land storage facility with a huge fork lift truck and a long float. A detailed chart or local knowledge are required before continuing beyond Dagmar's.

THINGS TO DO

1. **Boeing Aircraft Factory**. Take a 90-minute tour of the world's largest aircraft plant. Children must be at least 4 feet tall. A cab ride away.

2. **Flying Heritage Collection**. A remarkable collection of one-of-a-kind military aircraft from the past 75 years. Located at Paine Field, adjacent to the Boeing Factory.

3. **Tulalip Casino Resort**. Adult gaming and good restaurants. Call 360-716-6640 to arrange a free shuttle for groups of 4 or more.

4. **Seattle Premium Outlet Stores**. 125 outlet stores next to the Tulalip Casino.

5. **Imagine Children's Museum**. Hands-on activities for kids and many special events. About 1.5 miles from the marina.

6. **Port Gardner Bay Winery**. A boutique winery with relaxed tastings. They also offer classes in winemaking. About 1.5 miles from the marina.

7. **Everett Farmers Market**. Every Sunday at Port Gardner Landing, just up from the marina.

8. **Port Gardner Landing**. Concerts in the summer.

9. **Legion Memorial Golf Course**. Close to the marina.

⑩ **Port of Everett Marina**. P.O. Box 538, Everett, WA; (425) 259-6001; marina@portofeverett.com; www.portofeverett.com. Monitors VHF 16. Certified Clean Marina. Open all year, gasoline and diesel at fuel dock. The port guarantees guest moorage, or receive a complimentary one-night pass. Over 6000 feet of guest moorage with depths 10 to 16 feet, unoccupied slips used when available, 20, 30 & 50 amp power, restrooms, showers, laundry, multiple free pumpout stations, free portapotty dump, Beacon/BBX Wi-Fi.

Handicapped-accessible guest moorage available. Watch for strong currents when landing at the guest dock. Travelift haulout to 75 tons, with yard storage for repairs and maintenance. The Everett Marine Park, a 13-lane launch ramp (largest in the state) is just north of marina.

The Port of Everett's 12th Street Yacht Basin, or North Docks, opened in 2007, with its first-class 42-slip guest moorage dock. The concrete docks are wide, stable and heavily built, and the power is 30 & 50 amp, with 100 amp at the end moorages. A pumpout line is built into the main docks, with attachments at each slip. The basin has its own restrooms, showers, and laundry. The 75-ton Travelift is at the east end of the moorage.

The Port of Everett is a large, complete marina, with shops, full repairs, services nearby, and and two chandleries. An attractive marina village, with a hotel, shops and good restaurants, is adjacent to the south mooring basin. The wheelchair-accessible float is next to the street in the east end of the south basin. The new Waterfront Center Building has an inside coffee area, a brew-pub restaurant and a new distillery. Harbor Marine, a complete marine supply store and chandlery, is located on 10th Street, between the north docks and the Everett Marine Park launch ramps. They have added a snack bar and cafe with daily specials.

Everett Marine Park. On the Snohomish River, north of the Port of Everett Marina. Open all year, 700 feet of guest moorage, restrooms, pumpout, portapotty dump. No power, no showers. The park has a 13-lane launch ramp with boarding floats. An attendant is on duty summer and fall.

Jetty Island. (425) 257-8304; www.everettwa.org. Jetty Island is a lovely low sand island across the river from the Everett Marina and Everett Marine Park. Jetty Island is open all year for day use, with dock space for several boats. Boats can overnight at the dock. Jetty Island has toilets but no showers, no power, and no water for boats. The toilets are closed in winter.

River currents can make landing at the docks challenging. Before approaching the dock, be sure your boat is well fendered, with dock lines ready and contingency plans agreed upon.

Jetty Island is a wildlife preserve, with great birdwatching. The Parks Department offers nature programs during the summer,

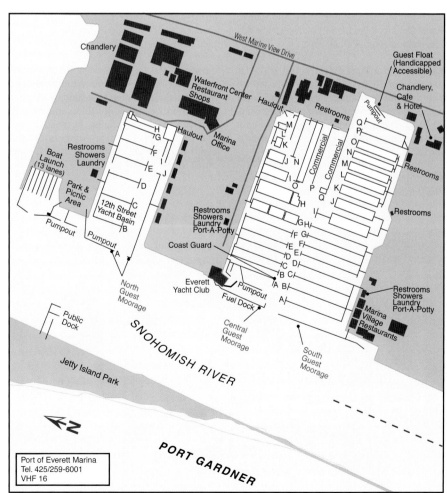

Port of Everett Marina

The long beach at Jetty Island is a favorite for families.

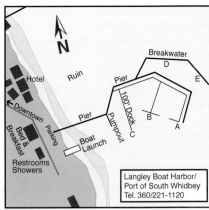

Langley Boat Harbor/
Port of South Whidbey
Tel. 360/221-1120

Langley Boat Harbor

and runs boats from the launch ramp to the island, no charge, July 4 through Labor Day.

Snohomish River Delta. The Snohomish River Delta has three main mouths—Steamboat Slough, Ebey Slough, and the main river—each of which is navigable for all or part of its length. Cautious boaters can cruise the delta.

Contributing Editor Tom Kincaid has cruised all of this area, some of it several times, in a 30-foot sailboat, a 36-foot powerboat, and an outboard-powered dinghy. The waters are subject to tidal action. Drying flats are off the river mouths. Enter only during the hours of highest tides. The Snohomish River Delta is a fascinating place, with wildlife, calm anchorages, and quiet.

Langus Waterfront Park. North shore of the Snohomish River. The park is open all year and has restrooms, but no guest moorage, power or showers. This is a City of Everett park, with a 2-lane concrete launch ramp and boarding floats. A wide concrete float is for fishing and launching rowing shells.

Port Susan. Port Susan is surrounded by Camano Island to the west and the mainland to the east. A swampy waterway connects the northern end of Port Susan with Skagit Bay.

Kayak Point in Port Susan is a Snohomish County Park. North of Kayak Point, Port Susan shoals to drying flats, through which meander the two mouths of the Stillaguamish River. At high tide it is possible to cross over these flats and enter South Pass to Stanwood, although the bridge just beyond Stanwood is very low.

Kayak Point County Park. 15610 Marine Drive, Stanwood, WA 98292; (360) 652-7992. Open all year, restrooms but no showers. Anchoring only, close to shore. The anchorage is exposed to southerly winds. Launch ramp with boarding floats. Fishing pier, no overnight moorage at the pier.

Saratoga Passage. Saratoga Passage separates Camano Island from Whidbey Island. The waters are better protected, and often smoother than Admiralty Inlet, and the current is less. Boats running between Seattle and the San Juan Islands often choose this inside route via Deception Pass or La Conner when the wind and seas are up in Admiralty Inlet.

This is not to say the waters are always smooth. One year, Bob and Marilynn Hale ran into uncomfortable seas while southbound in Saratoga Passage during a 25-knot southerly storm, and were forced to run back to Oak Harbor for shelter.

Saratoga Passage is relatively free of dangers, but it does have two tricks: Rocky Point(s) and Holmes Harbor. A study of the chart shows two Rocky Points in Saratoga Passage. One is on Whidbey Island at the entrance to Holmes Harbor; the other is at the north end of Camano Island.

Southbound boats may be tempted to go straight into Holmes Harbor instead of turning southeast past the Whidbey Island Rocky Point. If you're not watching your chart, the appeal is quite strong. Follow the Camano Island shoreline.

Cama Beach State Park. (360) 387-1550. Twelve miles southwest of Stanwood. Open all year, anchoring only. Restrooms, showers, small store, 15 miles of hiking and biking trails, 24 cabins, 7 deluxe cabins and 2 bungalows. The Center for Wooden Boats runs the boathouse and boat rental operation. Many classic rowboats and sailboats are available for hourly or daily rentals. The workshops

Langley has a charming shopping district.

Useless Bay Coffee Company, in Langley, is a pleasant stop.

Coupeville Wharf

Coupeville is an attractive small town with shops, galleries and restaurants.

on shore may have a boat building project or two underway. See the CWB website (www. cwb.org) for information on classes offered at Cama Beach and boat rentals.

Elger Bay. Elger Bay is a good anchorage, mud bottom, with surprisingly good protection from northerly winds. Watch your depths close to the head of the bay.

Camano Island State Park. (360) 387-3031. Fourteen miles southwest of Stanwood. Open all year for day use and overnight camping. Restrooms, showers, no power. Anchoring only. Launch ramp. Underwater park for scuba diving. Standard and primitive campsites.

⑪ **Langley.** The Langley Boat Harbor serves the delightful village of Langley. If the boat harbor is crowded, as it usually is during the summer, anchorage is good south of the harbor, unless strong northerly winds make the area uncomfortable. Before giving up, however, remember that the Langley Boat Harbor has a long history of being creative about getting another boat tied up. Their motto is, "We'll try to fit you in." *Be sure you have fenders set on both sides.* The town of Langley itself has streets lined with old buildings housing interesting shops, excellent galleries, fine restaurants, and a vintage 250-seat movie theater.

Langley is a good walking town. You'll find beautiful views of Saratoga Passage from the bluff above the marina. The streets are lined with old buildings housing interesting shops, excellent galleries, and fine restaurants. A couple blocks from the cozy commercial district the farms begin.

⑪ **Port of South Whidbey/Langley Boat Harbor.** P.O. Box 872, Freeland, WA 98249; (360) 221-1120; harbormaster@ portofsouthwhidbey.com; www.portofsouth-whidbey.com. Guest moorage year-round. Moorage in 35 slips or along each side of a 100-foot-long float, uninterrupted by pilings. End-tie to 70 feet. A new 400-foot

floating breakwater is scheduled to be completed in early 2014, creating a second basin for moorage.

Reservations accepted online. Restrooms, showers, 30 amp power, launch ramp (high tide only), pumpout barge, free Wi-Fi. Friendly service, staff tries to help every boat dock. Nearby groceries, post office, doctor, vet. Watch early morning minus tides if anchoring.

South Whidbey State Park. (360) 331-4559. On Admiralty Inlet on the Whidbey Island side, just south of Lagoon Point. Open all year, day use and overnight camping. Campground closed from October 15 to March 15. Restrooms, showers, no power. Anchoring in calm conditions or beaching only. Picnic sites, hiking trail, standard and primitive campsites, underwater park for scuba diving.

Fort Casey State Park. (360) 678-4519. Admiralty Head, adjacent to Keystone Harbor on Admiralty Inlet (Whidbey Island side). Open all year, day use and overnight camping, restrooms, no power, no showers. Has a 2-lane launch ramp with boarding floats. Not a good anchorage; beachable boats are best. Underwater park with artificial reef for scuba divers, picnic areas, standard and primitive campsites. Lighthouse and interpretive center. Historic displays and remains of the old fort to explore.

Fort Ebey State Park. (360) 678-4636. Open all year for day use and overnight camping. The park has restrooms and showers, no power. Anchoring only, or small boats can be beached. Standard campsites, picnic sites. Interesting bunkers and gun batteries are in the old fort.

Joseph Whidbey State Park. (360) 678-4636. Northwest shore of Whidbey Island on Admiralty Inlet. Open summers only, April through September, day use only. Toilets, no power, water or showers. Anchor or beach only. One mile of sandy beach on

Puget Sound. Picnic sites.

Holmes Harbor. Holmes Harbor indents the eastern shore of Whidbey Island for about 5 miles in a southerly direction. It is deep and relatively unprotected from strong northerlies. The harbor has a good launch ramp at the head and anchorage along either shore. Honeymoon Bay is a good anchorage. Holmes Harbor is subject to williwaws, the unusually strong gusts of wind that spill across the lower portion of Whidbey Island.

⑫ **Honeymoon Bay.** Honeymoon Bay is a favored anchorage on the west shore of Holmes Harbor. Private mooring buoys take up most of the good spots, but with a little diligence satisfactory anchoring depths with adequate swinging room can be found. Honeymoon Bay is exposed to northerly winds.

Penn Cove. Penn Cove is about 10 miles north of Holmes Harbor. The cove extends nearly 4 miles west from Long Point, with the town of Coupeville on the southern shore. Anchorage is good along both shores and toward the head of the bay, but be aware that strong winds from the Strait of Juan de Fuca can blow across the low neck of Whidbey Island at the head of the cove. This is where the famous Penn Cove mussels come from. Watch for mussel-growing pens.

⑬ **Coupeville.** The historic town of Coupeville is served by the Coupeville Wharf, a 415-foot-long causeway on pilings extending over the beach to deep water. Coupeville is quaint, old, and friendly, with a variety of shops, galleries, and restaurants. A good display of tribal canoes is just 200 feet from the head of the wharf.

⑬ **Coupeville Wharf.** P.O. Box 577, Coupeville, WA 98239-0577; (360) 678-5020; (360) 678-3625. Open all year, 400-plus feet of dock space. Watch depths at low and minus tides. Gasoline and diesel at the fuel dock. During the season 4 mooring buoys are installed northwest of the fuel dock. There is also room to anchor in front of town. Pumpout, restrooms, and showers are on the wharf, no power or water on the float. A gift shop and a restaurant are at the outer end of the wharf, along with KWPA radio station. The town's shops and restaurants are within easy walking distance. Island Transit, with stops nearby, offers free bus service to key points on Whidbey Island.

Captain Coupe Park. 602 NE Ninth St., Coupeville, WA 98239-0577; (360) 678-4461. Open all year with restrooms and nearby portapotty dump, no power, no showers. Anchoring only. A launch ramp with a float is installed in the summer. One-quarter mile by water from the wharf. It's better to anchor closer to the wharf. Mud flats surround the launch area at low tide.

NORTHEAST PUGET SOUND

⑭ **Oak Harbor.** Oak Harbor is a shallow and well protected port with a major, city-owned marina. The entrance channel is marked by red and green buoys and beacons, beginning with Buoy 2, offshore about 1 mile south of Maylor Point. From Buoy 2 the entry channel runs northward into Oak Harbor, and makes a 90-degree turn to the east for the final mile that leads to the marina.

Do not pass between Buoy 2 and Maylor Point. The water there is shoal, and littered with large boulders that have been known to tear stern drive units out of boats.

The only moorage is at the spacious Oak Harbor Marina. The marina has complete facilities, and park grounds ashore for dog-walking, games, or strolling. It's a bit of a walk to town, and the nearest grocery store is 1¾ miles away. Free bus service runs Monday through Saturday, or you can call a cab.

Anchorage can be found just outside the marina, close to the entry channel. The bottom is soft; be sure your anchor is well set. A small float for dinghies is in front of the business district, about a 1-mile walk from

Oak Harbor Marina, with picnic tables along the water, is a good place for gatherings.

the marina. The float dries at low tide.

Golf: The 18-hole Gallery Golf Course at the Whidbey Island Naval Air Station is open to the public year-round. The course overlooks the east end of the Strait of Juan de Fuca. Smith Island is clearly visible; (360) 257-2178. Also the Whidbey Golf & Country Club, open play after 1:00 p.m.; (360) 675-4546.

Taxi: (360) 682-6920 or (360) 279-9330.

LOCAL KNOWLEDGE

ENTRANCE CHANNEL: Shoals line each side of the channel all the way into Oak Harbor. At low tide especially, you will go aground if you stray.

⑭ **Oak Harbor Marina.** 865 SE Barrington Dr., Oak Harbor, WA 98277; (360) 279-4575; slee@oakharbor.org; www.whidbey.com/ohmarina. Monitors VHF 16, switch to 68. Open all year (closed Sundays & holidays, November through February), at

CHARTS	
18421	Strait of Juan de Fuca to Strait of Georgia (1:80,000)
18423 sc folio small-craft	Bellingham to Everett including San Juan Islands (1:80,000) Blaine (1:30,000)
18427	Anacortes to Skagit Bay (1:25,000)
18428	Oak and Crescent Harbors (1:10,000)
18441	Puget Sound – Northern Part (1:80,000)
18443	Approaches to Everett (1:40,000)
18445 sc folio small-craft	Puget Sound – Possession Sound to Olympia including Hood Canal

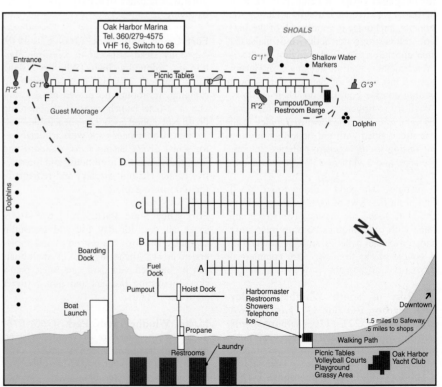

Oak Harbor Marina

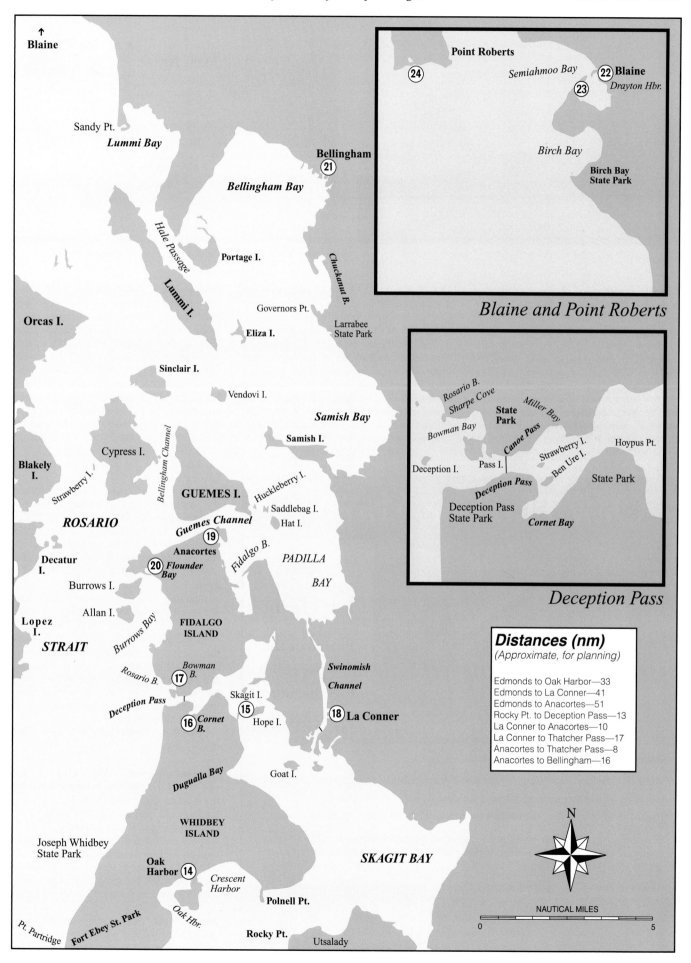

Blaine and Point Roberts

Deception Pass

Distances (nm)
(Approximate, for planning)

Edmonds to Oak Harbor—33
Edmonds to La Conner—41
Edmonds to Anacortes—51
Rocky Pt. to Deception Pass—13
La Conner to Anacortes—10
La Conner to Thatcher Pass—17
Anacortes to Thatcher Pass—8
Anacortes to Bellingham—16

This windmill is at Oak Harbor's City Beach Park.

Excellent docks make Oak Harbor an easy destination to visit.

least 20 slips of guest moorage, unoccupied slips used when available. Reciprocal moorage at Oak Harbor Yacht Club slips. Dredging completed in 2011 increased the guest moorage depth to 14 feet at zero tide. The fuel dock has mid-grade gasoline, diesel, and propane. Call ahead if your boat length is over 50 feet.

The marina has 20, 30 & limited 50 amp power, restrooms, showers, laundry, pumpout, portapotty dump, and Beacon/BBX Wi-Fi. Wi-Fi also is broadcast from the

Oak Harbor Yacht Club. The guest moorage dock has picnic tables along the breakwater. One set of restrooms and showers is on the lower level of the administration building at the head of the docks. Additional restrooms, showers, and laundry are in buildings a short distance away. A floating restroom facility is often located on the west end of the guest moorage dock. The nearby PBY museum has a new seaplane on exhibit. It is an easy walk. Military and retired military (with DoD I.D.) can walk onto the Navy base area and use

the Navy Exchange for shopping and provisioning. The Exchange is in one of the large buildings that formerly was a hangar.

A 100-foot-wide concrete launch ramp, built in 1942 to launch PBY Catalina patrol seaplanes, is at the south end of the marina. Extended parking for trailers and tow vehicles. Hoist to 6500 pounds. Mariners Haven has repairs and a chandlery. Kids' play area. Free bus service to town. Nearby doctor and post office. Guest moorage is not available during Whidbey Island Race Week, July 20 to 25, 2014.

Oak Harbor Marina is protected by a floating concrete breakwater. Guest moorage is in slips on the inside of this breakwater and along the long float leading to shore. A dredged channel, 100 feet wide with a least depth of 10 feet at zero tide, leads along the west face of the breakwater and around the end, to side-tie moorage on the float that leads to shore. Water outside the channel is shoal.

Entering Oak Harbor, keep red buoys and beacons close to starboard (see caution above).

If you plan to moor along the north side the marina, the safest approach is to head directly for the entrance light at the south end of the breakwater. When you reach the breakwater, turn to port and proceed along the outside (west side) of the breakwater to the north moorage.

The Oak Harbor Marina is well maintained, easygoing, and friendly.

Crescent Harbor. (360) 257-4842. Just east of Oak Harbor. The Navy facility along the western shore near the head of the bay has large old hangars that once housed PBY Catalina flying boat patrol aircraft. The docks at the recreation facility are for Navy and retired military use, reservations required: (360) 257-4842. Crescent Harbor is exposed to southerly winds, but in northerlies or westerlies it's a good anchorage.

Rocky Point. Tidal currents meet off Rocky Point. North of the point they flood south out of Deception Pass and Swinomish Chan-

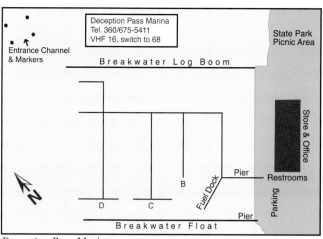

Deception Pass Marina
Tel. 360/675-5411
VHF 16, switch to 68

Deception Pass Marina

Note the currents in this view of Deception Pass looking west.

nel. South of the point they flood north out of Saratoga Passage

Skagit Bay. Skagit Bay extends from Polnell Point and Rocky Point to Deception Pass. The bay becomes increasingly shoal toward the east due to Skagit River outflow. The navigable channel parallels the Whidbey Island shore, and is well marked by buoys. Use caution in this channel; buoys can be dragged out of position by tugs with tows. The village of Utsalady, with a launch ramp, is on the Camano Island side of the channel. Anchorage there is not protected from northerly winds and waves, but Correspondents James & Jennifer Hamilton report anchoring through a southeast gale without difficulty.

⑮ Skagit Island, Hope Island, Similk Bay. Hope Island is a state marine park, with mooring buoys on the north side and good anchorage, particularly along the south shore. Check the depths before using the buoys. No power, water, restrooms or showers. Trails lead around and through the island. **Skagit Island**, just to the north, has 3 mooring buoys along its north side. **Similk Bay** is shoal, but navigable in shallow draft boats. Anchorage is possible anywhere.

Kiket Island/Kukutali Preserve. Located just east of Skagit Island. Kiket Island was acquired by Washington State Parks and the Swinomish Tribe in 2010 and renamed Kukutali Preserve. Until a management plan can be finalized, it is closed to visitor boat traffic. Even if it is opened to boat visitors, landing will be in human-powered craft only, at a designated location.

⑯ Cornet Bay. Cornet Bay, tucked in behind Ben Ure Island, indents the north shore of Whidbey Island just east of Deception Pass. A dredged channel marked by pilings leads to Deception Pass Marina and a state park, both of which offer visitor moorage. The passage west of Ben Ure Island should not be attempted except at high tide, and then only by shallow draft boats.

⑯ Deception Pass Marina. 200 West Cornet Bay Road, Oak Harbor, WA 98277; (360) 675-5411. Monitors VHF 16, switch to 68. Open all year. The marina has several slips reserved for visiting boats, and uses unoccupied slips as available. The docks have 30 amp power, but only limited room for larger boats. Gasoline, diesel, and propane at the fuel dock. The store carries groceries, bait, tackle, charts, books, beer and wine. Restrooms, no showers (showers are available at the state park next door). Call ahead for availability of guest moorage. Nearby laundry and haulout. Vessel Assist towing and emergency rescue office nearby.

⑯ Deception Pass Marine State Park, Cornet Bay area. Open all year for day use and overnight moorage. The park has 1140 feet of side-tie dock space, restrooms, showers and pumpout, but no power. Additional floats are anchored offshore and not connected to land. A 5-lane launch ramp has boarding floats. Hiking trails and picnic areas nearby. Groceries, laundromat and services are at Deception Pass Marina. Park has campsites, but not near this area.

LOCAL KNOWLEDGE

STRONG CURRENTS: Currents run to 8 knots in Deception Pass, with strong eddies and overfalls. Dangerous waves can form when a big ebb current meets strong westerly winds. It is best to time an approach to enter the pass at or near slack water. Try to travel single-file.

Deception Pass. Deception Pass narrows to 200 yards at Pass Island, one of the anchors for the spectacular 144-foot-high bridge that connects Whidbey Island and Fidalgo Island.

Tidal current predictions are shown under Deception Pass in the tide and current books. An even narrower pass, Canoe Pass, lies north of Pass Island. Kayaks use Canoe Pass, but lacking local knowledge we wouldn't run our boat through it.

From the west, the preferred route to Deception Pass is just to the south of Lighthouse Point and north of Deception Island.

North of Lighthouse Point, **Bowman Bay**, also known as Reservation Bay, is part of Deception Pass State Park.

⑰ Deception Pass Marine State Park, Bowman Bay (Reservation Bay). Open all year for day use and overnight camping and mooring. Four mooring buoys. Restrooms with showers, no power. Bowman Bay has a gravel 1-lane launch ramp. Standard campsites are on the north shore. The park has picnic sites and kitchens. An underwater park for diving is near the mouth of Bowman Bay, near Rosario Head. When entering take care to avoid Coffin Rocks and Gull Rocks, which cover at high tide. Safe entry can be made by staying fairly close to the Reservation Head side of the entrance.

A mooring float, approximately 100 feet long and not connected to shore, is located behind Reservation Head. On the east side of the bay the 40-foot-long float on the park dock is for dinghies.

Anchorage is also possible in the bay north of Rosario Head, but it is exposed to wave action from Rosario Strait.

Deception Pass Marine State Park, Sharpe Cove. Open all year for day use and overnight camping and mooring. The park has no power, but has a 50-foot floating dock. Restrooms, showers, portapotty dump, picnic sites, kitchen. Campsites are east of Sharpe Cove. The onshore facility is the Walla Walla University Rosario Beach Marine Laboratory.

Swinomish Channel. *In October, 2013, the U.S. Coast Guard changed the buoyage in Swinomish Channel. The "change point," noting the return to sea (Red Right Returning), was moved to the center of La Conner. It previously was about 2 miles north of La Conner. Old charts do not reflect this change. Buoy R22 has been changed to G35, G23 to R34, R26 to G31, and G25 to R32.*

The southern entrance to Swinomish Channel is just north of Goat Island. Do not turn into the channel until the range markers in Dugualla Bay, to the west, are in line. The channel is well marked but narrow, particularly if you meet a tug with a tow of logs. Check the range as you go. Rock piles lie immediately outside of the dredged channel. Tidal currents flow across the channel and can sweep a boat off course. At **Hole in the Wall** the channel bends sharply around a high rock outcropping. Swirling currents in this area can call for close attention.

From Hole in the Wall to the railroad swing bridge the channel is a no wake zone. Be particularly mindful of your wake when passing through the town of La Conner.

Red, Right, Returning: The buoyage system for Swinomish Channel south of the town of La Conner assumes "return" is from the south. In Padilla Bay, and north of La Conner, the dredged channel assumes "return" is from the north. Red navigation aids in Padilla Bay are on the west side.

Rainbow Bridge, located just south of La Conner, has an overhead clearance of 75 feet.

Swinomish Channel is dredged every few years, but it silts up between dredgings. A much needed dredging was completed in January 2013. Keep in mind that the silting occurs at the same locations each time, so at low tide the wary boater can avoid them. Here are the troublesome locations:

1. West of Goat Island, the very entrance to Swinomish Channel is shoal. Especially on a low tide, swing wide and don't cut any of the entry buoys close. The channel leading past Goat Island is quite shoal. On very low tides deep draft vessels such as sailboats should wait for more water.

2. South of town at Shelter Bay, a shoal extends from the west side of the channel, approximately in line with the southernmost house of the Shelter Bay development. Favor the center of the channel.

3. About midway along the main La Conner waterfront a shoal extends from the west side of the channel, approximately between the middle of the restaurants on the La Conner side and a tall pole with antennas on the west side. Favor the east side of the channel.

4. Just south of the highway bridges and the railroad swing bridge, at the location marked "Pipeline Area," sand accumulates on top of the pipeline to create another shoal.

5. The most troublesome shoal is opposite Buoy 29, north of the railroad swing bridge and the highway bridges. This shoal stretches across the entire channel.

Shelter Bay, with its private moorage, indents the western shore of Swinomish Channel just north of Hole in the Wall.

Then comes lovely Rainbow Bridge (now orange), vertical clearance 75 feet in the center. North of Rainbow Bridge the town of La Conner stretches along the eastern shore

of the channel. Across from La Conner the Swinomish Indian Reservation occupies most of the west side of the channel. On the La Conner side, several privately-owned floats serve restaurants and other businesses along the La Conner waterfront.

Just north of La Conner is another point where the flood and ebb currents meet, ebbing south past La Conner, and north toward Anacortes. The channel is marked by buoys and ranges, but follows a generally northerly direction until it passes under a swinging railroad bridge and fixed highway bridges to enter Padilla Bay. The highway bridges are high enough that they don't impede boating traffic. The railroad bridge is very low. If you are there at the wrong time consider dropping the anchor until the train is past. Currents can be strong.

⑱ **La Conner.** The Port of Skagit's La Conner Marina, with two large moorage basins, is a short distance north of downtown La Conner. Both moorage basins have guest moorage and full facilities for visitors. Fuel is available adjacent to the marina at La Conner Landing, and propane is available at Boater's Discount marine supply store, between the two basins. Current in Swinomish Channel can be strong and difficult to predict. Allow for current before landing anywhere along the channel.

The town of La Conner is thoroughly charming. It has excellent restaurants, galleries, museums, and shops. Public floats line the

---

AGROUND AGAIN

I have remained relatively grounding-free most of my boating life, until I got our last *Nor'westing*, a Romsdal trawler that draws 7½ feet. I recall a conversation with the late John Locke, whose 52-foot sloop *Angelica* also drew 7½ feet. John said he never had trouble with the first seven feet of draft, but the last half-foot always found the bottom. Me, too, John.

Sometimes it's just a little bump, like when we slid over a shallow spot just east of Goat Island, in Swinomish Channel. Or when we tied to a state park buoy at Hope Island and woke up the next morning thoroughly aground in mud. I hadn't checked the depth the night before. I thought the state would put its buoys where even I could float.

Sometimes it's more embarrassing, such as when I ran too close to the west side of the channel after a Stimson Trophy predicted log contest. One of the other boats passed me a line and pulled me off, but it was in full view of a whole passel of some of the most

experienced boaters in the area. Oh, my.

I've been fooled a few times by a peculiarity of many bays and coves in Alaska and northern British Columbia, such as misnamed Safety Cove on Calvert Island. Safety Cove is a nice little bay at the mouth of a river, a river that deposits silt into the deeper waters of the cove, creating a nearly vertical shelf. As I poked around looking for something a little less than 20 fathoms deep I bumped into the edge of that shelf, where the water went directly from 20 fathoms to no fathoms. I backed off okay, and decided I didn't like Safety Cove that much.

Do you suppose that if I had sawn a few inches off my keel I'd have stayed afloat better? After all, it's only that last inch or two that got me into trouble. Or maybe it's time to relearn an important lesson: When the depth of the keel exceeds the depth of the water, I am most surely aground—again.

– Tom Kincaid

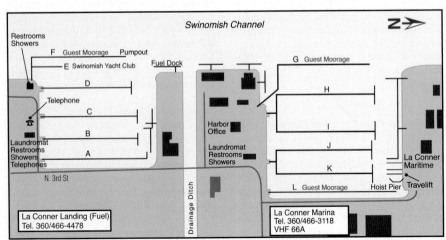

La Conner Marina

Currents in Swinomish Channel can make landing challenging. The La Conner fuel dock posts the direction of current to assist skippers.

Mt. Baker rises behind Swinomish Channel and La Conner.

business district. During the summer, hordes of visitors arrive by car and tour bus. Even when crowded, the town is enjoyable.

⑱ La Conner Marina. P.O. Box 1120, 613 N. 2nd St., La Conner, WA 98257; (360) 466-3118; www.portofskagit.com/la-conner-marina. Monitors VHF 66A. Open all year with 30 & 50 amp power, Beacon/BBX and free Wi-Fi, restrooms, showers, laundry, pumpout. Haulout to 82 tons. Complete repairs available.

All shopping and services are within walking distance. A monorail launch can handle boats to 14,000 lbs. Trailers must be roller style, no bunks. A paved, lighted storage yard is available for trailers and tow vehicles.

This marina, owned by the Port of Skagit, is where most visiting boats tie up. F dock at the south basin has 1200 lineal feet of side-tide guest moorage. G dock at the north basin has another 1200 feet of side-tide moorage. E dock, near shore in the south basin, has 450 feet of guest moorage for the Swinomish Yacht Club. Reservations accepted. Unoccupied slips are used when available. If the moorage appears full, call anyway. They try to fit everybody in.

⑱ La Conner Landing Marine Services. P.O. Box 1020, La Conner, WA 98257; (360) 466-4478. Open all year, 7 days a week in summer, 5 days in winter (call ahead, closed days vary). Fuel dock with gasoline and diesel. Portable toilets. The store has tackle, bait, ice, beer and wine, marine items, and snacks.

Padilla Bay. The well-marked channel through Padilla Bay is about 3 miles long, between drying flats. Don't take any shortcuts until north of Beacon 2, which marks the edge of Guemes Channel. Deeper draft boats, such as sailboats, should hold to a mid-channel course, especially at low tide. To the west of the channel are long docks serving ocean-going tankers calling at the two major oil refineries in Anacortes. Often, tankers, barges, or tug boats lie at anchor in the bay

awaiting room at the docks.

Red, Right, Returning: In Padilla Bay, Red, Right, Returning assumes "return" is from the north. Red navigation aids are on the west side of the channel from Padilla Bay to La Conner. South of La Conner, red navigation aids are on the east side of Swinomish Channel. Approaching La Conner from north or south, remember Red, Right, Returning.

Saddlebag Island Marine State Park. Open all year for day use and overnight mooring and camping. Boat access only. Anchorage is good off the north or south shore, mud bottom, but there is no float. Water depths are inconveniently deep on the west side, and inconveniently shallow on the east. Vault toilets, primitive campsites. Cascadia Marine Trail campsite. One-mile hiking trail. "Hot spot" for crabbing.

Huckleberry Island. North end of Padilla Bay, owned by the Samish Indian Nation. Open all year, day use only. No services. Undeveloped 10-acre island, with anchoring or beaching only. No fires or camping. Pack out all garbage. Attractive to kayakers and scuba divers. Gravel beach on the southwest side of the island.

⑲ Anacortes. www.anacortes.org. Anacortes is a major boating center, with fishing and pleasure craft facilities in Fidalgo Bay and along Guemes Channel. The city's marine businesses can provide for a boater's every need, including food, fuel, and repairs. With seven haulout yards, Anacortes has the marine trades for any repair.

U.S. Customs: Anacortes is a U.S. Customs port of entry, with an office in the Cap Sante Marina harbormaster's building. There is no U.S. Customs dock. Call the marina office for a slip assignment and proceed to the slip. Then call the Anacortes customs office at (360) 293-2331 for instructions. Between 1:00 p.m. and 3:00 p.m. during the summer agents are apt to be 4 miles away at the Washington State Ferry terminal, clearing arrivals on the international ferry from Sidney,

B.C. You'll have to wait aboard for the agents to return. Otherwise, they will ask the captain to walk up to the Customs office, Suite F, to the right of the harbormaster's office, for clearance.

Fidalgo Bay is shallow. At low water if you stray from the dredged and marked channels you could find yourself aground.

Four marinas are located on the Fidalgo Bay side of town. Three additional marinas are located on the west end of Fidalgo Island. From north to south on Fidalgo Bay, the first is Cap Sante Marina, owned by the Port of Anacortes, with guest moorage, fuel, water, electricity, and haulout facilities. Enter between the arms of a piling breakwater due west of Cap Sante.

The second is Anacortes Marina, where Marine Servicenter has fuel, haulout, and repairs. Permanent moorage only. Anacortes Yacht Charters and many bareboat charter boats are based in this marina.

Next is the 360-foot-long dock and haulout ramp for Pacific Marine Center. Limited moorage is available on their docks, typically reserved for repair or dry storage customers.

The fourth is Fidalgo Marina, where Cap Sante Marine and the haulout ramp for North Harbor Diesel are located. The marina is protected by a piling breakwater, and is entered through the dredged channel marked by pil-

CHARTS	
18421	Strait of Juan de Fuca to Strait of Georgia (1:80,000)
18423 sc folio small-craft	Bellingham to Everett including San Juan Islands and Blaine
18424	Bellingham Bay (1:40,000) Bellingham Harbor (1:20,000)
18430	Rosario Strait—Northern Part (1:25,000)
18429	Rosario Strait—Southern Part (1:25:000)

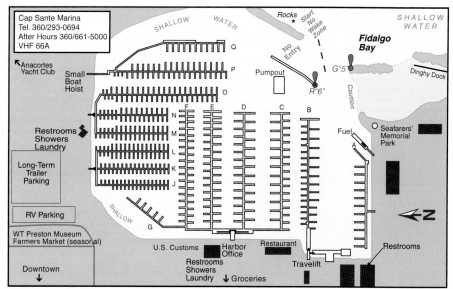

Cap Sante Marina
Tel. 360/293-0694
After Hours 360/661-5000
VHF 66A

Cap Sante Marina

ings extending from deeper water near Cap Sante.

Moving east to west, Dakota Creek Industries is a large shipyard on Guemes Channel with Syncrolift ship lift and drydock for vessels to 400 feet.

Just past the Guemes Ferry is Anchor Cove, a private marina with no transient moorage.

Lovric's Sea-Craft is on Guemes Channel with 2 marine ways for haulout, and a small dry dock.

Skyline Marina is in Flounder Bay on the west side of Fidalgo Island, 3 miles from downtown Anacortes. It has some transient moorage and a yard with haulout.

Farmers market: Saturdays 9:00 a.m. to 2:00 p.m. next to the Depot Arts Center.

Events: Anacortes Salmon Derby, March 29-30; Wine Festival, April 12; Trawler Fest, May 14-17; Anacortes Waterfront Festival, June 6-8 at Cap Sante Marina; Shipwreck Day, July 19; Anacortes Arts Festival, August 1-3; Oyster Run, September 28; Oktoberfest, October 3-4. www.anacortes.org; info@anacortes.org; (360) 293-7911.

THINGS TO DO

1. **Charming downtown**. Visit the shops, galleries, antique stores, and restaurants along Commercial Avenue.

2. **Marine Hardware and Supply**. Located at the end of Commercial Avenue. A classic marine chandlery in the old style.

3. *W. T. Preston*, an old snag boat, is now part of the Anacortes History Museum. Located across from the north end of Cap Sante Marina.

4. **Live music**. On Fridays and some Saturdays in July and August, the port hosts free summer concerts at Seafarers' Memorial Park.

5. **Skagit Cycle**. Rent a bike and ride the Tommy Thompson Trail, or just around town. Catch the Tommy Thompson Trail from R Avenue, at Cap Sante Marina.

6. **Cap Sante Park**. Walk to the top and

The entrance to Cap Sante Marina changed in 2011 with a new breakwater and esplanade.

rants, large Safeway and Marketplace grocery stores, well-stocked Ace Hardware and Sebo's hardware stores, and two marine stores (West Marine, Marine Supply & Hardware) are within walking distance. An esplanade leads from the marina to the new Seafarers' Memorial Park and building, and around the marina to Rotary Park. An Anthony's Restaurant fronts on the esplanade. A new dock for dinghies is behind a small breakwater at Seafarers' Memorial Park. The beach area is used as a kayak launch.

Cap Sante Marina is the third most popular marina (rated by marina moorage nights) in the state. It is considered the homeport of the San Juan Islands and is often used as a supply and provisioning jumping-off point for cruises into the islands and further north.

1207 Q Avenue
(360) 588-0333

view Mt. Baker and the marina from this scenic vantage point. Sunsets from here are particularly beautiful. A steep switchback trail leads up Cap Sante from the gazebo on the point.

7. **Seabear Smokehouse**. Learn the difference in taste between smoked pink, king and sockeye salmon.

8. **Crabbing**. Fidalgo Bay often has excellent crabbing.

⑲ **Cap Sante Marina/Port of Anacortes.** 100 Commerical Ave., 1019 Q Ave., Anacortes, WA 98221; (360) 293-0694; (360) 661-5000; marina@portofanacortes.com; www.portofanacortes.com. Monitors VHF 66A. Formerly Cap Sante Boat Haven. Open all year with moorage to 120 feet. Call or radio ahead for slip assignment. There is a $5 fee for reservations. No fee for same-day reservations. The 18×120-foot fuel dock, with gasoline, diesel and propane, is to port inside the breakwater. A high-volume fuel hose is available. The marina has 20 &

30 amp power with some 50 & 100 amp power available, 5 pumpouts (free), 2 porta-potty dumps, excellent restrooms, showers, and laundry. Shore power adapters available without charge. Free Wi-Fi throughout the marina. Complimentary bicycles with baskets for marina guests. A monorail launch can handle boats to 25,000 pounds. A small hoist and dry storage yard for hand launching small boats is in the North Basin on P-Q dock. Call (360) 293-7837 for more information. Haulout and propane nearby.

Most of the transient area marina floats been replaced by wide, stable concrete floats, with wide slips and wheelchair accessible ramps to shore. The new floats are first-class in every way.

Follow the dredged and marked channel, and enter between the arms of a piling breakwater due west of Cap Sante. The area to port just inside the breakwater, towards Seafarers' Memorial Park, is shoal and should not be attempted. The harbormaster's office and U.S. Customs office are just north of C & D floats.

This is a clean and popular stop, located in the heart of downtown Anacortes. Complete facilities, including several excellent restau-

Anacortes Marina. 2415 T Avenue, Anacortes, WA 98221; (360) 293-4543. Primarily private moorage. Marine Servicenter, with fuel dock, haulout, and repairs, is located there. Enter through the dredged channel to the south opening. Exit the marina through the north opening in the breakwater. Marine Servicenter's fuel dock and and Travelift are straight ahead when you enter the marina.

Marine Servicenter. 2417 T Avenue, Anacortes, WA 98221; (360) 293-8200; service@marinesc.com; www.marinesc.com. Open all year. Fuel dock with gasoline, diesel, propane, pumpout, portapotty dump, lubricants, engine oil. Complete repair facilities, haulout to 55 tons.

Pacific Marine Center. 2302 T Avenue, Anacortes, WA 98221; (425) 418-7658. Transient side-tie moorage on a space available basis. Haulout to 150 tons, full service repairs.

Fidalgo Marina. 3101 V Place, Anacortes, WA 98221; (360) 299-0873. No transient overnight moorage, but a number of marine

Cap Sante Marina

Located one block from beautiful historic downtown Anacortes.

Close to groceries, restaurants and shops.

Home of the oldest marine hardware supply on the west coast.

We welcome permanent and transient moorage, with 150-200 berths available for guest moorage.

The new 40', 46' and 57'monolithic / Uni-float docks offer stability, and room for ease of provisioning your vessel.

Accommodating Fairways offer the new and seasoned boaters the feeling of luxury and room, making your welcome home or entrance into Fidalgo Bay an ease.

Activity floats available.

20, 30 & 50 amp power to accommodate vessels up to 130' and water available

Visit Fido's Fuel Dock

Some of the <u>lowest</u> fuel prices in the Islands!
Propane, bait, ice cream and free treats for your pup.
We'd love to meet your four legged friends and post their photos on our wall of fame!

Harbor Office Telephone:

360-293-0694

AMENITIES

o RESERVATIONS ACCEPTED

o WELL MAINTAINED DOCKS AND SLIPS

o FOUR PORTABLE PUMP-OUTS/FLOATING PUMP-OUT AVAILABLE AT NO CHARGE

o HAUL OUT SERVICES AVAILABLE UP TO 25,000 LBS.

o FREE MARINA WIDE WI-FI

o WELL MAINTAINED RESTROOMS WITH SHOWER & LAUNDRY FACILITIES

o CLOSE TO PUBLIC TRAILS AND PARKS

o FREE SUMMER CONCERTS TWICE A WEEK IN SUMMER

o COMPLIMENTARY BIKES FOR GUESTS

YEAR ROUND WEEKLY EVENT CALENDARS SO YOU KNOW WHERE TO GO IN TOWN

Open seven days a week from 8:00am to 5:00pm
For slip assignment, call on VHF 66A, or 360-293-0694

E-mail: marina@portofanacortes.com | Web: www.portofanacortes.com/visit/the-marina
Fax: 360-299-0998 | Marina Office Telephone: 360-293-0694
1019 "Q" Avenue Suite C, 100 Commercial Ave., Anacortes, Washington 98221

MARINE SERVICES

TIPS FOR MAINTAINING YOUR BOAT

1. Change engine oil and filters every 100 hours.
2. Keep all raw water strainers clean and clear of grass and debris.
3. Keep bilge pumps and limber holes clear of debris.
4. Check coolant levels. Replace annually.
5. Annually, change fuel filters, transmission fluid, antifreeze, and impellers.
6. Check engine belts and pulleys. Replace if necessary.
7. Annually check the condition of batteries and top water if necessary.
8. Lubricate anchor and davit systems.
9. Annually check age of fire extinguishers and flares.
10. Maintain a list of all maintenance items from the boating season for your boat. At the end of the cruising season determine which items need to be addressed in the winter or can be deferred.

See more maintenance tips at WaggonerGuide.com/ maintenance.

Statue Photo Courtesy of Anacortes Chamber of Commerce, Steve Berentson, photographer

Mary LaFleur

ALT INSURANCE GROUP

An all lines broker with a specialty niche in yacht insurance, Mary LaFleur has twenty eight years in the insurance industry, represents over 30 insurance carriers, and is a life-long boater. "Most times we can save our boaters enough on their auto, home, commercial and RV insurance to put fuel in their tanks." Customer Service is second to none.
253-222-7519 • 360-899-4653
1019 Q Ave. Suite A - Anacortes, WA 98221
mary@altinsurancegroup.com
www.altinsurancegroup.com

ANACORTES RIGGING & YACHT SERVICES

Marine & Architectural wire swaging, including complete services for composite, wire & rod rigging. A large selection of rope in stock & custom splicing options with quick turn-around. Providing consultations, rigging inspections, spar refits, repairs & more!
360-293-2030 • 719-½ 28th St. (28th & R Ave)
www.AnacortesRigging.com

CELEBRATING 1979 Anacortes Yacht Charters 2014 35 YEARS

ANACORTES YACHT CHARTERS

AYC has established itself as the leading charter company with the largest selection of boats available for charter in the Pacific Northwest. Charter the San Juan or Gulf Islands or go as far North as Desolation Sound or Alaska.
2415 T Ave. suite #2 • www.ayc.com
1-800-233-3004 • 360-293-4555

ANDERS SIGNS

The two best days in a boater's life? We say they are the day you buy it and the day Anders Signs puts your new name on. At Anders we love boat lettering, and it shows. Boat lettering in Anacortes since 1990.
360-293-2452

CLASSIC UPHOLSTERY

We create beautiful Yacht Interiors: Cushions, Settees, Curtains, Sheets Pillows and Bedding. Located within blocks of 3 marinas, stop in and see our showroom. We have hundreds of fabric books to choose from.
360-293-1341 • 220 Commercial Ave.
classicupholsteryanacortes@gmail.com
www.classicupholsteryanacortes.com

EMERALD MARINE CARPENTRY

Specializing in classic wooden boat restoration and yacht joinery. Our shipwrights provide all manner of marine carpentry with passion for the craft, including wooden boat repair, teak decks, fabrication, interiors, and boat furniture. Inside work facilities are accessed by safe and convenient haulout.
360-293-4161 • 703 30th St.
emeraldmarine@earthlink.com
www.emeraldmarine.com

MARINE DETAIL SPECIALISTS

Washing, waxing, polishing and interior cleaning. It has been our mission to help Northwest boat owners "restore their hope" and "preserve their dreams" since 2001. Located in Anacortes just steps away from the marina office at Cap Sante.
206-617-4930
www.marinedetailspecialists.com

NORTH HARBOR DIESEL & YACHT SERVICE

North Harbor Diesel and Yacht Service has been in Anacortes Washington since 1985. Come see us for boat storage, engine services, hull and bottom repairs, maintenance and modernizing. Open year round Monday–Friday, we are the region's premier boatyard.
360-293-5551 • 730 30th St.
www.northharbordiesel.com

NORTH HARBOR YACHT BROKERS

North Harbor Yacht Brokers are friendly, responsive, and, above all, service oriented. Whether buying or selling, you'll receive expert, timely, market advice and research, and successful sales strategies to make your purchase or sale stress-free and fun! Come see us at our facility off R Ave. and you'll experience unmatched service and professionalism!
360-299-1919 • 409 30th St.
www.northharboryachtbrokers.com

OLYMPIC PROPELLER

• Third generation business 40 yrs. experience
• Sales/repair for all types of propellers
• National Marine Propeller Assoc. Member
• Hale Propeller Measurement Instrumentation
• No Charge check/advise, inboard propellers
• Pick-up/delivery Tacoma to Canada, I-5 corridor
866-790-7767 • 360-299-8266
kruger@olympicpropeller.com
www.olympicpropeller.com
www.getaprop.com

STEVE'S YACHT REPAIR

Providing installation and repair of all marine-related equipment and specializing in electrical repair, heating systems, alternators, inverters, anchor windlass systems, and watermakers.
360-333-2079 • 1903 12th St.
www.stevesyachtrepair.com

WEST YACHTS

FREE Boat Market Analysis
Buyer's Emissary • Seller's Agent
Power & Sail • 6 Experienced Yacht Brokers
Advertising in NW Boat Publications & Internet
Cap Sante Waterfront Office
Large Waterfront Display of Brokerage Boats
360-299-2526 • www.west-yachts.com
info@west-yachts.com • 1019 Q Ave. # D

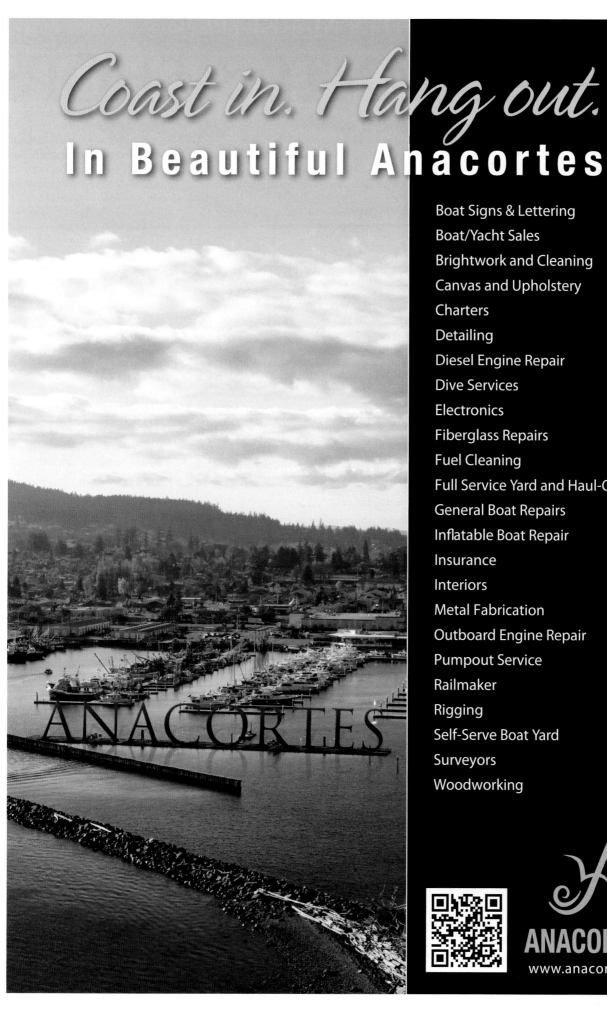

RESTAURANTS & SHOPS

CALENDAR OF EVENTS

MARCH
Spring Boat Show
Salmon Derby

APRIL
Spring Wine Festival
Spring Antique Show

MAY
TrawlerFest

JUNE
Waterfront Festival
Farmers Market
(Saturdays through
October)

JULY
4th of July Parade
& Celebrations
Shipwreck Day
Free Summer Concert
Series
(through August)

AUGUST
Anacortes Arts Festival
Workboat Races

SEPTEMBER
Taste Anacortes
Oyster Run
Fall Antique Show

OCTOBER
Oktoberfest
Fall Boat Show

DECEMBER
Holiday Parade
Lighted Boat Parade

For more info contact
the Anacortes
Chamber of Commerce

www.Anacortes.org
360-293-7911

THE MAJESTIC INN AND SPA

Discover a haven of elegance and charm. One of the most beautiful and romantic hotels in the region. Inspired NW cuisine and a luxurious spa to relax and rejuvenate the body and spirit.
360-299-1400 • 419 Commercial Ave.
www.majesticinnandspa.com

ANTHONY'S

Anthony's at Cap Sante Marina - Lunch and dinner served daily in a scenic waterfront setting, overlooking the marina. Serving fresh northwest seafood from our own seafood company along with seasonal local produce. Enjoy the view from our two decks, one of which is covered and has an outdoor fireplace. Restaurant is just steps from the marina.
360-588-0333 • 1207 Q Ave.
www.anthonys.com

THE BROWN LANTERN ALE HOUSE

Serving the locals & visitors to Historic Anacortes since 1933, just steps from the waterfront in the heart of oldtown.Featuring outstanding burgers, creative pub fare, 15 beers on draft, and over 50 different whiskies alone! See why we are voted the "Best Tavern in Anacortes" year after year.
360-293-2544 - 412 Commercial Ave.
www.brownlantern.com

CALICO CUPBOARD CAFÉ & BAKERY

Breakfast • Lunch • Baked Goods. Made-from-scratch bakery offering old-fashioned comfort foods using fresh, natural ingredients. Also providing tasty gluten-free options.
3 Locations: Near Cap Sante Marina in Anacortes 901 Commercial Ave., 360-293-7315
On 1st St. in La Conner 360-466-4451
Under the tulip in Mt. Vernon 360-336-3107
www.calicocupboardcafe.com

CAP SANTE INN

"The Best Value" and "Most Fun" in Anacortes. Located in Historic Old Town across the street from the Cap Sante Marina, restaurants, shops, & galleries. Walk to everything!
360-293-0602 • 906 9th St.
www.capsanteinn.com

FRIDA'S

Specializing in gourmet Mexican Cuisine. They offer both sides of Mexico, gourmet and traditional Mexican food. Their beautiful bar is home to an extensive selection of tequilas and serves excellent margaritas. Happy Hour daily 3 p.m. to 5 p.m. Te esperamos.
360-299-2120 • 416 ½ Commercial Ave.
www.FridasRestaurant.com

GERE-A-DELI

Family Owned Deli and Catering Company feeding Anacortes for the last 32 years, Traditional Deli Fare, Amazing Deli Sandwiches, Garden Fresh Salads, Pastas, In house Bakery. Voted Best Deli and Catering Company the last 25 years by locals. Take out and Box Lunches .
502 Commercial Ave. • close to Cap Sante Marina
360-293-7383 • www.Gere-a-Deli.com

H20

Anacortes' newest restaurant and bar features innovative food, a unique selection of cocktails using house made liquors, 24 craft beer handles (the largest selection in Skagit County), live music and a dance floor. Check website for a complete menu and event calendar.
360-755-3956 • 314 Commercial Ave.
www.anacortesH20.com

MAD HATTER'S ICE CREAM

42 flavors of soft serve and 24 flavors of hard ice cream. Malts, milkshakes, sundaes and more! Located within easy walking distance, just two blocks north of the Cap Sante Marina.
360-755-3799 • 801-6th St.

POTLUCK KITCHEN STUDIO

Gather, learn and create great food and memories by taking one of our scheduled cooking classes or by booking a private one! We offer Boater's Cooking Classes, Rendezvous Cooking Demos, and Floating Cooking Classes right in your own galley. Or saunter in for a sip of wine and browse our Pop-up Wine/Gift Shop.
360-393-2844 • 910-A 11th St.
www.potluckkitchenstudio.com

WATERMARK BOOK COMPANY

A locally owned, independent bookstore in the heart of downtown Anacortes. We carry books about boats and everything else and if we don' have the title you're looking for, we'll order it for you. (Most orders ship overnight). Open 7 days a week. Come on in if you need some literary ballast!
360-293-4277 • 612 Commercial Ave.
www.watermarkbookcompany.com

W.T. PRESTON STEAMBOAT TOURS & MARITIME HERITAGE CENTER

Step aboard this steamboat, and into the past. The *W.T. Preston* was the last sternwheeler to work in Puget Sound. Her crews removed navigational hazards from the bays and harbors of the Sound and from its tributary rivers. Call ahead or check website for schedule.
703 R Ave. • 360-293-1915
Just one block north of Cap Sante Marina
museum.cityofanacortes.org/preston.htm

The view of Mt. Baker from Anacortes.

Friday evening summertime concert at Cap Sante Marina.

businesses located there. Enter through the opening at the end of the dredged channel. First to starboard, is the dock with a 50-ton travelift for Cap Sante Marine, a full-service boatyard for repairs and refits (360) 293-3145.

Next are the staging docks with temporary moorage for the marine repair businesses. The city dock has marked temporary hourly moorage, but no overnight. The ramp at the end of the small basin is for the 45-ton capacity KMI Sea-Lift for North Harbor Diesel's repair yard and dry storage yards, and Banana Belt Boats brokerage storage yard.

Guemes Channel. On an ebb tide, waters in Guemes Channel can be very rough, especially west of the mouth of Bellingham Channel.

Watch for the Guemes ferry, a small car and passenger ferry that makes frequent crossings between Anacortes and Guemes Island.

Next to the ferry dock is Anchor Cove Marina, a private condo marina with covered and open slips.

Farther west is Lovric's Sea-Craft (360) 293-2042, a commercial shipyard and moorage with large marine ways for haul-out.

Ship Harbor was once the primary harbor for Anacortes and offers some protection and reasonable anchorage. Watch for ferry traffic from the busy Washington State Ferries ter-minal in Ship Harbor. Cross behind the ferries, not in front.

Guemes Island. Guemes Island has no facilities specifically for boaters, although anchorage can be found along the north shore. Anchorage also can be found on the eastern shore, in a tiny notch called Boat Harbor. A ferry connects Guemes Island to Anacortes.

Washington Park. www.cityofanacortes.org. West shore of Fidalgo Island on Guemes Channel. Open all year for day use and overnight camping. Restrooms and showers. Anchoring or beaching only. Two-lane launch ramp with parking area, picnic tables, picnic shelters, fireplaces, campsites. Playground equipment. The loop road is 2.2 miles in length, and is good for walking or jogging. The park has forested areas and viewpoints along the beaches overlooking Rosario Strait to Burrows Bay.

Flounder Bay. Flounder Bay has been dredged to provide moorage for Skyline real estate development. Skyline Marina and several charter companies are inside the spit. Also a small chandlery, Travelift, and other facilities, including a large dry storage building. Entry is from Burrows Bay, along a dredged channel marked by pilings.

⑳ **Skyline Marina.** 2011 Skyline Way, Anacortes, WA 98221; (360) 293-5134; marina@skylinemarinecenter.com; www.skylinemarinecenter.com. Monitors VHF 16, switch to 68. Open all year, guest moorage. Fuel dock with gasoline and diesel, propane, CNG, 30 amp power, laundry, showers, pumpout Beacon/BBX Wi-Fi. A seaplane float is at the fuel dock.

Complete boat repairs and services are available. The marina has a 55-ton Travelift for boat launching, haulout and repairs, plus two slings for boat launching. The yard has space for DIY repairs. Groceries (convenience store) nearby. Secure inside and outside storage for boats, vehicles, and trailers. Water taxi to the San Juan Islands. The marina is 4 miles from downtown Anacortes.

In 2010 the marina and its entry were dredged. No more groundings on low tides.

Burrows Island State Park. Open all year, no facilities. This is an undeveloped 330-acre state park. Anchor in Alice Bight on the northeast shore, or beach. No camping or fires. Pack out all garbage. Do not disturb wildlife or surroundings. Most of the shoreline is steep cliffs. The Burrows Island Lighthouse is on the west tip of the island.

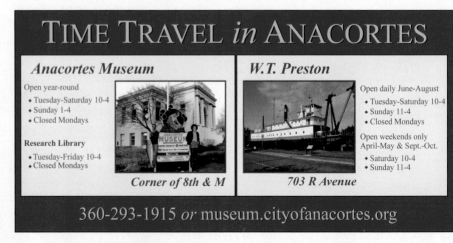

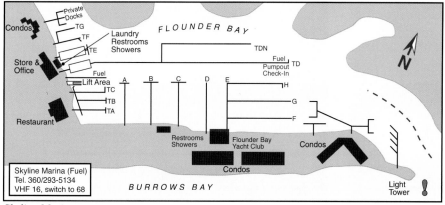

Skyline Marina

Allan Island. Allan Island is privately owned, but anchorage can be had in the little bight on the east shore.

Cypress Island. A park ranger told us he considers Cypress Island to be the "crown jewel" of the San Juans. This island, now largely in public ownership, is beautiful, and is an excellent place to stretch the legs. Access is hindered by a shortage of good anchorages, so you won't be bothered by large crowds. Several trails lead off from Pelican Beach at the northeast corner of the island. They can provide leisurely walks or vigorous hikes.

About a half-mile south of Pelican Beach, just past a small headland, two little coves are quite pretty, and have room for one or two boats each.

Pelican Beach Park. DNR park on the northeast side of Cypress Island. Open all year for day use and overnight camping and mooring. The park has 6 mooring buoys, a gravel beach, 4 campsites, clean vault toilets, picnic shelter, fire pit, information board. Many kinds of wildlife and birds can be observed. Public DNR beaches extend from the park around the north end of Cypress Island for 1.5 miles until just south of Foss Cove, and south of the park for 0.5 mile to Bridge Rock. The moorage is unprotected to the north. If anchored or moored to a buoy and the northerly wind comes in, you'll not want to stay. Current runs through the moorage, and it is subject to wake from passing traffic.

Eagle Harbor. East side of Cypress Island. Eagle Harbor is shallow, especially at low tide, but has several mooring buoys. Use care in approaching all but the outermost of these buoys. The bay's shallow spots are truly shallow. The innermost 4 buoys display red tags cautioning the user to verify depths at lower tide levels. Convenient beach access to the island's trails. No fires, no camping. If you have sufficient depth, Eagle Harbor is quite protected. Deepwater Bay, with its fish farms, is unattractive.

Cypress Head. East side of Cypress Island. Open all year for day use and overnight camping and mooring. The park has 5 mooring buoys and 5 campsites, picnic sites, vault

toilets, no other facilities. Three miles of public tidelands extend from the moorage/recreation area. Many types of birds and wildlife,

good fishing. Tide-rips ⟨...⟩ the island cause high wave⟨...⟩

Strawberry Island State P⟨...⟩ Cypress Island in Rosario Stra⟨...⟩ year. Anchoring or beaching on⟨...⟩ age in settled weather only. Strong and submerged rocks make landing d⟨...⟩ skiffs or kayaks are best for landing. Park three Cascadia Marine Trail campsites, va⟨...⟩ toilet.

Vendovi Island. The San Juan Preservation Trust purchased Vendovi Island in 2010. Daytime visitors are now welcome May 1 through September 30, 10:00 a.m. to 6:00 p.m. A 70-foot dock behind a rock breakwater is on the north shore. Anchoring is prohibited to protect eelgrass. Check in with caretakers upon arrival; they can answer

Saddlebag Island Marine State Park has good exploring on shore from several anchorages.

Cypress Island is close to Anacortes, La Conner, and Bellingham, but feels like a world away.

questions or direct you to the nearly 3 miles of hiking trails on the island. A public restroom is in the building at the top of the hill.

Sinclair and Eliza Islands. A piling breakwater protects a loading and unloading dock on the south shore of Sinclair Island, but there are no facilities specifically for pleasure boaters. Eliza Island is privately owned, with a private dock and float on the north side. Anchorage is possible several places around the island.

Larrabee State Park. (360) 676-2093. Seven miles south of Bellingham on Samish Bay. Open all year for day use and overnight camping. The park has restrooms and showers. This was Washington's first official state park, dedicated in 1923. It covers 2000 acres and is heavily used. Facilities include a launch ramp, kitchen shelters, picnic tables, standard, utility, and primitive campsites. Fishing, clamming, crabbing, scuba diving. Trails provide access to two freshwater lakes within the park. A 5.5-mile walking/bicycling trail connects with Bellingham.

Chuckanut Bay. Chuckanut Bay is a good anchorage, with protection from prevailing winds in the north or south arms. Enter close

to Governors Point to avoid extensive rocky shoals that partially block the entrance. The land around the bay is privately owned. Correspondents James and Jennifer Hamilton anchored in Pleasant Bay, just inside Governors Point, during a southeast gale. "The winds howled up to 49 knots, but the water was reasonably calm. Good holding over mud." [*Hamilton*]

㉑ **Fairhaven Moorage.** (360) 714-8891; www.boatingcenter.org. Mooring buoys and a side-tie linear mooring system at Fairhaven were installed by the Port of Bellingham, but are managed by the Bellingham Bay Community Boating Center. The buoys are for long-term moorage May through October, 35-foot maximum. The linear moorage is for visitor boats. Pay moorage at the BBCBC office ashore, and walk up to shops and restaurants in Fairhaven's lovely Victorian buildings. Just south of the business district you'll find a beautiful old park, with mature plantings and great expanses of lawn. Fairhaven moorage and boat launch are available May through October only. The boat ramp is in rough condition and is best suited to smaller boats. Water and garbage drop are at the dock. The dinghy dock is on the north side.

㉑ **Bellingham.** Bellingham is the largest city between Everett and the Canadian border, and has complete facilities for commercial and pleasure craft. Moorage, fuel, marine supplies, and repairs are available at the Port of Bellingham's Squalicum Harbor. Bellingham Yacht Club and Squalicum Yacht Club are nearby. BYC has moorage for members of reciprocal yacht clubs.

Charming Hotel Bellwether is near the mouth of the Squalicum Harbor south basin, adjacent to the Marina Restaurant and shops. The port runs a courtesy shuttle to grocery stores, to the historic Fairhaven area shops and restaurants, to downtown for more shopping, and to Bellis Fair Shopping Mall.

Mooring buoys and a linear moorage system are at Fairhaven, in the south part of Bellingham Bay. Fairhaven is a delightful stop, with turn-of-the-20th-century Victorian buildings, boutiques, a large bookstore and other interesting shops. Fairhaven is also the southern terminus of the Alaska Marine Highway Ferry System. As with Squalicum Harbor, you can take a bus or taxi to downtown Bellingham. Many shops, restaurants and a supermarket are within walking distance in this historic area.

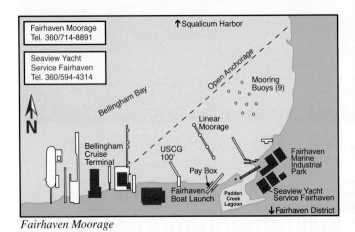

Fairhaven Moorage

Fairhaven has a linear moorage system as shown above.

Village Books, in Fairhaven, is an excellent bookstore.   *Exercise stations at Squalicum Harbor.*

THINGS TO DO

1. **Spark Museum of Electrical Invention.** Over 1,000 radios and many other electrical devices on display.

2. **Bellingham Railway Museum.** Model and actual trains, including a simulator.

3. **Whatcom Museum**. Art, photography, and a family interactive gallery. Downtown.

4. **Historic Fairhaven.** Good shopping and restaurants surrounded by period buildings. Peruse Village Books.

5. **Bellingham Farmers Market.** Held in Depot Square, a glass and steel building modeled after a railroad station, with beams and arches salvaged from a local highway bridge. Wonderful local vendors every Saturday. One of the largest markets in the state.

6. **Boundary Bay Brewery & Bistro.** Right across from the farmers market. Great beer garden, good food, and of course, very good beer.

7. **Mount Baker Theatre.** See a performance in this magnificently restored art deco theater built in 1927.

8. **Mindport.** Not quite a science museum. Exhibit themes are exploration, observation, creativity, play, and of course, fun.

9. **The Big Rock Garden.** More than 37 sculptures in this 2.5 acre park. Local and internationally acclaimed artists represented. Near the north shore of Lake Whatcom, a cab ride away.

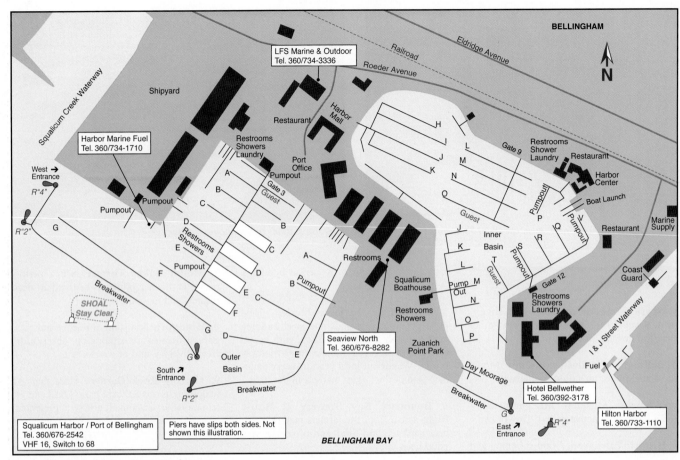

Port of Bellingham, Squalicum Harbor

LOCAL KNOWLEDGE

SHALLOW AREA: A shoal habitat enhancement bench (4-foot depth at zero tide) is along the breakwater protecting the western basin of Squalicum Harbor. The bench extends approximately 200 feet out from the breakwater and runs approximately 400 feet along the breakwater. White cylindrical can buoys mark the outer corners. From its outer edge, the bench slopes another 100 feet into Bellingham Bay until it meets the sea floor. Give the buoys a good offing when running along the face of the breakwater.

㉑ **Squalicum Harbor/Port of Bellingham.** 722 Coho Way, Bellingham, WA 98225; (360) 676-2542; squalicum@portofbellingham.com; www.portofbellingham.com. Certified Clean Marina. Monitors VHF 16, switch to 68. Open all year, guest moorage along 1500 feet of dock in two basins. Unoccupied slips are used when available. The marina has 20, 30 & 50 amp power (mostly 30 amp), restrooms, showers, laundry, pumpout, portapotty dump, and Beacon/BBX Wi-Fi. Internet also available in the harbor office. Three-day maximum stay in any 7-day period for visiting boats. The docks in both basins are gated for security. Restaurants and a snack bar nearby. Also chandleries,

The Web Locker Restaurant at Squalicum Harbor.

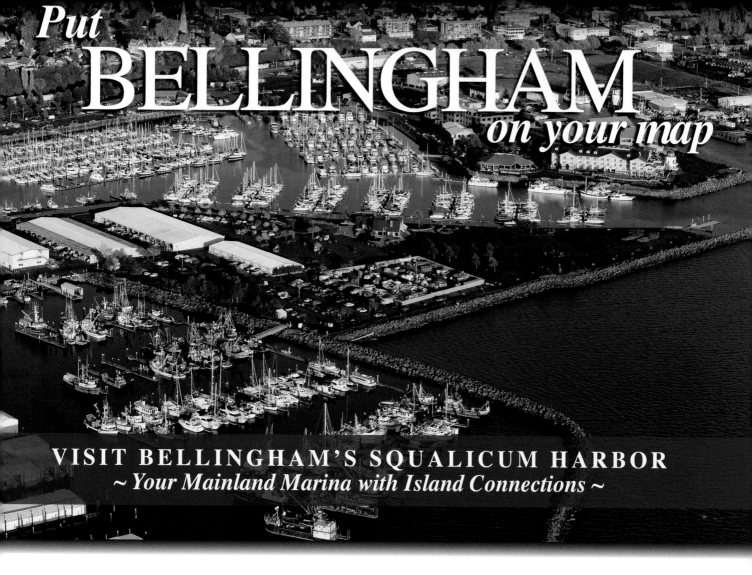

RESTAURANTS, SHOPS & SERVICES

SHIPSHAPE PROFESSIONAL YACHT CARE

We bring you integrity and excellence in all vessel maintenance and service. Create an annual maintenance plan today that provides a reliable schedule to manage your vessel, budget and maximize your cruising. Whether it is once, or time after time, ShipShape is here for you when ship hits the fan!

360-933-4656 • info@shipshapeyouryacht.com
www.shipshapeyouryacht.com

ANTHONY'S AT SQUALICUM HARBOR

Located in Bellwether on the Bay, offering spectacular views of the San Juan Islands. Serving fresh Northwest seafood from our own seafood company along with seasonal local produce - lunch, Monday through Saturday; Sunday brunch; and dinner served daily. Visitor moorage nearby on side-tie docks.

25 Bellwether Way • 360-647-5588 • www.anthonys.com

NW EXPLORATIONS

NW Explorations is a premier full service, brokerage, and charter company offering first class service in all areas. Whether you want to charter, buy/sell a vessel, or care for your existing boat, NW Explorations can help meet your needs.

2623 South Harbor Loop Dr.
360-676-1248 • www.nwexplorations.com

REDDEN MARINE SUPPLY INC.

Supplying paint & maintenance products, anchor & docking essentials, safety & survival gear to the boating public for over 50 years. Friendly knowledgeable staff. With over 50,000 items, we are your one-stop-shop for marine supplies. Open 7 days a week! In Squalicum Harbor.

1411 Roeder Ave. • www.reddenmarine.com
360-733-0250 or 800-426-9284

SEAVIEW NORTH BOATYARD

A full service and do-it-yourself boat repair facility for vessels up to 160 tons and 120'. We offer all disciplines of work including wood, fiberglass, topsides paint, fabrication, mechanical and general maintenance. Seasonal dry storage is also available.

2652 Harbor Loop Dr.
360-676-8282 • north@seaviewboatyard.com

SQUALICUM MARINE

Our friendly, professional crew has been serving the Pacific Northwest for over 45 years, providing top quality dodgers, covers, canvas and sail repair, and interior and exterior upholstery. We represent Neil Pryde Sails which are custom measured to fit your boat.

360-733-4353 • www.SqualicumMarine.com

SAN JUAN SAILING

A family run business for over 30 years, we strive to provide our guests with sail and power instruction, charters (sailboats, trawlers, motoryachts, sail and power catamarans), and brokerage services in a manner that consistently exceeds their expectations.

Gate 3, Squalicum Harbor, Bellingham
360-671-4300 • www.sanjuansailing.com

ANTHONY'S HEARTHFIRE GRILL

On Squalicum Harbor in Bellwether on the Bay, offering guests spectacular views of the San Juan Islands. Serving premier northwest beef and fresh northwest seafood, this high-energy restaurant specializes in hearthfire cooking. Lunch and dinner served daily. Visitor moorage nearby on side-tie docks.

7 Bellwether Way • 360-527-3473 • www.anthonys.com

TRI-COUNTY DIESEL MARINE

We're factory trained and authorized for top brands in maintenance, repair, and repower of marine propulsion and power generation. With over 100 years of combined experience, no job is too big or too small for our friendly team of professionals.

360.733.880 • care@tricountydieselmarine.com
www.tricountydieselmarine.com • 2696 Roeder Ave.

BITTER END BOATWORKS

Boat repair and maintenance, detailing, mechanical, electrical, bottom painting, haul-outs up to 30 ft. We are located on Bellingham's waterfront and can provide on-the-water service in the San Juan Islands area.

360.920.3862 • 1000 Hilton Ave.
www.bitterendboatworks.com

LFS MARINE & OUTDOOR

Located within easy walking distance of Squalicum Harbor docks. Boaters will appreciate the wide selection of fishing gear and crab pots, boat equipment and supplies, safety supplies, outdoor clothing, boots, and rain gear, plus Pacific Northwest gifts, nautical books, and cards. Open 8 to 5 weekdays, 9 to 4 Saturdays year round. Open Sundays during the summer.

851 Coho Way • www.LFSmarineoutdoor.com
800-426-8860 • 360-734-3336

Harbor Events

Charter Fest - Early spring, refer to website.
Ski-to-Sea - May 31st
Haggen Family Fourth of July - Fireworks & fair
Farmers Market - Every Saturday Railroad Ave.
Bellwether Art Market - August 15-17th
Bellwether Jazz Festival - September 6th
Holiday Port Festival - Dec. 5th-6th family fun
Lighted Boat Parade - December 6th

Contact the Port of Bellingham
www.portofbellingham.com • 360-676-2500

Maintenance tips

Basic engine service: Oil change, fuel filter change, refrigeration re-charge and diagnosis, battery maintenance, stuffing box adjustment, prop cleaning, and new zincs installed.

Inspect and service the tender: check for leaks in the inflatable, have the outboard serviced, ensure that all davit and hoist systems onboard are functioning.

Electronics: Ensure that all local charts are loaded onto nav gear, and or charts are procured. Keep an updated version of the Waggoner guide in the chart table.

Inspect and service all charging gear: High output alternator, regulator, inverter, and genset service.

Squalicum Harbor, Port of Bellingham

Bellingham has an active waterfront.

Hotel Bellwether, with moorage in front. The dock in the foreground is Squalicum Harbor's day dock.

electronics and engine repair shops.

Seaview Boatyard has taken over the long-idled shipyard adjacent to the western-most moorage basin, and has made major improvements to the facilities. The yard has a 150-ton Travelift and a 35-ton Travelift.

Squalicum Harbor is divided into two moorage basins, each with its own entrance and guest moorage. The westernmost has restrooms located about halfway out the main pier, and onshore at the top of the dock ramp. Portable pumpout carts are kept at the restroom station. Side-tie guest moorage is on the south side of the main pier, next to shore.

In the eastern basin, guest moorage is just inside the breakwater entrance. Hotel Bellwether, with its dock, is located on the east side, near the entrance. The hotel is part of a larger Port of Bellingham Bellwether development, with park grounds, restaurants, boutiques, and a coffee shop. Seasonally, you can buy fresh fish, right off the boat. A marine life tank (great for kids) also is near the streetside parking lot. A 4-lane launch ramp, with extended-term parking for tow vehicles and trailers, is just east of the east basin.

ANTHONY'S
AT SQUALICUM HARBOR
25 Bellwether Way
(360) 647-5588

Hearthfire
GRILL
7 Bellwether Way
(360) 527-3473

㉑ **Harbor Marine Fuel.** 21 Squalicum Way, Bellingham, WA 98225; (360) 734-1710. Open all year. Fuel dock with gasoline and diesel. Store carries motor oils. Located in northern Squalicum Harbor, behind the breakwater.

㉑ **Hotel Bellwether.** 1 Bellwether Way, Bellingham, WA 98225; (360) 392-3178; reservations@hotelbellwether.com; www. hotelbellwether.com. Open all year, side-tie moorage along 220-foot concrete float, 30, 50 & 100 amp power. Larger boats tie outside, smaller boats tie inside. This is a classy small hotel, done to 5-star standards. Outstanding dining. Located just inside the mouth of the Squalicum Harbor east basin. Reservations required. Dog friendly.

㉑ **Hilton Harbor.** 1000 Hilton Ave, Bellingham, WA 98225; (360) 733-1110; info@hiltonharbor.com; www.hiltonharbor. com. Fuel dock with gasoline only. Located at the south entrance to Squalicum Harbor at

Shops and restaurants are located above Squalicum Harbor.

the foot of Hilton Avenue. Travelift, repairs. Oil disposal available.

Lummi Island. Lummi Island is high (1480 feet), and has no facilities specifically for visiting boaters, although anchorage is good in several places, including Inati Bay and along both shores of Hale Passage. A ferry connects Lummi Island to the mainland, and a mooring float is alongside the mainland ferry dock. Restaurants and other businesses are near this dock. The Lummi Nation's people haul their boats, including reef net boats, on the beach south of the ferry dock.

Inati Bay. Inati Bay is on the east side of Lummi Island, approximately 2 miles north of Carter Point. It is the best anchorage on Lummi Island, protected from all but north-easterly winds (rare in the summer), with good holding. Members only allowed at the Bellingham Yacht Club property (change from earlier years, when all were welcome ashore).

When entering Inati Bay, leave the white cautionary buoy well to starboard, to avoid the rock that extends northward from the buoy. Stay close to the point of land on the south side of the entrance.

Lummi Island Recreation Site. Southeast shore of Lummi Island. Open all year, toilets, campsites.

Sandy Point. Sandy Point is a private real-estate development consisting of several canals with homes on them. No public facilities. Long docks serving a refinery and an aluminum plant extend from shore north of Sandy Point.

Birch Bay. Birch Bay is very shoal, but could provide anchorage in calm weather. Watch your depths. Birch Bay State Park has campsites, picnic and playground equipment, but no facilities for boaters.

Blaine Harbor's docks are wide and sturdy.

SHOAL ENTRY: The approach to Blaine through Semiahmoo Bay is shoal at all stages but high tide. Pay close attention to the buoys along the drying bank on the south side of the bay, and turn into the entrance channel before getting too close to the eastern shore.

㉒ **Blaine.** Blaine has two moorages in Drayton Harbor. One is owned by the Port of Bellingham; the other, Semiahmoo, is privately owned.

The Port of Bellingham's Blaine Marina is on the east (port) side as you enter. Entry to that marina is through an opening in the piling breakwater, with a fuel dock directly ahead. Once through the breakwater, and follow the signs to the guest moorage, in the middle of the harbor.

The Semiahmoo Marina is on the west side of the entrance channel. Both marinas have fuel, water, electricity, and other facilities ashore. The Port's marina gives access to the town of Blaine and a number of boating-related businesses. The Semiahmoo Marina has access to two fine golf courses. In the summer the classic foot ferry *Plover* operates between the two marinas.

㉒ **Blaine Harbor/Port of Bellingham.** PO Box 1245, 235 Marine Drive, Blaine, WA 98230; (360) 647-6176; blaine-harbor@portofbellingham.com; www.portofbellingham.com. Monitors VHF 16, switch to 68. Certified Clean Marina. Side-tie guest moorage along 760 feet of wide dock, unoccupied slips used when available. Services include 30 & 50 amp power, restrooms, showers, laundry, pumpout carts, portapotty dump, and Beacon/BBX Wi-Fi. Potable water, with good pressure, is on the docks. Repairs, haulout, supplies available. Waste oil disposal. Two blocks to town. Concrete launch ramp with parking. Restaurants nearby. Courtesy shuttle to grocery store.

The side-tie guest dock is served by a wide waterway for easy maneuvering. The shoreside facilities are built to a turn of the 20th century theme. The marina office is in the Boating Center building. A 65-person public meeting room, with kitchen, is also in this building. An attractive park is across the road, on the north side of the spit. Walking distance to the Peace Arch at the border.

㉒ **Blaine Marina Inc.** PO Box 1849, Blaine, WA 98231; (360) 332-8425; bmarinainc@yahoo.com. Open all year, gasoline and diesel. This is the fuel dock at the Blaine Harbor Marina.

㉓ **Semiahmoo Marina.** 9540 Semiahmoo Parkway, Blaine, WA 98230; (360) 371-0440; semimarina@comcast.net; www.semiahmoomarina.com. Monitors VHF 68. Open all year. Gasoline and diesel at the Semiahmoo Marina fuel dock, free pumpout. Guest

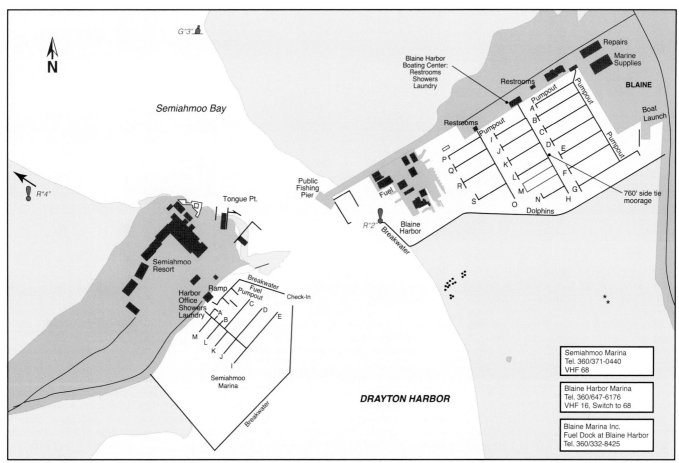

Drayton Harbor

moorage in unoccupied slips when available. One 50-foot slip is reserved for reciprocal yacht clubs. Call for availability for all guest moorage, reservations accepted. Services include 30 & 50 amp power, restrooms, free showers, laundry, pumpout, portapotty dump, Beacon/BBX Wi-Fi at the docks and free Wi-Fi in the café, gift and clothing shop with beer, wine and some marine items.

In 2013, the hotel, spa, and restaurants unexpectedly closed, but the marina remained open. A new ownership group reopened the resort in August 2013 and has been renovating the resort. All facilities are open again.

Golf: The par 72 Semiahmoo course is outstanding. Telephone (360) 371-7015.

㉔ **Point Roberts.** Point Roberts is a low spit of land extending south from Canada into U.S. waters. Although physically separated from the U.S., Point Roberts is U.S. territory and part of the state of Washington. The Point Roberts Marina is on the south shore. Enter via a dredged channel through drying flats.

MV Plover, *a passenger ferry, connects Blaine Marina and Semiahmoo Spit.*

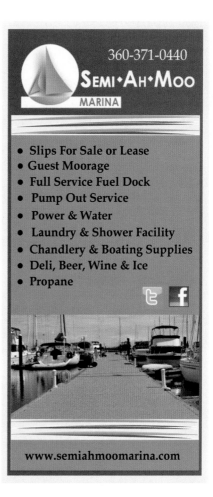

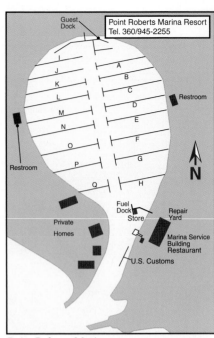

The Point Roberts customs dock.

Point Roberts Marina

㉔ **Point Roberts Marina Resort.** 713 Simundson Drive, Point Roberts, WA 98281; (360) 945-2255; prmarina@pointroberts-marina.com; www.pointrobertsmarina.com. Monitors VHF 66A. Open all year. Fuel dock with gasoline, diesel, propane, ice, beer & wine, fishing licenses, tackle, convenience items. Phone ahead for slip assignment, reservations required. Services include 30 & 50 amp power, restrooms, showers, laundry, pumpout, garbage drop, Beacon/BBX Wi-Fi. Pier Restaurant at marina, reservations recommended for large groups; (360) 945-7437. Other restaurants, golf and groceries are nearby. Haulout to 35 tons. Westwind

Marine Services, with repairs and a chandlery, is in the main building.

Point Roberts is a U.S. Customs port of entry, with a direct-dial telephone to customs on the Customs dock. Agents typically drive over from the Point Roberts border office. Consider calling ahead at (360) 945-2314.

Lighthouse Marine County Park. (360) 945-4911; lthouse@pointroberts.net; www.whatcomcounty.us. Open for day use and overnight camping in summer, day use only in winter. On the southwest corner of Point Roberts. Anchor north of the park and row in, or moor at Point Roberts Marina. Facili-

ties include campsites, picnic shelters, fire pits, barbecues, restrooms, showers, sand and gravel beach. Also a whale exhibit, playground, boardwalk, and picnic shelters. Whales can sometimes be seen from the park. A small public airstrip is along the eastern perimeter of the park.

STRAIT OF JUAN DE FUCA

CROSSING THE STRAIT OF JUAN DE FUCA
Sequim • Port Angeles • Clallum Bay • Neah Bay

The Strait of Juan de Fuca generally is 12 miles wide and 80 miles long. Depending on the weather it can be flat calm or extremely rough. The typical summertime pattern calls for calm mornings, with a westerly sea breeze rising by mid-day, increasing to 30 knots or more late in the afternoon. If this sea breeze opposes an out-flowing ebb current, the seas will be unusually high, steep, and close together. Often, however, the "typical" weather pattern does not prevail, and the wind blows around the clock. Or, it can be calm, even on a warm summer afternoon. Weather reports must be monitored. If wind is present or predicted, we stay off the strait.

Discovery Bay. Discovery Bay is west of Point Wilson on the Washington side. It is somewhat protected from the Strait of Juan de Fuca by Protection Island, a wildlife refuge. Discovery Bay is open and unobstructed, but is seldom used as an overnight anchorage by pleasure craft. Gardiner, halfway down the bay, has a launch ramp.

Sequim Bay. Sequim Bay is a beautiful, quiet anchorage with a public marina and a state park with floats. The bay is protected by Travis Spit, extending from the eastern shore. To enter, steer for the middle of this spit, then turn sharply west and run parallel to the spit.

Actor John Wayne, who visited Sequim Bay often aboard his yacht *Wild Goose*, donated 22 waterfront acres to the Port of Port Angeles, on condition that the Port build a marina on the site.

LOCAL KNOWLEDGE

SHOAL AREA: Sequim Bay has a large shoal in the middle, with passage around the eastern and western sides. The marked channel, which leads to the Port of Port Angeles John Wayne Marina, is on the west side. This route is best when approaching Sequim Bay State Park.

John Wayne Marina harbor office building also includes a restaurant with a deck overlooking the marina.

① **John Wayne Marina.** 2577 W. Sequim Bay Road, Sequim, WA 98382; (360) 417-3440; ron@portofpa.com; www.portofpa.com. Monitors VHF 16. Open all year, gasoline and diesel at the fuel dock, guest moorage in 22 slips and 200 feet of dock. Services include 30 amp power, restrooms, showers, laundry, pumpout, portapotty dump, and launch ramps. The Dockside Grill restaurant is ashore. Groceries, a picnic area, and beach access are nearby. Land at the first float inside the breakwater to check in.

① **Sequim Bay Marine State Park.** Sequim Bay Marine State Park occupies 92 acres along the western shore of Sequim Bay. Open all year, day use and overnight mooring and camping, 424 feet of dock space and 3 buoys. Facilities include restrooms, showers, portapotty dump, picnic sites, campsites, kitchen shelters, and launch ramp. No power. The mooring buoys are in deep water. The water around the dock and mooring float is shallower. Watch your depths at low tide. Boarding floats at the launch ramp are removed in the winter.

Dungeness Spit. Beautiful Dungeness Spit, 5.5 miles long, is the world's longest natural sand spit. It provides protection from westerly weather, and convenient anchoring depths along its inner edge before an attached cross-spit forces the channel south. Shallow draft boats can continue into the inner harbor, where there is a launch ramp and protected anchorage. Dungeness Spit is a wildlife refuge and open to hikers, but has no public facilities.

CHARTS	
18423 sc folio small-craft	Bellingham to Everett including San Juan Islands
18460	Strait of Juan de Fuca Entrance (1:100,000)
18465	Strait of Juan de Fuca – Eastern Part (1:80,000)
18468	Port Angeles (1:10,000)
18471	Approaches to Admiralty Inlet – Dungeness to Oak Bay (1:40,000)
18484	Neah Bay (1:10,000)
18485	Cape Flattery (1:40,000)

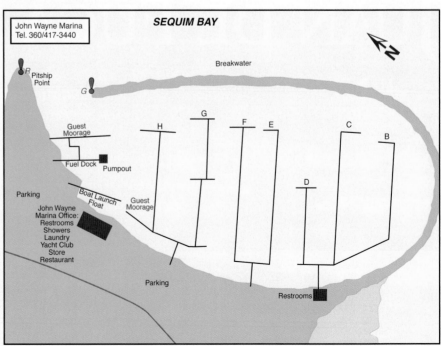

John Wayne Marina

The entrance to John Wayne Marina is a little unusual and requires close attention.

Port Angeles Boat Haven has a log yard outside the marina. Guest moorage shown above.

② **Port Angeles.** Port Angeles is a substantial small city on a bay protected by Ediz Hook. The Port Angeles City Pier, with visitor moorage, is near the south end of the business district. Guest moorage with full services is available at the breakwater-protected Port of Port Angeles Boat Haven marina at the southwest corner of the bay.

Port Angeles is a customs port of entry. The *Coho* car and passenger ferry runs from Port Angeles to Victoria (www.cohoferry.com).

The outer end of Ediz Hook is a Coast Guard station. Just west of the Coast Guard station is the Port Angeles Pilot Station, where ships bound to or from Puget Sound ports board and disembark pilots.

Port Angeles has a number of attractions. The Feiro Marine Life Center, on the city pier, focuses on the marine life in the Strait of Juan de Fuca. Open daily, 10:00 a.m. to 5:00 p.m. in summer and 12:00 p.m. to 4:00 p.m. in winter. In late June, free summer concerts begin on the pier, Wednesdays 6:00 p.m. to 8:00 p.m. The Juan de Fuca Festival, with music, workshops and crafts, is on Memorial Day weekend. For general tourist information see the North Olympic Peninsula Visitor & Convention Bureau website: www.olympicpeninsula.org.

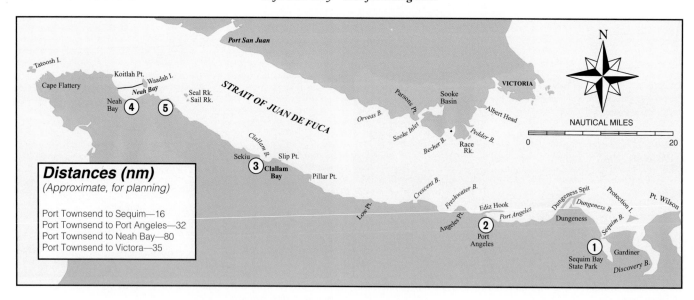

Port Angeles Boat Haven

Farmers market: A year-round farmers market runs Saturdays from 10:00 a.m. to 2:00 p.m at the corner of Front Street and Lincoln Street.

Olympic Discovery Trail: The Olympic Discovery Trail, for walking and bicycling, runs from Port Angeles to the town of Blyn. Eventually this trail will extend all the way from Port Townsend to La Push. Bike rentals are available in Port Angeles.

② **Port Angeles Boat Haven.** 832 Boat Haven Drive, Port Angeles, WA 98362; (360) 457-4505; pamarina@olypen.com; www.portofpa.com. Open all year, gasoline and diesel at the fuel dock, including certification and high-volume delivery for larger vessels. The marina has new concrete docks, side-tie guest moorage, and a new guest arrival float. Maximum boat length 164 feet. Wheelchair ramp to guest dock. Services include 30, 50, and 100 amp power, restrooms, Wi-Fi, showers, pumpout, portapotty dump. New security system with locking gates. Call ahead for after hours arrival. Excellent launch ramp with ample room for tow vehicles and trailers. Customs clearance is available, (360) 457-4311. The Fisherman's Wharf Café is open Monday through Saturday. Haulout on a 70-ton Travelift. Groceries, doctor, post office, and laundry are nearby.

② **Port Angeles City Pier.** Foot of North Lincoln St., Port Angeles, WA 98362; (360) 417-4550; www.cityofpa.us. Open Memorial Day through Labor Day with guest moorage in 35-foot and 80-foot slips. Day use only. Restrooms, no showers, no power.

Crescent Bay. Crescent Bay is a possible anchorage if conditions on the Strait of Juan de Fuca become untenable. Close to the western shore it offers a little protection from westerlies, but swells can still work into the bay and make for an uneasy stay.

Pillar Point. Pillar Point has a fishing resort with launch ramp and float, but is not available for transient moorage. In a westerly, the area close to and a little east of the point is a notorious windless spot–a "hole" in sailboaters' language. A Waggoner reader wrote to tell us anchorage is good along the eastern shore.

CLALLAM BAY AND SEKIU

Clallam Bay. Clallam Bay, with Sekiu on its western shore, is somewhat protected from westerlies, and has convenient anchoring depths along the shore. A serious reef, marked by a buoy at its outer end well offshore, extends from the eastern point. Leave the buoy to port when entering the bay. Three marinas offer transient moorage.

③ **Van Riper's Resort.** P.O. Box 246, 280 Front Street, Sekiu, WA 98381; (360) 963-2334; www.vanripersresort.com. Open summers, closed winters. Guest moorage along 2800 feet of dock space. Facilities include restrooms, showers, portapotty dump, campground, concrete launch ramp. No power. Boat and motor rentals, charter service, ice, groceries, charts, and books. Nearby post office, restaurant and bar, and marine supplies.

③ **Olson's Resort.** P.O. Box 216, 444 Front St., Sekiu, WA 98381; (360) 963-2311. Open February through September. Gasoline and diesel at the fuel dock. Guest moorage in 300 slips behind a breakwater, 40-foot maximum boat length. No power. Services include restrooms, showers, laundry, 3-lane concrete launch ramp, portapotty dump, and wireless internet near the office. Motel units available. Busy during salmon season. Boat and motor rentals.

③ **Curley's Resort.** P.O. Box 265, Sekiu, WA 98381; (360) 963-2281; (800) 542-9680; www.curleysresort.com. Open May through September, guest moorage along 750 feet of dock space, 30-foot maximum boat length. This is a resort with moorage, motel rooms, and cabins for rent. Pets must remain on the boat.

NEAH BAY

The Makah Indian town of Neah Bay is popular with sport fishermen, who trailer their boats in during the summer. It's also a good

---

Port Angeles Boat Haven
Tel. 360/457-4505
U.S. Customs Check-In:
Tel. 360/457-4311

Check-in dock for Port Angeles Boat Haven.

place to wait for a favorable weather window to round Cape Flattery and head down the Pacific Coast. Most boats bound to or from Barkley Sound, however, choose to stay along the Vancouver Island side of the Strait of Juan de Fuca. For cruising boats that do stop, moorage is at the Makah Marina docks, managed by Big Salmon Resort.

A long breakwater connects the mainland and Waadah Island, blocking ocean waves from getting in. Anchorage is good, sand bottom, throughout the bay. A second breakwater protects Makah Marina. The Coast Guard station at the entrance to the bay serves the west end of the Strait of Juan de Fuca and the northern Pacific Ocean coast.

Neah Bay is not a U.S. Customs port of entry, although entrants with Nexus cards can phone in from there. Those without Nexus must clear at a designated port of entry. Port Angeles is the nearest location.

The Makah Cultural & Research Center Museum features artifacts from the Ozette archaeological dig site. The museum is worldclass—a must see. The Ozette dig was a village buried by a mudslide 500 years ago, before contact with whites. It is a time capsule of coastal Indian life. The tools, clothing, furniture, weapons, and fishing implements are exquisitely preserved and displayed.

Neah Bay's general store is well-stocked, except for spirits. Neah Bay is dry.

④ **Makah Marina.** P.O. Box 137, Neah Bay, WA 98357; (360) 645-2374. Open all year, guest moorage, 30 & 50 amp power, Wi-Fi, potable water, restrooms, showers, laundry nearby, pumpout station, portapotty dump, 2-lane launch ramp with extended parking available for tow vehicles and trailers. Summertime visitor moorage is managed by Big Salmon Resort, listing below. Shopping (on the rough and ready side) and lodging are nearby. The extraordinary Makah Museum is an easy walk.

The marina is spacious and well-built. The concrete docks are extremely stable, and each mooring slip is served by sturdy mooring cleats. The slips are spacious and the fairways between docks are wide. On shore, the modern administration building has restrooms and showers. Summertime moorage can be crowded with commercial boats and

their gear, however, so don't expect a resort environment.

④ **Big Salmon Resort.** P.O. Box 140, 1251 Bay View Ave., Neah Bay, WA 98357; (360) 645-2374; (866) 787-1900; www.bigsalmonresort.net. Open April 1 to September 15. Gasoline and diesel at fuel dock. Pumpout. Haulout to 30 tons. Guest moorage at Makah Marina. They have a 2-lane concrete launch ramp with long-term parking. Small store carries tackle, some groceries, local charts. Motels, doctor, post office nearby.

If the fuel dock is closed for the season, fuel is available at the Makah Mini Mart's commercial dock just beyond the commercial fish offloading pier.

⑤ **Snow Creek Resort.** P.O. Box 248, Mile Marker 691, Hwy 112, Neah Bay, WA 98357; (800) 883-1464; snowcreek@gmail.com; www.snowcreekwa.com. Open from April 15 to October 1. Guest moorage for up to 40 boats and on 25 buoys. Maximum boat size 26 feet. Restrooms, showers, campsites and RV parking, cabins, limited groceries, diving air, haulout, beach launch, and hoist launch.

CROSSING THE STRAIT OF JUAN DE FUCA

Important: *Routes suggested below are approximate and for reference only. They assume good conditions and the absence of current. Since current always is present, appropriate course adjustments will be needed.*

Tugs with tows frequent the Strait of Juan de Fuca. Be especially vigilant in the fog to avoid passing between a tug and tow.

The Strait of Juan de Fuca has a well-earned reputation for being rough at times. It's true that a boat crossing the strait can take a beating its crew will not want to repeat, but often the crossing can be almost flat. If conditions truly are foul, alternate routes exist. The secret to an easy crossing lies in picking your times and not being foolhardy.

Summer weather pattern. During the high summer cruising season, the "typical" weather pattern calls for near-calm conditions in the early morning, when the air over the entire region is cool. As the summer sun heats the land, air over the land rises, and colder ocean air funnels down the Strait of Juan de Fuca to replace the rising land air. This is called a sea breeze, and it usually develops in the late morning or early afternoon. By late afternoon the sea breeze can be quite strong, creating short, high seas. After sundown, as air in the interior cools, the sea breeze dies away.

Given this pattern, early morning crossings are preferred. Carefully monitor the official weather reports and forecast. If the morning report says the wind already is blowing 15 to 20 knots, and more wind is expected, don't cross. Wait until the wind subsides or take an alternate route.

Fog can develop unexpectedly on the strait. Sometimes it is only a thin mist, other times it can be pea-soup thick. Normally when the wind moves in, the fog blows out.

Beware of the ebb tide. Ebbing tidal currents can set up dangerous tide-rips at Point Wilson, and at the south end of Rosario Strait, at Cattle Pass, and off Discovery Island. Do not underestimate the viciousness of these tide-rips. Whenever possible, plan your passage to transit these danger spots near the turn of the tide or on a flood.

Point Wilson to San Juan Channel. The most direct route from Point Wilson to Friday Harbor is via San Juan Channel. A direct course between the two intersects Smith Island. Shoals, covered with dense kelp, extend westward from Smith Island for nearly 2 miles. Partridge Bank, between Point Wilson and Smith Island, should be avoided. Heavy kelp is an obstacle, and if the wind is up seas are worse in the shallow water over the bank.

At Point Wilson you'll set a course of

approximately 301° magnetic until you're abeam the Smith Island light, where you'll turn to a course of 330° magnetic to fetch Cattle Pass. (From Cattle Pass to Point Wilson reverse the process: run 150° magnetic until the Smith Island light bears abeam to port, then turn to 121° magnetic to fetch Point Wilson.)

When using this route, it's best to time your arrival at Cattle Pass for shortly after the current turns to flood. Use the San Juan Channel current predictions.

If you do it right, you'll carry the last of a dying ebb out Admiralty Inlet, past Point Wilson, and well across the strait.

Just before reaching Cattle Pass, the current will turn to flood, flushing you nicely through the pass and into San Juan Channel. Since you can have 2 to 4 knots of current in Admiralty Inlet, and a couple knots of current in the strait, riding the ebb can save considerable time, even in a fast boat. The less time you're exposed, the less time you have to meet trouble.

The current can run hard through Cattle Pass, so it's best not to fight it.

The Point Wilson Lighthouse marks the northeastern tip of the Olympic Peninsula.

To Rosario Strait or Deception Pass. From the mouth of Admiralty Inlet, plot a course that leaves Point Partridge bell buoy off Whidbey Island to starboard. If you're bound for Rosario Strait, stay out of the traffic lanes as much as possible. As noted above, the mouth of Rosario Strait can be filled with dangerous tide-rips on an ebb tide. Be prepared to favor the eastern shore.

To Haro Strait (Roche Harbor). Leaving Point Wilson, run a course of approximately 301° magnetic until the Smith Island light is abeam to starboard. Then turn to approximately 305° magnetic to run toward Lime Kiln Point on the west side of San Juan Island. Once near Lime Kiln Point, follow the San Juan Island shoreline north.

If you're returning south from Roche Harbor, follow the San Juan Island coastline until you're a little south of Lime Kiln Point, then turn to approximately 125° magnetic until the Smith Island light is abeam to port. At Smith Island turn to 121° magnetic to fetch Point Wilson.

Both the flood and ebb currents run strongly along the west side of San Juan Island. Even in a fast boat it is best to make this passage with favorable current. The Canadian Hydrographic Service book *Current Atlas: Juan de Fuca Strait to Georgia Strait* illustrates these current flows in convincing diagram form. *Waggoner Tables,* published annually, provide the time schedule for the Current Atlas.

To Victoria. From Point Wilson, a course of approximately 275° magnetic takes you 30 miles to Victoria. Returning from Victoria, a course of about 095° magnetic should raise Point Wilson in time to make late-run corrections for the effects of current. In slow boats, the trip between Victoria and Point Wilson usually can be made on a single favorable tide. In all boats, utilizing favorable current can save significant time.

Even the best plan can go awry. While over the years we have made many easy crossings of the strait (only a few have been "memorable"), it's important to understand that conditions can change with little warning. When you're several miles offshore and the wind decides to kick up, you can't pull over until things improve.

The Strait of Juan de Fuca is not to be feared, but it should be respected. Be sure your boat is seaworthy, well-equipped, and in excellent condition. Carry plenty of fuel. Let the weather and tide and current tables set your plans. Don't be afraid to wait, but be confident enough to seize opportunities as they arise.

THE POINT WILSON RIP

One of the more frustrating pieces of water we face in the Northwest is the infamous Point Wilson tide-rip just off Port Townsend. The rip usually (but not always) forms on an ebb tide, and may or may not be accompanied by westerly wind. The patch of rough water can extend for several miles north and west of Point Wilson. We have learned three ways to avoid being bounced around by the Point Wilson rip.

The first is to round Point Wilson at or near slack water. Usually, the rip doesn't form until well into an ebb cycle, so timing your arrival to coincide with slack water should get the job done.

If, however, you must go that way while the rip is tearing the Strait of Juan de Fuca to shreds, you can pick one of two routes around it.

The first is to hug the Point Wilson shore as closely as you dare, keeping close to shore until you pass McCurdy Point, before heading across to the San Juan Islands or heading west to Victoria. The fact that the current runs more slowly close to shore prevents the tide-rip from having the same wild effect as farther out.

The other route is to stay close to the Whidbey Island shore (avoiding the shoal water off Partridge Point and staying east of Partridge Bank) until past Smith Island before turning toward your destination.

It doesn't take much ebb current to create the Point Wilson Rip. On July 26, 2001 we were returning to Seattle from the San Juan Islands, reaching Point Wilson at noon. Bush Point maximum ebb of 2.3 knots would not be until 1347, yet already the rip was visible and working its way eastward across the mouth of Admiralty Inlet. Although there was no wind and the water around us was calm, inside the rip ugly black seas reared up and broke.

A white powerboat entered the far side of the rip. The boat was about 40 feet long, perhaps coming down from Victoria. Once in, it was trapped. It rolled and plunged, taking water up to the fly bridge.

The longer it was in the rip, the bigger the rip became. Rolling and crashing, the boat had no choice but to carry on. The bow lifted out on the crests and disappeared in the troughs, burying in the waves ahead. Eventually the boat got through. We don't know if it suffered damage, but we're sure the people suffered. This rip should not be trifled with.

— Tom Kincaid and Robert Hale

SAN JUAN ISLANDS

SAN JUAN ISLAND
Friday Harbor • Roche Harbor • Garrison Bay

LOPEZ ISLAND
Fisherman Bay • Spencer Spit • Watmough Bay

ORCAS ISLAND
Eastsound • Deer Harbor • Rosario Resort

Blakely Island • Sucia Island • Jones Island
• Shaw Island • Stuart Island • James Island

The world-famous San Juan Islands are the dream destination for thousands of boaters each year. The scenery is stunning, the fishing is good, the anchorages are plentiful, and the amenities—marine resorts, settlements, villages and towns—are many and varied. The islands contain large flocks of bald eagles. Sailing in the company of porpoises and whales is almost commonplace.

The San Juans have a feel about them that is different from most other coastal cruising areas. In the San Juans we don't just head down the coast to another bay, or out to a little clutch of islets for the night. Instead, we are cruising among the peaks of a majestic sunken mountain range, and each island peak is different from the others. We've truly left the bustle of civilization behind, and found a corner of paradise.

The San Juans have so much to see and do that a first-time visitor can be overwhelmed. We have a short list of stops that we recommend. They are not the only places to experience, but they are unique. Nothing like them exists anywhere else. Our short list is as follows: Rosario Resort, Roche Harbor, English Camp (Garrison Bay), Stuart Island (Prevost Harbor and Reid Harbor), Sucia Island, and Friday Harbor. You will make many other stops as well. But these six are highly recommended, especially for the first-time visitor, or when you have guests.

Rosario Resort is a mansion and estate built in the early 1900s by Robert Moran, a turn-of-the-20th-century pioneer ship builder. The facilities were renovated beginning in 2008 and include a luxury resort hotel and marina.

Roche Harbor is another century-old monument, this one built around limestone quarrying. It's now a deluxe resort and a don't-miss experience. English Camp is at Garrison Bay, a short distance from Roche Harbor. This is where the British garrison

Roche Harbor Marina decorated for the Fourth of July.

was stationed during the historic 1859–1872 Pig War. The blockhouse, formal gardens, and several buildings remain. They are now a National Historical Park, with an interpretive center.

Stuart Island is a gem. In both Prevost Harbor and Reid Harbor you can anchor, tie to a mooring buoy, or moor on a dock. Whichever you do, you will be surrounded by beauty. A hike along a well-marked, up-and-down trail leads to the dirt road that runs out to Turn Point Lighthouse. Along the way are the Stuart Island one-room school, library, and museum.

Sucia Island, with its weather- and water-sculpted sandstone, its fossils and fascinating shoreline, is the definitive anchorage of the San Juans. The problem will be choosing which of Sucia Island's five bays to stay in.

Friday Harbor is a lovely little town where you can browse the shops, or stop in at one of the many restaurants or pubs. It's the commercial hub of the San Juans, with more services than any other destination.

No, we've not mentioned the charming village of Eastsound on Orcas Island, or Lopez Village on Lopez Island, or the Shaw General Store at the Shaw Island ferry landing, or Spencer Spit, or a dozen other delightful places to see, although we certainly describe them in detail later in the chapter. This is the problem with the San Juans. There's so much to do.

Although summertime tourism is a major industry in the San Juan Islands, the settlements have retained a small village atmosphere. Minutes out of town, you will be on winding roads in pastoral farm country. Island people are easygoing and friendly, and many of them are highly accomplished. Movie stars and industrialist families have estates there. The late author Ernest Gann lived on San Juan Island. One famous author's book bio

says simply that he lives on an island. What it doesn't say is that the island is in the San Juans.

Drinking water is in short supply in the San Juan Islands. In almost every case you'll find no water for boat washing. Go to the San Juans with full water tanks, and conserve while you are there.

Personal watercraft restriction: Because some people were hot-dogging on their PWCs and harassing whales and other wildlife, San Juan County has banned PWC use in the San Juan Islands.

Getting to the San Juan Islands. If you are approaching from the east, you'll enter the San Juans from one of four passes: Lopez Pass, Thatcher Pass, Peavine Pass, or Obstruction Pass.

At times the waters outside these passes can be turbulent, dangerously so, the result of tidal current and wind opposing each other. Be sure you have a complete tide and current book, and are able to read it. You can't go wrong with the official government publications, but our preferred tide books are *Captn. Jack's Tide & Current Almanac* and *Ports and Passes*, both available at marine supply stores. In an easy to understand page-a-day format, *Captn. Jack's* gives complete tide and current information for Puget Sound and the San Juan Islands in graph form. *Ports and Passes* is in a tabular format and covers the area from Olympia to the Alaska border. Examine both and determine what will work best for you.

① **James Island Marine State Park.** Open all year for day use, overnight mooring, and camping. James Island is a favorite spot. You can enjoy the hiking trails and watching wildlife. Visiting boats can use both sides of a 44-foot-long float and 1 mooring buoy on

CHARTS

18421	Strait of Juan de Fuca to Strait of Georgia (1:80,000)
18423 sc folio small-craft	Bellingham to Everett including San Juan Islands
18429	Rosario Strait, Southern Part (1:25,000)
18430	Rosario Strait, Northern Part (1:25,000)
18431	Rosario Strait to Cherry Point (1:25,000)
18432	Boundary Pass (1:25,000)
18433	Haro Strait – Middle Bank to Stuart Island (1:25,000)
18434	San Juan Channel (1:25,000)
3462	Juan de Fuca Strait to Strait of Georgia (1:80,000) (Canadian)

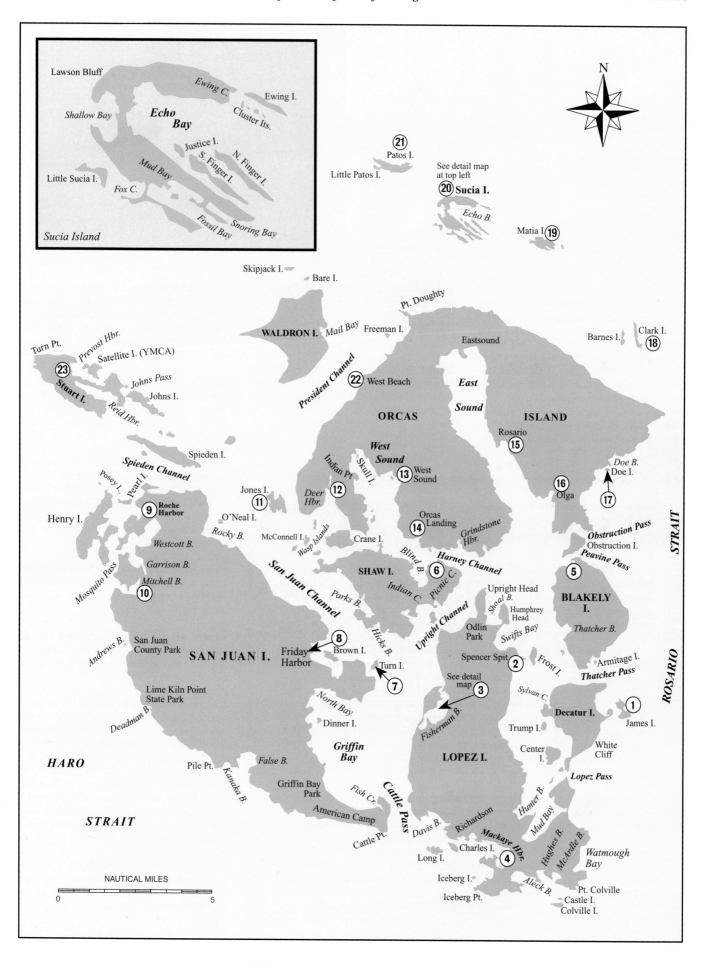

Sucia Island (inset, top left)

Lawson Bluff

Ewing C.

Ewing I.

Shallow Bay

Echo Bay

Cluster Its.

Justice I.

S. Finger I.

N. Finger I.

Little Sucia I.

Mud Bay

Fox C.

Fossil Bay

Snoring Bay

Sucia Island

㉑ Patos I.

Little Patos I.

See detail map at top left

⑳ **Sucia I.**

Echo B.

Matia I. ⑲

Skipjack I.   Bare I.

Pt. Doughty

Barnes I.   Clark I. ⑱

WALDRON I.   *Mail Bay*   Freeman I.

Eastsound

Turn Pt.   *Prevost Hbr.*

Satellite I. (YMCA)

President Channel

⑫ West Beach

East

Sound

Rosario

ISLAND

㉓ **Stuart I.**

Johns Pass

Johns I.

Reid Hbr.

ORCAS

West

Sound

⑮

Spieden I.

Doe B.

Doe I.

Spieden Channel

Indian Pt

Skull I.

⑬ West Sound

⑯ Olga

⑰

Posey I.   Pearl I.

Deer Hbr.

⑫

Henry I.

Jones I.

⑨ **Roche Harbor**

O'Neal I.

⑪

Orcas Landing

⑭

Grindstone Hbr.

Obstruction Pass

Obstruction I.

Peavine Pass

Westcott B.

Rocky B.

McConnell I.

Wasp Islands

Crane I.

Blind B.

Harney Channel

⑤

Garrison B.

Mitchell B.

⑩

Mosquito Pass

SHAW I.

Indian C.

Picnic C.

⑥

Upright Head

Shoal B.

Humphrey Head

BLAKELY I.

Thatcher B.

Andrews B.

San Juan County Park

SAN JUAN I.

Parks B.

Hicks B.

Brown I.   ⑧

Friday Harbor

Turn I.

⑦

Upright Channel

Odlin Park

Swifts Bay

Spencer Spit

②

Frost I.

Armitage I.

Thatcher Pass

Lime Kiln Point State Park

See detail map

③

Fisherman B.

Sylvan C.

Decatur I.

James I.   ①

Deadman B.

North Bay

Dinner I.

Trump I.

Center I.

White Cliff

HARO

Pile Pt.

False B.

Griffin Bay

Griffin Bay Park

Fish Cr.

LOPEZ I.

Lopez Pass

Kanaka B.

American Camp

Cattle Pass

Hunter B.

Mud Bay

Hughes B.

McArdle B.

STRAIT

Cattle Pt.

Davis B.

Richardson

Mackaye Hbr.

④

Aleck B.

Watmough Bay

Long I.

Charles I.

Pt. Colville

Castle I.

Iceberg I.

Colville I.

Iceberg Pt.

STRAIT (right side, ROSARIO)

NAUTICAL MILES

0   5

Sylvan Cove is a lovely anchorage, but the land ashore is all private.

Much of the area around Unnamed Island #3 dries at low tide.

the west side of the island. Toilets, no power or water. Anchoring can be difficult in the west cove. Use the float (removed in winter).

The east cove is exposed to wakes from passing traffic in Rosario Strait, but has 4 mooring buoys. The park has a picnic shelter and 13 primitive campsites. A Cascadia Marine Trail campsite is at Pocket Cove (high bank gravel beach). Excellent hiking, picnicking, scuba diving. Pack out all garbage. If at the dock, raccoons will go aboard unattended boats if food or garbage is left in the open. Best to stow food well and close the boat tight.

LOCAL KNOWLEDGE

TIDE-RIP: When the current is ebbing and the wind is blowing from the south, be particularly mindful of the tide-rips that form at the eastern entrance to Thatcher Pass.

CAUTION IN ROSARIO STRAIT

Lopez Pass, Thatcher Pass, Peavine Pass and Obstruction Pass all connect with Rosario Strait. Especially on an ebb, when current in Thatcher Pass and Lopez Pass flows east into Rosario Strait, expect rougher water off their mouths. If a big southflowing ebb in Rosario Strait is opposed by a fresh southerly wind, expect severe turbulence. The tide-rips and heavy seas can persist completely across the strait.

We have seen some vicious rips at the south end of Rosario Strait. Walt Woodward (*How to Cruise to Alaska without Rocking the Boat Too Much*) recalls that a rip outside Lopez Pass was the worst he had ever encountered.

The waters between Guemes Channel and Thatcher Pass can be rough or even dangerous in these conditions (southflowing ebb in Rosario Strait opposed by fresh southerly wind). Guemes Channel enters Rosario Strait from the east, and Thatcher Pass enters from the west. Bellingham Channel angles in from the northeast. The conflict of the four currents, combined with the opposing wind, creates confused, high and steep beam seas as you cross. It seems that all experienced local yachting families (ourselves included) have their own horror stories of crossings in such conditions.

We have learned to treat Rosario Strait with great respect. Thus, one year when a 20-knot southerly was blowing, we left the San Juans for Seattle via Peavine Pass, at the north end of Blakely Island. As we suspected, Rosario Strait was rough, especially to the south. We angled northward and eastward across the top of Cypress Island, and looked down Bellingham Channel. It too was a mass of whitecaps.

So we continued eastward, and found calm water on the east side of Guemes Island. Our route plan back to Seattle then went past La Conner and south through Saratoga Passage. It was longer and slower than a fast run across the Strait of Juan de Fuca and down Admiralty Inlet, but it was unruffled.

— *Robert Hale*

Thatcher Pass. Thatcher Pass runs between Blakely Island and Decatur Island and is one of the main entrances into the San Juan Islands. Currents can run strongly. Washington State Ferries use Thatcher Pass, so keep a sharp lookout.

Decatur Island. Decatur Island is east of Lopez Island and south of Blakely Island. Decatur Island has three vacation communities and about 50 full-time residents. No public services.

Sylvan Cove. Sylvan Cove, at the northwest corner of Decatur Island, has good holding bottom in convenient depths. The bay is truly beautiful, with New England-style buildings ashore. All the land ashore is private, as are the mooring buoys, the dock, and float that serves homeowners on the island.

Brigantine Bay. The area between Trump Island and Decatur Island is pretty and has anchorage in 24 to 42 feet, but the dock and all the land ashore are private.

Center Island. Good anchorage can be found by simply cruising around Center Island into **Reads Bay** until you find an area out of the prevailing wind.

Unnamed Island #3. This island, an undeveloped DNR park, is in the little bay at the south tip of Decatur Island, and joins Decatur Island at low tide. Open all year, day use only. Anchor out. No fires or overnight camping. Pack out all garbage. Do not disturb wildlife or alter the surroundings. This is one of Contributing Editor Tom Kincaid's favorite anchorages. When the Kincaid children were small, they used the concrete structure on the island as a fort.

Lopez Pass. Lopez Pass connects Rosario Strait to Lopez Sound. Currents can flow strongly through Lopez Pass and the area calls for careful navigation.

Lopez Island. Lopez Island offers a variety of anchorages and moorages. On the north-

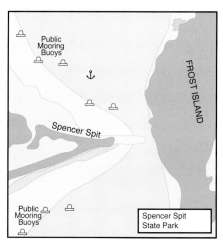

Spencer Spit State Park

ern end, sandy Spencer Spit is a favorite. Fisherman's Bay, on the west side, has the town of Lopez with marinas, a museum, a grocery store, and restaurants.

The southern end of Lopez Island is indented by several bays, and guarded by rocks and reefs. The geography is rugged and windblown, the result of the prevailing westerly winds from the Strait of Juan de Fuca. It's an interesting shore to explore when the wind is down. The village of Richardson used to be famous for its quaint general store (which stocked everything anybody might need, ever), but the store burned to the ground years ago and has not been rebuilt. The Richardson fuel dock, (360) 468-2275, with gasoline and diesel, is still operating, but you must lie next to a high pier while fueling. Most of its customers are fish boats and larger vessels. Anchorage at Richardson is marginal.

Lopez Sound. Lopez Sound, the body of water between Decatur Island and Lopez Island, has several anchorages. Among them, Mud Bay and Hunter Bay are good.

Mud Bay County Park. South end of Lopez Sound. Open all year, day use only, no facilities. Includes all of the southwest end of Mud Bay and the southeast shore of Mud Bay up to Shoal Bight, except some private tidelands on the southeast side of the bay. Anchor out at this undeveloped county park property. No fires or overnight camping. Most of the uplands are private. To go ashore, look for several boats pulled up on the shoreline on the southeast side of the bay. Pack out all garbage. Do not disturb the wildlife or alter the surroundings.

Hunter Bay. Southwest corner of Lopez Sound. Hunter Bay is a good place to anchor, mud bottom. It is surrounded by forest and protected from all but northeast winds. The small float is for loading and unloading only. No facilities are ashore, and the land is privately owned. Nice spot to put the hook down, though.

(2) **Spencer Spit Marine State Park.** 521

A. Bakerview Road, Lopez Island, WA 98261; (360) 468-2251; www.parks.wa.gov. On the northeastern shore of Lopez Island. Open all year, day use and overnight mooring and camping. The park usually has 16 mooring buoys. Mooring buoys typically fill up quickly during the summer, but anchoring is good. Restrooms are located upland, no showers. Restrooms are closed from the end of October to March. Water is available at the bottom of the trail to the uplands.

Spencer Spit is a popular park. A saltwater lagoon, fed from the north side, is in the middle of the spit. If you are on the north side, you must walk around the tip of the spit and back down the south side to get to the upland areas of the park. The park has standard and primitive campsites. Rabbits abound, and interpretive signs aid exploration. Spencer Spit is a Cascadia Marine Trail campsite. Although the pass between Spencer Spit and Frost Island is narrow, it is deep and safe.

Swifts Bay. Swifts Bay, behind Flower Island and Leo Reef, is shallow, but a usable anchorage in settled weather. Anchor on a sand bottom in 10 to 20 feet.

Shoal Bay. Shoal Bay indents the northern tip of Lopez Island between Humphrey Head and Upright Head, and offers good, fairly protected anchorage. We think the best spot

is behind the breakwater and off the private marina along the east shore. Numerous crab pot floats must be avoided in picking an anchorage.

 LOCAL KNOWLEDGE

SHOAL ENTRY: The entrance to Fisherman Bay should not be attempted by deep draft boats at less than half tide.

(3) **Fisherman Bay.** Fisherman Bay extends southward about 1.5 miles into the western shore of Lopez Island. The entrance is winding and shallow. About 200 yards off the entrance, a beacon marks the tip of a drying shoal. Leave this beacon to starboard, then follow the well-marked channel into the bay. Cutting any of the corners risks grounding.

The northernmost marina in Fisherman Bay belongs to Islands Marine Center. The docks next door belong to the Lopez Islander Resort. About one-half mile south of the Lopez Islander, the Galley Restaurant, (360) 468-2874, has two mooring buoys and a dock where moorage often can be arranged.

Anchorage in Fisherman Bay is shallow with a mud bottom. When entering or departing, resist the urge to cut inside any navigation marks. Departing, it's tempting to

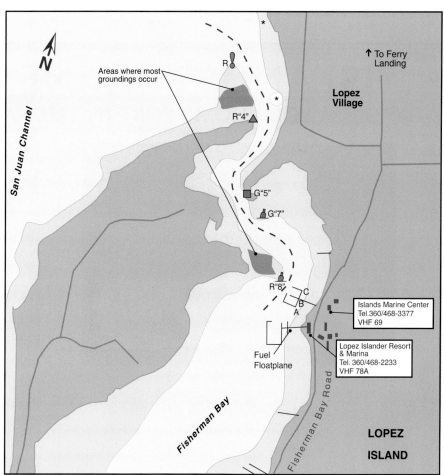

Fisherman Bay, Lopez Island

cut inside red nun Buoy 8, and there you are, aground. Remember: Red, Right, Returning, also means Red, *Left, Departing.*

Take a walk to Lopez Village, a little less than a mile away. You'll find excellent dining, a new, splendidly stocked grocery store, galleries, all the usual services, and the famous Holly B's Bakery.

The Lopez Historical Museum is open 12:00 p.m. to 4:00 p.m., Wednesday to Sunday, May through September, with exhibits inside and on the field outside. A farmers market takes up an entire field at the village, 10:00 a.m. to 2:00 p.m. on Saturdays, May through September. On the way to the village you'll pass the Lopez Island dump, where from 12:00 p.m. to 4:00 p.m. Wednesdays, Saturdays and Sundays, the Take it or Leave it Exchange takes place. They call the Exchange "Neil's Mall," after Neil Hanson, who runs the site. People bring the things they want to get rid of, and leave with treasures they discover.

Keep one hand free to wave to passing vehicles as you walk or cycle the roads. It's the custom on Lopez Island. Everybody waves.

Golf: The Lopez Island Golf Course, 9 flat holes next to the airport, is kept up entirely by volunteers. You'll need a ride to get there. (360) 468-2679.

③ **Islands Marine Center.** 2793 Fisherman Bay Rd., Lopez, WA 98261; (360) 468-3377; imc@rockisland.com; www.islandsmarinecenter.com. Monitors VHF 69. Open

Islands Marine Center in Fisherman Bay offers full-service repairs.

all year, Monday through Saturday. Guest moorage along 1000 feet of dock space, 30 amp power, Wi-Fi, restrooms, showers, and pumpout. Call ahead.

All shorepower receptacles are 30 amp, but some have only 20 amp breakers. Be sure you know how much juice is available before you start the heater, hair dryer, and microwave all at the same time.

This is a well-run, full-service marina, with haulout to 25 tons, launch ramp, repairs, and a fully stocked chandlery with fishing supplies. Two view rooms for rent. Good depth at all docks. Lopez Village shopping is nearby.

③ **Lopez Islander Resort & Marina.** P.O. Box 459, 2864 Fisherman Bay Rd., Lopez, WA 98261; (360) 468-2233; (800) 736-3434; desk@lopezfun.com; www.lopezfun.com. Monitors VHF 78A. Open all year. Gasoline & diesel at the fuel dock. Guest moorage in 64 slips plus 600 foot dock. Reservations recommended on busy weekends. Services include 30 & 50 amp power, Beacon/BBX Wi-Fi and free Wi-Fi in the lodge, new restrooms and showers, laundry, swimming pool (heated June through September), and a year-round Jacuzzi. The dock store has ice, beer, wine, and bait, along with basics like milk, eggs, cheese, and snacks. Nearby

Rental kayaks are available on the beach at the Lopez Islander Resort.

bicycle and kayak rentals.

The resort has a good restaurant with outdoor deck and a sports lounge, workout facility, spa, water-view lodging by reservation, and camping by reservation. Live music most weekends June through September. The docks are solid, and the management is attentive.

Odlin Park. 350 Court St. #8, Friday Harbor, WA 98250; (360) 378-8420; parks@ sanjuanco.com. West side of Lopez Island. Open all year. Located between Flat Point and Upright Head. Good bottom for anchoring, but exposed to northwest winds. Small float for dinghies, or they can be beached. Campsites, restrooms. Beach area and sea wall, baseball diamond, picnic sites and tables, cooking shelter, fire pits.

Upright Channel State Park. Northwest side of Lopez Island. Three mooring buoys, day use only. Restrooms, 4 picnic sites, no other facilities.

④ **Mackaye Harbor.** Mackaye Harbor and **Barlow Bay** at the south end of Lopez Island are a good overnight anchorage for boats planning an early morning crossing of the Strait of Juan de Fuca. Swells from a westerly wind can make their way into the harbor.

Dangerous wreck: A sunken boat is on the east side of the entry to Barlow Bay, approximately at the 2 fathoms, 5 feet sounding on Chart 18429. The wreck is visible at low tide. Mackaye Harbor is the site of a fishboat marina, and during the summer months a large fishboat fleet can be found in the harbor.

Iceberg Island. An undeveloped state park in outer Mackaye Harbor. Open all year, day use only. Anchor out. No facilities, no fires, no overnight camping. Pack out all garbage. Do not disturb wildlife or alter the surroundings.

Aleck Bay. Aleck Bay is not particularly scenic, but it is big and easy to get into. Anchor close to the head of the bay in 30 to 36 feet.

Hughes Bay. Hughes Bay is exposed, but Contributing Editor Tom Kincaid has anchored overnight as far into the bay as he could get and still have swinging room.

McArdle Bay. McArdle Bay provides good anchorage in 24 to 30 feet, but is completely exposed to southerly winds coming off the Strait of Juan de Fuca. Lovely homes are on the hills above the bay. Just outside, the chart shows a rock in the passage between Blind Island and Lopez Island. The rock is actually a reef.

Castle Island. An undeveloped state park off the southeast end of Lopez Island. Anchor out. No facilities, day use only. No fires or overnight camping. Pack out all garbage. Do not disturb wildlife or surroundings.

Watmough Bay. Watmough Bay has been one of Contributing Editor Tom Kincaid's favorites for 50 years, and it is one of our favorites, too. A beautiful high sheer rock wall is on the north side. The chart shows the bottom as rocky, but we have found excellent holding in blue mud in 12 to 18 feet about halfway in. Three public mooring buoys were installed in 2013 for boats 45 feet and under. They are free to use for up to 72 hours. Correspondents Bruce and Margaret Evertz report that wakes from passing traffic get into the bay.

A pretty trail leads back through the woods from the head of the bay. The head of the bay and the trail are part of a San Juan County Land Bank preserve, made possible by donations from private citizens.

LOCAL KNOWLEDGE

TIDE-RIP: Nasty tide-rips can form off the eastern entrance to Peavine and Obstruction Passes when the wind is blowing from the south and the tide is ebbing.

The Blakely Island Store & Marina lawn is a nice place to watch boats transit Peavine Pass.

Shaw General Store, next to the Shaw Island ferry landing serves ice cream sandwiches and more.

Obstruction Pass and Peavine Pass. Obstruction Pass runs between Obstruction Island and Orcas Island. Peavine Pass runs between Obstruction Island and Blakely Island. Both connect the inner San Juan Islands to Rosario Strait. Currents run to 6.5 knots, and can make these passes challenging. Peavine Pass is preferred, but be alert for occasional ferry traffic. They usually use Thatcher Pass. Peavine Pass is their storm route, but sometimes it is used in fair weather as well.

Blakely Island. Blakely Island is east of Lopez Island and Shaw Island. Both Blakely Island and tiny Armitage Island (off the southeast corner) are privately owned with no shore access. Anchorage is possible in Thatcher

Bay, and, with care, behind Armitage Island. The Blakely Island Store & Marina, at the north end of Blakely Island, has guest moorage. Blakely Island is private, including the roads. Confine your stays to the marina property.

⑤ **Blakely Island Store & Marina.** #1 Marina Dr., Blakely Island, WA 98222; (360) 375-6121; blakelymarina@comcast.net. Monitors VHF 66A. Moorage in 18 guest slips and in permanent slips as available. Phone reservations a must. Fuel dock has gasoline and diesel with a kiosk for credit card purchases. Facilities include excellent concrete docks, 30 amp power, wireless internet, water, restrooms, showers, laundry and covered picnic area.

The store is open from June until mid-September. It serves dinner on Friday and Saturday and breakfast and deli lunch daily. Beer on tap.

The channel leading to the boat basin is shallow, and may restrict deep draft vessels at the bottom of a very low tide. Other than those conditions, you should have plenty of water. If in doubt, call the marina office for guidance.

Shaw Island. The marina is adjacent to the Shaw Island ferry terminal. Resident boats occupy most of the dock space. Maximum length for short term guest moorage is 25 feet, call ahead. It's better to anchor in Blind Bay and take the dinghy over. Tie up in a place that doesn't block a permanent boat. Wakes make their way into the moorage, either from the ferries or boat traffic in the channel. Consider this when tying up to the dock.

Safety note: *Do not under any circumstances* run the dinghy under the bow of a ferry tied up at the landing.

LOCAL KNOWLEDGE

DANGEROUS ROCKS: Rocks obstruct the waters west of Blind Island. While it's possible to get through safely, our advice is do not pass west of Blind Island.

Blind Bay/Blind Island Marine State Park. Blind Bay, on the north side of Shaw Island, has good anchorage throughout the center portion. Blind Island is a minimally developed state park and Cascadia Marine Trail camp-

site, with 4 mooring buoys on its south side. Toilets are on the island. Pack out all garbage.

East of Blind Island a white daymark, installed and maintained by Bellingham Yacht Club since the 1950s, marks a rock that lies between Blind Island and the Shaw Island shore. Enter Blind Bay midway between that mark and Blind Island. The water shoals abruptly as you enter, but there's no danger unless you are close to the island.

⑥ **Shaw General Store.** P.O. Box 455, Shaw Island, WA 98286; (360) 468-2288; www.shawgeneralstore.com. Open 7 days a week in summer, Monday through Saturday in winter. Very limited short-term guest moorage, maximum 25 feet, call ahead. Groceries, beer and wine, ice, gift items, soup, sandwiches, ice cream cones in summer, local organic produce, and coffee roasted in-house. Restrooms adjacent to the ferry dock.

You'll enjoy anchoring in Blind Bay and taking the dinghy over to meet Steve and Terri Mason, who bought the store years ago. The back area of the store is a small cafe with lunch items. The store was built in 1924. It's as charming as can be, with its straight-grain wood floors, old shelving and displays, and posters and signs from days gone by. The store is a local hangout for Shaw Island residents.

Parks Bay. Parks Bay is a fine anchorage, but you can't go ashore. Except for three privately-owned parcels at the north end and a single parcel at the south end, the land surrounding Parks Bay is owned by the University of

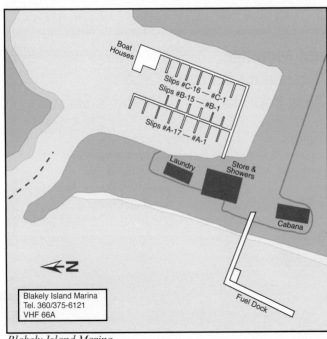

Boat Houses

Slips #C-16 — #C-1
Slips #B-15 — #B-1

Slips #A-17 — #A-1

Laundry

Store & Showers

Cabana

Fuel Dock

N

Blakely Island Marina
Tel. 360/375-6121
VHF 66A

Blakely Island Marina

Washington as a biological preserve, and is off limits to visitors. Stub pilings are at the closed end, but there is plenty of anchoring room, mud bottom, throughout the bay. Parks Bay Island, at the mouth of the bay, is no longer a state park.

Hicks Bay. Hicks Bay has good anchorage, although it is exposed to southerlies. When entering, take care to avoid a reef extending from the southern shore.

Indian Cove. Indian Cove, a popular anchorage area, is big and open feeling, somewhat protected from southerlies by nearby Lopez Island and Canoe Island. Watch for drying rocks between Canoe Island and Shaw Island, and a shoal 200 yards west of the southern point of Canoe Island. The Shaw Island County Park, with launch ramp, has an excellent beach.

Picnic Cove. Picnic Cove is immediately east of Indian Cove. It's a pretty little nook with room for a couple of boats. A mid-channel entrance is best, to avoid reefs on each side of the cove. The head

of the cove shoals to drying flats. Anchor in 20 to 25 feet. The mooring buoys in the cove are private.

SAN JUAN ISLAND

San Juan Island is the second largest of the San Juan Islands and the most heavily populated. Friday Harbor, the only incorporated town, is the seat of county government.

Cattle Pass. Cattle Pass is the local name for the narrow channel between the south end of San Juan Island and Lopez Island. It is the only southern entrance to the San Juan Islands, and connects with San Juan Channel. Whale Rocks lie just south of Cattle Pass. It's easy to get close to them if you're not careful. When we enter Cattle Pass from the south, we try to favor gong Buoy 3, marking Salmon Bank, to port, and make a course for the middle of the entrance. This avoids Whale Rocks.

After we clear Cattle Pass northbound we've felt a definite tendency to favor the Lopez Island shore. Maybe it's just us. In any case, this course leads dan-

gerously close to *Shark Reef*, about one-half mile north of Cattle Pass. We recommend sagging west a little toward Griffin Bay until past Shark Reef.

Tidal currents can run strongly through Cattle Pass. The waters can be turbulent with rips and eddies. Watch out for a big ebb current flowing out of San Juan Channel against a fresh westerly wind in the Strait of Juan de Fuca. We've seen this ebb current as much as a mile outside Cattle Pass. Against a fresh westerly it will create high, steep seas, the kind you definitely want to avoid. Current predictions are shown under San Juan Channel in the tide & current books.

In Cattle Pass, it's possible to run behind Goose Island and avoid foul current, but local knowledge is called for.

Fish Creek. Fish Creek is a tiny indentation near the southern tip of San Juan Island. It is lined with the docks and mooring buoys of the private homes along its shores. Fish Creek has no public facilities, and swinging room is very restricted between the homeowners' floats.

Griffin Bay. You can anchor in several places in Griffin Bay. A stretch of beach inshore from Halftide Rocks is Griffin Bay Park, a public campground. American Camp, maintained by the U.S. Park Service as an historical monument to the 1859-72 Pig War, is a short walk from the campground. The Pig War resulted in setting the boundary between the U.S. and Canada in Haro Strait, keeping the San Juan Islands in the U.S.

Griffin Bay Park. Next to American Camp. Open all year, 2 mooring buoys. Toilets, no other facilities. Four campsites and picnic area. Two inland campsites are exclusively for boaters arriving by human- or wind-powered watercraft. Vessels with motors are not allowed to moor at the park overnight. Watch for shallow water and pilings.

Unnamed Island #119. Griffin Bay, south of Dinner Island. Open all year, day use only, no facilities. Anchor out at this undeveloped state DNR property. No fires or overnight camping. Pack out all garbage. Do not disturb wildlife or alter the surroundings.

⑦ **Turn Island Marine State Park.** In San Juan Channel, at the southeast entrance to Friday Harbor. Turn Island is open all year for day use and overnight mooring. Outhouse and firepits. Boat access only. No camping. Pack out all garbage. Hiking, fishing, crabbing, birdwatching.

Turn Island is a beautiful park, completely wooded, with many trails. It's a popular stop for kayaks and beachable boats. Along the south side of the island the trees (madrona, cedar, hemlock, cypress) are bent and twisted, with much evidence of blowdown. The wind must howl though here in the winter.

Three mooring buoys are placed along the west side, at the mouth of the pass separating Turn Island from San Juan Island. Currents can be quite strong in this pass, but these buoys are located safely out of the current. If you anchor to seaward of them you will be in the current. We recommend the buoys.

Friday Harbor Seafood is on a float at the Port of Friday Harbor.

Spring Street in Friday Harbor has a wide variety of shops and restaurants.

Correspondents James and Jennifer Hamilton have anchored off the southwest tip of Turn Island in about 10 feet of depth at zero tide. Although the current ran noticeably the anchor held perfectly. Other boats, anchored farther out and closer to the eastern mouth of the pass, appeared to have less current.

Most of this park is a designated wildlife refuge. Do not disturb animals in their natural habitat.

⑧ **Friday Harbor.** www.fridayharbor.org. Friday Harbor is the government and com-mercial center of the San Juan Islands. It is a customs port of entry, and the terminus for ferries from Anacortes that also serve Sidney, B.C. The town swells with tourists during the summer months and has many boutiques, shops, galleries, restaurants and pubs to serve them. The post office is close to the marina. King's Market, a well stocked grocery store, is on the main street.

Kenmore Air flies in from Lake Union and Boeing Field in Seattle, with a shuttle to Sea-Tac Airport. Check their website for seasonal schedules.

You can moor at the Port of Friday Harbor marina or anchor out. Anchorage is good in the cove north of the marina, and behind Brown (Friday) Island. Do not anchor in the cable-pipeline area between San Juan Island and Brown Island. Our friend John Mifflin cautions that the water close to Brown Island contains several sunken wrecks, "requiring diver assistance when raising anchor."

Enter Friday Harbor around either end of Brown Island. An unlighted daybeacon marks the end of a drying reef off the southwest corner of Brown Island. Brown Island is privately owned, and has its own dock and floats.

Take care to avoid interfering with the ferries and the large number of float planes taking off and landing in the harbor. A fuel dock is located between the Port marina and the ferry dock. The floats just south of the ferry dock are owned by the condominium apartments ashore. Jensen's Marina, at the south end of the harbor, can handle repairs. Beacon/BBX Wi-Fi covers most of Friday Harbor, from Jensen's Marina to the Port of Friday Harbor Marina.

Dangerous wreck: A buoy marks the wreck of an old fish boat in the middle of the channel between Brown Island and Friday Harbor, approximately 100 yards or so south of the Washington State Ferry dock. Each year, the wreck feeds on unwary anchors.

Fire in 2013: A fire in August 2013 destroyed the waterfront building housing Downriggers Restaurant and Friday Harbor Marine, among other businesses. Check www.WaggonerGuide.com for updates.

Bus transportation: San Juan Transit, next to the ferry landing, has scheduled service all around San Juan Island; www.sanjuantransit.com; (360) 378-8887.

Taxi: Bob's Taxi, (360) 378-8388; Friday Harbor Taxi, (360) 298-4434; San Juan Taxi, (370) 378-8294.

Mopeds: Susie's Mopeds (800) 532-0087 (cars, mopeds, scootcars), Island Bicycles Transportation (360) 378-4941.

Golf: San Juan Golf & CC, 9 interesting holes with separate tee boxes for 18, par 71, is a short taxi ride away; (360) 378-2254.

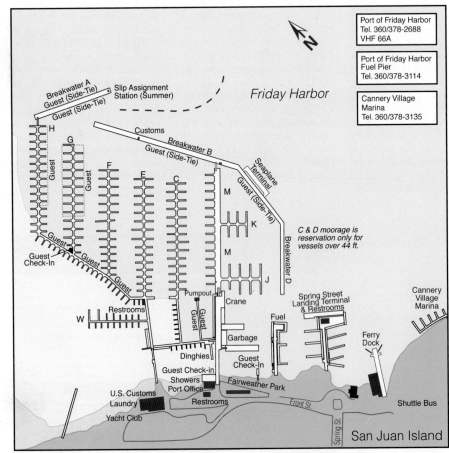

Friday Harbor

lean Marina
dership Award
ner...

Photo/Matt Pranger

Summer concerts: Live music Sundays at 2:00 p.m. and Fridays 5:00 p.m. to 7:00 p.m. July and August in the small park next to the marina.

Farmers market: San Juan Farmers Market Saturdays 10:00 a.m. to 1:00 p.m. mid-April through mid-October in the Brickhouse Plaza, 150 Nichols St., about 5 minutes from the marina.

Things to Do

1. **The Whale Museum.** In Friday Harbor learn about orca whales that frequent the San Juan Islands.

2. **Lime Kiln Point State Park.** Watch for orca and minke whales that often cruise by this park.

3. **Tastings.** San Juan Vineyards and Lopez Island Vineyards have tasting rooms in Friday Harbor. San Juan Island Distillery, with a variety of apple based spirits, has a tasting room within walking distance of Roche Harbor.

4. **Westcott Bay Sculpture Park.** More than 100 superb sculptures in iron, bronze, stone and wood displayed in a 20-acre park.

5. **Pelindaba Lavender Farms.** Walk through fields of purple lavender.

6. **San Juan Golf Course.** Beautiful 9 hole, par 71 course, with tee boxes for 18 holes.

7. **Saturday farmers market.** Fresh vegetables, flowers, plants, honey and more in Friday Harbor.

8. **English Camp.** See the gardens, hike the trails, learn the history.

9. **Roche Harbor Mausoleum.** Walk from Roche Harbor resort to this beautiful setting steeped in mythology.

10. **Blackberries.** In late summer they are everywhere, huge, tasty, and free.

11. **Krystal Acres Alpaca Farm.** See alpacas and what they can be used for.

12. **Suzie's Mopeds.** Rent mopeds or a bicycle. Rental offices in Friday Harbor and Roche Harbor.

13. The "**Retirement of the Colors**" ceremony at Roche Harbor at sunset is unforgettable.

14. **Friday Harbor Seafood.** Fresh shrimp, oysters, crab, or fish for sale on the dock.

15. **Shuttle Bus Tour.** Regular schedule in the summer. Ride the bus, getting on and off at locations such as the lavender farm, Lime Kiln Point, and English Camp.

---

⑧ **Port of Friday Harbor.** P.O. Box 889, 204 Front Street, Friday Harbor, WA 98250; (360) 378-2688; tamih@portfridayharbor.org; jeremyt@portfridayharbor.org; www.portfridayharbor.org. Monitors 66A. Certified Clean Marina. Open all year, gasoline and diesel at the fuel dock. Ample side-tie guest moorage along 1500 feet of dock, plus slips in guest docks and unoccupied slips. Reservations accepted. The slips handle a maximum length of 44 feet. Longer boats (to 200 feet) side-tie along the breakwater docks A, B, C, and D. Breakwater dock A has no power or water. Marina services include 120-volt 30 & 50 amp power, 240-volt 50 amp power, and some 240-volt 100 amp power, free Wi-Fi, newly renovated restrooms and showers, excellent laundry, garbage and recycling drop, pumpout. An ADA-compliant ramp connects the wharf with the floats. U.S. Customs clearance is available on the marked outside dock. A floating restroom is on the long float leading to guest moorage dock G. A covered activity barge is available for groups or rendezvous. Ten or more vessels earn a group moorage discount. Check their website for seasonal specials.

If you do not have reservations, call on VHF 66A for a moorage assignment, but wait until you are within sight of the marina before calling. In the summer, a slip assignment station is staffed at the end of the marina entrance. A dinghy float and day moorage are available. Nearby haulout and repairs.

This is one of the busiest marinas in the Northwest, and the pressure on staff and facilities is enormous. To their credit, they keep the docks, showers and restrooms up quite well. Because they are so busy, when you depart it is courteous to call the marina on VHF 66A to let them know your slip is available.

⑧ **Port of Friday Harbor Fuel Pier.** 10 Front Street, Port of Friday Harbor, Friday Harbor, WA 98250; (360) 378-3114; www.portfridayharbor.org. Open 7 days a week, all year. Fuel dock with gasoline and diesel. Carries oil, lubricants, propane, ice, and bait.

⑧ **Cannery Village Marina.** P.O. Box 1044, Friday Harbor, WA 98250; (360) 378-3135. Open all year, 30 amp power, no restrooms or showers. Best to call ahead. These are the docks east of the ferry landing.

Rocky Bay. Rocky Bay, close inshore from O'Neal Island, is a good anchorage and fairly well protected. Take care to avoid a drying shoal and a covered rock.

⑨ **Roche Harbor.** Roche Harbor is popular, attractive, and has a number of interesting anchorages and moorages. From the north (Spieden Channel), enter Roche Harbor

on the *west* side of Pearl Island. The passage east of Pearl Island is shallow, and is in line with dangerous rocks outside. From the south (Haro Strait), entry is through Mosquito Pass.

Roche Harbor is a busy U.S. Customs port of entry. During the summer months the customs office and the harbormaster's office are located in the center of the outer dock. The customs dock landing area is noted with signs on the pilings. Moor between the signs only when clearing customs. During busy summer periods, boats form an informal line on the water. Be patient. It can be a challenge to maintain a place in line among other boats at anchor, especially when a good breeze kicks up. One summer we watched as one of the area's large wooden sailing schooners pulled up to the dock to clear customs. The space was much too small to lie alongside. The captain commanded her crew of high school students to drop the anchor at the right time, as she turned stern-to the dock. With an audience watching, she backed down and tied off, stern-to. She placed a 133-foot vessel into less than 20 feet of dock space.

Note: During the winter, early spring or late fall months the customs and harbor offices are floated inshore to the dock area below the ramp to main dock. The customs landing area is designated across from the customs office. In winter, approach as though you are going to the fuel dock. The customs dock is to starboard, marked with signs, just below the ramp. Note: Once tied to the dock, all crew must stay on the boat until cleared. The U.S. Customs agents are particular about procedure here.

Many boats anchor in Roche Harbor, but we've heard of anchors dragging in strong winds. Check your set and use ample scope. Anchorage is also possible in Open Bay on Henry Island, although it is exposed to southerly winds. Dinghy docks are at the bottom of the ramp to the main wharf, or to port, just past the fuel dock.

Bus transportation: San Juan Transit has scheduled service all around San Juan Island. The pickup area is on the road across from the Roche Harbor store. Call (360) 378-8887; www.sanjuantransit.com. Moped rentals are available up near the airstrip.

ROCHE HARBOR
San Juan Island, Washington
Established 1886

Dining ✹ Lodging ✹ Marina
Air Strip ✹ Grocery & Shopping
Pool & Tennis ✹ Formal Gardens
Weddings ✹ Spa
Hiking ✹ Kayaking & Whale Watching

(800) 586-3590 Marina
(800) 451-8910 Lodging
www.rocheharbor.com

Roche Harbor is one of the most popular destinations in the San Juan Islands.

⑨ **Roche Harbor Marina.** P.O. Box 4001, Roche Harbor, WA 98250; (800) 586-3590; (360) 378-2155; marina@rocheharbor.com; www.rocheharbor.com. Monitors VHF 78A. Open all year, up to 250 guest slips, including moorage for boats to 150 feet. Call ahead for reservations. They work to fit everyone in, even on busy holidays. Last-minute holiday moorage may mean Med-tying stern-to on the cross docks. The dock crew provides plenty of help. Gasoline and diesel at the fuel dock. Services include 15, 20, 30 & 50 amp power, restrooms, showers, laundry, portapotty dump, propane, Beacon/BBX and free Wi-Fi. Pumpout is at the north end of the fuel dock, or call for the "Phecal Freak," for a courtesy pumpout at your slip (their motto: "We take crap from anyone..."). The moorage fee includes water, power, pumpout, trash disposal, and use of the pool and resort facilities. Excellent management. When we visited at the end of a busy day at the end of summer, we found all the facilities, including the showers, to be clean and in good condition.

This is one of the most popular spots in the islands, and in our opinion is a must-see destination. The historic Hotel de Haro, the heated swimming pool, formal gardens, tennis courts, Afterglow Spa, well-stocked grocery store, gift shops, and excellent restaurant and lounge are something apart from the usual tourist fare. An informal café also is available. Try the Roche Harbor donuts at the café, made fresh each morning.

Be sure to take a walk up to the Afterglow Vista Mausoleum. You've never seen anything like it. Another good walk is up the small mountain, past the limestone quarries, to a lookout. The trail is easy and well-maintained, and the view is excellent. The entire loop took us approximately a half-hour. If we had stopped to smell the flowers, it would have taken an hour. The hotel lobby

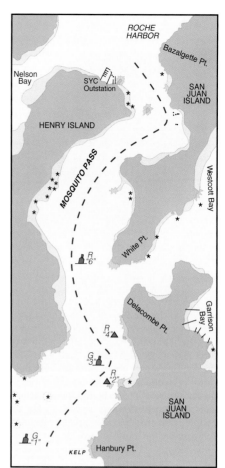

The restaurant and pub at Roche Harbor are popular for lunch or dinner, inside or out.

has complimentary walking tour maps. For $1.00 they also have a pamphlet detailing the remarkable history of Roche Harbor. See the guest registry on display and the pictures on the wall showing the history or Roche Harbor.

The Westcott Bay Sculpture Park is on the edge of Roche Harbor property, across the road from the airstrip. The park is a display of outdoor sculpture—approximately 100 pieces —set in a large grassy field and along several trails through the woods. This description completely understates how impressive the display is. We spent an hour in the park and should have spent three more hours. It's magnificent. The pieces are first-rate and the setting works.

Major development continues on the hillside up from the hotel. Great effort has been made to design the new construction in keeping with the classic century-old style of the existing buildings.

A lovely bell concert rings out from the church at 9:00 a.m., noon, and late afternoon. At sundown each evening during the summer season the marina conducts a formal retirement of the colors. The Roche Harbor flag is lowered, followed by the British flag to "God Save the Queen," and the Canadian flag to "O Canada." Then the cannon fires—BOOM!—and the U.S. flag is lowered to "Taps." Against a fiery sunset backdrop the ceremony is inspiring. It puts a lump in our throats.

Posey Island Marine State Park. www. parks.wa.gov. North of Roche Harbor. Day use and overnight mooring and camping. Pit toilet, no other facilities. Cascadia Marine Trail campsite (primitive). The island is less than 1 acre in size. Water surrounding the island is shallow. Motorized vessels are not permitted; anchor out and row in. Great sunset views on the west side.

Mosquito Pass. Mosquito Pass connects Roche Harbor to Haro Strait and provides access to Westcott Bay and Garrison Bay. The flood current sets north in Mosquito Pass and the ebb sets south, out of Roche Harbor. Currents can be strong at times. The channel is narrow but well-marked. Navigate carefully.

The route is shown on the chartlet at right.

Westcott Bay. Westcott Bay has good anchorage, but is partly taken up with a major shellfish culture business. Although the bay is shallow, adequate anchoring depths can be found throughout. The beach has excellent clamming.

Garrison Bay. Garrison Bay, the site of English Camp, is a popular and excellent anchorage, with room for a large number of boats.

English Camp National Historical Park. PO Box 429, 4668 Cattle Point Road, Friday Harbor, WA 98250; (360) 387-2240

Route through Mosquito Pass

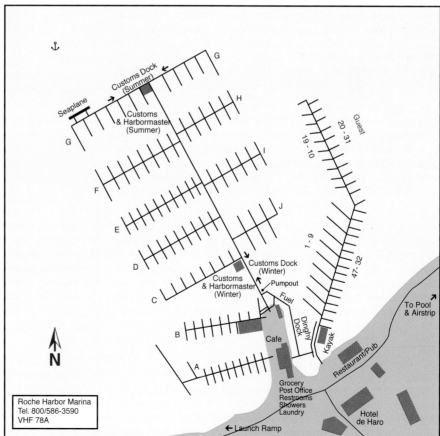

Roche Harbor Marina
Tel. 800/586-3590
VHF 78A

Roche Harbor Marina

Ample anchorage in Garrison Bay, site of English Camp.

ext. 2244; www.nps.gov. Open all year. Anchor in the bay and dinghy to the park dock. British troops were garrisoned here during the 1859-72 Pig War, and the U.S. Park Service has restored the buildings and grounds as an historical site. You can tour the grounds, several of the buildings, and the cemetery, where several people from that era are buried. Rangers are on duty to provide information, and an interesting film tells the history. It's a good stop for families with children. Restrooms, no other facilities. A steep trail leads to the top of 650-foot-high Young Hill, for a marvelous view.

Mitchell Bay. A shoal extends from the south shore of the entry almost to the middle. A rock is at the outer end. Leave this rock to starboard when entering. Large scale Chart 18433 shows the entrance clearly.

⑩ **Snug Harbor Resort.** 1997 Mitchell Bay Road, Friday Harbor, WA 98250; (360) 378-4762; sneakaway@snugresort.com; www.snugresort.com. Snug Harbor is open all year and welcomes visitors. Maximum boat length 60 feet. Depth at zero tide is 9 feet. No fuel at the dock but gasoline is available at the store. Services include 30 amp power, Wi-Fi, restrooms, showers, garbage drop, recycling, barbecues, fire pits. The on-site convenience store has ice and limited groceries, gifts, propane, fishing and boating supplies. Canoes and kayaks available for guest use free of charge. Reservations recommended.

The resort has been undergoing renovations. They've built 16 new cabins, with barbecues and fire pits.

Lime Kiln Point. Lime Kiln Point is a favorite place to watch for orcas, the so-called "killer whales," that often cruise within a few yards of shore. Anchorage offshore from this park would be very difficult and is not recommended. A small interpretive center with information about orca whales is in the park. Best visited by taking the San Juan Transit bus from Roche Harbor or Friday Harbor.

San Juan County Park. 380 West Side Road N., Friday Harbor, WA 98250; (360) 378-2992; www.sanjuanco.com. Open all year. Facilities include launch ramp and restrooms. No power, no showers. A popular park for kayak campers who can pull up on the beach.

Henry Island. A Seattle Yacht Club outstation (no reciprocals) is in Nelson Bay. Nelson Bay is shallow, so use your depth sounder and tide table before anchoring.

Unnamed Island #40. On the southwest side of San Juan Island, approximately 1 mile northwest of Pile Point. Open all year, day use only, no facilities. Anchor out at this undeveloped DNR property. No fires or overnight camping. Pack out all garbage. Do not disturb wildlife or alter the surroundings.

Unnamed Island #38. Southwest side of San Juan Island, near the center of Kanaka Bay. Open all year, day use only, no facilities. Anchor out at this undeveloped

BE WHALE WISE

Puget Sound and the San Juan Islands are filled with great anchorages, fascinating islands, and beautiful scenery. One of the best parts of cruising here, though, is the opportunity to see whales, most notably orcas.

"Whales" in regards to orcas is actually a misnomer: so called "killer whales" are, in fact, the largest members of the dolphin family. "Real" whales also frequent this area, including humpback, minke, and occasionally gray whales.

This story is all about respectful orca viewing.

As a cruiser, I've watched whales from our own boat. As a professional captain, I've run whale watch boats for San Juan Safaris in Friday Harbor and San Juan Outfitters in Roche Harbor. This background gives me insight into the issues cruisers run into when watching whales. As you might imagine, boaters have a lot of questions about viewing these magnificent animals.

Where are the whales? If I could answer that question with absolute certainty, I'd be buying lottery tickets. The Southern Resident Killer Whales, common to this area, are always on the move. No, they aren't always on the west side of San Juan Island. They can (and do) travel 70 to 100 miles per day searching for food. Their primary diet is salmon. Transient orcas are mammal-eaters.

When looking for whales, I follow the food. The "residents" (J, K & L Pods) are not always "in residence" in the San Juan Islands. If their food source is elsewhere, so are they.

No, whales are not "tracked." No radio transmitters, no spotting planes. As a professional whale watch operation, our company belongs to the Pacific Whale Watch Association. Members work together to find the whales. We report sightings and locations among our members. The captains are cooperative and work together to ensure guests on all member whale watch boats have the opportunity to view whales.

It's tacky to ask a professional whale watch captain, "Where are the whales?" If you want to utilize their knowledge, buy a ticket on a whale watch boat. The naturalists on our boats can explain the behavior you are viewing and answer questions, making the trip educational as well as entertaining. The captains position the boats for best viewing.

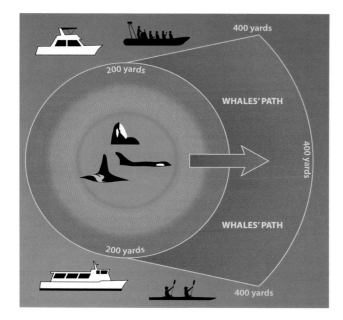

How close can we get to the whales? This is the most asked question when guests first board our boats. And, from what I see on a daily basis, many boaters are unfamiliar with laws governing operating near whales. Orcas are endangered and protected. Distance regulations are not suggestions. Violate them and you may be boarded by law enforcement, usually NOAA, Washington Department of Fish and Wildlife (WDFW), or the San Juan County Sheriff's Department.

A nearly million-dollar grant enabled more enforcement in 2013, and increased enforcement will likely continue in the future. The three resident pods collectively have fewer than 85 whales. Enforcement is a serious matter. The boating and whale watch businesses in the Pacific Northwest, and many local economies, depend on whale watching. We *all* want these animals around for future generations to see.

With that in mind, this graphic illustrates how close boats can get to whales. Laterally, vessels can approach no closer than 200 yards. Often, the whales are moving, and professional whale watch boats move along with them, always mindful of that 200-yard distance. That's two football fields. Binoculars are your friend.

Most professional captains use rangefinders to insure they maintain 200 yards of separation. If you aren't a good judge of distance, follow the lead of the professional operators, and stay at least as far away as they do.

No, you aren't allowed to "get ahead of the whales and shut down," with the idea that they will come to you. The law requires vessels give 400 yards of clearance in front of the whales, and vessels may not impede their progress.

Some of my fishing friends have questioned whether they have to move when they have lines in the water and they see whales moving towards them. I quote the, "200 yards laterally, 400 yards in front of" law. In the eyes of the law, a recreational boat with lines in the water is *not* a fishing vessel. Interpret that any way you want, but understand that if you are closer than the law allows, you may be cited and fined. I don't take the chance; my captain's license could be jeopardized, fines can be steep, and it's important to respect wildlife.

Despite the regulations, we see boaters run too close to whales almost every day during summer. Bad behavior is reported. If violators are lucky, they may just get an educational visit from the Sound Watch boat (or the Canadian equivalent, Strait Watch). If they're not lucky, they may get an expensive visit from NOAA or

WDFW. Learn the rules, follow the rules. The laws apply to all, whether you are a professional captain, a private boater (sail or power), or a kayaker.

Speed limits are also enforced. When within half a mile of whales, keep your speed to 7 knots or less. Have you seen someone speed right up to the whales? Yep, that's illegal. Don't be that guy.

In Canadian waters vessels must maintain 100 yards of separation.

What if the whales come up too close to me? Whales don't get the same memo we do. Sometimes they'll be running a straight course, then dive and change course.

The following is a *recommendation*, not the law. If whales surface unexpectedly within 100 to 200 yards, try to slowly move away perpendicularly to the whales' direction of travel. If they're within 100 yards, shut down until the whales are a safe distance away, then slowly move away. Even if the incident was not intentional, you can be cited.

Other respectful viewing tips:

· Turn off sonar (depth/fish finder) when close to the whales.

· Take turns. Limit your viewing time to 30 minutes or less.

· Do not cut in front of other boats that are viewing.

· Enter/exit the viewing area slowly.

· Do not approach whales from in front of or behind.

· Avoid getting caught between whales and shoreline

Seeing these mammals is breathtaking. You may see them milling or feeding, resting or on a hunt. You might see a calf learning new skills. If the timing is right, you may see a breach. Or two—they often breach a second time, so keep the camera ready.

Enjoy the whale viewing, but be whale wise.

– Captain Jim Bathurst

Be Whale Wise. Related info may be found at:
http://wdfw.wa.gov/conservation/orca/
http://www.bewhalewise.org/new-regulations/

Orca whales are often seen near the Lime Kiln Point lighthouse.

The deer on Jones Island are very tame. Please don't pet them.

DNR property. No fires or overnight camping. Pack out garbage. Do not disturb wildlife or alter the surroundings.

LOCAL KNOWLEDGE

DANGEROUS REEFS: Vessel Assist reports the Wasp Islands are the number-one area for groundings in the San Juan Islands. Navigate carefully.

Wasp Islands. The Wasp Islands on the east side of San Juan Channel are a rock- and reef-strewn area requiring careful navigation. The underwater hazards are charted but not all of them are marked, and the unwary can come to grief. Wasp Passage, however, is free of hazards, and the skipper who stays in the channel will have no problems.

All the major Wasp Islands are privately owned except Yellow Island, which is owned by The Nature Conservancy.

Northwest McConnell Rock. Northwest of McConnell Island. Open all year, day use only, no facilities. Anchorage only at this undeveloped state park property. No fires or overnight camping. Pack out all garbage. Do not disturb wildlife or alter the surroundings. At low tide McConnell Rock is connected to McConnell Island by a sandspit.

Unnamed Island #112. East of McConnell Island. Open all year, day use only, no facilities. Undeveloped DNR property; anchoring only. No fires or overnight camping. Pack out garbage. Do not disturb wildlife or alter the surroundings. A neighbor has complained that boaters often confuse his property with this island. Use care to avoid private property.

⑪ **Jones Island Marine State Park.** Open all year, day use and overnight mooring and camping. The bay at the north end of Jones Island is an excellent anchorage. Boats anchoring near the beach run stern-ties ashore, leaving swinging room for boats anchored in the middle. Currents can swirl through the bay, so leave ample room when you anchor.

Seven mooring buoys are in the bay. A seasonal 160-foot-long mooring float connects to a wharf that leads to shore. Composting toilet facilities are ashore. A well provides drinking water, but may run dry in late summer. Use the water sparingly.

A few mooring buoys are in the small bay on the south side of the island. In the middle of this bay, watch for a rock that lies awash at zero tide. The rock is shown on the charts, but the symbol is easy to overlook. Choose your anchorage based on which one provides the best protection from the wind. We've had a pleasant night in the south anchorage when the wind was blowing from the north, while cruisers anchored in the north bay reported a difficult night.

The south bay is the Cascadia Marine Trail site, with 24 primitive but excellent campsites, and toilet facilities. It's a popular kayak destination. Excellent view.

Jones Island suffered a blowdown of mature trees during a severe storm in 1990. For environmental reasons, most of the downed trees were left to rot on the ground, although campsites and trails were cleared and the logs bucked up for firewood. Ample evidence of the blowdown can be seen on the northeast side of the island.

This is a terrific park, popular for families with children. An easy trail connects the north and south moorages, with a 1.2-mile south loop trail branching off through forest and along rock headlands over the water. If you look carefully along this trail, you'll see low patches of prickly pear cactus growing along the way. At the north moorage especially, you probably will meet tame deer. If you dine at a picnic table they may try to join you. During the summer, mooring buoys and float space can be hard to get.

Caution: Raccoons will go aboard unattended boats at the dock if food is left in the open. Stow food well, and close the boat tightly.

Orcas Island. Orcas Island is the largest island in the San Juans, deeply indented by Deer Harbor, West Sound and East Sound. Various locations around the island offer services ranging from float plane flights to groceries to unique spa experiences. The island hosts a variety of festivals and has a seasonal Saturday farmers market.

Getting around: Orcas Rental Car (360-376-RIDE) has a variety of interesting cars available for rent. We spotted a 2 seater Miata with the company logo in a parking lot. For a taxi service, call (360) 376-TAXI. San Juan Transit has shuttle bus service around the island.

Golf: The 9-hole Orcas Island Golf Club is hilly but easily walked. During dry summer months even well-played shots can roll into oblivion. Fun course. (360) 376-4400.

Busy convenience store, with ice cream, at Deer Harbor Marina.

The pool at Deer Harbor is available for marina guests.

⑫ **Deer Harbor.** Anchorage can be found behind little Fawn Island, close to the western shore, but most of the harbor provides good anchoring.

⑫ **Deer Harbor Marina.** P.O. Box 344, 5164 Deer Harbor Road, Deer Harbor, WA 98243; (360) 376-3037; mbroman@deerharbormarina.com; www.deerharbormarina.com. Monitors VHF 78A. Certified Clean Marina. Open all year. Facilities include gasoline and diesel at the fuel dock, ample guest moorage to 120 feet, 30 & limited 50 amp power, free and Beacon/BBX Wi-Fi, restrooms and showers, pumpout, laundry, new barbecue floating dock for parties and rendezvous, and 2 buoys off D dock labeled "DHM."

The docks are excellent, and the restrooms and showers are clean and spacious. A small store at the outer end of the wharf provides groceries, espresso, and Lopez Island Ice Cream cones. A gift store is on the dock. Whale watching, kayaking, power and sail charters available. Electric bikes for rent. A 12-passenger van is available for day use, inquire at office.

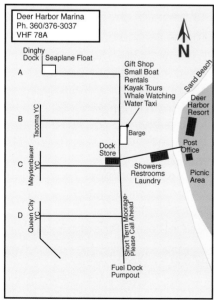

Deer Harbor Marina

Pole Pass seems much narrower than this photo suggests. To keep damaging wakes down, follow the 7-knot speed limit.

A beautiful sand beach next to the wharf will entertain the little ones. At the north end of the beach, a small but lovely park has been built. The Resort at Deer Harbor, across the road, is going through an extensive renovation. The marina has access to the swimming pool there. The Deer Harbor Inn Restaurant, a short one-half mile walk north, is excellent. If you don't want to walk, you can ride the restaurant's courtesy "limousine." The entire resort has an easy, relaxed "vacation" feeling. Even the quaint post office fits right in. During the busy months it's best to call ahead for mooring reservations.

LOCAL KNOWLEDGE

SPEED LIMIT: A 7-knot speed zone extends from just west of Pole Pass eastward almost to Bell Island and is marked by white cylindrical buoys.

Pole Pass. Boats transiting between Harney Channel and Deer Harbor usually go through Pole Pass, a narrow notch separating Crane Island from Orcas Island. Rocks obstruct the edges and approaches and currents can run swiftly through the pass. A

mid-channel course is safe. For most skippers, good sense dictates slow speeds. Unfortunately, not all skippers have seen it that way, and wakes have caused considerable damage to docks along the shoreline. So now speeds are limited to 7 knots maximum by county law. Sometimes the sheriff is there, ticketing speeders.

⑬ **West Sound.** West Sound is the middle inlet of Orcas Island, where the Wareham family's West Sound Marina offers limited overnight moorage and complete service facilities. Next to the marina is the Orcas Island Yacht Club, with reciprocal moorage for visiting members. A day use only public dock is west of the Orcas Island Yacht Club dock.

Good anchorage is available at the head of the bay (stay well clear of Harbor Rock, marked by a daybeacon). Anchorage is also good off the village of West Sound, and behind Double Island.

⑬ **West Sound Marina.** P.O. Box 119, 525 Deer Harbor Road, Orcas Island, WA 98280; (360) 376-2314; info@westsound-marina.com; westsoundmarina.net. Monitors VHF 16, switch to 09. Open all year, except closed Sundays in the winter. Facilities include gasoline and diesel at the fuel dock, propane, 400 feet of guest moorage, 30 amp power, restrooms, shower, pumpout. Haulout to 30 tons with full service and repairs, in-

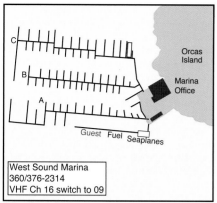

West Sound Marina
360/376-2314
VHF Ch 16 switch to 09

West Sound Marina

Plenty of shops to explore in the village of Eastsound.

cluding an enclosed area for major work. The chandlery has most boating supplies. When approaching, stay well off Picnic Island. A rock ledge extends into West Sound from the island. Once at the marina, stay close to the docks. The water shoals toward Picnic Island.

Victim Island. West side of West Sound. Open all year, day use only, no facilities. Anchor out at this undeveloped state park. No fires or overnight camping. Pack out all garbage. Do not disturb wildlife or alter the surroundings.

Unnamed Island #80. West of Indian Point in West Sound. Open all year, day use only, no facilities. Anchor out at this undeveloped DNR property. No fires or overnight camping. Pack out all garbage. Do not disturb wildlife or alter the surroundings.

Skull Island. North end of Massacre Bay. Open all year, day use only, no facilities. Anchor out at this undeveloped state park. No fires or overnight camping. Pack out all garbage. Do not disturb wildlife or alter the surroundings.

Unnamed Island #81. Near the West Sound Marina. Open all year, day use only, no facilities. Anchor out at this undeveloped DNR property. No fires or overnight camping. Pack out all garbage. Do not disturb wildlife or alter the surroundings.

⑭ **Orcas Landing.** Orcas Landing has a float next to the ferry dock, but stays are limited to 30 minutes. The grocery store at the head of the ferry dock is well stocked, and has a good selection of wine and cheese. Other shops in the village, aimed at serving the summer ferry lineup, are good. Great sandwiches and ice cream cones, too. Be well-fendered and securely tied to the dock at Orcas Landing. Passing boat and ferry traffic in Harney Channel throw a lot of wake towards the dock.

Grindstone Harbor. Grindstone Harbor is a small, shallow anchorage, with two major rocks in its entrance. One of these rocks became famous a number of years ago when the

Washington State ferry *Elwha* ran aground on it while doing a bit of unauthorized sightseeing. Favor the east shore all the way in. Private mooring buoys take up much of the inner part of the bay, but there's room to anchor if you need to.

Guthrie Bay. Guthrie Bay indents Orcas Island between Grindstone Harbor and East Sound. It's a pleasant little spot with private mooring buoys around the perimeter and homes on the hillsides. Anchor in 24 to 42 feet.

East Sound. East Sound, the largest of Orcas Island's indentations, extends about 6 miles north from Foster Point. The shores on both sides are steep, and offer few anchorage possibilities. Rosario Resort is on the east side, a short distance up the sound past the village of Olga. The village of Eastsound is at the head. Fresh winds sometimes blow in East Sound, while outside the air is calm.

Eastsound. The village of Eastsound, at the head of East Sound, is the largest settlement on Orcas Island. A small public mooring float is on the eastern shore. A 10-minute walk leads to town. Eastsound has several very good restaurants, a large grocery store, an excellent museum, many interesting shops, and on Saturdays during the summer, a busy farmers market.

Anchoring note. A sign on the county mooring dock announces that the bottom inshore, from a line between the dock and the small islet off the town, is sensitive eelgrass habitat. It asks that you anchor to seaward of that line.

⑮ **Rosario Resort & Spa.** 1400 Rosario Rd., Eastsound, WA 98245; (360) 376-2222; (800) 562-8820; harbormaster@ rosarioresort.com; www.rosarioresort.com. Monitors VHF 78A. Certified Clean Marina. Open all year, gasoline and diesel at the fuel dock (fuel dock by appointment October through April), 36 slips with unlimited water for filling tanks and boat washing, 30 & 50 amp power, 8 mooring buoys, garbage drop, restrooms, showers, car rentals from Orcas Island Shuttle, café, convenience store, Wi-Fi, seaplane service to Seattle via Kenmore Air.

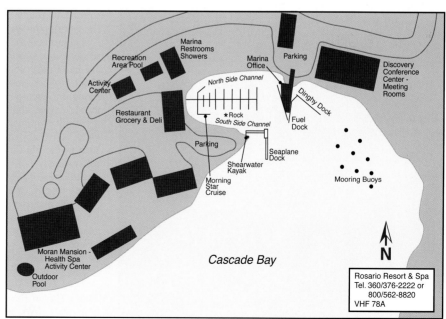

Rosario Resort

The Moran mansion is a distinctive landmark when approaching Rosario Resort.

Moorage includes use of the spa facilities, marina pool, restrooms, showers, power, and potable water on the dock. Boats on buoys or anchored out pay a landing fee for use of the marina pool, showers, and restrooms (spa facilities extra). The Cascade Grill and Store at the head of the dock is open from Memorial Day through mid-September and has snacks, sodas, beer and wine, and limited groceries. The Grill serves great burgers and hot sandwiches.

The center of the resort is the magnificent Moran Mansion, listed on the National Register of Historic Places. The mansion houses a restaurant, lounge and spa. The mansion itself also is a fascinating museum, a chronicle of Robert Moran's history as a shipbuilder, then as the builder of Rosario. Longtime resident artist and now resort manager Christopher Peacock presents a slide presentation on the history of the resort, with musical ac-

companiment performed on the giant Wurlitzer pipe organ. The concert begins at 4:00 p.m. Mondays through Saturdays mid-June through mid-September, and Saturdays through the winter. It's wonderful. Don't miss it. Golf and tennis are nearby. Moran State Park is about a 30-minute walk. Reservations for moorage are strongly recommended. Buoys are first-come, first-served, with room to anchor, though the sound is exposed to southerlies.

Although Rosario is world-renowned, it is also about a century old, with all the repair and maintenance challenges that go with an aging property. Renovations are underway and the resort is starting expansion and construction.

Figurehead: The beautiful carved figurehead on display on the walk above the marina is from the wreck of the *America*, a wooden clipper ship converted to barge use. The ship went aground near False Bay on San Juan Island in 1914 while under tow from Seattle to Vancouver. During periods of small tides and slack water the wreck's bones are still a dive site at False Bay (from *Northwest Dive News*).

⑯ **Olga.** Olga, a tiny pastoral village, is on the east shore of East Sound, near the entrance. Olga has a dock and 105-foot-long mooring float, but no power, restrooms, or showers. The float is removed in winter. A box for overnight moorage payment is at the bottom of the ramp. Good anchoring offshore, but exposed to southeasterly winds. The mooring buoys are private.

A sign above the dock lists local stores and locations. Olga Village has a post office. The Orcas Island Artworks and Café burned during the summer of 2013. It is not clear when the building will be rebuilt. Meanwhile, the Artworks and Café have been relocated to the old library building in Eastsound.

Twin Rocks. West of Olga. Open all year, day use only, no facilities. Anchor out at this undeveloped state park property. No fires or overnight camping. Pack out all garbage. Do not disturb wildlife or alter the surroundings.

Lieber Haven Resort. P.O. Box 127, Olga, WA 98279; (360) 376-2472; www.lieberhavenresort.com. In the middle of Obstruction Pass. Not your usual place. Overnight moorage is for cottage guests only. Store carries some groceries, beer and wine, and some marine supplies.

Obstruction Pass State Park. www.parks.wa.gov. Southeast tip of Orcas Island. Open all year, moorage at 3 buoys. Toilets, no power or showers. Good anchoring on a gravel bottom. Campsites with fireplaces, picnic tables, hiking trails.

⑰ **Doe Island Marine State Park.** On the southeast side of Orcas Island. Normally, open all year for day use and camping. This is a beautiful tiny island with a rocky shoreline dotted with tidepools. A trail leads around the island, through dense forest and lush undergrowth. Toilets, but no power, water, or showers. Pack out all garbage. Adjacent buoys are privately owned. Currents run strongly between Doe Island and Orcas Island. The 30-foot mooring float was damaged in a storm in 2010. Until repaired the pier is closed. The park is still open to small boats and kayaks.

Doe Bay Resort and Retreat. 107 Doe Bay Road, Olga, WA 98279; (360) 376-2291; office@doebay.com; www.doebay.com. Doe Bay is an interesting off-the-beaten-path destination with two guest buoys and anchorage space for 3 to 6 boats. Dinghy ashore to the rocky beach to visit the café or use the creek-side soaking tubs and cedar sauna. The café has an intriguing menu and is open for breakfast, lunch, and dinner with indoor and outdoor seating.

Smuggler's Villa Resort. PO Box 79, Eastsound, WA 98245; (360) 376-2297; smuggler@rockisland.com; www.smuggler.com. No transient moorage. Smuggler's Village has condos for rent, a swimming pool, and hot tubs. Reservations required. Good base for trailer boats who can rent a condo for overnights and explore the northern San Juans during the day.

⑱ **Barnes and Clark Islands.** These two beautiful islands lie parallel to each other in Rosario Strait, between Orcas Island and Lummi Island. Barnes Island is privately owned, but Clark Island is a state park, with mooring

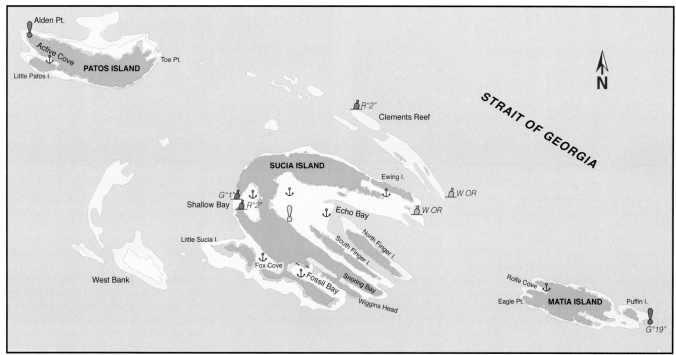

Sucia Islands Marine State Park

buoys installed during the summer. Camping and picnicking sites are ashore, and trails meander along the island.

⑱ Clark Island Marine State Park. Open all year, day use and overnight mooring and camping. Clark Island is exposed to Rosario Strait and the Strait of Georgia, and is best in settled weather. Mooring buoys are deployed between Clark Island and Barnes Island, and in the bay on the east side. The park has 9 mooring buoys for vessels to 45 feet: 6 on the east side and 3 on the west side. Toilets, picnic sites, fire rings, and primitive campsites. No power, no water. Pack out all garbage.

Note: A nasty rock is in the entrance to the bay.

Visitor report: Correspondents Bruce and Margaret Evertz spent a night on a buoy on the east side of Clark Island and ". . .woke up three times in the middle of the night hanging onto the mattress as we rolled in the wake of something big. Next time we'll try one of

the buoys on the west side."

⑲ Matia Island. Open all year, day use and overnight mooring. Facilities include a 64-foot-long moorage float in Rolfe Cove, 2 buoys, 6 campsites, toilet. No power, water or showers. The mooring float is removed in winter.

Those confident in their anchoring ability might try the little 1-boat notch between Rolfe Cove and Eagle Point, although you can't go inland from there. A stern anchor will be required to keep the boat positioned. High cliffs surround this cove. It's very secluded and serene.

There is some disagreement about the pronunciation of Matia. Bruce Calhoun's book, *Cruising the San Juan Islands*, says it's pronounced "Mah-TEE-ah." We've been told, however, that a number of genuine old hands have always pronounced it "Mah-CIA," as in "inertia" or "militia." However the name is pronounced, Matia Island is a popular destination, beautiful and interesting. The island

is part of the San Juan Island National Wildlife Refuge (run by the U.S. Fish and Wildlife Service). All access is restricted except the loop trail and the designated 5-acre moorage and picnicking area at Rolfe Cove. The rest of the island is off-limits to protect wildlife.

⑲ Rolfe Cove. The favored Matia Island anchorage is in Rolfe Cove, which opens from the west. Strong currents can run through Rolfe Cove and the bottom is rocky. Be sure the anchor is well set and swinging room is adequate. Anchorage is good in the bay indenting the southeast corner of the island. The remains of an old homestead are located at the head of that bay.

LOCAL KNOWLEDGE

DANGEROUS REEFS: A reef extends westward from Little Sucia Island nearly to the shoal water near West Bank. Sucia Island is surrounded by such hazards. We strongly recommend that vessels in these waters carry and use Chart 18431.

⑳ Sucia Island. Open all year, day use and overnight mooring and camping. For information call (360) 902-8844; for campsite reservations call toll-free (888) 226-7688. Facilities include dock space, 48 mooring buoys, toilets, portapotty dump. Water, but no power, no showers. This probably is the most heavily used marine park in the system. As many as 700 boats can visit on one weekend in the high summer season.

Like Matia and Patos Islands, Sucia Island is made of sandstone carved by water and wind into dramatic shapes. Many fossils can be found in Sucia Island's sandstone. It is il-

Though small, Matia Island has a cove for anchorage and a public dock.

Eroded sandstone on Sucia Island is remarkable.

Sucia Island has many trails for hiking—some easy, some challenging.

legal to disturb or remove them.

The park has 55 primitive campsites and 2 group campsites, which can be reserved. Camping is permitted in designated areas only. A day use/picnic area, with picnic shelters, is on the neck of land separating Echo Bay and Shallow Bay, and can be reserved. The park has several miles of hiking trails and service roads. Fresh water is available April through September at Fossil Bay and near Shallow Bay. The most developed facilities are at Fossil Bay.

Sucia Island has several fingers that separate small bays. Facilities are as follows: Fox Cove: 4 mooring buoys; Fossil Bay: 2 docks, 16 mooring buoys; Snoring Bay: 2 mooring buoys; Echo Bay: 20 mooring buoys, 2 linear moorings; Ewing Cove: 4 mooring buoys; Shallow Bay: 8 mooring buoys. The mooring buoy count can change based on winter weather and repairs.

Shallow Bay. Shallow Bay is an excellent, popular anchorage. Lots of room except on minus tides. Mooring buoys take most of the obvious good spots, so if they are taken you'll be looking at the south side of Shallow Bay. Check the tides before anchoring, and be sure you'll have enough water under the keel at low tide. Easy entry as long as you pass between the two buoys marking the entrance. The best place to beach the dinghy is on the narrow neck of land separating Shallow Bay from Echo Bay. Sunsets in Shallow Bay are beautiful.

Fox Cove. Enter Fox Cove from either side. Waters off the southern entry can be turbulent. At the west entry foul ground extends west farther than you expect. Tie to mooring buoys or anchor behind Little Sucia Island. A pretty spot with sandstone cliffs.

Fossil Bay. Fossil Bay is easy to enter, nicely protected, and beautiful. Anchor out, tie to one of the mooring buoys, or moor at the docks. In winter one of the docks is moved to a more protected area of the park. At the head of the outermost dock a plaque commemorates the yacht clubs that were members of the Interclub Boating Association of Washington, when Interclub worked to collect funds from ordinary citizens, then bought the

island and gave it to the state as a state park. One of the points of land overlooking Fossil Bay is named for Ev. Henry, the first president of Interclub, who conceived the idea and carried out the project.

Depths in Fossil Bay at zero tide are 6 feet at the outer end of the innermost dock, and they shoal rapidly toward the head of the bay. The park ranger told us depths are only 5 feet at zero tide near the outer dock. Be careful on low tides. A substantial day use shelter, excellent for group functions, has been built at the head of the dock. Call (360) 376-2073 for reservations.

Snoring Bay. Snoring Bay is easy to enter and has 2 mooring buoys. A good spot. As we understand the story, a park ranger was caught sleeping on duty in this bay, hence the name.

Echo Bay. Echo Bay is the largest of Sucia's bays. Although it is the most exposed, it is the most popular. Mooring buoys line the western shore, and 2 linear mooring systems are just outside the buoys. Picnic facilities are on the narrow neck of land separating Echo Bay from Shallow Bay.

The fine gravel beach at the head of Echo Bay is fairly steep, making dinghy landing much more convenient. We were able to step ashore without getting our feet wet.

The two long islands in Echo Bay (North Finger and South Finger Island) are privately owned. The south half of Justice Island (the

small island off South Finger Island) is park-owned but closed to the public as a nature preserve.

Caution: A reader reported that he grounded his Cal 39 sailboat, which draws 6 feet 8 inches, on an uncharted rock in Echo Bay. The grounding occurred in the area marked 1 fathom, 5 feet extending from the small islet northwest of South Finger Islet, as shown on large scale Chart 18431. He sounded the area carefully after the grounding, and found the depths to be somewhat less than charted. The keel of his boat confirmed the soundings. On low tides especially, give the tip of this islet a good offing.

Despite occasional stories of anchor dragging in Echo Bay, we have found the bottom to be heavy, sticky clay, with excellent holding.

No-anchor zone: A no-anchor zone is marked by buoys near the head of Echo Bay. They want to see if eelgrass can be established there. Mooring buoys are in the no-anchor zone and it's okay to use them. Just don't anchor.

Ewing Cove. In our opinion, cozy little Ewing Cove, tucked in behind Ewing Island on the north side of Echo Bay, is the most charming of Sucia Island's bays. The cove has 4 mooring buoys and a lovely beach at the western end. We have reports of a rock in Ewing Cove's southern entrance, from Echo Bay. The rock is east of a white can that marks a fish haven, shown on large scale Chart 18431.

Relaxing in Active Cove at Patos Island.

We're told the rock is black and hard to see, and feeds on propellers at low tide. Be extra cautious. Reader Bruce Farwell sent lat/lon coordinates of 48°45.794'N/122°52.924'W. We've found the narrow pass at the northwest end of Ewing Cove to be deep and easily run as long as you pay attention. Danger Reef lies just outside.

(21) **Patos Island.** Open all year, day use and overnight mooring and camping. Facilities include 2 mooring buoys in Active Cove, toilets, primitive campsites. The remains of the dock that served the lighthouse on Alden Point are still there, but barely recognizable. Pack out all garbage. The island is a breeding area for birds.

(21) **Active Cove.** The only possible Patos Island anchorage is in Active Cove, on the west tip of the island. The cove, with its sculpted sandstone walls, feels extremely remote. It is one of the most scenic spots in the San Juans. Considerable current activity is outside the entrances. Inside the cove the currents are reduced, but it's tight. Use the mooring buoys when possible. If the mooring buoys are taken, anchoring gets interesting. A stern-tie to shore probably will be called for.

Freeman Island. On President Channel. Open all year, day use only, no facilities. Anchor out at this undeveloped state park property. No fires or overnight camping. Pack out all garbage.

(22) **West Beach Resort.** 190 Waterfront Way, Eastsound, WA 9824; (360) 376-2240; (877) 937-8224; vacation@westbeachresort.com; www.westbeachresort.com. Open all

Prevost Harbor is one of the popular destinations in the San Juan Islands.

year, ethanol-free premium gasoline at the fuel dock, 10 mooring buoys in the summer and 3 in the winter, restrooms, showers. Larger powerboats and keel sailboats tie to mooring buoys. The store has a little bit of everything, including groceries, ice, beer, wine, espresso, and free Wi-Fi. Limited dock space in the off-season.

West Beach is a popular fishing resort, with cabins, children's activities, food service, private launch ramp (guests only) and parking. Be careful if you anchor out. The eelgrass bottom is not good in many places and you can drag.

Waldron Island. Waldron Island has no public facilities. In settled weather anchorage is good in Cowlitz Bay and North Bay. Mail Bay, on the east shore, is rocky but usable. The mail boat from Bellingham used to call there, leaving the mail in a barrel hung over the water.

(23) **Stuart Island.** The center portion of Stuart Island, including Reid Harbor and Prevost Harbor, is a state park, with campsites, potable water, and clean, spacious composting toilets. A trail and dirt road from Reid Harbor and Prevost Harbor lead out to the automated Turn Point lighthouse. The distance is about 3 miles, each way. It's an excellent walk, although the trail to the road goes over a mountain, and will have you puffing. The view down into Reid Harbor is excellent, however.

Once you get to the road, it's 0.7 mi. to the school house (1 room, K-8), library and museum, which in our opinion are on the must-see list. The school house is modern, but the library and museum buildings go back to earlier days. The museum is filled with information about island life, which, despite being close to big cities, is pretty primitive. There is no public electric power, for example. Every resident is responsible for his or her own electricity, and a few choose

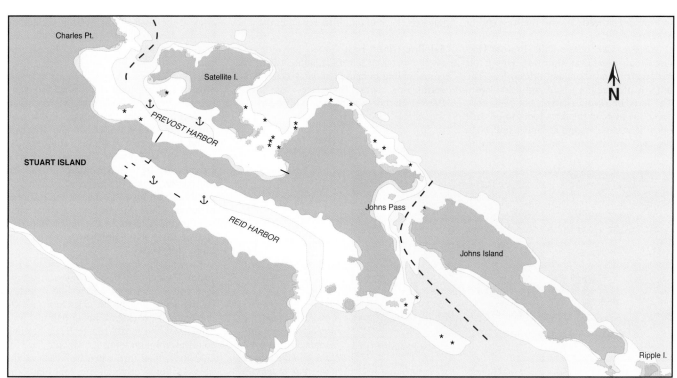

Stuart Island Marine State Park

TURN POINT SPECIAL OPERATING AREA

The Turn Point Special Operating Area was created in 2001 to manage the high volume of commercial ship and recreational boat traffic around Turn Point. Ships longer than 100 meters (328 feet) must call in to Victoria Traffic on VHF channel 11 prior to entering the area and report their intended navigation movements and any other information necessary to comply with standards of care.

Recreational vessels should monitor VHF channel 11 in this vicinity so they can be aware of any ships. If ships are in the Special Operating Area, stay well clear until they are past. In a crossing situation, *cross behind the large ship*, not in front of it.

Turn Point is a blind corner. A recreational vessel could be completely unaware of a fast approaching ship on the other side. Monitor VHF channel 11. We had a near-miss in fog a few years ago. It was scary.

Also see "What Recreational Boaters Need to Know about VTS" in Cruising Information section in the front of the Waggoner.

— *Robert Hale*

to do without. Ditto water and telephone, although cell phones have filled that void. Handmade postcards are for sale in the library, honor system.

One island family, Ezra and Loie Benson and their children, have created a small business called Boundary Pass Traders. They operate the Treasure Chest, near the schoolhouse. T-shirts, stationery, and the like have been enhanced with local scenes. Strictly the honor system. Select the items you like and mail a check for your purchases. We did it, and got a nice thank-you note in reply.

Prevost Harbor. Open all year, day use and overnight mooring and camping. Facilities include 256 feet of dock space, 7 mooring buoys, a linear mooring system, 18 primitive campsites, toilets. The favored entrance to Prevost Harbor is around the west end of Satellite Island.

Caution: Two reefs in the Prevost Harbor entrance cover at high tide. One is off the Stuart Island shore and dries 6 feet. The other is off Satellite Island and dries 4 feet. The reefs are clearly charted, but when they cover, the route to the dock looks to be wide open. If you're entering at higher tide when the reefs are covered, don't wrap tightly to

port around the tip of Satellite Island. That's where one of the reefs is. Proceed a short distance straight into the harbor (but not too far; that's where the other reef is), then turn to port.

Except for the reefs noted above, anchoring is good throughout Prevost Harbor. After dinner we took a slow dinghy ride around the shoreline. A grass airstrip is at the east end of the harbor, beyond the docks. As we putt-putted along we found the houses, rock forms, and beaches fascinating.

The passage to the east of Satellite Island is foul, and many people recommend against it. Contributing Editor Tom Kincaid, however, reports that with care these waters are passable at half tide or better, or by shallow draft boats. Use caution. Shoreside facilities are shared with Reid Harbor, on the narrow but steep neck of land that separates them.

Satellite Island East Cove. "The little cove on the eastern shore of Satellite Island has good holding in mud in about 40 feet. Wonderful view across Boundary Pass. Inside, Prevost Harbor was packed with boats; we were alone." [*Hamilton*]

Reid Harbor. Open all year, day use and overnight mooring and camping. The entrance is straightforward. A 192-foot mooring float is on the north shore, 15 mooring buoys dot the bay, and mooring floats and a linear mooring system are placed within easy dinghy distance of the landing pier. Facilities include toilets, pumpout, portapotty dump. Reid Harbor is long and narrow, and protected by high hills. The bottom is excellent for anchoring, and the harbor holds a great number of boats. It's a popular destination. The setting is beautiful. Shoreside facilities are shared with Prevost Harbor, on the narrow but steep neck of land separating them. The county dirt road leading to the Turn Point Lighthouse, with its museum (and the school house, museum and library along the way), begins at the head of Reid Harbor. No dock at the head of the bay, but if tides are favorable you could beach your dinghy there without having to carry it back through the mud.

Gossip Island. "Reid Harbor had too many boats for our taste. Preferring a view anyway, we dropped anchor just outside, in the cove formed by Gossip Island and the unnamed island immediately northwest of Gossip Island. It was very private, with two white sand beaches nearby. Good holding ground for the anchor. Southerly swells rocked us a couple times, but no worse than in the east cove of James Island. We had an excellent view through the islets to the Olympic Mountains, and of large ship traffic away off in Haro Strait." [*Hamilton*]

Johns Pass. Johns Pass separates Stuart Island and Johns Island, and is used regularly. At the south end of the pass foul ground, marked by kelp, extends about half of a mile southeast from Stuart Island. Boats heading southeast through Johns Pass should head for Gull Reef, then turn when well clear of the kelp. Anchorage is possible in Johns Pass and along the south side of Johns Island.

A trail and county road lead from Reid Harbor and Prevost Harbor to the school house and museum and library buildings.

CHAPTER 7

GULF ISLANDS

GULF ISLANDS
Victoria • Sidney • Butchart Gardens • Chemainus • Wallace Island • Pirates Cove • Nanaimo

SALTSPRING ISLAND
Ganges • Vesuvius • Fulford Harbour

NORTH & SOUTH PENDER ISLAND
Bedwell Harbour • Port Browning • Otter Bay

GALIANO ISLAND
Sturdies Bay • Montague Harbour

For convenience, the Gulf Islands section of this book includes the southern tip and the east side of Vancouver Island as far up-island as Nanaimo.

The Gulf Islands are British Columbia's answer to Washington's San Juan Islands, only they are different. The San Juan Islands are the peaks of a sunken mountain range. The Gulf Islands, for the most part, are a different geology, made of sandstone that has been folded and uplifted until it sticks out of the sea. Together, the San Juan Islands and Gulf Islands create a superb cruising area.

Like the San Juan Islands, the Gulf Islands are in the lee of mountains. They receive much summertime sun and little summertime rainfall. Water is in short supply. Boat washing is something that just isn't done, at least in the islands themselves.

The Gulf Islands are blessed with dozens of anchorages, from one-boat notches to open bays that hold dozens of boats. Provincial marine parks provide anchorage, mooring and docking possibilities, and facilities ashore. Private marinas run the spectrum from rustic to deluxe, many with excellent dining on-site or nearby.

The largest town in the Gulf Islands proper is Ganges. If your definition of the islands expands (as ours does) to include southern and eastern Vancouver Island, then Victoria, Sidney, Ladysmith and Nanaimo are larger than Ganges.

The best provisioning stops are Victoria, Sidney, Ganges, Ladysmith, and Nanaimo. Fuel is available throughout the islands.

Navigation is straightforward, but pay attention. It's easy to get confused, and the waters are dotted with rocks and reefs. You want to know where you are at all times. Unfortunately for those who use paper charts, no single chart sheet covers all the waters, so you will be working among the 1:40,000 scale Charts 3440, 3441, 3442 and 3443, plus several large-scale charts and plans charts. Plans charts are a collection of large-scale charts all

Victoria Harbour Authority's Causeway Floats are right in front of the Empress Hotel. The B.C. provincial parliament buildings are in the background

on one sheet.

The Canadian Hydrographic Service Chartbook 3313 is an excellent chartbook for the Gulf Islands. At $90 Cdn. this chartbook is not inexpensive, but it has everything.

Customs – Entering Canada. Vessels entering Canada are required to clear Canadian Customs at their first stop in Canada. Most boats will clear customs at Bedwell Harbour on South Pender Island, Victoria (includes Victoria Inner Harbour, Oak Bay, and Cadboro Bay), Sidney, or Nanaimo. Bedwell Harbour is just 4 miles north of Stuart Island in the San Juan Islands, but its station is open only from May 1 through September 30. See page 18 for more detailed explanations on the process of clearing Canadian Customs.

Gulf Islands National Park Reserve. The Gulf Islands National Park Reserve came into being in 2004. Many former provincial parks, and most of the uninhabited islands and islets south of Active Pass, were transferred to the

new national park, plus a number of other properties that were purchased. Land continues to be purchased and added to the Reserve. Park lands have green and white location signs, or small yellow boundary signs bearing the stylized beaver symbol of Parks Canada. Dogs must be on leash. Camping is in designated areas only. Nominal usage fees are charged, often collected through honor boxes on shore. Fees are slightly higher for 2014 but are still a good value.

For more information see www.pc.gc.ca/gulf; (250) 654-4000; (877) 841-1744. For emergencies or to report problems on park lands, call toll-free (877) 852-3100

VICTORIA AREA

Esquimalt Harbour. Esquimalt Harbour is a wonderful but often overlooked anchorage. Excellent holding in thick mud southeast of Cole Island, with room to swing. Protection is reasonable, even with big winds blowing in the Strait of Juan de Fuca. With this bottom you're not going anywhere, anyway. At night the lights from the shipyard reflect on the still water—magic. The Canadian Navy guards the entrance with a high speed inflatable, and will advise you to keep 100 meters away from their ships and property, but they are fine with anchoring.

The British Navy used Cole Island for munitions storage. The large brick buildings on the island are still intact and make interesting exploration. The land is apparently owned by the province and it's okay to go ashore. [*Hamilton*]

Our sister publication, *Cruising the Secret Coast*, by Jennifer and James Hamilton, devotes an entire chapter to Esquimalt Harbour and vicinity.

Security zone: All vessels entering or departing Esquimalt Harbour are requested to contact QHM Operations on VHF channel 10 or by telephone at (250) 363-2160.

Fleming Beach at Macaulay Park. West of Victoria Harbour, in Esquimalt. Open

	CHARTS				
3313 Small craft charts (chartbook)	Gulf Islands and adjacent Waterways		3477 Plans	Gulf Islands Bedwell Harbour to Georgeson Passage (1:15,000) Telegraph Harbour & Preedy Harbour (1:15,000) Pender Canal (1:4,000)	
3412	Victoria Harbour (1:5,000)				
3419	Esquimalt Harbour (1:5,000)				
3424	Approaches to Oak Bay (1:10,000)		3478 Plans	Saltspring Island Cowichan Bay to Maple Bay (1:20,000) Birds Eye Cove (1:10,000) Genoa Bay (1:10,000) Ganges Harbour & Long Harbour (1:20,000) Fulford Harbour (1:15,000)	
3440	Race Rocks to D'Arcy Island (1:40,000)				
3441	Haro Strait, Boundary Pass & Satellite Channel (1:40,000)				
3442	North Pender Island to Thetis Island (1:40,000)		3479	Approaches to Sidney (1:20,000)	
3473	Active Pass, Porlier Pass & Montague Harbour				

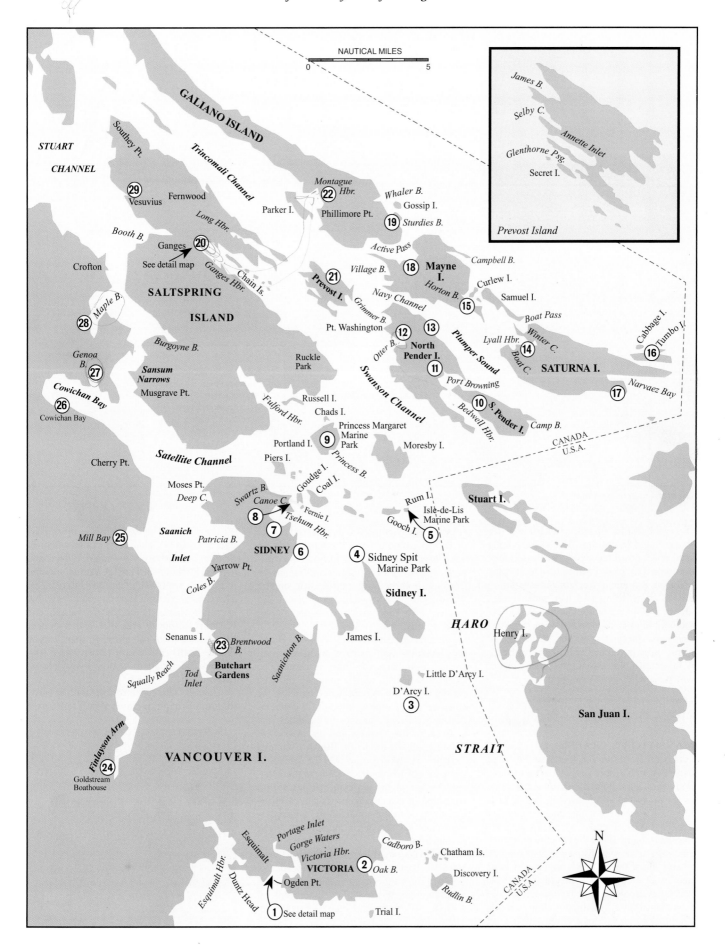

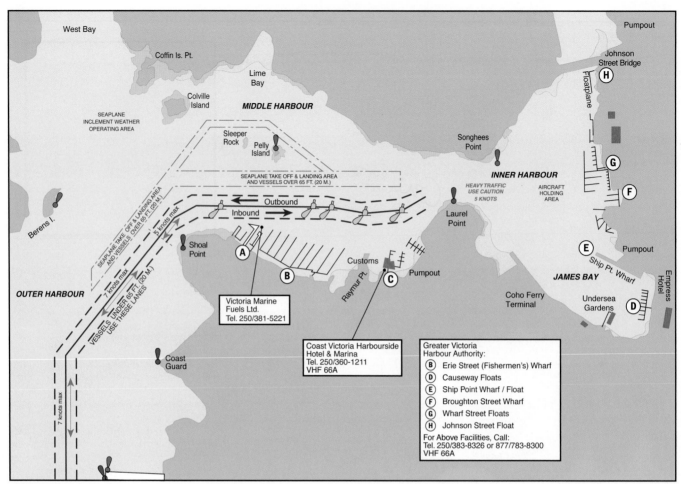

Greater Victoria Harbour

all year. Facilities include launch ramp (fee charged) and washrooms. This is a charming little cove, protected by a rock breakwater, overlooked by most boating people. It is the home of Esquimalt Anglers' Association, a private sportfishing and fish enhancement group. The launch ramp boarding floats have room for temporary moorage while shopping nearby, or you can anchor out. Walkways and picnic areas have been built. Fleming Beach is adjacent to old coastal gun emplacements, which make for good exploring.

LOCAL KNOWLEDGE

MANDATORY TRAFFIC LANES: All vessels 65 feet LOA and less must enter and depart Victoria's Inner Harbour between Shoal Point and Laurel Point along the south shore, as shown in the accompanying harbor map. Inbound vessels favor the docks; outbound vessels a little farther out. The traffic lanes are marked by buoys (keep the buoys to port when entering and exiting). The more open water in the middle of the harbor is used by the large number of float planes that land and take off constantly. Because of the volume of boat and float plane traffic, no sailing is allowed inside the breakwater. Sailboats under power must have sails lowered.

① **Victoria.** Victoria is the provincial capital of British Columbia and the largest city on Vancouver Island. Regular ferry service connects Port Angeles, Washington, Vancouver (through Swartz Bay), and Seattle on the Victoria Clippers. Scheduled float planes also connect with Vancouver and Seattle, among other destinations.

Victoria is beautiful. The Empress Hotel, for which the word "majestic" could have been created, dominates the Inner Harbour. The Empress is flanked on the south by the B.C. provincial parliament buildings, themselves the embodiment of dignity, thoughtful deliberation, and orderly progress—the buildings, that is. Between the Empress and the parliament buildings stands the Royal British Columbia Museum, a must-see, especially for families. A giant ice age mammoth dominates the entry, and the rest of the museum delights with a recreation of Capt. Vancouver's ship, a Victorian town, a west coast seashore, a First Nations bighouse and much, much more. *Highly recommended.*

The Maritime Museum of British Columbia, at 28 Bastion Square, is also outstanding.

The Visitor Information Centre is on top of the causeway at the head of the Inner Harbour, across from the Empress Hotel. It's easy to find. The entire Victoria Inner Harbour is covered by Wi-Fi.

Reservations: The docks in the Inner Harbour beneath the "blue" bridge (Johnson Street Bridge) are privately operated. The Coast Victoria Harbourside Hotel & Marina, adjacent to the Erie Street Wharf, accepts reservations. The Greater Victoria Harbour Authority now accepts reservations for any size vessel. The Harbour Authority asks that vessels greater than 65 feet LOA call ahead so space can be found: (250) 383-8326; (877) 783-8300; tbrooks@victoriaharbour.org; www.victoria-harbour.org.

Customs: The customs dock will be moving from Broughton Street Wharf to Raymur

Passenger ferries, like this one, operate in Victoria's harbor.

Street entertainers perform along the Inner Harbour waterfront in Victoria.

Point, just east of Fisherman's Wharf, in 2014. When arriving, check in using the dedicated phone at the customs dock, then call the Harbour Authority for a slip assignment. Check www.WaggonerGuide.com for updates.

The Harbour Authority has a "meet and greet" program for visiting boats. For all vessels, when you enter the Inner Harbour, call on VHF 66A and they will direct you to available guest moorage. Rafting is mandatory at the Harbour Authority moorages.

Inside Ogden Point, the Erie Street Wharf (Fishermen's Wharf) is reserved primarily for commercial fishboats and monthly pleasure craft moorage.

Next, you pass the new customs dock at Raymur Point. The dock is well marked. The phone on the dock is used for calling customs.

Then come the Coast Harbourside Hotel docks with pleasure craft moorage.

The Causeway Floats are to the south of Ship Point and in front of the Empress Hotel. These are the docks that fill up first. They are the most desirable location on the Victoria waterfront.

A seaplane float and moorage for government patrol vessels are at the same location. Showers, washrooms, and laundry facilities are available.

The Wharf Street wharf is north of the Broughton Street customs dock.

For an interesting side trip, take the dinghy through Gorge Waters to Portage Inlet. You'll travel first through the industrial part of the city, then through park and residential areas. It's about a 3-mile trip; currents are a factor if you intend to row.

Symphony Splash: On August 3, 2014 enjoy symphony music from a barge in the Inner Harbour, punctuated with cannons and fireworks. Something like 40,000 people turn out for the shows.

No discharge: Discharging raw sewage is prohibited in Victoria Inner Harbour, defined as beginning at the Ogden Point breakwater. This applies to "black water" only. "Gray water," such as from dishwashing or showers, is okay (if biodegradable). Pumpouts in the Inner Harbour are located at the Coast Victoria Harbourside Marina, at Ship Point, and at Fishermen's Wharf.

THINGS TO DO

1. **Butchart Gardens** in Brentwood Bay. A spectacular display of flowers and gardens. Fireworks on Saturdays in the summer. Take the bus from Victoria or anchor in Brentwood Bay and dinghy ashore.

2. **Shaw Ocean Discovery Centre** in Sidney. Learn more about the ecosystem of the these coastal waters.

3. **Bookstores**. Downtown Sidney has eight bookstores, from military, to kids, to collectors. Even a haunted bookstore. See why Sidney is called Booktown.

4. **Lochside Regional Trail** along the waterfront. Rent bikes for this flat and easy to ride trail from Victoria to Sidney.

5. **Royal British Columbia Museum**. True classical museum covering the human and natural history of British Columbia is just above James Bay in Victoria.

6. **B.C. Maritime Museum**. Displays on pirates, heritage vessels, and shipwrecks. It is also home to three historic sailboats — *Dorothy, Tilikum*, and John Guzzwell's *Trekka*.

7. **Afternoon tea at the Empress Hotel**. A special treat, high tea offers pastries and piano music in an elegant setting.

8. **Victoria Inner Harbour**. Watch street musicians, mimes, and artists. The waterfront comes alive in the summer. Great boat watching, too.

Ⓐ **Victoria Marine Fuels Ltd.** (250) 381-5221. Fuel dock with gasoline and diesel, located at Erie Street Fishermen's Wharf. Open all year, but with shorter hours in winter. Carries snacks, food items, charts. This is the only fuel dock in the Inner Harbour.

Erie Street Fishermen's Wharf bustles with tourists in summer.

Ⓒ **Coast Victoria Harbourside Hotel & Marina.** 146 Kingston Street, Victoria, V8V 1V4; (250) 360-1211; coastvictoria@ coasthotels.com; www.coasthotels.com. Guest moorage May through September, limited availability October through April; 30 & 50 amp power, potable water on the docks, holding tank pumpout. Marina guests have full access to the dining room and lounge, indoor/outdoor pool, Jacuzzi, sauna, and fitness facilities. Reservations accepted. Within walking distance of downtown.

Ⓓ **Greater Victoria Harbour Authority Causeway Floats.** (250) 383-8326 ext. 243; (877) 783-8300 ext. 243; moorage@ victoriaharbour.org; www.victoriaharbour. org. Monitors 66A. Open all year with 2000+ feet of side-tie dock space, 30 amp power, potable water, Wi-Fi, garbage and recycling drop. Limited transient moorage October 1 through May 15. No limit to length of stay, but maximum boat length is 57 feet LOA. Reservations available for all vessel sizes. The check-in kiosk, located beside the ramp to shore, is open June 15 through September 15. The docks are gated shut at night.

These are the picturesque and popular floats directly in front of the Empress Hotel. Downtown Victoria beckons with fabulous restaurants, shopping, hotels, museums, and sightseeing. Washrooms (no showers) are located under the Visitors Centre building. Private clean Harbour Authority operated showers, laundry,

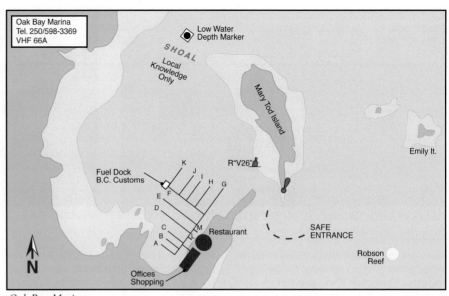

Oak Bay Marina

and washrooms are at the Wharf Street facility, a short walk from the floats.

Ⓔ **Greater Victoria Harbour Authority Ship Point Floats.** (250) 383-8326 ext. 243; (877) 783-8300 ext. 243; moorage@ victoriaharbour.org; www.victoriaharbour. org. Monitors 66A. Expanded docks can accommodate vessels to 280 feet. Reservations highly recommended. Water, 30, 50 & 100

amp power, Wi-Fi. Washrooms (no showers) are located under the Visitors Centre building. Private and clean Harbour Authority-operated showers, laundry and washrooms are at the Wharf Street facility, a short walk from the floats.

Ⓖ **Greater Victoria Harbour Authority Wharf Street Floats.** (250) 383-8326 ext. 243; (877) 783-8300 ext. 243; moorage@ victoriaharbour.org; www.victoriaharbour.org. Open all year, over 1000 feet of visitor dock space (limited guest moorage from October 1 to end of May), 30, 50 & 100 amp power, potable water, new washrooms and showers, laundry, garbage drop. Right downtown, to the left of the Seaplane terminal as you come in. Power availability varies, depending on location.

Victoria International Marina. (604) 687-2206; lhalgren@victoriainternationalmarina. ca; www.victoriainternationalmarina.ca. On the north shore of Victoria Harbour, two symmetrical one-story buildings sit on either side of this 29-slip marina designed to accommodate boats 65' to 150' in length. Slips available for purchase. The marina has received its approvals and is under construction. If all goes well, slips should be ready in late 2014.

Oak Bay. Oak Bay is on the east side of the south tip of Vancouver Island, west of the Chatham Islands. The channels between the various rocks and reefs are well marked. This is the route taken by many tugs with tows, and commercial fishing boats of all sizes. The Oak Bay Marina and a separate small repair yard are located behind the breakwater.

② **Oak Bay Marina.** 1327 Beach Drive, Victoria, BC V8S 2N4; (250) 598-3369; (800) 663-7090 ext. 247; obmg@obmg.com; www.oakbaymarina.com. Open all year with gasoline and diesel at the fuel dock. Customs clearance telephone at the fuel dock. Guest

moorage for boats to 80 feet, 15 & 30 amp power, washrooms, showers, laundry. Call ahead for availability.

The marina has excellent docks, a good restaurant, coffee house, and gift shop. A small chandlery carries essential boating supplies. Repairs are at the Gartside Marine boatyard in a neighboring building, no haulout. The Oak Bay Hotel is nearby for elegant dining. Complete shopping at quaint Oak Bay Village, a short distance away. Regular bus service to downtown Victoria.

Discovery Island Marine Park. Open all year. An undeveloped park suitable for beachable boats only. The island was once the home of Capt. E.G. Beaumont, who donated the land as a park. The northern part of Discovery Island, adjacent Chatham Island, and some of the smaller islands nearby are Indian Reserve lands: no landing.

Cadboro Bay. Cadboro Bay is entirely residential except for the Royal Victoria Yacht Club, which has a breakwater-protected marina on the western shore. Moorage at Royal Victoria Yacht Club is for members of reciprocal clubs only. Customs clearance is available.

Anchorage in Cadboro Bay is excellent, mud and sand bottom. A 100-foot-long concrete replica of Cadborosaurus, the elusive sea monster of Cadboro Bay, is prominent in the playground above the broad sandy beach at Cadboro-Gyro Park.

③ D'Arcy Island (Gulf Islands National Park Reserve). Open all year. This is an undeveloped island with no facilities other than some primitive campsites and a toilet. Dogs must be on leash. The island is surrounded by intimidating rocks, reefs, and shoals. Even if you study the chart carefully, kelp-covered rocks will pop up and surprise you. Approach with great caution.

As far as we are concerned, there are no "good" anchorages at D'Arcy Island, only acceptable spots in the right weather. If conditions allow, the cove on the west side of the island, south of the light, will work. Two coves on the northwest end look okay, but we didn't put the anchor down to confirm. The single Parks staff mooring buoy is in the cove on the east side of the island. This cove is closest to the island's campsites. We have not explored it ourselves.

D'Arcy Island was B.C.'s first leper colony; from 1891 until 1925 it housed Chinese lepers. The colony was closed in 1925 and the island reverted to provincial jurisdiction. Plans for the island as a federal penitentiary were never realized. D'Arcy Island remained undeveloped, and was established as a marine park in 1961. *A Measure of Value,* by Chris Yorath, provides a good history of D'Arcy Island.

To the east, Little D'Arcy Island is private property.

④ Sidney Spit (Gulf Islands National Park Reserve). Sidney Spit is exceptional. The park, open all year, occupies about one-

The opening of the breakwater at Port Sidney can be hard to see when approaching.

third of Sidney Island and all of the mile-long Sidney Spit extending northwest from the island. Anchor, tie to one of 21 mooring buoys, or moor on the well-maintained dock (dock is in place summer only). In the summer a passenger ferry runs to Sidney.

Picnic and camping areas are ashore. Dogs must be on leash. An easily walked 2-km loop trail winds around the island through a dense forest of cedar, hemlock, fir, big-leaf maple and vine maple. While we haven't seen them, a herd of fallow deer is supposed to be on the island. A large saltwater lagoon is habitat for many animal and plant species and is off limits; markers show its borders. The remains of a brick-making factory are near the lagoon,

and the beach there is covered with broken red bricks.

⑤ Isle-de-Lis at Rum Island (Gulf Islands National Park Reserve). Open all year, anchoring only, campsites and a pit toilet. This is a small, undeveloped, and very pretty park with a walking trail and beaches. Dogs must be on leash. Rum Island is located at the east end of Gooch Island, where Prevost Passage meets Haro Strait. Anchorage is on either side of the gravel spit connecting Rum Island and Gooch Island. The northern anchorage is preferred. Rum Island is said to have come by its name honestly during Prohibition. In 1995 the warship HMCS *Mackenzie* was sunk

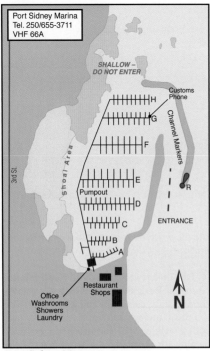

Port Sidney Marina
Tel. 250/655-3711
VHF 66A

SHALLOW – DO NOT ENTER

Customs Phone

H

G

F

Channel Markers

3rd St.

Shoal Area

E

Pumpout

D

R

C

ENTRANCE

B

A

Restaurant Shops

Office
Washrooms
Showers
Laundry

N

Port Sidney Marina

in approximately 100 feet just north of Gooch Island to create an artificial reef for divers. It is marked with 4 cautionary/information buoys.

Roberts Bay. Correspondent Pat Shera reports excellent anchorage in the middle of Roberts Bay, mud bottom. Protection is good from the south and west, but poor from the north and east.

Sidney. For boats crossing from Roche Harbor or the northern San Juan Islands, Sidney is a natural first stop to clear customs, stroll around, and restock with fresh produce, meat, spirits, and more. Downtown Sidney and nearby Tsehum Harbour have much to attract boaters, including excellent bakeries just up Beacon Avenue (Sidney's main street). The town also has good dining, art galleries, interesting shops, marine supplies, several bookstores, several liquor stores, and three supermarkets. A paved walkway stretches 2.5 km along the Sidney waterfront between Port Sidney Marina and beyond the Washington State Ferries terminal to the south. Summer concerts are held on the lawn at the base of Beacon Street.

Up at the corner of 4th and Beacon, the Sidney Historical Museum occupies the lower floor of the old Post Office Building. It has an excellent exhibit of early history in Sidney. Admission is by donation. Highly recommended, especially for families. The Shaw Ocean Discovery Centre in the Sidney Pier building has outstanding exhibits of marine life from local waters.

For an entirely different feeling from downtown Sidney, try Tsehum Harbour, a short distance north of downtown. The pace in Tsehum Harbour is much slower, and many of the moored boats are funkier. This is where

Port Sidney Marina is busy during summer.

the fishing fleet moors, and where the boat yards are. Van Isle Marina is the major marina.

Something about Tsehum Harbour attracts good restaurants, too. Tsehum Harbour's only disadvantage is the long walk to major shopping. Regular bus service runs into Sidney,

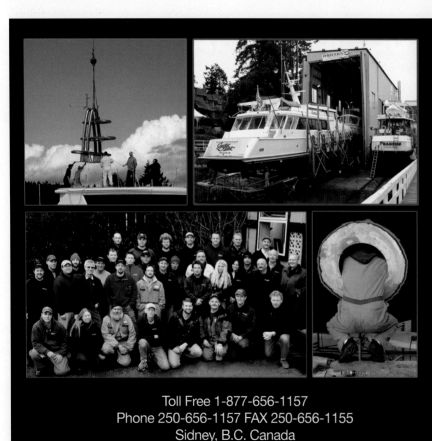

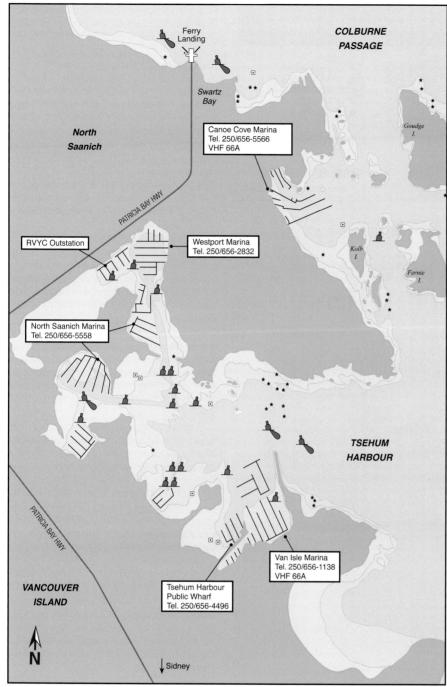

Tsehum Harbour

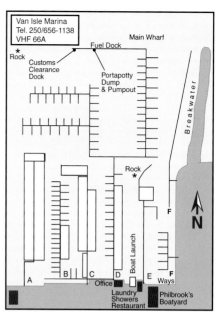

Van Isle Marina

or you could take a taxi or rent a car. Thrifty Foods charges $5 per order for delivery.

Market: The Sidney Summer Market takes over the lower part of Beacon Avenue Thursday evenings June through August, 5:30 p.m. to 8:30 p.m.

Customs: Sidney is the western terminus of the Washington State Ferries run from Anacortes and Friday Harbor, and is a Canada Customs port of entry. The customs check-in dock is inside the breakwater entrance at the Port Sidney Marina, just north of the public pier. Customs can be cleared by reporting in at the telephone on the dock. During summer months Customs officers may be stationed there for inspections after calling in. Van Isle Marina and Canoe Cove Marina also have

phone-in clearance from dedicated phones.

Wi-Fi: Shaw cable customers have free Wi-Fi throughout town.

Golf: Glen Meadows, 18 holes, (250) 656-3921; Ardmore, 9 holes (250) 656-4621. Both are said to be good courses.

⑥ **Port Sidney Marina.** 9835 Seaport Place, PO Box 2338, Sidney, BC V8L 3W6; (250) 655-3711; www.portsidney.com. Monitors VHF 66A. Open all year. Facilities include 30, 50 & 100 amp power, water, excellent washrooms, showers, laundry, Beacon/BBX Wi-Fi in the marina, free Wi-Fi in the marina lounge. The customs clearance phone is at the end of G dock, just inside the entrance. The pumpout, located between E and D docks, is

best suited to boats under 40 feet.

Call on VHF 66A low power before entering the breakwater. When approaching, pass between the two buoys just outside the breakwater entrance. The northernmost of these buoys marks a reef. Do not try to enter between the north end breakwater and shore. If you are directed to the shore side of the long, main pier, do not stray outside the marked channel. The bottom has been dredged alongside the shoreside dock, but shoal water lies just a few feet inshore. This is a popular marina, modern and well-maintained, adjacent to downtown.

Sidney Beacon Ave. Public Wharf. Sidney Beacon Avenue Public Wharf is used only for the summertime ferry to Sidney Spit Marine Park and does not have public dock space. A fresh fish market is at the end of the pier.

Tsehum Harbour. Tsehum Harbour (Tsehum is pronounced "See-um"), a shallow but navigable inlet about 1.5 miles north of downtown Sidney, contains a number of public, private, and yacht club moorages. Enter favoring the Armstrong Point (south) side to avoid a marked rock. This is the working waterfront of Sidney, with several excellent boat yards. Van Isle Marina, the first marina on the south side, has a customs check-in telephone, fuel, and guest moorage. Other moorages in Tsehum Harbour are Westport Marina, Capitol City and Sidney North Saanich yacht clubs, a Royal Victoria Yacht Club outstation, and private marinas.

Speed limit: A speed limit of 4 knots is in force in Tsehum Harbour. Watch your wake.

Repairs: Haulout and complete repairs are available.

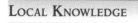
LOCAL KNOWLEDGE

ROCKS: Stay close to the end of the dock when rounding the west end of the fuel and

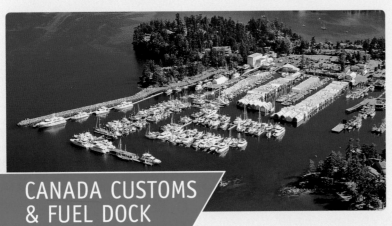

customs dock at Van Isle Marina. A substantial drying rock lies a short distance off, and each year a few boats manage to find it. The rock is marked by a beacon, but the rock extends toward the dock from the beacon.

⑦ **Van Isle Marina.** 2320 Harbour Road, Sidney, V8L 2P6; (250) 656-1138; info@ vanislemarina.com; www.vanislemarina.com. Monitors VHF 66A. Open 7 days a week, all year. Gasoline and diesel at fuel dock, customs clearance, free Wi-Fi, 15, 30, 50 & 100 amp 125-volt, 50 amp/125- & 208-volt power, excellent washrooms, showers and laundry, holding tank pumpout, portapotty dump, launch ramp for marina guests, oil pumpout.

A side-tie dock, 451 feet long and 15 feet wide, runs parallel to the breakwater on the east side of the marina. It is set up for the largest yachts, with 100 amp power, telephone, cable, and internet connections. Large boat or small, it's best to call ahead for guest moorage availability.

Van Isle is a large and busy marina, about a mile from downtown. Full repair services, haulout, and dry storage are available. The Sea Glass Waterfront Grill is at the head of the dock, call (778) 351-3663 for reservations. The famous Latch Country Inn Restaurant is a short walk away.

Van Isle Marina has been owned and managed by the same family for three generations. The family's long-term commitment to doing things right is evident. The staff is excellent.

⑦ **Tsehum Harbour Public Wharf.** (250) 655-4496. Open all year, 1043 feet of dock space, power, washrooms, no showers. This is a commercial fish boat harbor that accepts very limited transient moorage. Call in advance.

⑦ **Westport Marina.** 2075 Tryon Road, Sidney, BC V8L 3X9; (250) 656-2832; westport@thunderbirdmarine.com; www. thunderbirdmarine.com. Open all year, 15, 20 & 30 amp power, washrooms, free showers, Wi-Fi. Guest moorage in unoccupied slips, call ahead for availability. Well stocked chandlery, charts, limited groceries.

⑦ **North Saanich Marina.** P.O. Box 2001, 1949 Marina Way, North Saanich, BC V8L 3S3; (250) 656-5558; nsm@obmg.com;

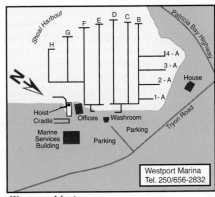

Westport Marina

www.northsaanichmarina.com. Open all year, gasoline and diesel at fuel dock. Permanent and visitor moorage to 70 feet, 15 & 30 amp power. Store carries charts, ice. Call ahead for moorage availability.

⑧ **Canoe Bay.** Canoe Bay, commonly called Canoe Cove, is tucked in behind a group of islands, only some of which have navigable passages between them. The clearest passage is **John Passage**, along the west side of Coal Island. From John Passage turn west into Iroquois Passage, and follow **Iroquois Passage** between Fernie Island and Goudge Island into Canoe Bay. From the south, **Page Passage**, west of Fernie Island, leads to Canoe Bay, and many boats use Page Passage. Canoe Bay has moorage with all amenities.

Caution: Page Passage should be run only with local knowledge or close study of large-scale Chart 3479. Tidal currents can run strongly, especially on spring tides.

⑧ **Canoe Cove Marina & Boatyard.** 2300 Canoe Cove Road, North Saanich, BC V8L 3X9; (250) 656-5566; (250) 656-5515; www.canoecovemarina.com. Monitors VHF 66A. Open all year, gasoline, diesel, propane at fuel dock, 30 amp power, washrooms, showers, laundry, 24-hour customs clearance at fuel dock, free Wi-Fi. This is a 450-berth marina with permanent and visitor moorage. Best to call ahead.

Canoe Cove Coffee Shop is in the center

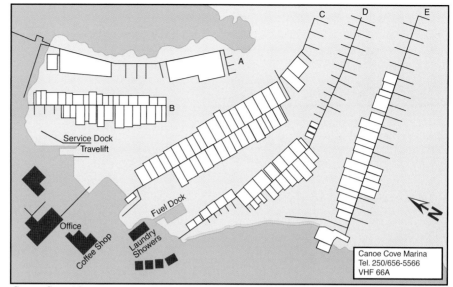

Canoe Cove Marina

of the marina, and the Stonehouse Restaurant is nearby. A short trail leads to the Swartz Bay ferry terminal. A harbor taxi shuttle connects the marina with Sidney. Navigate carefully on approach. A number of islands and rocks surround the entrance to Canoe Cove. They are well marked on the charts and easily avoided as long as you pay attention.

Canoe Cove's major thrust is its environmentally friendly full repair facility. They've added a new 83-ton Travelift for 2014, and they have extensive covered work areas and a well-stocked chandlery. The staff and management are friendly and competent. Together with Blackline Marine, Raven Marine, Sea Power Marine Centre, and Jespersen Boat Builders, they can do anything.

Swartz Bay Public Wharf. Open all year, adjacent to the ferry terminal, with 85 feet of dock space. No facilities. Watch for heavy ferry traffic near Swartz Bay.

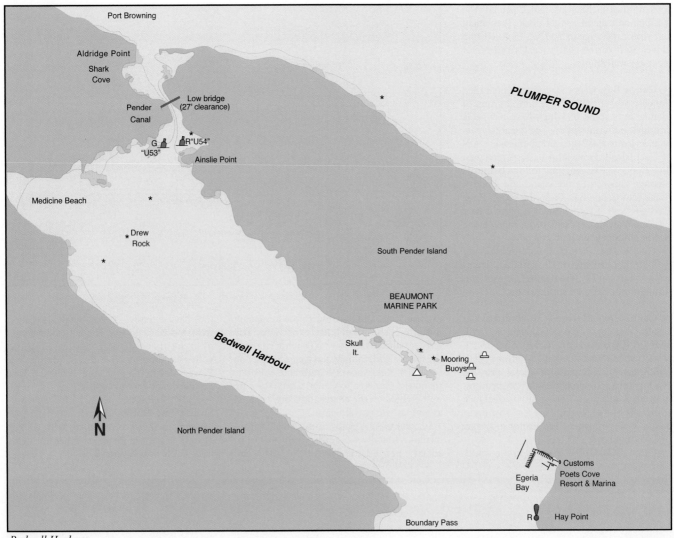

Bedwell Harbour

Piers Island Public Wharf. Open all year with 200 feet of dock space, no facilities.

⑨ Portland Island (Gulf Islands National Park Reserve). Formerly Princess Margaret Provincial Marine Park. Open all year, picnic and camp sites, toilets, no other facilities. Dogs must be

The Canadian Customs dock in Bedwell Harbour.

on leash and cleaned up after. In honor of her last visit to Victoria, Portland Island was donated to Her Royal Highness Princess Margaret, who later deeded the island to British Columbia. The park is now part of the Gulf Islands National Park Reserve.

Portland Island is wooded and hilly. Hiking trails follow the coastline. Easy-walking service roads and trails crisscross the center of the island. It would be easy to spend an entire day exploring. Reader Tyson Nevil says the coastline trail is easier to follow when walking in a counter-clockwise direction.

Anchor in Royal Cove (behind Chads Island) on the north side of the island, or in Princess Bay, behind Tortoise Island on the south side. The Royal Cove anchorage suffers mightily from the wakes of passing BC ferries, and Princess Bay also gets wakes. At Royal Cove you can have a quiet night if you can get well inside. Poorly marked stern-tie rings are along the high tide line in Royal Cove.

There's room for a couple boats behind Brackman Island, off the southwest corner of Portland Island. Watch your depths at low tide. Brackman Island is a protected wildlife and bird sanctuary. No access is allowed above the high tide line and no pets are allowed.

Princess Bay is roomier and far more popular, but somewhat exposed to southerly winds. In summer it usually is fine. With its shallow depths, not much anchor rode need be paid out, and the boats squeeze in pretty tightly. Watch your depths as you approach the head of Princess Bay. The bottom shoals rapidly, farther from shore than you might expect. Dinghy docks in Royal Cove and Princess Bay provide shore access.

The host float in Princess Bay is staffed by yacht club volunteers during the summer. They answer questions and give out information.

The *G.B. Church*, a sunken freighter off the southwest shore of the island, is an artificial reef for divers. The freighter lies in 100 feet and is marked with bow and stern buoys.

Bedwell Harbour. Bedwell Harbour has a luxury marina resort, Poets Cove, with docks that give

Poets Cove Marina

Poets Cove Marina has a pool for guests.

complete access to the facilities ashore. North of the resort, anchorage is good (except in a southeasterly) off the Beaumont/Mount Norman portion of Gulf Islands National Park Reserve. Anchorage also is good, if tight, in Peter Cove, on the west side of the harbor.

The Medicine Beach Market, Liquor Store and Café, a mini-convenience store, is located a short walk from Medicine Beach, at the north end of Bedwell Harbour. No dock, but easy anchoring just offshore, and a sandy beach for the dinghy.

Customs clearance: The Canada Border Services Agency (Canada Customs) dock is adjacent to Poets Cove Marina. Except for landing, only the skipper can leave the boat until customs is cleared. The procedure is for the captain to go up the ramp to the direct-line telephones along the wall of the customs office. Have all of your vessel's paperwork and crew's passport information ready. Call in for your clearance. In most cases the agent on the telephone will give you a clearance number. You may be asked to stand by for agents to inspect your vessel. Canpass or Nexus permits only from October 1 through April 30.

Peter Cove. Peter Cove is at the southern tip of North Pender Island. It is a well protected little anchorage, but permanently moored boats make anchoring a bit tight. A significant reef guards the mouth of the cove. Enter and depart north of the reef.

⑩ **Poets Cove Marina.** 9801 Spalding Road, RR #3, South Pender Island, BC V0N 2M3; (866) 888-2683; marina@poetscove. com; www.poetscove.com. Now open seasonally, the marina and resort will close November to March. Gasoline, diesel, and ice at the fuel dock. Guest moorage to 100 feet in 95 slips and side-tie, 30 amp power. If slips are filled, a floating dock is available at a reduced rate. Gourmet dining, pub, liquor store, café, heated pool, hot tub, spa, fitness center, free Wi-Fi.

This popular resort is a luxury getaway destination and it's first-class in every way, including the well-trained staff. The pool has a casual café and liquor store in the adjacent building. The showers and washrooms at poolside are some the finest we've seen on the coast. The coin-operated washing machines are located at the pool. The Aurora dining room is superb, and we enjoy the dress code: "We don't allow ties." The pub has seating indoors or out on the patio.

Poets Cove has plenty of activities. Rent a bike or kayak and explore the island, take a boat-based eco-tour of the area, play a round of golf, or try out the disc golf course. The resort now has a rental van available by the hour or day. Shuttle service to the farmers market is available on Saturdays.

Beaumont/Mount Norman Park (Gulf Islands National Park Reserve). West side of South Pender Island, in Bedwell Harbour. Open all year. Facilities include 15 mooring buoys (pay buoy fees at vault on shore at top of staircase, no charge before 6:00 p.m.). Toilets, no showers or fresh water. Walk-in campsites, picnicking, excellent walking and hiking trails. Dogs must be on leash. Hike to the top of Mount Norman, elevation 800 feet, for a memorable view.

Enter from Swanson Channel from the south, or from Plumper Sound and Port Browning through Pender Canal (27' clearance). The summertime host float is staffed by volunteers from the Sidney North Saanich Yacht Club. They are happy to provide park information.

Pender Canal. Pender Canal is a man-made dogleg channel between North Pender Island and South Pender Island, connecting Bedwell Harbour and Port Browning. The canal is crossed by a bridge with 27 feet of vertical clearance. Pender Canal is narrow, shallow, and often has a swift current running through it. Because of its dogleg shape, vessels approaching from opposite directions cannot see each other until they are in the narrowest section.

Before entering, signal your intentions on VHF 16, low power: *Securite, Securite, this is the 34-foot motor vessel Happy Days, northbound from Bedwell Harbour to Port Browning. Any concerned traffic please advise, channel one-six.*

Port Browning. Port Browning has a resort (Port Browning Marina) with moorage and other facilities. Anchorage is good throughout the harbor. The Driftwood Centre shopping area is about a half-mile walk from the marina. The center has a beautiful True Value Food Centre, a bank, gift shop, bakery, liquor store, pharmacy, post office, hair care, and laundromat. The gas station now has marine supplies.

⑪ **Port Browning Marina.** P.O. Box 126, North Pender Island, BC V0N 2M0; (250) 629-3493; info@portbrowning.com; www. portbrowning.com. Monitors VHF 66A. Canpass/Nexus-only reporting station. Open all year, 3000 feet of guest moorage, 15 & 30 amp power, Wi-Fi, fresh drinking water by request, excellent washrooms, laundry, launch ramp, seasonal swimming pool, beer & wine sales, family restaurant and pub, ATM, kayak and stand-up paddleboard rentals. The

For boats with clearance of less than 27 feet, Pender Canal is the shortcut between Bedwell Harbour and Port Browning.

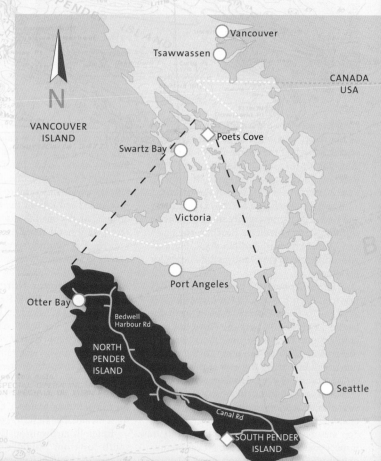

Overlooking the marina at Port Browning.

pub often has live music during summer weekends. On Saturdays during the summer, a fish boat sells fresh seafood on the docks mid-afternoon. Good shopping is a half-mile away at the Driftwood Centre, an easy walk.

Browning Harbour Public Wharf. Open all year, 89 feet of dock space, no facilities. Commercial fishing vessels have priority.

Shingle Bay (Gulf Islands National Park Reserve). This is a recent addition to the Gulf Islands National Park Reserve. Open all year, picnic tables, no other facilities. Dogs must be on leash and cleaned up after. See the remnants of the Shingle Bay fish reduction plant that operated intermittently between 1927 and 1959. It served as an important part of the local economy, employing 15 to 20 men at a time, mainly Pender Island residents.

Because the bay shoals rapidly, skippers must anchor well out, in line with the old reduction plant. Favor the north side, as a reef extends on the south. Anchorage is exposed to the southwest. The community park at the head of the bay is a welcome place to walk dogs, picnic, and access the island. A jungle gym is popular with children.

⑫ **Otter Bay Marina.** 2311 McKinnon Rd., North Pender Island, BC V0N 2M1; (250) 629-3579; info@otterbaymarina.com; www.otterbaymarina.ca. Monitors VHF 66A. Moorage open all year, full services open May 15 to September 30. Washrooms, showers, laundry, 15 & 30 amp power, 50 amp power on "A" dock, launch ramp, bistro, gazebo, children's play area, two heated pools, Wi-Fi.

Six mooring buoys are in the bay off the dock. Reservations recommended. The BC ferry is nearby.

The new upper pool is for families and is open mid-May through Labor Day. When both pools are operating, the lower pool is for adults. The showers, which take $1 coins (loonies) only, are excellent. The small convenience store carries fresh produce, baked goods, some groceries, frozen meat, poultry and fish, local art and gifts, clothing, and some boating supplies. Motor scooters available for rent.

This popular marina is on the west side of North Pender Island, facing Swanson Channel. Look for the tall flagpoles on the observation deck, just past the ferry landing.

In recent years the docks, electrical power, grounds, gift shop, and convenience store all have been upgraded. Look for the new seating areas overlooking the marina and other improvements to the ramp area.

For 2014, the activity center has been completely enclosed. With its stone fireplace and barbecue, it will be a nice setting for group events and rendezvous, even in the off-season.

The bistro is open for breakfast and lunch daily during the season, dinner on weekends. The resort now features a gourmet chef and hosts special food events such as pig roasts and lobster & steak nights on Saturdays throughout the summer. Check their website for the schedule.

Jess & Charlene Mansley are the very active managers.

Caution: A green spar buoy is off the corner of the marina docks. Red, Right, Returning means you leave this buoy to port as you enter. Especially at low tide, do not pass between the buoy and the dock.

Golf: The 9-hole Pender Island Golf Course is about a 15-minute walk from the marina. No tee times needed. For a small fee the marina will give you a ride up the hill to the course and back.

Roesland/Roe Lake (Gulf Islands National Park Reserve). Located on North Pender Island, deep in Otter Bay. Correspondent Deane Hislop reports: "We set the anchor, good holding, and took the dinghy to the park's dinghy dock. We discovered a former 1908 farmhouse that now serves as the Pender Island Museum, offering a glimpse into the island's past. This is also the location of Parks Canada's field office. We took the short walk to the end of Roe Islet to take in an amazing view of Swanson Channel, Saltspring Island, and Vancouver Island. Then it was back along the islet and up Shingle Bay road to the Roe Lake trail head and through the forest to beautiful Roe Lake, making for a full day of hiking and exploring."

Port Washington Public Wharf. On North Pender Island.

Open all year, 147 feet of dock space, unoccupied slips used when available. No facilities. Watch for a rock off the southeast dock. One float is designated for aircraft.

⑬ **Hope Bay Public Wharf.** (250) 813-3321. East side of North Pender Island, facing Navy Channel. Open all year, 226 feet of dock space, 1 day-use mooring buoy. Wakes from passing ferries make rafting undesirable, and depths on the inside of the dock are shallow at low tide.

After the historic 100-year-old Hope Bay Store above the dock burned in 1998, a group of 27 island residents bought the property and set about rebuilding. In 2005 Hope Bay reopened, with a café, an interior design and home decor boutique, hair salon, art gallery, a goldsmith, real estate, and other small businesses. The Café at Hope Bay is popular with the local Pender crowd. If the dock is full (it often is), tie to the one day-use mooring buoy and dinghy in.

Breezy Bay – Saturna Island Family Estate Winery. 8 Quarry Road, Saturna Island, BC V0N 2Y0; (250) 539-3521; (877) 918-

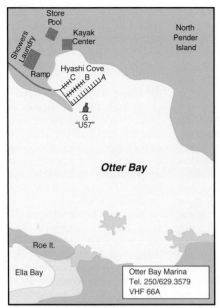

Otter Bay Marina

Otter Bay Marina, on North Pender Island.

3388; www.saturnavineyards.com. Open late spring to mid-September, check their website for hours. Access from a small dock in Breezy Bay, just north of Croker Point. When looking toward shore, two docks are visible. The winery dock is the one on the right; look for the sign on the ramp. Two orange and one white mooring balls (day-use only) are for winery visitors. Larger boats will find the mooring balls more suitable than the dock. A 15-minute walk past 60 amazing acres of vineyard takes you to the tasting room and lovely bistro overlooking the vineyard and the waters beyond.

Irish Bay. Irish Bay, on the west side of Samuel Island, is a good anchorage with scenic rock walls, but the island is privately owned. If you venture above the foreshore the caretaker will shoo you off.

Winter Cove. Winter Cove, between Samuel Island and Saturna Island, has an attractive park (part of the Gulf Islands National Park Reserve) on the Saturna Island side, and shal-low anchorage. We think the best anchorages are behind Winter Point, north of the cable line, or just off the national park reserve lands. The charts show shallow water in the middle of the cove, but you can patrol around—carefully—with the depth sounder and find anchoring sites away from the preferred spots. The mooring buoys in the southwest corner of the cove are private.

Minx Reef partially blocks the Plumper Sound approach to Winter Cove. Entering, we have found the best way to avoid the reef is to point the bow at the northern shore of Irish Bay, and run well past Winter Point before turning south into the cove.

The annual Canada Day (July 1) Saturna Island Lamb Barbecue at Winter Cove is a big event. The cove is packed with boats; islanders shuttle visitors ashore and back.

The annual Saturna Lions Club Dog & Dogs Show is in early September. Prizes for best dog and owner look-alike, best puppy, best tail wagger, and more. Bribes encouraged. Correspondents Bruce and Margaret Evertz happened upon the show and say it's wonderful. Bring your dog. For information see www.saturnalionsclub.net.

Boat Pass. Boat Pass connects Winter Cove with the Strait of Georgia. Currents in Boat Pass can run to 7 knots past several nasty rocks and reefs. Take this pass only at or near high water slack, preferably after seeing it at low water so you know where the rocks are.

Lyall Harbour. Lyall Harbour, on Saturna Island, is a large, well protected anchorage, with a ferry landing and store near the entrance. Nearby **Boot Cove** is a beautiful spot with anchorage in 12 to 18 feet, but it is crowded with resident boats on mooring buoys, and can be subject to williwaws blowing over a low swale on Saturna Island. Contributing Editor Tom Kincaid anchored there one afternoon, and before night his anchor line was stretched tight by 40-knot winds that were still blowing the next morning. "I dinghied to the nearest beach that afternoon and walked to the store for a loaf of bread," he reports. "I asked the proprietor if he'd heard when the wind was supposed to die down. 'Oh, you must be in Boot Cove,' he said. 'It always blows in Boot

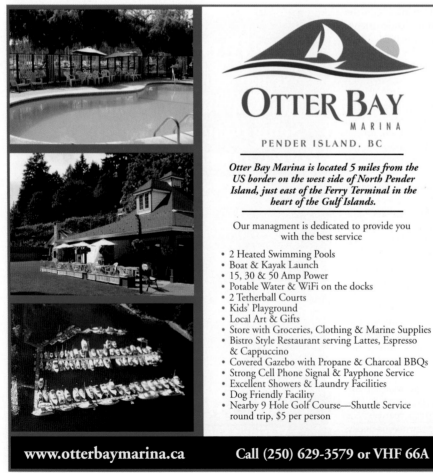

Cove.' So we weighed anchor, set sail, flew out the entrance and coasted to a stop, windless, just outside."

Lyall Harbour Public Wharf. Next to the ferry dock. Open all year, 200 feet of dock space. No power, water, washrooms, or showers. Commercial fishing vessels have priority. Gasoline and diesel at nearby fuel dock. Pay at the Saturna Point Store, just above the dock. The Lighthouse pub is in the same building. Wild Thyme Coffee House is up the road a bit in a cute converted double-decker bus, named Lucy. Wild Thyme is well known for their sweet and savory baked goods and organic coffee. Open for breakfast and lunch. Free Wi-Fi.

(14) **Saturna Point Store & Fuel.** 100 E. Point Rd., P.O. Box 80, Saturna Island, BC V0N 2Y0; (250) 539-5726. Open all year; open Thursday to Sunday October through Easter. Gasoline and diesel at fuel dock, washrooms, grocery store, ice, fishing gear, ATM and a small bookstore. The Lighthouse Pub downstairs offers sit down dining, take-out and off-premises sales. The pub has a new family dining area.

Georgeson Passage. Georgeson Passage, between Mayne Island and Samuel Island, is short and pretty. Currents, based on Active Pass, are about half as strong as those in Active Pass, both flooding and ebbing. Still, they run vigorously. See the Georgeson Passage secondary station under Active Pass in the Tide & Current Tables, Vol. 5 and Ports and Passes. If entering from the Strait of Georgia through the narrow pass between Campbell Point and Georgeson Island, be aware that a drying reef extends from Campbell Point into the pass. Favor the Georgeson Island side. Watch for rapids.

(15) **Horton Bay.** The public wharf is a Canpass/Nexus-only customs reporting station, and has room for a dozen 30-foot boats, plus rafting. Entering the area between Mayne and Samuel Islands requires some care, but is completely navigable. From the Gulf Islands side the best route is through Georgeson Passage, east of Lizard Island. Be careful of a kelp-covered rock in less than 6 feet, fairly close to Mayne Island. If entering west of Lizard Island, the rock is in the

middle of your path into Horton Bay. A reef extends from Curlew Island into Robson Passage, which separates Curlew Island from Mayne Island. Use Plans Chart 3477 (larger scale, much recommended) or 3442. A study of Chart 3477 shows a mid-channel course is called for. Several years ago we spent a quiet night at anchor in Horton Bay, and since then we've written positive things about it. In 2009, however, we received reports from two boaters who had bad experiences there. One was dragging anchor in high winds; the other said the only good spot was filled with private mooring buoys and the rest of the bay was subject to strong currents. [*Hale*]

(16) **Cabbage Island (Gulf Islands National Park Reserve).** Open all year, 10 mooring buoys, toilets, no water, no showers. Dogs must be on leash. This is a pretty anchorage between Cabbage Island and Tumbo Island, out on the edge of the Strait of Georgia.

The chart shows the entrance from the north, between two long reefs. Local knowledge advises to cross the reef on the Tumbo Channel side, between two patches of kelp, a short distance from the north tip of Tumbo Island. This should show 30 feet under the keel all the way across. Chartbook 3313 shows good depths at that location. The island has picnic sites, campsites, and a wonderful sandy beach. Crabbing is reportedly good.

Cabbage Island is interesting to explore. It isn't very big, so you can walk around the entire island in a reasonable time. Though tiny, the island is hardly dull. The beaches are different on every side, ranging from white sand, to sandstone reefs, to an aggregate of small rocks embedded in sandstone, to fine gravel.

Inland, you'll find forests of arbutus (madrona), Garry oak and western red cedar.

(16) **Tumbo Island (Gulf Islands National Park Reserve).** Tumbo Island, privately owned until recently, is now part of the Gulf Islands National Park Reserve. Dogs must be on leash. Trails lead through the island, although getting to them can be a challenge. The entire island goes straight up from the water, so you'll have to climb some rocks. Once there, you can find remnants of the island's commercial past in the forests

10 FAVORITE NORTHWEST GOLF PORTS

BY JOHN LUND

The northwest offers some of the world's best cruising. For us, the one thing that makes it even better is to combine boating with the ancient game of golf. Arranged from south to north, here are some of our favorite boating destinations and the golf courses near them.

WASHINGTON

THEA FOSS WATERWAY/TACOMA
Chambers Bay Golf Course

Chambers Bay Golf Course is Washington State's newest pure links course. From Thea Foss Waterway, Chambers Bay is a 30-minute taxi ride away. Chambers Bay is a walking-only track (caddies available) designed by Robert Trent Jones II. It is the site for the 2015 PGA Open Championship. A test of golf as the Scots intended, this tough course is softened somewhat by stunning views of Puget Sound.

> *Tacoma:* www.traveltacoma.com
> *Chambers Bay Golf Course:* 877-295-4657; www.chambersbaygolf.com

PORT ORCHARD AND BREMERTON
Gold Mountain Golf Complex, McCormick Woods Golf Course, and Trophy Lake Golf & Casting Club

The Port of Bremerton's two excellent marinas at Port Orchard and Bremerton offer Puget Sound's most varied golf selection. Within a cab ride are Gold Mountain's challenging Olympic and Cascade courses. Near Port Orchard is McCormick Woods Golf Course, a magnificent track ranked high on Washington's top ten lists, and the Trophy Lake Golf & Casting Club with its incredible views and chance to catch a trout.

> *Port of Bremerton:* 800-462-3793; www.portof-bremerton.org; www.goldmt.com; www.mccormick-woodsgolf.com; www.trophylakegolf.com

THE RESORT AT PORT LUDLOW
Port Ludlow Golf Course (shown above)

Port Ludlow's 300-slip marina is a terrific Puget Sound stop for boaters also passionate about golf. The 27-hole Port Ludlow Golf Course, designed by Robert Muir Graves, is consistently rated as one of the best resort courses in the

country by *Golf Digest* and *Golf* magazines.
　　The Resort at Port Ludlow: 877-805-0868;
www.portludlow-resort.com

SEMIAHAMOO RESORT
Semiahmoo Golf & Country Club and Loomis Trails Golf Club

Imagine a place where you can play golf at one of the northwest's top golf courses one day (Semiahmoo Golf & Country Club) and then play a different, equally excellent course the next day (Loomis Trail Golf Club) without ever moving the boat. Plus, you get to do it in a first-class resort where, golfer or not, you have a host of recreational and therapeutic activities. Semiahmoo Resort, located near Blaine, Washington, is just such a place.
　　Semiahmoo Marina: 360-371-0440; semiahmoomarina.com
　　Semiahmoo Resort: 800-770-7992; www.semiahmoo.com

FRIDAY HARBOR, SAN JUAN ISLAND
San Juan Golf & Country Club

Friday Harbor is the busiest town in the San Juan Islands. Combine it with the San Juan Golf & Country Club, one of the islands' best nine-hole courses, and you have a San Juanderer's favorite golf stop. The club is a short taxi ride away from the Port of Friday Harbor.
　　Port of Friday Harbor: 360-378-2688; www.portfridayharbor.org
　　San Juan Golf Club: 360-378-2254; www.sanjuangolfclub.com

BRITISH COLUMBIA

OAK BAY MARINA
Victoria Golf Club

Stay at the Oak Bay Marina on Victoria's east side and walk to the Victoria Golf Club, about half a mile away along Beach Drive. Built in 1893, Victoria Golf Club is Canada's oldest golf club still located at its original site. The course borders the windswept shores of the Strait of Juan de Fuca giving it extraordinary views of passing killer whales, Trial Island, and the Olympic Mountains. To play this private course, you must be a member of a reciprocal golf club or an invited guest of a Victoria Golf Club member. If you have the opportunity, play this course, often called Canada's Pebble Beach North.
　　Oak Bay Marina: 250-598-3369; www.oakbaymarina.com
　　Victoria Golf Club: 250-598-4322; victoriagolf.com

OTTER BAY MARINA, NORTH PENDER ISLAND
Pender Island Golf & Country Club

A rocky flag-decorated point acts as a navigational aid to one of the Gulf Islands' friendliest marinas. From Otter Bay's resort-like grounds you can catch a shuttle bus ride one mile up the hill to the excellent nine-hole Pender Island Golf & Country Club. Breakfast on the clubhouse deck comes with sweeping views of the rolling course and tree covered surrounding hills.

　　Otter Bay Marina: 250-629-3579; www.otterbaymarina.ca
　　Pender Island Golf & Country Club: 250-629-6659;
www.penderislandgolf.com

Pender Island Golf & Country Club

NANAIMO HARBOUR
Nanaimo Golf Club

Nanaimo boasts a spectacular natural and manmade harbor and is an excellent stopover for boaters. Nanaimo Golf Club, just minutes away from the Nanaimo Port Authority boat basin, is one of Vancouver Island's finest all-season golf courses. This semi-private club is located on a hillside overlooking the Strait of Georgia. To score well here, you must stay out of the trees and putt like a magician.
　　Nanaimo Port Authority: 250-754-5053; www.npa.ca
　　Nanaimo Golf Club: 250-758-6332; www.nanaimogolfclub.ca

SCHOONER COVE MARINA, NANOOSE BAY
Fairwinds Golf Club

It takes just five minutes to get from Schooner Cove Marina to Fairwinds Golf Club. It is not a long course, but Fairwinds demands straight drives and accurate irons as Garry oaks and rocky bluffs line the fairways. Throw in 70 sand traps and water hazards on 11 holes and you have a lovely yet tricky target course.
　　Schooner Cove Marina: 800-663-7060; www.fairwinds.ca
　　Fairwinds Golf Club: 888-781-2777; www.fairwinds.ca

BEACH GARDENS RESORT & MARINA, POWELL RIVER
Myrtle Point Golf Club

Northbound boating golfers can squeeze in one more round of golf before wilderness sets in by stopping at Beach Gardens Resort & Marina and playing the cut-from-the-woods championship Myrtle Point Golf Club. Designed by Les Furber, Myrtle Point, with its ocean, mountain and forest scenes, opened to rave reviews in 1991.
　　Beach Gardens Resort & Marina: 800-663-7070;
www.beachgardens.com
　　Myrtle Point Golf Club: 604-487-4653;
www.myrtlepointgolfclub.com

and fields.

Coal mining was attempted in the early 1900s, but the shafts flooded and the effort was abandoned. In the 1920s and 1930s foxes were raised. Horses were kept on Cabbage Island for feed for the foxes. At low tide the horses were brought across the sandbar between the two islands, then slaughtered and butchered. One horse, flesh and bone ground to mash, was consumed every three days.

The land owner who sold Tumbo Island to the reserve has a life tenancy for the house and a small area surrounding the house. If someone is in residence there, please respect their privacy.

The Strait of Georgia is visible from the Cabbage Island anchorage.

(17) **Narvaez Bay (Gulf Islands National Park Reserve).** Picnic tables and toilet, camping in 7 sites, ideal for kayakers. Dogs must be on leash. Beautiful Narvaez Bay indents the rock cliffs on the south shore of Saturna Island, and is open to southeasterly winds and the wakes of passing ship traffic in Boundary Pass. Parts of the bay's shoreline were added to the Gulf Islands National Park Reserve, including the small peninsula parallel to the western shore, a short distance in.

You can anchor in the little bight behind this peninsula and have shelter from wind and waves, although a reader wrote that in a northerly, they experienced williwaw winds of 20+ knots from the head of the bay. The wind in the Strait of Georgia was only 12 knots. The holding ground is not very good. It appears to be loose mud, the kind that washes off easily. It felt like a thin layer on top of rock—fine for a picnic in settled weather, but chancy for overnight.

The neck of land separating the peninsula from the rest of Saturna Island holds the ruins of an ambitious homestead. We didn't find any buildings, although fruit trees and the remnants of fences are there. A dirt service road runs the length of the peninsula and leads up the hill to a main Saturna Island road.

ACTIVE PASS AREA

Active Pass. Active Pass separates Mayne Island and Galiano Island, and has long been one of the most popular fishing areas in the Gulf Islands. It also is the route taken by commercial traffic, including BC Ferries that run between Tsawwassen and Swartz Bay. Currents in Active Pass run to 7 knots on a spring tide.

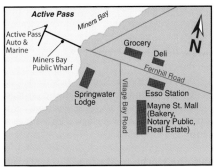

Miners Bay Public Wharf

They flood eastward toward the Strait of Georgia. See the Tide and Current Tables, Vol. 5 or Ports and Passes. Unless your boat is quite fast, slack water passage is recommended. If you are in the current, you can minimize turbulence by sagging into Miners Bay.

Dinner Bay. Dinner Bay, between Crane Point and Dinner Point, looks to be a good anchorage, but is exposed to ferry wakes and northwest winds.

Village Bay. Village Bay is wide and deep, with convenient anchoring depths near the head. The bay is open to northwest winds and waves, but well protected from everything else. Village Bay has a ferry terminal.

Miners Bay. A public wharf is in the bay on the south side of Active Pass, but it is subject to swirling tidal currents and the wakes from passing ferries. Fuel is available at a float alongside the public wharf. Convenient anchoring depths are close to shore—most of the bay is quite deep. The wharf is a Canpass/Nexus-only customs reporting station.

(18) **Active Pass Auto & Marine.** (250) 539-5411; www.activepassautoandmarine.com. Open all year. Propane, stove alcohol, tackle, bait, ice, confectionary with ice cream, marine supplies, haulout and 24-hour towing. Affiliated service station 200 yards from the dock has supplies.

(19) **Sturdies Bay.** Sturdies Bay, on Galiano Island toward the eastern end of Active Pass, is a landing for ferries coming to and from

---

NAMING NAMES

The early explorers got to name all the important places after themselves (Vancouver Island), officers on board (Puget Sound), or important friends back home (Mount Rainier). Many other places were given names adopted from the Indians (Stillaguamish River), or perhaps the first homesteader (Ebey Island). But we found we could name the less prominent places ourselves.

We were cruising in Desolation Sound with two youngsters on board, both named Michael. One was our son, Michael George. The other was Michael Edward Lust, the son of our neighbors across the back alley. With two Mikes on board, we quickly adopted the device of calling them by their middle names.

One day we dinghied to a little rock islet in Malaspina Inlet, and later tried to identify the islet on the chart. We found it didn't have a name. It quickly became George's Rock. The next place we discovered without a name became Edward's Point. In rapid succession over the next few days we discovered, named and officially entered on the chart such places as King Edward Bay, Prince George's Islet, Edward George Point, and George Edward's Reef, among many others.

Soon the kids were poring over the chart and discovering other places to name. Of course, we had to land on each rock or beach and officially declare its name, and then ceremoniously enter the name on the chart. Officialdom never recognized our efforts, so our names don't appear on anybody else's charts. But we decided that as explorers we had just as much right to name places as Capt. George Vancouver did. Those names still appear on an old, wrinkled, coffee-stained chart that lives in the bottom of the chart drawer.

– Tom Kincaid

Tsawwassen. A public float is alongside the ferry dock. The community of Sturdies Bay, just up the road, has a grocery store, shops and a post office. Galiano Oceanfront Inn & Spa is located there and has its own dock.

⑲ **Galiano Oceanfront Inn & Spa.** 134 Madrona Drive, Galiano Island, BC V0N 1P0; (250) 539-3388; info@galianoinn.com; www.galianoinn.com. Located in Sturdies Bay, north of the ferry landing. Open all year but dock in place May to October only, call for exact dates. Wi-Fi, but no power or water on the dock. The dock is subject to wakes from passing ferries in Active Pass. Set fenders accordingly. Reasonable dock rates; free if using spa, restaurant, or inn.

This is a high quality inn and spa, with casual fine dining, natural spa, and gardens. Pizza from a wood-fired oven is served for lunch and early dinner from a pizza terrace overlooking the bay (seasonal). Village shops are a block away with more choices for din-ing and shopping. The inn has year-round Smart Car rentals. A complimentary shuttle runs to and from Montague Harbour. If you're in Montague Harbour and want to dine at Galiano Oceanfront Inn, call for reservations, (250) 539-3388.

The Kunamokst Mural from the 2010 Olympic games is displayed in the Inn. The mural is made from individual tiles, each independently illustrated by a different artist. Collectively they form an image of an orca whale and calf. It's quite striking.

Whaler Bay. Whaler Bay is on the east side of Galiano Island, just north of Active Pass. It is full of rocks and shoal water. Enter carefully through a rock-strewn passage from the south, or through a more open passage around the north end of Gossip Island. Whaler Bay has a public wharf. Good protection is near the wharf, but there's very little swinging room.

Whaler Bay Public Wharf. (250) 539-2264. Open all year, 350 feet of dock space, no facilities except garbage drop. Commercial fishing vessels have priority.

MAYNE ISLAND, CAMPBELL BAY TO HORTON BAY

Campbell Bay. Campbell Bay, on the northeast side of Mayne Island, is entered between Edith Point and Campbell Point. It is open to southeasterly winds, but has anchoring depths near the head, mud bottom.

Bennett Bay (Gulf Islands National Park Reserve). Bennett Bay, south of Campbell Point, has good anchorage but is exposed to southeast winds. Curlew Island and Samuel Island are privately owned.

Note: Campbell Point, a portion of the waters of Bennett Bay, Georgeson Island, and the Belle Chain Islets including Anniversary Island, are part of Gulf Islands National Park Reserve. To protect sensitive ecosystems, access to Georgeson Island and the islets is prohibited.

SALTSPRING ISLAND, FULFORD HARBOUR TO LONG HARBOUR

Russell Island (Gulf Islands National Park Reserve). Russell Island is just outside Fulford Harbour. Anchor on the northwest side of the island, fair holding, with views of mountains above Fulford Harbour. A trail leads through open meadows and a forest of Douglas fir, arbutus (madrona) and Garry oak. The original house dates back more than a century. A caretaker lives on the island. A boater we trust reports, "Russell Island is wonderful!"

Fulford Harbour. Fulford Harbour is wide and open. Fulford Village, a public wharf, and the Fulford Harbour Marina (closed) are near the head, all adjacent to the ferry landing. A 52-foot-long public float is on the outside of the ferry terminal. It is exposed and has no services, and is used mostly for loading and unloading.

The charming village has a good grocery store (Salt Spring Mercantile), and an assortment of art galleries and stores specializing in crafts and country clothing. Everything feels very "island."

By all means take a 15-minute walk down the road to St. Paul's Catholic church (called the Stone Church), built in 1880. The graveyard, with island history chiseled into its headstones, is adjacent. On one visit we found the church's door unlocked, and stepped inside. It was lovely. "This is where God lives," we thought.

Bus transportation: Regular bus service on Saltspring Island connects Fulford Village, Ganges, Long Harbour, Vesuvius and Fernwood. For schedule see www.busonline.ca; (250) 537-6758.

Fulford Harbour Marina. #5-2810 Fulford-Ganges Rd., Salt Spring Island, BC V8K

ZACHARY ROCK

In 2007 one of our loyal Waggoner readers sent a note about an uncharted rock he had struck in Ganges Harbour. His sailboat draws 6.5 feet, and the incident occurred on a very low tide. What caught my attention was that the incident occurred about 50 feet from the Ganges Marina, in the middle of the likely approach route to Ganges Marina and Saltspring Marina. When I mentioned a possible rock in this area to others, I learned that deeper-draft sailboats had been bumping into it for some time.

We were scheduled to be in Ganges on September 12, when a low tide of 4.5 feet was predicted for 11:58 a.m. Our then 11-year-old grandson Zachary would be with us on this trip. It would be a good experience for Zachary. He could do some exploring and see firsthand the kind of research that goes into nautical charts.

At noon, Zachary, grandma Marilynn and I were in the dinghy, bouncing the leadline in the suspected area. Bump, bump: three fathoms, no rock. Bump, bump: no rock. Then bump, bump, BUMP: a little less than 12 feet. We'd found the rock. It was about 50 feet off C dock, the first dock behind the Ganges Marina floating breakwater.

We looked over the side, and through the water we saw it down there, partly exposed rock, partly mud. So, how big was it? We dropped the leadline off to all sides and the depths increased. The rock certainly isn't an isolated boulder, but as navigation hazards go the rock isn't all that big. It definitely isn't as big as Money Maker's Rock.

Our old Magellan GPS gave us a lat/lon location of 48°51.410'N/123°29.925'W. I don't know how reliable GPS was that day. The coordinates are close, but may be off slightly. The leadline, with knots tied every fathom (6 feet), suggested a least depth that day of around 10 feet. If we subtract 4.5 feet to reduce the depth to zero tide, we get 5.5 feet at zero tide. This would call for a + sign on the chart, meaning dangerous rock less than 2 meters beneath the surface. It would explain why our reader's boat, which draws 6.5 feet, hit on a low tide.

Clearly, sailboats need to be cautious in this area, especially at low water. Most powerboats draw less than 4 feet, which would put them clear of the rock, even on a zero tide. At high tide, everyone will clear.

Rocks don't have to be named, but many are. Since grandson Zachary was part of the exploration and helped run the leadline, the Waggoner will call it (drum roll, please) *Zachary Rock*.

— *Robert Hale*

1Z2; (250) 653-4467. Because of storm damage, no guest moorage until further notice.

Harbour Authority of Saltspring Island Fulford Harbour Wharf. Open all year, 120 feet of dock space with transient moorage on outer wharf.

Isabella Island (Gulf Islands National Park Reserve). A smallish anchorage is available behind Isabella Island, a short distance west of the mouth of Fulford Harbour. Although exposed to the west, it's a cozy little spot for one or two boats. Anchor in 24 feet.

Ruckle Park. Beaver Point on Saltspring Island. Open all year, day use and overnight camping. No mooring facilities, exposed anchorage on each side of Ruckle Point. Probably the best of these anchorages is in the first cove south of Ruckle Point. Swinging room is limited, and the cove is exposed to ferry wakes and southeast winds. The anchorage is pretty, though, and in settled weather could be a good day stop. This is an extensive park, with miles of shoreline and rocky headlands. Walk-in campsites. Great views of the southern Gulf Islands.

LOCAL KNOWLEDGE

ENTRANCE CHANNEL: There's only one safe way to get into Ganges by water, and that is to leave all the Chain Islands to starboard. This will put you in a safe fairway, amply wide and easily run. Do not cut through any of the islands, either. No short-cuts. Money Makers Reef, which extends northwest from Third Sister Island, is well-named, but Money Makers Reef is not the only problem. "It's a minefield out there," as one local put it.

The entry channel itself can be a minefield, too. It's filled with crab pot floats, and you have to pay attention every inch of the way to avoid them.

⑳ Ganges. Ganges, at the head of Ganges Harbour, is recommended. Marinas, good anchorage, and a bustling seaside village with shops, galleries, restaurants (including the exquisite Hastings House), a large Thrifty Foods supermarket (with dinghy dock), and Mouat's, a huge old hardware and house goods general store, plus separate gift shop and apparel store. The sprawling Salt Spring Island Saturday Market, also called the Farmers Market, is held in Centennial Park at Grace Point on Saturdays 8:30 a.m. to 3:30 p.m., mid-March through October.

While boats and tourists are important to summer trade, Ganges is not just a summer resort village. It's a bustling center of year-round local commerce.

The area is covered by Beacon/BBX Wi-Fi. Boats can anchor out in the bay or tie up at Saltspring Marina, Ganges Marina, or the town's Kanaka Wharf. Larger vessels might side-tie along the floating breakwater, 240 feet

Ganges during the summer. Kanaka Wharf, Ganges Marina, Saltspring Marina are in upper part. Harbour Authority docks, far left, are filled with local boats. Ample room to anchor.

long and 24 feet wide, that extends into the bay from the Coast Guard dock. An airplane float and pumpout station are on the breakwater. A ramp leads to shore. Because of the breakwater's high freeboard, it is best-suited to larger boats. If the wind blows (especially a southeasterly), expect some movement.

The Saltspring Island Sailing Club's docks, to port as you approach Grace Point, have some space for reciprocal clubs. It's about a 1-mile walk to town. The Centennial Wharf public dock behind Grace Islet is convenient to town and has some power and water, but usually is packed with resident boats. Off Mouat's, the Kanaka Visitors' Dock has water

and 20 amp power.

Anchoring is popular and there is plenty of room for visiting boats.

In the summer a cute electric-powered launch named *Queen of De Nile* runs between town and Saltspring Marina. It makes shopping at Thrifty Foods more convenient. Thrifty will deliver to the marinas.

More than 40 artists studios are in Ganges and scattered around Saltspring Island. They include artisan cheese makers, bakers, wineries, and now a microbrewery. Rental cars and vans are available at Saltspring Marina. A local map identifies stops, and hours.

Artspring: Locally supported arts and the-

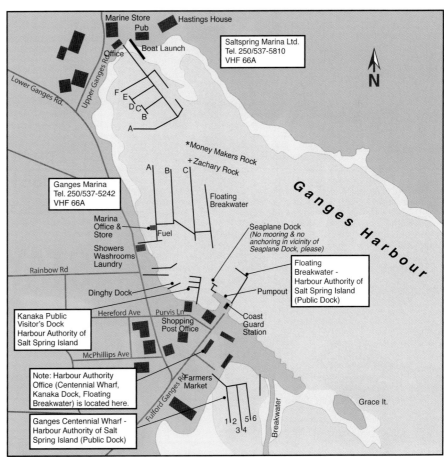

Ganges Harbour

The Salt Spring Island Saturday Market is a Gulf Islands favorite.   *Ganges Marina*

ater, an easy walk from the village. See www. artspring.ca.

Bird sanctuary: While you can anchor a short distance south of the Sailing Club's docks, Walter Bay and the spit that creates it are a sanctuary for black oystercatchers. Please leave the sanctuary area alone.

Golf: Salt Spring Island Golf & Country Club (250) 537-2121. Blackburn Meadows (250) 537-1707. Both courses are 9 holes.

Swimming pool: The recently opened Rainbow Road indoor public pool is an easy walk away. Call (250) 537-1402 for hours.

Bus transportation: Regular bus service on Saltspring Island connects Fulford Village, Ganges, Long Harbour, Vesuvius and Fern-

wood. For schedule see www.busonline.ca; (250) 538-4282.

Taxi: (250) 537-3030; (250) 537-3277
Car rental: (250) 537-3122

THINGS TO DO

1. **Studio Tour**. Map available at the Visitor Centre. Rent a car, van, or moped at the Saltspring Marina and visit some of the 40 artist studios. Most open every weekend.

2. **Salt Spring Island Cheese Company.** See the many steps needed to make artisan cheese. Then taste some 20 different cheeses.

3. **Wine Tasting**. Three wineries on Saltspring Island and they regularly have tastings.

4. **Salt Spring Island Saturday Market**. The largest farmers market in the islands.

5. **Hastings House**. Reserve for an elegant dinner or lunch. Exceptional food and service.

6. **Barb's Buns**. Delicious coffee and fresh baked goods. Bring some back to the boat. Their breakfasts and lunches are also very good.

GANGES & SALT SPRING ISLAND – FOODIE HEAVEN!

Salt Spring Island has been a foodie heaven since the late 1800s. Back then, fresh produce grown on the island was delivered to Hope Bay, where it was loaded on the ferry and shuttled to Vancouver.

Today, Salt Spring Island is home to brewers and vintners, farmers, cheesemakers, artisan bakers, and restaurateurs. If you love delicious food, Salt Spring Island is a fantastic destination.

Farmers Market

Ganges hosts the best farmers market in the Gulf Islands. Each Saturday from March through October, the "Market in the Park" at Centennial Park is open for business. More than 100 vendors sell their wares, ranging from fresh produce to seafood to pastries and crafts. The variety is outstanding and everything is made locally.

Another, smaller, market is held Tuesday afternoons at the same location.

Both markets are perfect places for provisioning. We've found fresh seafood, unusual mushrooms, heirloom tomatoes, ripe melons, berries, a variety of sprouts, and more. Four artisan bakeries—ranging from Rendezvous French Patisserie (superb desserts) to the Salt Spring Island Bread Company and the Bread Lady—attend the market. Fair warning: it's best to go early, since many items sell out by closing time.

Wine and Beer

Salt Spring has three wineries: Garry Oaks Estate Winery, Salt Spring Vineyards, and Mistaken Identity Vineyards. Each has a tasting room.

The wineries are beautiful. Both Garry Oaks and Salt Spring Vineyards require car transportation. Mistaken Identity Vineyards can be reached by walking 1.5 miles up Lower Ganges Road from Saltspring Marina.

Each winery hosts a variety of tasting events throughout the summer, some including food pairings or live music. Check their websites for a schedule of events.

The Sip and Savour festival in September celebrates Salt Spring Island's wineries.

If beer is your preference, stop by one of B.C.'s smallest breweries: Salt Spring Island Ales, outside of Ganges. You can enjoy beer on tap, or pick up a bottle or growler for later. The beer is organic and made with locally grown ingredients—even the hops are from Salt Spring Island.

Restaurants

Hastings House is one of the finest restaurants we've ever dined

at. They've hosted movie stars and sports stars, royalty and heads of state. Almost everything, including bread and crackers, is prepared fresh in their kitchen. They grow many of their ingredients on site, and the garden is open to patrons. We recommend wandering through, either before or after your meal. It's not uncommon to see the chef gathering herbs, fruits, or vegetables.

An optional cocktail hour in the Manor House precedes dinner. Recommended.

Just down the street is Harbour House hotel, which includes a restaurant and organic farm. Visitors to the farm are welcome. Enter through the wooden gate off the back parking lot. Be sure the gate closes behind you so the goats don't escape. Inside, three acres of raised beds, greenhouses, berry bushes, and fruit trees line the hillside. To the right is the chicken coop, filled with healthy, free-range chickens. Up the hill, in an old cabin, garlic dries in the sun. Trays of fresh-picked onions sit near the cabin's entry. Bees produce fresh honey.

This is a 2.3-acre garden producing fresh produce. A staff of 3-6 people manages three plantings throughout the year. The garden yields more than Harbour House can use, so they sell their products to many other restaurants on the island.

The farm honor stand, in the back of the parking lot near the entrance to the gardens, is open from 9:30 a.m. to 3:00 p.m. Pick out your favorite fruits and vegetables, baked goods, jams or even fresh eggs, total your bill, and leave money in the jar. If you visit Ganges when the farmers market isn't operating, this is an alternative.

The passion and commitment of the owners, chef, and staff of Harbour House comes through in the ever-changing menu for their restaurant. The chef and farm staff together plan plantings and arrange when crops will be harvested. A meal at Harbour House will send you into Foodie Heaven.

Other restaurants in Ganges get into the foodie spirit, too. Barb's Buns, Pomodoro Pizza, the Treehouse, Auntie Pesto's, the Salt Spring Inn, the three different places for sushi…they're *all* good.

Still hungry?

If you're willing to travel beyond walking distance from Ganges, another world opens up. Salt Spring Auto Rentals (250 537-3122) provides maps highlighting more than 40 destinations on Salt Spring Island. Many of these places are artisan food businesses, ranging from cheese makers to beekeepers.

One of our favorites is Salt Spring Island Cheese Company, near Fulford Harbour. A tour includes petting the goats and sampling some of their 20+ cheeses in a tasting room overlooking the production area. Afterword, customers can relax at outdoor tables and enjoy goat milk gelato.

Salt Spring Island's wide variety of food producers and restaurants, and their consistently high quality, make it the ideal destination for foodie boaters.

— Mark Bunzel

SALT SPRING ISLAND & GANGES HARBOUR MARKETPLACE

RESTAURANTS & SHOPS

SONIA STUDIO

At the Studio, find handcrafted, unique, chic, fun, functional aprons for the big and little chef, ladies handbags and totes for all occasions, and home décor. Product also at Waterfront Gallery, Art Craft and Winter Craft in Ganges. Studio Tour Map. Open daily 11-5

142 Woodland Dr. Salt Spring Island • 250-931-8215
www.soniastudio.ca

MISTAKEN IDENTITY VINEYARDS

Easy walking distance from marinas, friendly wine tasting experiences, licensed picnic grass area, local organic cheeses, crackers, and olives. Family, pet and bicycle friendly. Southern exposure patio overlooking vineyard. Call or see website for hours & events.

250-538-9463 • 164 Norton Rd., Salt Spring Island
www.mistakenidentityvineyards.com

LI READ SEA TO SKY PREMIER PROPERTIES

You love boating among the Gulf Islands. See Li Read to find your new dream home port. Visit Li for what is for sale, an island map and market conditions. Office located across the street from Ganges Marina, Salt Spring Island. Welcome!

250-537-7647 • LiRead33@Gmail.com
www.LiRead.com

BLACK SHEEP BOOKS

We are an independent, locally-owned shop dedicated to books and the people who love them. Here you will find two floors packed with volumes of enduring value, including familiar favorites, contemporary fiction, guides, books of local interest, and non-fiction titles covering everything from outer space to inner peace. We also have marine charts, art cards, unique prints, hand-crafted bags, and many other intriguing items.

250-538-0025 • Grace Point Square, Ganges Village

MOUAT'S CLOTHING CO.

Chart your course to Mouat's Clothing Co., a landmark business that offers an outstanding collection of clothing and footwear for landlubber and seafaring men and women. Located steps away from "The Dinghy Dock" this shopping destination always delights. We deliver to marinas.

250-537-5593 • 106 Fulford Ganges Rd.
www.mouatsclothingco.com

SALT SPRING ADVENTURES

We offer Kayak Day/Multi-Day Tours and Rentals, Bicycle and SUP Board Rentals, Mobile Yoga and Sailing. Come Adventure in the Gulf Islands with us!

www.saltspringadventures.com • 877-537-2764

SALT SPRING INN

A heritage site in Ganges Village, and one of Salt Spring Island's finest restaurants, offering seven tastefully appointed guest rooms. The Inn is steps away from the popular Saturday Market, many shops, galleries, cafés and marinas.

250-537-9339 • 132 Lower Ganges Rd.
www.saltspringinn.com

MOBY'S PUB

Moby's Pub offers a comfortable atmosphere. The friendly staff, great food, legendary live entertainment, waterfront patio, and excellent location make Moby's the best place on Salt Spring Island to meet people.

250-537-5559 • 124A Upper Ganges Rd.
www.mobyspub.ca • mobyspub@gmail.com

FRENCH COUNTRY FABRIC CREATIONS

We have taken a corner from the south of France and brought it home to Saltspring Island. Cotton fabrics from Provence, soft furnishings, table and bed linens. Hand bags, coated tablecloths and tapestries. Contact us for your pickup & return. Open Daily 10am -- 5pm

250-537-9865 • 109 Broadwell Rd. Saltspring Island
www.frenchcountryfabrics@shaw.ca

Salt Spring Island Community Calendar

Saturday Market March-October

All Summer Long
111 Nights of Music Under the Stars
Art Craft
ArtSpring Summer Performances

April
Salt Spring Blooms in April
Easter Art Tour

May
Round Salt Spring Sailing Race

June
Sea Capers

July
Canada Day Festivities
Classic Car Show
Lavendar Festival

August
Fulford Day Festival
Firefly Lantern Festival
Working Boat Festival

September
Pride Weekend
Fall Fair Weekend
Sip & Savour Salt Spring
Apple Festival

October
Harvest Grape Stomp

December
Christmas on Salt Spring
Christmas Craft Fairs:
WinterCraft at Mahon Hall
Beaver Point Hall
Fulford Hall

For more information contact:
Salt Spring Island Chamber of Commerce.
www.SaltSpringTourism.com • 250-537-4223

The Hastings House gardens are outstanding.

⑳ **Harbour Authority of Saltspring Island Ganges Centennial Wharf Boat Harbour.** 127 Fulford Ganges Road, Salt Spring Island, BC V8K 2T9; (250) 537-5711. This is the Grace Point facility. Open all year with 1070 feet of breakwater-protected dock space, 30 amp power, washrooms, showers, launch ramp, garbage collection, waste oil disposal, Beacon/BBX Wi-Fi. Telephone at dock. Mostly commercial and permanent boats; not much room for visitor boats.

⑳ **Kanaka Public Visitors Wharf.** Immediately north of the floating breakwater. Managed by the Harbour Authority of Saltspring Island. Has 1400 feet of visitor moorage May to September, water, 30 amp power, pumpout. Beacon/BBX Wi-Fi, and Wi-Fi from nearby cafés. Pay in the drop box at the head of the docks or at the office at Centenial Wharf. Office takes credit cards.

LOCAL KNOWLEDGE

TWO DANGEROUS ROCKS: A rock, 5 to 6 feet deep at zero tide, is approximately 50 feet off the end of C dock at Ganges Marina.

Money Makers Rock, a short distance off the Saltspring Marina entrance, is marked by two buoys. The rock is about 50 feet long, more like a short reef than a rock. Approach the Saltspring Marina on either side of the two buoys, not between them.

⑳ **Ganges Marina.** 161 Lower Ganges Road, Salt Spring Island, BC V8K 2L6; (250) 537-5242; gangesmarina@shaw.ca; www.ganges-marina.com. Monitors VHF 66A. Open all year, gasoline, diesel and limited lubricants at fuel dock, ample guest moorage. Facilities include 30 & 50 amp power, washrooms, showers, laundry, Wi-Fi, garbage drop. Groceries, restaurants, propane, and other services nearby.

A floating breakwater, 500 feet long and 24 feet wide, can handle vessels to 200 feet.

Renovations continue to repair, replace, and improve the docks at the Ganges Marina.

⑳ **Saltspring Marina.** 124 Upper Ganges Rd., Salt Spring Island, BC V8K 2S2; (250) 537-5810; (800) 334-6629; www.saltspring-marina.com. Monitors VHF 66A. Guest moorage for all sizes of boats, 15 & 30 amp power, washrooms, showers, laundry, water, ice, recycling and garbage drop, free Wi-Fi, concrete launch ramp. No long term parking.

Facilities include Moby's Pub (restaurant, take-out & offsales), Rendezvous Bakery, Harbours End full-service repairs and haulout to 40 feet. Car, van, scooter, bicycle, and kayak rentals. Fishing charters, sailing excursions, and whale watching. Harbor shuttle to the village aboard the electric powered *Queen of*

Departing Glenthorne Passage anchorage through the narrow pass between Secret Island and Glenthorne Point (Prevost Island).

A stunning sunset from Montague Harbour's Gray Peninsula.

De Nile during summer months.

For several years Saltspring Marina has been going through a challenging permitting process for new docks. Each year it appears things may start. Permitting was completed in 2013. The plan is to start construction of a new breakwater in 2014, and new expanded docks in 2015. Check www.WaggonerGuide.com for updates.

Long Harbour. Long Harbour lies parallel to Ganges Harbour,

but is much narrower. The ferry from Tsawwassen lands there. Good anchorage is beyond the ferry dock, taking care not to anchor over a charted cable crossing. Royal Vancouver Yacht Club has an outstation in Long Harbour.

PREVOST ISLAND

㉑ **Prevost Island.** Prevost Island is a favorite of many. Annette Inlet and Glenthorne Passage, on the northwest end, are particularly

attractive. The bays indenting from the southeast also look inviting, but with a southeaster always possible and with ferry traffic flying by in Swanson Channel, they might get a little lumpy.

Acland Islands. The passage between the Acland Islands and Prevost Island a pleasant and scenic anchorage, with dramatic sheer rock walls on the Prevost Island side. Anchor in 25 to 35 feet with enough room to swing, or stern-tie to Acland Island.

Glenthorne Passage. Glenthorne Passage is the westernmost of the northern bays on Prevost Island. Well protected anchorage in 15 to 30 feet, good holding. Even though cabins line Secret Island, the surroundings are agreeable and the anchorage is popular. In summer months the sun sets in the narrow passage between Glenthorne Point and Secret Island. The cover of this edition of the Waggoner was shot in Glenthorne Passage.

Annette Inlet. Annette Inlet is a little wider than Glenthorne Passage, with few houses and a good sandy beach at the head. As you approach, note the charted rock that dries 0.9 meter, off the mouth of the inlet. A rock at the point is marked by a small, private beacon. Approach from the Glenthorne Passage side and wrap around the point, leaving the beacon to starboard. The head of the bay shoals to drying flats. Anchor in 8 feet (zero tide) anywhere, gray mud bottom. Southeast winds can blow across the low swale separating Annette Inlet from Ellen Bay on the other side of Prevost Island, but there isn't enough fetch to build waves.

Selby Cove & James Bay. A house and dock are on the right side as you enter **Selby Cove**. Anchor in 18 feet and be sure of your set. We found poor holding in one spot. **James Bay** is the most northeast bay, open to northwesterlies. It is a little deep for anchoring until close to the head. The lands surrounding James Bay and a portion of the north shore of Selby Cove are part of Gulf Islands National Park Reserve, as are the lands surrounding Richardson Bay and the Portlock Point light station at the southeast corner of Prevost Island. Ferries do not serve Prevost Island, thus it is less populated than the larger islands.

MONTAGUE HARBOUR

㉒ **Montague Harbour.** *No Discharge Zone.* Gray water okay. Montague Harbour is a popular stopping spot in the central Gulf Islands. It is well protected and has an outstanding marine park. Depending on wind direction, you can find good anchorages around the bay.

Entry is unobstructed, either from the southeast, past Phillimore Point, or from the northwest, between Parker Island and Gray Peninsula.

Caution: A shoal extends southeast from the tip of Gray Peninsula into Montague Harbour. We've seen a boat thoroughly grounded on that shoal, awaiting a rising tide. Continue well into the harbor before turning east to anchor or pick up a mooring.

Montague Harbour will hold a huge number of boats. We have anchored there during high season surrounded by more than 100 boats, yet no one was crowded. If you are anchored out or tied to a buoy, leave the dinghy at the pub-

TOMMY TRANSIT

Tommy Transit, better known as Tommy T, is the most entertaining bus driver we've ever met.

Many years ago, after a couple of tough turns in life, Tommy decided to drive a transit bus in Vancouver, B.C. As a bus driver, Tommy realized he interacted with thousands of people every day. He aimed to make his passengers' lives better. He talked, joked, commented, and related to his customers. He made the bus commute fun, with snappy comments to his passengers and off the wall announcements to the entire bus. "That is a beautiful necklace you are wearing…" to the elderly woman struggling to get on the bus with her bags. "You are a sharp dresser," to the man in the suit.

This went on for years. Tommy's charm and wit brought happiness to his passengers and himself. He became a folk hero in Vancouver, appearing on TV and in newspaper articles.

Now "retired," Tommy drives the Hummingbird Pub bus on Galiano Island. The Hummingbird Pub bus is somewhat of an institution in Montague Harbour, shuttling customers from the marina and provincial park to the Hummingbird Pub. It's always been quirky, but Tommy has added his own twist.

Tommy greets each passenger with a big smile as they board the bus. His long gray hair flows out from under a large hat, and a Hawaiian shirt and bright red gloves establish a casual, relaxed vibe.

Soon the music begins. For an old school bus, the Hummingbird Pub Bus has a pretty awesome sound system. As the bus rolls on, Tommy hands back tambourines, maracas, shakers and even spoons. Passengers pass them around and start playing. A percussion section is mounted above Tommy's drivers seat, with cymbals, cowbells and drum boxes. Tommy drives with a drum stick in one hand, steering down the winding island road with the other.

Pretty soon the whole bus is playing along with Tommy. He quips and comments over the PA system. At one point he stops and fakes the bus stalling. Then an engine grinds to a start and the lead-in to Natalie Cole's classic song, "Pink Cadillac" blares through the speakers. The bus goes wild with percussion and rhythm.

All too soon the bus pulls to a stop at the Hummingbird Pub. Not to worry, though, since there's always the return ride.

---

lic dock, next to Montague Harbour Marina. Don't leave it at the marina. The marina has a fuel dock, store and seasonal restaurant.

Dining: Everybody enjoys the Hummingbird Inn Pub. In 2009 the Hummingbird received its restaurant license, so it's now family friendly. A visit to Hummingbird Pub begins with a memorable ride on the Hummingbird Pub bus. Catch the bus on the road above the marina, about 300 yards to the right to the intersection. Check the Hummingbird Pub website or signs at the marina for the scheduled times for bus pick-up.

For non-pub dining walk about one-half mile on Montague Road to La Berengerie Restaurant & Cafe Boheme. This is a French country inn in a wooded setting, offering a full restaurant and fine dining inside. Outside is lively Cafe Boheme with a more casual atmosphere and Mediterranean-Asian food. Open year round on weekends and 7 days a week in July and August.

㉒ **Montague Harbour Marine Park.** Montague Harbour Marine Park, at the north end of Montague Harbour, is beautiful and very popular. The park is open all year. It has excellent white sand beaches on the south side and astonishing rock beaches on the north and west sides. If you walk along the beach on the north side, opposite the head of the lagoon, you'll find a midden full of shells. There's no hint of the midden on the trail above, but it's obvious from the beach. A tiny, secluded beach is on Gray Peninsula, facing Parker Island. The park has walk-in campsites and toilets. A

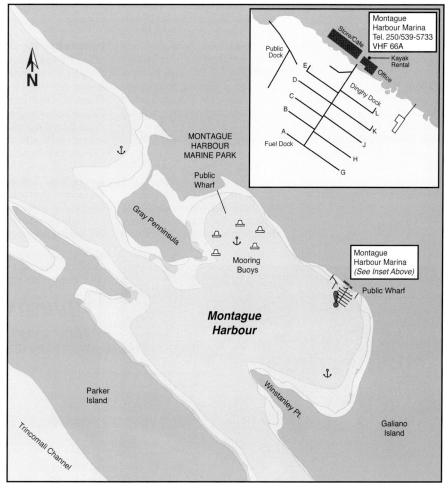

Montague Harbour Marine Park

dinghy dock and 300-foot-long mooring float extend into Montague Harbour, and approximately 35 mooring buoys are off the dock. The park has anchorage for many boats on both sides of Gray Peninsula, depending on wind direction.

㉒ **Montague Harbour Marina.** S17, C-57, RR #1, Galiano Island, BC V0N 1P0; (250) 539-5733; www.montagueharbour.com. Moorage open year-round. Canpass/Nexus-only customs clearance. Gasoline and diesel at the fuel dock, open May 1 to Sept. 30 and Saturdays during the winter from 10:00 a.m. to 2:00 p.m.

Facilities include guest moorage, 15 & 30 amp power, Wi-Fi, moped and kayak rentals, washrooms (but no showers because of severe water constraints), store, gift shop, and charts.

This is a popular stop. The store has convenience foods and ice cream cones, along with high-quality souvenir T-shirts and sweatshirts. The Sea Blush Cafe is licensed and has dining on the deck. Closed during the winter.

㉒ **Montague Harbour Public Wharf.** Open all year, 160 feet of dock space, no facilities. Tie dinghies here if not doing marina business.

Walker Hook. Walker Hook, on the west side of Trincomali Channel, has a beautiful beach on its eastern shore where it connects with Saltspring Island. Anchor in 24 feet. An approach between Atkins Reef and Saltspring Island takes the worry out of identifying just where the various rocks are.

Fernwood Public Wharf. Located on the Trincomali Channel side of Saltspring Island north of Walker Hook, opposite Victoria Shoal and just south of Wallace Island. Open all year, 44 feet of dock space, no facilities. Correspondents Fred and Judy Triggs visited and say they'd stop again. They enjoyed the locals who came down to visit, and concluded, "A pleasant and unexpected surprise was the Fernwood Road Café, located at the head of the pier, 50 meters up the road. Well stocked, good bakery items, sandwiches and pizza - excellent food." We visited last season, and agree.

SAANICH INLET

Saanich Inlet extends south into Vancouver Island for about 12 miles. The northern part of the inlet is fairly civilized, especially along the Saanich Peninsula shore to Brentwood Bay, where Butchart Gardens is located. For a beautiful and often-overlooked trip, continue south through Squally Reach and Finlayson Arm. Boat traffic usually is minimal.

Holding tank pumpout service: Pumpty-Dumpty, a mobile pumpout boat, serves the Brentwood Bay/Butchart Gardens area of Saanich Inlet. Because of a sill at the mouth of the inlet, Saanich Inlet does not exchange its water well and is growing increasingly lifeless along the bottom. Saanich Inlet is not a good place to pump overboard. Contact Pumpty-Dumpty at (250) 480-9292 or VHF 16 and 66A.

Restricted area: In Saanich Inlet, Area Whiskey Delta (WD) is restricted when the government is conducting certain operations. Listen to the continuous marine broadcast or call the Coast Guard

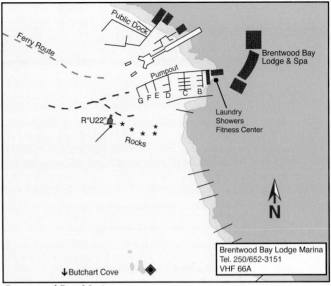

Brentwood Bay Marina

on VHF 83 to ensure the area is not restricted before entering.

Deep Cove. Wain Rock, with good water on both sides, lies about 0.2 mile off Moses Point. The remains of a public wharf are in the south part of the cove. The float was removed in 1978 and only the unused pier remains. Deep Cove Marina is adjacent to this pier.

Patricia Bay. Patricia Bay, locally called Pat Bay, is open, but all the facilities are reserved for the Canadian Government's Institute of Ocean Sciences. It is here that the Canadian Hydrographic Service develops and maintains charts and related publications for western Canada and the Arctic.

Coles Bay. Coles Bay is east of Yarrow Point. It is good for temporary anchorage but open to southerly winds. If approaching from the north, the Canadian

Small Craft Guide recommends that you give Dyer Rocks, off Yarrow Point, a 0.5-mile berth to avoid shoals extending south from the rocks.

LOCAL KNOWLEDGE

DANGEROUS ROCKS: A reef, marked by red nun buoy *U22*, is a short distance off the Brentwood Bay ferry dock. Approach Brentwood Bay Resort & Marina from the north, leaving buoy *U22* to starboard. Dangerous rocks lie on the other side of the buoy, and west and south of the lodge's docks. Locals report that these rocks are hit frequently.

㉓ **Brentwood Bay.** Although Brentwood Bay can be entered on either side of Senanus Island, prawn trap floats often clog the water between the north end of the island and Henderson Point.

Montague Harbour Marina has shops, restaurant and an ice cream bar.

The Brentwood Bay Marina is located next to the dock for the ferry to Mill Bay.

Butchart Gardens can be visited by boat or dinghy from Brentwood Bay.

Best to leave Senanus Island to port. The Mill Bay ferry departs a short distance south of Sluggett Point.

The village up at the highway has some shopping. Moorage is at Brentwood Bay Resort & Marina and Brentwood Bay Public Wharf.

㉓ **Brentwood Bay Resort & Marina.** 849 Verdier Ave., Brentwood Bay, BC V8W 1C5; (250) 652-3151; (888) 544-2079; marina@ brentwoodbayresort.com; www.brentwood-bayresort.com. The marina has 25 slips of guest and side-tie moorage for vessels to 100 feet, 15, 30 & 50 amp power, water, wash-rooms, laundry, pumpout (fee charged), free garbage, recycling, showers, adult pool with drinks and pub food service, sushi and sake bar, cold beer & wine off-sales in the pub, and free Wi-Fi. Reservations recommended.

This is a five-star rated resort and spa, with excellent views of Saanich Inlet, beautiful landscaping, a pub, and the casual Seagrille Seafood & Sushi restaurant. The docks have been improved and electrical power and lighting have been upgraded. A water shuttle makes runs to Butchart Gardens. They also offer kayak, canoe, and stand-up paddleboard rentals, guided diving trips, and eco-adventure tours.

㉓ **Angler's Anchorage Marina.** (250) 652-3531. Call before taking a slip. Mostly permanent moorage.

Nearby Blue's Bayou Café has Cajun/ Creole style food with views of the marina. Open for lunch and dinner, reservations recommended (250) 544-1194.

㉓ **Brentwood Bay Public Wharf.** On the north side of the ferry dock. Open all year, 72 feet of dock, no facilities.

㉓ **Butchart Gardens.** 800 Benvenuto Avenue, Brentwood Bay, BC V8M 1J8; (250) 652-5256; (866) 652-4422; www.butchart-gardens.com. Locally named **Butchart Cove** just outside the mouth of Tod Inlet is the back door to the celebrated and astonishing Butchart Gardens. The Gardens are a must-see attraction. They are lighted at night, creating

an entirely different effect from the day. On Saturday evenings during the summer a fire-works display is held on a large field in the gardens. Many people arrive early and have a picnic dinner while waiting for darkness. Bring blankets, cushions, and folding chairs or camp stools. Even for jaded viewers, it's worth the trip. The most interesting fireworks are done at ground level accompanied by music—you have to be at the field for the full experience.

The Gardens' dinghy dock is in tiny Butchart Cove, with 5 mooring buoys for overnighting yachts. Eyes for stern-ties are set into the rock wall. Most visitors put the anchor down in adjacent Tod Inlet and go by dinghy to the dinghy dock.

Tod Inlet. *No Discharge Zone.* Tod Inlet reaches back behind Butchart Gardens into Gowlland Tod Provincial Park, and has ample anchoring room. Anchor in water deeper than 20 feet to protect eel grass. Green can Buoy *U21* marks a rock. Leave it to port when entering. The inlet is narrow when seen from Brentwood Bay, but opens somewhat after a bend. In the narrow sections you should plan to run a stern-tie to shore. Boats in the more open sections around the bend often can swing without a stern-tie. On Saturday nights the inlet is crowded with boats that come to see the fireworks display at the Gardens.

The dinghy dock and nature house in Tod Inlet are run by First Nations students. Tod Inlet Nature House is open June to September and is free. Our friend Bruce Campbell recom-mends it. Correspondent Pat Shera reports that miles of forested hiking trails are accessible from the head of the inlet.

Finlayson Arm. Goldstream Boathouse is located at the head of Finlayson Arm, at the edge of drying flats off the mouth of the Goldstream River. The shoal water seems to be extending farther north, so come in close to the docks. If the approach is made from mid-channel, an unsuspecting skipper could find his ship aground.

㉔ **Goldstream Boathouse.** 3540 Trans-Canada Hwy, Victoria, BC V9B 6H6; (250) 478-4407; admin@goldstreamboathousema-

rina.com; www.goldstreamboathousemarina. com. Open all year, gasoline and diesel at fuel dock. Minimal guest moorage available. Much of the space is taken with resident boats, so it's best to call ahead. Complete repair facility and haulout to 55 feet, small chandlery, 2-lane concrete launch ramp, 15, 30 & 50 amp power, washrooms, no showers.

㉕ **Mill Bay.** Mill Bay is a good anchorage. The west shore provides a lee from the usual summer west or northwest winds. The bay is, however, open to southeast winds.

㉕ **Mill Bay Marina.** 740 Handy Road, Mill Bay, BC V0R 2P1; (250) 743-4303; contact@ millbaymarina.ca; www.millbaymarina.ca. Mill

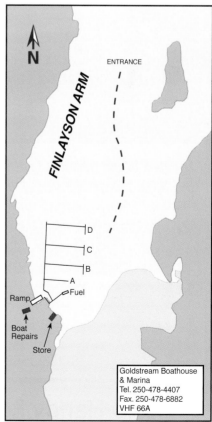

Goldstream Boathouse

On a clear day, Mt. Baker is visible from Mill Bay Marina.

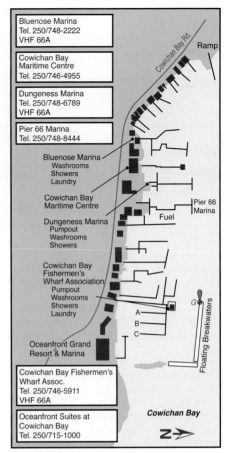

Bluenose Marina
Tel. 250/748-2222
VHF 66A

Cowichan Bay
Maritime Centre
Tel. 250/746-4955

Dungeness Marina
Tel. 250/748-6789
VHF 66A

Pier 66 Marina
Tel. 250/748-8444

Bluenose Marina
Washrooms
Showers
Laundry

Cowichan Bay
Maritime Centre

Dungeness Marina
Pumpout
Washrooms
Showers

Cowichan Bay
Fishermen's
Wharf Association
Pumpout
Washrooms
Showers
Laundry

Oceanfront Grand
Resort & Marina

Cowichan Bay Fishermen's
Wharf Assoc.
Tel. 250/746-5911
VHF 66A

Oceanfront Suites at
Cowichan Bay
Tel. 250/715-1000

Cowichan Bay Rd.

Ramp

Pier 66
Marina

Fuel

Floating Breakwaters

A
B
C

Cowichan Bay

N

Cowichan Bay

Bay Marina is now open after major renovations. The results are beautiful. New docks with 700 feet of transient moorage accommodate boats to 150 feet, 30 & 50 amp power, free Wi-Fi, water, gasoline, diesel, pumpout, laundry, showers. Reservations recommended in season.

Picnic tables and propane barbecues for guest use are on the docks. The Bridgemans Bistro restaurant is open for lunch and dinner and is a hit with locals and visitors alike. A small convenience store has espresso and breakfast, lunch, and snack items. The store also has an ATM, marine supplies, and kayak and stand-up paddleboard rentals.

The Mill Bay Shopping Centre is a short walk up the hill. The center has a supermarket, drug store, liquor store, hardware store, and gift stores. Several restaurants and the Visitor Centre are also located there.

A public launch ramp is on the north side of the marina.

㉕ **Mill Bay Public Wharf.** Open all year, 50 feet of dock space, no facilities, commercial fishing vessels have priority.

COWICHAN BAY & GENOA BAY

㉖ **Cowichan Bay.** www.cowichanbay. com. The picturesque waterfront village of Cowichan Bay is located near the southwest corner of Cowichan Bay. The Harbour Authority docks are behind a floating breakwater. The privately owned marinas are west of the public wharf. The expanded Cowichan Bay breakwater increased the size of the boat basin, and some private docks have been reconfigured.

At the other end of town, Hecate Park has a launch ramp with ample trailer storage.

In settled weather anchorage is good outside the breakwater, and we are told crabbing and prawning are good.

The village is full of life. It has numerous shops and businesses, including liquor stores and good restaurants, not one of them part of a major chain. Interesting little shops are tucked away everywhere. The bakery is superb. An excellent fish market is in town, as is an artisan cheese shop. Down at the end of the street, Morning Mist has some of the best ice cream on the coast.

The Cowichan Bay Maritime Centre, built on a wharf extending from shore, has many interesting displays. The new timber frame building was completed in 2012. It's beautiful.

The hotel is open and the pub has been remodeled. Visitors can use the hotel pool for a small charge. A grass tennis court, just like Wimbledon, is 3 miles away.

Water Taxi: The Genoa Bay Shuttle (250-812-7543) provides water taxi service between Genoa Bay Marina and Cowichan Bay Fisherman's Wharf.

㉖ **Cowichan Bay Fishermen's Wharf Association.** P.O. Box 52, Cowichan Bay,

Cowichan Bay Fishermen's Wharf

and diesel at the fuel dock. No transient moorage. Full-size convenience store with liquor store.

㉖ **Dungeness Marina & Rock Cod Cafe.** 1759 Cowichan Bay Rd., Box 51, Cowichan Bay, BC V0R 1N0; (250) 748-6789; info@dungenessmarina.com; dungenessmarina.com. Monitors VHF 66A. Moorage, shower & washroom facilities, 30 amp power, water, pumpout, Wi-Fi. Located just past the fuel dock. Open all year, guest moorage to 90 feet along 250 feet of outside dock and in unoccupied permanent slips. No laundry, but a laundromat is located at the public dock a short distance away. Carrie and Rob Hokanson are the owners. Carrie is one of the most enthusiastic people we know, a one-woman P.R. whirlwind for Cowichan Bay. Give her five minutes and she'll have you a believer.

The Rock Cod Café has very good food. We've heard it has some of the best halibut and chips in the area.

㉖ **Bluenose Marina.** 1765 Cowichan Bay Rd., P.O. Box 40, Cowichan Bay, BC V0R

1N0; (250) 748-2222; deven@ thebluenosemarina.com; www. thebluenosemarina.com. Monitors VHF 66A. Open all year. Guest moorage available, 30 & 50 amp power, washrooms, showers, laundry. Nearby launch ramp, public playground and kayak shop.

The Cow Cafe & Cookhouse serves seafood and steaks. An excellent ice cream shop is on site.

㉗ **Genoa Bay.** Genoa Bay indents the north shore of Cowichan Bay. Anchorage can be found off the marina docks. The Genoa Bay Marina has moorage.

Water Taxi: The Genoa Bay Shuttle (250-812-7543) provides water taxi service between Genoa Bay Marina and Cowichan Bay Fisherman's Wharf for touring the shops of Cowichan Bay village.

㉗ **Genoa Bay Marina.** 5000 Genoa Bay Rd., Duncan, BC V9L 5Y8; (250) 746-7621; (800) 572-6481; genoabay@telus.net; www.genoabaymarina.com. Monitors VHF 66A mid-May through end of October. Open all year, guest moorage in 30 slips and along 1200 feet of dock space, call ahead. Excellent washrooms,

BC V0R 1N0; (250) 746-5911. Monitors VHF 66A. Open all year, 900 feet of dock space for vessels to 100 feet, 30 amp power, Wi-Fi, clean washrooms, laundry, showers, pumpout, garbage drop, waste oil disposal. Short-term shopping stops are encouraged until 2:00 p.m.

㉖ **Oceanfront Suites at Cowichan Bay.** 1681 Cowichan Bay Rd., Cowichan Bay, BC V0R 1N0; (250) 715-1000; info@oceanfrontcowichanbay. com; www.oceanfrontcowichan-

bay.com. Full service resort hotel. Docks for guests and patrons, no power. Located immediately east of the Fishermen's Wharf dock. Spa, liquor store, and pet friendly rooms. Visitors can have pool and shower access for a small facilities charge. Watch your depths on very low tides.

㉖ **Pier 66 Marina.** 1745 Cowichan Bay Rd., Cowichan Bay, BC V0R 1N0; (250) 510-7711; (250) 748-8444; sales@pier-66marina.com; www.pier66marina.com. Open all year, gasoline

Genoa Bay Marina

This classic boat was spotted in Maple Bay.

showers, and laundry, 15, 30 & 50 amp power, limited water, launch ramp, covered picnic shelter, Wi-Fi. This is a popular summer stop. The Genoa Bay Café is busy, reservations recommended. The Genoa Bay Gallery has lovely paintings, prints, and sculpture. The new "breakfast cabana" offers self-service coffee, fresh baked goods, and other breakfast items served "all you can eat" buffet style during July and August.

The store carries convenience items, souvenirs, books, cruising guides and hand-dipped ice cream. Good crabbing in the bay.

Musgrave Landing. Musgrave Landing is on the southwest corner of Saltspring Island, at the mouth of Sansum Narrows. It is a popular stopover, although it has only a small public float for visitor moorage, no facilities, and very restricted anchorage nearby. Upland you'll find good hiking along miles of logging roads. On a pleasant roadside walk we picked a bouquet of thistle, foxglove, dandelion, fern, salal, nicotiana and pearly everlasting for the galley table. A housing development, with private dock, is on Musgrave Point.

SANSUM NARROWS TO DUCK BAY

Sansum Narrows. Sansum Narrows connects Satellite Channel to the south with Stuart Channel to the north, and leads between high hills on Saltspring Island and Vancouver Island. The wind funnels down the axis of the narrows, turning at the bends. It also funnels down the valleys leading to the channel, so wind directions can be erratic. Currents seldom exceed 3 knots; usually they are less.

Burgoyne Bay. Burgoyne Bay has ample anchorage in 18 to 30 feet at its inner end, but is subject to williwaws that blow across a low swale on Saltspring Island. Most of the bay is too deep for convenient anchoring. A 50-foot-long public wharf for visitor moorage is at the head of the bay, next to the anchorage.

㉘ **Maple Bay.** Maple Bay is a major pleasure boat center, with public moorages and all necessary facilities and services. Birds Eye Cove, off the southwest corner of Maple Bay, is home to the Maple Bay Marina and Birds Eye Cove Marina, both with fuel docks, and the Maple Bay Yacht Club, with reciprocal moorage. Anchoring is good in Birds Eye Cove, but avoid anchoring in the area just off the dock on the east side of the cove, opposite the marina docks.

Repairs: Maple Bay Marina has a 50-ton Travelift for haulout. See listing below.

Dining: Our lunches and dinners at Maple Bay Marina's Shipyard Restaurant & Pub have been good.

㉘ **Maple Bay Marina.** 6145 Genoa Bay Rd., Duncan, BC V9L 5T7; (250) 746-8482; (866) 746-8482; info@maplebaymarina.com; www.maplebaymarina.com. Monitors VHF 66A. Open all year. Gasoline, diesel, lubricants, and propane at the fuel dock. Mostly 15 & 30 amp power, some 50 amp power, washrooms, showers, laundry, water, Beacon/BBX Wi-Fi, ShawGo Wi-Fi, and free Wi-Fi. The Mariners Market & Espresso Bar has coffee, hot breakfast items, muffins, sandwiches, hot dogs, limited groceries and local art and crafts. A chandlery has marine supplies and charts. Call ahead for slip assignment, reservations recommended.

This is a popular stop, scenic and well protected from winds and seas, good for rendezvous and club cruises. The grounds are beautiful, with whimsical touches such as old marine engines, cleaned and painted red or white—they're unique.

A 55-ton Travelift provides haulout for repairs. It is run by Steve Lindstrom, who has

the small marine supply store at the marina. Do it yourself or hire tradesmen.

The washrooms are spacious, warm and clean, with good showers. The Shipyard Restaurant & Pub has good food, with daily specials and live music on Friday evenings. The marina has a courtesy shuttle van. A cooking school is nearby.

Harbour Air has scheduled float plane service to Vancouver Harbour. Saltspring Air has scheduled service to Vancouver Airport and Vancouver Harbour.

㉘ **Birds Eye Cove Marina.** 6271 Genoa Bay Rd., Duncan, BC V9L 5T8; (250) 746-5686; marina@birdseyecove.ca. Gasoline and diesel at fuel dock. Limited guest moorage with 15 & 30 amp power, washrooms. No showers. Coffee and snacks for purchase.

㉘ **Maple Bay Public Wharf.** Open all year. Located in Maple Bay, not in Birds Eye Cove, which extends from the south side of Maple Bay. Moorage along 300 feet of dock space, water to the bottom of the ramp but not out the dock, no power. Self-register at kiosk. A

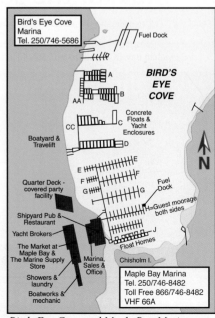

Birds Eye Cove and Maple Bay Marina

Genoa Bay Marina map:

E D C B

Overnight moorage Overnight moorage A

N

Office

Cafe

Washrooms ↓ & Laundry

Genoa Bay Marina
Tel. 250/746-7621
VHF 66A

Genoa Bay Marina

nice beach is nearby. An underwater park is about 200 feet off the end of the dock. The wharf is managed by the Chemainus Harbour Authority and checked daily.

Crofton Public Wharf. Open all year, 1000 feet of dock space, 20 & 30 amp power, washrooms, showers, laundry, garbage drop. Breakwater protected. Crofton is the pulp and paper mill town on the west side of Stuart Channel. The public dock is next to the terminal for the ferry to Vesuvius on Saltspring Island. Walking distance to all services including groceries, restaurants, fishing supplies and licenses. Playground two blocks away. Nearby outdoor swimming pool, tennis courts, hiking trails.

㉙ Vesuvius. North of Sansum Narrows along the Saltspring Island shore, Vesuvius has a public wharf for visitor moorage, and is the terminus for the ferry to Crofton. A small grocery store, a restaurant, and a pub are all a short walk from the public wharf.

Duck Bay. Just north of Vesuvius Bay, Duck Bay has good anchorage with steep, wooded cliffs rising on its east side.

NORTHERN GULF ISLANDS

Stuart Channel. Stuart Channel runs from Sansum Narrows to Dodd Narrows. It is bordered on the west side by Vancouver Island, and on the east side by Saltspring, Kuper, Thetis and De Courcy Islands. Stuart Channel tends to be littered with drift because of extensive log towing to Crofton, Chemainus, and Ladysmith. Keep a sharp watch ahead.

㉚ Chemainus. Chemainus is on the Vancouver Island side of Stuart Channel. It has a good public wharf and floats. The well-stocked 49th Parallel grocery store is near the head of the public wharf, only a few steps from the ferry landing.

Chemainus is filled with boutiques, galleries, antiques shops, and interesting-looking restaurants. More than 30 of the town's buildings have large, well-done murals painted on their sides, most of them depicting Chemainus's distant past as an Indian campground and its more recent history as a mining, logging, and mill town. The mural project is now focused on celebrating Canadian artist Emily Carr's work. The first new mural is a three-dimensional piece on the west side of the Chemainus Theatre Festival building. This is the initial step in a planned million-dollar outdoor gallery of Carr's art, both paintings and sculpture.

Chemainus has grown so popular that a large parking area has been built for tour buses, and in they roll, filled with visitors from around the world. Horse-drawn tours are available, and tours pulled by replicas of steam logging train locomotives—well, sort

The lunch menu changes daily at Maple Bay Marina's Shipyard Restaurant & Pub.

of replicas, good enough for effect.

A ferry crosses between Chemainus and Thetis Island, about a 10-minute walk from either Thetis Island Marina or Telegraph Harbour Marina. This is a good way to visit Chemainus. If you take in an evening show in Chemainus, be sure you can get to the ferry before the last departure.

Live theater. The Chemainus Theatre Festival mounts live matinee and evening performances

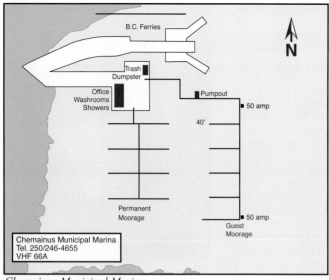

Chemainus Municipal Marina

Chemainus has horse and buggy tours to see the murals.

year-round. Highly recommended. Call for tickets: (250) 246-9820 or (800) 565-7738.

30 Chemainus Municipal Dock. P.O. Box 193, Chemainus, BC V0R 1K0; (250) 715-8186; (250) 246-4655; harmen.chemainus. munimarina@gmail.com. Monitors VHF 66A. Day and overnight moorage, 30 & 50 amp power, water, washrooms, excellent showers. Free garbage drop, pumpout and Wi-Fi. Good grocery shopping at 49th Parallel grocery is a few steps away. A nice laundromat is 1½ blocks away. This marina, with new docks, is next to the ferry terminal. Every two hours from morning to night the ferry arrives and rolls things around a little. It's not bad, but first-time visitors should be aware of it.

Visitor boats will tie along 175 feet on

CHARTS	
3313 Small craft charts (chartbook)	Gulf Islands and adjacent Waterways
3442	North Pender Island to Thetis Island (1:40,000)
3443	Thetis Island to Nanaimo (1:40,000)
3447	Nanaimo Harbour & Departure Bay (1:8,000)
3458	Approaches to Nanaimo Harbour (1:20,000)
3473	Active Pass, Porlier Pass & Montague Harbour (various)
3475 Plans	Stuart Channel Chemainus Bay, Ladysmith Harbour, Dodd Narrows to Flat Top Islands, Dodd Narrows, Osborn Bay
3477 Plans	Gulf Islands Telegraph Harbour & Preedy Harbour, Pender Canal, Bedwell Harbour to Georgeson Passage

the outside of the main dock or moor in slips on the inside of the main dock. Because Chemainus is a popular day stop, landing fees have been instituted—$6 under 40 feet; $12 over 40 feet. They found that the docks were full during the day then empty at night, and they need moorage income to maintain the facility. The irrepressible Harmen Bootsma is the manager.

Mooring buoys: Several mooring buoys have been installed off the park at the entrance to the bay. One boat per buoy, 45-foot maximum length. Cost is $12 per night if you pay at the harbor office; $20 if they have to come out and collect it.

30 Jones Marine Services Ltd. Box 29, Chemainus, BC V0R 1K0; (250) 246-1100. Diesel and mid-grade gasoline. Open 8:00 a.m. to 3:30 p.m. Monday through Saturday. Accepts cash and Visa/MasterCard. This dock services the 9-vessel Jones tugboat fleet, and offers fuel to pleasure craft as well. The docks may be taken up with Jones's own boats.

Evening Cove. Evening Cove, at the mouth of Ladysmith Harbour, is a possible anchorage. Correspondent Bruce Evertz reports: "We found good protection from northwest winds, but did have a few wakes from passing boats. There are several houses around the bay so it's not a good spot to take Fido ashore."

31 Ladysmith Harbour. Ladysmith is on Vancouver Island, approximately 6 miles north of Chemainus. Ladysmith is an active sawmill town. Logs are stored on the north side of the harbor and in front of the mill on the south side.

Ladysmith itself is about one-half mile from the Maritime Society's and the Fisherman's Wharf's moorages, up the hill and across the highway. It's a bit of a hike, but we think worthwhile. Before reaching the highway, the big blue building is the Ladysmith Waterfront Arts Centre, with interesting galleries, and the Ladysmith Maritime Society's office and

historical collection of outboard motors. The building used to be a railroad equipment repair facility. The tracks are still there.

The main street of Ladysmith looks as if time passed it by. Movie scenes have been filmed here. A large and friendly 49th Parallel Grocery is several blocks west from the main downtown area, and will deliver to the docks. A private liquor store is next door to the grocery.

The Old Town Bakery at 510 First Avenue (main street through town) is "to die for," with the widest variety of fresh baked cinnamon buns we've ever seen. We had an excellent and reasonably priced deli lunch there, too. Buoma Meats, at 412 First Avenue, is an old-fashioned butcher shop, all weights in pounds and ounces. In Beantime Coffee, you can watch employees roast beans while you enjoy their

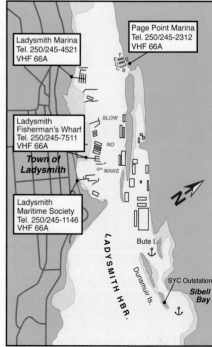

Ladysmith Harbour

coffee. A broad selection of restaurants are in town. Several restaurants will deliver to the marinas.

Ladysmith Maritime Society, behind Slag Point on the south side of the harbor, is the first major set of docks. Ladysmith Fisherman's Wharf is adjacent, followed by Ladysmith Marina, farther into the harbor. Page Point Marina, on the north shore, is open, and the restaurant is serving wonderful dinners. Near the mouth of Ladysmith Harbour the long float in Sibell Bay, on the north side of the Dunsmuir Islands, is a Seattle Yacht Club outstation, member boats only, no reciprocal moorage.

The best anchoring is either in Sibell Bay or just west of Sibell Bay, inside the westernmost of the Dunsmuir Islands. Because of shoal water between Sibell Bay and the latter anchorage, it's a good idea to loop around the west end of the Dunsmuir Islands.

Repairs: Ladysmith Marine Services offers marine repairs and haulout to 40 feet, (250) 714-6206.

③① **Ladysmith Maritime Society Community Marina.** P.O. Box 1030, Ladysmith, BC V9G 1A7; (250) 245-1146; wharfinger@lmsmarina.ca; www.ladysmithmaritimesociety.ca. Monitors VHF 66A. Best to phone or email for availability. Open all year, 750 feet of guest moorage with 15 & 30 amp power, free Wi-Fi, water, block and cube ice, pumpout. The new floating Welcome Centre with lounge, snack bar, washrooms, showers and laundry, opened in 2012. Reservations accepted. *No-Discharge Zone. Gray water okay.*

These are the first set of docks on the southwest side as you enter Ladysmith Harbour. The docks are very good and the historical displays, including restored museum boats and equipment, are fascinating. The new Harbour Heritage Centre and an art gallery are up the hill in the large blue building. The town of Ladysmith is about a 10-minute walk away, up the hill. Bus service runs to a nearby shopping mall outside of the town center.

The community is justifiably proud of this new facility and its large meeting spaces. It is one of the nicest on the coast. Picnic tables and grills are in a covered area outside. At the end of the day, it is not unusual for a group to gather round, some grilling their dinners and some visiting others. Sometimes potlucks are organized with the community. The Ladysmith Maritime Society Community Marina really is a community marina, run by a small staff and over 200 volunteers. As a guest, we could feel their enthusiasm.

③① **Ladysmith Fisherman's Wharf.** P.O. Box 130, Ladysmith, BC V9G 1A1; (250) 245-7511; lfwa@telus.net; www.ladysmith-fishermanswharf.com. Monitors VHF 66A. Open all year, 1200 feet of dock space, 20 amp power, garbage drop, telephone, washrooms, showers. Marine repairs, tidal grid and launch ramp. Commercial fishing vessels have priority and usually fill the docks. Stairs lead up the hill toward the town of Ladysmith, about one-half mile away.

This floating building at Ladysmith Maritime Society Community Marina has a lounge, restrooms, showers, and laundry.

③① **Ladysmith Marina.** 12335 Rocky Creek Rd., Ladysmith, BC V9G 1K4; (250) 245-4521; ladysmithmarina@obmg.com; www.ladysmithmarina.com. Monitors VHF 66A. Open all year, washrooms, showers, 30 & 50 amp power. This marina is mostly permanent moorage, but guest moorage is often available on the long linear dock on the east side behind the Ladysmith Yacht Club, and in unoccupied slips. The marina is part of Oak Bay Marine Group, a company that owns several marinas and fishing resorts throughout B.C.

③② **Page Point Marina Inc.** 4760 Brenton-Page Rd., Ladysmith, BC V9G 1L7; (250) 245-2312; (877) 860-6866; moorage@page-pointmarina.com; www.pagepointmarina.com. Monitors VHF 66A. Open all year. Permanent and guest moorage to 66 feet, 30 amp power, water, free Wi-Fi, restaurant, garbage drop, compost & recycling, Skye Marine Chandlery store for marine supplies. Can prearrange kayaks and bicycle rentals. Pet-friendly, community bonfire, yard games, barbecues on the deck. The docks are in good condition. Reservations recommended. The dinghy dock is next to the ramp at the head of G dock.

The award-winning Page Point Bistro has a beautiful view and is open year-round. The menu is casual, and has many local and specialty selections. A cozy inn is available for short or long-term accommodations.

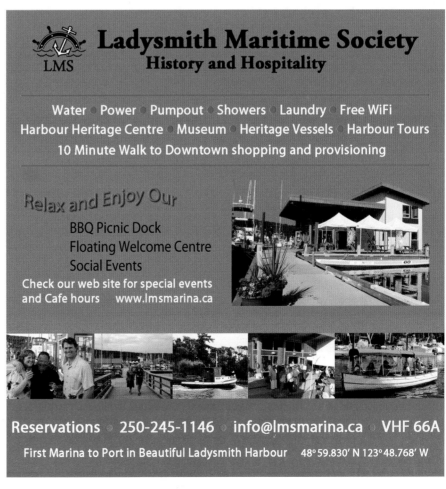

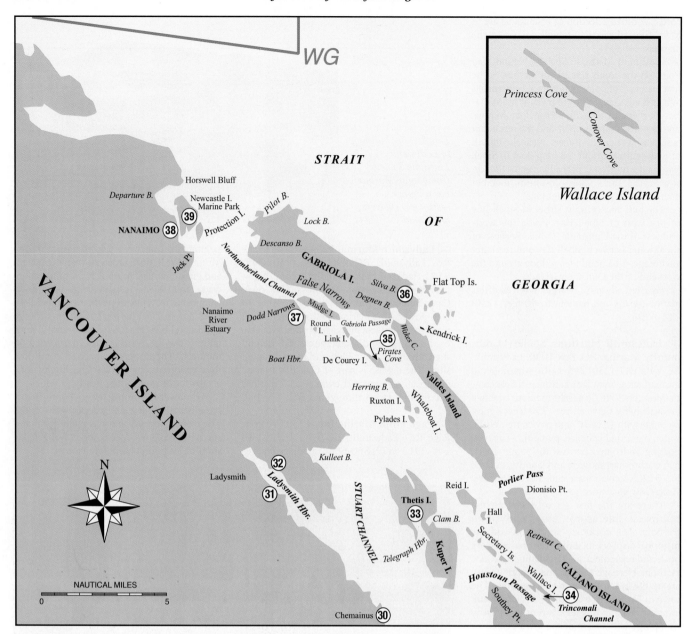

WG

Princess Cove

Conover Cove

Wallace Island

STRAIT

OF

GEORGIA

Horswell Bluff
Departure B.
Newcastle I.
Marine Park
㊴
Pilot B.
NANAIMO ㊳
Protection I.
Lock B.
Flat Top Is.
Jack Pt.
Descanso B.
Northumberland Channel
GABRIOLA I.
Silva B.
㊱
False Narrows
Degnen B.
Nanaimo
River
Estuary
Dodd Narrows
Mudge I.
㊲
Round
I.
Gabriola Passage
Wakes C.
← Kendrick I.
Link I.
㉟
Boat Hbr.
De Courcy I.
*Pirates
Cove*
VANCOUVER ISLAND
Herring B.
Valdes Island
Ruxton I.
Whaleboat I.
Pylades I.
N
Kulleet B.
㉜
Ladysmith
Reid I.
Porlier Pass
Dionisio Pt.
㉛
Ladysmith Hbr.
Thetis I.
Hall
I.
Retreat C.
㉝
Clam B.
Secretary Is.
STUART CHANNEL
Telegraph Hbr.
Kuper I.
GALIANO ISLAND
Houstoun Passage
Wallace I.
㉞
NAUTICAL MILES
Southey Pt.
**Trincomali
Channel**
0   5
Chemainus ㉚

Tent Island. Tent Island is off the south tip of Penelakut Island (formerly Kuper Island), at the junction of Houstoun Passage and Stuart Channel. The small bay on the west side of Tent Island is a popular anchorage in settled weather.

Preedy Harbour. Preedy Harbour indents the southwest corner of Thetis Island, due west of Telegraph Harbour. The ferry from Chemainus calls there. From the south, enter between Hudson Island and three long, thin reefs, marked with red (starboard hand) lights and day beacons. From Stuart Channel enter between Hudson Island and Dayman Island. Reefs, marked by green buoys on the Dayman Island side and a light on the Hudson Island side, extend from both these islands. Because the Hudson Island light is positioned upland from the toe of its reef, favor the Dayman Island buoys.

Entry from the north is clear as long as you stay mid-channel. For all three entries, check the chart carefully so you know where the reefs are, and how to avoid them.

A day use-only community dock is in the northwest corner of Preedy Harbour, near the ferry landing. Anchorage is good in this area, keeping in mind the ferry comings and goings.

㉝ **Telegraph Harbour.** Telegraph Harbour is one of the Gulf Islands' most popular stops. It is located across Stuart Channel from Chemainus, between Thetis Island and Penelakut Island (formerly Kuper Island). Two marinas are in Telegraph Harbour: Thetis Island Marina and Telegraph Harbour Marina. Both marinas are walking distance to an inter-island ferry to Chemainus. While you're at Telegraph Harbour, you may enjoy walking the roads of Thetis Island. You'll find a number of interesting stops, including the Pot of Gold Coffee Roasting Co.

White Restricted Operations buoys mark the edges of the anchoring area. Note the shoal areas on the starboard side of the channel and across from the Thetis Island Marina.

Penelakut Island (formerly Kuper Island) is an Indian Reserve.

Farmers market: A farmers market is held 9:00 a.m. to 1:00 p.m. on Sundays, May through September at Telegraph Harbour Marina.

LOCAL KNOWLEDGE

ENTRANCE CHANNEL: New channel markers indicate the channel between Thetis Island Marina and Telegraph Harbour Marina. Keep the marks to starboard when entering. On very low tides hug the breakwater outside the Thetis Island Marina fuel dock as you enter Telegraph Harbour. The channel has about 9 feet of depth at zero tide.

Thetis Island Marina

③ **Thetis Island Marina.** 46 Harbour Rd., Thetis Island, BC ; (250) 246-1443 (summer only); (250) 246-3464; marina@thetisisland. com; www.thetisisland.com. Monitors VHF 66A. To port, this is the first marina as you enter Telegraph Harbour. Open all year, gasoline, diesel, and propane at the fuel dock behind the breakwater, over 3000 feet of side-tie dock space, 15 & 30 amp power, washrooms, showers, laundry, ATM. The marina has three rental suites, and they're quite nice. This is a full-service marina with a liquor store, convenience groceries, snacks, ice, and post office. The fully-licensed pub has inside and outside

dining and separate areas for families. The pub has good food and an excellent selection of beers, porters, stouts, and single-malt scotches. Wi-Fi to the docks; get the password at the pub or the fuel dock. A cell phone booster covers the pub and deck areas. Large playground for kids. It's a 10- to 15-minute walk to the BC ferry to Chemainus.

The marina has its own water desalination system. Water is still precious because the system is expensive to operate, but the pub never runs out.

A covered picnic area is available for groups.

③ **Telegraph Harbour Marina.** Box 7-10, Thetis Island, BC V0R 2Y0; (250) 246-9511; (800) 246-6011; sunny@telegraphharbour. com; www.telegraphharbour.com. VHF channel 66A. This is the marina at the back of the bay. Although close to drying flats, the docks have at least 6 to 8 feet on all tides. Open 7 days a week, Easter through Canadian Thanksgiving. In the winter no facilities are available except moorage, water, and electricity. Gasoline & diesel, oil, alcohol, and kerosene at the fuel dock. Moorage along 3000 feet of dock, 15 & 30 amp power, washrooms, showers, laundry, free Wi-Fi, garbage drop, limited water.

The Bistro store carries convenience groceries, marine guides, books and gifts, and fresh-baked pies. The licensed Bistro, open weekends beginning after Easter and daily from mid-June through mid-September, serves breakfast, lunch, and dinner. Their pizzas and fresh pies can be delivered to your boat. The bistro is licensed for wine and beer. The marina is the exclusive outlet for Thetis Island's Pot of Gold coffee. They have an old fashioned soda fountain where you can still get guilt-filled hard ice cream milk shakes, sundaes, and ice cream specialties. For some, a cruise to the Gulf Islands is not complete without one of Telegraph Harbour's ice cream indulgences, or their delicious pie.

The marina is clean and well-maintained. Staff helps arriving boats land. They have a playground for kids, a large covered area for group functions, and a picnic area with tables and barbecues. It's a 10 to 15 minute walk to the BC ferry to Chemainus.

Rendezvous: Many rendezvous are held here in spring or early fall, best to call ahead for reservations on weekends. A few rendezvous (such as the Canadian Tollycraft event in mid-September) fill the marina, but most do not. Moorage space is usually available.

The Cut. The Cut is a straight and uncomplicated drying pass connecting Telegraph Harbour with Clam Bay. Red, Right, Returning assumes you are returning from Clam Bay. Cruising boats should only try The Cut at or near high water, with local knowledge. Signs at each end purport to show the depth, but they read approximately 3 feet too deep. We took the dinghy through at the bottom of a 4.3-foot tide, sounding the shallow spots with a leadline. Although the two signs said 6 feet of water was in the channel, we found only 2 to 2.5 feet in the shallow spots near the Telegraph Harbour entrance and in a couple thin places on the Clam Bay side.

North Cove. North Cove indents the north end of Thetis Island and is a good anchorage, although it is open to northwesterly winds. A substantial rock breakwater protects a private float and boathouse at Fraser Point, the entrance to North Cove. Camp docks are in the southwest corner of the cove. Anchor in 24 to 36 feet (zero tide) along the south shore. High tide covers fingers of rock that extend from the south shore, but the rock reappears when the tide drops. Don't get too close. Stay clear of the rocks in the middle of the entry. The charts show them as ++, for dangerous rocks 6 feet or less beneath the surface.

Cufra Inlet. Cufra Inlet, about a mile long, extends into Thetis Island from the southeast corner of North Cove. Most of the inlet dries, but is good for dinghy exploring at higher water.

Clam Bay. Clam Bay is a large, relatively open bay with good anchoring in convenient depths. Reader Jerry Williams, who lived there, says his favorite spot is the little bight on the north shore, between Leech Island and Thetis Island. The mouth of the Clam Bay is partly blocked by Centre Reef. Rocket Shoal is in the middle of the bay. Lacking familiarity, the safest entry is south of Centre Reef, between Buoy *U42* and Penelakut Spit, which extends from Penelakut Island (formerly Kuper Island). The charts show everything. Large scale Plans Chart 3477 is especially useful. Clam Bay is at one end of The Cut, the drying channel that separates Thetis Island from Penelakut Island.

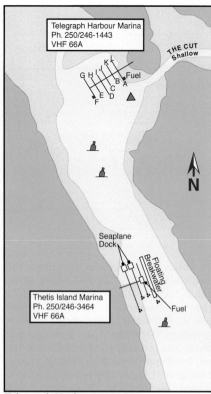

Telegraph Harbour

A stern tie is best for anchorage at Princess Cove on Wallace Island.

Southey Bay. At the north tip of Saltspring Island, tucked in beside Southey Point, is a little notch that Contributing Editor Tom Kincaid used as an anchorage in past years. An increasing number of private mooring buoys have restricted swinging room, but it's still a possible anchorage.

Secretary Islands. The Secretary Islands have several nice little anchorages, with emphasis on *little*. One of the easiest is in the notch on the Trincomali Channel side between the two Secretary Islands.

Mowgli Island. Mowgli Island, off the northwest tip of the Secretary Islands, has good anchorage in a cozy bay between it and the first Secretary island. Swinging room is limited. We suggest a stern-tie across the gravel beach to driftwood ashore. The island is surrounded by reefs. They are easily seen at low tide, but be cautious at high tide.

㉞ **Wallace Island Marine Park.** Open all year. Wallace Island, a marine park purchased with the help of the local boating community, is a low and beautiful tree-covered island in Trincomali Channel. Enter from Houstoun Passage. You'll find sheltered anchorage and a dock at Conover Cove, anchorage for many boats in locally-named Princess Cove, and room for a couple of boats just inside Panther Point. The park has toilets, campsites and picnic areas, and trails crisscrossing the entire island. It's a fine place to walk through the forest and stretch the legs. Old cabins set in an orchard near Conover Cove are locked shut, awaiting funds for restoration. Please respect the two private properties on the island.

㉞ **Conover Cove.** A reef directly offshore from the entrance to Conover Cove on Wallace Island can be avoided by going around either end. Especially from the southeast, give the reef ample room. When you leave, remember the reef is there. We are told that each year boats depart at high tide and drive up on the rocks. A dock, with room for several boats, gives access to the island. Conover Cove is fairly shoal at the dock and shoals even more toward both ends of the bay. You can anchor and stern-tie to rings set in the rocks on shore.

Be sure to check your depths. The entrance to Conover Cove is shallow at low tide.

㉞ **Princess Cove.** Princess Cove is just northwest of Conover Cove, and has room for quite a few boats to anchor. Mooring eyes for stern-ties, usually marked with yellow painted arrows, are set in the rock along the shoreline. Chain hangs from some of the mooring eyes. Absent the chains, at low water you have to be part mountain goat to get to several of those eyes. Set the anchor carefully in 18 to 24 feet (deeper toward the mouth of the cove), and maintain an anchor watch if the wind comes up. A dinghy dock is on the west side of the cove.

㉞ **Panther Point.** Panther Point is the southeast tip of Wallace Island. There's room for one or perhaps two boats in 30 to 36 feet just inside the mouth of the cove. If you anchor any farther inside, a rock on the north side will restrict your swing. The anchorage is exposed to southeast winds but protected from other winds.

Retreat Cove. Retreat Cove, a small notch protected by offlying Retreat Island, indents Galiano Island across Trincomali Channel from the south tip of Wallace Island. Enter only from the south. The approach around the north side of Retreat Island is shallow and foul with rocks and reefs. The head of Retreat Cove shelves sharply. Anchor in 18 to 24 feet,

but plan your swing to avoid the shelf. An 80-foot-long public dock, no facilities, is on the southern shore of the cove. Local boats take much of the space on the dock.

North Galiano. North Galiano is on the west side of Galiano Island. It lies to the northeast of Hall Island and has anchorage and a small public dock, no facilities.

Dionisio Point Park. Open all year, day use and overnight camping, toilets, no power, no showers. Anchor only. The park overlooks Porlier Pass. It has sandy beaches, rocky headlands and forested uplands.

Porlier Pass. Porlier Pass separates Galiano Island and Valdes Island. Several times a year, currents on large tides reach 9 knots. Current predictions are shown in the Tide and Current Tables, Vol. 5 and Ports and Passes. The current floods north into the Strait of Georgia, and ebbs south into the Gulf Islands. The best time to transit is at slack water. A study of the chart shows it is safest to transit Porlier Pass on the south sides of Black Rock and Virago Rock, staying toward the Galiano Island side of the pass.

From the Strait of Georgia, begin your approach near Lighted Bell Buoy *U41*. South of the buoy, pick up the range on Race Point and Virago Point. Follow that range into Porlier Pass to clear the rocks extending from the northeast tip of Galiano Island. Once clear of the rocks, you can turn to follow a mid-channel course between Virago Rock and Galiano Island. Charts 3442 and 3443 show the range and the rocks to be avoided on both sides, but the larger scale Chart 3473 really helps understanding. Chartbook 3313 also shows the pass in excellent detail.

De Courcy Group. The De Courcy Group has several interesting small anchorages. **Whaleboat Island**, just off the southeast shore of **Ruxton Island**, is a relatively undeveloped provincial park. The preferred anchorage is south of the island, taking care to avoid a drying rock. The north end of Ruxton Island has **Herring Bay**, one of the more attractive small anchorages in the northern Gulf Islands and frequently used when the

The entrance to Pirates Cove is narrow and should be carefully navigated.

Entering Pirates Cove, make the arrow near the shoreline point to the × on the tree near the house.

anchorage at **Pirates Cove** is full (which it often is in the summer).

Whaleboat Island Marine Park. Just south of Ruxton Island. No facilities. Whaleboat Island is undeveloped, but provides extremely limited alternate anchorage to Pirates Cove Marine Park. The preferred anchorage is south of the island, taking care to avoid a drying rock.

Pylades Island. Reader Jerry Williams, who grew up on Pylades Island, tells us the little hole just north of the dot islet off the northeast corner of Pylades Island is "magical." Most of the land is private. A drying shoal is between Pylades Island and the dot islet, so approach from the north. In Whaleboat Passage, between Pylades Island and Ruxton Island, note the drying rock a short distance off Pylades Island.

Herring Bay. Herring Bay indents the northwest end of Ruxton Island, off Ruxton Passage. The bay is bordered by weather-carved sandstone walls and has a beautiful sand beach on the southeast side. Good anchoring in 24 feet, much to explore.

A charted rock ledge that dries at 1 foot is in the west entrance to Herring Bay at 49°05.08'N/123°43.01'W. We use the north entrance exclusively.

LOCAL KNOWLEDGE

DANGEROUS REEFS: The entrance to Pirates Cove is guarded by a reef that extends parallel to the shoreline to a point a little beyond a concrete beacon. When entering, you must leave this beacon to port. A range, consisting of a white-painted arrow on the ground and a white × on a tree, shows where to make your approach. Align the × on the tree above the arrow on the ground and proceed slowly until just past the concrete beacon to port. Turn sharply to port and leave the red Spar Buoy *U38* to starboard. The entry is shallow. At lower tides deep-draft boats should be especially cautious.

㉟ Pirates Cove Marine Park. Pirates Cove is open all year, toilets, hand pump water on the south beach, no other facilities. It's a lovely little harbor, protected from seas but not all winds, with room for many boats (on a short scope). Iron rings for stern-ties are set into the sandstone cliffs that encircle the bay. Two dinghy docks are for shore access, but the dock to starboard as you enter is private.

Most of the land is a marvelous provincial park. The cove is surrounded by a forest of Douglas fir, Garry oak and arbutus (madrona). Well-maintained trails lead through the forest and along the rock shoreline, with its sculpted sandstone formations and tide pools.

Pirates Cove has only a fair holding bottom of sticky mud. If the wind comes up during the night, you can expect a fire drill as boats drag anchor. When departure time arrives, be prepared to spend extra time cleaning the anchor as it comes aboard.

On Ruxton Passage, the little notch at the south end of De Courcy Island is also part of the park, and you can anchor there. The beach is good for dinghy or kayak landing, and campsites are ashore. Additional anchorage is available at Whaleboat Island Marine Park, nearby. Another "Pirates Cove overflow" notch is just north of Pirates Cove off Link Island.

Boat Harbour. Boat Harbour, across Stuart Channel from the De Courcy Group, used to be home to a man named Ken Kendall, who looked and dressed like a pirate, and sometimes fired a brass cannon to herald your arrival in his lair. Actor John Wayne was a regular visitor. Kendall died some years ago. Beth Hill wrote engagingly of him in her book *Seven-Knot Summers* (now out of print).

Kenary Cove. In Boat Harbour. Pronounced "Canary," like the bird. The cove is almost fully occupied by mooring buoys, and has little room to anchor. The marina in the cove is private.

GABRIOLA PASSAGE TO NANAIMO

Gabriola Passage. Gabriola Passage (Gabriola is pronounced "GAY-briola") is the northernmost entrance to the Gulf Islands from the Strait of Georgia. From Bowen Island on the east side of the strait, it is 14 miles to Gabriola Passage, the shortest crossing between the lower mainland and the islands.

Tidal currents on spring tides can run to 8 knots in Gabriola Passage, both flood and ebb. Typical maximum currents are around 4 knots. Transiting is best at slack. The current sets east on the flood and west on the ebb. Times of slack and maximum currents are given in the Tide & Current Tables, Vol. 5 and Ports and Passes.

Degnen Bay. Degnen Bay, on the Gabriola Passage at the south end of Gabriola Island, is a good anchorage but a little crowded with boats on moorings. Entering Degnen Bay, favor the east side, close to Josef Point, to avoid rocks in the middle. An Indian petroglyph of a killer whale is on a slab of rock near the head of the bay. Correspondents John and Lorraine Littlewood report additional petroglyphs on the United Church grounds. A public dock provides access to Gabriola Island.

Degnen Bay Public Wharf. Has 190 feet of dock space, power, garbage drop, but no other facilities. Commercial fishing vessels have priority.

Wakes Cove. Wakes Cove, on Gabriola Passage at the north end of Valdes Island, has a beautiful new provincial marine park occupying almost the entire north end of Valdes Island. The park has trails and historical interpretation information. It is served by a small dock. Anchorage is a little iffy.

Shipyard Rock

Aptly named Shipyard Rock, at the entrance to Silva Bay, is big and menacing. Steer a course north of the rock. The open channel outside the docks is for float plane takeoff and landing.

Dogfish Bay. Kendrick Island, on the northeast side of Valdes Island, creates a narrow and shallow bay known locally as Dogfish Bay. Dogfish Bay is well protected and the holding ground is good. West Vancouver Yacht Club has an outstation on Kendrick Island, members only, no reciprocal moorage.

Drumbeg Provincial Park. South end of Gabriola Island overlooking Gabriola Passage. Open all year, day use only. Toilets, no other facilities. Has shelving sandstone rocks and a small sandy beach.

Flat Top Islands. The Flat Top Islands are appropriately named, and from the north or east they're a little hard to tell apart. If approaching from the Strait of Georgia, pass north of **Thrasher Rock Light**. The light marks the northern end of Gabriola Reefs. All the Flat Top Islands are privately owned.

LOCAL KNOWLEDGE

DANGEROUS ROCK: When entering Silva Bay between Vance Island and Tugboat Island, leave the beacon marking Shipyard Rock to port. Do not turn at once for the Silva Bay floats or other facilities. Shipyard Rock is larger than it appears on the charts. Continue instead until about halfway to Law Point before making your turn. A buoy marks the inner end of Shipyard Rock, but give the rock plenty of room anyway.

③⑥ Silva Bay. Silva Bay is a popular destination in the Flat Top Islands area, well protected, with good holding bottom. From the north, enter behind Vance Island; from the south, through Sear Island Passage, between Gabriola Island and Sear Island. Most boats, however, go through Commodore Passage, between Acorn Island and Tugboat Island, and enter Silva Bay between Tugboat Island and Vance Island. Notorious Shipyard Rock lies along the south side of this passage.

Silva Bay Shipyard, with marine railway and 12-ton Travelift, is next to Silva Bay Marina.

Anchoring: Over the last several years Silva Bay became so clotted with anchored derelict boats and other permanently anchored boats that little room was left for visitors to anchor. By 2012 civic pressure led to the removal of some of the derelicts and relocation of some of the permanently moored vessels closer to the edges. Anchoring is still tight. A float plane take-off and landing channel has been designated along the front of the docks, where anchoring is not allowed.

③⑥ Silva Bay Inn. 3415 South Rd., Gabriola Island, BC V0R 1X7; (250) 247-9351; info@silvabayinn.ca; www.silvabayinn.ca. No guest moorage at this time.

③⑥ Silva Bay Resort & Marina. 3383 South Road, Gabriola Island, BC V0R 1X7; (250) 247-8662 ext. 8; marina@silvabay.com; www.silvabay.com. Monitors VHF 66A. Open all year with guest moorage, 30 amp power, water, garbage drop, washrooms, showers, laundry, liquor store. Reservations recommended. Diesel and mid-grade gasoline at the fuel dock.

A Sunday market is held July and August 10:00 a.m. to 2:00 p.m.

Tofino Air has daily flights to Vancouver.

The Silva Bay Bar & Grill is a pub with a separate, quieter dining room (families welcome). It is open for lunch and dinner year-round.

The Silva Bay Shipyard School, the only full-time accredited wooden boatbuilding school in Canada, is located here.

③⑥ Page's Resort & Marina. 3350 Coast Road, Gabriola Island, BC V0R 1X7; (250) 247-8931; mail@pagesresort.com; www.pagesresort.com. Monitors VHF 66A. Open all year, mid-grade marine gasoline and diesel at the fuel dock, guest moorage in unoccupied slips and along both sides of a 150-foot extension to its docks, plus a 40-foot-long addition to the fuel dock. Facilities include 15 amp power, washrooms, showers, laundry, free Wi-Fi at most slips, and Beacon/BBX Wi-Fi throughout Silva Bay, bicycle and scooter rentals, ice. Cottages and tent sites for rent. The grounds are well maintained.

Cab service is required to get to Gabriola Island's shopping center, or you can rent bi-

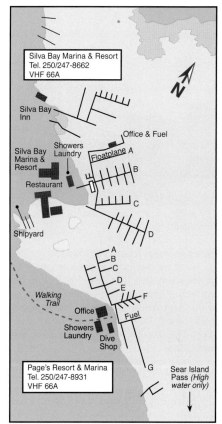

Silva Bay

You never know what you will see on the marine ways at the Silva Bay Shipyard.

At the Silva Bay Resort & Marina you can dine overlooking the boats and the water.

cycles or motor scooters at Page's.

For those interested in literature, Page's is an attractive stop. The office feels more like a peaceful library or book store (which it is), with an extensive range of titles, especially books about local subjects and by local authors. The shop also carries sundry items, bait, and charts.

Gloria and Ken Hatfield and their family are the owners.

㊱ **Silva Bay Shipyard.** 3445 South Road, Gabriola Island, BC V0R 1X7; (250) 247-9800; info@silvabayshipyard.com; www. silvabayshipyard.com. A do-it-yourself boat-yard with a 12-ton travelift and 80-ton railway. Ships chandlery, mechanical & electrical repairs, stern drive mechanics, and wooden boat repair.

False Narrows. False Narrows is east of Dodd Narrows, and is an alternate connection between the Gulf Islands and Northumberland Channel. Without local knowledge it's risky. If you choose to transit False Narrows, you will be traveling between reefs in a shallow channel that is best used at half tide or better. Local knowledge says if you strictly follow the two ranges shown on the chart you'll be okay. Go slowly to keep your wake down. Maximum currents in False Narrows are about half of those in Dodd Narrows, which is about the only reason to go this way.

㊲ **Dodd Narrows.** Currents in Dodd Narrows run to 9 knots as water swirls through the narrow but deep passage between cliffs. The narrows are best taken at slack water. For the hour or so before the predicted turn, boats collect at each end waiting for the right time. These boats include commercial craft, even tugboats with tows of logs, so the period around slack water can get pretty interesting. Generally, the boats on the upstream side go first, catching the last of the dying fair current. When they are through, boats on the other end go through, picking up the beginnings of the new (for them) fair current. It all works well as long as no one gets pushy.

Because Dodd Narrows is a dogleg, it's a good idea to broadcast a *Securité* before transiting (*Securité, Securité, this is the 34-foot motor vessel* Happy Days *entering Dodd Narrows southbound. Any concerned traffic please advise, channel one-six*). If you're dropping in behind a string of boats going through, you shouldn't need to broadcast a *Securité*. On busy days with a lot of traffic, redundant broadcasts clog up Channel 16. Be sure to use low power.

Don't be in a hurry, and don't try to pass a slower boat. Dodd Narrows is short. Travel single-file and leave room between your boat and the boat ahead.

Northumberland Channel. Northumberland Channel is the passage from the Gulf Islands to Nanaimo. It begins at False Narrows and runs northwest between Gabriola Island and Vancouver Island. Northumberland Channel exits in the Gulf of Georgia, or, at Jack Point, makes the turn to Nanaimo. Because of considerable log boom towing in the area, watch for floating debris. If you are not yet ready for civilization, you might lay over at Pilot Bay, on the north end of Gabriola Island.

Pilot Bay. Pilot Bay is on the north end of Gabriola Island. It's a good anchorage in a southeasterly, but is open to northwesterlies. Pilot Bay is a no-discharge zone. Gray water okay.

Gabriola Sands Park. North end of Gabriola Island. Open all year, day use only. Toilets, but no other facilities. This park fronts on Taylor Bay and Pilot Bay. It has a sandy swimming area and a playfield. Good for kids.

Sandwell Park. Northeast side of Gabriola Island. Open all year, day use only, toilets but no other facilities. This is a small seafront park with a sandy beach and forested uplands.

㊳ Nanaimo. As you pass Jack Point the city of Nanaimo opens up. Head for the prominent highrise condominium building, easily seen from Jack Point. The harbor is wide, and sheltered from the Strait of Georgia by Protection Island and Newcastle Island.

The Nanaimo Port Authority public marina is at the south end of the business district near Nanaimo's famous Bastion (blockhouse), with access to downtown Nanaimo. The Bastion was built in 1853 by the Hudson's Bay Company, and is Nanaimo's oldest man-made landmark still standing. A Thrifty Foods supermarket, ATM, and liquor store are in the shopping mall near the Port Authority marina. The Nanaimo Museum is in the Conference Centre, one block from the public marina.

The Canadian Customs dock is at the head of E dock on the north side. Other moorages, including the Nanaimo Yacht Club, are in Newcastle Island Passage, the channel leading behind Newcastle Island to Departure Bay.

The Bastion is Nanaimo's oldest standing building.

The Nanaimo Yacht Club has guest moorage for visiting members of reciprocal clubs.

Satellite Reef caution: Buoy *PS* is west of Satellite Reef, approximately where boats entering from Northumberland Channel would plan to turn to anchor at Newcastle Island or continue through Newcastle Island Passage. Satellite Reef dries at zero tide, and should be considered hazardous at all times. Stay west of Buoy *PS*.

Repair and haul-out facilities capable of handling any needed job are located along Newcastle Island Passage, known locally as Newcastle Channel.

Nanaimo is the natural point of departure for boats headed across the Strait of Georgia or north to Campbell River or Desolation Sound and beyond. It is the second largest city (behind Victoria) on Vancouver Island. Shops of all kinds line the narrow, winding streets. We've prowled through several impressive bookstores—new and used—in downtown. Nanaimo Maps & Charts on Church Street has an excellent selection of books, cruising guides, and an extensive stock of charts. Nanaimo offers excellent dining, from casual to elegant. Several restaurants are on the water in the marina. A winding promenade takes walkers along the waterfront. A busy casino is within an easy walk.

A cannon is fired at noon each day at the Bastion, beginning in May. It's a ceremony,

Every day at noon the cannon is fired from the historic Bastion above the moorage area.

complete with a piper in full regalia and a booming explosion and cloud of white smoke. Beginning in June the Brigadoon Dance Academy's highland dancers perform from 11:30 a.m. to 12:00 p.m. Get there early and bring your camera.

Chandlery: Harbour Chandler, south of the boat basin, is a an excellent chandlery.

Farmers market: Just north of the Bastion, a farmers market, often with entertainment, is open 10:00 a.m. to 2:00 p.m., Fridays mid-April to mid-October.

Golf: Pryde Vista (250) 753-6188 is a pretty and easily-walked 9-hole par 33 course, a short cab ride away. Nanaimo Golf & Country Club (250) 758-2451 is a first-class 18-hole course, a slightly longer cab ride away. Both are recommended.

Taxi: AC Taxi, (250) 753-1231

THINGS TO DO

1. **Nanaimo Bastion**. Located above the marina, the bastion is the oldest standing building in Nanaimo. You can explore it, or watch the cannon ceremony at noon.

2. **Newcastle Island**. Hike to the sandstone quarry or rent a kayak, stand-up paddleboard, or bike. The traditional tribal salmon bake happens most evenings. A children's playground was built in 2012. A foot ferry provides regular access to Newcastle Island from the Nanaimo waterfront.

3. **Fresh seafood on the dock**. Fishermen return to the Harbour Authority Marina and sell their catch. Prepare a fresh seafood dinner on your boat. Or, stop by Trollers for fish and chips.

4. **Nanaimo Museum**. Just up from the marina at 100 Museum Way. Learn the history of Nanaimo from its First Nation roots to the discovery of coal in the area.

5. **Petroglyph Provincial Park**. See carvings of animals and sea creatures immortalized in the sandstone hundreds and thousands of years ago. A taxi ride from the docks.

6. **Dinghy Dock Pub**. On Protection Island. Take your dinghy or the ferry ($9). Great sun deck, good food, and of course cold beer.

🕸 **Nanaimo Port Authority.** 104 Front Street, P.O. Box 131, Nanaimo, BC V9R 5K4; (250) 755-1216; (250) 754-5053; marina@npa.ca; www.npa.ca. During July and August call (250) 755-1216. Monitors VHF 67 (*not 66A*). Open year-round, except Christmas Day, Boxing Day, and New Years Day. In winter many commercial fishing vessels are in the basin, but pleasure craft moorage is available. Water at selected docks in the winter.

A floating breakwater dock is in the center of the marina entrance, and the Eco Barge pumpout and portapotty dump is tied to the inshore side. No charge for the Eco Barge. The harbor is a no-discharge zone. Arriving and departing vessels must pass south of the floating breakwater dock. The northern entrance is reserved for aircraft.

Marina facilities include 9000 feet of dock space, 20 & 30 amp power on all floats, some 50 & 100 amp power, washrooms, showers with heated tile floors, laundry, free Wi-Fi, and waste oil disposal. Customs clearance available. Three hours of moorage complimentary, but call on VHF 67 for slip assignment.

Nanaimo Harbour & Newcastle Island Passage

The Port Authority moorage is actually two facilities: the older, inner basin, and the newer Cameron Island docks inside the breakwater pier. We have used both and are happy either place. Large vessels and ships will tie on the outside of the Cameron Island breakwater pier, smaller boats on the inside. The wakes from boats headed for the fuel dock or the inner basin rock boats at Cameron Island. The Cameron Island docks are security-gated. The gates (and office) are open 7:00 a.m. to 11:00 p.m., but between 11:00 p.m. and 7:00 a.m. you'll have to call security to let you in.

Watch the current when landing at Cameron Island. Usually there's no problem, but be aware.

Reservations are accepted for Cameron Island. The basin can hold 250 to 300 boats at a time, depending on the size of vessels. Summertime turnover usually averages about 100 boats a day. Rafting is permitted. In summer, dock assistants can help you tie up.

Seasonally, fresh fish is sold on occasion at the Nanaimo Fisherman's Market dock at the entrance to the small boat basin. The dock is 250 feet long, 15 feet wide, and wheelchair accessible. With its flags and specially designed gazebos, you can't miss it. Fish & chips, Mexican food, and other delights are available at floating restaurants. Theaters, a waterfront promenade, and tennis courts are nearby. The seaplane terminal is adjacent to the marina. All of the Nanaimo commercial district is within a five-minute walk.

No designated dinghy dock. If coming by dinghy, call the marina office on VHF 67 for tie-up instructions.

The esplanade along the Nanaimo waterfront is an excellent place to stretch your legs.

③⑧ **Petro-Canada Coastal Mountain Fuels.** 6331 Cortu Drive, Nanaimo, BC V9R IP2; (250) 754-7828. Open all year, gasoline and diesel at the fuel dock. Lubricants, accessories, ice, and snacks. At the end of "E" dock. May to mid-June, 7:00 a.m. to 7:00 p.m.; mid-June to September, 6:00 a.m. to 8:00 p.m.; October to May, 8:00 a.m. to 5:00 p.m.

③⑧ **Waterfront Suites & Marina.** 1000 Stewart Ave., Nanaimo, BC V9S 4C9; (250) 753-7111; moorage@waterfrontnanaimo. com; www.waterfrontnanaimo.com. (Formerly Moby Dick Oceanfront Marina) At press time construction was underway and the marina was not open. The marina is scheduled to open after extensive renovation in 2014. Check www.WaggonerGuide.com for updates.

③⑧ **Departure Bay Gas N Go.** 1840 Stewart Ave., Nanaimo, BC V9F 4E6; (250) 591-0810. Open all year. Fuel dock with gas and diesel at north end of Newcastle Channel. Small store carries snacks, tackle, and some lubricants.

③⑨ **Newcastle Island Marine Park.** Open all year, moorage on 1500 feet of dock space, excellent washrooms and showers, no power. Anchorage is now prohibited in Mark Bay; 42 mooring balls are available at $12 per night, paid onshore. Extensive anchorage is still available just beyond Mark Bay and the docks. Several small bays, beaches, and playing fields. Many hiking trails. Walk-in campsites and picnic areas. Kayak, canoe, stand-up paddleboard, and bicycle rentals. In summer a passenger ferry connects the island with Nanaimo.

The pavilion houses a dance floor, snack bar, visitor center, and excellent interpretive displays on the natural and human history of the area.

This is an extraordinary park. Before European settlement, Newcastle Island was a summer campsite for First Nations. Since European settlement it has supported a shipyard and been mined for coal. In the early 1870s it was quarried for sandstone that built the San Francisco Mint. Between 1923 and 1932 its sandstone was quarried for pulpstones, giant

cylinders that ground wood into pulp for making paper. Before WWII, Japanese fishermen ran herring salteries here. Through it all, Newcastle Island has been a popular holiday spot.

You might see rare albino raccoons, and dozens of bunny rabbits. Arrive early enough to get literature from the visitor center. Try to spend the night. You can tie up at the excellent docks, moor in Mark Bay, or anchor just offshore. The lights of Nanaimo are beautiful.

The 1931 pavilion charms. The pulpstone quarry astonishes. The bays and beaches intrigue. We enjoy this park.

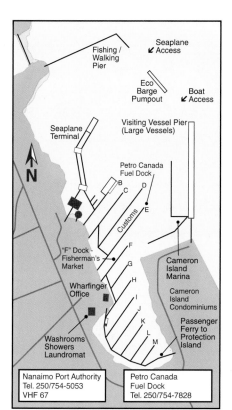

Nanaimo Port Authority

STRAIT OF GEORGIA

STRAIT OF GEORGIA
Schooner Cove · *French Creek* · *Denman Island*
· *Hornby Island* · *Comox* · *Oyster River*
· *False Bay* · *Squitty Bay*

CROSSING THE STRAIT OF GEORGIA

Crossing the Strait of Georgia. The Strait of Georgia is not to be trifled with. It's a big body of water, 110 miles long and 15 to 20 miles wide. Pleasure craft cross the strait all the time, but locals know better than to go out when the wind is blowing. They are especially careful when wind blows against strong currents.

When conditions are right, the strait need not be intimidating. The "typical" summertime fair weather wind pattern calls for calm mornings followed by a rising northwesterly sea breeze by early afternoon. By mid-afternoon the sea breeze can be 20 to 25 knots. In the evening the wind dies down. We have crossed early in the morning and in the evening and had no problems.

Frequently, though, the typical pattern doesn't hold. If a weak frontal system passes over the area, the higher pressure behind the front will produce northwesterlies of 20 to 25 knots, sometimes reaching gale force. These winds can blow around the clock for three days or even longer, effectively closing the strait to small craft.

Summer afternoon southwesterly winds known as Qualicums can blow across the strait between Qualicum Beach and False Bay, at the northern tip of Lasqueti Island. Qualicum winds resulting from the passage of a cold front can reach 40 knots, but are short-lived. When wind opposes current in Sabine Channel, between Lasqueti Island and Texada Island, 8-foot seas can result. Malaspina Strait can be rough, especially when wind is against current. Currents from Howe Sound and Burrard Inlet meet off Point Atkinson, and create rough seas. Wind makes them worse.

When the wind is up it produces a difficult 4- to 5-foot chop—sometimes higher—in the middle of the strait away from land influences. These aren't long, lazy ocean swells.

The Strait of Georgia on a nice day.

Strait of Georgia seas are steep and close together. In southeasterly winds, the largest seas are found near Chrome Island and Cape Mudge, both locations with significant fetch. When the wind blows from the northwest, the largest waves are found in Sabine Channel and near Sand Heads. A well-handled boat might run with these seas, but taken on the bow or beam they are no fun at all. As noted above, dangerous seas of 8 feet or even more are not unknown, especially off points (such as Cape Mudge) or in channels where mountains funnel and accelerate the wind.

Sometimes, the afternoon winds never materialize and the strait can be crossed all day. It's best to avoid being forced into crossing at a specific time or on a specific day. Wait for calm conditions and know that they don't always appear in the morning and evening. When the conditions are right, go. Be cautious yet decisive.

Even in calm conditions, you may find tide-rips off many of the points, and wherever passes or channels join the strait. When the current flows out of a pass or inlet into the strait, confusion results. Add wind, and big confusion results. While the ebb current flows from inlets into the strait, note that the *flood current* flows out of the Gulf Islands into the strait. At the eastern mouths of Active Pass, Porlier Pass and Gabriola Pass, look for rough seas on the flood, especially when the wind is blowing.

We list these cautions not to frighten the reader but to inform. Weather patterns do exist and the bad spots are known. The skipper who monitors the VHF continuous marine broadcast will gather a sense of what is happening, where it is happening, and why it is happening. Go and no-go decisions get easier.

Here are a few tips for a safe and comfortable crossing:
• Monitor the buoy reports for Halibut Bank (off Gibsons) and Sentry Shoal (between Comox and Campbell River and below Mitlenatch Island). These reports provide frequent updates on sea state and wind conditions. They can be found online on Environment Canada's website, on the

continuous marine broadcast, or by calling Dial-A-Buoy at (888) 701-8992.
• Monitor lightstation reports. Lightstations are at Chrome Island, Merry Island, and Entrance Island. The lightkeepers provide information on visibility, wind speed and direction, and sea state, updated every three hours.
• Based on the wind direction and sea state, choose the best angle and direction for your crossing. The most direct course may not be the most comfortable. Don't be afraid to change your destination if the weather isn't cooperating.
• The north-flowing flood current from Juan de Fuca Strait meets the south-flowing flood from Johnstone Strait near Mitlenatch Island. When travelling the length of the strait, time your departure to take advantage of currents flowing in the same direction as the wind. When crossing, especially in the south, try to time your departure to hit slack in the middle of the strait. Both strategies will minimize the effect of wind against the current.
• The area between Qualicum Beach and Lasqueti Island can be subject to southwesterly winds coming through the Alberni "notch" in the Vancouver Island mountains. Check Chrome Island for local southwesterly winds. Old salts also recommend checking winds at Cape Beale, on the West Coast of Vancouver Island. If a strong southwesterly wind is blowing there, often it will flow right over Vancouver Island through the Alberni "notch," affecting the waters off Qualicum Beach.
• Take advantage of lees along the way. For example, you may choose to go up one side or the other of Texada Island to stay in the lee of a southwesterly or northeasterly wind. Always be prepared to turn around and go back if things do not look right.

Whiskey Golf. Boats headed north from Nanaimo must navigate through or around "Whiskey Golf" (WG) restricted area. Whiskey Golf is a deepwater range operated by the Canadian and U.S. Navies, and is used to test torpedoes (always unarmed) and various

CHARTS	
3312 Small-craft chart (chartbook)	Jervis Inlet & Desolation Sound
3443	Thetis Island to Nanaimo (1:40:000)
3447	Nanaimo Harbour & Departure Bay (1:8,000)
3456	Halibut Bank to Ballenas Channel (1:30,000)
3458	Approaches to Nanaimo Harbour (1:20,000)
3459	Approaches to Nanoose Harbour (1:15,000)
3512	Strait of Georgia, Central Portion (1:80,000)
3513	Strait of Georgia, Northern Portion (1:80,000)
3527	Baynes Sound (1:40,000); Comox Harbour (1:15,000)
3536 Plans	Strait of Georgia (various scales)

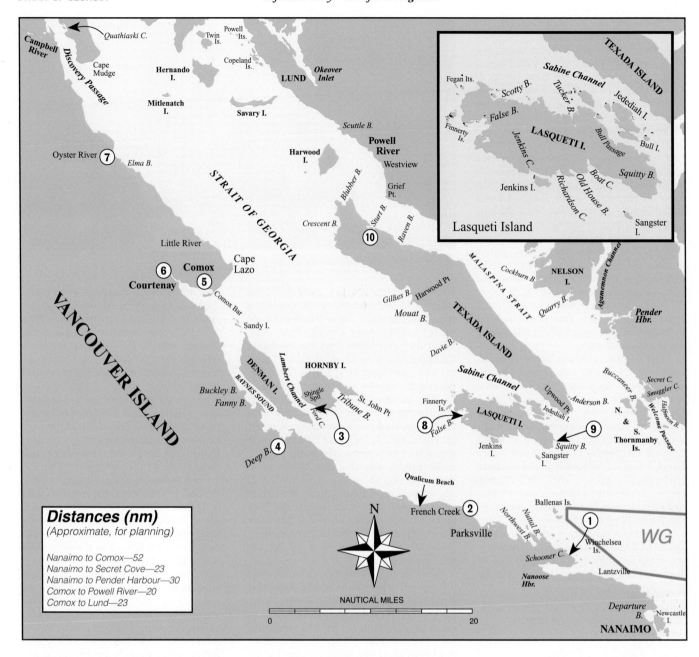

Distances (nm)
(Approximate, for planning)

Nanaimo to Comox—52
Nanaimo to Secret Cove—23
Nanaimo to Pender Harbour—30
Comox to Powell River—20
Comox to Lund—23

NAUTICAL MILES

0   20

ships' systems. The area consists of a network of underwater sensing devices joined by cables to a control site on Winchelsea Island. Torpedoes are fired from range vessels along a predetermined course, and are tracked from the Winchelsea control center. After the run the torpedoes are recovered, either by a helicopter or range vessels. Unauthorized craft are not permitted in the area while the range is in operation.

Typically, the range is active Mondays through Fridays, sometimes Saturdays, 7:00 a.m. to 5:30 p.m. Winchelsea Range Control monitors VHF channel 10 during operations. Notice of operation is included as part of the Canadian continuous marine broadcast on the weather channels. The Coast Guard (VHF channel 83A) also knows if the range is active. If unsure, contact Winchelsea Range Control or Canadian Coast Guard.

The Whiskey Golf restricted area is on the direct course across the Strait of Georgia from Nanaimo to Secret Cove, Smugglers Cove, Pender Harbour, and other destinations along the Sunshine Coast. Last summer we watched one oblivious skipper cross right through the active range. Winchelsea Control made multiple calls to the offending vessel but got no response. A patrol helicopter quickly flew over, hovered just in front of the offending vessel, and redirected it to safe water. Such encounters are best avoided.

The Canadian Navy established a safe transit route along the edges of the restricted area when the range is in use. After clearing Nanaimo Harbour or Departure Bay (being careful to avoid Hudson Rocks and Five Finger Island), head directly for the Winchelsea Islands. Pass to the east of Winchelsea Islands within 1000 yards. Turn to pass east of the Ballenas Islands within 1000 yards. Once well past the Ballenas Islands, steer a course for your destination on the mainland side of the strait, or northwest along the Vancouver Island side.

Nanoose Harbour. Anchorage is good just inside the sandy spit on the south side of the entrance. The docks and mooring buoys along the north shore are the base for Royal Canadian Navy and U.S. Navy vessels engaged in activity on the Winchelsea (Whiskey Golf) torpedo range.

Schooner Cove. Schooner Cove is north of Nanoose Harbour. It is open all year and has gasoline and diesel at the fuel dock.

① **Fairwinds Schooner Cove Marina.** 3521 Dolphin Dr., Nanoose Bay, BC V9P 9J7; (250) 468-5364; (800) 633-7060; marina@fairwinds.ca; www.fairwinds.ca. Monitors VHF 66A; winters monitors channel

16, switch to 66A. Schooner Cove is open all year with gasoline and diesel at the fuel dock. Guest moorage, 30 & 50 amp power, pumpout on G dock. Reservations recommended.

The hotel building is now closed. The marina office, washrooms, showers and laundry are in a temporary building at the top of the dock while the marina property is redeveloped.

Watch for a rock marked by a red buoy just inside the breakwater. Keep the buoy well to starboard when entering. The outstanding Fairwinds Golf club with the Pub House restaurant and lounge is part of the resort. A courtesy shuttle takes you there. No charge for rental clubs for overnight moorage guests (they encourage drop-in golfers).

Schooner Reef. Schooner Reef is a short distance northward off the mouth of Schooner Cove, and has caught a number of boats unaware. The light marking the reef is on the southernmost of its rocks. More rocks lie up-island from the light.

Nuttal Bay. Nuttal Bay is protected from southeasterly winds but exposed to northwesterly winds. To enter Nuttal Bay, leave Dorcas Rock Buoy *P27* to port. Do not pass between Dorcas Rock Buoy *P27* and the land south of it. Buoy *P27* lies a good deal farther out than one might expect. If you are traveling up- or down-island, locate that buoy and pass to seaward of it.

Mistaken Island. Privately owned and posted with "No Trespassing" signs.

Schooner Cove on a beautiful day.

Parksville. Parksville has a nice beach, but shoal water extends out some distance. Except for the marina at French Creek at the north end of Parksville, no facilities are available for boaters.

② **Harbour Authority of French Creek.** 1055 Lee Rd., Parksville, BC V9P 2E1; (250) 248-5051; hafc@frenchcreekharbour. com. Monitors VHF 66A. Open all year with gasoline & diesel. Commercial vessels have priority for moorage, but room is available for pleasure craft. Washrooms and shower, 20 & 30 amp power, waste oil disposal. Office hours are 8:00 a.m. to 5:30 p.m. Restaurant, pub, marine supplies, nearby launch ramp and haulout. A fish market sells fresh seafood. Groceries are at the mall, a 15-minute walk away.

French Creek is the only breakwater-protected harbor in the 25-mile stretch between Northwest Bay and Deep Bay. The breakwater has been moved out and the entrance changed recently, and additional docks are planned for the future. French Creek is the western terminus of the passenger ferry to Lasqueti Island.

Hornby Island. Hornby Island has anchorages in Tribune Bay, Ford Cove, and south of Shingle Spit (where a little ferry runs to Denman Island). Tribune Bay and Shingle Spit are exposed to southeast winds.

Tribune Bay. Tribune Bay is a wonderful place to visit and justifiably popular. Anchor offshore in 18 to 30 feet and dinghy to a splendid sand beach. Visit Tribune Bay Provincial Park. Take the 3-mile hike to Helliwell Provincial Park, on St. John Point.

Tribune Bay has excellent protection from northwesterlies, but in a southeasterly the bay gets rough. For a more private nook, try the little cove near St. John Point. Anchor in 20 to 30 feet.

③ **Ford Cove.** Upgraded harbor with greater capacity at the public dock. A green spar buoy marks the southern end of Maude Reef. You'll see a rock breakwater and a floating breakwater. To enter, leave the rock breakwater to starboard.

③ **Ford's Cove Marina & Store.** (250) 335-2169; info@fordscove.com; www.fordscove.com. Open all year. The well-stocked general store has been under the same ownership for nearly 40 years. It carries groceries, tackle, and general merchandise. Take-out pizza year round, fish and chips July and August. Art gallery, cottages, campsites, RV parking. No fresh water available. Good anchorage on rocky bottom.

③ **Ford Cove Harbour Authority.** P.O. Box 2-6, Ford Cove, Hornby Island, BC V0R 1Z0; (250) 335-0003. Open all year, guest moorage along 1550 feet of dock space, 15, 20 & 30 amp power, toilets, garbage drop.

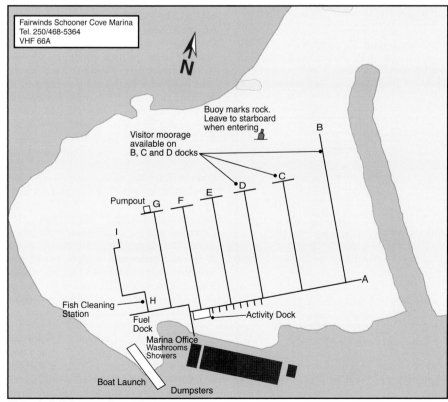

Fairwinds Schooner Cove Marina
Tel. 250/468-5364
VHF 66A

N

Buoy marks rock.
Leave to starboard
when entering

B

Visitor moorage
available on
B, C and D docks

C

D

E

Pumpout   G   F

I

A

Fish Cleaning
Station   H

Fuel
Dock

Activity Dock

Marina Office
Washrooms
Showers

Boat Launch

Dumpsters

Fairwinds Schooner Cove Marina

Fish boats have priority at the Harbor Authority of French Creek, but there is often room for recreational boats.

The Chrome Island lighthouse off the south end of Denman Island is a dramatic landmark.

Baynes Sound. Chart 3527 shows navigation aids not shown on Chart 3513. These aids are buoys marking extensive shoals off Gartley Point, Union Point, Denman Point and Base Flat (Buckley Bay); 2 buoys near Repulse Point; and 2 buoys marking the shoal off Mapleguard Point. Baynes Sound, a 12-mile-long refuge, is protected from the Strait of Georgia by Denman Island. A ferry to Denman Island crosses from Buckley Bay. Comox is at the north end of Baynes Sound and Deep Bay is at the south end. The northern entry to Baynes Sound is across the Comox Bar, marked by buoys and a lighted range on the Vancouver Island shore. The southern entry is past Chrome Island.

LOCAL KNOWLEDGE

NAVIGATION NOTE: A considerable shoal extends into the mouth of Baynes Sound outside Deep Bay. The shoal, and shoaling along the shoreline of Denman Island, opposite, are marked by buoys shown on Chart 3527 but not on Chart 3513.

④ **Deep Bay.** Anchorage is good in Deep Bay, though in deeper water than most boaters like. Ship & Shore Cafe and Store with convenience supplies, fishing tackle, hardware, laundry and a lunch counter, is near the head of the public wharf. The store has gasoline available upland and delivered dockside.

④ **Deep Bay Harbour Authority.** 164 Burne Rd., Bowser, BC V0R 1G0; (250) 757-9331; deepbaymgr@shawcable.com; www.dbha.ca. The public wharf and floats are open all year with moorage along 1130 feet of dock. Garbage drop, 20 & 30 amp power, free Wi-Fi, free pumpout, waste oil disposal, tidal grid, rafting dock, washrooms, showers. The pumpout is located at the loading zone on the main pier. Space is limited, call ahead to see what is available.

Fanny Bay. Fanny Bay is primarily a camping area, but does have a small public mooring float.

Denman Island. A public dock and float once were alongside the landing for the ferry that runs to Buckley Bay, on Vancouver Island, but they are gone. The Denman Gen-

eral Store, with groceries, post office, and liquor store, is a short distance from the ferry dock. The Chrome Island lighthouse off the south end of Denman Island is a dramatic landmark. The north end of Denman Island peters out into a long spit, dotted with small islands and rocks. One of these islands, Sandy Island, is a provincial park.

Sandy Island Marine Provincial Park. This park includes the Seal Islets, and is accessible only by boat. Anchor in Henry Bay, south of Longbeak Point. Picnic areas, swimming, fishing, hiking trails, and wilderness campsites. Sandy Island is a popular overnight stop for kayakers. At low tide it is possible to walk along the sandy spit all the way to its end—halfway to Comox.

LOCAL KNOWLEDGE

NAVIGATION TIP: If you follow the buoyed channel over the Comox Bar in a fresh southeasterly you will have 4- to 5-foot seas on your beam. In these conditions it's better to ignore buoys *P54* and *P52* and instead work your way south until you can turn to fetch the inner Buoy *P50* while running with the seas. The chart indicates ample depths. Large scale Chart 3527 shows Buoy *P50*, but small scale Chart 3513 does not.

Comox Bar. The Comox Bar nearly joins Denman Island and Cape Lazo, with a shallow channel (least depth 15 feet) across the bar. A lighted range—white, with vertical red stripes—is on the Vancouver Island shore. The range's lights are clearly visible in cloudy weather and at night, but in sunlight they can be hard to see. Lighted red Bell Buoy *P54* marks the Strait of Georgia end of this channel. Red Buoys *P52* and *P50* show the course across the bar.

⑤ **Comox.** If you plan to go to Comox, we urge that you have Chart 3527 (1:40,000), with its 1:15,000 inset of Comox Harbour and the Courtenay River up to the Lewis Bridge. Chart 3527 shows the various ranges and other navigation aids in excellent detail

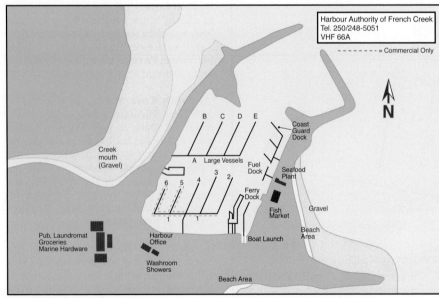

French Creek Boat Harbour

and could save you from much uncertainty.

Comox is a busy little city, population 13,600, with breakwater-protected marina docks. HMCS *Quadra*, a Canada Sea Cadet camp, is across the bay from Comox on Goose Spit.

The Comox Valley is a popular retirement area. Albertans from the oil patch can take daily flights to the Comox airport and enjoy golf and skiing within an hour of one another, right on Vancouver Island.

From Baynes Sound the entrance to Comox is well marked, but be careful of drying flats off Gartley Point and in the inner half of the bay. The breakwater in front of the town will be clearly visible. As the harbor map shows, the breakwater shelters four sets of docks: the Comox Bay Marina; the Gas N Go fuel dock and marina; the municipal marina; and one set of Comox Harbour Authority public docks, used entirely by commercial fish boats. A launch ramp and two tidal grids are behind the breakwater. The other set of Harbour Authority public docks, where pleasure craft are welcomed, is around the east end of the breakwater.

Showers and laundry are located in the Harbour Authority's new building at the head of its docks.

Comox has good shopping and a number of restaurants. The downtown area includes a supermarket and chandlery. A hospital overlooks the bay. Regular bus service runs from Comox Mall to the town of Courtenay with more shops, restaurants and a museum. You can also go by dinghy up the slough to Courtenay. See the Courtenay section for more information.

SEARCHING FOR THE BAR

Many years ago my then-teenage daughter and I were coming south along the Vancouver Island side from Desolation Sound. A southeast gale was blowing, with flying haze that obscured the shoreline. I had just about given up trying to find the outer buoy to the channel across Comox Bar and was prepared to jog offshore all night, when a small Canadian troller passed me close aboard, and almost immediately turned west onto the heading (222 degrees true) of the channel. Feeling lucky to have local knowledge so close at hand, I immediately followed him, and eventually wound up in Comox safe and sound, although thoroughly wet.

After getting secured, I walked up the dock where the troller was tied to thank its skipper for leading me in. "Hell," he said, "I bought this boat yesterday and have never been here before. I was totally lost and just guessing where that damn bar was. But when I saw you turn right behind me, I figured I must be in the right place!"

The halt leading the blind.

— Tom Kincaid

When you're in Comox, take the short walk to the Filberg Heritage Lodge & Park. It's a 9-acre estate built in the 1930s by logging baron R. J. Filberg, furnished and maintained in its original splendor. The heavy wood construction, fabulous gardens, and interesting outbuildings (root cellar, chicken coop, dairy barn, potting shed, and so forth) are must-see attractions. Weddings and art shows are held there.

Float planes: A float plane landing and takeoff zone is southwest of the marina breakwaters, with regularly scheduled flights. It does not affect anchoring behind Goose Spit or the approach to the marinas.

Golf: The Comox Golf Club, a well-maintained, flat and fun 9-hole course, is within walking distance of the docks. Call (250) 339-4444. A number of other courses (from good to outstanding) are a taxi ride away, or rent a car and have complete mobility.

Festival: The Filberg Festival, an arts, crafts, food, and enter-tainment celebration, draws 20,000 to 25,000 visitors each year. It's held at Filberg Park, east of the public floats in Comox Harbour. Dates coincide with Comox Nautical Days and B.C. Day long weekend. The park will be closed the week prior to the festival and the week following. Special events also can result in closures. Call first to confirm they are open (250) 339-2715. www.filbergfestival.com.

⑤ **Comox Bay Marina.** 1805 Beaufort, Box 20019, Comox, BC V9M 1R9; (250) 339-2930; manager@comoxbaymarina.com; www.comoxbaymarina.com. Dedicated guest moorage side-tie dock and moorage in available permanent slips. Water, 15, 30,

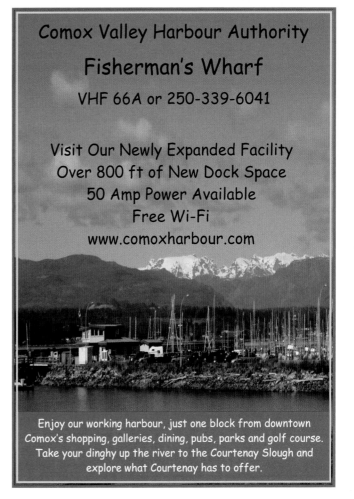

The Comox boat ramp makes a good launching point for trailerable boats heading to Desolation Sound from Vancouver Island.

Comox's nautical theme extends to the residential areas.

& 50 amp power, shower, washroom, free wireless internet, 24-hour access to laundry, garbage, and nearby floatplane service. The floating amenities building at the base of the ramp was new in 2012.

⑤ **Gas N Go Marine Ltd.** 11 Port Augusta St., Comox, BC V9M 7Z8; (250) 339-4664; (888) 575-4664; gasngomarine@gmail.com ; www.gasngomarine.com. Monitors VHF 66A. Open all year. Fuel dock with gasoline & diesel, four 40-foot slips, 15 amp power, washrooms, small store, wireless internet. As you approach, look for the Gas N Go sign.

⑤ **Comox Municipal Marina.** 1809 Beaufort Avenue, Comox, BC V9M 1R9; (250) 339-2202; (250) 339-3141. Permanent moorage only. Sublets available, call caretaker. Water, 15 & 20 amp power, garbage, cardboard and oil recycling, launch ramp, tidal grid, nearby washrooms and park, long-term pay parking.

⑤ **Comox Valley Harbour Author**ity. 121 Port Augusta St., Comox, BC V9M 3N8; (250) 339-6041; info@comoxharbour. com; www.comoxharbour.com. Monitors VHF 66A. Located at east end of the Comox breakwater. Guest moorage available on 2100 feet of docks, 20, 30 & 50 amp power. Holding tank pumpout, garbage drop, cardboard recycling, waste oil disposal, free Wi-Fi (get the password at the marina office). Clean washrooms, showers, laundry, and an air-conditioned lounge with a bucket of biscuits for visiting boat dogs.

This is a working waterfront facility, only two blocks from downtown Comox. In the summer, harbor staff move the fish boats to one float and reserve the other dock for overnight pleasure craft. Fresh seafood is available "off the boat." The Harbour Authority staff works hard to make visiting pleasure boaters feel welcome and comfortable.

Note: The dock configuration changed in 2012 with the addition of a new D dock connected to a steel floating breakwater. The marina diagram on pg. 215 shows the new configuration.

Caution: The shoreside of D dock is not dredged and dries at low tide. Do not go outside the floating breakwater.

⑥ **Courtenay.** For a pleasant diversion, take the dinghy a short distance up the Courtenay River to the town of Courtenay. A dredged channel, marked by ranges, leads through the delta to the river mouth. The river is an interesting break from the saltwater experience out on the strait.

Just before you reach Lewis Bridge (vertical clearance 10') Courtenay Slough leads off to the right. Inside, an extensive Comox Valley Harbour Authority float parallels the shore, and a city float is at the head. Enter the slough at high tide only. The mouth is blocked by a weir that dries 8 feet; without the weir the slough would empty completely at low tide.

The slough's Harbour Authority dock is gated and locked. Pick up a re-entry key at the office at the dock in Comox. An imposing restaurant dominates the view at the head of the slough. Excellent shopping and several restaurants are within easy walking distance.

Museum: We highly recommend a visit to the Courtenay & District Museum, a 4-block walk from the slough. There, hung from the ceiling, is the 40-foot-long skeletal reconstruction of an 80-million-year-old elasmosaur, excavated from the banks of the nearby Puntledge River. This is the most dramatic exhibit in an outstanding paleontological display. Other things you will see are dinosaur footprints, an extinct marine reptile that resembles a 15-foot-long alligator, and an ancient fish they call a "sabre-toothed salmon." We toured the museum and were impressed. Families with inquisitive children will be richly rewarded. There's much more than we can cover here. The museum is in the old brick post office building at 4th St. and Cliffe Avenue. From Comox you can get to the museum by bus or cab, or take the dinghy to Courtenay. Call for information: (250) 334-0686.

Cape Lazo. Cape Lazo is marked by a high cliff. Be sure to stay to seaward of Buoys PJ and PB. The buoys are well offshore, but shoals studded with boulders reach almost all

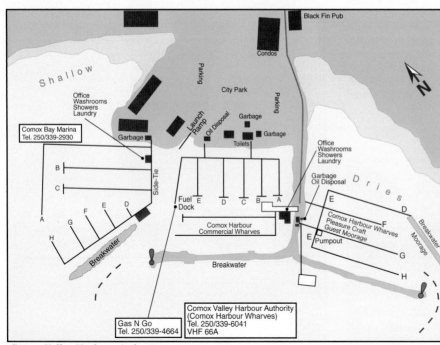

Comox Valley Harbour Authority

See a 40-foot-long 80-million-year-old elasmosaur at the Courtenay & District Museum.

This is one of the anchorages at Jedediah Island.

the way out to them.

Somewhere just north of Cape Lazo is the point at which the tidal currents change direction and begin flooding south from the north end of Vancouver Island, rather than north from Victoria.

Little River. Little River, 3 miles up-island from Cape Lazo, is the western terminus for the ferry to Westview/Powell River. Marginal moorage for a few small craft can be found behind the ferry dock.

Oyster River. A channel, dredged annually and marked by pilings, leads to the protected Pacific Playgrounds Marina next to the mouth of the Oyster River.

⑦ **Pacific Playgrounds International.** 9082 Clarkson Drive, Black Creek, BC V9J 1B3; (250) 337-5600; www.pacificplaygrounds.com. Open all year, 15 amp power, washrooms, showers, laundry, portapotty dump, launch ramp. This marina, for boats to 36 feet, is entered via a dredged channel, shallow at zero tide. Store carries marine supplies, some groceries.

LASQUETI ISLAND

Lasqueti Island is often overlooked by pleasure craft as they hurry across the strait between Nanaimo and the Sunshine Coast, or run along the Vancouver Island shore between Nanaimo and Campbell River. It has a number of good anchorages, and a convenience store at the village of Lasqueti, in False Bay at the northwest corner.

The south and west shores of Lasqueti Island are indented by a number of bays that invite anchorage. Along the south shore are Boat Cove, Old House Bay,

Richardson Cove, and Jenkins Cove, all of which are somewhat open to southerlies, but offer good protection from northerlies or in settled weather. This part of the Lasqueti shoreline is rugged and beautiful. On the southeast end is Squitty Bay—tiny, but with a public float. Several little dogholes for anchoring can be found in Bull Passage. Little Bull Passage, between Jedediah Island and Bull Island, has a number of good anchorages in both ends and is passable for most boats. Other anchorages are Boho Bay, Tucker Bay, and Scottie Bay. Spring Bay is only partially protected from the north by a group of small islands offshore.

⑧ **False Bay.** False Bay is the primary settlement on Lasqueti Island, with a public float with limited dock space and a float plane tie-up. A passenger-only ferry runs from False Bay to French Creek on Vancouver Island. Anchorage is possible off the public float, but the preferred anchorage is the north shore of the bay. On warm summer afternoons strong winds, called Qualicums, can blow through False Bay and make anchoring unpleasant.

⑨ **Squitty Bay.** Squitty Bay is a tiny, narrow, and shallow notch at the southeast corner of Lasqueti Island. It would be harrowing to enter Squitty Bay in a roaring southeasterly, but at other times entry should be easy. Rocks border the north side of the entrance; favor the south side. The public dock, 150 feet long, may be largely occupied by local boats. Rafting is permitted. Ashore, the trees in this area are bent and broken, obviously by strong winds. Tall trees are rare.

A walk along the roads is fascinating.

Bull Passage. Bull Passage and the islands that lie off the south end of Jedediah Island are rugged and scenic.

Little Bull Passage. Between high rock cliffs, Little Bull Passage is narrow and beautiful. Watch for the charted rock on the Jedediah Island side. It hides at high tide. Our notes say, "The east end of Little Bull Passage is absolutely fabulous. So much variety and strength in the rock walls and islands. Worth a side trip just to see the sights."

Jedediah Island. Jedediah Island is a marine park. Although good anchorages are scarce and tight, Jedediah Island is increasingly popular. One of the best anchorages is in the little notch opposite the south end of Paul Island, where chains have been installed along the north shore to facilitate stern-ties. The bay just south of the notch is usable, too. Long Bay goes dry a short distance inside the mouth. If nothing looks good on Jedediah Island itself, Boho Bay, about 1 mile away, is an alternative.

One interesting spot is the narrow and protected steep-sided notch at the southeast end of Jedediah Island. Although its sheer walls might discourage much on-shore exploration, it is possible to scramble from the head of the notch up the bluffs on the north side. You will be rewarded not only with access to the rest of the island but also an excellent view toward Texada Island. [*Hamilton*]

TEXADA ISLAND

Texada (pronounced "Tex-AY-da") Island has three main anchorages: Anderson Bay on Malaspina Strait at the south end; Blubber Bay at the northern tip of the island; and Sturt Bay, a couple of miles south along the Malaspina Strait (eastern) side. Although it has a ferry landing and public float, **Blubber Bay** is dominated by an enormous quarry and is not inviting. Anchorage, if needed, is possible.

Anderson Bay. Anderson Bay is at the south end of Texada Island, on Malaspina Strait. It is a beautiful spot, lined with sheer rock walls. Anchor in 24 feet near the head.

The quarry at Blubber Bay is uninviting, but a refuge in a southeaster.

At Sturt Bay, on Texada Island, moor at The Texada Boat Club floats. It offers good protection if things get rough on Malaspina Strait unless the wind is out of the southeast.

The safest approach is from the southeast. In our opinion, the pass between Texada Island and the unnamed 20-meter island is not as open as the charts suggest. We explored this pass at the bottom of a 1.6-foot low tide, and found rock shelves extending from the Texada Island side well into the pass. Be especially careful of the reef that extends from the southwest point of Texada Island. The reef dries at low tide, but at higher stages of tide it could be a nasty surprise.

⑩ **Sturt Bay.** Locally called Marble Bay, on Malaspina Strait near the north end of Texada Island. Sturt Bay has the best anchorage and moorage on Texada Island. The Texada Boat Club has extensive floats, visitors welcomed. The floats have water and 15 amp power. Bob and Maggie Timms are the wharfingers, (604) 486-0274. Anchorage is elsewhere in the bay.

Hiking trails are close to the docks. The Texada Island Inn (604-486-7711) has Wi-Fi, as does the Centenial Service Garage (gas station), a block beyond the inn. The gas station also has laundry facilities. A new RV campground just up the hill from the garage has laundry facilities and coin-operated showers. The full service grocery store has liquor and good meats. Correspondents Al and Becca Symanski tell us the Texada Island Museum, housed in a wing of the local school, is "must see."

We overnighted at Sturt Bay a few years ago and walked up to the the Texada Island Inn. The restaurant, with themed nights, closes at 8:00 p.m. The pub closes at 11:00 p.m. on weekdays, 2:00 a.m. on weekends. It was about a 15-minute walk and we had to ask for directions. This turned out to be a good thing, because Texada Islanders are a relaxed, friendly lot, with equally friendly dogs.

As mentioned above, you can anchor out in Sturt Bay. Our notes, however, say, "You'd save the moorage fee, but you'd miss everything." [*Hale*]

Caution: Sturt Bay is a welcome haven if a northwesterly is kicking up Malaspina Strait, but not suitable in a fresh southeasterly. Swells from a southeasterly bounce back from the north shore of the bay, making it and the guest moorage dock lumpy. Blubber Bay is a better anchorage in a southeasterly.

Vananda/Sturt Bay Public Wharf. Dock has 98 feet of mooring space. Exposed and not very interesting. Nearby Sturt Bay is preferred.

Harwood Point Regional Park. Gillies Bay, Texada Island. Anchor out only and dinghy in to a 40-acre park. Grass fields, picnic tables, campsites, pit toilets.

DOGS ON BOARD

There are really only two types of boaters—those who cruise with dogs, and those who don't. Those who don't think cruising with dogs is for the birds. The rest of us know cruising with dogs is best.

There are many reasons why this is so. The main reason lies at the heart of why we cruise in the first place. Muttless cruisers scoff at the thought of going ashore two, three or more times a day to attend to the hound's needs. They may scoff at going ashore altogether. But cruising is about exploring, and on those routine shoreside jaunts, dog people come to know the terrain with an intimacy one wouldn't have thought possible. When our fellow-cruisers are still abed, listening to the coffee perk while cold rain drums on the deck above them, we're ashore in full foul-weather gear, hiding under the dripping trees while Buddy sniffs out the perfect spot to lift a leg.

Led by The Nose, we hike to the ends of obscure trails—and beyond. We scramble over slippery rocks and dig up the coast's finest beaches. We come to know this extraordinary place in all its moods.

Dogs initiate us into the world of wildlife, living and dead. In Jedediah Island's Deep Bay, my wife Jan took our dachshund Rosie ashore for her evening visit. Suddenly, Spouse was leaping over rocks and crashing through bushes in hot pursuit of Hound, who was in hot pursuit of one of Jedediah Island's rank-smelling wild goats. To Rosie, a city beast with a hunter's heart, the goat's scent trail must have seemed as wide as the I-5 freeway.

Dead wildlife also has its attractions, especially if it's decaying and smelly. If you are a canine, getting in touch with your Inner Hunter means disguising your scent so your prey can't smell you coming. A beach walk is not complete without a roll on a dead crab, a seagull or fish carcass . . . or worse.

On Wallace Island, for example, it was my turn to chase Rosie as she bounded over logs and disappeared into Cabin Bay. From afar I watched in horror as she sniffed the rotting remains of a seal, then looked at me for permission to roll. All I could do was yell "Nooooo!" at the top of my lungs. Rosie looked mighty put out but, incredibly, she left her prize untouched.

Aboard the boat, settling down with Rosie in my lap gives me an ironclad excuse for not moving when my mate asks me to do something. In fact, it allows me to issue orders: "Could you pass up my sweater (my binoculars, my wine glass, my dinner . . .)?" It's not unknown for the crew of our little ship to have a debate about whose knee gets Rosie. These arguments are more frequent on chilly off-season cruises, when Rosie gives off the warmth of a modest cabin heater.

What dogs really teach us is how to enjoy the simple things. When the trails have been walked, the beaches dug and the goats chased, it's time for us all to sit down together, to listen to the sounds or the silence, feel the tide turn, watch the birds fly and the sun set, and savor life on this coast in all its perfection.

Yes, cruising with dogs is best.

— *Duart Snow*

Duart Snow is a former editor of Pacific Yachting *magazine and current editor of* Canadian Yachting West *magazine.*

CHAPTER 9

VANCOUVER, MAINLAND B.C. & THE SUNSHINE COAST

WHITE ROCK TO VANCOUVER

The coastline between Boundary Bay and Vancouver is an uninteresting river delta and the waters are often rough. Sediment from the Fraser River has created shoal depths for some distance offshore. The prevailing winds tend to blow against the river current in the shallow water, and steep seas build quickly. Stay well off in deeper water, but even there, a 20-knot wind can make for a rough ride.

We listened on the radio one day when a storm front blew through, and we sympathized with a terrified woman aboard a chartered 45-foot powerboat caught in steep seas near Roberts Bank. She kept repeating their lat/lon coordinates from the GPS and begging for help. The boat wasn't taking on water and no one was injured, but conditions were awful and they were scared. There was nothing another boat could do.

A few weeks earlier we had spoken with a couple who had gone up that shore to Vancouver and had a very rough ride of it, the kind of ride they never wanted to repeat— period. We have run that coast in calm conditions and had no problems. If you decide to go that way, be sure conditions are favorable. [*Hale*]

Most pleasure craft choose to go north through the Gulf Islands, then pick a patch of good weather to cross the Strait of Georgia to Vancouver or Howe Sound. The shortest distance across the strait, from Gabriola Pass to Howe Sound, is 14 miles. Even slow boats can make the crossing in 2 or 3 hours; faster boats can cross in an hour or less.

Boundary Bay. The U.S./Canada border runs through Boundary Bay. Delta, B.C. is located on the northwest shore. Point Roberts, Washington, is to the southwest. White Rock and the Semiahmoo First Nation's reserve are on the southeast shore. The southeastern section of Boundary Bay, straddling the U.S./Canada border is known as Semiahmoo Bay. The northern tip of Boundary Bay is known as Mud Bay.

① **White Rock.** White Rock, in Canada, is almost due north of Blaine, in Boundary Bay. A long pier crosses tide flats, with floats at the

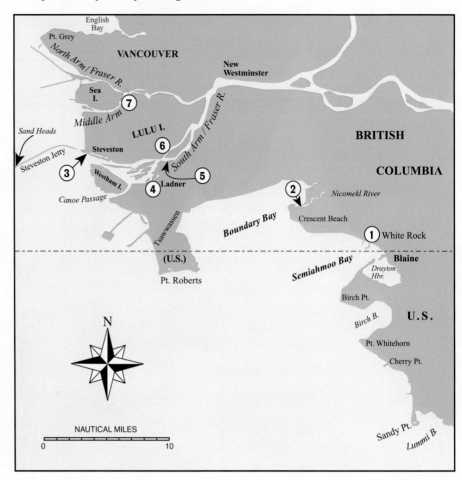

CHARTS

3463	Strait of Georgia, Southern Portion (1:80,000)
3488	Fraser River, Pattullo Bridge to Crescent Island (1:20,000)
3489	Fraser River, Crescent Island to Harrison Mills (1:20,000)
3490	Fraser River, Sand Heads to Douglas Island (1:20,000)
3491	Fraser River, North Arm (1:20,000)
3492	Roberts Bank (1:20,000)

outer end. The village has interesting shops and galleries.

① **City of White Rock Pier**. White Rock is a Canada Customs port of entry; call (888) 226-7277. The south side of the eastern float is reserved for transient moorage.

② **Crescent Beach.** North of White Rock, the Nicomekl River empties into Boundary Bay, creating a channel that leads to the village of Crescent Beach and the Crescent Beach Marina. The channel is marked by port and starboard daymarks. The marina is located just beyond the Burlington Northern Railway swing bridge that crosses the river to Blackie Spit. Depending on tide, bridge clearance ranges from 9 to 20 feet. The bridge is manned 7 days a week, from 6:30 a.m. until 10:30 p.m., and will open to 3 whistle blasts. Call the bridge at (604) 538-3233 or call the Crescent Beach Marina at (604) 538-9666, and they will contact the bridge tender.

② **Crescent Beach Marina Ltd.** 12555 Crescent Road, Surrey, BC V4A 2V4; (604) 538-9666; info@crescentbeachmarina. com; www.crescentbeachmarina.com. Open all year, gasoline & diesel at the fuel dock. Guest moorage for boats to 50 feet; call first. Haulout on hydraulic trailers to 35 tons, 15, 20 & 30 amp power, washrooms, ice, repairs, chandlery, launch ramp, showers, laundry, pumpout.

Canoe Passage. Canoe Passage is the southernmost mouth of the Fraser River. The seaward entrance is marked by a government buoy, but private dolphins mark its winding path through Roberts Bank. Although mainly used by commercial boats with local knowledge, Canoe Passage can be used by small craft, especially at half tide or better on a rising tide. The swing bridge connecting Westham Island with the mainland is manned 24 hours a day, and opens to 3 whistle blasts. Contact the bridge tender on VHF 74 or by telephone at (604) 946-2121. In 1997 the Canadian Hydrographic Service published large scale Chart 3492 (1:20,000) showing Canoe Passage, but we are skeptical. Locals who use the passage re-mark the channel yearly, after major runoff has moved the sand bars.

South Arm Fraser River. Sand Heads marks the mouth of the South Arm (also called the **Main Arm**) of the Fraser River. The South Arm is the Fraser's major entry, and is protected on its north side by the Steveston Jetty. Currents in the Fraser River can run to 5 knots, depending on the volume of water in the river, which in turn depends on rain and snow melt upstream. Large flood tides will at times slow or reverse the current.

Caution: An on-shore wind meeting an ebb current, combined with heavy outflow from the river, will create dangerously steep and high seas in the river mouth. Friends

An excursion boat roars past a tug with a tow entering Steveston.

A busy day on the Steveston waterfront. Lots of choices for shopping and dining.

who keep their boats on the river tell of their entire boat being airborne in these conditions.

The lower part of the Fraser River is delta country, low and flat. The marshlands are havens for wildlife, and you'll see many eagles. The river itself contains much drift. The river is used heavily by fish boats, tugs towing barges or log booms, Coast Guard boats, work boats of all description, and freighters. Water-oriented industrial companies are located along the shores.

Relatively few cruising boats go up the Fraser River, in part because the entire coast between Point Grey and Point Roberts is uninteresting to view, and hostile in any kind of wind. Most of the marinas on the Fraser River exist primarily for permanent moorage tenants, with few facilities for visitors.

③ **Steveston.** The first stop on the Fraser River is Steveston, a long, slender harbor on the north side of Cannery Channel, protected by a sand island (Steveston Island). Although Steveston is primarily a fishing town with moorage and other services for commercial fishermen, it has become a lively tourist destination as well. Pleasure craft may use the moorage when the fishing fleet is out. Steveston has a fuel dock. Chandleries, antiques shops, bookstores, plenty of dining and all the other facilities of a small city are ashore. The streets of Steveston are quaint; the local

movie industry sometimes films scenes there.

③ **Steveston Harbour Authority Wharf.** 12740 Trites Rd., Richmond, BC V7E 3R8; (604) 272-5539; www.steveston-harbour.com. Open all year, 20 & 30 amp power, water, washrooms, showers. Pleasure craft may use inside pier, east of fish sales float, reservations required. Commercial vessels have priority. Wakes from passing traffic make the outside face of the dock a little bumpy.

③ **Steveston Chevron.** (604) 277-4712. Fuel dock with gasoline, diesel, washrooms. Limited marine supplies, lubricants, snacks.

④ **Ladner.** Ladner is a pretty town. Leave the main branch of the Fraser River and take Sea Reach to Ladner Harbour, fronted by float homes. A fish boat moorage is on the port side. Pleasure craft are welcome when the fleet is out. Strongly favor the south shore as you enter Ladner Harbour, skirting the docks of marinas and businesses located along River Road. A drying mud bank, studded with deadheads, extends a considerable distance from the north side of the harbor.

④ **Ladner Yacht Club.** (604) 946-4056; www.ladneryachtclub.ca. Reciprocal boats only if space is available. Water, restrooms, 30 amp power, secured marina.

Deas Slough. Deas Slough is home to Captain's Cove, located behind Deas Island, a little farther up the river from Ladner. A low bridge (Hwy. 99) blocks passage any farther up Deas Slough, except for small boats with no masts.

⑤ **Captain's Cove Marina & Pub.** 6100 Ferry Rd., Ladner, BC V4K 3M9; (604) 946-1244; info@captainscovemarina.ca; www.captainscovemarina.ca. Open all year, guest moorage available for boats from 28 to 60 feet, best to call ahead. The fuel dock has gasoline and diesel. Washrooms, showers, laundry, water, 30 & 50 amp power, waste oil disposal, pumpout, Wi-Fi. The facility is large and well cared for. Pub on site, haulout to 60 tons, and a yard for repairs.

Golf. Cove Links, a pretty (and pretty challenging, we're told) 9-hole par 29 golf course next to Captain's Cove Marina, is part of development that includes homes and condos.

⑥ **Shelter Island Marina Inc.** 6911 Graybar Rd., Richmond, BC V6W 1H3; (604) 270-6272; www.shelterislandmarina.com. Open all year, some guest moorage, call ahead. Washrooms, showers, laundry, water, 15, 30, & 50 amp power, Travelift for boats to 220 tons, full service chandlery. Restaurant and pub, beer and wine store. Free wireless in restaurant.

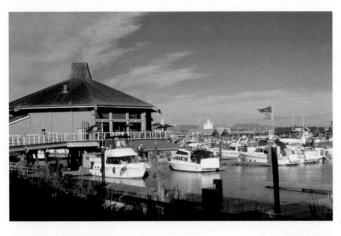

Delta River Inn has excellent docks. The building on the left houses a good restaurant.

Shelter Island Marina is behind Don Island at the south entrance to Annacis Channel. It is a busy facility with a number of boat repair companies.

New Westminster. New Westminster is located at the confluence of the North and South Arms of the Fraser River, and is heavily industrialized along the waterfront.

Contributing Editor Tom Kincaid has run the river past New Westminster to the Pitt River, where he spent the night at the Pitt Meadows Marina. A few friends have continued to the Harrison River, running up the Harrison River to Harrison Lake and Harrison Hot Springs. All recommend having a fast boat and a knowledgeable pilot aboard before attempting to run either of these rivers. The Fraser River beyond Richmond is poorly marked, with sand bars that are con-

stantly changing. The river is navigable as far as Hope during high water stages, but mariners should rely on local knowledge before attempting this run.

North Arm Fraser River. The North Arm of the Fraser River is lined with boatbuilding and repair yards and other businesses that serve the marine community. A jetty runs through Sturgeon Bank along the south side of the North Arm, parallel to the Point Grey shoreline. A dredged basin, known locally as "Coward's Cove" or the "Chicken Hole," is on the north side of the channel, just before the North Arm enters the Strait of Georgia. The basin gives good protection to skippers while they assess conditions out on the strait.

⑦ **Richmond Chevron.** 7891 Grauer Rd., Richmond, BC V7B 1N4; (604) 278-2181.

Beneath Arthur Laing Bridge. Open all year, gasoline, diesel, kerosene, lubricants and waste oil disposal.

Middle Arm Fraser River. The Middle Arm of the Fraser River runs along the south side of Sea Island, which is almost entirely taken up by Vancouver International Airport. The west entrance is blocked by Sturgeon Bank, with no marked channels. We have seen a small, fast cruiser enter the Middle Arm, but the tide was high and perhaps the skipper had local knowledge (or maybe he was just lucky). Prudence dictates entry from the North Arm only. The Delta River Inn Marina and Vancouver Marina are on the Middle Arm, near a low swing bridge connecting the city of Richmond with the airport.

⑦ **Delta River Inn Marina.** 3500 Cessna Drive, Richmond, BC V7B 1C7; (604) 278-1241. Located 8 miles up the North Arm of the Fraser River in Moray Channel at Delta Vancouver Airport Hotel. Open all year, limited guest moorage, call ahead. The marina has 20 & 30 amp power, customs clearance, haulout to 50 tons, and full service shop on site. The marina is operated by Delta Charters. The hotel has several restaurants, a bar, and a pool. They run a bus to the local shopping mall.

⑦ **Vancouver Marina.** #200-8211 River Road, Richmond, BC V6X 1X8; (604) 278-9787; (604) 278-3300; mooring@vancouvermarina.com; www.vancouvermarina.com. Monitors 66A. Open all year, call ahead for guest moorage. Gasoline & diesel at the fuel dock, 15, 20 & 30 amp power, garbage, recycling and waste oil disposal, washrooms, no showers. They carry marine supplies, snacks, bait, and ice. Restaurant, mechanic and parts department, haulout to 30 feet. Located in the heart of Richmond on the Middle Arm of the Fraser River.

⑦ **Skyline Marina.** 8031 River Road, Richmond, BC V6X 1X8; (604) 273-3977; www. skylinemarina.ca. Open all year, no transient moorage. The marina has a 30 ton haulout.

VANCOUVER

Vancouver is the largest city in British Columbia, and the major deepwater port on the west coast of Canada, handling cargo from across Canada and around the world. The city is clean, safe, and thoroughly cosmopolitan. Its architecture is exciting. Vancouver's parks, museums, hotels, and dining are wonderful.

If you are approaching Vancouver from the south, you could go up the North Arm of the Fraser River to a number of marinas in the Richmond area, and take a bus into the city. If you are approaching from the north, you could tie up at Horseshoe Bay or at Snug Cove, on the south side of Bowen Island. From Snug Cove you would take the ferry to Horseshoe Bay, then board a bus for the trip into Vancouver—or as far south as White Rock if that's where you wanted to go. The Vancouver bus system is excellent and affordable.

For moorage in Vancouver proper, choose either the Vancouver Harbour area or the False Creek area. Each has advantages, and each is good. Once you're settled, Vancou-

The Vancouver skyline is the backdrop behind Coal Harbour.

ver's bus system allows you to get around the entire area with minimum delay.

Anchoring restriction: Pleasure craft may anchor in False Creek (free permit required) but not in English Bay.

Point Grey. Point Grey marks the southern entrance to Burrard Inlet. When approaching from the south, cutting too close to Point Grey risks grounding on Spanish Bank. Leave the buoys to starboard when entering.

Spanish Bank. Spanish Bank is an extensive drying bank off the north shore of Point Grey. The outer edge of the bank is marked with buoys. Royal Vancouver Yacht Club has its main clubhouse and sailboat moorage about 3 miles from Point Grey along the south shore of English Bay. A launch ramp is close to the former Kitsilano Coast Guard station near the entrance to False Creek.

FALSE CREEK

Anchoring permits: After years of effort, the squatters have been removed from False Creek and visiting boats can anchor there easily. Anchoring permits (free) are required for day anchoring longer than 8 hours and

overnight anchoring. Permits can be picked up at the Vancouver Boating Welcome Centre on the dock at False Creek Yacht Club (at the Welcome Boat on the water), or if after hours, by self-registering at Stamps Landing on the south side of False Creek. Boats without permits are subject to ticketing and fines up to $500.

False Creek Yacht Club, on the north shore of False Creek, usually has guest slips available. Quayside Marina, also on the north shore, has excellent facilities and some guest moorage. Fishermen's Wharf marina on the south shore has transient moorage and very good facilities. The marina is managed by the False Creek Harbour Authority. It is a short walk from there to the Granville Island Market, shops, and restaurants. False Creek is covered by Wi-Fi.

Blue Pacific Charters (604-682-2161), on the west side of Granville Island near the Granville Market, sometimes has moorage available. To reach these docks turn just before the Bridge Restaurant, on the south side when you enter False Creek, and work your way towards the docks. On the east side of Granville Island the Pelican Bay Marina, next to the Granville Island Hotel, has some guest moorage.

CHARTS

3311sc Small craft charts (strip charts)	Sunshine Coast to Desolation Sound
3463	Strait of Georgia – Southern Portion (1:80,000)
3481	Approaches to Vancouver Harbour (1:25,000)
3493	Vancouver Harbour, Western Portion (1:10,000)
3494	Vancouver Harbour, Central Portion (1:10,000) Second Narrows (1:6,000)
3495	Vancouver Harbour, Eastern Portion (1:10,000) Indian Arm (1:6,000)
3512	Strait of Georgia, Central Portion (1:80,000)
3526	Howe Sound (1:40,000)
3534 Plans	Howe Sound: Mannion Bay, Snug Cove, Fishermans Cove, Horseshoe Bay, Shoal Channel, Squamish Harbour

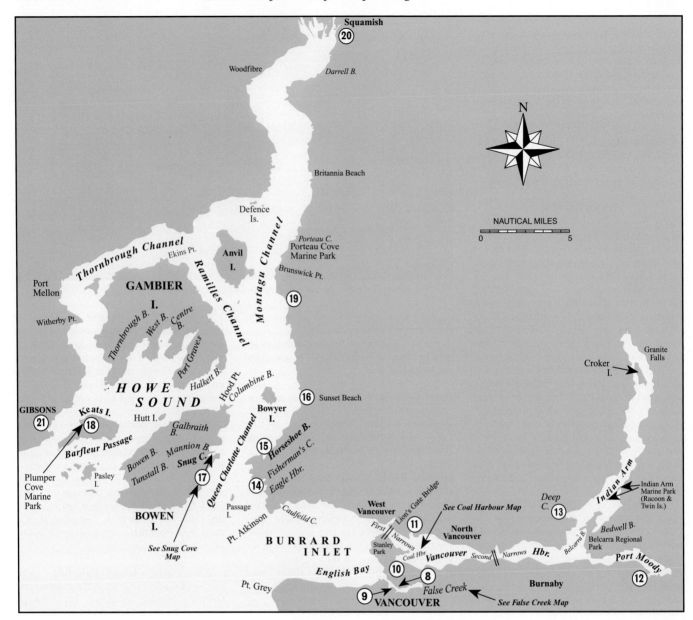

Granville Island is an active and vibrant place, full of people. You'll find a busy food market (smaller, but similar in many ways to Seattle's Pike Place Market), many restaurants, galleries, shops, and a variety of marine supplies, both on the island and a short walk away. Docks face the waterway, and are posted for 3-hour maximum stay.

Two harbor foot ferry franchises serve False Creek. If anchored, you can hail a passing ferry for transportation around the creek. Great for a tour of the harbor too.

Fuel: Fuel is available at the False Creek Fuel Dock.

Pumpouts: Pumpouts are located at Burrard Bridge Civic Marina, False Creek Harbour Authority Fishermen's Wharf, Heather Civic Marina (under the large "Monk's" sign), and Quayside Marina.

THINGS TO DO

1. **Granville Market**. On Granville Island, a delight to the senses with flowers, spices, teas, fruit and other food markets, restaurants and crafts.

2. **Aquabus Foot Ferries**. Crisscross the water from False Creek. Travel to different attractions or stay aboard to tour the entire harbor area. Some ferries allow bicycles.

3. **Vancouver Maritime Museum**. Learn more about B.C. maritime history from Vancouver to the Arctic. See tugboats, fireboats and even pirates. Easily reached by Aquabus.

4. **Stanley Park**. Rent a bike and ride the trail along the seawall. Several bike rental shops are on Denman Street, near Coal Harbour. Or, take a walk around the park. While in Stanley Park, learn more about B.C.'s First

Nations people in Klahowya Village.

5. **Vancouver Aquarium**. Located in Stanley Park. Excellent. Don't miss the white Beluga whales.

6. **Spirit Catcher Miniature Train**. Take a ride and see the story of Sasquatch.

7. **Science World**. The distinctive domed glass building on False Creek with imaginative exhibits and hands-on experiments for young and old.

8. **Bloedel Floral Conservatory**. Tropical plants and colorful birds flying about. In Queen Elizabeth Park.

9. **Museum of Anthropology**. On the University of British Columbia campus. Study of First Nations people and other B.C. cultures.

10. **Deeley Motorcycle Exhibition**. Over

The False Creek Yacht Club and the Vancouver Boating Welcome Centre are located under the Granville Street Bridge.

The Granville Market has a colorful array of flowers, fruit, vegetables, fish and other items.

250 motorcycles on exhibit, spanning 115 years and 59 different manufacturers.

11. **Yaletown** or **Gastown**. Key shopping areas with many shops and boutiques.

⑧ **Vancouver Boating Welcome Centre.** 1661 Granville St., Vancouver, BC V6Z 1N3; (604) 648-2628; welcome@fcyc.com. Monitors VHF 66A. Open 7 days a week all year. Hours 9:00 a.m to 7:00 p.m. The Boating Welcome Centre is in a clearly marked boat tied to the outside dock at False Creek Yacht Club. Permits for False Creek anchoring (no charge) are issued there. They provide local marine information.

⑨ **False Creek Fuel Dock.** 1655 Whyte Avenue, Vancouver, BC V6J 1A9; (604) 638-0209; fillup@falsecreekfuels.com; www.falsecreekfuels.com. Just west of the Burrard Street Bridge, the 120-foot float carries gas, diesel, oil, lubricants. Open 7 days a week. The store has drinks, snacks, ice cream, sand-wiches (seasonal), and a coffee bar. It also has ice, bait, tackle, marine supplies, guidebooks.

⑨ **False Creek Harbour Authority Fishermen's Wharf.** 1505 W. 1st Ave., Vancouver, BC V6J 1E8; (604) 733-3625; info@falscreek.com; www.falsecreek.com. Monitors VHF 66A. This is a 4-Anchor Clean Marina, open all year, around the clock. It is on the south shore of False Creek, west of Granville Island. *Contact the wharf office for tie-up instructions before landing.* Customs clearance at the outer end of the fish sales dock. Mostly 30 amp power with some 20 amp; water, washrooms, showers, laundry, ice, pumpout, recycling, waste oil disposal, 24-hour security, Wi-Fi. The ramps to shore are 75 feet long and 5 feet wide, and fitted with transition plates at each end to make them fully handicap compliant. Go Fish is a popular take-out. Expect long lines at noontime. Dine outside on picnic tables.

Fishing vessels have moorage priority, but transient moorage is available in the summer. A fish sales dock is just east of the main dock.

Fresh fish and prawns right off the boat are sometimes available. Do not tie to the fish sales dock, even if it is empty.

⑨ **Blue Pacific Yacht Charters.** 1519 Foreshore Walk, Vancouver, BC V6H 3X3; (604) 682-2161; info@bluepacificcharters.com; www.bluepacificcharters.com. Open all year, moorage in unoccupied slips as available, 30 & 50 amp power, washrooms, showers, haulout and repairs. Located on the west side of Granville Island.

⑨ **Pelican Bay Marina.** 1708 W. 6th Ave., Vancouver, BC V6J 5E8; (604) 729-1442; pelicanbaymarina@mail.com. Open all year, adjacent to the Granville Island Hotel on the east end of Granville Island. Moorage in un-occupied slips when available, 15, 30 & 50 amp power, water, washroom, ice.

⑧ **False Creek Yacht Club.** 1661 Granville St., Vancouver, BC V6Z 1N3; (604) 682-3292; www.fcyc.com. Open all year on the north side of False Creek, directly under

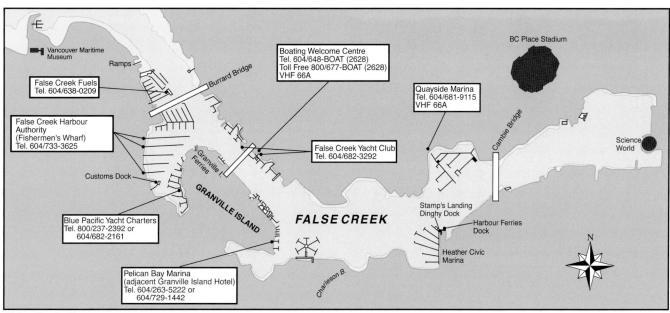

False Creek, Vancouver

Visitors can watch artists carving totem poles on Granville Island.

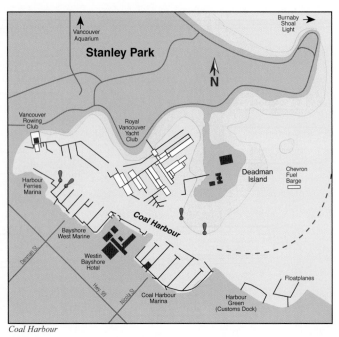

Coal Harbour is in the middle of downtown Vancouver.

the Granville Street Bridge. Guest moorage in unoccupied slips. Slips usually are available. Call the dock master, (604) 648-2628, before arriving. Washrooms, showers, laundry, pumpout, Wi-Fi, lounge, 30 amp power. A passenger foot ferry runs regularly to Granville Island. This is where False Creek anchoring permits can be obtained.

⑧ **Quayside Marina.** 1088 Marinaside Crescent, Vancouver,

BC V6Z 3C4; (604) 681-9115; (604) 209-6456; qsmarina@ ranchogroup.com; www.rancho-van.com/marina. Monitors VHF 66A. Open all year, 30, 50 & 100 amp power, water on the docks, washrooms, showers, laundry, pay telephone, pumpout, garbage and recycling, ice, security. Wheelchair accessible.

The Quayside (pronounced "Keyside") Marina is on the north shore of False Creek, in the middle of Vancouver's cosmopolitan

Yaletown district. It is approximately opposite the prominent Monk McQueen's restaurant on the south shore. Most of the slips are for permanent moorage, but guest moorage is available on a 500-foot-long float extending from shore, or in vacant slips. Colorful Aquabus foot ferry boats come and go from their spot near the head of that float. Moorage reservations are essential during high season and requested year-round. Although it's a bit of a walk from the guest dock to the office, check in promptly after you arrive.

Vancouver Maritime Museum. 1905 Ogden Avenue in Vanier Park, Vancouver, BC V6J 1A3; (604) 257-8300; www.van-couvermaritimemuseum.com. If you can, spend some time at the

Vancouver Maritime Museum. It's on the south shore of English Bay at the entrance to False Creek. The museum's docks are for display boats only. The vessel *St. Roch*, which explored the Northwest Passage across the top of Canada between the Atlantic and Pacific Oceans, is on display in its own building. The Aquabus ferries include the museum on their water route in the harbor.

STRONG CURRENTS: Currents run strongly in both First and Second Narrows. Use caution, especially because of the heavy traffic that frequents the area.

Coal Harbour

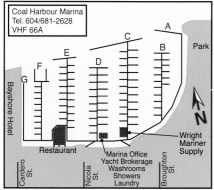

Coal Harbour Marina

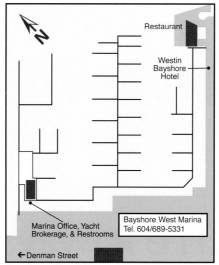

Bayshore West Marina

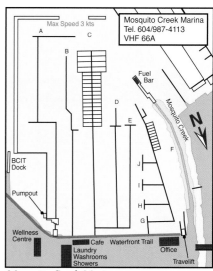

Mosquito Creek Marina

Vancouver Harbour (South). Vancouver Harbour is entered under the Lions Gate Bridge through First Narrows, in the northeast corner of Burrard Inlet. Because of heavy commercial traffic, strong currents and narrow channels, sailing craft must be under power from westward of First Narrows until well into Vancouver Harbour. No sailing is permitted through Second Narrows, either. In First Narrows, a strong ebb current meeting a fresh onshore breeze can create high, steep seas. Current predictions are shown in the Tide and Current Tables, Vol. 5 and Ports and Passes. Monitor VHF 12 for Vancouver Vessel Traffic Services (VTS) information.

Watch for drifting logs, float plane traffic,

and Vancouver Rowing Club rowers in Vancouver Harbour. Approaching Coal Harbour, leave Burnaby Shoal and the Chevron fuel barge to starboard. Observe a 5-knot speed limit.

Once into Vancouver Harbour, your best bet for moorage is along the southern shoreline in the Coal Harbour area. Vancouver Rowing Club, located adjacent to Stanley Park, has moorage for members of reciprocal yacht clubs. The Coal Harbour area, from

the Vancouver Rowing Club to Coal Harbour Marina, is covered by Wi-Fi. Stanley Park is nearby.

Bayshore West Marina, next to the Harbour Ferries docks, has all new facilities.

Coal Harbour Marina, just east of the Bayshore Hotel, makes a visit to Vancouver a real pleasure. It is first class in every way, and is an excellent base for a few days in town.

These marinas are close to downtown Vancouver, a pleasant walk or short cab ride

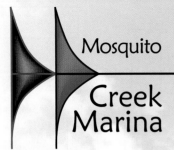

away. Wright Mariner Supply, occupying a floating structure in the Coal Harbour Marina, sells a complete range of marine supplies, clothing, charts, and books.

Robson Street's shops, galleries and wide range of restaurants are just a few blocks away.

Anchoring restriction: Pleasure craft may not anchor in Vancouver Harbour between First Narrows and Second Narrows.

Customs dock: The customs dock is a Parks Board dock called "Harbour Green," east of Coal Harbour Marina. Day moorage is okay, but not overnight. The dock is managed by The Mill Marine Bistro.

⑩ **Coal Harbour Chevron.** (604) 681-7725. Fuel barge in Coal Harbour open 7 days a week 7:00 a.m. to 11:00 p.m., gasoline & diesel, washrooms, showers. They do oil changes and have waste oil disposal.

⑩ **Coal Harbour Marina.** 1525 Coal Harbour Quay, Vancouver, BC V6G 3E7; (604) 681-2628; guestservices@coalharbourmarina.com; www.coalharbourmarina.com. Monitors

VHF 66A. Open all year, guest moorage for boats to 330 feet, reservations recommended. Facilities include 30, 50, & 100 amp single/three-phase and 150 amp three-phase power, Wi-Fi, pumpout, washrooms, showers, laundry. This is a first-class marina, with wide concrete docks, 24-hour staff, security gates, a restaurant, marine supply store, and easy access to downtown Vancouver.

⑩ **Bayshore West Marina.** 450 Denman St., Vancouver, BC V6G 3J1; (604) 689-5331; bayshorewest@thunderbirdmarine.com; www.thunderbirdmarine.com. Open all year, limited guest moorage to 115 feet. They have 30, 50, & 100 amp power, garbage, Wi-Fi, washrooms, and pumpout. Located between the Westin Bayshore Resort in Coal Harbour and Stanley Park. Restaurants and shopping within easy walking distance. The slips and fairways are wide for easy maneuvering.

Vancouver Harbour (North). The north shore of Vancouver Harbour is mostly heavy com-

mercial, although Mosquito Creek Marina is an excellent stop close to downtown North Vancouver. SeaBus foot ferry service runs from North Vancouver to downtown Vancouver at Lonsdale Quay. The crossing takes 12 minutes and connects with other transportation options in downtown Vancouver. For more information see the Vancouver Transit planning website: www.translink.ca.

A number of good repair shops are in Mosquito Creek Marina and at Lynnwood Marina, just west of Second Narrows.

St. Roch Dock. (604) 982-3910; www.cnv.org. This is a day-use pleasure craft float adjacent to the newly-developed 700-foot-long Burrard Dry Dock Pier in North Vancouver. Hours at St. Roch Dock are 6:00 a.m. to 11:00 p.m., no overnight moorage. Allow ample time to walk up to North Vancouver's downtown for sightseeing or dinner. The moorage is east of the Lonsdale Quay public market. Lonsdale Quay is easily recognized by the large rotating "Q" on top of a red tower.

Saturday Summer Concerts: July through August at Shipbuilders Square at the foot of Lonsdale.

Caution: The SeaBus north terminus is just west of Lonsdale Quay, with frequent arrivals and departures of two foot-passenger catamaran SeaBus ferries.

⑪ **Mosquito Creek Marina.** 415 West Esplanade, North Vancouver, BC V7M 1A6; (604) 987-4113; donny_mekilok@squamish.net; www.mosquitocreekmarina.com. Open all year with guest moorage to 160 feet, reservations recommended, 15,

30 & 50 amp power (100 amp on Dock A), new washrooms and laundry, cafe, Wi-Fi, 50-ton Travelift, potable water, pumpout, marine repairs, security locks on the dock gates, 24-hour security, and general store. Fuel dock with gasoline and diesel.

The marina is close to Lonsdale Quay shopping, a marine chandlery (Martin Marine), restaurants, and tourist stops. Several boat repair companies, with complete services, are on-site. It's a 10-minute walk to the SeaBus foot ferries to downtown Vancouver. The annual "Boat Show at the Creek" is in September.

⑪ **Lynnwood Marina.** 1681 Columbia St., North Vancouver, BC V7J 1A5; (604) 985-1533; info@lynnwoodmarina.com; www.lynnwoodmarina.com. Moorage for repair customers only. The marina has 15 & 30 amp power, complete repairs, and haulout to 60 tons. Shopping is about a 10-minute walk away.

BURNABY, PORT MOODY, INDIAN ARM

Second Narrows. To proceed eastward from Vancouver Harbour to Burnaby and Port Moody, you first must go through Second Narrows. On spring tides, flood currents can reach 6.5 knots and ebb currents 5.5 knots. The narrows are not to be treated lightly. Wind and current opposing each other can create standing waves and difficult seas. The best advice is to go through near times of slack, although on small tides the current should present few problems for boats with adequate power. Current predictions are shown in the Tide and Current Tables, Vol. 5 and Ports

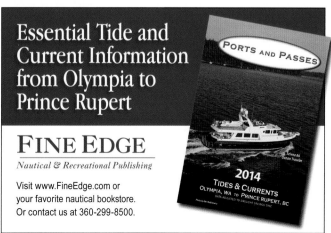

and Passes. Because of extensive, heavy displacement commercial traffic, monitor Vessel Traffic Service on VHF channel 12. Sailing is not permitted in Second Narrows.

Cates Park. Cates Park is at Roche Point, near the entrance to Indian Arm. The park has a paved launch ramp, beach, trails, playground, changing room, and picnic shelter. Temporary anchorage only.

Burnaby. The park at Burnaby is the site of an old sawmill. The park has no public float, but anchorage is good just east of the fishing pier.

Port Moody. Port Moody ends in drying flats, but a dredged channel on the south shore leads through the flats to Rocky Point Park. The park has a launch ramp, swimming pool and picnic areas, and is the location of the Port Moody Museum. Further development is underway. The Reed Point Marina, with moorage for about 900 boats, has a guest float, fuel, and the usual amenities associated with a large marina.

⑫ **Reed Point Marina.** 850 Barnet Highway, Port Moody, BC V6H 1V6; (604) 937-1600; office@reedpoint.com; www.reedpoint.com. Open all year, mid-grade gasoline and diesel. Washrooms, showers, pumpout, haulout to 55 tons, chandlery, sundries, seasonal concession stand, marine supplies and service.

INDIAN ARM

Indian Arm extends 11 miles into Coast Range mountains soaring to 5000 feet. Indian Arm is largely unpopulated beyond Deep Cove, because Deep Cove is the end of the road from North Vancouver. The waters in Indian Arm generally are calm, but can be ruffled by local downdraft winds off the mountains. Indian Arm is a little secret that Vancouver boaters have. It feels remote, yet it is close to the city.

Indian Arm Marine Park. In 1996 the Indian Arm Marine Park was expanded from the Twin Islands and Racoon Island to include most of the fjord. Croker Island and Granite Falls are part of the park.

Belcarra. Belcarra Regional Park is located on the east shore of Indian Arm, near the entrance. The public float is for loading and unloading only. Anchorage is good in Belcarra Bay. The park has 2 lakes, 4 miles of shoreline, and complete facilities. It's a popular stop.

Strathcona. The small Strathcona municipal float is at the mouth of Indian Arm across from Belcarra, behind White Rock and the Grey Rocks Islands. The float dries at low tide.

The Union Steamship Marina combines old world charm and modern amenities.

Deep Cove. Deep Cove is a city of about 5,000 people. The public float provides access to shopping in the town of Deep Cove, but no overnight moorage is permitted. The commercial village, adjacent to the public float, is upscale. Deep Cove is the location of the Deep Cove Yacht Club. Seycove Marina at the north end of Deep Cove has moorage, fuel, and other amenities.

Deep Cove Public Wharf. The dock is 145 feet long, and is within walking distance of grocery stores, restaurants, live theater, and other facilities. Day use only, no overnight moorage.

⑬ **Seycove Marina.** 2890 Panorama Drive, North Vancouver, BC V7G 1V6; (604) 929-1251. Open all year, gasoline and diesel at the fuel dock, limited guest moorage. Call ahead. Facilities include washrooms, showers, laundry, and convenience store. Deep Cove Village with restaurants and shopping is nearby.

Bedwell Bay. Bedwell Bay has the best anchorage in Indian Arm. The bay is sheltered from southerly winds.

Twin Islands and Racoon Island. The larger of the Twin Islands has a dinghy float on its east side, and picnic and sanitary facilities ashore. Anchorage offshore is quite deep (between 80 and 150 feet). Both Twin Islands and Racoon Island are used by kayakers and canoeists who pull their craft ashore.

Granite Falls. Granite Falls, the largest of the falls entering Indian Arm, tumbles off a cliff along the east bank. A small day dock makes access easy and serves campsites ashore. Anchorage is fair just offshore. The climb up the cliff is good exercise for cramped muscles. Because of the questionable anchoring bottom, overnight anchoring is not recommended if outflow winds are expected.

Wigwam Inn. The Wigwam Inn, at the head of Indian Arm, was a luxury resort whose rich history goes back to 1906. Today it is a Royal Vancouver Yacht Club outstation. RVYC members only. Burrard Yacht Club and Deep

Cove Yacht Club have outstations nearby—members only, no reciprocals.

POINT ATKINSON TO
HORSESHOE BAY

Caulfeild Cove. Caulfeild Cove is a tiny bight, protected from nearly all winds and seas, tucked into the shoreline just east of Point Atkinson. A 52-foot public float lies along the east side of the cove, with 6 feet of depth alongside.

Point Atkinson. Point Atkinson is the north entrance to Burrard Inlet. The waters just off Point Atkinson can be very rough, especially on a large ebb flowing against a fresh onshore wind. Often, a course well to seaward is called for, and even that can be heavy going. Point Atkinson is well known to Vancouver boaters, who give this area great respect.

Eagle Harbour. Eagle Harbour is the home of the Eagle Harbour Yacht Club. No guest moorage.

Fishermans Cove. Fishermans Cove, the home of West Vancouver Yacht Club, is filled with Thunderbird Marina. West Vancouver Yacht Club has some guest moorage for members of reciprocal clubs.

Important: Enter on the northwest side of the 39-meter island and Eagle Island, leaving the flashing red light to starboard. A "false entrance" between the 39-meter island and Eagle Island could put you in real trouble.

The passage from Eagle Harbour east of Eagle Island is shown clearly on Plans Chart 3534 but not on smaller scale Chart 3481.

The daymark in the northern mouth of the passage east of Eagle Island has been changed from port hand to starboard hand. This daymark relates to craft approaching from the north side of Eagle Island. Those craft should leave that daymark to starboard, to stay between the daymark and the docks on the north side of Fishermans Cove. Vessels northbound from Eagle Harbour should leave the daymark to port.

⑭ **Thunderbird Marina.** 5776 Marine Drive, West Vancouver, BC V7W 2S2; (604)

921-7484; thunderbird@thunderbirdmarine.com; www.thunderbirdmarine.com. Open all year. Haulout to 25 tons. Repairs available. Thunderbird Marine Supplies carries marine supplies and hardware.

HOWE SOUND

Howe Sound, about 12 miles from Vancouver, is the "backyard" for Vancouver area boaters. Stunning Coast Range mountains surround Howe Sound. Since the sound is largely unpopulated, it provides a wilderness setting close to the city.

Watch for the considerable drift floating in Howe Sound.

Horseshoe Bay. Horseshoe Bay is the eastern terminus of ferries serving the Gulf Islands, Sunshine Coast, and Vancouver Island. Sewell's Marina, a large, breakwater-protected public marina, is located to the west of the ferry docks. Boaters transiting this area are urged to use caution because of the steady procession of large ferry boats.

⑮ **Sewell's Marina Ltd.** 6409 Bay St., West Vancouver, BC V7W 3H5; (604) 921-3474; www.sewellsmarina.com. Open all year, gasoline and diesel fuel, limited

Union Steamship Marina's docks are busy in summer.

15 & 30 amp power, concrete launch ramp, frozen bait. Limited guest moorage for boats 40 to 45 feet, call ahead. Restaurants, groceries, and a post office nearby.

⑮ **Horseshoe Bay Public Wharf.** Dock is 210 feet in length, commercial vessels have priority.

⑯ **Sunset Marina Ltd.** 34 Sunset Beach, West Vancouver, BC V7W 2T7; (604) 921-7476. Open from March 1 to October 15. Gasoline, guest moorage to 30 feet, haulouts to 25 feet (power boats only), repairs, launch ramp with long term parking, washrooms. They carry marine

supplies, tackle, and bait.

Bowen Island. Bowen Island is served by ferry from Horseshoe Bay. Snug Cove has a public wharf and two marinas. It's a wonderful destination, with shops, a number of good restaurants, and a 600-acre park. A co-op store up the hill from the harbor has provisions. On the northeast corner of Bowen Island, Columbine Bay and Smugglers Cove offer good anchorage. Galbraith Bay has a public float. Anchorage is in Bowen Bay and Tunstall Bay.

⑰ **Snug Cove.** Snug Cove, on Bowen Island, is a favorite stop. It has a public dock and two marinas, and is served by ferry from Horseshoe Bay. From there you can take a bus to downtown Vancouver. The commercial village at Bowen Island has several boutiques, restaurants, a co-op grocery store, bakery/coffee house, pharmacy, wine store and liquor agency, and a couple of pubs. One of the pubs is part of Doc Morgan's, the restaurant at Union Steamship Marina. The other pub is a short distance up the hill. Bowen Island residents are artistic, interesting, and eclectic. The local shopping reflects the character of the population.

Rock the Dock: The annual Rock the Dock, a benefit dance for the local volunteer firefighters, will be held Saturday, August 2, 2014. Participants take over the dock at Snug Cove for a dance party that literally rocks the dock with music and dancing.

Golf: The new 9-hole par 35 Bowen Island Golf Club is challenging and beautiful, with greens that are devilishly hard to read. Call (604) 947-4653. Union Steamship Co. provides

transportation for its guests.

Ferry Noise: Ferry propellers make underwater noise that can sometimes be heard throughout Snug Cove. If you hear what you think is an onboard pump cycling ON whenever a ferry is at the dock, realize that it may actually be noise transmitted from the ferry's props to your hull.

⑰ **Bowen Island Marina.** 375 Cardena Dr., RR 1 A-1, Bowen Island, BC V0N 1G0; (604) 947-9710; norma@bowen-island.com; www.bowen-island.com. Open all year, limited guest moorage, reservations required, 15 & 30 amp power. Located on the starboard side when entering Snug Cove. Historical display, ice cream, tacos, kayak rentals, pies, pastries.

⑰ **Snug Cove Public Wharf.** This wide concrete dock, with 350 feet of space, is next to the ferry landing in Snug Cove, and exposed to ferry wash. No water or electricity.

⑰ **Union Steamship Co. Marina.** P.O. Box 250, Bowen Island, BC V0N 1G0; (604) 947-0707; marina@ussc.ca; www.ussc.ca. Monitors 66A. Open all year, ample guest moorage, pumpout, 30 & 50 amp power, new floating washroom and shower building, laundry, free Wi-Fi. The new washroom and shower building also includes a comfortable lounge with big screen TV and a computer station, all near the showers and laundry. Reservations recommended.

This is an excellent place to stop. Rondy Dike, an architect by training, and his wife Dorothy have restored the Union Steamship Co. landing into a wonderful destination resort. Shops, a good

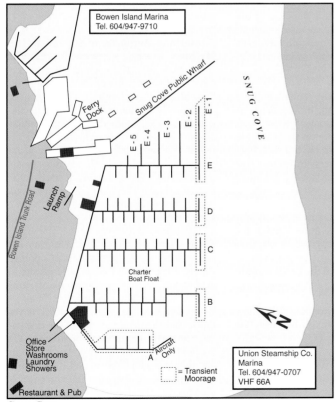

Bowen Island Marina
Tel. 604/947-9710

Snug Cove Public Wharf

S N U G   C O V E

Ferry Dock

E-5 E-4 E-3 E-2 E-1

E

D

C

Charter Boat Float

B

Launch Ramp

Bowen Island Trunk Road

A   Aircraft Only

Office
Store
Washrooms
Laundry
Showers

Restaurant & Pub

N

☐ = Transient Moorage

Union Steamship Co.
Marina
Tel. 604/947-0707
VHF 66A

Snug Cove

Plumper Cove Marine Park has an excellent dock, but no power and no water.

restaurant and pub, boardwalks, a small chandlery, a 600-acre park to explore, and more. It seems that everyone who stays at Union Steamship has a good report.

The marina has a small number of cottages available, reasonable rates. Take the ferry to Horseshoe Bay and ride the bus to enjoy Vancouver. A seasonal foot ferry runs to Granville Island for day excursions.

Mount Gardner Park Public Dock. Galbraith Bay, northwest side of Bowen Island. Has 110 feet of space.

Gambier Island. Gambier Island has three significant inlets, all opening from the south: West Bay, Centre Bay, and Port Graves. A smaller inlet, Halkett Bay, is at the southeast corner of the island. Thornbrough Bay, on the west side of the island, has a public dock. We are told that boats often tie to log booms on the western (Port Mellon) side of the island. In the summertime the water around Gambier Island can warm to swimming temperatures.

Gambier Harbour Public Wharf has 100 feet of dock space.

Burrard Yacht Club and Thunderbird Yacht Club have outstations at Eakins Point at the north end of Gambier Island. Members only, no reciprocals.

West Bay. Favor the west shore when entering West Bay to avoid the reef extending from the eastern shore. West Bay once was a major log booming site and the bottom is apt to be foul with old cable and equipment.

Anchorage in West Bay is in at least two places. The first is on the north side of the reef, close to the reef. The second is in the bight at the northeast corner of the bay. Easy anchoring depths are close to shore in this bight, but because of real estate development, you probably shouldn't run a stern-tie to shore.

Centre Bay. Most of Centre Bay is deep, but the little bight on the west side, just inside the entrance, has 18- to 24-foot anchoring depths, and is delightful. Royal Vancouver and West Vancouver yacht clubs have outstations in Centre Bay. The docks belonging to the Centre Bay Yacht Station are at the head of the bay.

Port Graves. Port Graves is definitely the most scenic of Gambier Island's inlets, and has good anchoring depths at the head. Because of real estate development in West Bay and Centre Bay, Port Graves is the best anchoring spot on the island. A public wharf with small float is located at the head of the bay, and a private dock is a short distance to the west. Anchor in the area off the docks and between them to avoid logging cable on the bottom.

Halkett Bay. Halkett Bay, at the southeast corner of Gambier Island, has room for 4 to 5 boats, but can be somewhat active in southerly winds. Rocks are on the west side of the bay. Approach along the east shoreline. A small float provides access to Halkett Bay Marine Park, with its pit toilets, primitive campsites, and trails.

Brigade Bay. Brigade Bay is on the eastern shore of Gambier Island. Anne Vipond, reporting in Pacific Yachting, suggests that because of deep water fairly close to shore, a stern anchor be set toward the beach and the main anchor set offshore.

Thornbrough Bay. The New Brighton Public Wharf in Thornbrough Bay has 390 feet of dock space.

⑱ **Plumper Cove Marine Park.** Plumper Cove Marine Park is in a cove formed by Keats Island and two small nearby islands. The park has 400 feet of dock space and several mooring buoys. The bay has anchorage for quite a few boats. A rock, marked by a buoy, lies a dozen yards off the dock.

Porteau Cove. Porteau Cove is on the east shore of Howe Sound in Montagu Channel, at latitude 49°33'N. The park is open all year, with toilets, launch ramp, walk-in campsites, hiking trails and a picnic area. Tiny Porteau Cove itself has 1 mooring buoy. Sunken ships and man-made reefs provide excellent scuba diving. White caution buoys mark the yellow-buoyed diving area. Watch your depths; some of the cove dries at low tide.

⑲ **Lions Bay Marine Ltd.** 60 Lions Bay Ave., P.O. Box 262, Lions Bay, BC V0N 2E0; (604) 921-7510. Open all year, except closed December 15 to January 15. Gasoline, diesel and propane available. In summer they have 400 feet of dock space. Haulout to 30 feet (powerboats only) with repairs on site. Groceries and a post office are nearby.

⑳ **Squamish.** www.squamish.ca. The town of Squamish, pop. 15,000, is nestled against the Coast Range mountains at the north end of Howe Sound, on the road between Vancouver and Whistler. Since the 2010 Winter Olympics at nearby Whistler, Squamish has become a pretty vibrant place. A bus runs to Whistler, or you can rent a car. Shopping and two golf courses are an easy drive away. The superb Furry Creek course is a little farther, but if you have a car, give it a try. The shopping district is about one-quarter mile from the docks, and the pub is closer. Summertime inflow winds usually begin between 11:00 a.m. and 12:00 p.m. By 2:00 p.m., the wind can make landing tricky. Best to go to Squamish in the early morning.

⑳ **Harbour Authority of Squamish Boat Harbour.** P.O. Box 97, Squamish, BC V8B 0A1; (604) 892-3725. Open all year. Located on the west bank of the east arm of the Squamish River with 600 feet of dock space divided between the Harbour Authority section and the Squamish Yacht Club. Pumpout, 15 amp power, boat launch. The docks are full in the winter, but open up a little in the summer; definitely call ahead. Best to approach at high water. Expect a relaxed, informal experience. They don't get many visitor boats. The SYC number is (604) 892-3942; leave a message.

Shoal Channel (The Gap). The Gap is a sandy shoal with a least depth of approximately 5 feet at zero tide, between Keats Island and Steep Bluff, at the mouth of Howe Sound. Although waves off the Strait of Georgia tend to break on this shoal, if you know your draft and the state of the tide you can approach Gibsons from the strait via The Gap and have no problems—unless it's rough, and then you should go around Keats Island. Stay mid-channel. Boulders line the edges of the passage. The distance to Thrasher Rock, outside Gabriola Pass in the Gulf Islands, is approximately 16 miles. Use Chart 3463 for the crossing, changing to Chart 3526 as you approach Popham Island. This approach, with Howe Sound islands backed up by the Coast Range mountains, is magnificent.

Correspondent Pat Shera says you can cross at anything but low tides using a natural range. Keep the FlG (flashing green) light located east of the Gibsons Harbour entrance just barely visible in line with the base of Steep Bluff in the foreground. This transit takes you across the shoals with a minimum depth of 7 feet at zero tide. Travel along the 20- to 30-foot depth contour from either side until this natural range lines up, then stay on the range until you reach 20- to 30-foot depths on the other side. Not recommended when a strong southerly is blowing.

This long pier in Gibsons connects shops and a boardwalk to shore.

㉑ **Gibsons.** Gibsons is a charming seaside village, a good place to take the day off and stretch your legs. The lower Gibsons downtown area is filled with shops, restaurants ranging from elegant to funky, and a pub. The Sunshine Coast Museum & Archives is excellent. Hours are 10:30 a.m. to 4:30 p.m., Tuesday through Saturday.

The nearest supermarket is Super Valu, in upper Gibsons. You'll need a ride. Be sure to see Fong's Market in lower Gibsons, one of the more unexpected places on the coast. They have many of the essential grocery items and a good selection of Asian foods.

As you approach the marina complex at Gibsons you will see the Hyak Marine fuel dock just ahead. Gibsons Marina is south of the fuel dock, and the Gibsons Landing Harbour Authority public dock is to the north. A shoal extends from the shore between the public dock and the fuel dock. Approach each moorage directly from seaward. Avoid the water between them.

Some boats anchor outside the breakwater and to the east of the pier, in front of the townside. This is unprotected and probably suitable only in settled weather.

Sea Cavalcade: The Sea Cavalcade festival, featuring food, dancing, fireworks, and other events, is held each July. See www.seacavalcade.ca for details.

㉑ **Gibsons Marina.** P.O. Box 1520, Gibsons, BC V0N 1V0; (604) 886-8686. Monitors VHF 66A. Open all year except Christmas Day. Limited guest moorage, call ahead for availability, 15 and some 30 amp power, washrooms, showers, well-stocked chandlery, laundry, pumpout, concrete launch ramp, marine repairs.

㉑ **Hyak Marine.** P.O. Box 948, Gibsons Harbour, BC V0N 1V0; (604) 886-9011. Open 7 days per week, April through October, closed Mondays November through March. Hours 8:00 a.m. to 8:00 p.m. June through August, 9:00 a.m. to 5:00 p.m. the rest of the year. Gasoline and diesel fuel. Limited moorage, call ahead for availability.

㉑ **Gibsons Landing Harbour Authority.** PO Box 527, Gibsons, BC V0N 1V0; (604) 886-8017; info@gibsonsha.org; www.gibsonsha.org. Monitors VHF 66A. Open all year, guest moorage, 30, 50 and 100 amp power but mostly 15 amp with 20 amp receptacles, 3-ton crane, washrooms and showers, laundry, pumpout, garbage dumpster, Wi-Fi. The public wharf has been upgraded with beautiful new offices, improved shoreside amenities, and television security. Much of the moorage space is taken by permanent tenants, but they work to fit visitors in. Call ahead for availability, reservations not accept-ed. In the summer an 80-foot-long float for short-term day stops is on the opposite side of the wharf, outside of the breakwater. In 2013, a new drive-on commercial dock was added next to the short-term moorage float for loading and overnight moorage.

GOWER POINT TO SECHELT INLET

From Howe Sound to Pender Harbour the coast is largely a barren run. The exceptions are Buccaneer Bay, Secret Cove, Smuggler Cove, and to a lesser extent Halfmoon Bay. When the weather gets up the going can be

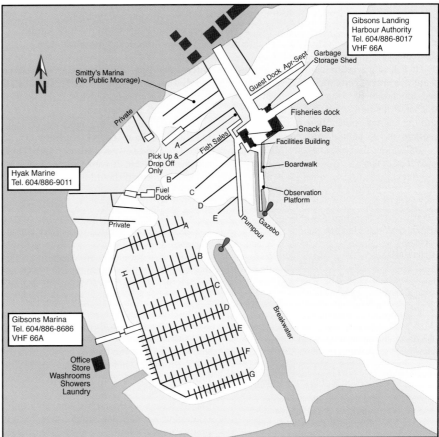

Gibsons Landing

wet and slow. But with a weather eye, the passages can be easy.

Trail Bay. A rock breakwater protects a small moorage at **Selma Park** on the south shore of Trail Bay. We once waited out a nasty southeasterly, riding on the hook in this hideout.

LOCAL KNOWLEDGE

STRONG CURRENTS: Currents run to 3 knots at the north end of Welcome Passage and 2 knots off Merry Island at the south end. When wind and current oppose each other, the waters can be rough and uncomfortable. Watch for drift.

Welcome Passage. Welcome Passage separates South Thormanby Island from Sechelt Peninsula and is used by boats of all types bound up or down the Sunshine Coast. The passage west of Merry Island is deep and easily navigated.

Halfmoon Bay. A public dock with 170 feet of mooring space is at the head of Halfmoon Bay, with a store (a longtime landmark) a short distance away. Henry Hightower, a resident of Halfmoon Bay and a Grenfell 32 owner, provided us with the following insider's view of the facilities and anchorage possibilities. He writes:

"The store at the Halfmoon Bay government wharf is well stocked, and has the best bacon and free-range eggs, as well as fresh and packaged meat, fruit, vegetables and staples, fishing gear, beer, wine and liquor, convenience store stuff, and a gift shop.

"If a strong wind is blowing or forecast, there will almost certainly be at least one tug and log boom fixed across the open south side of Priestland Cove, between the shore and the charted rocks. There is quite a bit of room to anchor behind its shelter."

Halfmoon Bay also has a coffee house with fresh bakery.

CHARTS	
3311 Small craft charts (strip charts)	Sunshine Coast to Desolation Sound
3312 Small craft chart (chartbook)	Jervis Inlet & Desolation Sound
3512	Strait of Georgia, Central Portion (1:80,000)
3514	Jervis Inlet (1:50,000); Malibu and Sechelt Rapids
3535 Plans	Malaspina Strait: Pender Harbour, Secret Cove/ Smuggler Cove, Welcome Passage

The fuel dock at Buccaneer Marina & Resort.

Priestland Cove is southeast of the government dock.

㉒ **Smuggler Cove.** Smuggler Cove has a tricky entrance, but opens to a beautiful anchorage that is protected from all weather. Before entering, first-timers should have in hand Sheet 3 from Sunshine Coast Strip Chart 3311 or Plans Chart 3535. Both charts show Smuggler Cove clearly, but Chart 3311's scale of 1:6000 is even clearer than Chart 3535's 1:10,000 scale. As both charts show, the channel is very close to the Isle Capri side of the entrance, to avoid rocky shoals extending from the south shore. Inside is Smuggler Cove Marine Park, which has no facilities for boaters or campers, but does have trails through the park's 400 acres of woodlands. A favorite diversion is paddling the dinghy among all the little islets and coves. Reduce swinging room by taking a stern-tie to rings set in the rock ashore.

No Discharge Zone. Gray water okay.

Buccaneer Bay. Buccaneer Bay is between North Thormanby and South Thormanby Islands and has a beautiful white sand beach at the south end and west side.

Be careful to enter Buccaneer Bay by leaving the Tattenham Ledge Light Buoy *Q51* to port. The buoy is well north of South Thormanby Island, but it marks the end of Tattenham Ledge and should be respected.

Once in Buccaneer Bay, you can anchor in 30 to 40 feet behind the Surrey Islands or in 20 to 30 feet in Water Bay. The Surrey Islands anchorage is particularly cozy and attractive.

A private moorage is in Water Bay. During the day small boat traffic to and from the dock will rock you some, but it dies down at night. The dock is posted for loading/unloading only, 2-hour maximum.

Watching your depths, you can also snug up to the shoaling waters off Gill Beach, at the south end of the bay. In a southeasterly, you'll get some wind but no seas. There's no protection from a northwesterly, however. One year we anchored in calm conditions, only to have a northwesterly come in around midnight and ruin our night's sleep. It was pretty bouncy.

Secret Cove. Secret Cove has three branches, each with excellent weather protection and easy anchoring depths. Unfortunately, the Secret Cove bottom is notorious for anchor dragging in strong winds, so be sure you are well set if you do anchor.

Enter Secret Cove north of a light on a small rock in the middle of the entrance. Inside are the three arms. The southern arm has a very narrow entrance but adequate depths inside. This arm is surrounded by private docks that restrict swinging room in the middle. You can find room, however, off the Royal Vancouver Yacht Club outstation docks about halfway in. Correspondents James and Jennifer Hamilton have anchored there and report the holding ground is excellent. The center arm has Buccaneer Marina. The north arm is occupied almost entirely by Secret Cove Marina, but there is still plenty of room for anchoring, using stern-ties to shore if needed. A public float is adjacent to Secret Cove Marina. It is primarily used by local commercial fish boats.

㉓ **Buccaneer Marina & Resort Ltd.** 5535 Sans Souci Rd., Halfmoon Bay, BC V0N

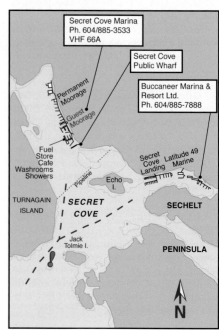

Secret Cove

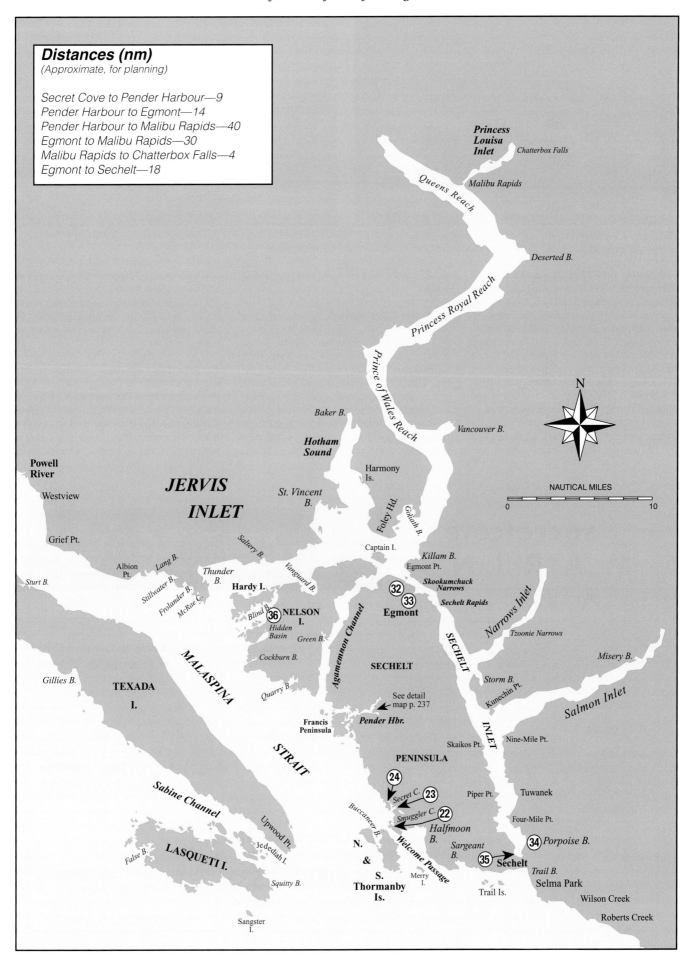

Distances (nm)
(Approximate, for planning)

Secret Cove to Pender Harbour—9
Pender Harbour to Egmont—14
Pender Harbour to Malibu Rapids—40
Egmont to Malibu Rapids—30
Malibu Rapids to Chatterbox Falls—4
Egmont to Sechelt—18

The Secret Cove Marina has a popular restaurant on the second floor of the marina floathouse.

At Fisherman's Resort & Marina signs tell how far you are from just about anywhere.

1Y2; (604) 885-7888; buccaneermarina@ telus.net; www.buccaneermarina.com. Open all year, gasoline and diesel fuel, limited guest moorage with 15 amp power, chandlery, engine and outboard repairs (weekdays), propane, haulout to 40 feet, paved launch ramp with long term parking. Fishing tackle and one of the few places with live herring bait. Water taxi to Thormanby Islands. Located in the center arm of Secret Cove. Owned and operated by the Mercer family since 1968.

Secret Cove Public Wharf. Dock has 144 feet of moorage with 20 amp power, no water. Primarily used by local commercial fish boats.

㉔ **Secret Cove Marina.** 511 Secret Cove Road, Sechelt, BC V0N 3A0; (866) 885-3533; info@secretcovemarina.com; www. secretcovemarina.com. Monitors VHF 66A. Open April 1 through Canadian Thanksgiving. This is a full service marina in the north arm of Secret Cove, with gasoline and diesel fuel, guest moorage, 15 & 30 amp power, washrooms, clean showers, liquor agency, restaurant, store with groceries, block and cube ice, fishing tackle, and Wi-Fi. Fishing charters

and golf shuttles, moped, canoe, paddleboat and bike rentals. Reservations requested. The marina continues to receive excellent reviews.

The store has a wide range of foods and other essentials, including a good liquor and wine selection.

Bargain Bay. Although its entry is actually off the Strait of Georgia, Bargain Bay is properly a part of the complex of bays that make up Pender Harbour. Enter between Edgecomb Island to the east and Francis Peninsula to the west. The entry is easy and open until you are part way inside, where a drying

reef and an underwater rock extend from the west shore to the middle of the channel. Another underwater rock lies off the east shore. Pass between the two rocks and proceed into the bay.

Bargain Narrows, called Canoe Pass, is a drying channel spanned by a bridge with 4 meters (13.12 feet) vertical clearance. The pass runs between Bargain Bay and Gerrans Bay inside Pender Harbour.

PENDER HARBOUR

Pender Harbour is a natural stopover for boats heading north or south in the Strait of Georgia. For northbound boats, it's just the right day's run from Nanaimo, Silva Bay, or Howe Sound. For boats southbound from Desolation Sound, it's a good place to prepare for the long, exposed legs across the Strait of Georgia or down the Sunshine Coast. Boats bound to or from Princess Louisa Inlet often use Pender Harbour both going and coming.

Pender Harbour has good marinas, good anchorages, good eating, and good shopping. It has fuel and a haulout and repair facility. The harbor is nestled against steep mountains; the scenery is beautiful. It's a good place for walking and hiking. If you carry trail bikes, the Madeira Park Public Wharf has a map of the nearby Suncoaster Trail, built and maintained by volunteers.

Pender Harbour is not a single large bay. It is a complex of coves, each with its own

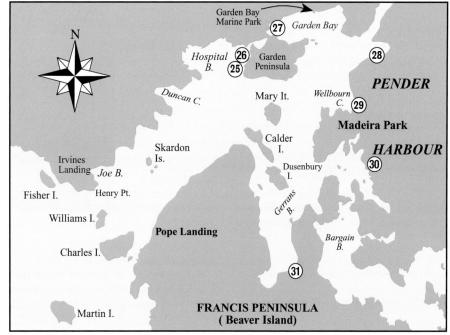

Pender Harbour

personality. Most cruisers will go down the north side. At the back, Hospital Bay and Garden Bay have marinas, fuel, shopping, and dining. The best anchorage is in Garden Bay. Madeira Park, in the southeast corner of Pender Harbour, has moorage, haulout and repairs, and the most complete shopping just

a short walk from the dock.

Pender Harbour has several drying and underwater rocks throughout, but most of them are marked. With Chart 3535 (or good electronic charts) and a little care, you should have no problems.

Pender Harbour Blues Festival: Early June,

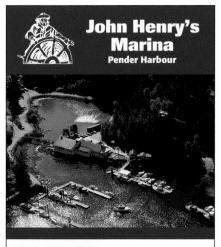

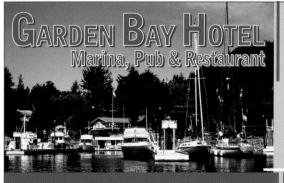

www.penderharbourbluesfestival.com.

Pender Harbour Jazz Festival: September 19-21, 2014. Musicians and audiences from around the world. Performances in venues all around Pender Harbour. About one-quarter of the events are ticketed, the rest are free. *Pender Harbour Chamber Music Festival*, mid- August. For both festivals and more see www.penderharbourmusic.ca.

Transportation: There's no bus or taxi service. Use your dinghy, or try the **Slo-Cat Harbour Ferry**, based in Madeira Park, for excursions or shopping trips. Call Slo-Cat on VHF 68.

Golf: The Pender Harbour Golf Club 9-hole course is terrific, but you'll have to find a ride to get there. If you walk the course you'll get a workout. The par 5 number 4 hole is blind and over a mountain, which you get to climb. Call (604) 883-9541. Tell them you read about them in the Waggoner.

Irvines Landing Marina & Pub. Closed.

Hospital Bay. Hospital Bay is on the west side of Garden Peninsula, facing the mouth of Pender Harbour. The harbor is home to Fisherman's Resort and Marina, John Henry's store and fuel dock, and a public dock. John Henry's store is not quite a supermarket, but it is very well stocked. Hospital Bay is also

The Garden Bay Hotel & Marina's Pub deck overlooks the docks.

the site of the St. Mary's Columbia Coast Mission Hospital building, built in 1929.

A narrow isthmus divides Hospital Bay from Garden Bay with a walkway between the two. LaVerne's, a local favorite "diner," is located here. The milkshakes are legendary.

㉕ **Fisherman's Resort & Marina.** P.O. Box 68, Garden Bay, BC V0N 1S0; (604) 883-2336; fishermans@dccnet.com; www.fishermansresortmarina.com. Monitors VHF 66A. Open April 1 to September 30, guest moorage along 2300 feet of dock, 20 & 30

amp power, washrooms, showers, laundry, Wi-Fi, garbage, recycling, water, ice, launch ramp, kayak rentals. Fisherman's is located in Hospital Bay, adjacent to John Henry's fuel dock. David Pritchard and Jennifer Love are the owners. This is a quiet, well-cared-for marina with beautiful lawns and flower gardens, cottages and RV sites, and good docks. Kenmore Air and charter float plane service. They handle boats of all sizes, including large motor yachts on the outside dock. A pub is a short walk away in Garden Bay.

㉖ **John Henry's Marina, Inc.** P.O. Box 40, 4907 Pool Lane, Garden Bay, BC V0N 1S0; (604) 883-2253. Open all year. John Henry's, in Hospital Bay, has a fuel dock with gasoline, diesel, CNG and propane. No transient moorage. The well-stocked store has fresh produce, meats, grab and go pizzas, sandwiches, charts, liquor agency, post office, ATM, and a dedicated internet and email computer for visitors. The store also carries tackle, bait, ice, and scoop ice cream. John Henry's is where the locals on the north side of Pender Harbour gather. Wayne and Lucy Archbold are the owners.

Hospital Bay Public Wharf. Across from the fuel dock in Hospital Bay, 150 feet of overnight moorage, 20 & 30 amp power on all floats, water. Close to the pub in Garden Bay and LaVerne's.

Garden Bay. Garden Bay is at the northeast corner of Pender Harbour. It has two marinas: the Garden Bay Hotel & Marina, which has ample visitor moorage, and The Pilothouse Marina. The Garden Bay Hotel hasn't been a hotel for a long time, so don't look for rooms to rent. The restaurant and pub are good, with indoor and outdoor seating.

Seattle Yacht Club, Burrard Yacht Club, and Royal Vancouver Yacht Club have outstations in Garden Bay—members only, no reciprocals. Many boats anchor out in Garden Bay and dinghy either to the marinas and John Henry's, or to Madeira Park. The Garden Bay holding ground is good and the protection is excellent in most weather. Garden Bay Provincial Park has about 50 feet of frontage on the north shore. The park has

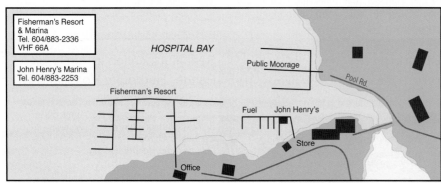

Fisherman's Resort & Marina
Tel. 604/883-2336
VHF 66A

John Henry's Marina
Tel. 604/883-2253

HOSPITAL BAY

Public Moorage

Pool Rd.

Fisherman's Resort

Fuel   John Henry's

Store

Office

Hospital Bay

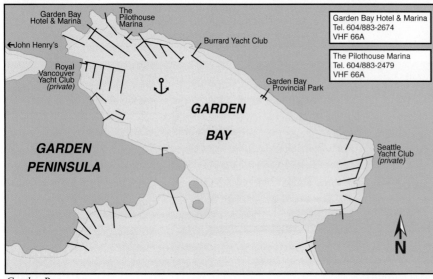

Garden Bay Hotel & Marina

The Pilothouse Marina

←John Henry's

Burrard Yacht Club

Royal Vancouver Yacht Club (private)

Garden Bay Provincial Park

Garden Bay Hotel & Marina
Tel. 604/883-2674
VHF 66A

The Pilothouse Marina
Tel. 604/883-2479
VHF 66A

GARDEN BAY

GARDEN PENINSULA

Seattle Yacht Club (private)

N

Garden Bay

Coffee, pastries and sandwiches at the top of the dock at Madeira Park Public Wharf.

A great way to relax at the Sunshine Coast Marina overlooking the Pender Harbour.

a dinghy dock, toilets, and a network of excellent walking trails, but no other facilities for boaters.

㉗ Garden Bay Hotel Marina & Pub. P.O. Box 90, Garden Bay, BC V0N 1S0; (604) 883-2674; gbhm@dccnet.com; www.gardenbaypub.com. Monitors VHF 66A. Open all year, 1200 feet of well-maintained dock, 15 & 30 amp power, washrooms, showers, Wi-Fi, nearby liquor store. This is a large, full-service marina with a popular pub and separate dining area. The pub is open 7 days a week all year, live bands on most weekends.

We've had good lunches and dinners in the pub, and we've heard positive reports about the dining room. On a beautiful day, the deck overlooking Garden Bay is pleasant. A road and walking trail leads from the pub to Hospital Bay and John Henry's store. The Pender Harbour Blues Festival is at Garden Bay Pub in early June. Moorage is free for ticket holders. The Garden Bay Pub is a venue for the Pender Harbour Jazz Festival in September.

㉗ The Pilothouse Marina. P.O. Box 6, Garden Bay, BC V0N 1S0; (604) 883-2479; (877) 856-2479; office@thepilothousemarina.com; www.thepilothousemarina.com. Monitors VHF 66A. Open all year with side-tie guest moorage to 145 feet along 1400 feet of docks, 15, 30, & 50 amp power, water, showers, laundry, free recycling, garbage, launch ramp, boat rentals, Wi-Fi. Complimentary kayaks and bicycles for guests. Dog-friendly and family-friendly. Three waterfront cabins, one cabin with guaranteed moorage to 50 feet. Morgane Ojer (pronounced "O-Jay") is the

owner and Shawn and Shannon are the marina managers.

A diver is on site and mechanics are on call. The marina can also help arrange for parts to be delivered from just about anywhere.

Gunboat Bay. Gunboat Bay, surrounded by high, steep mountains, is entered through a narrow channel with a least depth of 4 feet. An underwater rock lies just to the north of the centerline of the entry channel. Currents in the entry channel are quite strong except at slack water. Although the bay is open and good for anchorage before it peters out into drying flats, few boats anchor there because Garden Bay is so much easier.

㉘ Sunshine Coast Resort & Marina. P.O. Box 213, Madeira Park, BC V0N 2H0; (604) 883-9177; (888) 883-9177; vacation@sunshinecoast-resort.com; www.sunshinecoast-resort.com. Monitors VHF 66A. Open all year with moorage for boats to 100 feet, call for reservations, 30 amp power, water, washrooms, showers, free Wi-Fi, jacuzzi, laundry, bait, small boat and kayak rentals, and a new lodge with 16 truly outstanding rooms.

The entire property is tidy and well-maintained. Owner/manager Ralph Linnmann is committed to providing outstanding customer service.

A steep mountainside rises above the docks. The laundry, showers, and road to town are a considerable climb up the hill, although the office and additional showers are in the new lodge about halfway up. The marina is in the small bay to the right as you approach Gunboat Bay, about

a half-mile north of Madeira Park shopping. You can walk to Madeira Park down the hill (and back up to return) or take the dinghy (we'd take the dinghy). Free transportation to the challenging Pender Harbour Golf Club.

㉙ Pender Harbour Authority Madeira Park Public Wharf. P.O. Box 118, Madeira Park, BC V0N 2H0; (604) 883-2234; penderauthority@telus.net. Monitors VHF 66A. Open all year, 600 feet of dedicated visitor moorage space, 15, 20, 30 and 50 amp power, washrooms, showers, garbage drop, pumpout, aircraft float, free Wi-Fi. The dinghy dock faces shore, adjacent to the launch ramp. No dinghy check-in is needed and no charge for daytime dinghy tie-up. Marine repair, chandlery, and mechanics nearby. Fresh crab and prawns are available from a fish boat during the summer.

If you want to reprovision,

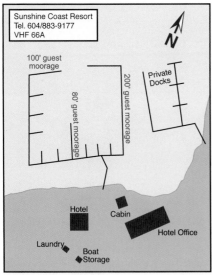

Sunshine Coast Resort

Madeira Park is where you'll do it. The docks are close to two grocery stores (the well-stocked IGA Marketplace, and the Oak Tree Market with excellent meats and cheeses). The IGA is open 7 days a week 8:00 a.m. to 7:00 p.m., and 9:00 a.m. to 8:00 p.m. in July and August. A drugstore, liquor store, post office, bank with ATM, bakery, hairdresser, book store, and veterinarian are close by. No laundromat. Madeira Park has a full-service medical clinic. Eight-minute walk to Painted

Boat Restaurant.

In recent years considerable upgrading has been done to make Madeira Park not just a dock for the dinghy but a destination in its own right. With donations from local businesses and mostly volunteer labor, walls were built, walkways laid, landscaping installed, new offices constructed with washrooms and showers, a gazebo added, and the docks improved.

㉙ **Madeira Marina.** P.O. Box 189, Madeira Park, BC V0N 2H0; (604) 883-2266; madeiramarine@dccnet.com. Open all year. Marine railway with haulout to 40 tons, complete marine repairs, parts. We get continued reports of prompt, competent repair service.

Gerrans Bay. Gerrans Bay is dotted with rocks, but all of them are marked. It is mostly residential, with some of the homes obviously in the commercial fishing business. Two resorts, the Coho Marina (no guest moorage) and the new and lavish Painted Boat Resort & Marina, are in Gerrans Bay.

㉚ **Painted Boat Resort Spa & Marina.** P.O. Box 153, 12849 Lagoon Rd., Madeira Park, BC V0N 2H0; (604) 883-2456; (866) 902-3955; reservations@painted-boat.com; www.paintedboat.com. Formerly Lowe's Resort. Open all year with guest moorage to 70 feet, reservations recommended. The docks are tight. The approach winds

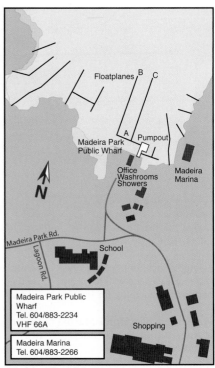

Madeira Park Marinas

through rocks and reefs. We suggest entering carefully with a bow watch. The docks have 15, 30 & 50 amp power. It's not really a marina; it's a high quality resort with moorage. It has been completely redeveloped

into 31 deluxe rental quarter-share condos. The upscale but relaxed Restaurant at Painted Boat is open seasonally for lunch and dinner with 280 feet of short term moorage for restaurant patrons. It is elegant with a great view. The full-service spa is beautiful and has eight treatment rooms, two pools and hydrotherapy. Resort amenities are for guests of resort only.

(31) **Whiskey Slough Public Wharf.** Guest moorage along 60 feet of dock, 20 & 30 amp power, no facilities or services. Mostly commercial fish boats here.

Agamemnon Channel. Agamemnon Channel runs northeast between Nelson Island and the mainland, and is the shortest route for those heading for Princess Louisa Inlet, Egmont, or Sechelt Inlet. The only reasonable anchorage is at Green Bay. A private marina is in Agamemnon Bay.

Green Bay. Green Bay is a lovely spot, just don't trust the charts to show you the rocks. The prime anchorage, in 30 feet or less, is in the cove on the west side of the bay, in front of the lake shown on the chart. A stream with waterfall runs from the lake to the cove. A drying reef nearly closes the pass to the back bay and we did not attempt it.

A vacation cabin is on a point midway on the northeast side of Green Bay, and a large uncharted rock lies off this cabin. A course

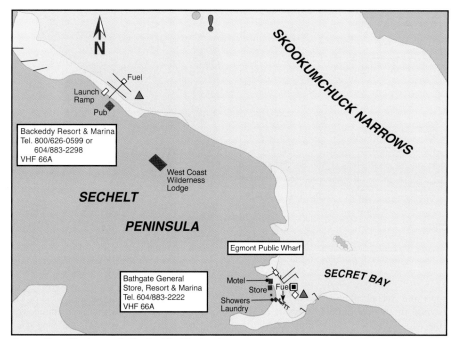

Secret Bay (Bathgate & Backeddy Marinas)

west of midchannel will clear the rock easily. Sailing Directions warns of rocks on the east side of the entry to Green Bay. An aerial photo in Sailing Directions suggests rocks in the middle of the channel as well. "After investigating, we think the 'rocks' in the photo are sunlight reflections. We hugged the west

shore going in, but departed midchannel. We looked for rocks but saw none." [*Hale*]

SECHELT INLET

Egmont. Egmont, on the Sechelt Peninsula, is near the entrance to Skookumchuck Nar-

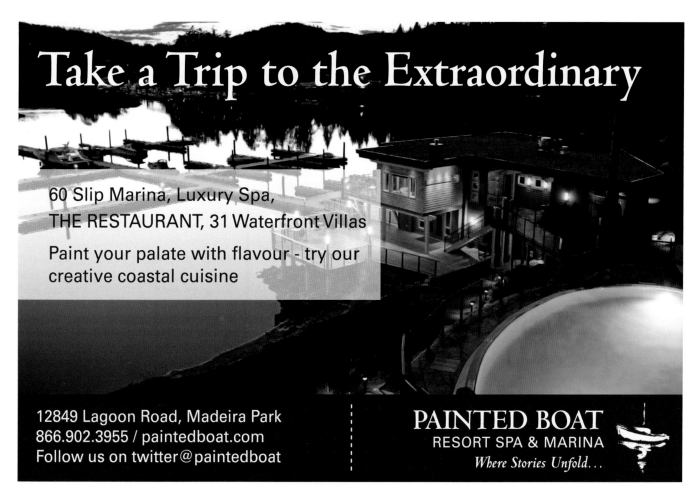

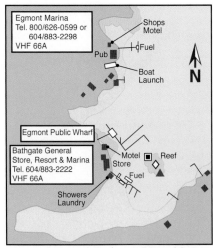

Egmont Marina & Bathgate General Store

The view from the West Coast Wilderness Lodge, Backeddy can be seen below.

rows and Sechelt Rapids. Sechelt Inlet lies beyond the rapids. Backeddy Resort & Marina and Bathgate General Store & Marina both have fuel. Backeddy Resort & Marina fronts on Skookumchuck Narrows; Bathgate is closer to the rapids, behind a well-marked reef in Secret Bay. The public dock is adjacent. Beautiful West Coast Wilderness Lodge, with fine dining and more, is immediately south of Backeddy Resort & Marina. It's an easy walk between the two and the view from the dining room at West Coast

Wilderness Lodge is a knockout. One of our correspondents reports that their dinner was as good as the view—world class, they said.

The Egmont Heritage Centre is a short walk up the main road from the marinas.

LOCAL KNOWLEDGE

STRONG CURRENTS: Strong currents can whip through Backeddy Marina. Watch the current as you approach the dock, al-

though dockhands are usually available to assist. Sechelt Rapids currents will give you an idea of the current direction and force.

DANGEROUS ROCKS: The red triangle day beacon off Backeddy Marina's south docks means Red, Right, Returning for the channel outside. Approaching the docks, leave the beacon to port or you will run up on a rock shelf that extends from shore.

(32) **Backeddy Resort & Marina.** 16660 Backeddy Rd., Egmont, BC V0N 1N0; (604) 883-2298; (800) 626-0599; info@backeddy.ca; www.backeddy.ca. Monitors VHF 66A. Open all year with guest moorage and services, reservations accepted. Gasoline and diesel fuel, moorage to 120 feet, 15 & 30 amp power, Wi-Fi, pub and restaurant, cabins, inn rooms, camping, washrooms, showers, laundry, gravel launch ramp, float plane access for Kenmore Air and West Coast Air. Small convenience store on site. Pub open for lunch and dinner, hours vary between October and April, call ahead.

The marina is located opposite the Sutton Islets. Tours for Princess Louisa Inlet leave from the Backeddy dock. Water taxi service available. The Backeddy fuel dock is just off the route to, or from, Princess Louisa Inlet.

(33) **Bathgate General Store, Resort & Marina.** 6781 Bathgate Rd., Egmont, BC V0N 1N0; (604) 883-2222; info@bathgate.com; www.bathgate.com. Monitors VHF 66A. Open all year, gasoline and diesel at the fuel dock, limited guest moorage, 15, 20 & 30 amp power, free Wi-Fi, sparkling clean showers, washrooms, laundry. The store has fresh produce and a full line of groceries, propane, marine supplies, liquor agency. It's the only well-stocked store for miles. Deluxe wheelchair-accessible waterfront motel unit available. Short and long term parking.

The reef in Secret Bay can confuse a first-time visitor, especially one who isn't that familiar with navigation aids. Remember: Red, Right, Returning. When entering, leave the

red daymark well to starboard and you'll have no problems. If you still aren't sure, just remember to go around the ends, not between the two beacons.

㉝ Egmont Public Wharf. 500 feet of dock space. The outer end of the eastern float is reserved for float planes.

Sechelt Inlet. Beautiful Sechelt Inlet, with few anchorages and limited facilities for pleasure craft, is often passed by—especially with Princess Louisa Inlet at the end of nearby Jervis Inlet. Sechelt Rapids also serve as a gate to keep out all but the determined.

To explore Sechelt Inlet and its arms, use Chart 3512 (1:80:000) or Chartbook 3312. The inlet is shown at 1:40,000 in Chartbook 3312. Sechelt Inlet extends about 15 miles south of Sechelt Rapids. It ends at Porpoise Bay, the back door to the village of Sechelt, where there is a public float and easy anchorage. Two arms, Salmon Inlet and Narrows Inlet, run from the eastern side of Sechelt Inlet into the heart of the Earle mountain range. A number of provincial park sites are in Sechelt Inlet, most of them best suited to small boats that can be pulled up on the beach.

Inflow winds can blow from south to north in Sechelt Inlet and up Salmon Inlet and Narrows Inlet. Even when the northern part of Sechelt Inlet is near calm, the southern part can be increasingly windy. In Salmon Inlet and Narrows Inlet, the inflow winds will grow stronger as the inlets deepen and narrow. Outflow winds can develop at night, but in the summer they often don't unless a strong southeasterly is blowing out on the strait.

The tidal range does not exceed 10 feet in Sechelt Inlet, and the times of high and low tide are 2 to 3 hours after Point Atkinson. Two secondary ports, Porpoise Bay and Storm Bay, are shown in Tide & Current Tables, Vol. 5. Current predictions for Tzoonie Narrows, in Narrows Inlet, are shown under Secondary Stations in Tide & Current Tables, Vol. 5 and Ports and Passes.

For a complete description of Sechelt Inlet cruising, including excellent hiking trails, see our sister publication, *Cruising the Secret Coast,* by Jennifer and James Hamilton.

LOCAL KNOWLEDGE

DANGEROUS CURRENTS AND INCORRECT TIDE DATA: Sechelt Rapids can be extremely dangerous except at or near slack water. At full flow the rapids are boiling cauldrons with 8-foot overfalls and 12- to 16-knot currents. Even an hour before slack, when many other rapids may have calmed down, the Sechelt Rapids can be menacing. Traverse the rapids only at slack water.

We've had reports that some current tables contained in electronic navigation programs don't agree with the printed tables for Sechelt Rapids. Use the Canadian Hydrographic Service or Ports & Passes tables.

View from the Lighthouse Pub in the village of Sechelt.

Sechelt Rapids. Sechelt Rapids, also known as the Skookumchuck Rapids (Sechelt is pronounced "SEE-shelt"; skookum means "big" or "strong," and chuck means "body of water"), provide the only water access to Sechelt Inlet.

Times of turn and maximum current are shown in the Tide and Current Tables, Vol. 5 and in Ports and Passes. On neap tides the maximum current can be as little as 1 to 2 knots. But the next exchange could have a 7.4-knot current and be very dangerous. You may meet tugs with tows in the rapids. Check the tide and current tables and plan accordingly.

Lacking prior experience, do not go through without accurate charts for Sechelt Rapids and Secret Bay. Sailing Directions says the best route through the rapids is west of Boom Islet (choked with kelp, but safe) and west of the Sechelt Islets light.

We, however, have run a dogleg course without discomfort through the middle of the channel, between the Sechelt Islets and the unnamed islet directly north of the Sechelt Islets. This area is where dangerous whirlpools can develop on ebbs, so be careful. Give Roland Point a wide berth, especially on a flood.

Either direction, Sechelt Rapids are just fine at slack, and if you time it well (easily done) you'll slide through with no problems at all. But when the rapids are running, their roar can be heard for miles. Live have been lost there.

Before making your own entrance it can be instructive to walk to the rapids from the public dock in Egmont to watch the channel in full boil. Locals tell us that at night on a spring flood tide, the water glows with phosphorescence. The sight, we are assured, is amazing.

㉞ Poise Cove Marina. 5991 Sechelt Inlet Rd., Sechelt, BC V0N 3A3; (604) 885-2895. Open all year with limited guest moorage for boats to 25 feet, limited 15 amp power, concrete launch ramp for boats 25 feet or less. No long term parking. Located on the east side of Sechelt Inlet near Porpoise Bay Marine Park.

㉞ Choquer & Sons Ltd. 5977 Sechelt Inlet Rd., Sechelt, BC V0N 3A0; (604) 885-9244; choquerandsons@telus.net. Good docks with guest moorage for boats to 75 feet, deep enough for sailboats, 15 & 30 amp power. Launch ramp and trailer lift. No showers. Their primary business is a machine and metal fabrication shop upland.

㉟ Lighthouse Pub & Marina. 5764 Wharf Rd., Sechelt, BC V0N 3A0; (604) 885-9494; moorage@secheltmarina.com; www.secheltmarina.com. Located at the south end of Sechelt Inlet with easy access

to Sechelt village. New docks with slips from 16 to 40 feet plus side-tie moorage, 30 amp power, showers, laundry, washrooms, garbage drop. Call ahead for moorage. Three 2-bedroom "Bed & Boat" cottages are available for rent. Gasoline and diesel at the fuel dock. We've heard the food at the pub is excellent. Look for the lighthouse on top of the pub.

㉟ Royal Reach Marina & Hotel. 5758 Wharf Rd., Sechelt, BC V0N 3A0; (604) 885-7844. Open all year, moorage to 30 feet is for hotel guests only, limited 15 amp power, must call ahead. Located at the head of Sechelt Inlet. Watch your depths at low water.

㉟ Sechelt Public Dock. Located at the head of Sechelt Inlet next to the Lighthouse Pub & Marina. This dock usually is completely taken by local boats. Depths at the head of the inlet are shallow enough for easy anchoring, however, and the dinghy can be squeezed in at the public dock. The long and often empty dock extending from the pub is reserved for West Coast Air and their float planes. The fuel pumps are for their aircraft.

Narrows Inlet. Narrows Inlet is mostly 150 to 180 feet deep except at the head, where the Tzoonie River makes a delta. Tzoonie Narrows, about a third of the way along, is a spectacular cleft in the high mountains that surround the inlet. Tidal currents run to a maximum of 4 knots through Tzoonie Narrows, but the passage is free of hazards. All but the slowest or lowest-powered boats could run them at any time. Arguably the best anchorage in this area is in Storm Bay, at the mouth of Narrows Inlet. Storm Bay is very pretty, with a dramatic rock wall on its eastern shore. Anchor behind the little islets at the entrance or near the head of the bay.

Tzoonie Narrows Park. This park takes in both sides of the narrows, and is good for swimming, fishing, diving, and picnicking. Walk-in campsites. The 1-meter islet shown on the chart is a long, narrow reef, with large extensions under the surface. You can anchor inside the reef, or in the deep bight on the other side of Narrows Inlet.

Salmon Inlet. Salmon Inlet is very deep, although anchorage is good in Misery Bay, where the water is warm enough for swimming. A drying shoal almost blocks the passage across the inlet at Sechelt Creek. The shoal can be passed safely by staying close to the north shore.

Quarry Bay. Quarry Bay faces the Strait of Georgia and is too deep and exposed to be a destination of first choice. If you must anchor there, you could work your way in among the rocks in the southeast corner of the bay. It would be a good idea to run a stern-tie to keep from swinging onto a rock. At the north end of Quarry Bay a little cove, surrounded by homes, is well protected and has good an-

At anchor in Hardy Island Marine Park.

choring depths. It would be a good hideout. Chart 3512 (1:80,000) and Chartbook 3312 (1:40,000) show a stream connecting this cove with Quarry Lake. Three rocks in this cove are shown in Chartbook 3312.

Cape Cockburn. An unmarked drying rock is a short distance off Cape Cockburn. Give the cape a good offing.

Cockburn Bay. Cockburn Bay is completely plugged by drying rocks and is accessible only by small craft at or near high water.

Hidden Basin. Hidden Basin is blocked by drying shoals and rocks, and currents run strongly through the restricted entrance. Chartbook 3312 (1:40,000) shows Hidden Basin better than Chart 3512 (1:80,000). Entrance to Hidden Basin should be made—carefully—at high water slack. Secure anchorage is available once inside.

㊱ Blind Bay. Blind Bay once had a number of good anchorages, especially along the Hardy Island side. Most of them now are taken with private homes and their docks, so the choices are fewer. One good spot on the south side is popular Ballet Bay. On the north side, Hardy Island Marine Park (formerly Musket Island Marine Park) has anchoring.

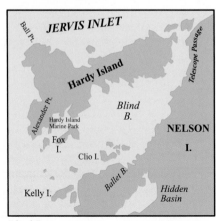

Blind Bay

Nearly all anchorages require a stern-tie. Use your chart and depth sounder, watch for rocks, and go slowly.

㊱ Ballet Bay. Ballet Bay, on Nelson Island, is a popular, well-protected anchorage in Blind Bay.

Ballet Bay can be entered from the north, but many rocks obstruct the path and close attention is called for. The easier entry is from the west, between Nelson Island and Clio Island. If you do enter from the west, the rock shown at the point before you turn into Ballet Bay truly is there, and farther offshore than you might expect. Give it a wide berth. Many rocks in the area around Ballet Bay are marked with sticks or small floats, but don't count on all of the rocks being marked. Not all the rocks are charted, either. Go slowly and pay attention.

The center of Ballet Bay is good-holding mud, but the bottom grows rockier toward shore ("a boat-eating rockpile" —*Evertz*). A trail reportedly connects Ballet Bay and Hidden Basin, although all Evertz found were "No Trespassing" signs.

Hardy Island Marine Park. Formerly Musket Island Marine Park. Located behind Fox Island, near the western entrance to Blind Bay. The upland area of the park is on Hardy Island. A beautiful spot. Anchor behind the tiny islet, or in the bay that opens up to the north of the islet. In most cases you'll stern-tie to shore. The bottom can be rocky, so be sure you have a satisfactory set. You also can anchor in the narrow, vertically sided, almost landlocked cove indenting Hardy Island immediately northwest of the park itself. A reader who dove this cove to recover a lost item reports a mud bottom. Rock is being quarried on the peninsula high above the cove. It's quite dramatic.

Telescope Passage. Telescope Passage connects Blind Bay with Jervis Inlet, but is partly blocked by underwater rocks that extend from the 70-meter island at the north entrance. Strongly favor the Nelson Island side until past the 70-meter island. Then trend toward the middle of the passage to avoid charted and uncharted rocks along the Nelson Island side. When approaching Telescope Passage from Jervis Inlet, you might be confused (we were) by the presence of a tiny islet almost 100 feet high, just outside the entrance. Check the chart closely; the islet is shown as the smallest oval imaginable, with (26), for 26 meters high, directly beside it.

JERVIS INLET

Jervis Inlet extends 46 miles into Coast Range mountains, and is the route to fabled Princess Louisa Inlet. Jervis Inlet is 1 to 1.5 miles wide and often more than 600 feet deep. Steep-to shores, with mountains rising directly above, make for few good anchorages. Currents in Jervis Inlet are light, and are often affected by winds. Watch for drift. Heading up-inlet, Backeddy Resort & Marina and Bathgate Marina in Egmont are the last fuel stops.

Once beyond Foley Head and Egmont Point, you'll find only indifferent anchorages at Vancouver Bay, Deserted Bay, and Killam Bay. The 30 miles of Princess Royal Reach, Prince of Wales Reach, and Queen's Reach do not have useable anchorages. Unlike the other deep fjords that penetrate from the sea, however, Jervis Inlet has a spectacular prize at the end: Princess Louisa Inlet.

Pictograph: Correspondent Pat Shera reports a good pictograph of what appear to be a group of salmon and other figures on the north side of Princess Royal Reach, midway between Osgood Creek and Patrick Point, 50°03.42'N/123°50.65'W.

Thunder Bay. Thunder Bay, immediately inside the north entrance to Jervis Inlet, has anchorage in the protected cove on the south shore, and in the open cove at the northwest corner. Correspondent Capt. Fred Triggs reports that in the southern cove, the rock drying 2.1 meters appears to be farther offshore than charted. The cove looks a little small on the chart, but Capt. Triggs says it has room for several boats and good holding. The shores are lined with vacation cabins. Mooring floats restrict anchoring room. Rocks ex-

tend from the point as you approach. Give the point a good offing. At low tide the charted rock looks like a small haystack. If you stay off the west shore you'll be fine.

Saltery Bay. Saltery Bay has a public float, a boat launch, and picnic sites. It is the ferry landing for road travel along the Sunshine Coast.

Saltery Bay Public Wharf. Adjacent to the ferry landing. Visitor moorage available along 435 feet of dock space. Garbage pickup. Commercial vessels have priority.

Saltery Bay Provincial Park. Open all year, anchor only or moor at the public wharf, a 1-km walk from the park entrance. Picnic facilities and a dive rinse station are located above the small sandy beach. Most of the shoreline is rock, however, and very impressive. In Mermaid Cove, scuba divers can look for the underwater statue of the mermaid. The dive reef is marked by white buoys. A launch ramp is a short distance west of Mermaid Cove.

St. Vincent Bay. Much oyster culture activity. Sykes Island and Junction Island may have anchorage.

Hotham Sound. Hotham Sound is a beautiful, 6-mile-long body of water, surrounded by high, rugged mountains. The sound is sheltered from most strong winds, and in the summertime the water is warm enough for swimming. Friel Lake Falls tumble 1400 feet down sheer mountainside near the Harmony Islands. Unfortunately, good anchorages in Hotham Sound are few.

Wolferstan (*Cruising Guide to British Columbia Vol. 3, Sunshine Coast,* now out of print) devotes an entire chapter, with superb aerial photos, to Hotham Sound, but for the most part even his advice comes down to finding little niches along the shoreline. Baker Bay, at the head of Hotham Sound, is an anchorage.

Harmony Islands Marine Park. The Harmony Islands in Hotham Sound are a lovely spot. The best anchorage is in locally-named Kipling Cove, a nook surrounded by the three northern islands that make up the Harmony Islands. The bottom is rocky, so be sure you have the right ground tackle and it's well set. You'll run a stern-tie to shore.

Two of the three islands that make up Kipling Cove are privately owned and posted with "Private Island, No Stern Ties, No Fires, No Kayakers" signs. The signs mean what they say, and private property must be respected. The northeasternmost island that makes up Kipling Cove is owned by B.C. Parks, however, with no restrictions on going ashore or stern-tying. The southernmost of the Harmony Islands (separate from Kipling Cove) is also part of the marine park.

Because anchoring inside Kipling Cove can be tight, some boats choose to put the hook down in the channel on the east side of the islands. Close to the islands the depths are fine, but the channel itself is around 100 feet deep. As long as you are set up for deeper anchorages, you should be okay. Rings were added along the high tide line in 2011 to run stern ties through.

We have been told that williwaws can blow down out of the mountains and make anchoring interesting. And we have heard that flies can be aggressive. Our visits have been in late June. On our one overnight we were troubled by only a few flies in the evening—but they were definitely determined.

Dark Cove. Dark Cove is a little notch between Foley Head and Goliath Bay, and was recommended to us by an experienced sailboater we met at Princess Louisa Inlet. We motored through Dark Cove the next day but didn't stop. At 90 feet deep, Dark Cove isn't ideal for anchoring, although protection behind Sydney Island is excellent.

Malibu Rapids. Malibu Rapids mark the entrance to Princess Louisa Inlet. The rapids

CHARTS	
3311 Small craft charts (strip charts)	Sunshine Coast to Desolation Sound
3312 Small craft chart (chartbook)	Jervis Inlet & Desolation Sound
3512	Strait of Georgia, Central Portion (1:80,000)
3514	Jervis Inlet (1:50,000) Malibu Rapids (1:12,000) Sechelt Rapids (1:20,000)

The scale of Princess Louisa Inlet is hard to capture in a photograph. Note the dock, filled with boats, in the lower right corner.

Young Life's Malibu Club, at the mouth of Princess Louisa Inlet, overlooking Malibu Rapids.

The setting at Princess Louisa Inlet is breathtaking.

are narrow and dogleg-shaped, and boats at one end cannot see boats at the other end. It is courteous—and wise—to warn other vessels via VHF radio that you are about to enter the rapids, and the direction you are traveling. Most boats use channel 16 because it is the one VHF channel everyone is supposed to monitor. The transmission can be brief: "*Securité, Securité. This is the 34-foot motor vessel Happy Days, inbound to Princess Louisa Inlet. Any opposing traffic please respond on channel one-six.*"

Currents in Malibu Rapids run to 9 knots and create large overfalls. Run this passage at slack water. High water slack occurs about 24 minutes after high water at Point Atkinson, and low water slack about 36 minutes after low water at Point Atkinson. High water slack is preferred because it widens the available channel somewhat. High slack or low, before entering or leaving Malibu Rapids, local knowledge says to wait until the surf created by the overfall subsides entirely.

Important: Use the Volume 5 Canadian Hydrographic Service or Ports and Passes tide tables for Point Atkinson tides. Through 2013, the NOAA tide tables for Point Atkinson did not agree.

Princess Louisa Inlet. Princess Louisa Inlet, 4 miles long, is the "holy grail" for cruising people from all over the world. Entered through Malibu Rapids, the inlet is surrounded by 3,000-foot-high mountains that plunge almost vertically into 600-foot depths below. Entering Princess Louisa Inlet is like entering a great cathedral. The author Earle Stanley Gardner wrote that no one could see Princess Louisa Inlet and remain an atheist. It is one of the most awesome destinations on the coast. What words can describe this place? All the superlatives have been used up on lesser subjects.

Please observe a no-wake speed limit. Larger wakes bounce off the sides of the inlet.

Malibu Club, a Young Life Christian summer camp for teenagers, is at the entrance to the inlet, just inside Malibu Rapids. The kids and staff are welcoming and polite. Tours are

possible. It's probably best to visit by dinghy after your boat is settled at MacDonald Island or the park dock at Chatterbox Falls.

As you clear Malibu Rapids and motor up Princess Louisa Inlet, you will be treated to waterfalls streaming down the mountainsides. About halfway along, 5 mooring buoys are behind MacDonald Island.

Princess Louisa Park is at the head of the inlet, surrounded by a bowl of high, sheer cliffs that astonish even repeat visitors. The 500-foot-long park dock will hold a large number of boats. The dock is available at no charge; stays are limited to 72 hours. Maximum boat length at the dock is 55 feet. Snug up close to the boat in front, to leave room for others.

The best anchorage is directly below Chatterbox Falls, which drops in a series of cascades from the mountains above. Keeping the stream outlet in front of you, take your boat as close as you dare and drop the anchor in 10 feet of water. Then back down to set the hook. The current will hold your boat facing the falls. It's elegant.

If the dock is full and spots near the outlet from the falls are taken, you'll be forced to anchor in deep water to the north. Boats patrol around, not liking what they find, but in the end their anchors go down. On our mid-summer visit, the stars in the sky were mirrored by the anchor lights from what must have been a dozen boats out there. Another option, of course, is the five mooring buoys at MacDonald Island.

Since most people don't stay longer than a day or two, there's ample turnover. A boat at anchor need only wait for the twice-daily departure of boats from the dock. Space then can be found before the next fleet arrives from Malibu Rapids. Water (not potable, unfortunately) is available all the way out the dock, but no electricity. Up-inlet thermal winds can develop on warm afternoons. Be aware if you're out in the dinghy.

The park is beautifully developed and maintained. Use the shoreside toilets. *Do not discharge sewage at any time.* Also, limit gen-

erator use to 9:00 a.m. to 11:00 a.m. in the morning and 6:00 p.m. to 8:00 p.m. in the evening. Quiet hours are 11:00 p.m. to 7:00 a.m. The water is warm enough for swimming, even by adults who usually don't go in anymore.

There's a covered fire pit for group get-togethers. For those who wish, a short walk to the pools near the base of Chatterbox Falls will yield a bracing bath/shower. A shampoo followed by a power rinse from the chilled spray will make you tingle.

A delightful waterfall-fed pool is hidden in the forest on the north side of the inlet. From the dock you can see a large boulder that marks the spot. Land the dinghy on the small beach just beyond the boulder and walk a few steps to the pool. A bather we met yelped when he jumped in, but a moment later said the water was fine.

No hook-and-line fishing. Princess Louisa Inlet is a rockfish conservation area.

Trapper's Cabin is about a 2-hour very demanding hike from the dock area. The cabin is now completely collapsed. The trail is steep. It is often muddy and slippery. We're not kidding about the hike being demanding. In 2007 a man in his early 20s slipped and fell, broke his leg, and ultimately died.

With a fast boat, Princess Louisa Inlet could be seen in one day. Zoom up for the morning slack at Malibu Rapids, see the sights for a few hours, and zoom out on the afternoon slack. That, however, would be seeing Princess Louisa Inlet but not experiencing it. Something good happens to people when they're at Princess Louisa Inlet. We suggest at least three days for the trip: one day up 46-mile-long Jervis Inlet; the next day at the park; and the third day back down Jervis Inlet on the morning slack.

Princess Louisa Society. The Princess Louisa Society was formed to buy and preserve the area around Chatterbox Falls for perpetuity. The Society gave the property to B.C. Parks, but maintains an active role in the care of the facilities. Fundraising continues to

CHARTS

3311sc Small craft charts (strip charts)	Sunshine Coast to Desolation Sound
3512	Strait of Georgia, Central Portion (1:80,000)
3513	Strait of Georgia, Northern Portion (1:80,000)
3536 Plans	Strait of Georgia (various scales)
3538	Desolation Sound and Sutil Channel (1:40,000)

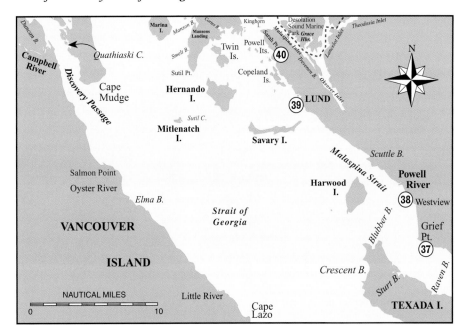

maintain and develop the facilities at docks and in the area. Annual memberships are $40 U.S or Cdn.; life memberships are $200 U.S. or Cdn. The Society website is www.princesslouisa.bc.ca.

MALASPINA STRAIT TO SARAH POINT

Malaspina Strait, 36 miles long, separates Texada Island from the mainland. Although the strait looks protected from the open water of the Strait of Georgia, storms can create high seas. Especially on an ebb tide, confused seas often build up off the mouth of Jervis Inlet and extend almost to Texada Island. Grief Point, at the north end of Malaspina Strait, is another bad spot in a southeasterly. Other than the mouth of Jervis Inlet, however, Malaspina Strait poses no threat in settled weather.

McRae Cove faces Malaspina Strait, just west of Scotch Fir Point at the mouth of Jervis Inlet. The cove is well protected but shallow. The charts show a straightforward entry between the 27- and 29-meter islands, then along a 36-meter island. Anchoring is in the vicinity of the 36-meter island in 6 feet at zero tide. Don't go much farther in—the bottom shoals quickly.

㊲ Beach Gardens Resort & Marina. 7074 Westminster St., Powell River, BC V8A 1C5; (604) 485-6267; (800) 663-7070; beachgardens@shaw.ca; www.beachgardens.com. Monitors VHF 66A July & August. Open all year, moorage, 15 & 30 amp power, free Wi-Fi, washrooms, showers, coin laundry, fitness center, indoor pool, ice, well-stocked beer and wine sales store. Gasoline, diesel, and lube oil at the fuel dock, open summer only. This is a breakwater-protected marina with good docks, just south of Grief Point. Deluxe waterfront rooms and cottages are available.

Beach Gardens Resort features a new building overlooking the marina and fronting the older buildings of the resort. The laundry, beer and wine store and the Savoury Bight Seaside Restaurant and Pub are on the bottom level of the new building, with a beautiful view of Malaspina Strait. Free shuttle service to Town Centre Mall in July and August.

The Myrtle Point Golf Course is nearby and will pick up marina guests.

Grief Point. Grief Point marks the northern end of Malaspina Strait on the mainland side. The seas around Grief Point get particularly rough when the wind blows.

㊳ Westview/Powell River. The breakwater-protected public wharf at Westview is the pleasure craft moorage for the town of Powell River. The north section of the marina is primarily permanent moorage; the south section is reserved for commercial and transient boats. The marina was renovated recently. The breakwater was extended and the moorage area enlarged with new docks. Fuel, water and power are available, and nearby stores have supplies. Grocery stores and a major shopping center are a taxi or a free seasonal shuttle from the marina.

The section adjacent to the ferry loading area between the two basins has been redeveloped and now houses the harbor office, new washrooms, showers, and laundry. The new docks and new facilities make Westview a destination worth visiting again.

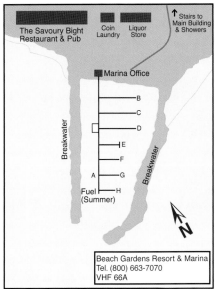

Beach Gardens Resort & Marina

The hotel at Beach Gardens is easily spotted from the water.

An excellent stock of marine and fishing supplies is available at nearby Marine Traders. Shops and restaurants are on the main commercial streets, a short walk away. The Town Centre Mall, with Save-On Foods, Shoppers Drug Mart, WalMart, liquor store and other shops, is located some distance away, up a steep hill (they call it Cardiac Hill). It's a hike. Another shopping center has a new QF grocery store that will deliver to the marina.

The original Powell River townsite is a couple of miles up the road from Westview.

It's a pleasant walk. Many of the houses and buildings in Powell River date from the first half of the 20th century.

The historical museum along the main road is definitely worth a visit. The Blackberry Festival is the second Friday in August. Check the town's website (www.discoverpowellriver.com) for a schedule of activities.

Golf: The 18-hole Myrtle Point Golf Club is a short distance south of Westview. Call (604) 487-4653.

(38) Westview Harbour. 6910 Duncan, Powell River, BC V8A 1V4; (604) 485-5244. Monitors VHF 66A. Open all year, guest moorage in the south section (no reservations), potable water, 30 & 50 amp power, washrooms, new large showers, laundry, garbage drop, recycling, waste oil disposal, Wi-Fi. Pumpout by appointment. Leave the beacon inside the entry to port when entering the harbor.

Westview went through a significant expansion in 2011. The breakwater was extended south, and new docks (Southview) added to the enlarged basin. Southview docks are more spacious and accommodate boats over 100 feet. A new trail connects the two facilities. The Westview Fuels fuel dock is now in the middle of the south moorage. When calling the marina on the VHF, call "Westview."

Two-hour complimentary moorage, please call ahead. Seasonal free shuttle to the mall picks up at the docks. The message is clear — recreational boats are welcome in Westview/Powell River.

(38) Westview Fuels. P.O. Box 171, Powell River, BC V8A 4Z6; (604) 485-2867. Monitors VHF 66A. Gasoline, diesel, lubricants, washrooms, and ice. Located in the south basin of the Westview Harbour. Joe and Debbie Hooper are the owners and they're great.

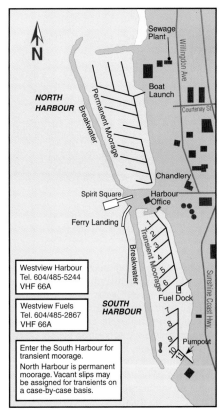

The Rocky Mountain Pizza & Bakery Company is just above the Westview Harbour.

Westview Harbour
Tel. 604/485-5244
VHF 66A

Westview Fuels
Tel. 604/485-2867
VHF 66A

Enter the South Harbour for transient moorage.
North Harbour is permanent moorage. Vacant slips may be assigned for transients on a case-by-case basis.

Westview Harbour

Dinner Rock. Dinner Rock, exposed at all tides, is approximately 0.2 mile off the mainland shore, slightly southeast of Savary Island. In 1998 a 1000-lb. cross was erected on the rock. It is a memorial to the five people who died there in October 1947, when the vessel *Gulf Stream*, proceeding in darkness with rain falling, struck the rock and sank.

Savary Island. Savary Island is a 4-mile-long sandy island that lies approximately east and west, and is served by water taxi from Lund. The small public dock on the north shore is for loading and unloading only. Anchorage is good, sand bottom, within easy dinghy distance of shore. Although Savary Island has no real protected harbor, the beaches are awesome. In summer months a licensed restaurant and general store are open. Bicycles can be rented. A number of years ago Bob Hale anchored off the north shore for the night and "got away with it." By contrast, Contributing Editor Tom Kincaid once anchored overnight in the same area, but by morning the wind had come in from the north and he was on a lee shore. Visiting by water taxi from Lund might be a better idea.

Nearby **Hernando Island** is surrounded by rocky shallows, and is seldom visited by cruising boats. Renowned authors Lin and Larry Pardey, however, report excellent anchorage with protection from southeast

winds in Stag Bay, northwest of the pier. Anchor in 18 to 24 feet on a firm sand bottom.

Mitlenatch Island. Roughly west of Hernando Island, Mitlenatch Island appears to be an uninviting rock out in the middle of the Strait of Georgia. It is in fact a thriving and ruggedly beautiful wildlife refuge, with a small, protected anchorage on its east side. Park volunteers spend a week in turn each year on the island, doing trail maintenance and guiding tours. Visitors are asked to stay on the trails to avoid disturbing birds. Those who visit will be rewarded, as this note from Correspondents John and Lorraine Littlewood suggests:

"If you can get there on a calm clear day in September, you'll see an incredible variety of wildlife, from Goshawks to huge sea lions. An additional benefit is water so clear that we could actually watch our Bruce anchor deploy. It hit the bottom in about 20 feet, flipped over, bit, and buried itself. This was on only 2:1 scope, although we later paid out to our normal 3:1."

We thank reader Sharl Heller for increasing our awareness of Mitlenatch Island.

③⑨ Lund. Lund is the north end of the road that leads all the way to the tip of South America. Lund is a busy place in the summer, a jumping-off point for Desolation Sound

with fuel, provisions, and pumpout.

The historic Lund Hotel, with restaurant and pub, is at the head of the fuel dock. The small but well-stocked store, in the same building as the hotel, has a good deli, fresh (often local) vegetables, ice cream, frozen meats, liquor agency with good wine selection, pet supplies, prawn bait, frozen herring, camping and picnic supplies, and more.

Lund is the mainland's closest launch site to Desolation Sound. Long-term auto, trailer and tow vehicle storage are available at Dave's Parking and Lund Auto & Outboard. Nancy's Bakery is in the modern, larger building overlooking the public docks. Nancy's pastries, pizzas, and other specialties are famous. Nancy's also has Wi-Fi. Pollen Sweaters, specializing in locally made sweaters, is upstairs from Nancy's.

The Lund Small Craft Harbour has recently been expanded. It's a jumping-off point for Desolation Sound.

Nancy's Bakery, Pollen Sweaters and other shops are located just above the harbour.

The Boardwalk Restaurant in Lund.

The town assumed operation of the public docks following divestiture by the federal government several years ago. With commercial fishing in decline, these docks and shoreside facilities were upgraded to make them more inviting to visiting pleasure craft. The docks were expanded in 2011, and the floating breakwater was expanded and moved out. When the docks are full, you can moor along the inside of the breakwater and dinghy to the dinghy dock. There's a good launch ramp, and modern public washrooms with excellent showers.

Over on the north side of the bay a public float, with no access to shore, is in the middle of Finn Cove.

Fuel: The busy Lund Hotel fuel dock has gasoline and diesel.

Haulout: Jack's Boatyard in Finn Cove has haulout and boat storage.

About Finn Cove: Sailing Directions and the charts call it Finn Cove, but the locals call it Finn Bay. The road that leads from the village to the cove is named Finn Bay Road. The Waggoner will call it Finn Cove, however, to be consistent with the charts.

㊈ Lund Small Craft Harbour. P.O. Box 78, Lund, BC V0N 2G0; (604) 483-4711; lundharbour-wharfinger@twinncomm.ca; www.lundharbourbc.wordpress.com Monitors VHF 73. Open all year, more than 1700 feet of breakwater-protected dock space, 20, 30 & some 50 amp power, pumpout, seasonal garbage. No oil disposal. Excellent washrooms and showers. Wide concrete launch ramp with 4 lanes, good for most launch-

ings down to about 5 feet above zero tide. (Some say 3 feet, but that's cutting it close.) The docks were expanded in fall of 2011 by moving the breakwater out and lengthening the docks. The new configuration provides 600 more feet for this popular harbor. The best Wi-Fi coverage is up at Nancy's Bakery.

Enter north of the floating breakwaters. Inside, the northern dock is reserved for pleasure craft, rafting required. Don't give up if the docks appear full. Office hours are 8:00 a.m. to 11:00 a.m. and 3:00 p.m. to 5:00 p.m. October to May, 8:00 a.m. to 5:00 p.m. June and September, 8:00 a.m. to 8:00 p.m. July 1 to Labour Day. Moorage is free for the first

hour, 1 to 3 hours are charged at the half-day rate.

The floating concrete breakwater noted above (no power or water) protects the inner docks. You can tie inside of these floats and dinghy to the marked dinghy dock area below the ramp. Overnight moorage is charged on the breakwater.

A green buoy marking a shallow ledge is near the launch ramps. Local knowledge says to be aware of a high spot there, about 3 feet at its shallowest.

㊈ Lund Hotel. 1436 Highway 101, Lund, BC V0N 2G0; (604) 414-0474; (877)

Lund Small Craft Harbour

Wing on wing up Thulin Passage.

569-3999; info@lundhotel.com; www.lundhotel.com. The hotel, which dates back to 1905, has been restored and remodeled with a pub and separate dining area. The hotel has 31 rooms, ranging from budget-sensitive to four "boutique superior ocean-front" rooms overlooking the water. The fuel dock has gasoline and diesel. Limited overnight moorage. The store and deli are well stocked. The laundry facility is clean, with good machines.

Wi-Fi is available. Tug-guhm Gallery & Studio, a very nice art studio, is in the lower part of the hotel.

(39) **Lund Water Taxi.** (604) 483-9749. Scheduled service to Savary Island. Can deliver parts or people to Desolation Sound and surrounding areas.

(39) **Dave's Parking.** P.O. Box 94, 1440 Lund Rd., Lund, BC V0N 2G0; (604) 483-3667. Daily and long-term vehicle and trailer parking in secure lots. Call ahead for reservations.

(39) **Lund Automotive & Outboard Ltd.** 1520 Lund Hwy, Lund, BC V0N 2G0; (604) 483-4612. Long-term tow vehicle and trailer parking in secure lots. Call ahead for reservations. Mechanics are on staff for mechanical and electrical repairs and they are an authorized service facility for several engine brands. Haulout to 30 feet.

(39) **Jack's Boatyard (Finn Cove).** 9907 Finn Bay Road, PO Box 198, Lund, BC V0N 2G0; (604) 483-3566; info@jacksboatyard.ca; www.jacksboatyard.ca. Haulout to 60 tons, storage available. Can haul sailboats.

Owner Jack Elsworth blasted the boat storage yard out of solid rock and welded up the darndest haulout machine imaginable. Think Travelift, then make it completely different. You have to see it.

In 2013 a massive construction project closed the dock all summer long. A new dock was built to support a 60-ton Travelift and a lower yard was cleared to allow for blocking 4 or more medium to large boats. The old lift will still be used to haul boats to 30 tons to the expansive upper yard.

Copeland Islands. The Copeland Islands (locally known as the Ragged Islands) are a provincial park, with no facilities specifically for boaters. Anchorage is possible in several nooks and coves among the islands, although some of the coves are exposed to wakes of boats transiting Thulin Passage. Because of remnants of booming cable on the bottom, a buoyed trip line to the anchor crown is a good idea. Check your swing when you anchor. On low tide a few years ago we saw a Grand Banks 42 high and dry, propped up with driftwood.

(40) **Bliss Landing Estates.** (604) 414-9417. Located in Turner Bay, north of Lund. Open all year. Guest moorage usually available but call ahead. The docks belong to the development and space cannot be guaranteed. Washrooms, showers, laundry, 30 & 50 amp power, limited fresh water, Wi-Fi and landline internet. The docks are exposed to westerly winds; moor bow-out. It's about a 15-minute dinghy ride to Lund. Limited to boats under 60 feet LOA.

WE ALMOST DIED FROM SHELLFISH POISONING

My husband and I manage a beautiful marina on an island in British Columbia. The exact location doesn't matter, because what happened to us could have happened anywhere along the coast.

After a very busy summer, at last the final weekend of the season arrived. It was October 11, 1997, and luckily the weatherman was wrong again. We had a beautiful autumn day—a perfect day for a barbecue. Many of our permanent moorage tenants already had arrived to enjoy a seafood extravaganza.

Two of them were experienced divers, and one had been in the scuba charter business for many years. They would show us their secret spot for harvesting scallops. The seas were calm and in no time we were at our destination. It wasn't long before the divers had harvested enough scallops for all of us.

When we got back to the dock a six-year-old boy questioned the divers about how and where they got the scallops, and begged to try just a couple. How could we look in those big eyes and say no? With two scallops in his tight little fists he ran back to his boat and talked his mother into cooking them right away. One of the divers, knowing that the red tide shellfish ban had been lifted a few weeks earlier, teased the boy's mother that if her son's lips didn't go numb in the next half-hour the scallops would be safe for the rest of us to eat.

Our feast began around nine in the evening, after the children were fed and settled down with a movie. We started off with freshly harvested crab legs, followed by steak, salad, potatoes, and of course the delectable scallops. Somebody suggested that we try a little Tabasco sauce on the scallops. We thought we had died and gone to heaven.

And we almost did.

In a little while my lips began to feel numb. My husband said his lips were numb too, and a few others said their lips were numb. We decided it was the Tabasco sauce, and had the rest of the scallops plain. My husband was eating as if he hadn't eaten in days, and loving every mouthful. I was close behind. Cheers for the divers and the cooks! Great food, great wine and great friends. I couldn't think of anyplace I would rather be.

The air was getting cold and my fingers and toes were growing numb. We called it a night, and told our friends we would see them in the morning for coffee. Little did we suspect that our nightmare was about to begin.

When we got home my husband said his feet and hands were so cold that he was going to take a hot bath. I just wanted to snuggle under the covers to get warm and go to sleep. I must have fallen asleep because the next thing I knew my husband was yelling that he could hardly walk and was I all right? I realized my head felt as if it was in a fog, and I couldn't feel my body.

I tried to get up and go to him, but I couldn't feel my feet touch the floor. I tried to tell him this, but the words were so hard to come out. Everything was moving in slow motion. My husband said, "I think we have shellfish poisoning. What do we do now?"

I wasn't sure how serious our situation was, but I knew that I was having trouble breathing and my condition was growing worse. We called the doctor's emergency number, feeling sorry to waken him at 2:00 a.m. The doctor asked if we could make it to the clinic on our own or did we need an ambulance. My stubborn husband said that we could make it on our own.

Getting down the stairs and into the car was easier said than done. We had to concentrate on our feet touching the ground, and it seemed to take forever to get to the car. Luckily it was late and no other cars were on the road. I'm sure the doctor thought we were drunk when we walked into the clinic. It must have been quite a sight to see the two of us holding onto each other, trying to keep our balance.

Once we told the doctor what had happened, all we could think about was the others on the boats. Were they in the same shape or even worse? What if they couldn't get to a phone? What about the little boy? The doctor called the poison control center and then the ambulance and police. We told them the boat names and locations of the 11 other people who had eaten the scallops. Fortunately, only a few of them had symptoms, and they were minor. Other than having been shaken from their sleep at 4:00 a.m., everybody else was all right.

There is no antidote for this type of toxin. All the doctor could do was start us on I.V.s, monitor our vital signs, and wait. I began to get sick. My heart felt as if it was going to jump right out of my chest. My blood pressure was out of control. I was afraid to close my eyes, because I didn't think I would wake up again.

My husband began to pass out. Somehow, between the doctor and myself, we got him onto a bed. Later, my husband told me that he felt he was floating above us, watching what was happening, everything in slow motion. And he could hear the doctor shouting, "Stay with us!"

Once again the doctor called the poison control center, and they decided that we had to be transported to a hospital in Victoria.

It was our first helicopter ride, and it wasn't supposed to be like this. I was so scared that we were going to die and never see our children again. We were taken to the emergency room, hooked up to heart and blood pressure machines, and monitored very closely. We were given liquid charcoal to drink, to absorb anything left in our stomachs.

By this time it was 7:00 a.m. We were still in the emergency room and I was so tired. But I was afraid to close my eyes. We were seen by a neurologist, who explained that we were suffering from Paralytic Shellfish Poisoning (PSP). He said the reason that we had been affected more than the others could have been that we had eaten more, or that only some of the scallops held the toxin. He told us that death usually occurs within a half-hour of consumption. Since we were still here we should be all right. It would just take time for the toxin to flush out of our systems.

Usually the symptoms last for about 12 hours, but sometimes they last longer. Everyone reacts differently. The doctor tested our reflexes and hand-eye coordination. When I tried to touch my finger to my nose, my arm would fly into the air. My legs would not do what I wanted them to do. I was frustrated and frightened. The doctor decided to admit us to the hospital.

While we were in the emergency room a friend arrived with clothes for us (we were still in our pajamas). When he saw us his face went ashen. We must have looked pretty scary, with the charcoal still on our lips and teeth. At least we were alive, and he could take that good news back to the others.

At last we were admitted and taken to our rooms, and I felt safe enough to close my eyes. But nightmares of what could have happened robbed me of my sleep.

By the next afternoon my husband had recovered enough to go home, but I was still in bad shape. I learned the hard way how we take simple things for granted—things such as feeding myself, sitting, walking, even talking. The nurses wanted me to eat something, but the thought of food made me sick. They said that was all right, the soup

of the day was clam chowder. It felt good to be able to laugh about it.

The next day I agreed to try to eat. It proved to be quite an ordeal. When the bed was raised to a sitting position I got dizzy, and I had to lie on my side. The next step was to get the fork from the plate to my mouth. My hand and my brain were not communicating, and I had more food on the bed than in my mouth. At last I found that if I used two hands I could manage. It took more than an hour to eat just half of what was on the plate.

As each day passed I got stronger. I could feed myself and sit up in a chair. By the fifth day, with the help of physiotherapists and a walker, I was walking. That night I practiced and practiced with the walker. I knew I couldn't go home until I proved to the doctor that I could walk on my own. On the sixth day I showed the doctor that I could walk to the door. He agreed to let me go home.

I'm writing this three weeks since that eventful night, and every day I count my blessings that my husband and I are alive. It could have been very different.

This deadly PSP toxin can remain in bivalve shellfish for as long as a year. (When does the year begin?) Some shellfish might contain the toxin while others might not, even if they have been harvested from the same area. The toxin cannot be killed by cooking or freezing.

Typically, symptoms begin with numbness or tingling of the lips and tongue. The numbness and tingling spread to the fingers and toes. These symptoms can be followed by nausea, a floating feeling, and a loss of muscular coordination. Danger of death occurs when the breathing muscles are affected, which necessitates the use of a respirator.

We, and others, have always believed that in the absence of a red tide alert bivalve shellfish were safe to eat. The lifting of this red tide alert brought a false sense of security. Our experience has proven that there is always a risk.

— *Kay Spence*

Editor's note: Despite a fierce battle, in 2002 Kay Spence succumbed to lung cancer.

For latest information on Paralytic Shellfish Poison (PSP) closures, call:

Washington State	*(800) 562-5632*
British Columbia	*(866) 431-3474*

CHAPTER 10

DESOLATION SOUND & DISCOVERY PASSAGE

DESOLATION SOUND
Prideaux Haven • Homfray Lodge • Pendrell Sound • Refuge Cove • Teakerne Arm

CORTES ISLAND
Squirrel Cove • Cortes Bay • Von Donop Inlet • Gorge Harbour

QUADRA ISLAND
Rebecca Spit • Heriot Bay • Octopus Islands • Okisollo Channel

DISCOVERY PASSAGE
Campbell River • April Point • Brown Bay • Small Inlet

Captain George Vancouver had it all wrong when he explored and wrote about this area during his cruise in 1792. He named it Desolation Sound, saying, "there was not a single prospect that was pleasing to the eye." Granted, his crew did have a challenging time with weather, fleas, and even shellfish poisoning. In reality, Desolation Sound, located literally just beyond the end of the road, is a place of extraordinary beauty. It's one of the Northwest's most dreamed-about and sought-after cruising destinations.

Officially, Desolation Sound is the body of water north of Sarah Point and Mary Point, and south of West Redonda Island. When most people think of cruising these waters, however, they consider Desolation Sound to include the entire area north of Cape Mudge and Sarah Point, and south of Yuculta Rapids and Chatham Point, including Discovery Passage (Campbell River).

For those departing from the Seattle or Vancouver areas, the trip to and from Desolation Sound might take as long as a week, depending on boat speed, weather, and stops along the way.

Desolation Sound is not a huge area. Even slow boats can go from one end to another in a day. But Desolation Sound offers a wilderness setting, generally easy waters, many bays and coves to explore and anchor in, and marinas where fuel and supplies are available. On the west side of these cruising grounds, Campbell River, on Vancouver Island, is a vibrant small city. Campbell River has complete supplies and even a shipyard for haulout and repairs. Lund, on the B.C. mainland, is at the eastern entry to Desolation Sound. Lund

Teakerne Arm is deep, but anchorage is possible in front of Cassel Falls by tying a stern line to hooks in the rock wall.

is only a village but has several services vacationing boaters are apt to need. Lund also is the northern terminus of Highway 99, the road that ends at Tierra del Fuego, the tip of South America. Small marinas scattered throughout Desolation Sound offer fuel, water, and limited supplies.

Since it is close to the point where the tidal currents meet, the water in Desolation Sound is not regularly exchanged with cold ocean water. During the summer, water temperatures of 70° to 80°F are not unusual in some of the bays, making for comfortable swimming.

Navigation is straightforward, with few hazards in the major channels. Closer to shore it's a different story, but the rocks and reefs are charted.

The most popular time to cruise Desolation Sound is from mid-July through the end of August, when the prospects for sunny, warm weather are best. It's also when the anchorages and facilities are most crowded. June weather can be cool and rainy, but crowds are not a problem. It's then that the waterfalls are most awesome and the resorts and businesses, while open and stocked, are the least harried.

If your calendar permits, the very best time to cruise Desolation Sound might be early- to mid-September. By then the high-season crowds have departed, yet summer usually hangs on for a last and glorious finale. Stock in the stores may be thin and the young summertime help has headed back to school, but the low slanting sunlight paints the hills and mountains with new drama, and the first colors of autumn make each day a fresh experience. Watch the weather closely. Leave before the fall storm pattern begins, although usually that's not before October.

Navigation note: Tide information for locations in Desolation Sound is shown in Ports and Passes and Canadian Tide and Current Tables, Vol. 5 (they are shown as secondary ports based on Point Atkinson Tides). Currents for Beazley Passage, Hole in the Wall,

and Discovery Passage are shown in Vol. 6, as are corrections for Upper Rapids and Lower Rapids in Okisollo Channel. Owen Bay tides and Okisollo Channel secondary port tide corrections also are in Vol. 6.

Sarah Point. For boats running north through Thulin Passage, Sarah Point, at the tip of the Malaspina Peninsula, is the dramatic entrance to Desolation Sound. The high hills of the Malaspina Peninsula hide the Coast Range mountains. But on a clear day, once Sarah Point is cleared, the mountains come into magnificent view.

MALASPINA INLET

Malaspina Inlet, Okeover Inlet, Lancelot Inlet and Theodosia Inlet all are entered between Zephine Point and Myrmidon Point. On a spring flood tide you will most likely find current at the mouth of Malaspina Inlet, all the way up to Grace Harbour. Much of Gifford Peninsula, to the east of Malaspina Inlet, is Desolation Sound Marine Park. Several good anchorages are in this area. You'll also find rocks and reefs, most of which are covered by kelp during the summer and easily identified. They'll keep you alert, though.

Aquaculture occupies several otherwise inviting anchorages, but there are still plenty of choices in this area. Many of the aquaculture sites indicated on charts are no longer active, but debris left behind can foul ground tackle.

Malaspina Inlet is popular with kayakers. Be mindful of your wake.

① **Grace Harbour.** Grace Harbour is a popular anchorage. The inner bay is surrounded by forest and almost completely landlocked, with anchorage for quite a few boats. Many of the anchorages are along the shore, so be prepared to run a stern-tie. A fire pit is in a little, parklike area at the north end. A rock, shown on the charts, is in the middle of this

CHARTS	
3312 Small craft chart (chartbook)	Jervis Inlet & Desolation Sound
3513	Strait of Georgia – Northern Portion (1:80,000)
3537 Plans	Okisollo Channel (1:20,000); Whiterock Passage (1:10,000)
3538	Desolation Sound and Sutil Channel (1:40,000)
3539	Discovery Passage (1:40,000) Seymour Narrows (1:20,000)
3540	Approaches to Campbell River (1:10,000)
3541	Approaches to Toba Inlet (1:40,000)
3542	Bute Inlet (1:40,000)
3555 Plans	Vicinity of Redonda Islands & Loughborough Inlet
3559	Malaspina Inlet, Okeover Inlet & Lancelot Inlet (1:12,000)

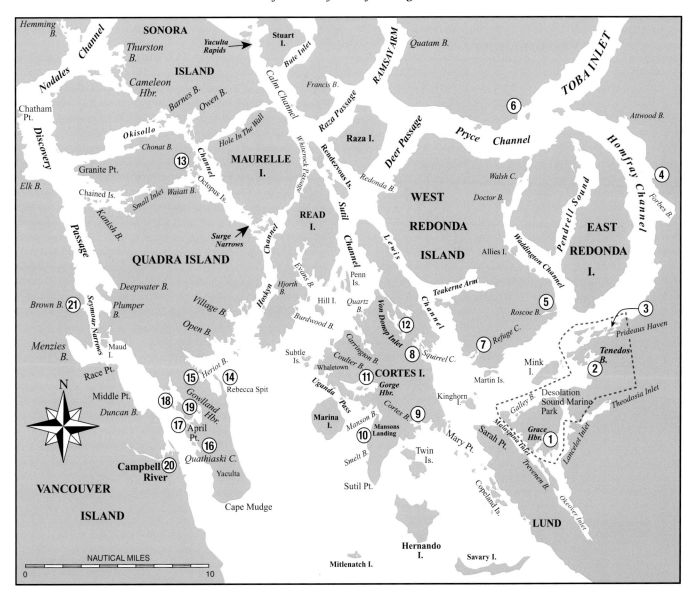

innermost bay. The anchor just skids across the rock before finding holding ground on the other side. On a crowded summer weekend, the empty spot in the middle is there for a reason.

Trevenen Bay. The head of Trevenen Bay looks like a good anchorage on the chart, but the bay is largely taken by aquaculture.

Penrose Bay. Anchorage at the head of the bay. The Okeover Marina is on the west shore to the south.

Okeover Inlet. South of Penrose Bay a public float gives access to the road to Lund, with a natural launching ramp alongside. Oysters and other seafoods are grown in several places along Okeover Inlet, and are on private property.

The public dock in Okeover Arm usually has room for a few visitors. This is a working dock; no power or water.

The Laughing Oyster Restaurant (604-483-9775) is above the public float. It is an excellent restaurant with lovely surroundings

and a stunning view. Reservations recommended. A float is available below the restaurant, making it easy to visit in the mother vessel instead of the dinghy.

Lancelot Inlet. Isabel Bay in Lancelot Inlet is popular. The best anchorage is behind Madge Islands, with a beautiful view and room for 1 or 2 boats. Good anchorage is also in Thors Cove. The bay is deep until close to shore or in the nooks.

Correspondent Pat Shera, from Victoria, wrote to tell us that in Isabel Bay he fouled his anchor on a section of bulldozer track at the head of the anchorage, just west of the north tip of Madge Island. If you have Chartbook 3312, it's where the 4.2-meter sounding is shown. He says another section of track was high and dry on a nearby rock.

Theodosia Inlet. Theodosia Inlet has a narrow, shallow, and kelp-choked entrance, but is navigable by most boats at all stages of the tide. Once inside, the bay opens up. Logging activity takes away from the remote feeling of the bay and boomed logs can oc-

cupy much of the shoreline. Anchorage is in a number of gunkholes along the shoreline.

MINK ISLAND AREA

Galley Bay. Galley Bay is just east of Zephine Head. It is a good anchorage, particularly in the eastern end.

Mink Island. Mink Island is private property, but you'll find excellent anchorage in the bay that indents the southeast shore, particularly if you work in behind the little island in the center of the bay. You'll probably run a stern-tie to shore.

Curme Islands. Wolferstan describes navigation in the Curme Islands, east of Mink Island, as "challenging." Bailey and Cummings, in their *Gunkholing* book (now out of print), described the Curme Islands as extremely tight with shallow waterways, but with anchoring possibilities if the boat uses 4-way ties to hold position. For most people, dinghies and kayaks are probably the way to go.

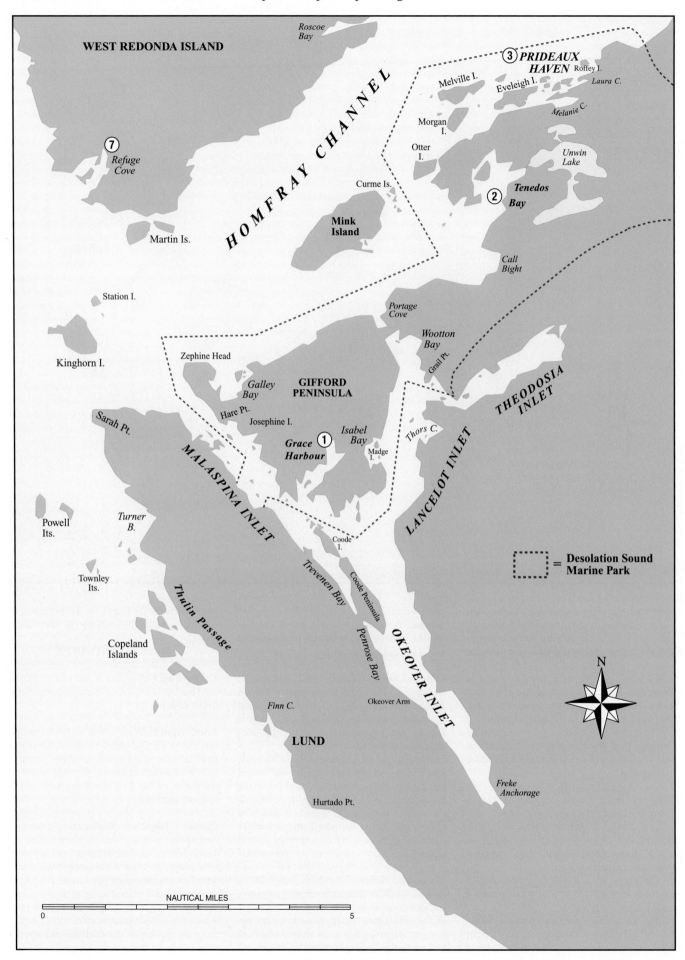

WEST REDONDA ISLAND

Roscoe Bay

③ *PRIDEAUX HAVEN*   Roffey I.

Melville I.

Eveleigh I.   *Laura C.*

Melanie C.

Morgan I.

H O M F R A Y   C H A N N E L

Otter I.

Unwin Lake

⑦ *Refuge Cove*

Curme Is.

② *Tenedos Bay*

Mink Island

Call Bight

Martin Is.

Station I.

Portage Cove

Wootton Bay

Kinghorn I.

Zephine Head

Grail Pt.

THEODOSIA INLET

Galley Bay

GIFFORD PENINSULA

Hare Pt.

Josephine I.

Isabel Bay

Thors C.

Sarah Pt.

Grace Harbour ①

Madge I.

LANCELOT INLET

MALASPINA INLET

Powell Its.

Turner B.

Coode I.

Townley Its.

Trevenen Bay

Coode Peninsula

Penrose Bay

OKEOVER INLET

⌐ ¬
┊   ┊ = **Desolation Sound Marine Park**
└ ┘

Thulin Passage

Copeland Islands

Okeover Arm

N

Finn C.

LUND

Hurtado Pt.

Freke Anchorage

NAUTICAL MILES

0   5

Prideaux Haven, with jaw-dropping mountain views, is the quintessential Desolation Sound anchorage.

Melanie Cove is one of the most popular anchorages in Desolation Sound.

② **Tenedos Bay.** Tenedos Bay (also called Deep Bay) is a favorite, for a couple of reasons. First, it's a good, protected anchorage, with a landlocked basin behind the island off the northwest shore. This island is joined with the mainland by a drying shoal, shown on the charts. Second, it's just a short dinghy ride to the mouth of the stream that runs from Unwin Lake, a popular freshwater swimming hole. A path beside the stream leads to the lake. Several of the stream's pools, screened by vegetation, make good bathing places.

In addition to the landlocked basin noted above, you'll find anchorages in coves along the shore of Tenedos Bay. We like the little notch at the northernmost corner. Stern-ties to shore are the norm. The center of Tenedos Bay is too deep (300 to 600 feet) for anchoring.

Caution: As you enter Tenedos Bay, a nasty rock lies submerged off the south side of Bold Head. Especially if you are headed to or from Refuge Cove, Mink Island, or around Bold Head to Prideaux Haven, this rock is right on your probable course. The rock lies farther offshore than you might expect. Give it an extra wide berth, just to be sure. Remember to study your charts before proceeding in these waters. A number of rocks are shown. All are easy to avoid if you are aware of them.

Otter Island. A very narrow but navigable channel runs between Otter Island and the mainland. Space for a few boats to anchor, using stern-ties to shore.

PRIDEAUX HAVEN AREA

The coves that make up the area generally known as Prideaux Haven are the most popular spots in Desolation Sound, with several requiring stern-ties to increase the number of boats accommodated. The area is described in great detail by M. Wylie Blanchet in her classic book *The Curve of Time.*

At the head of Melanie Cove you can find the remains of Mike's place, and in Laura Cove traces of old Phil Lavine's cabin site are visible (both from *The Curve of Time*). The evidence, however, is getting pretty faint.

The entire clutch of islands and shallow waterways invites exploration by dinghy or kayak. The narrow pass between Scobel Island and the William Islands, for instance, is beautiful. During high season, the only thing missing is solitude. You'll have lots of company.

No Discharge Zone. Gray water okay.

③ **Eveleigh Island.** Anchorage is in Eveleigh Anchorage, the western cove behind Eveleigh Island. A drying reef connects Eveleigh Island with the mainland. Entry to the other Prideaux Haven anchorages is around the east end of Eveleigh Island. A reef almost, but not quite, closes this entrance. Use Chart 3555 (recommended) or Chartbook 3312. Smaller scale Chart 3538 (1:40,000) shows the entry but with too little detail to inspire confidence. Strongly favor the Eveleigh Island side of the passage to clear the reef.

③ **Prideaux Haven.** Inside Eveleigh Island is the main Prideaux Haven anchorage and also Melanie Cove. Except in the very middle of Prideaux Haven and Melanie Cove, stern ties are the rule during the summer. *No Discharge Zone. Gray water okay.*

③ **Melanie Cove.** Melanie Cove is perfectly protected with ample room along both shores for boats to anchor and stern-tie. A few boats can anchor in the middle without a stern-tie. An overgrown apple orchard and the remains of Mike's cabin, warmly described in *The Curve of Time*, are at the head of the cove. A small creek on the south shore, near the head, has a flowing hose. The water is untreated, and not recommended for human consumption.

Correspondent Gil Flanagan tells us a trail runs between Melanie Cove and Unwin Lake with a new section that bypasses an earlier hand-over-hand section. He says the first half-mile is easy, and has a nice view at the end.

③ **Laura Cove.** Laura Cove has a fairly narrow entrance with a least depth of approximately 10 feet at zero tide. Rocks extend from both sides. Enter cautiously. Once you're inside, the bay is beautiful. Traces of Old Phil the Frenchman's cabin site, mentioned in *The Curve of Time*, are at the head of this bay. Anchorage is to the east of Copplestone Point; the west end of the bay is a maze of rocks and reefs.

Roffey Island. If you can't find a place at Prideaux Haven, Melanie Cove, or Laura Cove, try the little bay behind Roffey Island. Room for one or more boats away from the crowd.

Homfray Channel. Homfray Channel curves from the south end of West Redonda Island around East Redonda Island until it merges with Toba Inlet. The only bays of consequence are Forbes Bay and Atwood Bay. Atwood Bay is too deep and exposed for convenient anchoring, but Bob Stephenson of Desolation Sound Yacht Charters says Forbes Bay can be good for anchoring.

On p. 100 of his book, Wolf-

erstan tells of two Indian pictographs on the west shore of Homfray Channel, one of a single fish, the other unidentified. Actually, there are several pictographs, located about 10 feet above the high water line. Correspondent Pat Shera gives coordinates of 50°11.698'N/124°39.514'W.

④ **Homfray Lodge.** (604) 740-6032; info@homfraylodge.com; www.homfraylodge.com. New lodge in Homfray Channel, just north of Forbes Bay. Beautiful and remote location with 250 feet of moorage. Good, potable water, showers, Wi-Fi. No power or food service. The three Macey brothers have been actively developing this property. The lodge and a small store opened in 2013. Cabins are available for rent. Fishing and sightseeing charters.

WADDINGTON CHANNEL

⑤ **Roscoe Bay/Roscoe Bay Marine Park.** Roscoe Bay, on West Redonda Island where Waddington Channel meets Homfray Channel, is an excellent, protected, and popular anchorage. The bay is divided into an inner cove and an outer cove, separated by a drying shoal easily crossed by shallow draft boats at half tide or better. If in doubt, go in on a rising tide. At high tide most sailboats can get in.

The inner cove is pretty, and except for the other boats enjoying the bay with you, it's a good example of what cruising in these waters is all about. Dinghy ashore and take the short hike up to the knob dividing the two bays.

At the head of the inner bay a short stream connects with Black Lake. An old logging road leads to the lake. During summer months the water in Black Lake is warm and excellent for swimming or bathing. Trout fishing is reportedly good. If you carry your dinghy up the road you can launch it along the lake's shoreline.

On the west side of Roscoe Bay a large red float (a "scotsman") hangs in a tree and marks the beginning of trail to the top of a 2200-foot-high mountain. A rock cairn has been built at the summit, and on the cairn is a bottle with pencil and paper inside. Write

your name on the paper and add it to the collection. The hike is demanding and a round trip takes several hours, so use your judgment.

No Discharge Zone. Gray water okay.

LOCAL KNOWLEDGE

SPEED LIMIT: Seed oyster growers in Pendrell Sound ask for a 4-knot speed limit in the vicinity of their operations to prevent damage.

Pendrell Sound. With summer water temperatures dependably in excess of 68°F, Pendrell Sound has been called the "warmest saltwater north of Mexico." Major oyster culture operations are in the sound, providing seed oysters to growers all over the coast.

Strings of cultch material (often empty oyster shells) are suspended from floats in the bay until the oyster spat adheres to them, at which point they are shipped.

The favored anchorage is at the very head of the sound, probably stern-tied to trees ashore. Wear good shoes and sturdy gloves when you're clambering around on the rocks.

Another anchorage is on the western shore, about three-quarters of the way up the sound. It's tucked in behind a small islet at the outfall from a saltwater lagoon. "We tried this anchorage in deteriorating weather a few years ago, but found the best spots, close to the islet, taken. With nightfall approaching and conditions worsening, we got creative. The charts show the shore on the north edge of this cove as reefs, but we found a nice opening, perhaps 50 feet wide, between two fingers of reef. We were able to set the anchor in front of the opening and back in. A long stern-tie was run to rocks on shore. It took several changes in the stern-tie termination point to align the boat just right, but once done, the anchorage was snug and safe for the night—a windy night filled with rain, thunder and lightning. We were rather proud of ourselves." [*Hale*]

Elworthy Island. A delightful anchorage lies behind Elworthy Island, a mile north of

Church Point, roughly across Waddington Channel from the entrance to Pendrell Sound. The aquaculture noted on charts no longer is present. The island is called Alfred Island by Wolferstan, but in 1992 it was renamed Elworthy Island for seaman Richard Elworthy, who died serving freedom in 1942. A handsome plaque is set into rock on the northeast corner of the island. Enter the anchorage from either end, but watch for a drying rock near the north entrance. The island's shoreline is covered with oysters.

Allies Island. Allies Island is connected to West Redonda Island by a drying reef. The north cove is pretty well choked with aquaculture; anchorage is possible in the south cove.

Doctor Bay. If it weren't taken up by aquaculture, Doctor Bay would be a good anchorage.

Walsh Cove Marine Park. Walsh Cove Marine Park is a beautiful little spot with room for a few boats to anchor on a rocky bottom. Enter Walsh Cove from the south. At the north end of the cove, a rock-strewn reef connects Gorges Island to West Redonda Island. The middle of the cove is deep. Most boats anchor near shore with stern-ties to rocks or trees. The cove is well protected from down-channel winds but open to up-channel winds from the south. Two sets of Indian pictographs are at Butler Point.

⑥ **Toba Wildernest Marina.** Box 9, Munson, AB T0J 2C0; (250) 830-2269; tobawildernest@lincsat.com; www.tobawildernest.com. This is a small marina and resort located behind Double Island at the mouth of Toba Inlet. The views up Toba Inlet are breathtaking. The marina has 350 feet of moorage, campground, 5 km of hiking trails, three cabins, Wi-Fi, excellent block ice, and a shower. Unlimited water on the dock, but no power. The resort's electricity is provided by an incredibly-engineered home-built hydro-electric plant. The cabins are German in style and decor. Excellent new docks have recently been installed.

Call ahead on VHF 66A for instructions

Homfray Lodge is easy to spot when transiting Homfray Channel.

At Roscoe Bay there is enough depth to enter at high tide, but at lower water note rocky bottom in lower right corner.

The docks at Refuge Cove look open in this photo, but they get busy in the summer.

Disposing of garbage can be a challenge in Desolation Sound. At Refuge Cove, Dave's Garbage Service takes garbage for a fee.

on where to tie up.

Please don't swim in the pool up by the falls. It's the source of the property's drinking water.

The owners are Kyle and Andrea Hunter and their daughter, Rowan.

Toba Inlet. Toba Inlet extends 20 miles into the 8,000-foot-high Coast Range mountains until it ends in drying flats at the mouth of the Toba River. The water is very deep right up to the rock wall shores. Magnificent waterfalls crash into the sea, especially early in the season when the snowpack is melting rapidly. Toba Inlet reminds us of the inlets north of Cape Caution. Limited anchorage is possible at the head of the inlet, and in Brem Bay off the mouth of the Brem River.

After being unused for some time, lately we found the log dump in Brem Bay active again. A sign on the barge said "Welcome to Paragon Camp." Correspondent Gil Flanagan reports that he has anchored, stern-tied, on the northeast side of Brem Bay, at the mouth of a cove created by a rock breakwater not shown on the chart. The views were beautiful.

LEWIS CHANNEL

Lewis Channel runs between West Redonda Island and Cortes Island.

⑦ **Refuge Cove.** Refuge Cove, with a public marina, fuel dock, shops and well-stocked store, is a good resupply port in the heart of Desolation Sound. The busiest times are between 11:00 a.m. and 3:00 p.m. For easiest moorage and fuel dock use, early morning and late afternoon are recommended.

Several homes, joined by boardwalks, surround the cove. Ample moorage is available. Dogs should be on a leash. A pet path is beside the used book stand. Anchorage is possible toward the head of the bay.

During high season traffic can be heavy. Approach slowly, and wait your turn for dock space or fuel. Turnover is rapid; you shouldn't have to wait long.

Refuge Cove is a scheduled stop for float plane service.

Garbage barge. Around mid-June, an enterprising chap named Dave Cartwright moors a barge near the mouth of Refuge Cove. For a reasonable fee he accepts bagged garbage and responsibly takes it away. If you have accumulated garbage from several days in Desolation Sound, this is one of the few places to dispose of it.

⑦ **Refuge Cove General Store.** General Delivery, Refuge Cove, BC V0P 1P0; (250) 935-6659; refcov@twincomm.ca. Guest moorage along 2000 feet of side-tie dock space. The fuel dock has gasoline, diesel, and propane. Washrooms, showers and laundry are up by the store. Potable water, 15 amp power, fee-based Wi-Fi.

The store carries groceries, fresh produce, deli items including cheeses and meats, a complete liquor agency with interesting wine selections, some marine supplies and gear, charts, cube and block ice, a good selection of books and magazines. It is also a post office. If Judith Williams' delightful book *Dynamite Stories* is in stock, pick up a copy. The stories are a blast, literally. The store has limited operating hours in the fall.

Most businesses, including the art gallery and gift shop, are open

June through August. The cafe has bakery items and fresh bread that quickly sell out.

Teakerne Arm. Teakerne Arm is a deep inlet extending from Lewis Channel into West Redonda Island. Anchorage is just inside the entrance on the south side, or in front of the waterfall from Cassel Lake at the head of the north arm, or in the south arm. Both arms are deep, except very close to shore.

The area near the waterfall is a provincial park, with a dinghy float connected to shore by an aluminum ramp. Anchorage is in 90 to 150 feet. A cable in fair but serviceable condition hangs down the rock wall west of the waterfall for stern-ties, and several rings are set in the rock just above the high tide line on either side of the dinghy dock. The waterfall is stunning, about 2½ stories high. Taking the short, vigorous hike from the dinghy float to

Squirrel Cove Store has food, supplies and a selection of marine hardware.

The Squirrel Cove anchorage is protected with plenty of room to anchor.

Cassel Lake for a swim is a popular pastime. The water warms in the summer.

Other than the park, much of the water near shore in the remainder of Teakearne Arm is filled with log booms. Some vessels tie to the log booms.

CORTES ISLAND

Recommended book: *Destination Cortez Island,* by June Cameron, describes the early days on Cortes Island. In our opinion this book joins *The Curve of Time* as essential and entertaining background reading about the B.C. coast. After reading *Destination Cortez Island* you will have an entirely different outlook about your explorations of Cortes Bay, Squirrel Cove, Von Donop Inlet, Whaletown, Gorge Harbour, Mansons Landing, and the entire Desolation Sound area.

Published in Canada by Heritage House and in the U.S. by Fine Edge Nautical Publishing.

⑧ Squirrel Cove. Squirrel Cove is made up of two bays.

In the outer bay, a public float gives access to the Squirrel Cove Trading Co. general store. The inner bay has better protection, and during the summer is often full of anchored boats. A saltwater lagoon is at the head of the inner bay. A connecting rapids that runs into the lagoon at high tide and out of the lagoon at low tide. Be sure to plan an exit strategy if you enter the lagoon by dinghy.

At one time the inner bay was used for log booming. June Cameron wrote an article in Pacific Yachting telling of a tangle of sunken logs on the bottom. At least one tough old log might still be down there. Friends once anchored between the two islands in the inner bay and snagged a large log with their anchor. It took three hours and much effort to work the log to the surface, and then it slipped free and sank back to the bottom. Until we get an accurate report from a diver, we would be cautious about anchoring between the two islands.

Another spot to be wary of is the small bay south of the lagoon outlet, east of the little bare islet.

Correspondent Pat Shera wrote to tell us he saw one boat foul its anchor on an old engine block and another boat pick up some old cable. "The catches were released," he reported, ominously. As far as we know, they're still down there.

A trail leads from the northwest corner of Squirrel Cove to Von Donop Inlet.

The large new building on the west shore is a Native Cultural Centre and offices.

No Discharge Zone. Gray water okay.

⑧ Squirrel Cove Public Wharf. Guest moorage with 15 amp power along 200 feet of dock. The dock is close to the Squirrel Cove Trading Co. store, The Cove Restaurant and the Flying Squirrel Take-Out window. Garbage drop (charge assessed) and pay telephone available.

At very low tides the ramps from the wharf to the floats are quite steep. Local boats often take much of the dock space, although by being patient we've found room. There's always room for a dinghy. A full-time diver is onsite for maintenance and recovery. The phone number is posted at the top of the dock.

⑧ Squirrel Cove Trading Co. Ltd. P.O. Box 1, Squirrel Cove, BC V0P 1T0; (250) 935-6327; squirrelcovetrading@yahoo.ca; www.squirrelcove.com. Open all year. Washrooms, showers, and laundry are in a separate building just west of the store. Gasoline, diesel, propane and kerosene available upland; gas and diesel lines run to the dock, but it can only be used at higher tides. Tent sites with water and picnic tables available. This is a good provi-

sioning stop with fresh produce, meat and fish, groceries, ice, charts, books and videos, marine hardware, post office, pay phone, Wi-Fi, liquor, ATM. The hardware section has just about anything a person might need.

A crafts shop and gallery is next to the store, stocked with island-made (or designed) goods. Artists take turns staffing the shop. A Sunday market, with crafts, local produce, baked goods and musicians, runs from 11:00 a.m. to 3:00 p.m., summer only.

The Cove Restaurant, with indoor or outdoor dining, is open seasonally. The food is very good. It also has a kids' menu, including mac & cheese. The Flying Squirrel is a take-out restaurant serving fresh fish, bannock "native fry bread," and several gluten-free options.

⑨ Cortes Bay. Cortes Bay is well protected, but in some places the soft mud bottom doesn't hold well. Use Chart 3538 when approaching. Several charted rocks and reefs near the entrance have claimed the inattentive. These include Central Rock, north of Twin Islands, several rocks around Three Islets, and a rock off the headland midway between Mary Point and the entrance to Cortes Bay. To be safe, we always pass south of Three Islets.

Pay close attention to the beacon in the middle of the narrow entry to Cortes Bay. This beacon, with its red triangle dayboard, marks the south end of a nasty reef. Leave the beacon to starboard (Red, Right, Returning) as you enter. If you doubt the existence of this reef, one look at low tide will convince you. A small public wharf is at the head of

Cortes Bay. It is usually full during the summer. Rafting is required.

Seattle Yacht Club has an outstation on the south shore of Cortes Bay, at the location of a former marina. Royal Vancouver Yacht Club has an outstation on the north shore. No reciprocals at either outstation.

Local knowledge says the best holding ground is east of the Royal Van outstation, off the mouth of a small drying cove. During a 30- to 40-knot southeasterly blow, however, we did see boats anchored successfully off the SYC outstation as well.

No Discharge Zone. Gray water okay.

Twin Islands. Twin Islands, located off the southeast side of Cortes Island, are really a single island divided by a drying spit. Anchorage is possible close to the drying spit on either side, but a better anchorage is opposite the islands on Cortes Island.

Sutil Point. Sutil Point is the south end of Cortes Island. A long, drying spit dotted with boulders extends south from the point, almost to buoy *Q20*. Give this buoy plenty of sea room.

A fresh southeast wind, especially if it is blowing against an ebb current (see Point Atkinson tides), will set up high steep seas south of Sutil Point and east past Mitlenatch Island. We found steep 6-foot seas in this area one year, and vowed to never repeat the experience.

Correspondent Gil Flanagan sent a note that in 2009, with 20-30 knot winds, "These were the steepest waves we have experienced in 20 years." On 8- to 10-foot waves, Flanagan says the crests seemed only 20 feet apart. Conditions such as these are more than difficult—they are dangerous. Don't challenge this area in a southeaster.

Smelt Bay Provincial Park. One mile north of Sutil Point on the west side of the peninsula. Good temporary anchorage is close to shore. The park has 23 campsites, picnic tables, and a white sand beach.

⑩ **Mansons Landing.** The historic store at Mansons Landing has been closed and the building moved about three-quarters of a mile up the hill. It is now a co-op with a broad selection of organic foods and a coffee shop with Wi-Fi. An excellent small bookstore is next to the co-op. The post office, community center and library, snack stand and a small market are across the street. A farmers market is held Fridays from 12:00 p.m. to 3:00 p.m at Manson's Hall.

The 177-foot public dock is still there, and garbage can be left for a fee. Anchorage is good north of the public dock. The entire area is exposed to the south.

No Discharge Zone. Gray water okay.

⑩ **Mansons Landing Marine Park.** Open all year, 117 acres. The park has no dock of its own, but can be reached from the Mansons Landing public dock or you can an-

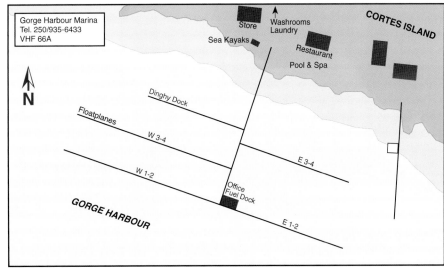

Gorge Harbour Marina

chor out. Hague Lake, with warm water and swimming beaches safe for small children, is a 10-minute walk from the public dock.

⑪ **Gorge Harbour.** Gorge Harbour is a large bay with many good spots to put the hook down. The entry is through a narrow cleft in the rock cliff. Orange-colored Indian pictographs, including a stick figure man, a man on what appears to be a turtle or fish, and several vertical lines, are on the rock wall to port as you enter. You have to look closely to identify them. Current runs through the entrance, but boats go through at any time. Inside you'll find good, protected anchorage. An aquaculture operation is to starboard just inside the entrance. The Gorge Harbour Marina Resort, on the northwest shore, has many amenities, including an outstanding restaurant.

No Discharge Zone. Gray water okay.

⑪ **Gorge Harbour Marina Resort.** P.O. Box 89, Whaletown, BC V0P 1Z0; (250) 935-6433 ext. 4; moorage@gorgeharbour. com; www.gorgeharbour.com. Monitors VHF 66A. Open all year, gasoline and diesel at the fuel dock, guest moorage along 1750 feet of dock. Facilities include 15, 30 & 50 amp power, water, swimming pool, hot tub, barbecue areas, washrooms, showers, laun-

dry, Wi-Fi, pay phones. A well-stocked convenience store has fresh vegetables, meats, dairy products, liquor, ice, propane, and DVD movie rentals. Four lodge rooms and a poolside cottage for rent. Cell phone coverage is in a small zone near the marina office on the side of the store building. Garbage disposal is available for a fee, no charge for recycling. Complete recycling instructions available. The resort has an RV park, campground, lodge accommodations, and float plane service. Boats, kayaks, stand-up paddleboards, and cars for rent.

The resort features attractive landscaping around the pool and hot tub, a fireplace patio and barbecue area for guest use. Both overlook the harbor. There is an elaborate childrens' play area for kids.

The Floathouse Restaurant always gets excellent reviews. The atmosphere is cozy and conducive to multi-table conversations. Open from April to October, with reduced hours in winter. During peak season the restaurant offers a continental breakfast, lunch, dinner and a Sunday brunch. Year after year, they have a great chef. Limited seating, with reservations recommended in the high season.

⑪ **Gorge Harbour Public Dock.** Located a short distance east of the Gorge Harbour Marina; commercial vessels have priority.

Gorge Harbour Marina has excellent docks that lead to landscaped grounds ashore.

The pool and spa at Gorge Harbour are a favorite for kids and adults.

Uganda Passage. Uganda Passage separates Cortes Island from Marina Island. The pass is narrow and winding, but well marked and easy to navigate as long as you pay attention. Red, Right, Returning assumes you are returning from the south. See the map showing the route through the passage. Shark Spit is long and low with a superb sand beach. Swimming is good. Anchorage is south of the pass on either the Cortes Island or Marina Island side.

Whaletown. Whaletown is the terminus of the ferry between Cortes Island and Quadra Island. The ferry dock is on the north side of the bay and a small public float is on the south side. Watch for several marked and unmarked rocks, normally covered by kelp. The small post office is open limited hours, but outgoing mail can be deposited anytime.

Subtle Islands. The two Subtle Islands are separated by a drying shoal. Good anchorage is off this shoal on the east side, particularly in settled weather. The little bay on the north side is very deep except at the head. It has a lovely (and exposed) view to the north. The islands are privately owned and marked with "stay off" and "keep away" signs.

Coulter Bay. Coulter Bay is quite pretty, but as the chart indicates, much of the bay is too shallow for anchoring. Most of the good spots are taken by local boats on mooring buoys. You could anchor in the tiny nook behind Coulter Island, beside a little unnamed islet to the west. Some cabins are nearby, but they are screened from view and you won't feel as if you're in their kitchens.

Carrington Bay. Carrington Bay is pretty and well protected except from the north. The bottom is reportedly rocky, so be sure your anchor is properly set before turning in for the night. Carrington Lagoon, at the head of the bay, is interesting to explore. Drag the dinghy across the logs that choke the entrance to the lagoon. June Cameron, in *Destination Cortez*, says the lagoon entrance was blasted out of rock, with amazingly smooth sides—a tribute to the skills of the man who did the blasting. A good anchorage is to the right, near the entrance to the lagoon, with a

stern-tie ashore. We've seen other boats anchored in the little bight a short distance to the left of the lagoon entrance and behind the tiny island just off the eastern shore of the bay.

No Discharge Zone. Gray water okay.

Quartz Bay. Quartz Bay is unusually pretty with good holding bottom. The eastern cove of the bay has several homes and two private docks along the shoreline. Near the head, you can anchor in 30 to 42 feet with swinging room, but you're in their front yards. The western cove has some aquaculture, one cabin on the shore, and anchoring depths near the south and west shores. You may have to run a stern-tie to shore. It is exposed to north winds, but it's a nice spot.

LOCAL KNOWLEDGE

DANGEROUS ROCK: About halfway into Von Donop Inlet, a rock lies in the narrowest part of the channel. Look for two prominent rock outcroppings covered with lichen, moss and grass on the left side of the channel. The rock is opposite the second, or inner, of these outcroppings. Hug the right side, and keep that rock to port, even if tree branches try to brush the starboard side of the boat or rigging.

⑫ **Von Donop Inlet.** Von Donop Inlet, on the northwest corner of Cortes Island, is en-

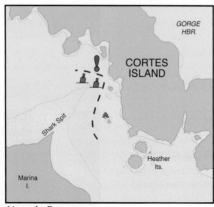

Uganda Passage

tered through a narrow, 2-mile-long channel through the trees. Once inside, several coves provide protected anchorage. The largest of these coves takes up the entire head of the inlet and has room for many boats. The bottom in this area is sticky mud. It is ideal for holding, but requires extra cleaning time when the anchor is brought aboard. Several maintained trails lead from the head of Von Donop Inlet to lakes, other destinations, and Squirrel Cove.

⑫ **Von Donop/Háthayim Provincial Marine Park.** This 3155-acre park includes Von Donop Inlet, Robertson Lake, and Wiley Lake.

Read Island. The east side of Read Island is indented from the south by Evans Bay, where several little notches are worth exploring as anchorages. Most have drying flats at their heads. Bird Cove is probably the best protected, although Contributing Editor Tom Kincaid has spent a quiet night behind the little islets in the bay just to the north of Bird Cove. A small public float is near the entrance to Evans Bay.

Hill Island. Hill Island is privately owned. According to Sailing Directions, a private lodge with a floating breakwater is in Totem Bay. The island is not open to the public.

Burdwood Bay. Burdwood Bay has several possible anchorages, particularly on the lee side of the little islands that extend from the south side of the bay, and in a notch in the north end. Burdwood Bay is not particularly pretty, but could be a hideout in a storm.

Hoskyn Channel. Hoskyn Channel runs between Read Island and Quadra Island and connects at the north with Whiterock Passage and Surge Narrows.

Bold Island Anchorage. Bold Island is just north of Village Bay on the west side of Hoskyn Channel, conveniently located at the intersection of 50°10.00'N/125°10.00'W. Correspondent Carol-Ann Giroday reports that they enter through Crescent Channel, and have good anchorage in the basin at the northwest corner of Bold Island, approximately between the two drying reefs. She says two oyster farms are in the area, but there is room for several boats to anchor, and that a wonderful oyster and clam beach is in the green-colored drying nook on Quadra Island. She adds, "We have gone ashore at this location and walked along Surge Narrows Road to nearby Village Bay Lake, where we enjoyed a fresh water swim. From the anchorage, the view southward across to Read Island and Dunsterville Islet is spectacular." This anchorage might be exposed to southerlies.

Hjorth Bay. Hjorth Bay, on Hoskyn Channel along the west side of Read Island, is a good anchorage except in a strong southerly.

Anchor in 50 to 60 feet, probably with a stern-tie to shore. A small cabin is on shore behind the island.

Whiterock Passage. Whiterock Passage is narrow, and the dredged channel is bounded on both sides by drying shoals studded with angry boulders. Least depth at zero tide is 5 feet. Maximum currents are 2 knots. Running Whiterock Passage at half tide is a good idea—it exposes the shoals on both sides but provides a little extra depth. The uninitiated tend to avoid Whiterock Passage, but it's easy to run if you pay attention and know how. Here's how:

Carefully study Plans Chart 3537, or Chartbook 3312, both of which detail Whiterock Passage at a scale of 1:10,000. As the charts show, two ranges are on the Read Island side of the passage. Going either direction, one will be a leading range as you enter, and the other a back range as you depart. Approaching, find the leading range and stay exactly on it. Proceed slowly and watch astern as the back range comes into view. When the back range lines up, turn the appropriate direction and let the back range keep you on course as you complete your transit.

Remember that the course lines on the charts are true, not magnetic. You must subtract the magnetic variation from the true heading to get the magnetic course.

"I steer when we go through in our little ship *Surprise*. As the back range comes into view, Marilynn Hale turns to stand back-to-back with me and calls the turn when the back range lines up. If I drift to either side of the back range, Marilynn taps my left shoulder or right shoulder as needed, to indicate the direction toward which I must alter course. Touching the shoulders avoids any port/starboard verbal mix-ups that might occur when each of us is facing a different direction." [*Hale*]

Rendezvous Islands. The Rendezvous Islands have a number of homes along their shores. Anchorage may be possible in a bight between the southern and middle islands, but a private float and dolphins restrict the room available.

CALM CHANNEL

Calm Channel connects Lewis Channel and Sutil Channel to the south and with Bute Inlet and the Yuculta Rapids to the north. It is appropriately named, often being wind-free when areas nearby are breezy.

Frances Bay. Earlier editions referred to Frances Bay, located just off Calm Channel at the entrance to Ramsay Arm, as a good anchorage, but the Hales don't think so anymore. The head of the bay has been the site of recent logging and they fouled their anchor on a length of logging cable—very heavy, greasy logging cable. The cable is back down on the bottom, about where you'd

want to drop your anchor. The rest of the bottom is rocky.

Church House. Church House is an abandoned Indian Reserve opposite the entrance to Hole in the Wall on Calm Channel, and near the mouth of Bute Inlet. The white-painted church, an often-photographed landmark, has collapsed in a heap.

Redonda Bay. Redonda Bay has the ruins of an old wharf left over from logging days, but otherwise is not a good anchorage. The wharf is no longer usable and the ramp leading from the float to the wharf is gone. Several rocks in the bay are charted.

Bute Inlet. Bute Inlet, approximately 35 miles long, is very deep. Except in small areas near the mouths of rivers and at the head of the inlet, it is not good for anchorage. Usually, the bottom drops away steeply, making a stern-tie to shore necessary. Anchorages should be chosen with an eye to strong inflow winds during the afternoon, followed by calm, then by icy outflow winds in the morning. Correspondents Gil and Karen Flanagan explain:

"The glaciers around Bute Inlet were melting and there are a lot of them. The water was milky by Stuart Island, and got darker and darker the farther up we went, turning from light green to gray to brownish. We saw considerable drift, including complete trees with roots sticking 8 feet or so into the air. At times we had to slow to idle, shift to neutral and coast through bands of drift. Jack Mold, the caretaker at Southgate Camp, said what we experienced was normal.

"There are three logging camps before Purcell Point. A family lives in a house at Bear Bay. Two more logging camps are at Bear Harbour, although they weren't active when we were there.

"Waddington Harbour, at the head of Bute Inlet, has a lot of good anchoring spots in 10 to 50 foot depths. We anchored as close to the northeast shore as we could get, and still were at least 100 yards from the beach (don't bother trying to stern-tie). There is no

protection from wind, but we had no wind. We didn't see much driftwood on the beach, either. We doubt if inflow winds blow hard or long, probably because even on hot days the massive ice fields in the mountains above preclude high land temperatures.

"Because of the ice fields, we had an overnight low in the upper 40s on September 1. It was 10 to 20 degrees lower than temperatures we had been experiencing in Desolation Sound. The morning air was cold enough that we needed heavy coats, even in the sun.

"Mountains 6,000 to 7,000 feet high rise directly from the head of the inlet. They have snowfields, and are spectacular.

"The milky water, drifting logs, huge harbor and high mountains create an environment that felt wild and different from anywhere we have been on the coast. We spent only 19 hours in Waddington Harbour, which wasn't long enough to take the dinghy up either river. We did see a grizzly bear on the beach near our anchorage. We definitely will go back." [*Gil Flanagan*]

Reader Richard McBride sent a note about a tiny anchorage he calls "The Nook," just outside Orford Bay:

"It is a small crack in the mountain wall about 100 feet wide at the opening and about 150 feet deep, with a little waterfall at the head. This is a terrific spot for a couple of small boats to tuck in. Lat/lon 50°34.368'N/124°52.439'W."

OKISOLLO CHANNEL/ SURGE NARROWS

Owen Bay tides and Okisollo Channel Secondary Port tide corrections are contained in Canadian Tide & Current Tables, Vol. 6 and Ports and Passes. Okisollo Channel runs along the east and north sides of Quadra Island, from Surge Narrows to Discovery Passage.

Surge Narrows & Beazley Passage. Surge Narrows and Beazley Passage should be run at or near slack water. Spring floods set eastward to 12 knots and ebbs set westward to 10 knots. Current predictions are shown un-

Calm Channel is often isolated from wind that blows elsewhere in Desolation Sound.

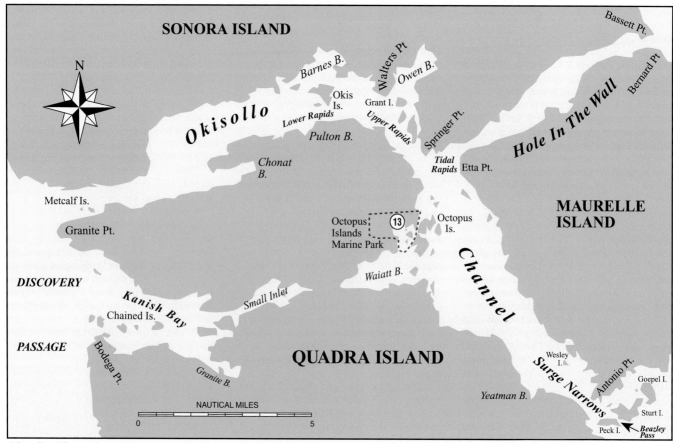

Okisollo Channel

der Beazley Passage in the Canadian Tide & Current Tables, Vol. 6 and Ports and Passes.

Although Beazley Passage, between Peck Island and Sturt Island, has the strongest currents in the Surge Narrows area, it is the preferred route between Hoskyn Channel and Okisollo Channel. Especially on an ebb current in Beazley Passage, watch for Tusko Rock, which dries 5 feet, on the east side of the pass at the north end. Stay well clear of Tusko Rock.

According to Sailing Directions, the duration of slack at Surge Narrows varies between 5 and 11 minutes. According to Contributing Editor Tom Kincaid, the passage north of the

Settler's Group is useable, but notorious for rocks. Local knowledge is required.

⑬ **Octopus Islands Marine Park.** This is a beautiful, popular anchorage and exploration area, wonderfully protected. You can enter from Waiatt Bay, but the usual entry is by a narrow channel from the north. Anchor in any of several coves and run a stern-tie to shore.

At the end of the channel as you enter from the north, a rock, clearly shown on Plans Chart 3537, obstructs part of the entry to the first cove on the right. This rock is easily seen as a white smear under the water.

You'll be going slowly anyway; watch for it and you'll have no trouble.

Waiatt Bay. Waiatt Bay is broad and protected, with convenient anchoring depths behind the Octopus Islands. The bay's entrance is choked with islets and rocks. Sailing Directions (written for large vessels) warns against entering. With the aid of large scale Plans Chart 3537 (1:20,000), however, a small boat can pick its way in along the south shore, or in the middle of the islets, or along the north shore. The chart shows the possibilities. You might anchor in a notch along the shore, or at the head of the bay.

A trail connects the head of Waiatt Bay with Small Inlet. The trail splits about halfway along. Both branches go through, but Correspondent Pat Shera says the branch to the northwest is the drier of the two. Correspondent Carol-Ann Giroday adds that the trail continues along the south shore of Small Inlet to beautiful Newton Lake and to Granite Bay, beyond. She cautions hikers not to confuse a pond along the way with substantial Newton Lake.

Hole in the Wall. Hole in the Wall connects Okisollo Channel with Calm Channel to the east. Boats accumulate on each side of the rapids at the western entrance to Hole in the Wall, waiting for slack water. In general, boats on the upstream side will catch the last of the fair current when the rapids calm down, leaving room for the boats on

Octopus Islands. These boats are anchored in the mouth of the largest bay close to Waiatt Bay.

If you think tidal current rapids are unimportant, this photo of Okisollo Channel's Upper Rapids at full song should change your mind. Courageous photo by David Helland.

the other side to pick up the new fair current in the opposite direction. Slacks occur 50 to 55 minutes before Seymour Narrows, and last about 4 minutes (Seymour Narrows currents are shown in Canadian Tide & Current Tables, Vol. 6 and Ports and Passes). The flood current sets northeast. Maximum currents run to 12 knots on the flood and 10 knots on the ebb.

LOCAL KNOWLEDGE

DANGEROUS CURRENTS: Upper Rapids and Lower Rapids in Okisollo Channel can be dangerous and should be run at or near slack. Slacks occur 50 to 55 minutes before slack at Seymour Narrows.

Upper Rapids. These are the first rapids in Okisollo Channel north of Hole in the Wall, and they are dangerous unless run at or near slack water. Slack occurs 55 minutes before Seymour Narrows (Seymour Narrows currents are shown in Canadian Tide & Current Tables, Vol. 6 and Ports and Passes). At full rush on a spring tide, the rapids, running at 9 knots, are frightening to watch. A wall of white water stretches nearly across the channel almost until slack. When it's time to go through, steer a little east of mid-channel to avoid Bentley Rock. The chart makes the course clear.

Barnes Bay and several small indents in this part of Okisollo Channel could be good anchorages, except for the large amount of log booming and aquaculture. Owen Bay is the preferred anchorage.

LOCAL KNOWLEDGE

STRONG CURRENTS: Currents run strongly through the islands that separate Owen Bay from Upper Rapids. If you explore these islands, exercise caution to avoid getting sucked into the rapids.

Owen Bay. Owen Bay is large and pretty. Our recommended anchorage is in the second little notch on the west side of the bay. This notch is quite protected, and has room for

about 5 boats if the spots are well chosen and stern-ties are used. Correspondent Pat Shera adds that there is good holding and shelter near the small public float on the east side of the bay. Shera also says that the northeastern head of Owen Bay has "acres of good holding on a flat bottom." That area, however, is subject to being hit by strong (and cold) outflow winds from Bute Inlet. He was "kissed by the Bute" one sleepless night and knows what he's talking about.

A trail leads from the public float to Hole in the Wall. Correspondent Bruce Evertz informs us that for most of the distance the trail is a road that passes several homes and homebuilding sites, and then gets overgrown. Shortly before reaching the water in Diamond Bay, it becomes a plank road that turns 90 degrees to the right. Don't turn. Continue ahead, onto a foot path, which leads to a good view of Hole in the Wall rapids, part of Upper Rapids, and the Octopus Islands.

Enter Owen Bay through a narrow channel between Walters Point and Grant Island. A reef, marked by kelp, extends from Walters Point nearly halfway across this channel. It will inspire you to hug the Grant Island side.

Lower Rapids. Lower Rapids turns at virtually the same time as Upper Rapids—55 minutes before Seymour Narrows (Seymour Narrows currents are shown in Canadian Tide & Current Tables, Vol. 6 and Ports and Passes). Currents run to 9 knots on spring tides, and you must steer a course to avoid Gypsy Shoal, which lies nearly in the middle. Transit at slack water only.

We recommend avoiding Lower Rapids

SPRING TIDES, NEAP TIDES

Spring tides are large tides that occur around the times of new moon and full moon. Neap tides are small tides that occur around the times of half moon.

This is a complex subject and not easily summarized. The 2002 Bowditch, for example, has a chapter titled "Tides and Tidal Currents" that runs 21 pages. It's heavy going.

Still, if you are cruising a boat on Inside Passage waters you need at least a basic understanding of spring tides and neap tides and how they affect you.

Tides are created by the gravitational pull of the moon and to a lesser extent the sun. The sun and the moon's gravitational attractions combine to pull a bulge of the earth's water toward them. This bulge is the tide. At times of full moon and new moon the sun, earth and moon are in alignment—stacked up, you might say, one behind the other—and the bulge is large. These are spring tides.

At half moon, the sun and moon are approximately at right angles to each other. Their gravitational pulls tend to offset one another and the bulge of water is small. These are neap tides.

It takes only a week to go from new moon to half moon and another week to go from half moon to full moon. Thus it takes only a week to go from spring tides to neap tides and another week to get back to spring tides. Depending on other factors, some spring tides can be quite large, while some neap tides can actually be nonexistent. If you're interested in why, read Bowditch.

Typically, in the Northwest, we get two high tides and two low tides each day, but they aren't uniform. The difference between high and low water is much greater on one of the two tides than the other. So it's not only a matter of high tide and low tide, but how high and how low.

With this knowledge, you'll know if you can anchor in a shallow bay. You'll know if you can beach the dinghy and go for a walk, assured that the dinghy will be easy to relaunch when you return. You'll know if tidal rapids, such as Deception Pass or Gabriola Pass, are apt to be flowing fast or slow.

With this knowledge in place, the tide and current tables begin to make more sense. The cruise takes on an entirely new dimension—that of working with the forces of Nature, not against them.

—Robert Hale

Anchorage can be found on the Drew Harbour side of Rebecca Spit Provincial Marine Park, with dinghy access to the long beaches.

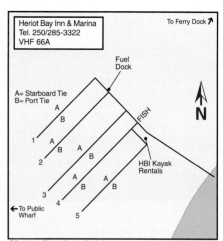

Heriot Bay Inn & Marina

altogether by going through Barnes Bay, north of the Okis Islands. At times other than slack you will still see considerable current, but you will avoid the hazards of Lower Rapids.

Barnes Bay. Barnes Bay and several small indents in this part of Okisollo Channel could be good anchorages, except for the large amount of log booming and aquaculture. Anchorage may be possible in **Chonat Bay** and in the notch behind **Metcalf Island**.

QUADRA ISLAND, SOUTH

⑭ **Drew Harbour/Rebecca Spit Marine Park.** Drew Harbour is large and in the right winds the open harbor can be lumpy. The preferred anchorage is in the bight immediately inside the north tip of Rebecca Spit. A drying shoal defines the south side of this bight. The shoal extends a considerable distance from shore, and it could fool you at high tide.

If the preferred bight is full, anchor in 24 to 36 feet south of the drying shoal, although it isn't as protected. Rebecca Spit

Marine Park is popular. The Drew Harbour side of the spit has a lovely sand beach. The exposed Sutil Channel side has a beach of remarkable small round boulders.

Bill Wolferstan's cruising guide to Desolation Sound contains an excellent section describing silvered tree snags on the spit, the result of subsidence during a 1946 earthquake. Wolferstan also describes the mounded fortifications, thought to be defenses built 200 to 400 years ago by the local Salish Indians against Kwakiutl Indian attacks.

⑮ **Heriot Bay.** Heriot Bay has a public wharf, a supermarket, the Heriot Bay Inn & Marina, and the Taku Resort. During the summer high season the public dock usually is full with boats rafted several deep. The Heriot Bay Inn & Marina is between the ferry dock and the public dock. Just south of Heriot Bay, in Drew Harbour proper, Taku Resort has excellent new docks and facilities. Heriot Bay Tru-Value Foods, a short walk from Heriot Bay or Taku Resort, is the best-stocked grocery store in Desolation Sound, with complete groceries, including fresh vegetables and meats, a post office, gift shop, and

liquor store. Free delivery to the docks. Bicycles can be rented from a shop on the road above Taku Resort.

⑮ **Heriot Bay Public Wharf.** Open all year, 670 feet of dock space, garbage drop, telephone, launch ramp. Watch for ferry wash on the outer face.

⑮ **Heriot Bay Inn & Marina.** P.O. Box 100, Heriot Bay, BC V0P 1H0; (250) 285-3322; (888) 605-4545; info@heriotbayinn.com ; www.heriotbayinn.com. Monitors VHF 66A. Open all year, gasoline, diesel, propane, ice. Guest moorage available on 1800 feet of side-tie dock, mostly 15 amp power with some 30 amp, washrooms, showers, laundry, Wi-Fi. Reservations recommended June through August. The docks still need replacement, but they have been improved from their earlier, quite "rustic" condition. The outer docks and fuel dock are subject to wakes from passing ferries.

This is a historic old hotel with cottages, restaurant, and pub. They offer sea kayaking lessons and rentals, whale watching, and rapids tours. The hotel gift store, off the lobby, has charts, local guide books, local artisan jewelry, crafts, and souvenirs. Fishing guides and other services available. Heriot Bay Tru-Value Foods is a short walk up the hill. A bicycle rental shop is nearby.

The hotel is old and funky, and a challenge to maintain. In 2008 a group of 20 Quadra Island residents ("old hippies," one of them said) bought the property and set about making it right. Among them they have all the needed skills: carpentry, electrical, painting, administrative, whatever else is required. In recent years the Heriot Bay Inn's public areas have been upgraded. The lobby fireplace hearth is very inviting. The dining room is warm and nice. The laundry is new and the washrooms and showers were recently remodeled.

⑮ **Taku Resort & Marina.** P.O. Box 1, Heriot Bay, BC V0P 1H0; (250) 285-3031; info@takuresort.com; www.takuresort.com.

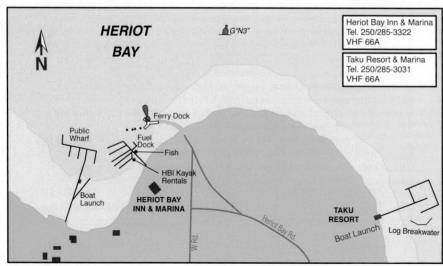

Heriot Bay

The Heriot Bay Inn & Marina has a pub, restaurant, and gift shop.

Monitors VHF 66A. Open all year. The docks have 30 & 50 amp power, potable water and Wi-Fi. Washrooms, showers, laundry and a 14-room resort are ashore, as are RV sites, tennis, volleyball, badminton and horseshoes. The docks are some of the nicest in the area. Although they are exposed to southeast winds across the bay, the inside moorage is protected. A shopping center and Tru-Value Foods grocery store is a short walk away. A kayak tour operator is on site and a bicycle rental store is just up the road. The resort offers cooking classes and paddleboard rentals; see their website for more information. The facilities and service are high quality. Lynden McMartin is the manager.

DISCOVERY PASSAGE

Discovery Passage is approximately 20 miles long, and separates Quadra Island and Sonora Island from Vancouver Island. It is the main route for commercial traffic north and south along the east side of Vancouver Island. Cape Mudge is the south entrance to Discovery Passage. At the north end, Discovery Passage connects with Johnstone Strait at Chatham Point. An enormous amount of water flows through Discovery Passage, flooding south and ebbing north. Tide-rips are frequent.

LOCAL KNOWLEDGE

TIDE-RIPS: A strong southeasterly wind blowing against a large, south-flowing flood tide can set up high and dangerous seas. Lives have been lost off Cape Mudge in such conditions. Cape Mudge, at the south end of Quadra Island, has been a graveyard for vessels of all sizes, particularly in the winter months. If a southeaster is blowing, Sailing Directions recommends entering at or after high water slack. Good advice.

Cape Mudge. The area around Cape Mudge and Wilby Shoals is a famous hot spot for salmon fishing, and often during the summer months it is full of small craft. Several resorts in the area cater to sport fishermen. Guides are available for hire in Campbell River.

On a flood tide, a backeddy often sets up at Cape Mudge, running north along the western edge of Wilby Shoals all the way to the Cape Mudge Lighthouse.

Yaculta. The Native settlement of Yaculta, located on the east side of Discovery Passage at latitude 50°01.4'N, is the site of the Nuyumbalees Cultural Centre with its splendid collection of potlatch regalia and historical artifacts and photos. Open 7 days a week,

May to September. The Centre is a 3-block walk south from the new public dock. We urge a visit. **Cape Mudge Boatworks** is located here.

Murray Abercrombie, who runs Cape Mudge Boatworks, cautions against mooring overnight at the public dock. He says the steady stream of large ships tend to run faster at night, and some put out powerful wakes.

⑯ **Quathiaski Cove.** Quathiaski Cove is the Quadra Island landing for the ferry to Campbell River. A public dock is next to the ferry landing and may be rolly from ferry wakes. A seasonal snack stand is in the ferry parking lot and a pub and restaurant are a short walk away. A shopping center, with a good grocery store, a tasty informal café, bank with an ATM, and a variety of stores to peruse is a few blocks from the ferry landing. The grocery store will deliver to the dock. The Visitor Centre is next to the bank. Because of ferry traffic, the best anchorage is farther north, in the cove behind Grouse Island. Fingers of current from Discovery Passage work into Quathiaski Cove at some stages of the tide, so be sure the anchor is well set.

⑯ **Quathiaski Cove Public Wharf.** Adjacent to the ferry landing. The dock has 20, 30 & 50 amp power and non-potable water. Above the dock are new washroom and shower facilities with a number to call for the keycode after hours. The dock has considerable mooring space that might be taken up with commercial fish boats. Waste oil disposal is available.

⑰ **April Point Resort & Marina.** P.O. Box 248, Campbell River, BC V9W 4Z9; (250) 285-2222; aprilpointmarina@obmg.com; www.aprilpoint.com. Monitors VHF 66A. Open mid-April to mid-October. Call ahead. Ample marina guest moorage along 4500 feet of dock, 15, 30 & 50 amp power, Wi-Fi at the resort, laundry, cable TV hookup, kayak, bike and scooter rentals, picnic area ashore. Although this marina is where the very large yachts tie up, all boats are welcome.

April Point Resort & Spa is a deluxe desti-

It's time for kayak lessons at the Taku Resort & Marina.

nation fishing resort. It has everything for the most demanding guest, including excellent rooms, a beautiful new spa, fishing guides, renowned dining, and scheduled air service by three different floatplane companies.

Approaching, you will see a red spar buoy in the entrance to the bay. The buoy marks a shoal, and must be left to starboard as you enter (Red, Right, Returning). The proper channel will appear narrow. Especially at low tide, you will be strongly tempted to leave the buoy to port, which might put you aground. Entering, *leave the buoy to starboard.*

The marina is owned by Oak Bay Marine Group, which operates a number of high-quality resorts on the coast. Painter's Lodge, just north of Campbell River on the west side of Discovery Passage, is also an Oak Bay property. April Point moorage guests have full access to the amenities at Painter's—pool, hot tub, tennis courts and fitness room. A free water shuttle crosses Discovery Passage between April Point and Painter's.

The marina is hidden back in the cove that extends south of April Point, and as noted above, is set up to handle larger boats. You also can find limited anchorage in the cove. A passage leads between the cove and adjacent Gowlland Harbour, but the passage is shallow and littered with rocks. Lacking local knowledge, the general advice is to stay out of this passage.

⑱ **Steep Island Lodge.** P.O. Box 699, Campbell River, BC V9W 6J3; (250) 830-8179; info@steepisland.com; www. steepisland.com. Open May 15 to October 15. Limited guest moorage by reservation only, 15, 30 & 50 amp power, no water. This is a beautiful resort with private cabins. It is on the east side of Steep Island, off the northwest corner of Gowlland Island. Fishing and kayak charters available. Float plane service. Jacuzzi. Dinner is all-inclusive and by reservation only.

Gowlland Harbour. Gowlland Harbour is a large, protected bay behind Gowlland Island, with considerable log booming activity along the shoreline. Before entering, study the chart so you can avoid Entrance Rock, north of Gowlland Island.

You'll find good anchoring depths at the north end of the bay, but it's much prettier at the south end, especially behind Stag Island. Although homes and docks are on the shores, we didn't feel closed-in-upon. Good anchoring is also behind Wren Islet, Crow Islet, and the Mouse Islets, all of them a little to the north of Stag Island. These islets, which are protected as provincial park preserves, make good picnic spots.

⑲ **Seascape Waterfront Resort.** P.O. Box 250, Quadra Island, BC V0P 1N0; (250) 285-3450; seascapequadra@gmail.com; www.seascapewaterfrontresort.com. Located north of Stag Island. Open all year, 1000 feet of guest moorage, 15 & 30 amp power, washrooms, showers, laundry, kayak rentals.

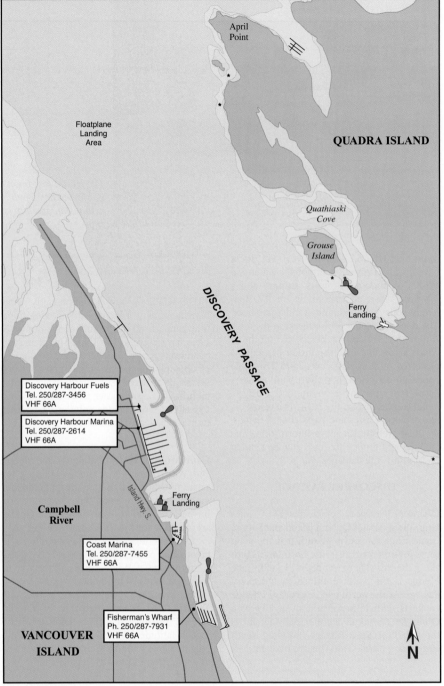

Campbell River

The resort is tucked back in a beautiful location, but still close to Campbell River.

CAMPBELL RIVER

The city of Campbell River is working to become an important tourist destination, especially for sport fishermen. The city calls itself the "Salmon Capital of the World." While dozens of guideboats take sportfishermen to prime fishing areas in Discovery Passage and off Cape Mudge, lunker-size salmon are still caught from marina breakwaters and the public fishing pier.

Campbell River has complete shopping, dining, and marine facilities, all close to the waterfront. Fisherman's Wharf and the Coast Marina are close to Tyee Plaza, with supermarket, drugstore, liquor store, excellent laundromat, and more. Discovery Harbour Marina is part of the extensive Discovery Harbour Centre, with more grocery and general merchandise stores, liquor store, fast food, restaurants, and pubs.

An attractive promenade leads from the Fisherman's Wharf marina to the ferry dock. The promenade is scheduled to be extended to the Discovery Harbour Marina; for now follow the sidewalk along the highway. At the north end of Discovery Harbour Marina, a Native-owned cruise ship terminal has been built.

The Discovery Harbour Fuel Dock serves both recreational and commercial boats with the capability for high-volume fueling.

Crabby Bob's, on the dock at Campbell River Fisherman's Wharf, sells fresh seafood.

As you approach Campbell River from the south you will find three marinas, each protected by its own breakwater. The southernmost marina is Fisherman's Wharf (formerly the Government Dock, now Campbell River Harbour Authority).

The second breakwater protects the Coast Marina, which has guest moorage. The ferry to Quathiaski Cove, on Quadra Island, lands adjacent to the Coast Marina. Of the three marinas, this is closest to downtown Campbell River.

The third marina is the Discovery Harbour Marina, with a fuel dock and considerable moorage. The 52-acre Discovery Harbour Centre adjoins the marina. Ocean Pacific Marine Supply, a well-stocked chandlery, is in this shopping center, and a 110-ton Travelift haulout and repair yard is adjacent.

All three marinas monitor VHF 66A.

Marine Parts & Supplies: In addition to its excellent stock, Ocean Pacific has overnight delivery from a major supplier in Vancouver for just about anything.

Museums: The Campbell River Museum & Archives, at 470 Island Hwy, is in the "don't miss" category. The care and imagination of the exhibits remind us of the Royal British Columbia Museum in Victoria, only smaller, and without the giant ice age mammoth.

The Maritime Heritage Centre, a short walk south from Fisherman's Wharf, features a number of fishing and maritime exhibits.

The new Discovery Passage Aquarium is just above the docks at Fisherman's Wharf. It is small, but the exhibits are well done.

Campbell River's Maritime Heritage Centre is located just south of Fisherman's Wharf.

Younger crew will enjoy it.

Farmers market: Sundays, May through September, 10:00 a.m. to 2:30 p.m., in the fishing pier parking lot at the Fisherman's Wharf docks. Fresh farm produce, baked goods, fresh fish, all the things you'd expect.

Golf: The 18-hole Story Creek golf course, south of town, is outstanding, a must-play for serious golfers. Call (250) 923-3673. Sequoia Springs, a short cab ride from the marinas, is a flat but serious 18-hole course with lots of water and deep rough, well maintained and fun to play. Call (250) 287-4970.

Salmon Point Resort. Gas, propane, launch ramp, store, laundry, pool, jacuzzi and kids' activity areas. Located 2.5 miles south of Campbell River on the western shore of Discovery Passage, this marina, built behind a rip-rap breakwater, has room for powerboats up to 32 feet. The entrance is very shallow, especially at low tide. Stay aboards are not permitted. The resort is an RV park primarily serving recreational fisherman with 1 to 2 bedroom cottages, rental RVs, and a licensed restaurant and pub on site.

20 Fisherman's Wharf (Campbell River Harbour Authority). 705 Island Highway, Campbell River, BC V9W 2C2; (250) 287-7931; fishermans@telus.net; www.fishermanswharfcampbellriver.com. Monitors VHF 66A. Open all year, water on docks, 20, 30, limited 50 & one 100 amp power, pumpout, ample dock space, washrooms, showers, 3 tidal grids, Wi-Fi, garbage, recycling. Reservations accepted. All but one of the docks are side-tie only, rafting permitted. The pumpout is on dock C in the north basin, in the area marked "Loading Zone." At press time a new office and laundry facility are under construction for 2014.

This was almost entirely a commercial fish boat moorage until locals took over operation. Several improvements have been made to attract pleasure craft. All the docks have been recently re-decked, and the washrooms and showers renovated. Crabby Bob's on finger 6 on the south wharf has fresh and frozen seafood on the dock. Other boats sell fresh fish on the floats between fingers 2 & 3. Call the office for a heads-up on what's available. Office hours are 8:00 a.m. to 5:00 p.m., 7 days a week. If the office is closed, take an empty space and register in the morning.

20 Coast Marina. 975 Shoppers Row, Campbell River, BC V9W 2C4; (250) 287-7455; coastmarina@gmail.com; www.coastmarina.ca. Monitors VHF 66A. The Coast Marina is located behind the middle of Campbell River's three breakwaters, and has facilities for boats to 180 feet in length. Open all year, guest moorage, 30, 50 & 100 amp power, washrooms, showers, excellent laundry in the plaza, Wi-Fi. Water taxi, boat rentals, whale watching. Diver on standby.

The marina is under new ownership and is no longer connected with the Coast Discovery Inn. The marina has wide concrete docks with power and water to each slip. The marina is just steps away from Foreshore Park and downtown Tyee Plaza shopping. Dick's Fish & Chips on the docks at the marina is a local favorite.

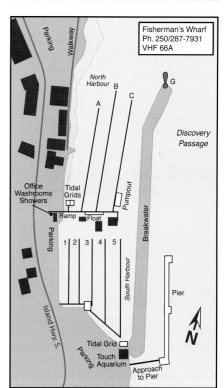

Fisherman's Wharf, Campbell River

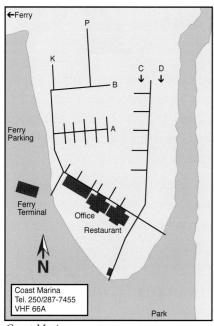

Coast Marina

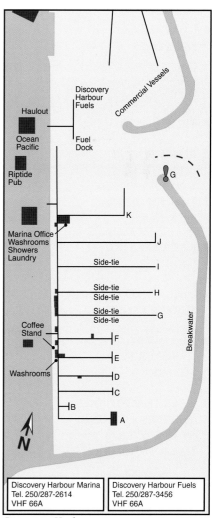

Discovery Harbour

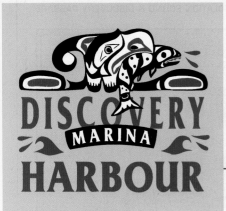

DISCOVERY HARBOUR M·A·R·I·N·A

CAMPBELL RIVER, BRITISH COLUMBIA

COMPLETE SHOPPING AVAILABLE

A Great Marina Destination
In A Great Little City
With Great Shopping Next Door

- OCEAN PACIFIC HAULOUT
- WIRELESS INTERNET
- MODERN GUEST DOCKS
- POWER & WATER
- WASHROOMS & SHOWERS
- LAUNDRY FACILITIES
- GARBAGE DISPOSAL
- TELEPHONES
- BLOCK & CUBE ICE
- FISHING GUIDE SERVICES
- FISH CLEANING FACILITIES
- 24HR VIDEO SURVEILLANCE
- DISCOVERY HARBOUR FUELS FUEL DOCK
- WALK TO SHOPPING, SERVICES & DINING AT DISCOVERY HARBOUR CENTRE

The huge 52-acre, 50-store Discovery Harbour Centre adjoins our marina, and has everything you need. Groceries at Real Canadian Superstore. Target. Canadian Tire. Several restaurants, from fast food to fine dining. Starbuck's Coffee. Ocean Pacific haulout, repairs and marine supplies. Two banks, even an optometrist. And Wei Wai Kum House of Treasures, Vancouver Island's largest native-owned gallery and gift shop.

Our breakwater-protected wide concrete docks can take everything from the smallest boats to the largest mega-yachts. Our friendly staff will help you land. With unmatched shopping, services and dining right next door, let us be your stop in Campbell River.

WWW.DISCOVERYHARBOURMARINA.COM

PHONE (250) 287-2614 ▮ FAX (250) 287-8939 ▮ VHF 66A
E MAIL TARA@DISCOVERYHARBOURMARINA.COM
#392 - 1434 IRONWOOD ST. ▮ CAMPBELL RIVER, B.C. ▮ V9W 5T5

⑳ Discovery Harbour Marina. Suite 392-1434 Ironwood St., Campbell River, BC V9W 5T5; (250) 287-2614; tara@discoveryharbourmarina.com; www.discoveryharbourmarina.com. Monitors VHF 66A. Open all year. Fuel dock with gasoline and diesel. Washrooms, showers, laundry, garbage drop, ample guest moorage, 20, 30, 50 & 100 amp single-phase and three-phase power, Wi-Fi. The G, H, I and J floats have side-tie moorage that can handle megayachts. Customs clearance available. This is the northernmost and largest of Campbell River's three breakwater-protected marinas. The marina has excellent docks, landing assistance and friendly people.

The marina office, with showers, washrooms, and laundry, is in a 2-story floating facility at the foot of the north ramp on K dock. New floating washrooms were added in 2013 near E dock to save the long walk to the main washrooms.

The extensive Discovery Harbour Centre shopping plaza is adjacent to the marina, with everything you would expect to find in a major center.

⑳ Discovery Harbour Fuels Sales. Box 512, Campbell River, BC V9W 5C1; (250) 287-3456; dhfs@telus.net; www.discovery-harbourfuel.com. Monitors VHF 66A. Fuel dock open all year, gasoline, diesel, self-service oil change system. Located straight ahead as you enter the Discovery Harbour Marina breakwater. A full line of cruising guides, maps, fishing gear, marine parts, ice, kerosene and convenience supplies.

⑳ Campbell River Public Wharf (north, behind Discovery Harbour breakwater). (250) 287-7091. Campbell River Small Craft Harbour is open all year with 4000 feet of dock space behind the same breakwater that protects the Discovery Harbour Marina. This is primarily commercial vessel moorage. Washrooms and showers, tidal grid, waste oil disposal, telephone.

Seymour Narrows. Currents in Seymour Narrows run to 16 knots on the flood and 14 knots on the ebb, flooding south and ebbing north.

Northbound, you can wait for slack either in Menzies Bay on the Vancouver Island side, or in the good-size unnamed bay behind Maud Island on the Quadra Island side. South of Maud Island, the flood forms a backeddy along Quadra Island, sweeping northbound boats more easily toward Maud Island. Southbound, Plumper Bay is a good waiting spot on the east side, as is Brown Bay on the west side. Brown Bay has a floating breakwater and a marina with a fuel dock and restaurant.

Both **Deepwater Bay** and **Plumper Bay** are too open and deep to be attractive as anchorages. **Menzies Bay** may have good anchorage, being careful to go around either end of a drying shoal which almost blocks the entrance. This area is used as a booming

SEYMOUR NARROWS

Seymour Narrows is a wide pass, clear of hazards, and offers a direct route north past the important provisioning town of Campbell River. It is the easiest connection from the Strait of Georgia to Johnstone Strait or Cordero Channel.

Most commercial vessels stay clear of Seymour Narrows except at slack. A ship or barge-towing tug cannot afford to go sideways for even a few seconds.

Small fishboats and recreational vessels, however, often transit Seymour Narrows within an hour of the turn, especially if going with the current. We always take Seymour Narrows going with the current and we've rarely had an anxious moment.

Smaller tides, where maximum current is predicted at six knots or less, can be taken at any time for most boats (again, going with the current). Larger tides should be taken within a half-hour of the turn. If it's a strong current cycle, in the 14- to 16-knot range, arrive at the pass within 15 minutes of slack water and the current will be manageable. The strongest current doesn't extend very far in either direction, so the transit past whirlpools lasts only a few minutes.

Hydrographers say the strongest currents at the Narrows are in the vicinity of Ripple Rock (slightly west of mid-channel, directly beneath the hydro lines strung between Vancouver Island and Maud Island). On a flood, the strongest turbulence will be along the west wall and in the area south of Ripple Rock. On an ebb, the turbulence and the set starts between Maud Island and Ripple Rock. The ebb current sets northwest to the west wall.

Northbound vessels: On small tides, northbound vessels should arrive off the Maud Island light an hour before the end of the ebb, or an hour prior to high water slack, before the ebb begins. Once into the narrows, steer toward the tongue of the current stream (east of mid-channel) to avoid the whirlpools and eddies north of Maud Island up to North Bluff. On big tides, low-powered vessels will find it prudent to be at the Maud Island light at high water slack, or just a few minutes into the north flowing ebb.

If the slack is at low water, arrive at the pass before the end of the ebb. Slack on large tides is not very long, five to ten minutes at most. You'll want to be past Brown Bay before the southflowing flood gets underway. It can be brutal in a slow-moving boat. You may find a back eddy along the eastern shore. On a large flood, Seymour Narrows can reach 16 knots, no place to be in any kind of boat.

Southbound vessels: Southbound boats should be opposite Brown Bay within an hour of the beginning or end of a neap (small) flood. On a large spring flood, it would be wise to be opposite Brown Bay within a half-hour of its end or beginning. Keep well off the sheer rock wall on the west shore of the narrows. Current turbulence can set a vessel onto that wall. The worst turbulence is usually south of Ripple Rock, especially if wind is against current. Stay on your side of the channel (i.e. to starboard) to be clear of any tugs or large ships headed the other way. The good news about Seymour Narrows is that there are no obstructions and just one strong, main stream.

– Bill Kelly

Anne Vipond and Bill Kelly are the authors of *Best Anchorages of the Inside Passage.*

Brown's Bay Marina has fuel, a small store, and a seasonal restaurant.

ground for the pulp mill in Campbell River.

Seymour Narrows is the principal route for northbound and southbound commercial traffic, including cruise ships. Give large vessels ample room to maneuver. Before going through, we urge you to read the Sailing Directions section on Seymour Narrows. Especially on a flood, Sailing Directions counsels against the west side because of rough water. Monitor the passage times of commercial traffic on VHF 71, the area Vessel Traffic Services (VTS) frequency.

The warship HMCS *Columbia* was sunk off Maud Island to create an artificial reef.

㉑ **Brown's Bay Marina & RV Park.** 15021 Brown's Bay Road, Campbell River, BC V9H 1N9; (250) 286-3135; marina@brownsbayresort.com; www.browns bayresort.com. Monitors VHF 12 & 66A. Open all year, gasoline and diesel, side-tie moorage to 100 feet along 2000 feet of dock, 50 slips for boats to 24 feet, 15, 30 & 50 amp power, free Wi-Fi, washrooms, showers, laundry, ice, cable television, phone, garbage drop, marine & RV store. Three rental cabins available.

This marina is located on Vancouver Island at the north end of Seymour Narrows. Enter around the north end of the breakwater. Strong currents can sweep through the marina; be sure to take the current into account when maneuvering, and tie your boat to the dock securely.

The store has a variety of snack items, clothing, and fishing gear. The seasonal floating restaurant is newly remodeled and quite pleasant. All-you-can-eat crab feed specials are a signature event in season. Call or check their website for the schedule.

Kanish Bay. Kanish Bay has several good anchorages. You could sneak behind the **Chained Islands**, and with some thought and planning find a number of delightful spots, especially in settled weather. **Granite Bay** is well protected with a good bottom, but houses are on the shoreline and it's not very cozy feeling. The small bay between Granite Bay and Small Inlet offers protection from westerlies. An aquaculture

operation is in the mouth of this bay.

Correspondents James & Jennifer Hamilton anchored in the cove behind Bodega Point, just south of the 2-meter rock. "Really beautiful. Birds calling. Good holding in sticky mud."

Small Inlet. A narrow but easily-run channel with a least depth of 8 feet leads from the northeast corner of Kanish Bay to Small Inlet. This inlet, surrounded by steep, wooded mountains, is beautiful, although we can confirm that a strong westerly from Johnstone Strait can get in and test your anchor-

ing. Once through the kelp-filled entrance channel, a number of good anchorages can be found along the north shore. A couple of boats can fit behind a little knob of land near the southeast corner. The chart shows 3 rocks in this anchorage—actually, they're a reef with 3 high points. You also can anchor in the cove at the head of Small Inlet, behind 2 small islands.

A trail runs from the head of Small Inlet to Waiatt Bay. Correspondent Carol-Ann Giroday adds that at Small Inlet the trail continues along the south shore and leads to Newton Lake. The trail is well marked, but Carol-Ann cautions hikers not to confuse a smaller pond along the way with the substantial (and lovely) Newton Lake. The trail continues to Granite Bay.

Granite Point. If you are traveling between Discovery Passage and Okisollo Channel, you can safely steer inside Min Rock, north of Granite Point, and run close to Granite Point itself. You will be treated to the sight of some extraordinary rock on Granite Point.

Rock Bay Marine Park (Otter Cove). Otter Cove is just inside Chatham Point. It's a useful little anchorage with convenient depths and protection from seas rolling down Johnstone Strait. If you need a place to hide until the wind or seas subside, it's a good spot.

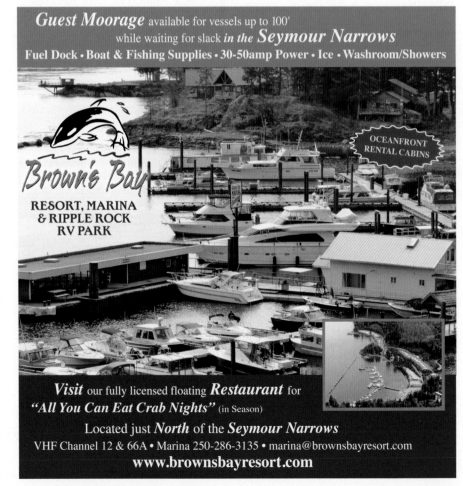

JOHNSTONE STRAIT

JOHNSTONE STRAIT
*Yuculta Rapids • Stuart Island • Cordero Channel
Nodales Channel • Blind Channel • Greene Point
Rapids • Whirlpool Rapids • Sunderland Channel
Johnstone Strait*

The southern tip of Stuart Island marks the northern boundary of Desolation Sound. North of Desolation Sound you'll find colder water, harsher weather, fewer services, and a greater number of rocks, reefs and tidal rapids. You should have good ground tackle and know how to use it.

Fewer boats venture north of Desolation Sound. A greater percentage of those boats are 32 feet in length and larger. Many stay out for four to eight weeks or more, and the larger boats provide more comfortable accommodations. On average the occupants are older, too. The farther north you go, the more remote conditions become, all the way to Alaska.

It is possible to do a quick two- to three-week trip from Seattle to this area, although it might require long days on the water. The reward is experiencing beautiful cruising grounds few others will see.

Garbage Drops. While occasionally you will find a lack of garbage drops in Desolation Sound and south, garbage becomes a much greater problem farther north. Garbage must be hauled from marinas and settlements to authorized dumps, usually on Vancouver Island. Since marinas must pay for hauling and disposal, most charge a fee for garbage, if they accept it at all. Those that do will sometimes take recyclables at no charge. Use as little glass as possible, wash and flatten cans, and pack paper out.

Fresh Water. Fresh water can be a problem even in Desolation Sound, and northward the supplies are fewer. The resorts have access to water for drinking, cooking and cleaning, but few have enough for boat washing. Some stops, such as Lagoon Cove or Blind Channel, have sweet spring water. Shawl Bay wa-

The Stuart Island Community Dock is in a gorgeous setting.

ter is highly regarded. In some places, water has a brown cast from cedar bark tannin. We don't know of anybody who has had a bad experience from it.

Prices. The season is short and the costs are high. Everything must be brought in by water taxi, barge, or air. Don't be upset when prices are higher than at home. Remember too that during the season the marina personnel's workday starts early and ends late, and calls for a smile at all times.

Recommended books. Peter Vassilopoulos's cruising guide, *Broughton Islands Cruising Guide*, is excellent. The book covers the waters from Yuculta Rapids to Port Hardy, and is packed with maps, history, and hundreds of aerial color photos.

A second book, *Local Knowledge: The Skipper's Reference, Tacoma to Ketchikan* by Kevin Monahan, is a compilation of useful navigation and trip-planning information, including mileage and conversion tables. It has a comprehensive section on tidal rapids, including recommended strategies for transit. We use the mileage charts every day. Monahan's excellent Johnstone Strait diagrams have been reproduced on page 279.

THE INSIDE ROUTE TO THE BROUGHTONS

Most cruisers heading north choose the sheltered inside route through Cordero Channel, Chancellor Channel, Wellbore Channel and Sunderland Channel rather than face a long, possibly rough passage in Johnstone Strait. The inside route runs from the north end of Calm Channel (the south tip of Stuart Island), through five sets of rapids: Yuculta Rapids, Gillard Passage rapids, Dent Rapids, Greene Point Rapids and Whirlpool Rapids. The route includes an open stretch of approxi-

mately 13 miles in Johnstone Strait (which cannot be avoided) between Sunderland Channel and the safety of Havannah Channel, after which the currents of Chatham Channel must be negotiated. Careful planning is paramount. You need to know the times of slack water at each rapids, and you need to know how long it will take to get to each rapids.

Up-to-date charts and a copy of the Canadian Tide and Current Tables, Vol. 6 or Ports and Passes are critical for safe navigation. Using the corrections shown in the Reference and Secondary Current Stations in the front part of the Tide and Current Tables (back of the book for Ports and Passes), you must be comfortable calculating the times of slack water at the various rapids. For anchoring or transiting shallow channels, use the corrections in the Reference and Secondary Ports pages to calculate times and heights of tides.

The calculations can be daunting at first, but an evening spent reading the excellent instructions will clear matters considerably. For clarifications, don't be shy about asking a few old salts on the docks. They (we) love to help.

Since the waters north of Desolation Sound flood southward from the top of Vancouver Island and ebb northward, the northbound boat (if it wishes to clear a number of rapids in one run) has a timing problem. Assuming a start with Yuculta Rapids, all the rapids to the north will have already turned before slack water occurs at the Yucultas. It is best to approach Yuculta Rapids before the southbound flood current turns to the northbound ebb, and utilize two backeddies (described below) to help your way against the flood for the two or so miles to Gillard Passage and Dent Rapids. Done correctly, you'll go through Dent Rapids against the last of the flood current, and let the new ebb current flush you out Cordero Channel.

The ebb will already have been run-

CHARTS	
3312 Small-craft chart (chartbook)	Jervis Inlet & Desolation Sound
3539	Discovery Passage (1:40,000)
3543	Cordero Channel (1:40,000) Greene Point, Dent, & Yuculta Rapids (1:20,000)
3544	Johnstone Strait, Race Passage & Current Passage (1:25,000)
3545	Johnstone Strait, Port Neville to Robson Bight (1:40,000)
3546	Broughton Strait (1:40,000)
3555 Plans	Vicinity of Redonda Islands & Loughborough Inlet
3564 Plans	Johnstone Strait; Port Neville, Havannah Channel & Chatham Channel

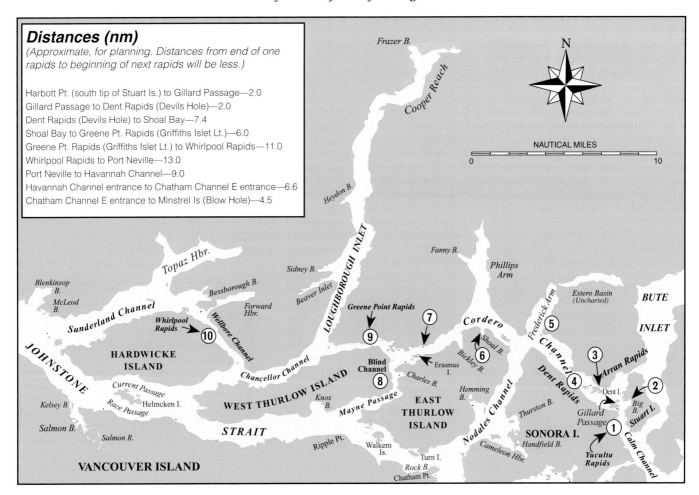

Distances (nm)

(Approximate, for planning. Distances from end of one rapids to beginning of next rapids will be less.)

Harbott Pt. (south tip of Stuart Is.) to Gillard Passage—2.0
Gillard Passage to Dent Rapids (Devils Hole)—2.0
Dent Rapids (Devils Hole) to Shoal Bay—7.4
Shoal Bay to Greene Pt. Rapids (Griffiths Islet Lt.)—6.0
Greene Pt. Rapids (Griffiths Islet Lt.) to Whirlpool Rapids—11.0
Whirlpool Rapids to Port Neville—13.0
Port Neville to Havannah Channel—9.0
Havannah Channel entrance to Chatham Channel E entrance—6.6
Chatham Channel E entrance to Minstrel Is (Blow Hole)—4.5

ning 13 miles away at Greene Point Rapids, which turned earlier. Depending on your boat's speed, the ebb could be at full force when you arrive. Rather than go through in these conditions, many cruisers choose to overnight either at Cordero Lodge or Blind Channel Resort. Both have excellent restaurants. Shoal Bay and the Cordero Islands are other good places to wait for Greene Point Rapids to turn to slack.

The next day you can depart before high water slack and push through Greene Point Rapids in the dying flood current. Then you'll hurry to Wellbore Channel, to take Whirlpool Rapids early in the favorable ebb current. If this is done early in the morning, it is possible the wind will not have started increasing for the stretch in Johnstone Strait. With luck it can be a pleasant run down Sunderland Channel and into Johnstone Strait, for the 13-mile stretch to Havannah Channel. How well this works depends on the speed of your boat, the time of day, the conditions, and the flexibility of your schedule.

Southbound, the options are greater. Take your first rapids against the last of the dying ebb, and let the new flood current flush you south. Each rapids in succession turns at a later time. Given the right conditions, even a slow boat can take all the rapids on one tide, with only a few hours' wait if the boat arrives at any given rapids when they are running too hard to risk transit.

Caution: A tight schedule is not justifica-

tion for taking a chance with bad conditions. The dangers are real.

Note: Canadian Tide and Current Tables do not adjust for Daylight Saving Time.

We suggest that you carry and use the guidebook *Exploring the South Coast of British Columbia,* 3rd ed., by Don Douglass and Réanne Hemingway-Douglass. You might also want to consult Peter Vassilopoulos' *Broughton Islands Cruising Guide,* formerly called North of Desolation Sound. Vassilopoulos effectively uses aerial photos to provide a clearer understanding of the waterways.

① **Yuculta Rapids.** The Yuculta (pronounced "YEW-cla-ta") Rapids run between Stuart Island and Sonora Island. Taken at slack they are benign, but at full force on a spring tide, especially against an opposing wind, they can be extremely dangerous. Northbound, Sailing Directions recommends that slow and low-powered boats arrive at the rapids an hour before high water slack, and use a backeddy along the Stuart Island shore until off Kellsey Point. Then cross to the Sonora Island shore to use a prevailing northerly current. This should position the boat to go through Gillard Passage and Dent Rapids satisfactorily. If you are late and unsure about transiting Dent Rapids, wait in Big Bay for the next slack.

② **Big Bay (Stuart Island).** For decades, Big Bay on Stuart Island has been a major

fishing resort center. The public floats are behind a plank and piling breakwater at the head of Big Bay. The pub near the head of the public dock is closed. The Big Bay Marina has been closed for several years. The Stuart Island Community dock has moorage and a store on shore.

② **Stuart Island Community Dock.** P.O. Box 5-6, Stuart Island, BC V0P 1V0; (250) 202-3625; postmaster@stuartisland.info; www.stuartislandca.info. Monitors VHF 66A. Moorage, water, liquor, laundry, post office, store, ice, community kitchen, fishing guides, good cell phone coverage. No power, no fuel.

The docks were rebuilt and expanded to accommodate boats to 100+ feet. A store was built, and it has a large deck with covered picnic area. The store carries locally-made goods as well as the usual convenience items. It is a liquor agency. Store hours may be "on call" with a cell phone number posted.

A well-marked road and trail lead to Eagle Lake, where a leaky skiff is kept. It's a good walk, through beautiful forest.

Shoal: An important shoal lies a short distance off the dock. Approach from the south. Also, we are told kelp can be a problem in the marina at low tide.

Gillard Passage. Currents run to 13 knots on the flood and 10 knots on the ebb. Transit near slack water. Times of slack are shown in Canadian Tide and Current Tables, Vol. 6

RUNNING THE RAPIDS

The cautious advice—the first rule of thumb—for transiting tidal current rapids is to wait for slack water and go through then. This rule of thumb is fine but imperfect. There you sit, watching other boats go through before slack and after slack.

A second rule of thumb is a corollary of the first. It says that boats should arrive at a rapids an hour before predicted slack, so they're ready to go through as soon as the rapids grow quiet. Like most rules of thumb, this one doesn't always work either. Sometimes it appears as if the rapids would be safe much longer than an hour before or after. Sometimes one look tells you it's smarter to wait. With a little study, however, it's possible to predict when the window of opportunity will be wider or narrower.

Before going further, two definitions:

Slack water. Slack water is the time when rapids cease flowing one direction but haven't begun flowing the opposite direction. Another word for slack is turn, meaning the time when the water's flow turns from one direction to the other.

Window, or window of opportunity. For purposes of this article, window means a time when most boats can transit a rapids safely, without too much excitement.

This article gelled with me in Malibu Rapids at the mouth of Princess Louisa Inlet. It has its origins in the successful running of the Pacific Northwest's tidal current rapids over a span of nearly four decades.

Understand that my wife and I are the original cautious and conservative boaters when it comes to rapids. Several years ago we hiked from Big Bay, on B.C.'s Stuart Island, to Arran Rapids, one of the most deadly rapids on the coast. We arrived in what must have been the middle of a large tide exchange, with its frightening whitewater overfalls, upwellings and whirlpools that no sensible boat could be expected to survive. White water is full of air, and less buoyant than green water. Boats float lower, with less freeboard. Rudders lose effectiveness and propellers lose their bite. We got the message: Rapids are not to be trifled with.

With experience, we have developed a loose sense of when a rapids could be run at times other than slack. Until our transits of Malibu Rapids, however, this sense was not refined to any kind of structure.

For what it's worth, here's our thinking. But first,

Caution: Every rapids has its own personality and characteristics. What follows is general in nature, and may not apply to any given rapids. It is a way of looking at things, an approach to the problem. It is not a guarantee.

The determining factors are 1) high water slack vs. low water slack; 2) neap tides vs. spring tides; 3) the size of the exchange on each side of slack.

High water slack vs. low water slack. We entered Princess Louisa Inlet through Malibu Rapids without drama nearly two hours before high water slack. When we departed two days later we found definite swirls, overfalls and whirlpools only 20 minutes before low water slack. The two transits were entirely different.

Our entry to Princess Louisa Inlet was at high water, when the narrow, shallow channel was full. Our departure was at low water, when the channel was much less full and much narrower. The less water in the channel, the faster the current must run.

General Rule: The window of opportunity is wider at high water slack. The narrower and shallower the channel, the more this is true.

Neap tides vs. spring tides. Neap tides are small tides that occur around the times of half moon. Neaps often show only a small dip from one high water to the next. The widest windows of opportunity occur on that small dip.

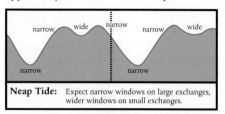

narrow   wide   narrow   narrow   wide

narrow   narrow

Neap Tide: Expect narrow windows on large exchanges, wider windows on small exchanges.

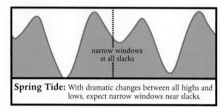

narrow windows
at all slacks

Spring Tide: With dramatic changes between all highs and lows, expect narrow windows near slacks.

Spring tides occur around the times of full moon or no moon. Low tides can be very low and high tides very high. On springs even the dip between two high tides can be significant. The windows of opportunity are narrower on spring tides than on neap tides.

Since it takes only a week to go from neap tide to spring tide (and another week to go from spring tide to neap tide), the experience from just a few days earlier has no bearing on the day you're going through. Each day, each transit, must be evaluated on its own.

Size of the exchange. Imagine this exercise. Using a garden hose, fill a five-gallon container in a minute. Then fill a one-gallon container in a minute. You had to turn the flow of water way down for the one-gallon can. Our neap tide entry through Malibu Rapids was near the top of a fairly small rise from lower low water to high water. The smaller the rise or fall, the less the current.

Conclusions

1. The window is narrowest at lower low water slack. The tide has dropped a long way and will be rising a long way. The farther the tide has dropped and the farther it is to rise, the narrower the window. Also, the shallower and narrower the rapids, the narrower the window at lower low water. At lower low water, plan to go through fairly close to slack.

2. The window at high water slack is wider on neap tides than on spring tides. The window is widest in the "dip" between the two high waters on neap tides.

3. At high water slack, the window is narrower on the rise from lower low water. The window is wider between the next two high waters.

Disclaimer. Skippers are responsible for the welfare and safety of their vessels and passengers. The purpose of this article is to provide tools for evaluating situations. It is not the purpose of this article to tell a skipper when he should transit a rapids before or after slack water, or how much before or after. When in doubt, the safest course is to transit at slack water, regardless of what other boats are doing.

— Robert Hale

MONAHAN'S LOCAL KNOWLEDGE

LEGEND
- 🐾 Boils (upwelling)   ⊚ Whirlpool   ∿ Turbulence (Tide Rip)
- ← Direction of ebb current   ⇀ Direction of flood current

LOCAL EFFECTS – EBB

West of Port Neville, the ebb begins along the mainland shore and takes almost two hours to completely cover the strait from one side to the other.

Turn to flood occurs in Sunderland Channel 1h 40m before Johnstone Strait Central and 1h 20m before Camp Point.

To avoid heavy weather in Johnstone Strait (especially when wind opposes currents) Sunderland, Wellbore and Cordero Channels offer calmer conditions.

Current Passage turns to ebb 50m after Johnstone Strait Central, but 1h 15m before Camp Point.

Turn to ebb at Vansittart Point occurs up to 30m before Current Passage, almost two hours before Camp Point.

Freshet conditions in mainland rivers may encourage a premature turn to ebb in the vicinity of Mayne Passage.

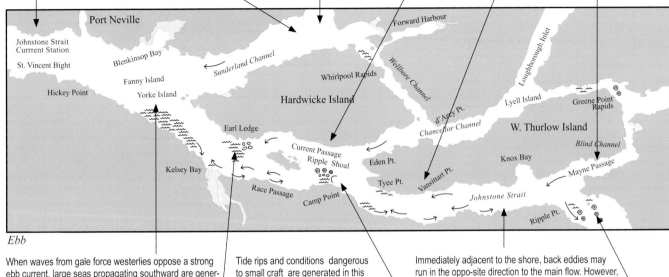

Ebb

When waves from gale force westerlies oppose a strong ebb current, large seas propagating southward are generated in this area. In this case, smaller boats should seek shelter at Port Neville or enter the harbour at Kelsey Bay and wait for the contrary current to moderate.

Tide rips and conditions dangerous to small craft are generated in this area during large tides, especially when strong westerlies oppose the ebb current.

Immediately adjacent to the shore, back eddies may run in the oppo-site direction to the main flow. However, at headlands between back eddies, the ebb current is strong right up to the shore.

A steep underwater ridge extends southward from Earl Ledge across the channel to the Vancouver Island shore. Deep tidal currents meet this steep topography and are deflected to the surface, causing extreme turbulence west of Helmcken Island during large tides.

Stay clear of Ripple Shoal. Dangerous whirlpools form to the west of the shoal during the ebb.

Tide rips and turbulent conditions are generated in this area during large tides, especially when strong westerly winds oppose the ebb current.

LOCAL EFFECTS – FLOOD

Near Port Neville, the mainland and Vancouver Island shores turn to flood up to one hour before the center of the channel.

In Current Passage, turbulence is weaker near the north shore.

To avoid heavy weather in Johnstone Strait (especially when wind opposes currents) Sunderland, Wellbore and Cordero Channels offer calmer conditions.

Stay clear of Ripple Shoal. Dangerous whirlpools form to the east of the shoal during the flood.

First ebb current in eastern Johnstone Strait begins between Mayne Passage and Vansittart Point, up to two hours before turn to ebb at Camp Point.

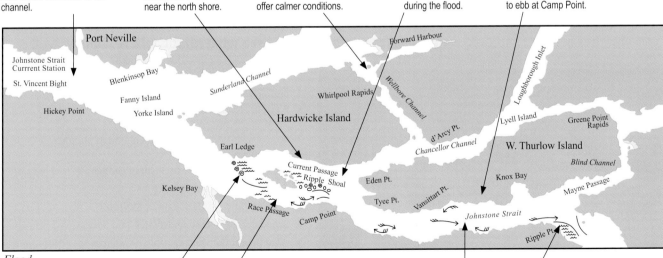

Flood

Tide rips and conditions dangerous to small craft are generated in this area during large tides, especially when strong southeasterlies oppose the flood current.

The ebb current in Current and Race Passages persists approximately 1h 20m longer than in Sunderland Channel.

Immediately adjacent to the shore, back eddies may run in the opposite direction to the main flow. However, at headlands between back eddies, the flood current is strong right up to the shore.

Tide rips and turbulent conditions are generated in this area during large tides, especially when strong southeasterlies oppose the flood current.

and Ports and Passes. Pass south of Jimmy Judd Island. Big Bay is a good place to wait if the current is too strong.

If you're lucky, you might find the trees on and near Jimmy Judd Island filled with eagles that swoop down to the swirling waters to feed on hake, whose air bladders have brought them to the surface. It's a real sight.

③ **Morgan's Landing Retreat.** P.O. Box 5-3, Stuart Island, BC V0P 1V0; (250) 287-0237; morganslanding@hotmail.com. Monitors VHF 66A. Guest moorage along 350 feet of dock, limited 15, 30 & 50 amp power, washrooms, laundry, ice, meals by reservation, accommodations, showers, guided fishing. Reservations suggested. This is a deluxe fishing lodge located at the mouth of the little bay that separates Dent Island from the mainland. Bob Morgan is a third generation resident of Stuart Island, with more than 40 years experience as a fishing guide. Jodé (pronounced "Jody") Morgan is a baker by trade and has been a fishing guide for 27 years. Fishing charters are their specialty. They also offer eco tours and can arrange just about anything you need. Floatplane and water taxi service available.

③ **Dent Island Lodge.** P.O. Box 8, Stuart Island, BC V0P 1V0; (250) 203-2553; info@dentisland.com; www.dentisland.com.

Reversing rapids in Canoe Pass beside Dent Island Lodge are fascinating to watch.

Monitors VHF 66A. Open late May to mid-September, guest moorage for boats to 200 feet on wide, stable concrete docks, 30 & 50 amp power at every dock pedestal, plus single-phase power 100 amp power upon request. Potable water on the docks, Wi-Fi, fishing guides. Gift shop, sauna, showers, exercise room, hot tub.

Dent Island Lodge is first class with moorage rates and dinner prices to match. The staff is professional. They treat you as if you are a guest in a small, quiet, private retreat. At the end of the day, after the guide boats have returned from fishing, an elegant appetizer table is set out. The dinner menu

is limited but very well done. A less formal tapas-style dining area with a dramatic view over the rushing waters is available when reservations allow. A hiking trail, rough in places, is a good place to work off some of the calories.

The lodge is at the back of a little bay separating Dent Island from the mainland. It is next to Canoe Pass Rapids, where 10- to 12-knot whitewater tidal currents churn. A spacious deck overlooks the pass. Another deck, screened by forest, holds a hot tub. It is utterly beautiful.

The lodge has a fast jet boat for eco-explorations. Manager Justin Farr can take you

The Dent Island Lodge is tastefully decorated and beautifully landscaped.

for a thrilling ride in the rapids. They offer tours to the head of Bute Inlet, including runs up the rivers in the inlet. Justin is an experienced fishing guide in these waters, and he knows every swirl, overfall and calm spot. The boat turns in its own length and dances through rough waters.

Schedule your arrival and departure to coincide with slack water in Gillard Passage, and approach from the southeast. The 1:20,000 inset on Chart 3543 shows it well, even the dock. As the inset shows, a shoal area 0.9 meter deep at zero tide is on the east side of the entry. Stay mid-channel. It is best to make reservations, even in the less-busy weeks of the season, and reservations are just about essential during high season.

Justin and Trish Farr are the managers, with their children Olivia and Ty.

④ **Dent Rapids.** Currents run to 9 knots on floods and 8 knots on ebbs. Time corrections are shown under Reference and Secondary Current Stations in Tide and Current Tables, Vol. 6 and Ports and Passes. Per Sailing Directions, "In Devils Hole, violent eddies and whirlpools form between 2 hours after turn to flood and 1 hour before turn to ebb." People who have looked into Devil's Hole vow never to run that risk again. Favor the Sonora Island shore of Dent Rapids.

Tugboat Passage, between Dent Island and Little Dent Island, avoids the potential problems of Devils Hole, and the current is less. Use the large-scale inset on Chart 3543, and favor the Little Dent Island side.

Arran Rapids. Current predictions for Arran Rapids are shown in Canadian Tide and Current Tables, Vol. 6 and Ports and Passes. Arran Rapids separate the north side of Stuart Island and the mainland, and connect Bute Inlet with Cordero Channel. Arran Rapids are unobstructed, but tidal streams run to 13+ knots. These rapids have a long history of killing the unknowing or foolhardy. *Run Arran Rapids at slack water only*, if at all. We have hiked from Big Bay to Arran Rapids, and watched the water during a spring tide. The enormous upwellings, whirlpools and overfalls were impressive and frightening.

Frederick Arm. Frederick Arm is deep, with almost no good places to anchor. You can anchor in several nooks along the eastern shoreline, or near the head, where the bottom shoals rapidly. A log booming ground is located near the head of the inlet. If nothing is going on, it looks as if you could tie off there.

⑤ **Oleo's.** (250) 203-6670; monitors VHF 66A. Oleo's is an unlikely little floating restaurant with moorage for a few boats, located

about three-quarters of a mile up the east shore of Frederick Arm, behind the 49-meter island. Call on VHF channel 66A or by phone for reservations. They don't take credit cards. Go without preconceptions; this is different from what you're accustomed to. We suggest calling ahead for reservations; last year when we tried to visit in mid-August they were already closed for the season.

Estero Basin. Estero Basin, off the head of Frederick Arm, is uncharted. If the crowds are getting to you, Estero Basin is where you can avoid them. The narrow passage into the basin, called "The Gut," is passable only at high water slack (very high water slack, we now are told), and slack doesn't last very long. A dinghy with outboard motor is a good way to go. You may have to drag it part of the way. We have not been in Estero Basin, but Wolferstan has. He writes convincingly about the strong currents in The Gut and the eerie stillness of the 5-mile-long basin with its uncharted rocks. Friends tell us that Estero Basin is absolutely beautiful, usually deserted, with small islands, sheer cliffs, and water that grows fresher the farther you go. "Bring your lunch and shampoo," we're advised.

Waggoner reader Patrick Freeny reported that he had just enough water for his inflatable dinghy on a 13 foot tide. On a 10 foot tide, the dinghy had to be dragged in. Dinghies or skiffs only, no larger boats.

NODALES CHANNEL

Thurston Bay Marine Park. Thurston Bay Marine Park is large enough to hold many boats without feeling too crowded and has good anchorages with exploring ashore.

We had good overnight anchorage in 36 feet behind Block Island and in Handfield Bay.

The landlocked inlet behind Wilson Point, on the south side of Thurston Bay, is best entered at half tide or higher. Wolferstan calls this inlet Anchorage Lagoon. At the entrance, least depth at zero tide is 2 feet or less. We tiptoed in near the bottom of a 2.9-foot

The jet boat tours at Dent Island Lodge illustrate why transiting Dent Rapids should be done only near slack water.

The Gut that leads to Estero Basin is narrow and passable only at high water in a small boat. Photo by David Helland.

The view up Phillips Arm from Shoal Bay.

low tide with the depth sounder showing 6 feet (our boat drew 3 feet). Inside we found four boats at anchor in a pretty setting, with 9 to 10 feet of depth. This is a good place to know your vessel's draft and the tidal range during your stay.

Be bear aware when ashore.

Handfield Bay. Handfield Bay is entered from Binnington Bay, located to port as you enter Cameleon Harbour. Chart 3543 (1:40,000) makes it clear that you should enter Handfield Bay leaving Tully Island to port. Once inside, you'll find excellent protection, good anchoring depths, and shore access for dog-walking. From the upper helm the rock north of Tully Island was easy to spot at half tide. Handfield Bay is a favorite stop for many cruisers. Note that in the entrance to Cameleon Harbour, Douglas Rock, which dries 1.5 meters, is detached from Bruce Point. Give Bruce Point ample room.

Cameleon Harbour. Cameleon Harbour is a big, open bay with ample protected anchorage, depending on where you need the shelter. Note that in the entrance to Cameleon Harbour, Douglas Rock, which dries 1.5 meters, is detached from Bruce Point. Give Bruce Point ample room.

Hemming Bay. Hemming Bay is pretty, especially at the north end, near the head. Enter leaving the Lee Islands well to starboard

to avoid Menace Rock in the middle of the bay. Most of the Hemming Bay is deep, but you can find anchoring depths near the head. Correspondent Carol-Ann Giroday reports that the land at the head of Hemming Bay is private, and posted with no-trespassing signs.

⑥ **Shoal Bay.** Shoal Bay has a public float with good anchorage off the outboard end. The water shallows dramatically at the head of the bay. Shoal Bay is protected from most winds blowing down Cordero Channel, but is open to wakes from passing boats. It has a beautiful view up Phillips Arm. It's a good place to wait for slack water at rapids north or south. Rafting is mandatory; set out fenders on both sides. The docks fill quickly during the summer, so arrive early or be prepared to anchor out. No power or water at the docks. Mark MacDonald is the wharfinger and moorage fees are collected at the Shoal Bay Pub, just up from the head of the wharf.

⑥ **Shoal Bay Pub.** General Delivery, Blind Channel, BC V0P 1B0; (250) 287-6818; shoalbay@mac.com; www.shoalbay.ca. Open May 1 to October 1. Free Wi-Fi, washrooms, showers, laundry, guest cabins. The pub has cold beer. Saturdays are pizza day. Bring whatever toppings you have from your boat; pizza dough is provided for a small charge.

A large vegetable patch is available for garden-deprived cruisers who like to get their hands dirty. All tools are provided. Ap-

ple, plum, pear, and cherry trees have been planted, and visitors can pick fruit. You can offer a donation for what you pick.

For exercise, you can take the sometimes challenging hike up the mountain to the gold mine.

The 2014 Shoal Bay International Blues Festival will be held Saturday, August 9. The event has grown over the years. What started out as a bunch of friendly folks jamming now has a stage with a schedule of acts. In 2013, the dock and anchorage filled. During the afternoon they roast a pig and offer dinner for a nominal charge. After dinner the music goes on into the wee hours.

In addition to the Blues Festival, owners Mark and Cynthia MacDonald have added activities like pig and lamb roasts throughout the summer. See their website for the schedule.

Phillips Arm. Phillips Arm is deep, with little protection along the shores. **Fanny Bay** looks good on the chart, but has log booming activity. A northwest wind can blow through a saddle in the mountains at the head of the bay. On an earlier visit we found a stiff breeze in Fanny Bay; in Phillips Arm the air was calm. Large logging operations are located near the head of the inlet. A friend, much experienced, tells us not to anchor in the area of Dyer Point. The bottom there is foul with a tangle of sunken logs. [*Hale*]

Bickley Bay. Bickley Bay on Cordero Channel has anchoring depths toward the head of the bay. Favor the east shore to avoid a shoal area. Friends who have cruised in the area extensively warn of poor holding ground, however, and won't go in anymore. Phil Richter at Blind Channel Resort also warns of poor holding. Caution advised.

⑦ **Cordero Lodge.** Cordero Lodge, General Delivery, Blind Channel, BC V0P 1B0; (250) 287-0917; info@corderolodge.com; www.corderolodge.com. Open end of May to mid-September. Cordero Lodge is on log floats behind Lorte Island, a short distance east of Greene Point Rapids. The lodge has rooms, a cozy restaurant, and nearly 800 feet

The public dock at Shoal Bay.

of dock space. Currents at the docks can be deceptively strong. Washrooms, guest rooms, limited Wi-Fi. No power.

Reinhardt and Doris Kuppers sold the resort to Lorrie Tangway in 2013. When we visited, the resort was freshly painted and changes were underway.

The fully licensed restaurant serves lunch and dinner. Some of the items are based on Doris Kuppers' original German recipes. It still has a warm, inviting atmosphere. You may start your meal alone, but by the time you finish everybody in the place will have become friends, swapping information and exchanging addresses and phone numbers back home. Best to email or call ahead on the VHF to determine the dinner plan and menu.

Please, please slow down. Passing boat traffic in Cordero Channel can put out damaging wakes that roll into boats moored at Cordero Lodge. As you approach the lodge location, throttle back to no-wake speed and hold that speed until you're past. It's only a short distance.

Crawford Anchorage. Crawford Anchorage, between Erasmus Island and East Thurlow Island, is chancy at best, with a rocky and poor holding bottom. Friends, however, report they have anchored in Crawford Anchorage successfully, using a Bruce anchor and a stern-tie to Erasmus Island. We tried anchoring with indifferent results. Enter Crawford Anchorage from the west—rocks lie in the eastern entrance. Rocks also lie southeast of Mink Island.

Mayne Passage (Blind Channel). Mayne Passage connects Cordero Channel with Johnstone Strait. From Johnstone Strait the entrance can be hard to spot, hence the local name "Blind Channel." The current in Mayne Passage reaches 5 knots at springs, flooding north and ebbing south. Chart 3543 (1:40,000) shows rips in the northern part of Mayne Passage, and Sailing Directions warns of whirlpools and overfalls. Passages near slack are recommended. Blind Channel Resort, on the west shore of Mayne Passage, is popular. On the east side of Mayne Passage, Charles Bay is a good anchorage.

Charles Bay. On the east side of Mayne Passage, Charles Bay has convenient anchoring depths around Eclipse Islet, in the center of the bay. Just east of Eclipse Islet, however, the bay shoals to drying flats.

⑧ **Blind Channel Resort.** Blind Channel, BC V0P 1B0; (888) 329-0475; info@ blindchannel.com; www.blindchannel.com. Monitors VHF 66A. Open all year, gasoline, diesel, propane. Ample moorage on 2400 feet of dock, 15, 30 & some 50 amp power, washrooms, showers, laundry, UV-treated spring water, garbage drop for fee, credit card pay phone, free Wi-Fi. Float planes stop here. This is a complete, well-run, and popular marina and resort, with water taxi, adventure tours, accommodations, excellent

Blind Channel's docks are sturdy, but watch for current when docking.

fully-licensed restaurant open June through Labour Day, well-stocked store, fresh-baked goods during high season, post office, liquor agency, and gift items. In July and August they have daily lunch barbecues on the patio. The new gazebo overlooking the marina is a welcome addition in rainy weather.

Current runs across the face of the floats and landing can be a little tricky. At the fingers themselves, the current runs from north to south about 90 percent of the time, regardless of the current in the middle of the channel. A short distance off the fingers, however, the current usually runs from south to north. You can verify the current direction at the docks by observing which way the fingers press against the pilings at the outer

ends. Call on the VHF for docking instructions. One of the staff always comes down to help you land, which helps a lot. They know what to do.

The resort is surrounded by hiking trails, developed and maintained by Interfor. One trail leads to an 800-year-old cedar, 16 feet in diameter. It's a good hike and a splendid old tree. Recommended.

The Cedar Post Restaurant is excellent, akin to something you might find in Whistler or Vancouver. The servers are well-dressed, the tables are covered in linen, and the menu is varied.

This is a real family enterprise, now spanning four generations. Edgar and the late Annemarie Richter bought Blind Channel in

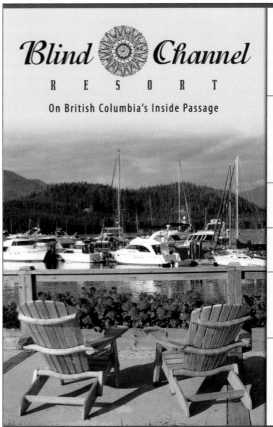

The meals at Blind Channel Resort are colorful and delicious.

the 1970s. Edgar designed and built all the buildings, and Annemarie's distinctive and lovely artwork decorates the dock and the restaurant. What they built, with long hours and hard labor, is a long way from what they bought 40 years ago.

Their son Phil Richter is general manager. Phil's wife Jennifer gets up early to bake her wonderful pies, bread, and other items offered for sale in the store. Phil and Jennifer's sons Eliot and William grew up working on the docks and in the dining room. Eliot is now a partner in the business and lives on-site. You will most likely see Eliot's children running around the docks, learning and having fun.

⑨ Greene Point Rapids. Currents run to 7 knots on spring tides in Greene Point Rapids. Sailing Directions warns of "considerable overfalls, whirlpools and eddies," and recommends transiting near slack. On small tides currents are much less. Slack water occurs about 1 hour and 30 minutes before slack water at Seymour Narrows. Current corrections are shown under Seymour Narrows in the Secondary Stations section in Tide and Current Tables, Vol. 6. and in Ports and Passes. When eastbound on flood tides, low-powered boats and boats with tows are cautioned against being set against Erasmus Island.

Loughborough Inlet. Loughborough (pronounced "Loch-brough") Inlet, off Chancellor Channel, is deep, with steep-to sides and few good anchorages. The best anchorage used to be a short distance from the mouth on the western shore, in **Beaver Inlet**. Beaver Inlet is now a log booming ground with significant commercial activity, making it ill-suited to pleasure boats. Edith Cove in Beaver Inlet is occupied by a float home and log raft, so it's not an anchorage.

WELLBORE CHANNEL

⑩ Whirlpool Rapids. Whirlpool Rapids on **Wellbore Channel** has currents to 7 knots. The time of turn is based on Seymour Narrows, and the corrections are shown under Secondary Current Stations in the Tide

and Current Tables, Vol. 6 and Ports and Passes. The flood sets southeast and the ebb sets northwest. When the current is running, expect strong whirlpools, upwellings and backeddies on the downstream side. The turbulence occurs south of Carterer Point on the flood, and north of Carterer Point on the ebb. It is best to transit within a half-hour of slack, although on small tides boats seem to go through anytime. At low tide you might see bears on the beach near the south entrance to Wellbore Channel.

Forward Harbour. The entrance to Forward Harbour is narrow but unobstructed. Most of the harbor is 60 to 90 feet deep. Douglas Bay is a pretty anchorage, sheltered from Johnstone Strait westerlies that turn and blow through Sunderland Channel. The bottom of Douglas Bay drops off quickly, and you may find yourself anchored in 60 feet of water—a good reason to carry at least 300 feet of anchor rode. We've had a report that a southeast wind can make for a rough time for boats anchored along the northern shore.

A trail leads from Douglas Bay to a white sand beach at Bessborough Bay. In the past the trail was well marked and easy to walk, but we received a report that winter blowdown has made the trail much more challenging.

If Forward Harbour is too full, good anchorage can be found in the little bay on Hardwicke Island, directly across from the mouth of Forward Harbour.

Bessborough Bay. Although you can find anchoring depths in the southeast corner, the entire bay is open to strong westerlies blowing up Sunderland Channel.

Topaze Harbour. Big and pretty enough, but little shelter for small boats.

Sunderland Channel. Sunderland Channel connects Wellbore Channel with Johnstone Strait. If the westerly is blowing and whitecaps are in Sunderland Channel, it will likely be worse in Johnstone Strait. Many boats wait out these conditions in Forward Harbour.

All of the channels north of Yuculta

Rapids—Nodales Channel, Mayne Passage, Chancellor Channel, and Sunderland Channel—lead to Johnstone Strait. Each provides some protection and a chance to observe conditions on Johnstone Strait before venturing out. A strong westerly wind opposed by an ebb current can make Johnstone Strait difficult.

JOHNSTONE STRAIT

Johnstone Strait is a seductive and difficult body of water. The strait begins at Chatham Point in the east, and stretches 54 miles along the northeast side of Vancouver Island to Blinkhorn Peninsula. It is the shortest route up- or down-island. Especially on the Vancouver Island side, Johnstone Strait is bounded by steep, high and beautiful mountains. On a clear day the scenery is awesome.

That is the seductive part. The difficult part is what the wind and current in Johnstone Strait do to each other. The flood current flows eastward, down-island, toward Discovery Passage and Campbell River. The ebb current flows westward, up-island, toward Queen Charlotte Strait and the North Pacific Ocean. A residual ebb surface current exists in Johnstone Strait, increasing the west-flowing ebb current's strength and duration. In the summer, the prevailing wind in Johnstone Strait is a westerly, often a gale-force westerly, funneled by the mountains. The result is a classic wind-against-current heaping up of the seas.

Conditions are worst where the meeting of currents creates tide-rips, even in calm conditions. This stretch begins at Ripple Shoal, east of Kelsey Bay. It extends westward past Kelsey Bay, through Race Passage and Current Passage, and across the mouth of Sunderland Channel. Especially on an ebb, when the westerly is blowing you don't want to be there—period. Leave the heroics to others. Johnstone Strait can take all the pleasure out of a pleasure boat. Kevin Monahan's excellent diagrams on page 279 illustrate Johnstone Strait's trouble spots.

Despite the potential problems, we have run the length of Johnstone Strait, both directions, and had an excellent ride each time. But we listened to the weather and went when conditions were calm or near-calm. If the wind had come up, we were prepared to run for cover in a bay or seek out a friendly point to hide behind until conditions improved. We always keep a bail-out point in mind. Conditions can change quickly.

Watch for drift in Johnstone Strait. There's considerable current activity, and many shear lines where scrap wood, tree limbs, logs, and even entire floating trees accumulate.

Turn Island. Turn Island is off the southern tip of East Thurlow Island at the intersection of Johnstone Strait and Discovery Passage. Anchor behind Turn Island, about where the 5.8-meter sounding is shown on the chart, with good holding and room to swing. The anchorage has nice views to Johnstone Strait and the mountains on Vancouver Island. [*Hamilton*]

Knox Bay. Knox Bay is located near the mouth of Mayne Passage on the north side of Johnstone Strait. It would be a poor choice for an anchorage, but a good hideout to escape a strong westerly in the strait. The northwest corner of the bay is best protected. Unfortunately it is deep, and devoted to log booming.

Fanny Island. When the Environment Canada weather station was moved from Helmcken Island to Fanny Island a few years ago, Johnstone Strait weather reports improved dramatically (Helmcken Island could report 8 knots of wind when it was blowing 30). We're told, however, that while Fanny Island reports of northwest winds are fairly accurate, south and east winds can be reported less than what's actually going on.

Helmcken Island. Helmcken Island has protected anchorage on its north side in Billygoat Bay. Currents in this part of the strait run at 5 knots. When opposed by wind from the opposite direction, large, dangerous seas can build rapidly. Billygoat Bay is a good place to hide out. Anchor in approximately 30 feet, although Correspondents James and Jennifer Hamilton found only poor holding over rock. Instead, they recommend the cove northwest of Billygoat Bay. They go up to the head of the cove, where they have found calm water, with an "awesome" view eastward. The cove is unnamed in Sailing Directions or on the chart. The Hamiltons call it Helmcken Cove.

Kelsey Bay. Kelsey Bay, on the north side of Vancouver Island, has a breakwater past the harbor made of old ship hulks—the Union Steamship *Cardena* and three WWII frigates: HMCS *Runnymede*, HMCS *Lasalle*, and HMCS *Longueil*. Enter leaving the new breakwater to starboard and tie to a 150-foot-long public float. Limited power and water. Quieter moorage can be found farther inside, at a second public wharf with power and water.

The store at Port Neville dates back to 1924, and was closed up in 1960.

Moorage is paid at the honor box at the top of the ramp.

Some shopping is available in the village of Sayward, a short distance up the road.

Blenkinsop Bay. Blenkinsop Bay has reasonably protected anchorage along the north shore of Johnstone Strait, but swells from westerly winds work into the bay. The chart shows tide-rips off Blenkinsop Bay. The chart isn't kidding. McLeod Bay and an unnamed bay inside Tuna Point are possible temporary anchorages.

Port Neville. Port Neville is an 8-mile-long inlet, a popular hideout for the fishing fleet, and an excellent spot to duck into if the weather in Johnstone Strait deteriorates. The inlet is a good anchorage, with a government dock and float a short distance inside, along the eastern shore. Boomed logs are stored in several places toward the inner end of the inlet. No public facilities are in the vicinity. The current can run swiftly past the government float, so plan your approach carefully. Remember, there's no shame in making several attempts before you get your landing right.

For years Olaf "Oly" Hansen, at the government dock post office, could be reached by radio for a report on conditions on Johnstone Strait. Oly died in January, 1997 at age 87, another legend gone from the coast.

Oly's widow Lilly lived on in the family house for a few years, but finally had to move down-island. In 2003, shortly after her 90th birthday, she too left us. Their daughter Lorna (Hansen) Chesluk raised her daughter Erica in the house at the head of the wharf. Lorna was the postmaster, and she happily looked out on the strait and gave a report if you called on the radio.

The post office was closed in 2010, and Lorna moved to Campbell River to be closer to family. The Hansen family had lived at Port Neville since 1891. Until it closed, the Port Neville post office was the longest continuously-operating post office in the province. Yet another page of coastal history is turned. A caretaker now looks after the property, although Lorna comes up from time to time. The wonderful old store building is at the head of the wharf. Occasionally tour and whale watching groups stop by to see the old post office, still frozen in time.

If you go ashore, keep pets on a leash. Wild animals (grizzly bears and black bears) and protective mother deer are in the area.

Anchoring: Correspondents James and Jennifer Hamilton recommend Baresides Bay. "Anchor directly south of the *MSh* symbol on Charts 3545 and 3564. You will be in 15 feet of water at zero tide, about 200 feet from shore. Excellent holding. Not super-protected, but out of the teeth of the westerly, so no worries." [*Hamilton*]

LOCAL KNOWLEDGE

RESTRICTED AREA: Robson Bight, on the Vancouver Island side near the north end of Johnstone Strait, is an Ecological Reserve, a gathering place for Orcas. Unauthorized vessels (meaning yours and ours) are not allowed.

Robson Bight. The Robson Bight restricted area runs .5 mile offshore and for 5 miles off Robson Bight. It is not centered on the Bight and extends more to the east. If you stray into the restricted area, wardens will intercept your boat and instruct you to leave immediately.

Kelsey Bay is full of local fishing boats and some recreational boats, but it is a welcome duck-in point on Johnstone Strait.

CHAPTER 12

THE BROUGHTONS

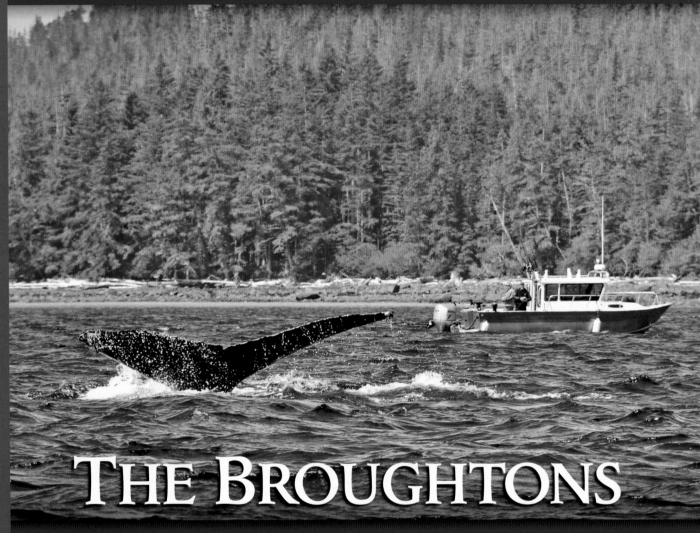

THE BROUGHTONS

THE BROUGHTONS
Port Neville • Port Harvey • Lagoon Cove
• Kwatsi Bay • Echo Bay • Shawl Bay •
Sullivan Bay • Jennis Bay • Monks' Wall

"The Broughtons" is an all-encompassing term for the inlets, islands and waterways on the mainland side of Queen Charlotte Strait, north of Johnstone Strait. This area includes the islands adjoining Blackfish Sound and Fife Sound. It also includes Knight Inlet, Kingcome Inlet, Tribune Channel, Drury Inlet, and Mackenzie Sound. For convenience we include Port Neville, Havannah Channel and Chatham Channel. Locals call this area the Mainland, to distinguish it from the Vancouver Island side from Sayward (Kelsey Bay) to the top of Vancouver Island, which they call North Island.

The Broughtons, or the Mainland, is one large, complex cruising ground. It offers anchorages from raw and wind-swept Fife Sound and Blackfish Sound, to the gentler waters of Simoom Sound, Greenway Sound and Drury Inlet. Small, family-owned resorts—no two of them alike—are spread throughout the Broughtons. Most cruisers anchor out some of the time and enjoy the social side of marina life the rest of the time. Cruisers usually stop at or overnight at all the marinas during their cruise: Port Harvey, Lagoon Cove, Kwatsi Bay, Pierre's at Echo Bay, Shawl Bay, Sullivan Bay and Jennis Bay.

Resupply and repairs are on the North Island side, at Port McNeill, Alert Bay, Sointula, and Port Hardy. North Island is described in a separate chapter.

The rich history of the Broughtons begins with Native habitation dating back thousands of years. On Mound Island, 14 depressions in the earth are evidence of Native Big Houses and Long Houses, each of which held extended families. We're told that trading beads, the colorful glass beads exchanged for valuable pelts by early traders, still can be found on beaches throughout the Broughtons.

The Broughtons were homesteaded in the late 1800s and early 1900s. Families were raised on crude farms. The men rowed across Queen Charlotte Strait to Alert Bay, or rowed—*rowed*—200 miles south to Vancouver or Victoria to conduct business and bring back supplies.

In most cases, the forest has erased all

The beautiful Lacy Falls in Tribune Channel near Watson Cove and Kwatsi Bay.

traces of the homesteaders' now-abandoned efforts. One notable exception is remarkable "Monks' Wall," at the north end of Beware Passage. There, hidden in the trees, are the remains of a rock archway and other rock walls, all that are left from William and Mary Anne Galley's wilderness trading post that was active from the late 1800s until after the First World War.

The Broughtons are a destination. Take your time and don't hurry through. See Billy Proctor's museum in Shoal Harbour. Marvel at Lacy Falls on Tribune Channel. Anchor out. Visit the marinas and meet the families who run them.

Ask questions, read the history, and take time to explore. If you spend your entire cruise in the Broughtons, you might scratch the surface.

Marinas: Marinas in the Broughtons are different from marinas elsewhere on the coast. They're small and often family run. Some cruisers develop friendships with the owners, and come back year after year to catch up. The marinas may be a little rough around the edges, but that's part of their charm. These are wilderness marinas, and the owners make do with what they have.

Potluck hour: Many of the marinas in the Broughtons have a potluck hors d'oeuvre—or even a potluck dinner—gathering around 5:00 p.m. Bring your own beverages, leaded or unleaded. It's an ideal time to meet other boaters and exchange information. Kids usually are more than welcome, although if they're the only ones, they might get bored with grownups' chit-chat. You'll want to carry a stock of suitable fixings for your hors d'oeuvre or potluck contribution. The fixings don't have to be fancy. If you're down to Doritos and salsa, they'll be hoovered into mouths in short order. If you enjoy doing something special, this is a good time to show your stuff.

Exceptional book: Bill Proctor's *Full Moon,*

Flood Tide, edited and illustrated by Yvonne Maximchuk and published by Harbour Publishing, ought to be required reading before cruising in the Broughtons. If you are hungry for a little more, consider Yvonne's recently released book *Drawn to Sea* for more insights on life and the people of this area.

HAVANNAH CHANNEL

Havannah Channel leads northward toward Knight Inlet and other channels to the north and west.

① **Port Harvey.** Port Harvey is large, and although it is open to westerlies from Johnstone Strait, it is an excellent anchorage. If you're planning an early morning run on Johnstone Strait it's a good place to overnight. You'll find anchorage in several notches along the east side before you reach the head of the bay, and at the head.

A big logging operation is on the west side of Port Harvey. A permanent house with private mooring floats is on the shore. The wind blows through Cracroft Inlet, and a gentle, low surge can come in if the wind is blowing on Johnstone Strait.

The Port Harvey Marina opened in 2009 with good docks, a well-stocked store, and a cafe. They charge a fee for landing the dinghy.

Caution: Do not attempt the narrow canal that leads between Port Harvey and Cracroft Inlet. The channel dries and is studded with boulders.

① **Port Harvey Marina Resort.** Box 40, Minstrel Island, BC V0P 1L0; (250) 902-9003; portharveymarine@gmail.com; www.portharvey.blogspot.com. Monitors VHF 66A. Guest boats welcomed, well-stocked store, licensed cafe, gift shop, good cell phone coverage, Wi-Fi, Visa & MasterCard accepted. Ample moorage along good docks

Reference Only – Not for Navigation

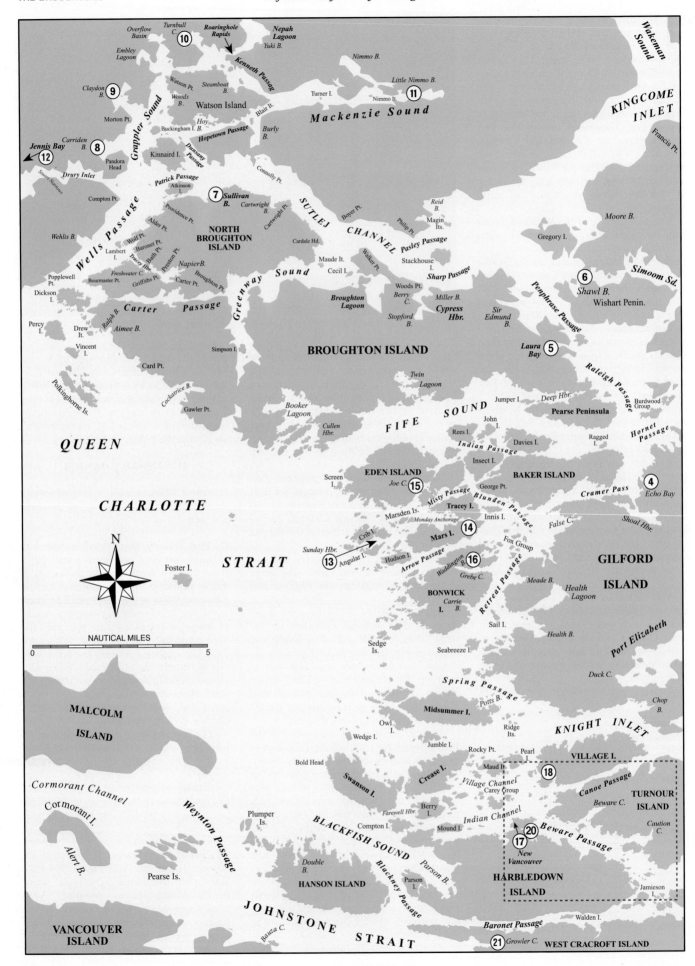

NAUTICAL MILES

0 _____ 5

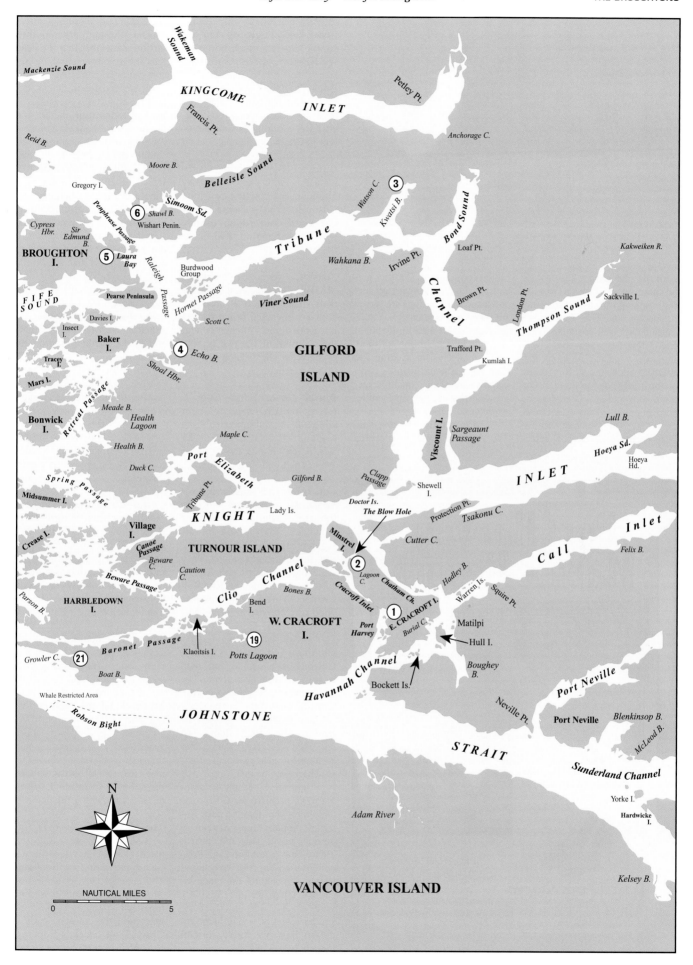

The docks at Port Harvey Marina Resort.

with 30 amp power. Easy access to shore for walking the dog or trail walking through the forest.

George and Gail Cambridge opened this well-positioned marina a few years ago and it was instantly popular. The store and the Red Shoe Pub & Restaurant are on a barge tied to shore. Bring a red shoe and get a free dessert. Cinnamon buns are made fresh every day. The restaurant can be busy during prime season, reser-vations encouraged. Weather per-mitting, fireworks are set off and free chili and hot dogs are served on July 1 (Canada Day).

Nothing is fancy. Rustic might be a good word—rustic but solid, and attentively run. George and Gail are warm and helpful, dedi-cated to providing a quality expe-rience. They improve the facilities every year.

The marina isn't visible until you get all the way to the head of Port Harvey, beyond Range Island, so don't give up. You will see the log camp first. Port Har-vey Marina is just across the bay.

Bockett Islets. Contributing Editor Tom Kincaid has anchored for a few hours among the Bock-ett Islets awaiting favorable cur-rent in Chatham Channel.

Boughey Bay. Anchorage is to-ward the south end of Boughey (pronounced "boogie") Bay. John Chappell (*Cruising Beyond Desola-tion Sound*) says strong easterly winds can spring up suddenly in the bay.

Matilpi. Matilpi (pronounced MAT-il-pi) is an abandoned In-dian village site. It is beautiful, with a white shell beach backed by dense forest. Anchor behind the northern of the two islands, or between the islands. Protec-tion is excellent.

Burial Cove. Burial Cove is pretty, though open to most winds. It is well-protected from seas and has good holding in 25 feet. A few houses are on shore. We've anchored there twice.

Call Inlet. Call Inlet is approxi-mately 10 miles long, and runs through beautiful, steep-sided mountains. You can find anchor-ing depths in the Warren Islands, near the mouth of the inlet. They are a pretty spot to wait for the current to change in Chatham Channel. A stern-tie to shore is a good idea for overnight anchor-age.

Chatham Channel. Chatham Channel is easier to run than it appears from the chart. The southern section is the narrowest, with the least room in the chan-nel, and requires the greatest at-tention. The current floods east and ebbs west. Near slack water is the most pleasant time to tran-sit Chatham Channel.

Slacks are based on Seymour Narrows predictions. Correction factors for the times of slack wa-ter are found under Secondary Stations in the Tide and Current Tables, Vol. 6 and Ports and Pass-es. Chart 3545 (1:40,000) shows the area, including the range lo-cations. Chart 3564 (1:20,000), with its 1:10,000 insert of the southern section, really helps un-derstanding. We highly recom-mend Chart 3564.

If you are running compass courses through the southern section, remember that the head-ings shown on the chart are true, and must be corrected to mag-netic. We have found that in some lighting conditions the ranges are hard to locate from the far ends of the lower channel. Going ei-ther direction, a sharp-eyed crew should sight astern at the back range until it grows difficult to see. By then the leading range should be visible. Maximum cur-rents in the southern section run to 5 knots at springs, with no significant swirls or overfalls. In our experience, the current usu-ally is much less than shown (but not always; twice, we have found considerable current). Chatham Channel can be taken at times other than slack water, but you should know what you are doing, and in the southern section *keep your boat lined up on the range*. The current is strongest in the narrow section, then diminishes when moving to the wider areas of the channel.

North of this area a small re-sort, with docks, is on the east side of Chatham Channel. Slow to no-wake speed when passing this resort.

Cutter Cove. Cutter Cove, lo-cated across from Minstrel Island Resort (now closed) at the north end of Chatham Channel, is very pretty and a good anchorage. A fresh west or northwest wind can enter the cove. No swells, but ag-gressive little whitecaps. The bot-tom looks flat, as if it's pure mud. "At least one noisy old rock is down there, though, because the anchor chain dragged across it all night long." [*Hale*] Anchor in 24 feet (zero tide).

Minstrel Island Resort. The sad story of this once great stop continues. The buildings appear abandoned and vegetation con-tinues growing on the docks. You may see several boats moored there, but keep in mind there is no one maintaining the docks.

The Blow Hole. The Blow Hole is a short, shallow, easily-navi-gated channel between Minstrel Island and East Cracroft Island. The channel gets its name from strong westerly winds that some-times blow through. Near the west end a reef, shown clearly on Chart 3564, extends from East Cracroft Island on the south side

Lagoon Cove is a popular destination. The managers work hard to squeeze every boat in.

People frequently gather on the dock to socialize at Lagoon Cove.

of the channel. Brave the kelp and favor the north side of the channel and you'll have no problems.

② **Lagoon Cove.** Lagoon Cove has good anchorage along the shorelines, although the middle of the bay is a little deep for most boats. Lagoon Cove Marina is on the east side of the bay. Locals recommend against anchoring on the west side of the bay, which they say is foul with logging cable. We got a note from a reader who said at least one cable can be found on the east side as well.

② **Lagoon Cove Marina.** c/o Minstrel Island P.O., Minstrel Island, BC V0P 1L0; www.lagooncovemarina.com. Monitors VHF 66A. Open all year. Lagoon Cove has gasoline, diesel, propane, stove oil, 15, 30, & 2×30 amp power, water, washroom & showers, gift shop, wired internet connection in the workshop. Mechanic on site for many repairs. Kenmore Air and NW Seaplanes ser-

vice to Seattle.

A do-it-yourself burn barrel is available for burnable garbage (no fair just dropping a bag of garbage in, for someone else to deal with). The fuel dock office carries fishing tackle, prawn and crab traps, ice, charts, a few essentials. A separate store with the grand name "Edgewater Emporium" carries Lagoon Cove branded clothing.

The entire property has a whimsical quality about it. The workshop is an "historic" workshop. A totem pole is made from pieces of outboard motors and all sorts of other junk. Two "exercise stations," one of them a pile of wood with an axe, the other a brightly painted lawnmower, invite the eager. Several hiking trails are maintained. a pet path is available for the four-legged crew.

Lagoon Cove Marina is one of most popular stops on the coast. You may have to raft, but they work to fit everyone in. Owner Jean Barber and managers Pat and Bob provide personal, attentive service and introductions.

Happy hour appetizer potlucks for marina guests are held almost every day in the "historic" workshop. Guests bring treats from their boats. For many years, Jean's husband, Bill, provided fresh prawns for happy hour. Bill passed away in 2013, and marina guests now often volunteer to set and retrieve the marina's prawn traps. Weather permitting, an occasional marshmallow roast might be organized at sunset. Over the years singing around the campfire has been a big part of Lagoon Cove. Bring your instrument and join in.

Everybody, by the way, goes up to the happy hour and marshmallow roasts. "This is summer camp for adults," an enthusiastic lady said to us.

Bill Barber died in in April 2013. We will miss his famous "long tale" stories at the happy hours and campfires. Jean is now seeking the right new owners for the marina. Inquiries invited.

CRUISING TIPS – RAFTING DOGS

Sooner or later, rafting dogs come in handy. As the photo shows, a rafting dog is a crude iron casting with an eye at one end and a point at the other. It is designed to be driven into a log so a line can be passed through the eye. Rafting dogs (also called log dogs) are just the thing for tying mid-way along a log boom, where nothing can be found to pass a line through.

If you use rafting dogs, be sure to drive them into the perimeter boomsticks (the logs that are chained to one

another to hold the boom together). Do not put rafting dogs into logs that are bound for the sawblade. And remove all rafting dogs before you leave.

Rafting dogs are available from Marine Supply & Hardware, 202 Commercial Ave., Anacortes, WA 98221; (360) 293-3014; www.marinesupplyandhardware.com.

— Robert Hale

Knight Inlet. Knight Inlet (locally called Knight's Inlet) extends from its mouth, at Midsummer Island, to its head at the mouth of the Klinaklini River. Knight Inlet is about 70 miles long and 2 miles wide, the longest of the fjords indenting the B.C. coast. Along most of its length the shores rise steeply to 6,000-foot-high mountains. Anchorage is iffy at best, so for many, the inlet's upper reaches are explored mainly by fast boats able to make the round trip in a single day. Boats with limited fuel capacity should top off at Lagoon Cove before making the trip. Extensive logging activity has put considerable debris in the water. Watch carefully.

The section above Glendale Cove is reported to be more dramatic than Jervis or Bute inlets. Reader John Tyler reports, "Even with the distances involved, it's well worth the time to cruise up there."

In Knight Inlet, **Tsakonu Cove** is a pretty anchorage, protected from westerlies but exposed to the east. Several years ago we anchored near the head of Tsakonu Cove for a quiet lunch, while outside a 20-knot inflow wind blew Knight Inlet into an uncomfortable chop. Correspondents Bruce and Margaret Evertz report that a large drysort and booming operation now occupies the head of the bay. Driftwood logs on the shore suggest that outflow winds in Knight Inlet probably roar into Tsakonu Cove, accompanied by substantial seas.

Hoeya Sound. Hoeya Sound is pretty, but deep and completely exposed to the westerly winds that are prevalent in the summer.

Glendale Cove. The cove offers minimal protection from strong northeast winds that often blow down the inlet. "We anchored on a sloping bottom off the east side, just north of some old pilings. The second night four other pleasure boats were there. Every place else seemed to be less than 6 feet or more than 150 feet." [*Evertz*] Another boat reports being kept awake all night by the rumble of anchor chain rubbing on rocks.

In 2013 Knight Inlet Lodge, which specialises in grizzly bear adventures, took over the abandoned logging camp and cannery. They monitor VHF 68.

Wahshihlas Bay. Located at the mouth of the Sim River, Wahshihlas Bay is a possible anchorage. Although we've never tried it, Correspondents Bruce and Margaret Evertz have. "It was settled weather and we anchored in the northwest corner, just off the shoal. There were some snags to avoid. If we expected any winds we could have moved away from the shoal a little and anchored with a stern tie to shore or to some old pilings. The bay is far from 'bomb proof,' but we felt secure with the weather we had." [*Evertz*]

Port Elizabeth. Port Elizabeth is a great big bay bounded on the west by low hills that let westerlies in. A substantial log booming operation is in the cove in the northwest corner. You can find good anchorage near the booming site and along western shore, west of the largest of the three islands. The two smaller islands are joined on the west by drying flats.

Correspondents John and Lorraine Littlewood provided us with the following extra information:

"The unexpected difficulty with the anchorage in Duck Cove at the west end of Port Elizabeth is that in any winds from 0 to 180 degrees you will feel the full force. We were getting gusts to 30 knots in a southeaster, supposedly sheltered. The only real shelter is in the extreme southeastern end of Port Elizabeth, except for in a northwest blow." [*Littlewood*]

Sargeaunt Passage. Sargeaunt Passage connects Knight Inlet and Tribune Channel, and has anchorage at either end of the narrows. The passage runs between steep-sided mountains, and is beautiful. The shoal in the middle extends from the east shore across much of the passage. Favor the west shore. We found the depth at the narrow part was less than shown on the chart.

Tribune Channel. Tribune Channel borders the east and north sides of Gilford Island. Kwatsi Bay is one of the most dramatic anchorages on the coast. Lacy Falls can be stunning.

Kumlah Island Anchorage. Kumlah Island is in Tribune Channel, roughly across from the mouth of Thompson Sound. Waggoner reader Joel Erikson found suitable anchorage in 16 to 24 feet behind between Kumlah Island, between it and Gilford Island. We haven't spent the night, but would consider anchoring there in settled weather. The view is beautiful.

Thompson Sound. Thompson Sound is surrounded by forested mountains so steep that the hillsides are scarred by many landslides. Earlier editions of the Waggoner said Thompson Sound has no good anchorages, but Correspondents John and Lorraine Littlewood set us straight with this email: "There is excellent anchorage at the head of Thompson Sound, on the shelf between the mudflats at the mouth of the Kakweiken River. You can explore the river for a couple miles at high tide; there is lots of bear sign, and we don't mean black bears, either!"

A reader reported that when they tried to anchor they found the shelf dotted with crab trap buoys, leaving no room. They anchored briefly in the lee of Sackville Island, with a stern-tie to shore.

Bond Sound. In the past, we reported that Bond Sound had no good anchorages. But inspired by Bill Proctor's wonderful book, *Full Moon, Flood Tide*, readers Jim and Marsha Peters anchored their Grand Banks 42 *Dev's Courage* at the head of the sound in settled weather and took the dinghy some distance up the Ahta River. They said it was beautiful. Correspondents Steve and Elsie Hulsizer say to go up about two hours before high water. Another reader (Bill Cooke, Eastbay *Pop Pie*) told us that cutthroat trout fishing is good at the head of the sound. Correspondents John and Lorraine Littlewood add this note from an early September cruise:

"Bill Proctor's book, *Full Moon, Flood Tide*, led us to the Ahta River at the head of Bond Sound, an absolutely pristine salmon spawning river teeming with every sort of wildlife, from very large, dead salmon that have just completed their life cycle, to very much larger hairy brown mammals that feed on them (and just about anything else they want to). The place is like something from a fairy tale. It is not all that easy to find and explore, but very much worth it. Anchorage is tricky just off the drying bar at the mouth of the rivers (there are two: Ahta Creek on the left as you face the estuary and pretty well destroyed by clearcut logging, and the Ahta River on the right). The Ahta River, with a

Kwatsi Bay fills quickly during the summer cruising season.

Viner Sound is a beautiful anchorage. Two mooring buoys are available.

smaller opening, is deep, fast and clear. Don't tell a soul."

③ Kwatsi Bay. The inner cove of Kwatsi Bay on Tribune Channel is a stunning anchorage, one of the most impressive on the coast, surrounded by a high, sheer bowl of rock. Sunrises and sunsets are magnificent. Our log says, "Wow!" The bay is deep, though, over 100 feet deep in much of the inner cove. We had a peaceful night in 60 feet with good holding off the two streams that empty into the western bight of the inner cove. The next morning, we found several other possible places to anchor in 48 to 72 feet. We have been told that the spot we anchored in is rocky and we should have anchored on the south side of the back bay, east of the entrance. [*Hale*]

③ Kwatsi Bay Marina. Simoom Sound P.O., Simoom Sound, V0P 1S0; (250) 949-1384; kwatsibay@kwatsibay.com; www.kwatsibay.com. Monitors VHF 66A. Water, shower, small gift store, Wi-Fi, but no shore power. Visa and MasterCard accepted.

In 1998 a new marina, owned by Max Knierim and his wife Anca Fraser, was established in Kwatsi Bay. They and their daughter Marieke and son Russell carved out a place to live in the bush, and offer moorage services to passing boaters. Marieke and Russell have grown up and are now off in their own lives at university and summer jobs. Max and Anca are empty nesters, except for the many friends and guests who visit Kwatsi Bay during the summer.

The store is small, but classy, with a selection of local arts and crafts ranging from pottery to woodwork. It also carries souvenir T-shirts, caps and sweatshirts. Reservations recommended for July/August, email is best. Short hiking trails are nearby, reached by dinghy. One leads to a beautiful waterfall. Max or Anca can provide directions. Kwatsi Bay often hosts a potluck happy hour in the evening.

This is not a luxury resort; this is the wilderness, at its gentle but hardworking best. Recommended.

Watson Cove. Watch for a rock in the entrance, and favor the north shore when entering. Watson Cove is surrounded by beautiful rock, stunning waterfalls, and dense forest. A fish farm and floathouse have been moved from inside the cove to just outside. This makes the cove accessible for anchoring (60 feet, about halfway in), although we've heard the bottom is foul with logging debris. Don't tie to the aquaculture float; a barge is moored there overnight.

At the head of Watson Cove a dinghy can be tied to a length of large logging chain and you can scramble up the rock to a trail leading to a 1000-year-old cedar tree. This is the tree mentioned on p. 164 of Bill Proctor's *Full Moon, Flood Tide*. On an otherwise quiet afternoon at Kwatsi Bay, Anca took a bunch of us over in the speedboat to see the tree. The forest was beautiful and the tree was a memorable sight.

Lacy Falls. Just west of Watson Cove, Lacy Falls washes down an expanse of smooth black rock and tumbles into the sea. The boat can be brought up close, but not too close. The bottom at the base of the falls is rocky. *Note*: During dry periods water does not fan across the rocks.

Wahkana Bay. The inner cove of Wahkana Bay is attractive, but 120 feet deep except near shore. The south shore has spots where you can anchor in 48 to 72 feet with swinging room, however. Parts of the east shore are reported to be foul with logging debris and old pilings beneath the surface. The head of the inner cove shoals rapidly so watch out. Wind can blow through the saddle that reaches to Viner Sound.

Viner Sound. Viner Sound is pretty, but narrow and shallow. An indent on the north side, a short distance down the narrow channel, will hold one boat near the opening. Just inside that indent the water shoals immediately. Two public mooring buoys are in the little cove on the north side. The long shoaling area shown on the chart at the head of Viner Sound is real. Watch your depths as you explore.

Scott Cove. Scott Cove once was a busy logging camp, but the camp is now closed.

It's worth the trek through the forest to see the 1000-year-old cedar tree at Watson Cove.

Pierre's at Echo Bay is popular, especially during meal events.

The docks at Pierre's at Echo Bay are excellent.

LOCAL KNOWLEDGE

POWELL ROCK WARNING. A nasty drying rock lies off Powell Point, the southwest corner of Scott Cove. A boat running between Tribune Channel and Echo Bay or Cramer Passage could easily run up on this rock. Give Powell Point (and the rock) a big, wide offing.

④ **Echo Bay.** Echo Bay has moorage, fuel, cabins, the most complete store in the area, and a provincial park. The concrete breakwater at the mouth of the bay is a section of the old Lake Washington Floating Bridge. People have caught good-sized salmon and halibut from the breakwater.

A short but steep trail leads from Pierre's at Echo Bay Marina to Billy Proctor's museum.

The deep midden at the head of Echo Bay is easily investigated from the beach. An abandoned schoolhouse with playground is on high ground a short distance from the beach. If you have kids on board, it might be a fine place to let them run. Unfortunately, the school-age population of the area has fallen below the threshold needed to keep the school open. It closed in 2008. A good hike begins behind the schoolhouse, and leads back into the hills past two dams, across a couple of bridges, and onto a logging road. The logging road is heavily overgrown with alder, however, and you probably won't go much farther.

A little history: Echo Bay has been a gathering place for thousands of years (hence the midden at the head of the bay), and for more than 100 years it has been a center for loggers, fishermen, and now summertime boaters. In 2008 Pierre and Tove Landry bought the Echo Bay Resort and moved Pierre's Bay Marina from nearby Scott Cove to Echo Bay. The Echo Bay Resort docks were scrapped and new docks, with upgraded power, were built and installed. The store was refurbished and restocked. A new fuel dock was built. In a span of about three months the resort was transformed—a remarkable achievement in a remote location where help is scarce and everything must be barged in.

Since then Pierre has continued expanding and improving the facilities. The events building, on the concrete breakwater, is the first sight upon entering. Meal events at Echo Bay are now inside this building instead of under the old tent. What used to be called Windsong Village, under the cliff opposite Pierre's, is now part of Pierre's, known as The Cliffside.

Slow down: The wakes from passing vessels and the following wake from approaching vessels can get inside the bay and set things a-rocking. Please slow down well outside the marina when approaching.

Caution: See Pym Rocks warning.

④ **Echo Bay Marine Park.** The dock has been condemned and is now closed. The holding bottom is poor; anchoring is not a good idea. The park has walk-in campsites and picnicking. A nice beach is often used as a landing for kayakers.

④ **Pierre's Echo Bay Lodge & Marina.** c/o General Delivery, Simoom Sound PO, BC V0P 1S0; (250) 713-6415; info@ pierresbay.com; www.pierresbay.com. Monitors VHF 66A. Phone coverage is spotty in the area. Best to contact the marina by email. Open all year, gasoline, diesel, propane, 15, 30 & 50 amp power, rental cabins, store, ice, water, washrooms, showers, laundry, Wi-Fi. Ample guest moorage, reservations recommended mid-July through mid-August, credit cards accepted.

This is a busy destination in the Broughtons, with wide, sturdy docks, ample electric power, a well-stocked store, and fuel dock. Pierre and Tove (pronounced "Tova") Landry have made Echo Bay a popular destination. The setting is beautiful in a protected bay. It is also a social place. Happy hour gatherings are common, and sometimes lead to potluck dinners. Check their website for the many food events, such as such as Italian night, fish n' chips night, prime rib dinner night twice a week, Christmas in July, etc. From the last weekend in June to the first weekend in September, Saturday-night themed pig roasts are signature sell-out events. Many visitors arrive on Fridays to get a good spot on the dock. Reservations are just about essential. Check their website for themes, some of which merit a costume or funny hat. Floatplane service by Kenmore Air and NW Seaplanes.

This might sound too structured and busy for some people, but Pierre and his delightful wife Tove, along with Maddog Mike and the rest of the crew, make it pure fun.

④ **Pierre's Echo Bay - The Cliffside.** Formerly Windsong Sea Village. Pierre and Tove Landry acquired this facility in early 2013. The Cliffside offers overflow moorage for

The pig roasts at Pierre's draw big crowds. Reservations are best.

Billy Proctor's remarkable museum draws more than a thousand visitors each year.

Billy Proctor built this replica of an early hand logger's cabin from a single cedar log.

Pierre's at Echo Bay. Water, no power. For cruisers who prefer less hustle-and-bustle, The Cliffside is a good alternative to the main docks at Pierre's. There is a ramp to shore and a trail to Billy Proctor's Museum.

Shoal Harbour. Shoal Harbour has good, protected anchorage, mud bottom. We would anchor just to the right, inside the entrance. Wherever you anchor, check the depths before retiring—parts of the bay are quite shoal.

④ **Billy Proctor's Museum.** Open 10:00 a.m. to 5:00 p.m. A trail, rough in places, leads from Pierre's at Echo Bay. By boat, if you leave Echo Bay and turn left toward Shoal Harbour, you can follow the shoreline around the peninsula and into a cozy bay with a home, small dock and marine railway haulout. This is where legendary Billy Proctor, who has logged, trapped and fished on the coast all of his 75-plus years, lives and has his museum.

Over a lifetime, Billy Proctor has collected a treasure of Chinese opium bottles, Chinese and Japanese beer bottles, engine plates, tools, arrowheads, bone fish hooks, a 1910 mimeograph machine from Minstrel Island, a crank telephone, a scale from the old Simoom Sound post office, and thousands of other artifacts of the coast's past.

Finally, in a structure he built from lumber he milled himself, the remarkable collection is displayed. Out the back door is a fish pond. Out the front door is another building he put up himself, housing a small gift shop and more treasures. Everything has a story, even the windows and doors. A few years ago, Billy built a replica of a hand logger's cabin, circa 1900. All the wood came from a single cedar log Bill found floating. No admission charge for the museum, but a box marked "donations," which go to salmon enhancement, is next to the door. Billy also has an excellent selection of books on the area, including his own.

If you want to call ahead, try *Ocean Dawn* on VHF 16. Hike the occasionally challenging trail from Pierre's, or the alternate trail from the schoolhouse, or tie up at the small dock. Meet Billy and go have a look. We think you'll be glad you did.

Pym Rocks. *Caution:* When crossing from the vicinity of Echo Bay bound for Simoom Sound, Shawl Bay, Greenway Sound and so forth, Pym Rocks, off the northeast tip of Baker Island, lie very close to your probable course. We know of one experienced skipper whose attention wandered briefly and he went right up on the rocks. We had a close call with the rocks ourselves, but steered clear in time. The rocks are farther out than they ought to be, and unless you're on autopilot they keep drawing the boat toward them. [*Hale*]

Burdwood Group. The Burdwood Group is a beautiful little clutch of islands, a gunkholer's dream. The group is dotted with rocks and reefs, and Chart 3515 (1:80,000) doesn't show a lot of detail. With a sharp lookout, however, small boats can maneuver among the islands on slow bell. Anchorages are scarce, deep and rocky, and recommended in settled weather only. Given the opportunity, the cruising boat should at least patrol through these islands.

Simoom Sound. Simoom Sound is a dogleg inlet, very scenic, but most of it is too deep for convenient anchoring. The best anchorages are in **O'Brien Bay** at the head of Simoom Sound, and in **McIntosh Bay** and the bays adjacent, along the north shore. You'll be in 48 to 60+ feet in O'Brien Bay, and 18 to 36 feet in the McIntosh Bay area. We spent a quiet night in McIntosh Bay. In an emergency you could find anchorage off the northeast corner of Louisa Islet, and near the mouth of a creek on the Wishart Peninsula side.

Hayle Bay. After a visit to Hayle Bay our log reads, "Too deep, too exposed." [*Hale*]

⑤ **Laura Bay.** Laura Bay is a pretty, popular anchorage. Anchorage is in two sections: one, with a challenging entry, is in the long neck that extends westward behind the outer anchorage; the other is the outer anchorage in the cove between Trivett Island and Broughton Island. The cove behind Trivett Island is lovely. A little islet is in the cove, but the chart incorrectly shows good water all around. A rock is in the narrow passage to the east of the islet. Entering the cove, leave the islet to starboard.

Caution: A major drying reef lies a short distance inside the entry to the neck that extends westward from the outer anchorage. This reef is shown on small scale Chart 3515, but without enough detail to indicate how to get around it. Our observations indicate that the reef extends from the south shore until somewhat past the middle of the channel. Approaching the reef, favor the north side at dead slow with an alert bow watch. (Don Douglass's chartlet in the popular *Exploring the South Coast of British Columbia, 2nd and 3rd ed.* shows a reef attached to the north shore at the mouth of this anchorage, but that reef does not exist. A corrected map is available for download on www.FineEdge.com in the updates section for the book).

The diagram here is courtesy of longtime Northwest cruising couple Fred and Mike Hayes, who felt their way in and anchored. Fred suggests a familiarization run by dinghy before taking the bigger boat in. Low tide would be best, when the rocks are visible.

Sir Edmund Bay. Sir Edmund Bay should

A MEAL IN THE WILD

One of the special memories from a recent trip to Echo Bay was an opportunity to explore the world of edible plants with Nikki van Schyndel of Echo Bay Eco Ventures. Nikki will take you deep into the forest to show you another world. Nikki grew up like any other girl, until one day she realized that there was a whole world around her that she really did not understand. There were trees and plants and wildlife. Many were edible and could sustain life. After this turn in her life she studied the outdoors and edible plants and wildlife for 10 years in the Bellingham area until she and a friend determined they could sustain themselves in the wild. They lived on a remote island near the San Juans for 18 months, building shelter, harvesting plants in the wild, and hunting wildlife. They even learned to create their own soaps and remedies, roughing it, but finding plenty in the world around them.

More recently, Nikki fell in love with the Broughton Archi-

pelago and Echo Bay. She built her own house there in 2007, on land near local legend Billy Proctor. During the summer she offers several programs for guests, including kids and families. She takes you out in her boat to a remote island, tying the boat up against barnacle-encrusted rocks. She bounds ashore with her guests in tow and within 10 feet she has found edible plants you probably always looked at and thought were weeds. She begins to collect the plants, talking all the time with an easy manner, instructing and exploring with you. She hands you leaves and tells you what they will taste like, and they do. She will point out the poisonous or bitter ones to avoid. She grabs a handful of berries, hands you some, and they are great. Pretty soon her basket is full and it is time to stop, as she calls it, "grocery shopping." The basket has Sea Plantain, Black Gooseberries, Wild Strawberries, Nodding Onions and Silverweed - a root that tastes like sweet potato. While boarding the boat she grabs a couple of pods of Bladder Rack kelp floating on the surface of the water and squeezes out the gel. You see this kelp all the time, even around the San Juan Islands. She points out that you can boil this and it makes a fantastic skin cream.

We grab other kelp and munch on it—pretty good. She has some kelp with her she has already dried, along with salmon she recently caught and smoked. Soon we are off to another island, bound by secrecy not to reveal its location. Nikki takes

us through a dense canopy of old growth forest on this hidden island. It is softly raining but we don't feel it down on the forest floor. Soon we break out into her remote "camp," a clearing under the forest canopy with a fire pit and several rustic structures she has built, suitable for an overnight or protection from the rain.

She chops up the ingredients we foraged and adds her salmon, dried kelp and brown rice in a cast iron skillet. Next, she sets about starting a fire with thin cedar bark tinder. Using a board with holes started with her knife and a strategically placed "V" cut, she uses a bow and a string to quickly spin the wood in the hole. While it took a few tries, a hot coal, less than the size of a fingernail, emerges from the sawdust generated by the drill. As the little coal gets more oxygen it begins to glow red hot. Soon she adds a little dry cedar tinder and within a

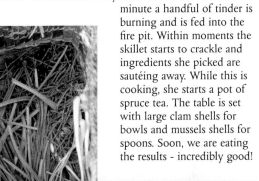

minute a handful of tinder is burning and is fed into the fire pit. Within moments the skillet starts to crackle and ingredients she picked are sautéing away. While this is cooking, she starts a pot of spruce tea. The table is set with large clam shells for bowls and mussels shells for spoons. Soon, we are eating the results - incredibly good!

And the spruce tea is equally good. All the while Nikki is telling us about all of the food around us and how easy it is to find natural ingredients for food and medicinal purposes.

Soon it is time to leave this incredible place in the forest and head back to Echo Bay. On the way back, racing through the islands in her boat, Nikki talks about how she loves to get to Vancouver or Seattle to shop or have a pedicure. She is a survivalist expert who can still enjoy the big city and a few creature comforts.

— *Mark Bunzel*

Laura Bay has room for several boats to anchor.

be entered east of Nicholls Island to avoid a rock west of the island. This rock is farther offshore than you might expect. Fish farms take up considerable space, but anchorage is possible in a cove at the northwest corner of the bay, and in another cove at the south corner.

The northwest cove is 48 to 60 feet deep until well in. Then it shoals to 30 feet before the shelf is reached. An all-chain anchor rode would yield a small enough swinging circle; boats with combination chain and rope may need to stern-tie to a tree. The cove is not very pretty and wouldn't be our first choice.

The southern cove has anchorage behind a charted drying rock. Some years ago, we visited near the bottom of a 7-foot low tide and failed to locate the rock. Others who have anchored there say the cove is a good spot, however. Until we know more we neither recommend nor discourage anchoring.

⑥ **Shawl Bay & Moore Bay.** Shawl Bay and Moore Bay are a short distance inside the entrance to Kingcome Inlet on the east side. Shawl Bay is a friendly stop with moorage and lots of amenities. Shawl Bay is connected to Moore Bay by a narrow canal that is reportedly navigable at half tide or better. Anchorage is behind Thief Island in the south part of Moore Bay, or in 36 feet close behind the 55-meter island near the north shore. Two other nooks along the east shore

might also be workable anchorages, depending on the weather. Along the north shore, near where a stream from Mt. Plumridge enters the bay, the Ministry of Forests installed a dinghy dock and 4 campsites with picnic tables and an outhouse.

⑥ **Shawl Bay Marina.** Simoom Sound P.O., Simoom Sound, BC V0P 1S0; (250) 483-4169; shawlbaymarina@gmail.com; www.shawlbaymarina.com. Monitors VHF 66A. Guest moorage along 1000 feet of dock, 15 & 30 amp power, internet terminal, Wi-Fi, pay telephone, washroom, showers, and laundry. Cash or check only, no credit cards. Shawl Bay connects with Moore Bay by a channel navigable at half tide or higher.

Shawl Bay's history goes back several generations. The float houses and rental cabins are old but brightly painted, and include free moorage for boats to 26 feet. Lorne and Shawn Brown have made the marina into one of the popular stops in the area.

Carol "The Bead Lady" Ellison has moved her gallery from Shawl Bay Marina to a nearby float home camp. Visitors can take the dinghy over, or tie the big boat alongside the front deck.

The covered community float has picnic tables and room for large groups. A "K-9 Yacht Club," with genuine lawn, accommodates visiting boats' dogs. The free daily pancake breakfasts for guests on the community

float are their signature event. Kenmore Air and NW Seaplanes provide service to the Seattle area.

Reid Bay. Reid Bay, on the western shore just inside the entrance to Kingcome Inlet, is open, deep, and uninteresting. It is no place to anchor. Just south of Reid Bay, however, an unnamed cove has possibilities. It is rather pretty and has good protection from westerlies. The chart indicates depths of approximately 6 fathoms throughout the bay, but our depth sounder showed 60 to 80 feet, except about 36 feet close to the head. If you go into this cove, give a wide berth to the point at the south entrance. We saw one uncharted rock just off the point; Chappell says there are two.

KINGCOME INLET

Kingcome Inlet extends 17 miles inland between high and beautiful mountains, terminating at the delta of the Kingcome River. The water is milky from glacier runoff and the surface band of water can be surprisingly fresh. Just beyond Petley Point at the head of the inlet, a magnificent new pictograph, a real work of art, is painted high on a rock cliff on the north shore. It is the work of Native artist Marianne Nicolson. The pictograph is brilliant red in color, and measures 28 feet wide and 38 feet high. The book, *Two Wolves at the Dawn of Time*, describes the project. The book's prose is a bit rich, but the story is interesting.

Kingcome Inlet's great depths and sheer rock walls allow virtually no suitable anchorages in the upper portions, except in settled weather.

Wakeman Sound. Wakeman Sound branches off Kingcome Inlet and extends about 7 miles north into the mountains. Although

At the head of Kingcome Inlet artist Marianne Nicolson painted this huge pictograph of a native copper.
Photo by James Hamilton.

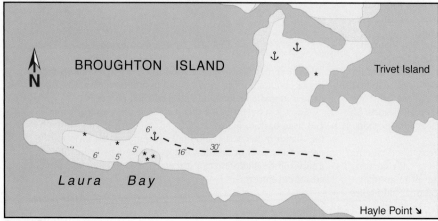

BROUGHTON ISLAND

Trivet Island

6' 6' 5' 5' 16' 30'

Laura Bay

Hayle Point ↘

Laura Bay

Stopford Bay is a peaceful anchorage with a little-developed marine park ashore.

it has no good anchorages, on a clear day the scenery is beautiful. Wakeman Sound is a center for logging activity. Watch for drift in the water.

Belleisle Sound. Belleisle Sound branches off Kingcome Inlet to the south. Entry is between two high green mountains — the kind that make you feel small. Belleisle Sound is beautiful and remote-feeling, but generally too deep for easy anchoring. Only a small area just inside the entrance is usable. Chappell and Sailing Directions warn that strong westerlies can blow through. On the day of our visit the surface was mirror-calm. The water was warm and people on another boat took a swim, right out in the middle. Way back in 1981 we spent the night in Belleisle Sound without difficulty, anchored and stern-tied to the little islet across from the entrance. [*Hale*]

SUTLEJ CHANNEL

Cypress Harbour. Cypress Harbour is a pretty spot, but a large fish farm occupies part of Miller Bay, and an old logging operation is in Berry Cove farther in. Good anchorage, removed from the fish farm and logging, is in lovely Stopford Bay, in the southeast corner of Cypress Harbour. Be sure to avoid the charted rock. We've had a report of a stretch of logging cable lying on the bottom a short distance before the rock is reached. Correspondent Gil Flanagan reports that a pleasant ¼-mile walk leads from the campground to a rock grotto and pond. The old road continues to a meadow about a mile farther along, and keeps going. Watch the depths in Stopford Bay; the

bottom grows increasingly shoal until it becomes drying flats. Recommended if you want a quiet, tucked-away anchorage.

Broughton Lagoon. "The entrance to Broughton Lagoon is a reversing tidal rapids. At Alert Bay high slack, water pours in through the narrow passage, trying to fill the lagoon. At Alert Bay low slack, water pours out at a ferocious rate. The calmest time to enter Broughton Lagoon is about 1 hour 15 minutes after Alert Bay high slack. For about 30 minutes around that time the rapids are at their least flow. Use the north entry channel only. The other channel often dries. This is a beautiful lagoon. It has plenty of width and depth for powerful dinghies. Not recommended for larger craft without local knowledge." [*Tom Taylor*]

Greenway Sound. Greenway Sound has several good anchorages and the now-closed Greenway Sound Marine Resort. The bay behind Broughton Point, at the east end of Carter Passage, is pretty.

Depending on conditions, anchorage is in a number of little nooks on both sides of Greenway Sound and behind Simpson Island, near the head of the sound. Leave Simpson Island to starboard when approaching the head of Greenway Sound. For exercise, Broughton Lakes Park, with access from a dinghy dock on the west shore of the bay due east of Greenway Point, received much work in recent years and has excellent hiking. The bay itself is a little deep for anchoring, so anchor elsewhere and take the dinghy over. Good trout fishing at the lakes, beautiful views.

PLANNING FOR HAPPY HOUR

The primary social gathering when cruising in the Broughtons is Happy Hour. This ritual typically begins around 4:00 to 5:00 p.m. and can extend well past dinnertime. I am told a movement underway at some marinas to move the start of happy hour to 3:00 p.m., or maybe sometime after lunch.

If a Happy Hour is not scheduled it could happen spontaneously when a group is hanging around the dock with nothing to do. All of a sudden someone gasps, "Hey, we ought to have a Happy Hour!" The drinks start flowing and food emerges.

During our early years of cruising the Inside Passage, we never seemed to have the right provisions for a proper Happy Hour contribution. We once showed up at an impromptu Happy Hour with a plate of store bought Oreo cookies (oh, the horror!), though the Oreos always disappeared. No one had briefed us on Happy Hour etiquette, and our cruising guides lacked this critical information.

With a few seasons under my belt I now begin preparing for Happy Hour at the beginning of the cruising season. In addition to making sure we have an adequate supply of oil, filters, and belts, I make sure we have plenty of items for whipping up a jaw-droppingly impressive Happy Hour hors d'oeuvre, preferably something that will stack or mound to 8-12 inches high or more.

What is my secret? A good supply of cream cheese and crackers!

At the beginning of the season I make a special trip to my local warehouse store for bricks of cream cheese. In order to carry sufficient quantities, I purchased and installed a dedicated refrigerator. I also buy a variety of crackers, boxes of them. I stock onion soup mix, different spice combinations, canned smoked salmon, canned crab, and even canned shrimp. Just in case I end up cruising to multiple locations with the same people, I also have a number of sweet mixes for cream cheese to change things up. Dried cherries, cran-raisins, dried apricots, and a few syrups to add color and flavor.

Now, cream cheese adaptations go over well, but I have noticed some captain and first mate teams look for extra points in the unspoken Happy Hour competition. They bring a dip with fresh caught crab (sometimes even artfully arranged in the shell) with chunks of crabmeat. Or, they show up with a bowl of fresh prawns caught that morning, still warm from a spiced boil. I really hate the guy who shows up with his salmon caught that morning and hot smoked on the dock next to his boat. How does he do this? He is one competitive Happy Hour cruiser!

Other Happy Hour recipes show up too. I long for the pea salad like my mother used to make, or the spicy coleslaw someone brings in an antique bowl. Sometimes someone will bring a simple green salad with fresh tomatoes and basil brought over from Vancouver Island that morning, garnished with pine nuts. Fresh brownies are a wonderful contribution, and yes, I might even sneak an Oreo cookie or two when one of the newbies joins the party on the dock.

Our best galley advice for cruising in the Broughtons? Be ready and go bold for Happy Hour. Mix it up, mound it high, and watch it fly. My fellow cruisers love the end result!

– Anonymous

The facilities at Sullivan Bay are complete, with a store, fuel dock, liquor agency, showers, laundry, and a restaurant.

Greenway Sound Marine Resort. The marina is closed and for sale. It is not clear what the future holds for the resort. The owners ask that cruisers not tie to the docks. See www.WaggonerGuide.com for updates.

Cartwright Bay. This bay is open to the wakes from passing traffic in Sutlej Channel, but offers easy anchorage at its inner end.

⑦ **Sullivan Bay Marina Resort.** Box 6000, Port McNeill, BC V0N 2R0; (604) 484-9193; sullivanbaymarina@gmail.com; www.sullivanbay.com. Monitors VHF 66A. Fuel and store open year-round, moorage seasonal. Services include gasoline, diesel, propane, 15 & 30 amp & 240-volt 50 & 100 amp power, water, washrooms, showers, large laundry, Wi-Fi. Accepts Visa, MasterCard and CDN cash.

Everything except the fuel storage tanks is on floats, in cozy float houses that date from a half-century ago. The docks are named like streets. During the season the fully-licensed Town Hall floating restaurant serves lunch and dinner. Check the website for scheduled dinner events such as prime rib night, turkey dinner, and international nights. Visitors often gather around 5:00 p.m. for drinks and appys at the "Happy Hour Square" float, next to the Town Hall restaurant. Golfers can try their hands on the re-installed 1-hole golf course. Depending on tide and wind, the target is 100 to 140 yards out.

Sullivan Bay is legendary among cruising boaters. It has ample moorage (3000 feet) for even the largest vessels, a well-stocked store with liquor agency, bait and tackle. Now, they also offer fresh-baked pastries, pies, and cinnamon buns. Last season they added an exercise room. This is a popular turnaround point for Broughtons cruisers. The annual July 4th celebration and parade on the docks is hugely popular. Reservations are highly recommended for this event.

Boatsitting available. Daily air service to Seattle and elsewhere makes attending to matters at home easy.

A community of handsome vacation float homes occupies a portion of the Sullivan Bay moorage. Improvements continue every year. Debbie Holt and Chris Scheveers are the attentive managers. Debbie and Chris's enthusiastic Yorkie, "Buddy," is the assistant manager.

Atkinson Island. Find anchorage in either end of the passage south of Atkinson Island.

GRAPPLER SOUND

Grappler Sound, north of Sutlej and Wells Passages, has several good anchorages.

Kinnaird Island. The bay in the northeast corner of the island is reported to be good in settled weather.

Hoy Bay. Some anchorage is possible in Hoy Bay, behind Hopetown Point, west of Hopetown Passage.

LOCAL KNOWLEDGE

DANGEROUS CURRENTS: If Hopetown Passage is attempted at all, it should be done cautiously, at high water slack in a shallow draft boat.

Hopetown Passage. The eastern entrance to Hopetown Passage is blocked by a drying reef. Strong currents and shallow depths make this a challenge. Explore by dinghy first.

⑧ **Carriden Bay.** Carriden Bay is located just inside Pandora Head at the entrance to Grappler Sound. The holding is reportedly good, if a little deep when away from the shoreline. One reader calls Carriden Bay "a special spot." As you look in, the spectacular knob of Pandora Head rises on the left, and when you're in, you see a beautiful vista of mountains out the mouth of the bay. This vista makes Carriden Bay exposed to east winds, however. It could be an uncomfortable anchorage in such winds.

⑨ **Claydon Bay.** This is a popular anchorage. Entering or leaving, favor the Morton Point side. Foul ground, shown on the chart, extends from the opposite side of the entry. In Claydon Bay you can pick the north arm or south arm, depending on which way the wind is blowing. An islet lies in the entry to the north arm. Leave this islet to starboard when entering. Note also that the drying reef surrounding the islet extends a considerable distance southeast of the islet. We are told aggressive flies can be a problem in Claydon Bay, especially in the north arm. Crabbing is reportedly good.

Woods Bay. Woods Bay is deep until close to the shore and exposed to westerly winds. This bay has been reported to be a good spot in settled weather, but we think other anchorages in the area are more appealing.

Embley Lagoon. Too shallow for anything but dinghies, but an interesting exploration.

Overflow Basin. Dinghies only.

⑩ **Turnbull Cove.** Turnbull Cove is a popular, large, and beautiful bay with lots of room and good anchoring in 30 to 50 feet. Avoid the areas in front of recent slides. The bottom there probably is foul with debris. Chappell warns that an easterly gale can turn the entire bay into a lee shore, so be aware if such winds are forecast.

The Ministry of Forests built a trail from Turnbull Cove over a mountain to Huaskin Lake. A large float for swimming, a picnic table, a tent platform, and a fire pit are at the lake. It's really nice. The trail goes straight up and straight back down, and it's muddy in places. Steps and even a handrail are on the lake side. They make a big difference. The lake is scenic and looks as if it goes forever.

Approach: Currents of 2+ knots flow through the channel leading to the entry. The currents are not hazardous, but they can come as a surprise. The west side of the entry to Turnbull Cove is charted as clear, but lots of kelp is growing there. A mid-channel course is recommended.

Nepah Lagoon. The adventuresome might want to try Roaringhole Rapids into Nepah Lagoon. Transit, by dinghy with an outboard motor, should be attempted only at high water slack, which lasts 5 minutes and occurs 2 hours after the corresponding high water at Alert Bay. The channel is only 3 feet deep at low water. Nepah Lagoon doesn't appear to have any useable anchorages, except possibly a little notch about a mile from the rapids.

MACKENZIE SOUND

Kenneth Passage. Kenneth Passage has sufficient depths at all stages of tide, being careful of a covered rock off Jessie Point. Currents can be quite strong and whirlpools sometimes appear. Slack water entry is advised, especially on spring tides. The best advice is to take a look and decide if conditions suit you and your boat.

Steamboat Bay. Steamboat Bay is a good anchorage, with room for a few boats. The bay shoals to drying flats all around. Watch for the drying rocks along the east shore at the entrance.

Burly Bay. Burly Bay is a good anchorage, mud bottom, but the muddy shoreline makes going ashore difficult. The little notch just to the west of Blair Island is better. Chappell (*Cruising Beyond Desolation Sound*) was not excited about Burly Bay. Bob and Marilynn Hale noted in their log, "Spectacular scenery,

Ansel Adams photograph stuff, with rock wall on eastern shore falling straight into the sea." We've heard reports of grizzly bears on shore at Burly Bay. Guidebooks often are influenced by who visited, and what kind of day was had.

Little Nimmo Bay. Little Nimmo Bay is a pretty anchorage, and the rock-strewn entrance is not as difficult as it appears on the chart—except on a low tide. The Nimmo Bay Wilderness Resort is located there. Anchor in 24 feet, mud bottom. Several small waterfalls tumble through the forest. Grizzly bears are reported to be in the area. Make lots of noise if you go ashore. With care it is possible to go through to Nimmo Bay, also a good anchorage.

⑪ **Nimmo Bay Wilderness Resort.** Box 696, Port McNeill, BC V0N 2R0; (800) 837-4354; (250) 956-4000; heli@nimmobay.com; www.nimmobay.com. Monitors VHF 10. If you're looking for a high-end experience in the Broughtons, this is it. They have hosted presidents and prime ministers, movie and sports stars, captains of industry, and appeared in the popular TV show *Boston Legal.* Their hospitality is unsurpassed. The main draw for their guests are helicopter trips into the mountains for guided fishing, enjoying the scenery, or even a wedding on a glacier.

Meals are unique, with everything, including the crackers, made in their own kitchen. Dinners are pricey but all-inclusive, beginning with appetizers down on the dock followed by the main meal and dessert in the beautiful dining room, then drinks by the fireplace back on the dock. Visiting boats are welcome—with reservations.

This is the kind of place where you go to treat your significant other, or crew, at the mid-point of a summer cruise. Inquire to see if a massage is available or if you can try the hot tubs next to the waterfall. Heli-tours or wilderness excursion day trips with gourmet picnic lunches are also available with reservations.

Dock space is limited, no power. Water is available at the end of two of the floathouses. Larger vessels can anchor in Mackenzie Sound and take the tender to the resort's

Nimmo Bay Wilderness Resort is the most luxurious destination in the Broughtons.

dock. Floatplane service available from Kenmore Air, NW Seaplanes, and Pacific Coastal Airlines.

DRURY INLET

Drury Inlet is surrounded by logging-scarred low hills that become lower near the head of the inlet. Drury Inlet is much less visited than other waters in the area. The entrance, off Wells Passage, is clearly marked on the charts, as is Stuart Narrows, 1.5 miles inside the entrance. Good anchorage is in two arms of Richmond Bay (choose the one that protects from the prevailing wind); near Stuart Narrows; in Jennis Bay; and in Sutherland Bay, at the head of Drury Inlet. Approach Sutherland Bay around the north side of the Muirhead Islands, after which the bay is open and protected.

We anchored for the night in the southwestern cove of Richmond Bay, near Stuart Narrows, and found it superb. The cove was protected, tranquil and private. Our notes read, "Best if enjoyed without other boats." [*Hale*]

Our sister publication, *Cruising the Secret Coast*, by Jennifer and James Hamilton, devotes an entire chapter to Drury Inlet and Actaeon Sound, with details about interesting hikes.

Helen Bay. Helen Bay is just east of Stuart Narrows. It is reportedly a good anchorage. Halibut are said to be caught in the area.

Stuart Narrows. Currents in Stuart Narrows run to a maximum of 7 knots, although on small tides they are much less. Times of slack are listed under Alert Bay, Secondary Current Stations, in the Tide & Current Tables, Vol. 6 and Ports and Passes. The skipper of a tug towing a log boom through Stuart Narrows advised us that he times slack for 10 minutes after both high and low tides at Alert Bay, which is in line with the tide and current tables information. The only hazard is Welde Rock. You will most likely see the kelp. Get way over to the south side of the channel. The current flows faster south of Welde rock, although passage can be made north of the rock as well (we haven't tried). Leche Islet should be passed to the north. A study of the chart shows a rock patch to the south.

Note that Stuart Narrows is well inside the mouth of Drury Inlet.

⑫ **Jennis Bay.** Jennis Bay is the site of a logging camp and booming ground, with good anchorage in the cove north of Jennis Bay Marina.

⑫ **Jennis Bay Marina.** P.O. Box 456, Port McNeill, BC V0N 2R0; (250) 230-3076; info@jennisbay.com; www.jennisbay.com. Monitors VHF 66A. Moorage available all year, with other services during the boating season. Free Wi-Fi, cell phone service with a signal booster in the cookhouse. No power. Cabin rentals, washroom and shower, kayaking, mountain biking, Huaskin Lake tours, and miles of logging roads and trails for exploring. A small store sells gift items. Dock space for 8 to 12 boats, others anchor off the docks in the protected bay.

Excellent hospitality. Kim and Kent, as your hosts, continue the tradition of this family-style resort. Check their website or Facebook page for the latest information and event schedule for the season. Several fascinating videos illustrating history in the Broughtons are in the cookhouse. Served by Pacific Coastal Airlines, NW Seaplanes, and Vancouver Island Air.

Enter Jennis Bay around either end of Hooper Island. Keep to a mid-channel course to avoid rocks along the shores. Leave the floating log breakwater to starboard to enter the marina.

Davis Bay. Davis Bay looks inviting on the chart, but is not very pretty and is open to westerlies. Enter on the south side of Davis Islet, strongly favoring the Davis Islet shore.

Jennis Bay is off Drury Inlet. It's a quiet, friendly place to stop.

Muirhead Islands. The Muirhead Islands, near the head of Drury Inlet, are rock-strewn but beautiful. They invite exploring in a small boat or kayak. The cove on the northeast side, behind the dot island, is a suitable anchorage, as is the cove on the south side, immediately west of the 59-meter island.

Actress Passage and Actaeon Sound. Actress Passage, connecting Drury Inlet with Actaeon Sound, is rock- and reef-strewn, narrow, and twisting. Careful navigation is required. There are two theories: some feel high water slack is best to have more water; others feel low water slack is best to allow a better chance of seeing the rocks and hazards in the water. One approach is to enter Actress Passage between Dove Island and the mainland to the north, avoiding the charted rock. Tugs and tows and other commercial traffic, however, use the shorter channel east of Dove Island, splitting rocks marked with sticks at the entrance to Drury Inlet.

Once into Actress Passage, the overriding navigation problem is the area between Skene Point and Bond Peninsula, where a careful S-shaped course around the rocks is required, hence the local name Snake Passage. Another choice is to follow Chappell's suggestion of crossing from Skene Point to Bond Peninsula, and working past the charted hazards around the corner.

In our sister publication, *Cruising the Secret Coast*, the Hamiltons have extensively explored this area and present specific directions for this passage and the area.

Tracey Harbour. Tracey Harbour indents North Broughton Island from Wells Passage. It is pretty and protected. No anchorage is viable, however, until near the head of the bay. There, you can find anchorage on mud bottom in Napier Bay, or on rocky bottom in the bay behind Carter Point. You're apt to find log booms in Napier Bay, and leftover buildings from an old logging operation. Anchor near the head of the cove behind Carter Point. The cove is beautiful and cozy-feeling, but the bottom feels like a thin layer of mud on top of rock and it wouldn't take much to drag the anchor.

Carter Passage. Since Carter Passage is blocked in the middle by a boulder-strewn drying shoal it is actually two harbors, one off Wells Passage and one off Greenway Sound, with good anchorages in each end. The west entrance has tidal currents to 7 knots, and should be taken at or near high water slack. A reef extends from the south shore, so keep north of mid-channel. Two pleasant anchorages are in this west end.

The east entrance, off Greenway Sound, is somewhat easier, in terms both of tidal currents and obstructions. John Chappell's *Cruising Beyond Desolation Sound* describes the explorations needed to safely transit the drying shoal between the two ends of Carter Passage.

Dickson Island. Dickson Island is near the mouth of Wells Passage. The small anchorage on the east end of the island provides good protection from seas, but the low land lets westerly winds blow across the bay. Two other bays along the west side of Broughton Island are too exposed to westerly weather to be good anchorages.

Polkinghorne Islands. The Polkinghorne Islands are outside the mouth of Wells Passage. A channel among the islands is fun, particularly on the nice day. The anchoring bottom we've found is not too secure, so an overnight stay is not recommended. [*Kincaid*]

FIFE SOUND

Cullen Harbour. Cullen Harbour is on the south side of Broughton Island, at the entrance to Booker Lagoon. It is an excellent anchorage, with plenty of room for everyone. You might rock a little if the wind is blowing from northwest. The bottom is mud, and depths range from 24 to 50 feet.

LOCAL KNOWLEDGE

UNCHARTED ROCK: Correspondents John and Lorraine Littlewood did some independent chart surveying in Booker Lagoon, and found a ledge of rock not shown on the charts (see Booker Lagoon map). Its presence was confirmed by two bent props, one bent skeg and one bent rudder— "a real boat-eater," according to John.

Booker Lagoon. The entrance to Booker Lagoon is from Cullen Harbour through **Booker Passage**, a narrow channel bounded by reefs on both sides. The channel is about 50 feet wide and has ample depths. Best to transit at slack water. Opinions vary about the time of slack water. Usually it's somewhere between 30 and 60 minutes after the high or low water at Alert Bay, give or take a little. On big tides the duration of slack water is about 10 minutes, and the stream can build to 7 knots or more. The aquaculture pens that once occupied the four arms of Booker Lagoon have been removed, so it's a good anchorage again on a sticky mud bottom. Don't enter Booker Lagoon through the passage on the west side of Long Island. The passage is shoal and choked with kelp.

Once in Booker Lagoon you'll be in a secluded coastal paradise. The lagoon is quite large, and deep in the middle. Explore around, then anchor in one of the arms— away, we suggest, from other anchored boats. It's that kind of place.

Deep Harbour. In the past the inner part of Deep Harbour was blocked by boomed logs and the center of the bay taken over by aquaculture pens. It is now clear and there are little nooks around the edges with room for one boat.

BROUGHTON ARCHIPELAGO

Much of the Broughton Archipelago is now a marine park. Some of the islands are private, however, so use discretion when going ashore.

Our journal, written while at anchor after a day of exploring, reads, "A marvelous group of islands and passages, but few good anchorages. We navigated around Insect Island and through Indian Passage. Very pretty—many white shell beaches. Rocks marked by kelp. A different appearance from Kingcome Inlet or Simoom Sound. The trees are shorter and

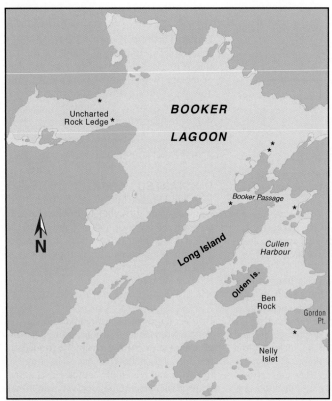

Booker Lagoon

more windblown. The west wind is noticeably colder than farther east. Fog lay at the mouth of Fife Sound; a few wisps blew up toward us. Great kayaking, gunkholing country." [*Hale*]

This large group of islands west of Gilford Island does have anchorages, including Sunday Harbour, Monday Anchorage, and Joe Cove. The area is dotted with rocks, reefs, and little islands, which in total provide good protection, but also call for careful navigation.

M. Wylie Blanchet (*The Curve of Time*) was blown out of Sunday Harbour, and we've heard mixed reports about Monday Anchorage. Chappell wasn't impressed with either one. Joe Cove is considered to be a good anchorage. Chart 3546 (1:40:000) should be studied carefully before going into these waters, and kept close at hand while there. Currents run strongly at times through the various passages.

⑬ **Sunday Harbour.** Sunday Harbour is formed by Crib Island and Angular Island, north of the mouth of Arrow Passage. The bay is very pretty, although exposed to westerly winds. We would anchor in the middle for a relaxing lunch on a quiet day. The little cove in the northeast corner looks attractive but is full of rocks.

⑭ **Monday Anchorage.** Monday Anchorage is formed by Tracey Island and Mars Island, north of Arrow Passage. It is large and fairly open. Chappell says you can anchor behind the two small islands off the north shore of the bay. When the Hales visited they anchored for lunch fairly deep in the first large cove on the south shore. The anchor bit easily in 40 feet, and they had good protection from the westerly that was blowing.

⑮ **Joe Cove.** Joe Cove, perfectly protected and private feeling, indents the south side of Eden Island. The best anchorage is near the head. A little thumb of water extends southeast near the head of the cove, but access is partially blocked by several rocks. It is possible, however, to feel your way in by hugging the shore to starboard as you enter. The passage is narrow but clear. Tie to the float in the cove.

Lady Boot Cove. Lady Boot Cove is what Douglass calls this nice little anchorage and we'll stick with that name. The cove indents the northeast corner of Eden Island, with Fly Island directly off the mouth. As the chart shows, the southern indent is shoal and foul with a drying reef. The northern indent is beauti-

fully protected with room for a couple of boats.

RETREAT PASSAGE

Seabreeze Cove. This otherwise unnamed lovely little anchorage in Gilford Island was suggested by Correspondents James and Jennifer Hamilton. It lies behind the 70-meter island due east of Seabreeze Island, at the western entrance to Retreat Passage. Their report: "We anchored in 18 feet south of the 70-meter island and held very well in sticky mud. Some southwest winds did blow through, but nothing major. The water was barely rippled. Caught three big Dungeness crabs overnight."

Be aware that the bottom shoals rapidly once past the 70-meter island.

Bootleg Bay. South of False Cove, a thumb-like island protrudes northwest from Gilford Island. The cove south of that island has about 30 feet at the entrance, shoaling gently toward the head. No name appears on the charts. According to Chappell it is known locally as Bootleg Bay. When we visited in 2012, a wrecked fish boat was at the head of the bay.

⑯ **Waddington Bay.** Waddington Bay indents the northeast corner of Bonwick Island. The bay is popular, with room for several boats. It has good holding in 18 to 30 feet. The approach is off the little pass that connects Retreat Passage and Arrow Passage. Turn to leave the 46-meter island to starboard, and go on in. Be sure you have the right island; they all look alike. The approach is wide enough, but rocks are all around and careful piloting is called for. Know your position at all times. Waddington Bay shoals at the head. The wind direction and your depth sounder will tell you where to put the hook down. Wind will get in when the westerly is blowing, but there's no fetch for seas to build. This is a good anchorage.

Grebe Cove. Grebe Cove indents the east side of Bonwick Island off Retreat Passage. The cove shallows to 40 to 50 feet about 200 yards from the head, and 30 to 40 feet near the head, mud bottom, with good depths side to side. A saddle in the hills

at the head might let westerlies in, but the seas would have no fetch. On one visit, a couple in a 20-foot pocket cruiser called out, "Great anchorage! The otters will entertain you!"

Carrie Bay. Carrie Bay indents Bonwick Island across Retreat Passage from Health Bay. The head of the bay is pretty and protected from westerly winds. The bottom shoals rapidly from 40 to 50 feet in much of the bay to around 20 feet at the head.

Health Bay. The Health Bay Indian Reserve, with dock, fronts on Retreat Passage. Health Bay itself is strewn with rocks. Anchorage is best fairly close to the head of the bay, short of the first of the rocks.

BLACKFISH ARCHIPELAGO

The name Blackfish Archipelago does not appear on the charts or in Sailing Directions, but generally refers to the myriad islands and their waterways adjacent to Blackfish Sound.

Goat Island Anchorage. You'll find a good anchorage in the cove that lies off the southeast corner of Crease Island.

Clarification: Two islands make up this cove, a larger island to the north and a much smaller one to the south. Chart 3546 seems to label the smaller, southern island as Goat Island, but until now we—and Chappell and Douglass—have meant the larger island to be Goat Island. In their book, Vipond and Kelly label the smaller, southern, island as Goat Island. A careful study of the chart shows Vipond and Kelly to be correct. Whatever the islands are named, the entry suggestions are unchanged.

Enter Goat Island Anchorage between Crease Island and the larger, northern island, leaving the northern island to port. The chart makes the preferred entry clear. Anchor in 12 to 18 feet on a sometimes rocky bottom, wherever it looks good. The cove is excellent for crabbing. Weed on the bottom might foul some anchors. A reader reported that their anchor found a large diameter line on the bottom, probably left over from earlier logging. Where there's one cable there might be more. It would be a good idea to rig a trip line to the crown of the anchor.

The view to the southeast is very pretty.

Leone Island. A bay lies between Leone Island and Madrona Island. Contributing Editor Tom Kincaid has anchored there and recommends it. "'Friends, with extensive experience, also recommend it. We, however, tried to set our anchor four times over a 2-day period, and failed each time. Twice the anchor did not penetrate large, leafy kelp. Once it refused to set in thin sand and reedy weed. On the last try the anchor seemed to set, but it dragged with only moderate power in reverse." [*Hale*]

Mound Island. The cove behind Mound Island is a good anchorage, paying mind to the rocks (shown on the chart) that line the shores. Tom Sewid at Village Island told us that 14 depressions in the earth were once the sites of big houses. Correspondent Pat Shera reports that the depressions are obvious, just inland from the beach at the western end of the island.

⑰ **New Vancouver.** New Vancouver is on the north side of Harbledown Island, a short distance west of Dead Point, the entrance to Beware Passage. The location is marked IR on the chart, for Indian Reserve. It is the ancestral home of the Da'naxda'xw Native band, who were moved off the land in the 1960s. Now the band is resettling the village. A concrete dock has been installed, along with 30 amp power, washrooms, and showers. Call the band office in Alert Bay, (250) 974-2703, for more information.

Farewell Harbour. You'll find good anchorage in Farewell Harbour close to the Berry Island side. The **Farewell Harbour Yacht Club**, shown on the chart, is actually a luxury fishing resort and doesn't cater to visiting yachties.

Chiefs Bathtub. The Chiefs Bathtub is located on Village Channel on the north side of Berry Island, at approximately 50°36.45'N /126°39.56'W (NAD 83). It's a sculpted-out depression in a rock cliff, a little below

The panoramic view to seaward from Village Island is stunning.

the high water line. According to Tom Sewid, up-and-coming chiefs had to sit in this bathtub four times a day for four days as the cold waters of the tide washed in. If you take the dinghy to see the tub more closely, don't touch the pictographs on the rock. Skin oils attack the paint.

⑱ **Village Island.** (250) 668-9359; tom. sewid@gmail.com; www.aboriginaladventurescanada.com. A site on the western shore of Village Island is often known incorrectly as Mamalilaculla. This site is an abandoned, collapsing Indian village. Anchor in the bay north of the village (be sure of your set). Mooring buoys have been installed at Village Island, and in Farewell Harbour on the east side of Compton Island.

Many years ago Tom Sewid was the watchman for the Mamalilaculla Qwe'Qwa'Sot'Em' First Nations and he conducted interpretive tours at the village site. After a 4-year leave of absence Tom is back leading tours at Village Island.

Accommodations are available, as well as traditional feasts.

First Nations Watchmen are ready to assist 24 hours a day during the cruising season. Contact the watchmen on VHF 79A.

A fee is charged for entering the Indian Reserve on Village Island to see the old fallen totem pole and big house remains. All fees go towards the cleanup of village site and support for the Native Watchmen.

Native Anchorage. Native Anchorage is located at the southwest corner of Village Island. It's no place to be in a southerly storm, but in all other winds it's a fine anchorage. Put the hook down in 18 to 24 feet. Excellent mud bottom.

Canoe Passage. Canoe Passage runs roughly east-west between Turnour Island and Village Island. The waterway dries at low tide, but can be transited at higher tides, depending on a vessel's draft.

CLIO CHANNEL

Cracroft Inlet. Cracroft Inlet is on the south side of Dorman and Farquharson Islands. While we have not anchored there (yet), it is reportedly well protected, with good holding bottom on either side of the large charted rock. Lagoon Cove, on the other side of Farquharson Island, can be reached by taking the dinghy around the east end of the island. The passage is shallow, so check the tides and be sure of your depths. Crabbing is reportedly good.

Waddington Bay is peaceful and well protected.

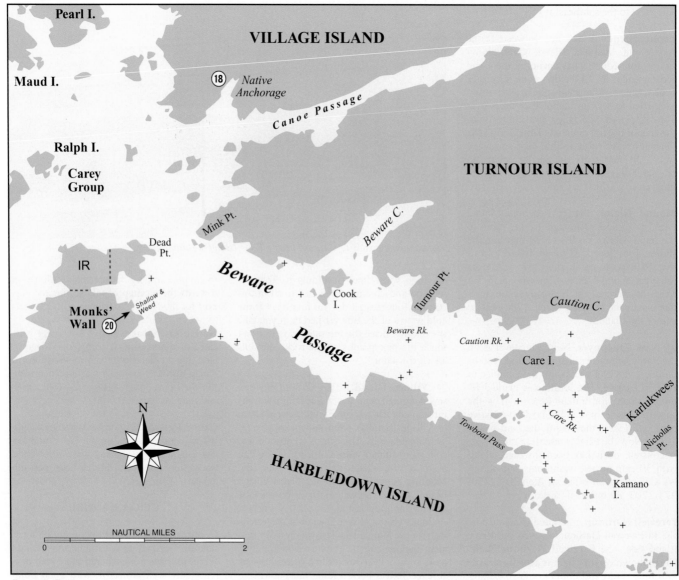

Beware Passage

Bones Bay. The entire bay is fairly open, although you may find temporary anchorage behind the islets along the south shore. Watch for rocks around the islets. A floating fishing lodge is moored behind these islets.

Bend Island. Bend Island is connected to West Cracroft Island by a drying ledge, but good anchorage is in either end. Friends have anchored in the tiny nook just east of Bend Island, with a stern-tie to shore.

⑲ Potts Lagoon. The outer bay, hidden behind the 119-meter headland, is a good anchorage. Most boats, however, pass on the west side of the 41-meter island to anchor in 18 to 24 feet in the protected, scenic and spacious inner bay. Several float homes are moored in the inner bay. Even with the presence of float homes, this is a nice anchorage.

Klaoitsis Island. Anchorage might be found in the bay northwest of Klaoitsis Island and in a notch on the south shore of Jamieson Island. Currents can run through these an-chorages. For most boats, Potts Lagoon is a better choice.

Beware Passage. If you read the place names from Chart 3545 (1:40,000), Beware Passage will scare you to death. The first fright is the name itself: Beware Passage. Then Care Rock, Caution Rock, Caution Cove, Beware Rock, Beware Cove, and Dead Point. Beware Passage is aptly named, but you can get through safely.

Sailing Directions recommends that lacking local knowledge, Beware Passage be transited at low water, when the rocks are visible. Assuming a passage from east to west, Chappell (*Cruising Beyond Desolation Sound*) mentions a route across the abandoned Turnour (pronounced "Turner") Island village of Karlukwees, somehow avoiding all the rocks, and skirting the shore of Care Island, but he doesn't provide details. Chappell's second alternative is to go through "Towboat Pass."

The Care Island Route, provided by the late Trev Roote and his wife Susie, longtime coast cruisers, is shown on the Beware Pas-sage reference map. We have run it and it worked very well. We did have to pay attention to our course, however. Repeat visits will remove much of the anxiety, and this is the way we plan to go in the future.

The Towboat Pass route is courtesy of a couple from Nanaimo with nearly 20 summers' experience cruising these waters, and requires a little instruction. It may be helpful to have Chart 3545 at hand, to identify place names as the instructions proceed. This route is also shown on the reference map.

Towboat Pass route, east to west: From the east, enter Beware Passage close by Nicholas Point on Turnour Island, and continue until Karlukwees is abeam to starboard. You'll recognize Karlukwees by its abandoned buildings, decaying pier, and white shell beach.

When Karlukwees is abeam, turn to a course of 250° magnetic. This course will take you across Beware Passage to the Harbledown Island side, and south of a pair of small islands that lie just offshore from Harbledown Island.

Towboat Pass, marked 3 meters, runs

between these small islands and Harbledown Island. The pass has kelp in it, but is reported safe at all tides. Go close to Harbledown Island, turn northward, and proceed through the pass. We go through at dead slow bell, one set of eyes on the water, another set on the depth sounder. Kelp and all, we have no problems.

Exit Towboat Pass on a course of approximately 292° magnetic. While underway, watch astern to starboard until you see three islands apparently spread across the water behind you. Turn to port, to run on a line that connects the middle island of these three islands with Dead Point, at the far end of Beware Passage. At the time of your turn, the middle island should be a little less than 0.5 mile away. Assuming good visibility, Dead Point, now off your bow, will be easily identifiable on a course of approximately 270° magnetic. This course will put you a little close to a rock that lies of Harbledown Island, but you should clear it easily.

We drew the entire course on the chart before entering Beware Passage, marking all headings and agreeing on our plan. It went so smoothly that when we exited Beware Passage we wondered what all the fuss was about.

We recommend the Towboat Pass route. From the east, enter Beware Passage close by Nicholas Point on Turnour Island, and continue until Karlukwees is abeam to starboard. You'll recognize Karlukwees by its abandoned buildings, decaying pier, and white shell beach.

Caution Cove. Caution Cove is open to prevailing winds, but the bottom is good. Caution Rock, drying 4 feet, is in the center of the entrance. The rock is clearly shown on Chart 3545, as are the rocks just off the drying flats at the head of the cove. An extensive logging operation may be operating in the cove. Beware Cove might be a better option.

Beware Cove. Beware Cove is a good anchorage, very pretty, with protection from westerlies but not southeasterlies. Easiest entry is to the west of Cook Island, leaving Cook Island to starboard.

20 Monks' Wall. The ruins of a massive and mysterious rock wall and archway lie hidden just inside the treeline on Harbledown Is-

This 1910 photo at Harbledown Island shows William Galley, a teacher named Miss Monro, and added to the photo, Mary Anne Galley. The child at left is not identified.

land, at the north end of Beware Passage. Chinese Buddhist monks are reported to have been on the island a century ago, and some have speculated that they are the ones who built the wall. It makes an intriguing story: far from their homeland, devout Buddhists in their robes carrying and positioning huge stones for what?—a temple, perhaps.

The real story is not as intriguing, but it is at least as inspiring. The wall was not built by monks. It was built by white settlers, William Herbert Galley and his wife Mary Anne Galley. In the late 1800s Galley acquired 160 acres on Harbledown Island and built a trading post there. According to Galley's great-granddaughter, great-grandfather Galley married Mary Anne Wharton in 1889. Together they cleared the land, planted 125 fruit trees, and kept cows, pigs, chickens, ducks and sheep. The homestead was defined by carefully-built rock walls, straight and solid. The archway marked the entrance to the trading post. It is said that Mary Anne Galley carried rocks in her apron. Those rocks are big. Some apron. Some great-grandmother.

The Monks' Wall is located on the west side of Beware Passage, a short distance south of Dead Point. It is on the point of land separating two large, shallow bays, at lat. 50°35.40'N. (This latitude was measured on the chart, and is approximate.) Anchor in the bay north of that point of land and row the dinghy in. The bottom shoals when approaching the cove, and is dense with weed that could foul a propeller. Working from north

to south, identify the third little nook on the point of land. It's a definite indent. At the treeline, a tangled rootball from a blown-down tree marks the entry. The ruins of the magnificent archway are just inside.

If you hike through the woods around the area you'll find more walls. They aren't as dramatic as the archway, but taken together they're impressive. All built by hand. Straight and true. Enveloped now by the relentless forest.

Although Monks' Wall is a misnomer, it looks like the name will stick. Our thanks to Galley great-granddaughter Kathy Young, for her historical background, and to Billy Proctor, for his quickly-drawn map that showed us exactly where to find the site.

Request: The wall and the lesser walls in the surrounding forest are a treasure. Please, no souvenirs, no destruction, no litter.

Note: We've heard the top of the arch has fallen.

Dead Point. The unnamed cove just inside Dead Point offers protection from westerlies.

CURRENT DIRECTIONS: Current in Baronet Passage floods west and ebbs east, the opposite of the flows in Johnstone Strait a mile south and in Knight Inlet 4 miles north.

Baronet Passage. Baronet Passage is very pretty. It's partially obstructed by Walden Island, with the preferred passage in the

Eileen Galley, age 22, sits with her 7-year-old brother Sykes in front of the store in this 1913 photo. Note the chicken hanging from a wire to keep it away from cougars.

deeper channel to the north of Walden Island. This is a well used passage for boats heading to and from Blackfish Sound.

21 Growler Cove. Growler Cove, on the west end of West Cracroft Island, is an excellent anchorage, with ample room and good protection from both westerlies and easterlies. It is popular with commercial fishermen who work Johnstone Strait and Queen Charlotte Strait. During the prime commercial fishing months of July and August, Growler Cove is apt to be full of commercial boats, with little room for pleasure craft.

If you're approaching from the east, enter along West Cracroft Island, favoring the island as you work your way in. We saw an extensive kelp bed, not shown on the chart, off the point that leads to the entrance. We would keep clear of that kelp. If you're approaching from the west, enter between Sophia Islands and Baron Reef, both shown on the chart. Inside, keep a mid-channel course, favoring the north side to avoid a charted rock about halfway in. Good anchoring near the head in 18 to 24 feet.

Hanson Island. The rugged and beautiful north shore of Hanson Island is indented by a number of bays and coves that are a gunkholer's paradise. The most popular anchorage is in Double Bay, also the location of the Double Bay Resort, a private fishing lodge. Enter only along the west side of the bay. The bay behind Sprout Islet, to the east of Double Bay, is also a good anchorage.

CHAPTER 13

NORTH VANCOUVER ISLAND

WEYNTON PASSAGE
Bauza Cove • Telegraph Cove • Beaver Cove • Pearse Islands

BROUGHTON STRAIT
Port McNeill • Alert Bay • Sointula

QUEEN CHARLOTTE STRAIT
Beaver Harbour • Port Hardy • Bear Cove

N orth Island refers to the eastern side of Vancouver Island from Sayward (Kelsey Bay) to the top of the island. North Island is served by Highway 19 and is the center of commerce for both sides of the Inside Passage in this area. Port McNeill and Port Hardy are the principal towns. Alert Bay on Cormorant Island and Sointula on Malcolm Island also have facilities.

Boats cruising the Broughtons or continuing farther up the coast usually stop at one or more of the North Island towns for supplies, repairs, fuel, and water. For this reason, the North Island chapter opens with comments about crossing Queen Charlotte Strait.

Kelsey Bay and Robson Bight are covered in the Johnstone Strait section.

Hospitals: Port McNeill and Port Hardy have fully-staffed hospitals. The Cormorant Island Community Health Centre is located at Alert Bay in a new building located behind the U'mista Cultural Centre. It has a doctor on duty every day.

Queen Charlotte Strait. Queen Charlotte Strait is about 15 miles wide. The prevailing winds are from the northwest in the summer and the southeast in the winter. In the summer, morning is usually the best time to cross.

Typically, by late morning or early afternoon a sea breeze will begin, and by mid-afternoon it can increase to 30 knots with very rough seas. The sea breeze usually quiets at sundown.

Tom Taylor, owner of the now-closed Greenway Sound Marina Resort, has crossed the strait between Wells Passage and Port McNeill hundreds of times, and tells us that in good weather he could go (in a fast boat) as late as 2:00 p.m. Any given day can go against the norm, however. Skippers should treat Queen Charlotte Strait with great respect.

Weather information: The wind report from Herbert Island, in the Buckle Group, can be a good reference for approaching northwesterly winds. If it's not blowing at Herbert Island, there's a good chance Queen Charlotte Strait will be okay. If Herbert Island is windy, however, Queen Charlotte Strait probably will be next.

Bauza Cove. Bauza Cove is an attractive but deep bay, with good protection from westerly swells. It is open to the wakes of passing traffic in Johnstone Strait.

Totems in the 'Namgis burial ground at the south end of Alert Bay.

① **Telegraph Cove.** Telegraph Cove is postcard picturesque. The boardwalk is lined with old, brightly painted buildings on pilings, including a good restaurant and pub. The place is the embodiment of the word "charming." The old homes are now cottages for resort guests. A whale museum is located at the end of the docks and a whale watch excursion boat leaves several times each day. Tide Rip Grizzly Tours takes groups up Knight Inlet by fast boat to see grizzly bears. Charter fishing boats head out to fish for salmon and a kayak operator takes groups out to the islands and Johnstone Strait.

The Telegraph Cove Resort moorage is restricted to resort guests only, but has some room for larger boats at the dock near the entrance. To port as you enter, Telegraph Cove Marina has some side-tie guest moorage for larger boats, and a considerable number of guest slips for boats to 30 feet.

Be advised, though, that Telegraph Cove isn't very big. There's room to maneuver, but "spacious" is not the word that comes to mind.

① **Telegraph Cove Marina.** Box 1-8, 1642B, Telegraph Cove, BC V0N 3J0; (250) 928-3163; reservations@telegraphcove.ca; www.telegraphcove.ca. Monitors VHF 66A. Open all year, 130 slips to 30 feet, limited side-tie moorage to 65 feet. Some slips have 15, 30 & 50 amp power and potable water. Concrete launch ramp. Showers, laundry, and washrooms close by. Reservations requested.

It's an easily walk around the cove to amenities and tour operators, such as whale watching, grizzly bear viewing, and kayak tours. Rooms for rent are adjacent to the marina. The Seahorse Cafe has good food and a great view over the marina.

① **Telegraph Cove Resort.** Box 1, Telegraph Cove, BC V0N 3J0; (250) 928-3131; (800) 200-4665; tcrltd@island.net; www.telegraphcoveresort.com. Open seasonally with gasoline, launch ramp, restaurant, pub, general store with gifts and fishing tackle. No power or water. Moorage slips are for resort guests. Cabins or campsites available for rent. They do have room for larger vessels at the main dock. The restaurant and pub are good.

Beaver Cove. Fairly deep anchorage can be found along the shores of Beaver Cove, the site of an old sawmill. Logs may be boomed in the bay, and the bottom of the bay is almost certainly foul with sunken logs and debris.

CHARTS	
3546	Broughton Strait (1:40,000); Port McNeill & Alert Bay (1:20,000)
3547	Queen Charlotte Strait, Eastern Portion (1:40,000)
3548	Queen Charlotte Strait, Central Portion (1:40,000); Blunden Harbour & Port Hardy (1:15,000)

The main dock at Telegraph Cove Resorts will handle larger vessels by reservation.

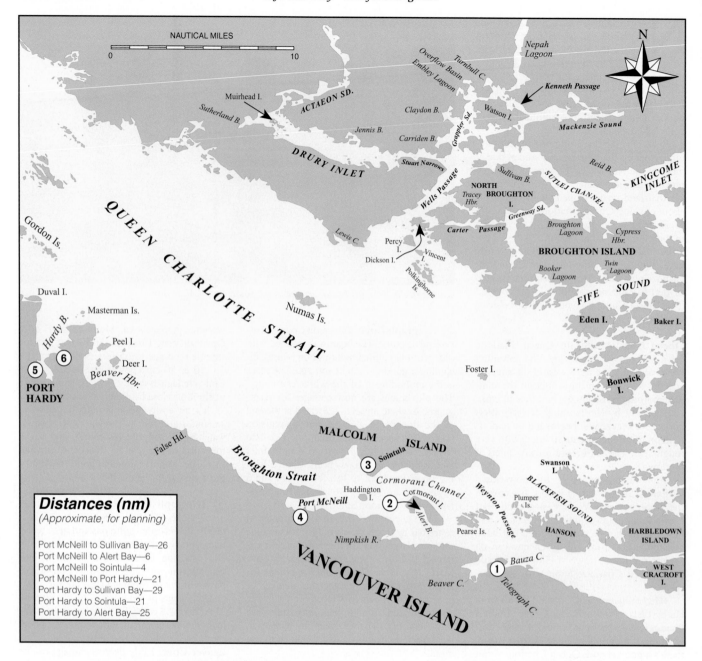

Distances (nm)
(Approximate, for planning)

Port McNeill to Sullivan Bay—26
Port McNeill to Alert Bay—6
Port McNeill to Sointula—4
Port McNeill to Port Hardy—21
Port Hardy to Sullivan Bay—29
Port Hardy to Sointula—21
Port Hardy to Alert Bay—25

Pearse Islands (Cormorant Channel Marine Park). Careful piloting is called for when exploring this area because of rocks, reefs, and strong currents in the narrow channels between the islands. Correspondents James and Jennifer Hamilton report:

"We anchored in 30 feet (zero tide) just north of the 72-meter islet, about where the 9.8-meter sounding is on Chart 3546. A little wind blew through from the northwest, but we saw very little boat traffic. It was a lovely spot with an excellent view down Broughton Strait. Good holding—the anchor set instantly with 150 feet of rode out. It looks like excellent dinghy-exploring country, but it had been a long day and we didn't have the strength.

"The next morning the current was really whipping through the passage, but we held just fine. When we left we found the current very strong off the tip of the 88-meter island,

with whirlpools and upwellings." [*Hamilton*]

Correspondent Pat Shera reports that when the current is flooding east in Broughton Strait, a strong westward countercurrent is present when approaching the Pearse Islands from the south.

② **Alert Bay.** One can learn more about native culture here, in less time, than anywhere on this part of the coast.

Study Chart 3546 before taking your boat to Alert Bay. Note the 3-knot currents shown throughout the area. While summer weather usually is quiet, be aware of rough water when wind opposes current. Note also the various shallows and other hazards, and plot your course to stay well clear.

A small public float is in front of the main part of town. It is exposed to all winds, and current can run swiftly, but it is convenient when provisioning at the nearby grocery.

Deeper in the bay, the breakwater-protected Boat Harbour basin, northwest of the ferry landing, has moorage.

The Alert Bay village, with shopping and services, is about a half-mile walk from the Boat Harbour. At the top of the dock, take a right and walk along the waterfront. The Native side, including the U'mista Cultural Centre, is about a mile from the dock in the opposite direction. Five pavilions along the way represent the five Native clans in Alert Bay. The Ecological Park is a get-the-heart-going hike up the hill.

The Visitor Centre is on the water side of the road, about midway into the commercial area. It's open 7 days a week during the season. On weekdays you'll probably meet Norine, the manager. She's terrific. Regardless of who's on duty you will get good information about the attractions in Alert Bay: the world's tallest totem pole (whose top blew off in a

Alert Bay
Discover our World

Arts, Culture and Heritage

U'Mista Cultural Centre
Alert Bay Visitor Centre and Art Gallery
Alert Bay Museum
Big House & World's Tallest Totem Pole
'Namgis Burial Ground with stand of totems

Activities

Whale watching
Fishing
Nature Trails
Traditional Canoes
Tennis Courts

Health

Hospital and Health Centre
Personal Care Services

Business

Full service Marina
Accommodations – Hotels, B&B's, Cabins
Restaurants
Campground
Grocery store
Liquor Store
Post Office
Pharmacy
Pubs
Churches
Banking
Hair Salon
Bike Rentals

The Alert Bay town dock is convenient to shopping, grocery stores, and restauarnts. Current can run strongly at the dock.

2007 winter storm); the U'mista Cultural Centre and gift shop; the Ecological Park, where you can see culturally modified cedar trees (trees partly stripped of bark to make baskets, regalia, and clothing); the burial grounds; the Anglican church that dates back to 1879. Brochures give information and map routes for self-guided tours. Interpretive displays have been installed. Occasionally, pocket cruise ships stop at Alert Bay.

Alert Bay has a grocery store, pharmacy, pub, liquor store, restaurants, bike rentals, salon and spa, bank, ATM, and a post office. Marine mechanics are available. The new hospital and dental clinic is located behind the U'mista Cultural Centre. The hospital has an emergency room and can do lab work and x-rays. It does not do surgery.

Cruisers moored at Port McNeill can walk-on the BC ferry to Alert Bay. Catch the 8:40 a.m. ferry to Alert Bay and return on the 5:55 p.m. or 8:25 p.m. ferry. Bring your camera. The entire town of Alert Bay is walkable and photogenic.

Alert Bay's delicious drinking water comes from a well more than 300 feet deep. The water is absolutely pure—no additives.

If you can, schedule your visit to see the T'sasala Cultural Group dance performance, Thursdays through Saturdays at 1:15 p.m. in the 'Namgis Bighouse, $15 adults, $8 under 12. They explain and perform traditional dances, complete with regalia and masks. Adults, teens, and little children share equal roles. The audience joins in a joyful dance at the end. Afterward, a visit to the U'mista Cultural Centre takes on greater importance. The artifacts on display are extraordinary. Recently they added storytelling on Saturday afternoons.

If you want to experience more of the 'Namgis culture, a local business, Culture Shock (www.cultureshockgallery.ca), offers a number of interactive experiences, including local eco tours, a traditional salmon barbecue, storytelling, and a class on cedar weaving.

Hiking trails: Cormorant Island has an extensive system of predator-free hiking trails. Ask for a map in the Visitor Centre.

Seafest: Fourth weekend in July along the boardwalk. Table vendors, music, fun contests, and Artfest.

360 Eco Paddle: B.C. Day is the first Monday in August. That weekend, observe or participate in this paddling race around Cormorant Island.

② **Alert Bay Boat Harbour.** 15 Maple Road, Bag 2800, Alert Bay, BC V0N 1A0; (250) 974-5727; boatharbour@alertbay.ca; www.alertbay.ca. Monitors VHF 66A. Good docks, water, 20 & 30 amp power, Wi-Fi. This is the breakwater-protected public wharf and floats in Alert Bay, located next to the ferry landing. During the summer season space is reserved for visiting pleasure craft on docks C, D and F. It's a good idea, though, to call ahead by radio or telephone to assure a place to tie up. Rafting is mandatory. The new harbor manager's office features showers and flat-rate laundry. Eric Gregory is the harbor manager. Alert Bay ice cream, with handmade waffle cones, is available in the lobby. The ice cream stand is run by village children.

② **U'mista Cultural Centre.** P.O. Box 253, Alert Bay, BC V0N 1A0; (250) 974-5403; info@umista.ca; www.umista.ca. We doubt

that anyone could see this collection of coppers, masks and other ceremonial regalia without being affected. Open daily 9:00 a.m. to 5:00 p.m. in summer and Tuesday through Saturday, 9:00 a.m to 5:00 p.m. in winter. Admission is $8 adults, $7 seniors, $1 children under 12.

The displays portray the history of the area and the significance of the potlatch. In 1884 the government attempted to outlaw potlatch ceremonies, but the law was generally ignored and unenforced. In 1921, however, 45 people in the village were charged with violating a revised version of the law. Twenty-two people received suspended sentences, in an agreement where potlatch paraphernalia and ceremonial regalia, including masks and coppers, were turned over to the Indian Agent at Alert Bay. The items were sent to Canadian museums; some ended up in the personal collection of a government official. The people of Alert Bay successfully negotiated the return of their property in the 1960s, with the stipulation that museums be constructed for their display in Alert Bay and in Yuculta, near Cape Mudge. The result in Alert Bay is the U'mista Cultural Centre.

Mitchell Bay. Mitchell Bay, near the east end of Malcolm Island, is a good summertime anchorage, protected from all but south winds.

③ **Sointula.** Sointula is an pleasant stop, with amenities including an Info Centre, Coop grocery store, and restaurant. The Harbour Authority marina has space in the summer for visiting boats in both the north and south sections. The Sointula Co-op, across the road from the south docks, carries charts and a good selection of marine hardware. A Co-op grocery store in the village, closed

The totem poles displayed outside of the U'mista Cultural Centre all tell a story.

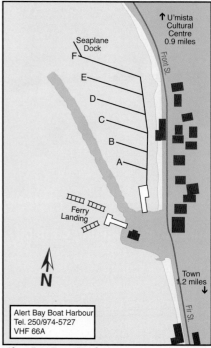

Alert Bay Boat Harbour

ALERT BAY — THE SPIRIT OF U'MISTA

The heritage of the Inside Passage is a rich tapestry of man's life on the land and his utilization of its waters for both transportation and sustenance. Today we enjoy the beauty of the islands and animals, the fjords and waterfalls. And, occasionally, nature's bounty, hauled to the surface in a crab pot or caught on the end of a fishing line. But for thousands of years, since long before Europeans arrived, the area was carefully occupied by First Nations people.

Their culture is different than ours. They depended on the environment around them in ways often lost in modern life. Their beliefs and customs are inextricably linked to the Inside Passage. A glimpse into their culture reveals a belief in family and clan and an interest in preserving life and land. They believe in sustaining their people by maintaining nature's balance.

They are also a giving people, always ready to share. Perhaps there is no better example of their culture of sharing than their potlatch ceremonies.

Potlatches bring together neighboring families and nearby tribes. Cultural traditions, like songs and dances, are performed and ceremonial regalia, like coppers, masks and robes, are shown off. Feasts are prepared. Gifts, ranging from blankets to berries, are given. Successful potlatches can be reminisced about for years. Potlatches may celebrate marriage, birth, death or other rites of passage. Regardless of the reason for celebration, potlatches are a vehicle for giving. The more a family shares, the better the event is remembered.

In 1885, the government of Canada banned potlatches. Unwilling to give up centuries old traditions, the celebrations secretly continued. But in the early 1920s a new Director of Indian Affairs gave orders to enforce the potlatch laws. First Nations members were arrested and some were jailed for up to two months. Regalia was confiscated, packed and shipped to Ottawa for storage. Some masks were kept for the personal collection of the Superintendent General of Indian Affairs.

Beginning in the 1960s the Canadian government slowly repatriated the items they had taken. They reached an agreement where the regalia would be returned and placed on display in two museums, the Nuyumbalees Cultural Centre near Cape Mudge, and the U'mista Cultural Centre in Alert Bay. When a person returns from enslavement, they are said to have "u'mista," and the same can be said for the potlatch regalia that has now been returned to the First Nations people.

Today, the spirit of u'mista is alive in the coppers, robes and masks on display in the U'mista Cultural Centre.

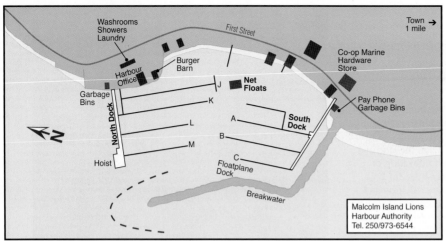

Malcolm Island (Sointula)

Sundays, has a small liquor agency. The Co-op does not use plastic bags. Bring your own bags for purchases. A Saturday farmers market at the Info Centre is open from 10:00 a.m. to 1:00 p.m. every other weekend from the first weekend in July until September. A coffee shop and bistro are in the new building across from the Co-op.

Sointula means "place of harmony" in Finnish, and was settled by Finnish immigrants as a utopian cooperative shortly after the turn of the 20th century. Utopia didn't last, but the Co-op store is a reminder of earlier days. There's no doubting the Finnish influence as you walk around; the town is clean, well-maintained and orderly. You'll find well-tended lawns and gardens, and it seems every fence is unique.

Schedule time to see the museum. It's lovingly done, and volunteers on duty are full of information.

Sointula is a place where drivers wave as they go by, and are apt to stop and ask if you'd like a ride. It's a place where people put down what they are doing to chat briefly and exchange a small joke or two.

You can also visit Sointula by walking on the BC Ferry from Port McNeill.

Note: the concrete float that used to be next to the BC Ferry dock in front of the town center has been removed.

③ **Sointula (Malcolm Island Lions Harbour Authority).** P.O. Box 202, Sointula, BC V0N 3E0; (250) 973-6544; milha@cablerocket.com. Excellent docks with 20 & 30 amp power, water, laundry, showers, garbage drop, Wi-Fi. Office hours are 8:30 a.m. to 12:30 p.m. in the winter, all day in the summer. Visa and MasterCard accepted. ATMs are a mile away, at both the credit union and the Co-op store in the village.

Sointula's extensive public docks are behind a rock breakwater at the head of Rough Bay, 1 mile north of the ferry landing. The docks are divided into north and south sections. Both sections are available to visiting boats and it's an easy walk on the road between the two. Each set of docks has a garbage drop and pay phone. The north docks also have washrooms, showers, and laundry, built and maintained by the Malcolm Island Lions Club. Solar panels on the roof provide the hot water. Both sections have potable water on the docks. All moorage is first-come, first-served, side-tie only, no reservations. Rafting possible. Moor where it makes sense. Pay at the office in the north section. Lorraine Williams is the manager. The office staff is happy to provide you with more information on the town.

The Tarkanen Marine shipyard, capable of major work, is located near the boat basin.

④ **Port McNeill.** Port McNeill is a modern small city on Highway 19, complete with banks, stores, hotels, restaurants, and transportation to the rest of Vancouver Island. With nearly all services located within easy walking distance of the boat harbor, Port McNeill is an excellent resupply point for boats headed north, south, or into the Broughton Islands.

Port McNeill has two marinas: the Town of Port McNeill Harbour docks and North Island Marina, formerly Port McNeill Fuel Dock and Marina. Both are protected by an extensive breakwater. The Town docks are the first, and to port as you round the end of the breakwater. North Island Marina is immediately beyond. Both facilities are close to shopping, restaurants and a modern laundromat with 8 washers, 8 dryers and 2 extractors. The laundromat also has a free Wi-Fi.

A large, drive-on loading float was installed between the town docks and the North Island Marina fuel dock, reducing maneuvering room, particularly at low tide.

The well-stocked IGA and Super Valu grocery stores are in a shopping center a few blocks from the docks. The IGA has a van and will deliver to the dock. Fishing tackle, post office, large liquor store, drug store, marine supplies and more are within a few minutes' walk. A hospital is nearby. The Shop-Rite marine and logging store near the marina

The Burger Barn at Sointula is popular and very good.

A dramatic end to the day at North Island Marina.

carries just about everything and handles outboard repairs. There is a good selection of restaurant and pub dining.

Regular floatplane service connects down-island. Kenmore Air and NW Seaplanes fly to Seattle from North Island Marina, and Pacific Coastal Airlines flies to Vancouver. The Port Hardy International Airport, with air service north and south, is a 30-minute taxi ride from town.

If the town marina and the North Island Marina are full, anchorage is possible. The preferred spot is across the bay from the marinas. Good holding in thick, sticky mud.

Be sure to see the Port McNeill and District Museum, which showcases the history of logging in the area. It is a short walk from the docks. Nearby, the world's largest burl is on display.

Golf: Seven Hills Golf & Country Club, par 35, 9 interesting and hilly holes halfway between Port McNeill and Port Hardy, on the road to Port Alice. If you walk you definitely will get your exercise. Call (250) 949-9818; they may be able to arrange a ride. Also the Cedar Park 9-hole par 3 course just outside Port McNeill. Tougher than it looks: pitching wedge, sand wedge, and putter are all you need. Call (250) 956-2270.

④ **Town of Port McNeill Harbour.** 1594 Beach Drive, P.O. Box 1389, Port McNeill, BC V0N 2R0; (250) 956-3881; pmharbour@telus.net; www.portmcneillharbour.ca. Monitors VHF 66A. When approaching, call on the VHF for a slip assignment. Open all year, guest moorage, 20, 30, 50 & 100 amp power, water, washrooms, showers, pay phones, pumpout, waste oil disposal, garbage drop. This is a comfortable marina, with friendly management and room for all sizes of boats. Reservations are now accepted in July and August. The marina office is in the Visitor Centre building, above the marina.

The BC Ferry landing, with service to Alert Bay and Sointula, is next to the marina.

The marina has a unique policy for showers. When checking in at the office, pay $10 for a key. Take as many showers as you like and return the key before departing. The marina keeps $5 for the showers and returns $5 to you.

Note: In 2012 the docks were extended to increase the capacity of the marina. The change can be disconcerting if you are used to the old configuration. Large vessels may be side-tied to the new dock and on the new fingers very close to the breakwater.

④ **North Island Marina.** P.O. Box 488, Port McNeill, BC V0N 2R0; (250) 956-4044; info@portmcneill.com; www.portmcneill.com. Monitors VHF 66A. Formerly Port McNeill Fuel Dock and Marina. Open all year with 2000 feet of guest moorage, 20, 30, 50 (120/208 volt) and 100 amp power, water, free Wi-Fi. Garbage and recycling at the head of the dock. A security gate was installed in 2012; get the passcode from the marina office. Reservations accepted.

The fuel dock has gasoline, diesel, stove oil, 100 LL and Jet A aviation fuel, propane. In 2013, they installed a long fuel hose and reel, allowing in-berth fueling. A small dock store has charts, ice, and some marine parts. An

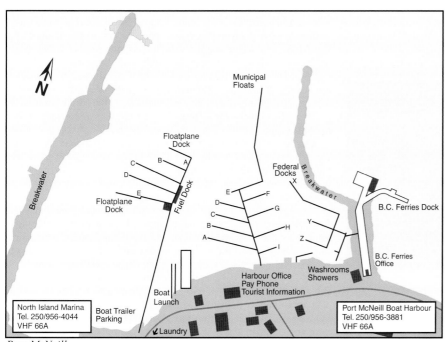

Port McNeill

The Town Docks at Port McNeill were expanded in 2012. Note the new configuration above with the extended dock inside the breakwater. Commercial moorage at left; pleasure craft moorage in middle; fuel dock and marina at right. A new loading float is near shore between the Town Dock and the fuel dock.

auto parts store is above the dock. Diver available. This is a friendly and well-staffed marina located adjacent to the town docks.

A first-rate laundromat is across the street. Port McNeill grocery stores, shops and restaurants are all within walking distance. Look for the new "happy hour" float with the large white tent. It is becoming the place to be at the end of the day. Long-time cruisers will recognize the

tent as the site of many of the Pierre's Bay pig roasts over the years. Exhalatte, a coffee and snack shop on the docks, opened in 2013.

North Island Marina offers many services, including a courtesy car and pick-up and drop-off at the airport. They can arrange for heli-tours, golf, or other services, including boat watch. For those who need to return home, North Island Marina is a good

spot to leave your boat. The marina staff can drive you to the Port Hardy Airport or you can depart via Pacific Coastal, Kenmore Air and Northwest Seaplanes directly from the North Island Marina dock.

Beaver Harbour. The islands in Beaver Harbour are picturesque. The west side of the Cattle Islands is protected; anchor on a mud bottom in 30 to 45 feet. Patrician Cove has been recommended to us. Several white shell midden beaches are located throughout the islands. Reader Jack Tallman reports fresh northwesterly winds get in and can make for a "troublesome night."

Our sister publication, *Cruising the Secret Coast*, by Jennifer and James Hamilton, devotes a chapter to Beaver Harbour and the Native village of Fort Rupert.

Fort Rupert. Just past Thomas Point, in the bay with some protection from the Cattle Islands. No marina, but there is a beach for landing and a trail to the general store.

Fort Rupert is the site of the Hudson's Bay Company fort built and commanded by William Henry McNeill in 1849. Today,

this is the village of the Kwagu'ł and the Kwakiutl First Nation. You may see native carvers working on totem poles or other artwork and traditional crafts.

Anchor off the beach in 16 to 30 feet and dinghy to the beach. A public gazebo is on the beach. A trail leads to the road and the Fort Rupert General Store. For complete information see our sister publication, *Cruising the Secret Coast*, by Jennifer and James Hamilton.

⑤ **Port Hardy.** Port Hardy is the northernmost community on Vancouver Island. Moorage is at the City Dock (summer only), Quarterdeck Marina, and Port Hardy Harbour Authority.

The City Dock is adjacent to the Coast Guard wharf. If the City Dock floats are full, you can anchor out and take the dinghy in. The City Dock has easiest access to shopping.

The Quarterdeck Marina and fuel dock are a mile or so farther into Hardy Bay, past a narrow entry channel. The Harbour Authority floats are to the right of the Quarterdeck Marina. From this inner bay to downtown is a bit of a walk, but not bad.

A large Overwaitea supermarket is at Thunderbird Mall. For items with Overwaitea's "Regular price/Member price" shelf tags, we found that non-members can get the Member price by asking the checker for a tourist card. Overwaitea will pay the cab fare to deliver large orders to the City Dock, Harbour Authority, and Quarterdeck Marina. They didn't give us an exact amount, but something around $100 probably would qualify.

Port Hardy has a park at shoreside, with a seaside promenade past tidy waterfront homes. In the park, be sure to read the sign commemorating completion of the Carrot Highway. The Visitor Centre is next to the park. The town is clean and friendly. The library houses a museum and artifacts section.

Port Hardy is not fancy but has city amenities, including a hospital and airport, with scheduled flights to and from Vancouver. Being a commercial fish boat center, almost any kind of boat problem can be repaired. Nearby Bear Cove is the terminus for the ferry that runs to Prince Rupert during the summer. Coastal Mountain Fuels is in Bear Cove.

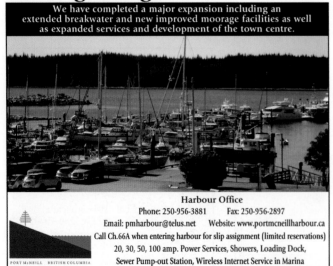

FORMERLY "THE PORT MCNEILL FUEL DOCK & MARINA"

NORTH ★ ISLAND MARINA
PORT MCNEILL
BRITISH COLUMBIA

RESERVATION LINE: 1.855.PORT.MAC
MARINA OFFICE: 250.956.4044
VHF: 66A

www.portmcneill.com
email: info@portmcneill.com

50° 35.49 N
127° 5.43 W

MARINE DIESEL - MARINE GAS - AVGAS - JET FUEL - PROPANE
*IN BERTH FUELING - BAIT - ICE - CHANDLERY - GATED MARINA
TRANSIENT MOORAGE - COURTESY VEHICLES - FREE WIFI
MARINA MEMBERSHIP BENEFITS - MOORAGE RESERVATIONS
WHALE WATCHING - PROVISIONING SERVICES - LAUNDROMAT
*OUR NEW CAFE "EXHALATTE" - HELI TOURS - PARKING
GUEST AND CREW EXCHANGE SERVICES
DIRECT FLIGHTS TO SEATTLE & VANCOUVER

PORT MCNEILL
BRITISH COLUMBIA

BROUGHTON ARCHIPELAGO
POKER RUN

"GATEWAY TO THE BROUGHTON ARCHIPELAGO"

A large wind farm was constructed on the north end of the island and offers tours.

Dining: Port Hardy has several good restaurants. We've had a good lunch and dinner at the Quarterdeck Pub at the Quarterdeck Marina. In town, breakfast at Captain Hardy's is a local favorite, complete with oversized portions. Cafe Guido has excellent coffee and baked goods. The Book Nook and the West Coast Community Craft Shop are co-located with Cafe Guido. These are not the kind of places you would expect up north. Local favorite, The Sporty Bar & Grille, is downtown. A sushi restaurant, an Asian wok-styled restaurant, and several cafes are scattered throughout Port Hardy.

Museum: The museum on the main street in town is small but superb. It also houses the finest collection of local history and local interest books we've seen. We recommended it.

Golf: Seven Hills Golf & Country Club, par 35, 9 hilly holes halfway between Port Hardy and Port McNeill on the road to Port Alice. A nice course. Call (250) 949-9818; they may be able arrange transportation.

Fuel: Fuel is available on the east side of Hardy Bay at Coastal Mountain Fuels in Bear Cove and farther in at Quarterdeck Marina.

Walkway & Nature Trail: A walking trail with picnic tables and viewpoints starts near the Quarterdeck Marina, leads past the Glen Lyon Inn and continues along the edge of Hardy Bay. At the head, you can turn north and walk to the Quatse River estuary, or you can take the Quatse River loop through the woods to the Quatse River Salmon Hatchery (www.quatsehatchery.ca or call (250) 949-9022 to arrange a tour). The trail is very easy, and much of it is wheelchair-accessible. It's a great side-trip that offers a different perspective of Port Hardy. [*Hamilton*]

LOCAL KNOWLEDGE

DANGEROUS REEF: South of the Port Hardy City Dock in the outer bay, yellow buoys mark a large drying reef. If proceeding to the inner bay, pass well east of this reef.

⑤ **Port Hardy Harbour Authority.** 6600 Hardy Bay Rd., Port Hardy, BC V0N 2P0; (250) 949-6332; (250) 949-0336; phfloats@cablerocket.com; www.porthardy.ca. Monitors VHF 66A. The finger floats have mostly 20 amp power, some 30 amp. The main float has increased the number of 30 amp outlets. Although this basin is primarily for commercial fishing vessels, there is limited room for pleasure craft in the summer when the fleet is out. The facility has a launch ramp, washrooms, holding tank pumpout and garbage drop.

⑤ **Quarterdeck Inn & Marina Resort.** 6555 Hardy Bay Rd., P.O. Box 910, Port Hardy, BC V0N 2P0; (250) 949-6551; (250) 902-0455; info@quarterdeckresort.

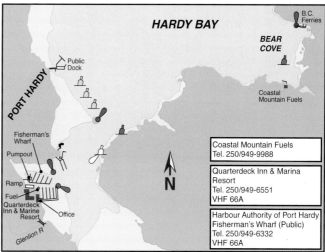

The Port Hardy City Dock is installed in summer and is the nearest moorage to shopping.

Port Hardy

net; www.quarterdeckresort.net. Monitors VHF 66A. Open all year, gasoline, diesel, propane, guest moorage, 15, 30 & 50 amp power, washrooms, showers, laundry, Wi-Fi access, liquor store. The fuel dock carries Delo lubricants. During winter the fuel dock and marina office are closed on Sundays.

This is a busy marina with a well-stocked marine supplies and fishing tackle store, fuel dock, and haulout and repair. The Quarterdeck Pub & Restaurant is on the same prop-erty. The repair yard has a 22-foot-wide, 60-ton Travelift, the only Travelift between Campbell River and Shearwater. Do it your-self or have the pros do it. A launch ramp is adjacent.

Quarterdeck's 40-room hotel is attractive and well-appointed. It has full wheelchair ac-cess, ocean views, and a covered walkway to the pub, with a nice area for families.

Quarterdeck is well managed. The people are friendly, accommodating, and efficient.

⑥ **Coastal Mountain Fuels (Bear Cove).** 6720 Bear Cove, Port Hardy, BC V0N 2P0; (250) 949-9988. Monitors VHF 09. Open all year, gasoline, diesel, kerosene, propane. Despite commercial appearance, they welcome pleasure boats. Washrooms, showers, bait, ice, waste oil disposal. Located near the BC Ferries terminal. Launch ramp and convenience store.

CHAPTER 14

WEST COAST OF VANCOUVER ISLAND

HARDY BAY TO QUATSINO SOUND
God's Pocket • Goletas Channel • Nahwitti Bar • Cape Scott • Sea Otter Cove

QUATSINO SOUND TO KYOQUOT
Winter Harbour • Quatsino Narrows • Coal Harbour • Brooks Peninsula • Bunsby Islands

KYOQUOT SOUND TO ESPERANZA INLET
Clear Passage • Zeballos • Esperanza • Tahsis Narrows

NOOTKA SOUND TO HOT SPRINGS COVE
Tahsis • Critter Cove • Friendly Cove • Estevan Point

CLAYOQUOT SOUND
Bacchante Bay • Ahousat • Lemmens Inlet • Tofino

BARKLEY SOUND
Ucluelet • Broken Group • Port Alberni • Bamfield

Cruising the west coast of Vancouver Island. For many, the area from Port Hardy, at the top of Vancouver Island, down the west coast to the mouth of the Strait of Juan de Fuca, is the finest cruising ground in the Northwest—except, perhaps, Alaska. Little can compare with the variety, beauty, ruggedness, remoteness, and sheer satisfaction of a voyage down the outside of Vancouver Island. Please allow enough time when you make the trip. Plan for three weeks, two weeks at a minimum. This is a lot of area to cover and you have to allow for being weathered in.

The area is broken down into five inlets and sounds that snake their way into the heart of Vancouver Island. Mountains rise all around. Rocks lurk in the waters. Fish and wildlife abound. Only the hardy (and occasionally the foolhardy) are out there with you. This is Northwest cruising writ large.

Except for the rounding of Cape Scott and the long run down the Strait of Juan de Fuca, the distance between inlets and sounds of the West Coast is in the 30- to 40-mile range. Wait for good weather and dash around. Once inside, let the wind outside blow. You're safe.

Clockwise or counter-clockwise? Most boats navigate the west coast of Vancouver Island traveling counter-clockwise. For sailboats, the prevailing summertime westerly winds combine with the westerly swells of the Pacific Ocean. They create some splendid downwind sailing on the offshore passages. Most powerboats have an easier time running with the seas than into them, so they prefer the prevailing conditions.

The difficulty with a counter-clockwise trip is the time it takes. To go down-island on the outside, you first must go up-island on the inside, and the weeks go by. Those who do not have the luxury of time to circumnavigate Vancouver Island can cruise the West Coast by running out the Strait of Juan de Fuca to Barkley Sound. They begin their explorations from Barkley Sound, traveling clockwise up the coast, perhaps only as far as Nootka Sound and then back down the coast. They must pick their weather for outside passages up-island into the prevailing swells, but that can be done. And if weather delays a passage for a day or even a few days, at least the time is spent on the West Coast, not in traveling up the Inside Passage.

Strait of Juan de Fuca. For boats coming from Puget Sound or Vancouver/Victoria, the Strait of Juan de Fuca can be a difficult body of water. The typical summer weather pattern calls for calm conditions in the early morning, with a sea breeze building by afternoon, often to 30+ knots. When wind and tidal current oppose, large, steep seas result.

On the American side, boats can leave Port Townsend at first light and get to Sequim Bay or Port Angeles before the wind builds. From there they can cross to the Canadian side for the run to Ucluelet Customs the next day. Weather permitting, a fast boat can make it in one day.

On the Canadian side, boats can depart Victoria or Sooke at first light, and reach Port San Juan or even Barkley Sound, conditions and boat speed permitting. The distance from Victoria to Bamfield is approximately 92 nautical miles.

These thoughts are for typical conditions. Variations often change typical conditions. We have seen the strait windy all day and calm all day. Listen to the weather broadcasts, watch the barometer and sky, and be cautious.

The boat. Large or small, a boat for the West Coast should be seaworthy, strong, and well-equipped. The seas encountered on the coastal passages will be a test, especially at Cape Scott, Brooks Peninsula, Tatchu Point, Estevan Point, the entrance to Ucluelet, Cape Beale, and in the Strait of Juan de Fuca.

The wind accelerates as it is funneled at the capes and points, and the ocean's currents grow confused. Between wind and current, the seas grow noticeably higher and steeper. Even on moderate days, a boat can be suddenly surrounded by whitecaps. At Cape Scott and off Brooks Peninsula, pyramid-shaped waves can appear, break (or crumble into foam), and sweep past.

Often these "rogue" waves come from a direction different from the prevailing seas. Assuming a summertime westerly wind and a course in following seas, these waves can grab the broad sterns of many powerboats and make broaching a hazard. A double-ender, especially a double-ended sailboat with a large rudder, will not be affected as much. In fact, sailing in these seas with a 25-knot breeze from astern could be high points of the trip. But a planing-hull powerboat skipper will pay close attention to the waves and their effect on his boat.

It is at times such as these that the skipper and crew know they are in serious water, and that their boat and equipment must be dependable. It is no place for old rigging, uncertain engines, sticky steering, intermittent electrical power, broken antennas, small anchors, unswung compasses, or clogged pumps. For a lifelong city-dweller, the West Coast is a wild coast with open seas and rocks a mile offshore. It pays to be prepared.

Most consider radar all but essential. The local boats, even the little ones, have radar. A GPS chartplotter will add to your navigational peace of mind. Even on clear days in mild conditions, GPS can identify turning points and confirm visual navigation. A chartplotter can take the anxiety out of navigating among ugly black rocks. In thick weather or fog, radar and electronic navigation will raise the comfort level aboard dramatically.

Weather. Winter on the West Coast is stormy, and not a place for pleasure craft. In early spring the weather begins to improve, and by June or July the pattern of calm early mornings followed by rising westerly winds establishes itself. In the evening the winds subside. That said, even in summer, serious storms can hit the West Coast.

Fog can be a problem, particularly in August and September. We've heard the month of August referred to as "Foggust." The typical fog forms in early morning and burns off in late morning or early afternoon—just as the westerly fills in. If an outside passage is planned but the morning is blanketed in fog, the skipper will appreciate having radar and a chartplotter. He also will be glad he did his chart navigation the day before, with waypoint coordinates plotted and loaded, distances measured, and compass courses laid.

Plan for rain and cool temperatures as well as sunshine during a visit of two to four weeks or more.

Lennard Island Lighthouse along the west coast of Vancouver Island. Photo by John Forde, The Whale Centre.

The Coast Guard broadcasts continuous weather information from several locations along the way. The reports are limited in scope to weather that affects the West Coast only, and include wind and sea state reports from lighthouses and weather-monitoring stations. In surprisingly short time, a visitor who's paying attention learns how to interpret the weather broadcasts and decide whether the time is right for an outside passage.

Lighthouse weather reports are particularly valuable. These reports include visibility, wind speed and direction, human-observed sea state, and swell height and direction. Reports are issued every three hours, but light keepers can often be reached on VHF 82 for up-to-the-minute weather information.

Fuel. Although the West Coast is a wilderness, it is a wilderness with fuel. Gasoline and diesel are available all along the way, within workable ranges for virtually any boat capable of safely being out there. The fuel stations exist to serve the fishing fleet, logging camps, and the pockets of permanent residents, especially Native communities. Fuel can be found at Winter Harbour, Coal Harbour, Fair Harbour, Zeballos, Esperanza, Tahsis, Critter Cove (gasoline only), Moutcha Bay, Ahousat, Tofino, Ucluelet, Bamfield, Poett Nook (gasoline only), Port Alberni, Port San Juan (gasoline only), Sooke, and Victoria.

Note: The above list of fuel stops is subject to change. Check our website www.WaggonerGuide.com for updates.

Ice. Block ice can be a problem. If commercial fishing is allowed, the fish processing plants may have flaked ice for the fish boats, which take it on by the ton. A polite inquiry usually will yield enough ice for the icebox or cooler—sometimes for a charge, often not. Fish ice is "salt ice," and not recommended for the cocktail hour.

Water. Always check with locals before filling the water tank.

Fresh vegetables. Uneven quality. Best to plan ahead and stock accordingly. Port Alice, Tofino, and Ucluelet are the only towns with real supermarkets.

Public docks. Every community has a public dock with moorage fees collected by a local resident. At some of the docks the local resident isn't around, or doesn't bother to come collecting. Accept the no-charge tie-ups where you find them, pay gladly where the charge is collected.

Reference books and guidebooks. The Canadian Tide and Current Tables, Vol. 6 (blue cover) gives tides and currents south to Port San Juan. Vol. 5 (green cover) covers the Strait of Juan de Fuca and inland waters of Strait of Georgia and Puget Sound. *Sailing Directions,* B.C. Coast, South Portion, is the official government publication, and should be considered essential. Note that *Sailing Directions* is intended for large vessels. A cove listed as good for anchoring may be too deep or exposed for small craft, but a passage listed as tortuous may be easily run by small craft.

New book: Voyages to Windward by Elsie Hulsizer. Well-told stories of West Coast adventures. Excellent photos.

Three good guidebooks exist, and we carry all three.

The first is Don Watmough's *Cruising Guide to the West Coast of Vancouver Island.* It was published in 1984 as part of the Pacific Yachting series on British Columbia cruising, and republished (unrevised) in 1993 by Evergreen Pacific Publishing Co. The rocks have not moved since 1984, and the excellent aerial photos by George McNutt will help with navigation. The book was written before boats had GPS and radar. Its dependence on traditional coastal navigation skills is instructive.

The second is Don and Reanne Douglass's *Exploring Vancouver Island's West Coast,* 2nd ed., published in 1999. The book is clear, easy to understand, and describes a large percentage of bays and coves along the West Coast. Not every bay described is

a desirable anchorage, but Douglass tells the reader what to expect if he is forced to enter.

The third and newest is Anne and Laurence Yeadon-Jones' *Dreamspeaker Cruising Guide, Vol. 6: The West Coast of Vancouver Island,* published early 2009 by Fine Edge in the U.S. and Harbour Publishing in Canada. It has the most up-to-date information of the cruising guides.

Charts. The Canadian Hydrographic Service has more than 30 charts that cover the coast between Port Hardy and Trial Island. Buy them all. Let the few that you don't use be insurance that you will have the chart you need, regardless of where you are. The charts are of excellent quality and easy to read. The West Coast is no place for approximate navigation. If a $20 chart can take even a moment's anxiety out of a passage, the $20 is well spent.

Helpful maps. Correspondents James and Jennifer Hamilton recommend the Coast Recreation Maps (www.coastalwatersrec.com). The maps cover all the major inlets.

Coast Guard. The Canadian Coast Guard stationed along the West Coast is simply incredible. They watch like mother hens over the fleets of fish boats, pleasure boats and work boats, ready to deploy helicopters and rescue craft instantly. They know what the weather is doing and where the traffic is. They know where help can be found. A call to the Coast Guard brings action.

Local communities often can get help out even faster than the Coast Guard. In the area off Kyuquot Sound, for example, we were told that a call to Walters Cove on VHF 06 or 14 would bring help a-running. Be sure to call the Coast Guard on channel 16, too.

Insurance. Insurance policies for most inshore boats do not cover the west coast of Vancouver Island. Read your policy and check with your agent about extending the coverage for the period of your trip.

Oregon's Secret. Many of the boats cruising the West Coast come from Oregon. For years it's been their playground, their little secret. The reason is obvious. After the trip along the Washington coast, their first stop is the west coast of Vancouver Island. In good weather it's a long but easy run. Boats from the population centers of Puget Sound or Vancouver/Victoria must fight the Strait of Juan de Fuca or go around the top of Vancouver Island. Often, it is easier for them to enjoy cruising in the protected waters inside Vancouver Island.

Trailer Boats. Trailer boats can be towed on Vancouver Island to each of the sounds and inlets along the West Coast, where launch ramps are available. There are also a great many kayakers, who get to see whatever part of the West Coast they choose, without making a summer of it. The West Coast truly is kayak country.

Bears can sometimes be seen at waters' edge.

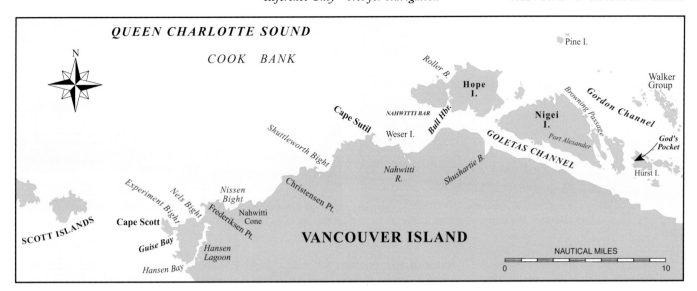

HARDY BAY TO CAPE SCOTT

Goletas Channel stretches west-northwest 23 miles between Duval Point (entrance to Hardy Bay) and the western tip of Hope Island. At the west entrance of Goletas Channel the notorious Nahwitti Bar blocks westerly swells from entering. Goletas Channel's shorelines are steep-to. Winds can funnel between them and grow stronger, but in usual summer conditions the channel, while it can get pretty choppy, is not known for dangerous seas. Be alert, however, for turbulence and debris in the water where Christie Passage, Browning Passage and Bate Passage join Goletas Channel. The mouth of Hardy Bay can be slow going as you pick your way through drift. Bull Harbour indents Hope Island, at the west entrance to Goletas Channel. It is the usual waiting point for slack water on Nahwitti Bar.

God's Pocket is a favorite layover in Christie Passage on the west side of Hurst Island, just off Goletas Channel. Boats bound around Vancouver Island probably will not see God's Pocket unless to escape a chop in Goletas Channel. But boats planning a di-

rect crossing of Queen Charlotte Sound to the Queen Charlotte Islands, or boats bound past Cape Caution, find God's Pocket to be a good jumping-off spot. God's Pocket is a local name, not shown on the chart. The harbor is marked on the chart with a marina symbol and the notation, "2 buoys." The mooring buoys no longer are there, however.

God's Pocket Resort. P.O. Box 130, Port Hardy, BC V0N 2P0; (250) 949-1755; info@godspocket.com; www.godspocket.com. This is primarily a diving resort with friendly people. Room for a few boats at the dock, or anchor out. No power or water on the docks. Washrooms and showers. Breakfast, lunch and dinner are available for the resort's diving guests; others can be accommodated on an as-available basis, with reservations.

Port Alexander. Port Alexander, indenting Nigei Island from Browning Passage, is a good anchorage for boats bound for Cape Scott or around Cape Caution. Anchor near the head in 50 to 60 feet. The beach is good for dog walking. The westerly wind blows in across the island, but has no fetch for seas to

build. The west side of the bay seems more protected than the east. The accumulation of large logs on the beach indicates that this is no place to be in a southerly storm.

Clam Cove. Clam Cove is a local name, not shown on the chart, for an anchorage on the Gordon Channel side of Nigei Island, where Browning Passage meets Gordon Channel. The entrance is approximately 0.7 miles southeast of Hougestal Point. The entrance is guarded by rocks, but Correspondent Bruce Evertz reports that with attention entry isn't a problem. Correspondents Carol-Ann Giroday and Rick LeBlanc tell us the entry is wider than it appears on the chart and kelp marks the shallow spots. The basin has room for several boats, with protection from all winds. An easily-walked trail leads from the south end of Clam Cove to Port Alexander.

Shushartie Bay. "We stopped for breakfast in Shushartie Bay after rounding the top end of Vancouver Island (clockwise circumnavigation). A 30-knot southeasterly wind was blowing against a strong flood current, making Goletas Channel very rough. We went deep into the bay and dropped the hook in

CHARTS	
3549	Queen Charlotte Strait, Western Portion (1:40,000)
3598	Cape Scott to Cape Calvert (1:74,500)
3605	Quatsino Sound to Queen Charlotte Strait, 1:150,000
3624	Cape Cook to Cape Scott (1:90,000)
3625	Scott Islands, 1:80,000
3679	Quatsino Sound (1:50,000)
3681 Plans	Quatsino Sound
3686	Approaches to Winter Harbour (1:15,000)

God's Pocket Resort has space for a few boats and is a good jumping-off point when rounding Cape Scott.

The public dock at Bull Harbour. Moorage is collected by the care-taker.

When the wind and current are calm, Nahwitti Bar can be easily negotiated.

50 feet just inside the 30-meter line, west of some dolphins marked *'Dns'* on the chart. Holding was good in thick mud. This is no Prideaux Haven, but considering the conditions outside, the swell that came in wasn't too bad. Douglass's description of Shushartie Bay is fairly negative, and we don't know how it would be in a westerly. But it worked for us that day." [*Hamilton*]

Bull Harbour. Bull Harbour is a lovely bay almost landlocked in Hope Island. It is the place to wait for weather and for slack water on Nahwitti Bar.

Enter Bull Harbour around the east side of Norman Island, which blocks the southern entrance. Parts of Bull Harbour grow quite shoal on a low tide. Check the depths and tide tables before anchoring for the night. The bottom is mud and holding is excellent. Sailing Directions says the southern portion of the harbor is reported to be foul with old chain and cable. During the fishing season commercial fish boats often crowd the harbor.

All of Hope Island, including Bull Harbour, at the west end of Goletas Channel, is the property of the Tlatalsikwala Native band. Depending on the time of year, between two and 30 band members are apt to be on Hope Island. Visitors are welcome, but must be scrupulous about leaving no trash, damaging nothing, and "respecting Mother Earth."

A public float, not connected to shore, is in the southern part of Bull Harbour. A public dock is on the east shore, north of Norman Island. The band charges for tie-up. If time allows, go ashore and cross the narrow neck of land at the north end of the harbor and watch the seas come into Roller Bay. It is always polite to ask permission to enter band property. In 2013, two young men drove to the dock to collect moorage and landing fees (cash only) shortly after we tied up.

Westerly winds can enter Bull Harbour, as can southeast gales. If you are anchored, be sure the anchor is well set, with adequate scope. In crowded conditions, achieving adequate scope can be a problem.

Nahwitti Bar. Nahwitti Bar should be attempted only at or near slack. Slack water and current predictions are shown in Tide and Current Tables, Vol. 6. Maximum tidal currents over the bar reach 5.5 knots. From seaward, the bar shoals gradually to a least depth of approximately 35 feet. When ocean swells from deep water hit the bar, friction from the shallowing bottom slows the water there, while the top of the swell continues its pace. As a result the waves grow high and steep. If a strong ebb current opposes westerly winds, dangerous and heavy breaking seas will develop.

It is often said that the ideal time to cross Nahwitti bar is at high slack water, when the typical westerly wind blows with the flood current. This tends to keep seas down and permits crossing a few minutes before the slack. The subsequent ebb current flows as fast as 3 knots along the coast all the way to Cape Scott.

A crossing at high slack is not without its disadvantages, though. First, the ebb that follows will oppose the prevailing westerly wind, and could build a steep chop along the run to Cape Scott. Second, if you cross Nahwitti Bar at slack, you are almost guaranteed to arrive at Cape Scott around mid-tide, when currents there could be kicking up the seas. One alternative is to take the inner route around Nahwitti Bar prior to high or low slack at the bar, timing your arrival at Cape Scott for high or low water.

Thus the wise skipper considers all factors before crossing Nahwitti Bar: current, weather, time of day, and the speed and seakeeping qualities of his vessel. At least 30 minutes should be allowed to get through the swells on the bar. Even fast boats usually must proceed slowly. At slack water in windless conditions, we found impressive swells extending 2.5 miles out to Whistle Buoy *MA* before they died down.

Nahwitti Bar Inner Route. A September 1992 *Pacific Yachting* article by June Cameron describes a quieter inner route that avoids Nahwitti Bar altogether. While in Bull Harbour an old and grizzled commercial fisherman told us we were nuts if we didn't take it. He said he hadn't gone across the bar in

years. Cross to the bay on the south shore of Goletas Channel and work in behind Tatnall Reefs. Follow the Vancouver Island shoreline around the bay, passing on either side of Weser Island. If the westerly is blowing, you can hide in the little nook behind Cape Sutil. We did it and it works. We don't plan to cross Nahwitti Bar again. [*Hale*]

Cape Sutil to Cape Scott. Sailing Directions says the distance from Cape Sutil to Cape Scott is 15 miles, but this understates the actual running distance after crossing Nahwitti Bar. A more realistic distance would be measured from Whistle Buoy *MA*, and would be approximately 16.5 miles. Although the run across the bottom of Queen Charlotte Sound is exposed to westerlies, except for the relentless Pacific swell the early morning conditions are often quiet. Rocks extend as much as a mile offshore all along the way. Stay well off.

According to Sailing Directions, temporary anchorage can be found in Shuttleworth Bight, Nissen Bight, Fisherman Bay (southwest corner of Nissen Bight), Nels Bight, and Experiment Bight. Study the chart before entering, and watch the weather.

Cape Scott is the westernmost point of Vancouver Island. Dangerous rocks extend 0.5 mile offshore, northward and westward. The cape itself is a low piece of land connected by a narrow neck with the main body of Vancouver Island. The Cape Scott Light, on a square tower 13 feet high, is on higher ground about a quarter-mile inland from Cape Scott.

Currents flowing on both sides of the cape meet at Cape Scott. Especially when opposed by wind, the currents can produce heavy seas and overfalls, dangerous to small craft. Even in calm conditions, seas can emerge seemingly from nowhere, the result of colliding currents. With its seas, rocks, and shortage of convenient hidey-holes, Cape Scott is not a place to treat lightly. A vessel in trouble at Cape Scott could be in serious trouble, and quickly.

It is with good reason that guidebooks (including this one) and magazine articles emphasize the dangers and cautions at Cape

Scott. The waters can be treacherous. Yet in settled summer conditions, a well-managed seaworthy vessel, with a good weather eye, can make a safe and satisfying rounding. The standard advice is to round Cape Scott at slack. Other factors may persuade a skipper to round at times other than slack. Each situation, each boat, is different. What worked yesterday may not work today. A careful skipper, fully aware that the safety of his vessel and crew truly are at risk at Cape Scott, must judge conditions and make the right choices.

Weather information: The Cape Scott lighthouse weather report is regularly updated with wind speed and direction, sea conditions, and visibility information. The automated weather station on Sartine Island provides wind speed and direction. Listen to the continuous marine broadcast for the latest weather information.

CAPE SCOTT TO QUATSINO SOUND

Depending on the courses chosen, the run from Cape Scott to the entrance of Quatsino Sound is approximately 28.5 miles. To stay clear of off-lying rocks and reefs, the general advice is to follow the 20-fathom curve all the way down the coast. Douglass says

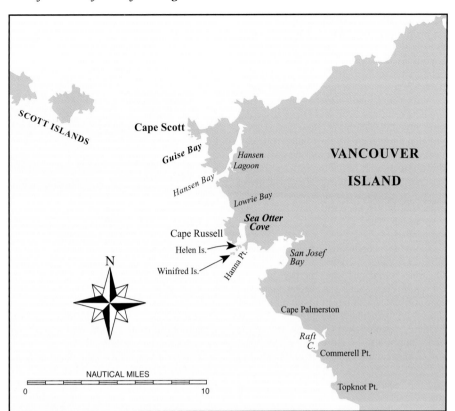

CAPE SCOTT

For 25 years Cape Scott, the remote far north tip of Vancouver Island, had been a dream of mine. Cape Scott is exposed to weather and current, and to seas that could have begun thousands of miles away. It is the most significant landmark in a circumnavigation of Vancouver Island—one of the events that marks a *compleat* Northwest boatman.

Cape Scott can be rough. At their worst, Cape Scott's seas have capsized and sunk substantial vessels. Even quiet days can be uncomfortable, the result of swells that sweep in from the Pacific to meet colliding currents. Rocks lie offshore. If you find yourself in trouble off Cape Scott, you are in trouble.

Mrs. Hale, ever stalwart before, refused to face Cape Scott. So longtime friend Tom Hukle came aboard for my first voyage around the north face of Vancouver Island and down the West Coast. Tom is a former sailboat skipper of the year at Seattle Yacht Club, an excellent seaman, knowledgeable navigator, and superb shipmate (but lousy cook).

On a breakfast of buns from the bakery and hot coffee, Tom and I departed Port Hardy at first light and ran out Goletas Channel. *Surprise*, a well-equipped Tollycraft 26 repowered with a "big-block" 454 V-8 Crusader engine, cruised at an easy 15 knots. We made all 15 knots in the flat water of a windless Goletas Channel, and reached Bull Harbour an hour and 15 minutes before the predicted turn at Nahwitti Bar. With time to kill, we inspected and took pictures at Bull Harbour. A few minutes before the turn, we followed two fish boats into the up-and-down rollers of the bar.

We rolled across at slow speed, steering a course for Whistle Buoy *MA*, 2½ miles away. A short distance beyond the buoy

the bottom grew deeper and the seas flattened. We powered back up to 15 knots for the run to Cape Scott, confirming major landmarks as we progressed: Cape Sutil, Northwest Nipple, Christensen Point, Nahwitti Cone, Frederickson Point. At last Cape Scott lay ahead, with the uninviting Scott Islands offshore. Cape Scott itself was uninviting. Rocks extended from the land. Seas broke heavily on the shore. A low salt mist hung over all.

Out where we were, in only 10 to 15 knots of wind, the seas began to lump up. They were not towering, but for a small boat their closeness and steepness made even modest height significant. It had to be the currents. At first *Surprise* shouldered into the seas well, but after a brief time Tom Hukle, who was on the helm, said, "I'd like to slow down."

Tom and I agreed that if this is what Cape Scott was like in good conditions, it could be unrelenting hell in foul. Speed reduced, we bucked along. Charts slid onto the cabin sole, and a few books rearranged themselves. The wipers cleared spray from the windshield.

At last, at 10:15 that morning, in erratic writing clearly affected by the motion of the boat, I made the log entry I had waited 25 years to make: "Cape Scott abeam to port 1.5 miles. Light wind. Confused 4 to 6 foot seas. We're going home. A major moment."

A major moment indeed. Tom turned chatty, but I stared out the side window at Cape Scott, watching it move past as we began our voyage down the west coast of Vancouver Island. "Give me a few minutes," I said to Tom. "I know it's corny, but I've waited a long time for this. I want to savor it."

– Robert Hale

he prefers the 30-fathom curve for an extra margin of safety. We are inclined toward Douglass's 30-fathom standard. In moderate conditions with excellent visibility we felt comfortable in 25 to 30 fathoms. Had conditions worsened, we would have moved out.

With the summer westerly in place, the run between Cape Scott and Quatsino Sound is a downhill sleighride. Powerboaters, especially those with planing hulls, will have to saw away at the helm and play with the throttle to stay in harmony with the relentless procession of rollers. They will arrive tired. The sailboaters will have all the fun, especially if the boat and crew can handle a spinnaker. They too will arrive tired, but exhilarated.

Given the conditions, many boats make a direct passage between Cape Scott and Quatsino Sound, and leave the bays between for another day. Sailboats, after a long passage at 6 knots, will be apt to put into one of those bays, particularly Sea Otter Cove. Boats heading counter-clockwise, toward Cape Scott, might also be more apt to investigate the shoreline, choosing to spend the night in

Looking seaward at the mouth of Sea Otter Cove. If this photo looks rugged, wait 'til you see it in person.

PAST & PRESENT: SEA OTTER COVE

For boats rounding Cape Scott heading down the West Coast, the first fully protected harbor is Sea Otter Cove. Kayakers and rowers sometimes stop in Hansen Lagoon, where they can more easily pull their boats up on the beach. But for boats that need to anchor, Sea Otter Cove is a welcome retreat, safe from whatever might be going on out on the ocean.

Boats can enter and leave Sea Otter Cove from either the north or south. The south entrance to Sea Otter Cove is protected by a group of small islands, each one of which is surrounded by a reef. Using care, entry can be made on either side of these islands. If you choose the southernmost route, a single red light kept to starboard (Red, Right, Returning) provides a reference point for the very narrow channel between the reefs. The northernmost route is broader and deeper, but more exposed to the ocean swells until you're well into the bay.

Once inside, you'll note that the entire bay is quite shallow, in many places less than 5 feet at zero tide. Be very careful during extreme low tides. One of the two rows of government mooring buoys shown on the chart has been removed.

Sea Otter Cove. They could make an early departure the next morning and round Cape Scott before the westerly fills in.

Weather information: At the north end, the Cape Scott lighthouse weather report informs mariners of wind and sea conditions. At the south end, the Quatsino lighthouse report does the same. Listen to the continuous marine broadcast for the latest weather information.

Guise Bay. Guise Bay is just south of Cape Scott. Sailing Directions says the entrance to Guise Bay is encumbered with rocks, and local knowledge is called for. The chart suggests that entrance is possible, but Douglass says that the rocks are often covered with foam and a strong heart is called for. Correspondents Gil and Karen Flanagan, however, put in to Guise Bay, and here is their report:

"Guise Bay is a great anchorage. The shore is so interesting we would consider overnighting there. The walk to the lighthouse is well used, and pretty easy. The anchorage area is about 600 yards long by 600 yards wide. The swell that day was only a few inches. Behind the island, the main south entrance channel is 1000 feet wide and 42 feet deep. If it is a reasonably nice day, don't pass it by." [*Flanagan*]

Hansen Bay. Hansen Bay was the location of a Danish settlement around 1900. Supply vessels could anchor in good weather only. The settlement failed. Sailing Directions says Hansen Bay "affords no shelter," although commercial fish boats do hole up there.

Sea Otter Cove. Sea Otter Cove, south of Cape Scott, is described in Sailing Directions as "indifferent shelter." Nevertheless, Sea Otter Cove is a favorite of fish boats, and well-known to yachtsmen. The rocks and islets outside the entrance are awesome in their ruggedness. Inside, you feel safe but surrounded by hostile ground. Sea Otter Cove is an exciting place to be. We recommend it.

Enter from the south, between Hanna

Point and the Helen Islands. Watmough's book shows swells breaking almost across the entrance, but careful attention to the chart will bring you through. The channel is narrow, and grows shallower as you go in. Contributing Editor Tom Kincaid says he stopped watching the depth sounder because it scared him. Deep draft sailboats, especially, should be careful if they anchor there. There is a story of a fish boat that anchored in Sea Otter Cove and at low tide found itself perched on a rock.

San Josef Bay. San Josef Bay is protected from northerly winds, but open to westerly and southerly winds. Anchor in settled weather.

QUATSINO SOUND

Quatsino Sound is the northernmost of the five sounds that indent the west coast of Vancouver Island. Despite fish farms, logging operations, a pulp mill and former mining sites, Quatsino Sound still provides scenic coves and interesting anchorages. With the exception of North Harbour and Winter Harbour on the north side near the entrance, Quatsino Sound is probably the sound least explored by cruising yachts.

Quatsino Sound is, however, the first quiet anchorage after the 50-mile run from Bull Harbour and a welcome sight it is after anxiety at Cape Scott and hours of rolling seas. The entrance is straightforward. Using large-scale Chart 3686, identify South Danger

CHARTS	
3624	Cape Cook to Cape Scott (1:90,000)
3679	Quatsino Sound (1:50,000)
3681 Plans	Quatsino Sound
3686	Approaches to Winter Harbour (1:15,000)

Rock and Robson Rock (both of them well away from land), stay close to Kains Island, and proceed into Forward Inlet. North Harbour and Browning Inlet are good anchorages, or you can continue to Winter Harbour.

For those coming from Haida Gwaii or the Central Coast, Quatsino offers the opportunity to do major provisioning, either at Port Alice or by taking a bus to Port Hardy from Coal Harbour.

VHF: We are told the fishermen work on channels 73, 84, and 86.

Cell phones: In 2013, we found good Telus service throughout most of Quatsino Sound.

① **Winter Harbour.** Winter Harbour once was a commercial fishing outpost. B.C. Packers owned the first major set of docks as you enter, including the fuel dock. With the closing of fishing, their docks and fuel facility have been taken over by the company that owns and runs the Outpost store.

Beyond the Outpost and its facilities is the campground of the Winter Harbour Lodge, followed by the Qualicum Rivers Fishing Resort (the large white building), and finally, the Winter Harbour Authority public dock.

The library, located above the public dock, has irregular hours. Pay phones are on the far side of this building. A post office and book exchange is located in a small building to the right of the public wharf. Pay-for-use Wi-Fi is available throughout Winter Harbour.

① **Outpost at Winter Harbour, Grant Sales Ltd.** Grant Sales, c/o General Delivery, Winter Harbour, BC V0N 3L0; (250) 969-4333; winterharbour@telus.net; www.winterharbour.ca. Monitors VHF 19. Open all year, moorage, gasoline, diesel, oil, laundry, washrooms & showers, general store, water at fuel dock. The showers, which once were at the public dock, now are in a small building on a dock near the Outpost. The general store has frozen foods including some frozen meat, canned goods, packaged foods and fixings. Produce is limited. Grocery availability may depend on delivery schedules. The Outpost also carries liquor, clothing, charts and fishing equipment. The liquor agency has

a decent wine selection. Greg Vance is the owner. You might also meet Ron Lust, who looks after the place.

Ice is available at the Winter Harbour Lodge next door.

① **Winter Harbour Harbour Authority.** Moorage, 15 & 30 amp power, water, waste oil disposal, garbage drop. A pay phone is at the top of the dock and Wi-Fi can be purchased. A tidal grid is available. Qualicum Rivers, the fishing lodge next door, sells flaked ice to cruisers and has a restaurant.

A sign on the dock asks shallow draft boats to allow deeper draft boats priority on the outer side. Larger boats also anchor to the north of the public dock and at the head of Winter Harbour.

North Harbour. North Harbour, north of Matthews Island in Forward Inlet, is an excellent anchorage, popular with boats planning a morning departure from Quatsino Sound. A small float house is moored close to shore and does not significantly interfere with anchorage. North Harbour is sheltered and quiet, yet close to the mouth of Quatsino Sound.

Browning Inlet. Browning Inlet is narrow and sheltered from seas and swells, with good holding in 18 to 30 feet. Crabbing is reportedly good. In strong northwesterlies, winds blow from the valley to the north. In those conditions North Harbour or Winter Harbour are preferable.

Koskimo Bay. Koskimo Bay has a couple of anchorages, one behind Mabbot Island and one at Mahatta Creek. The Koskimo Islands are at the east end of Koskimo Bay.

Mabbott Island. The little area behind Mabbott Island would be a cozy spot to drop the hook if the large fish farm and float house didn't take much of the anchorage.

Mahatta Creek. In Koskimo Bay. Work your way east of the mouth of the creek, anchor in 30 to 45 feet. At high tide you can explore the creek. During strong northwesterlies,

waves can build across the sound. On those days it's best to move north to East Cove.

Koskimo Islands. Explore by dinghy. The narrow passage between the largest of the islands and Vancouver Island can be run (carefully), but with safe water just outside the islands we see no need to.

Koprino Harbour. Most of Koprino Harbour is too deep for pleasure craft, but the area of East Cove, near the northeast corner of Koprino Harbour, is excellent.

East Cove. East Cove is tranquil, snug and tree-lined, with good dinghy access to shore—cruising as it should be. If East Cove were in Desolation Sound instead of Koprino Harbour, it would be filled with 25 boats every night, all stern-tied to shore. But because East Cove is on the west coast of Vancouver Island, you will probably be the only boat at anchor and you won't need a stern-tie. Another cove, almost as delightful, is just to the north, behind a group of little islets. The largest of these islets is identified on the chart as Linthlop Islet.

Pamphlet Cove. Pamphlet Cove, part of a provincial recreation reserve, is located on the north side of Drake Island, about 3.5 miles west of Quatsino Narrows. Pamphlet Cove is scenic and protected, an ideal anchorage. You can go ashore and enjoy the reserve. At high tide several small lagoons make for good exploring by dinghy or kayak. Watmough reports a trail leading from Pamphlet Cove to the south side of Drake Island, but we couldn't find it in 2013.

Julian Cove. Southeast of Drake Island and east of Kultus Cove. Protection is excellent and holding is good. Probably the most pristine cove in Quatsino Sound, Julian Cove has room for four or five boats. Beautiful forested hills surround it without a clear cut in sight. At the head of the bay a stream crosses a marsh and salmonberries grow along the shore. Watch for bears. Entry is direct and easy.

Winter Harbour was hit hard by the decline in commercial fishing, but the fuel dock and a small store are open for visiting boaters.

Julian Cove is an outstanding anchorage.

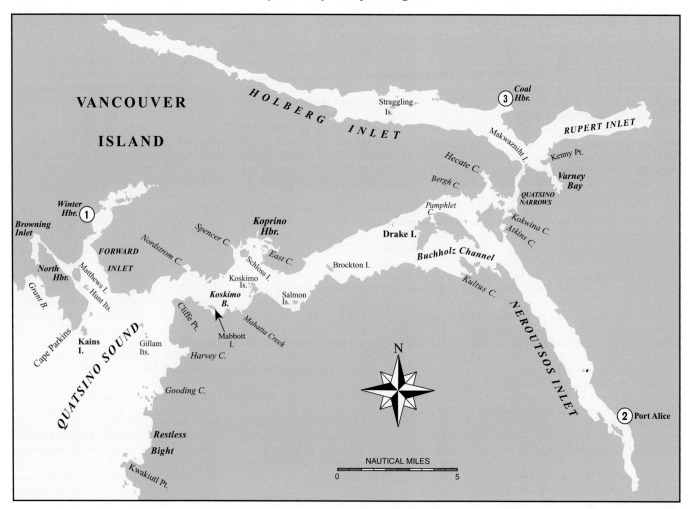

Smith Cove. In 2013, a large float and separate float house with cables running to shore occupied much of Smith Cove. Nearby Julian Cove is a better choice.

Atkins Cove. Atkins Cove is well protected from all directions except south. Good holding over a mud bottom.

"Early Bird Cove," Douglass's name for the almost-landlocked cove accessed through the narrows on the north side of Atkins Cove, is also a good anchorage. We went through the narrow, shallow entrance strongly favoring the west shore. On an 8.5-foot high tide we saw depths of 6.5 feet. In 2013 a float was anchored inside, near the entrance, but there is still plenty of room for anchoring.

Neroutsos Inlet. "The wind blows hard every afternoon in Neroutsos Inlet," one knowledgeable local told us. Neroutsos Inlet is long and straight-sided, with little diversion along the way. An important pulp mill is at Port Alice near the south end.

② **Port Alice.** Port Alice, properly Rumble Beach but locally called Port Alice, is a friendly, prosperous-looking cellulose-mill town. There's a public dock at the north end of town, although it's designed for smaller boats, the Port Alice Yacht Club, and the new

Rumble Beach Marina. Restaurants, liquor store, grocery market that almost qualifies as a supermarket (and the best grocery shopping between Port Hardy and Tofino). Fuel is available from a service station near the public dock at the north end of town for a $20 fee. A tricky 9-hole golf course is located at the mill, the *real* Port Alice, about a mile south of the town. Showers and laundry are available at the campground half a mile south of the yacht club and Rumble Beach Marina.

Visitors are warmly welcomed in Port Alice. It is a delightful stop and a good alternative to a bus ride into Port Hardy from Coal Harbour for provisioning.

② **Rumble Beach Marina.** (250) 209-2665; (250) 284-3391. Open all year with moorage to 100 feet. This brand-new marina, just south of the Port Alice Yacht Club, is the best moorage prospect in Port Alice. Potable water and garbage drop. No power.

The marina is operated by the city and is within walking distance of all Port Alice amenities.

② **Port Alice Yacht Club.** You don't have to belong to a yacht club with reciprocal privileges to tie up here. A log breakwater protects the yacht club and the new public dock/launch ramp to the south. Moorage is

available in members' vacant slips. Slips are generally not available in July and August. Boats that have been trailered to Port Alice cannot stay at the yacht club.

Although the yacht club is designed primarily for smaller boats, it may have room for larger boats if two adjacent moorage spaces are open. A volunteer worker may point you to your slip, help you tie up, then show you around town. Good water and 20 amp power on the docks. If you come in after hours, the gate is locked but the phone numbers of volunteers are posted. A public park with picnic tables and playground equipment is immediately to the north. We were told that boats can anchor south of the Frigon Islets.

Quatsino Narrows. Quatsino Narrows connects with Rupert Inlet and Holberg Inlet, and the village of Coal Harbour. With tidal streams near Makwazniht Island running to 9 knots on the flood and 8 knots on the ebb, it is best to take the narrows near slack. Predictions for Quatsino Narrows are shown in Tide & Current Tables, Vol. 6. You'll find considerable turbulence near Makwazniht Island. The range on the eastern shore of the narrows is for large ships with 30-foot drafts; small boats need not stay on the range. Turbulence, though less than that found near Makwazniht Island, is present near the south

The entrance to Early Bird Cove is narrow and shallow.

The museum at Coal Harbour houses memorabilia from Coal Harbour's military and whaling days.

entrance to Quatsino Narrows. At slack water watch for tugs with log boom tows.

Varney Bay. Varney Bay, at the mouth of the Marble River and east of the north entrance to Quatsino Narrows, is scenic, tranquil and protected. A dinghy ride up the Marble River is worth a trip through Quatsino Narrows. Anchor inside Kenny Point behind the 3-meter island, and watch for rocks and deadheads as you enter. Varney Bay is a fish preserve. No fishing. Correspondents Gil and Karen Flanagan add this report: "After you cross the rather large delta, the Marble River flows through a canyon. The river has undercut some of the canyon walls, forming fantastic caverns. We went up the river about 2.7 miles to a rapids, where we found a huge cavern, measuring at least 30 feet by 30 feet. A must-see." To ensure enough water to safely cross the delta and reach the cavern, plan to be at the rapids as close to high tide as possible.

Rupert Inlet. Rupert Inlet is the site of the giant Utah Mines open pit copper mine, now closed and flooded. Not much reason to go there.

③ **Coal Harbour.** Coal Harbour has a small village with launch ramp, marina, small general store, and museum. It is 8 miles by road from Port Hardy.

Twice-daily bus service to Port Hardy, with connections to Port McNeill, leaves from the Whales Reach development.

During World War II, Coal Harbour was as a Royal Canadian Air Force seaplane base. The large building on the waterfront was the hangar. The Coal Harbour Whaling Station, the last whale-processing site on the West Coast, later operated out of these same facilities. Whaling operations ceased in 1967. The hangar and adjacent land now serves as seaplane storage, launching facilities, and water taxi service.

One room in the hangar is a museum, with artifacts, newspaper clippings and photographs from Coal Harbour's years as an air force base and a whaling station. Ask at

the desk to see it. If you're lucky you'll get a guided tour. No charge. The large whale jawbone shown in photos of Coal Harbour has been repaired and is on display. Recommended.

The old assembly building for the air base has been renovated as the Whales Reach Development to include a restaurant, general store, and lodging. In June 2013 the general store was open and the restaurant slated to open within weeks.

③ **Quatsino First Nations Dock.** 322 Quattishe Road, Coal Harbour, BC V0N 1K0; (250) 949-6870; qcswharf@recn.ca. Moorage, gas, diesel, water, some 20 amp power. Showers and laundry facilities available beyond the wharfinger office. Pay-for-use Wi-Fi is available. The floats can be busy with commercial boats.

Holberg Inlet is 18 miles long, narrow and deep, a classic fjord. It has few places to anchor, and not much for the cruising yachtsman. With its 36-mile round trip and no facilities or attractions, it is seldom traveled by cruising yachts.

Quatsino Village. There is a public dock at Quatsino Village, mostly for smaller boats and loading/unloading. We tucked into the only larger space available and were yelled at by a taxi boat operator who had plenty of room to maneuver. We walked into the village and to the 1898 Anglican church, open for visitors. A small museum and snack shop are open one hour per day several days a week. Chart 3681 shows the details for entry. Room to anchor off the dock if necessary.

BROOKS BAY

Brooks Bay is between Quatsino Sound and Brooks Peninsula. It's about 19 miles from a departure point south of Kains Island (at the entrance to Quatsino Sound) to a point about 2 miles west of Solander Island. Solander Island to Walters Cove is another 22 to 25 miles depending on the course chosen—a

total of at least 40 miles in the open sea. If wind and seas are favorable, those heading south will want to seize the opportunity to round Brooks Peninsula. They can be excused for not exploring Brooks Bay. If the weather is unfavorable, Brooks Bay is a good place to explore while waiting for a weather window. If you have the time, it is recommended.

Two inlets, Klaskino Inlet and Klaskish Inlet, are beautiful and have good anchorage, although portions of Klaskino Inlet have been logged. Brooks Bay is dotted with unmarked (but charted) rocks and reefs that make navigation exciting. Plot courses carefully.

④ **Klaskino Inlet.** Assuming an approach from the north, leave Lawn Point approximately 2 miles to port. (Lawn Point's grassy-looking slopes are in fact covered with low bushes). Continue, to leave Scarf Reef to port. Then turn to leave Rugged Islets to starboard. Turn to pass midway between Buoys *M17* and *M18*, then turn to enter Klaskino Inlet.

For a quick anchorage, skirt around Anchorage Island into Klaskino Anchorage (the mooring buoys shown on the chart were removed in early 2009, along with their associated ground tackle). The small bight north of the now-removed charted buoys also will hold you. Although the surrounding hillsides

CHARTS	
3623	Kyuquot Sound to Cape Cook (1:80,000)
3624	Cape Cook to Cape Scott (1:90,000)
3651	Scouler Entrance and Kyuquot
3677	Kyuquot Sound, 1:40,000
3679	Quatsino Sound (1:50,000)
3680	Brooks Bay (1:38,300)
3683	Checleset Bay (1:36,500)

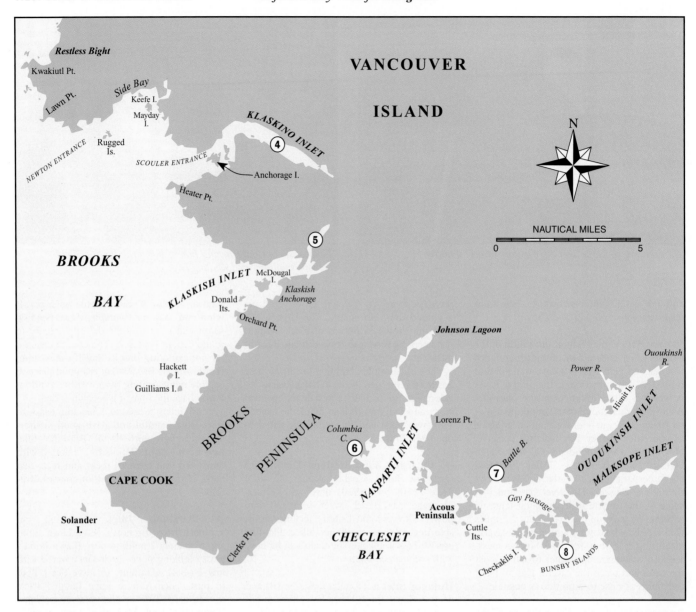

have been clear cut, the islands in the anchorage still appear pristine.

If you'd like to explore further, go through Scouler Pass. Use the more open northern channel, leaving Buoy *M23* to port. The kelp will be close enough to hold your attention. Anchor in the bight between the 67- and 53-meter islands, in the area shown as 7 meters at zero tide. The drying flats of the river mouth come up sharply. Be sure you don't swing onto them.

Correspondent Gil Flanagan went all the way to the head of Klaskino Inlet (about 4 miles from Scouler Pass), and recommends the anchorage behind the little island near the head. He says shore access is excellent, with logging roads for walking. Make noise; bears frequent the woods.

Leaving Klaskino Inlet, the safest route is back between Buoys *M17* and *M18*. Although it's possible to take a route westward through Steele Reefs, we're not sure we'd do it again. Our course took us directly over the word "Steele" on the chart. We had good depths, but even on a quiet day the surf

crashing on the rocks seemed closer than we expected. [*Hale*]

⑤ **Klaskish Inlet.** If you run from Quatsino Sound directly to Klaskish Inlet, your probable course will take you very near to Hughes Rock, which dries 5 feet. Hughes Rock is clearly shown on the chart. Don't run over it.

Consider anchoring in magnificent Klaskish Basin, reached through a knockout, must-see, narrow gorge with vertical rock sides, overhung with dense forest. Once through, you are separated from the rest of the world. All the mooring buoys shown on the chart have been removed.

Brooks Peninsula. Brooks Peninsula and the waters off Cape Cook are, together with Cape Scott, the most hostile on the west coast of Vancouver Island. Like rounding Cape Scott, rounding the Brooks is a milestone in a circumnavigation. The peninsula itself is a mountainous, rectangular promontory that extends 6 miles out from Vancouver

Island, like a growth on the side of an otherwise handsome face. Rocks and reefs guard much of the shoreline. Tangles of driftwood make beaches impassable. Cliffs rise from the beaches. At the tops of the cliffs, wilderness. Much of the peninsula is a provincial park, preserved for its wildness. Twenty thousand years ago, when glaciers covered most of Vancouver Island, the Brooks Peninsula remained ice-free. Plant species wiped out in glaciated areas are still found here. Park status helps preserve those species.

Cap on the Cape: When a cloud forms on top of Brooks Peninsula over Cape Cook, it often means that strong northwesterly winds will follow.

Cape Cook & Solander Island. Cape Cook is the northwestern tip of Brooks Peninsula. Rocks and shoals extend offshore from Cape Cook nearly to Solander Island.

The Cape Cook/Solander Island area can be a dangerous patch of water. When conflicting currents meet accelerating winds, conditions can sink a boat. Cape Cook has driven back large steamships. The marine weather broadcasts often talk of "local winds off the headlands" of 35 knots. The headland they have in mind is Cape Cook. While no headland on the West Coast should be taken lightly, Cape Cook (and Cape Scott) should be given the greatest respect. Listen to the weather broadcasts. If conditions sound questionable, wait. When your opportunity comes, seize it.

On all but the quietest days, the safe route past Cape Cook is well offshore from Solander Island. If you are one of the rare lucky ones to round the Brooks on a quiet day and can approach Solander Island more closely, you'll see Steller sea lions hauled out on the base of the island and puffins swimming near your boat.

Weather information: An automated weather station on Solander Island provides wind speed and direction, updated hourly. Listen to the continuous marine broadcast for the latest weather information.

Clerke Point. Clerke Point marks the southeast corner of Brooks Peninsula. Shoals extend at least 0.5 mile offshore. Following the 20-fathom curve will leave ample room for safety. The pyramid-shaped seas we had battled at Solander Island disappeared completely by Clerke Point.

Once past Brooks Peninsula the winds slacken, the weather warms and conditions improve.

CHECLESET BAY

Checleset Bay has a number of anchorages, including the Shelter Sheds, Columbia Cove and the Bunsby Islands. If you have just rounded Brooks Peninsula, Shelter Sheds or Columbia Cove are good stops. Columbia Cove is exceptional.

Shelter Sheds. The Shelter Sheds are lines of reef extending from Brooks Peninsula into Checleset Bay. Fishermen have found shelter in their lee, hence the name. Correspondent Gil Flanagan reports that Shed 4 has by far the finest beach his family has found—better even than West Beach at Hakai. The water was near 70° F. A trail leads to Columbia Cove, but Correspondents Steve and Elsie Hulsizer report that windfall has made the trail difficult, especially the first 200 yards.

⑥ **Columbia Cove.** Beautiful Columbia Cove is known locally as Peddlers Cove. Neither name is on the chart. It is immediately north of Jackobson Point, snugged up against the base of Brooks Peninsula.

Be sure to enter between Jackobson Point and the 215-foot island. Columbia Cove is a voluntary no-discharge zone. Please volunteer. The mooring buoys and associated ground tackle were removed in early 2009, so it's anchoring only. The cove has experienced some silting over the years and anchoring room has become limited. The mouth of the cove, between Jackobson Point and the

Brooks Peninsula is famous for high winds and rough water. It demands respect.

215-foot island, is safe in a northwesterly. In southerlies, winds and waves make this area uncomfortable, leaving room for only about three boats in the cove itself.

The name Columbia Cove comes from Captain Robert Gray's ship *Columbia*, which overnighted here twice. If you think Columbia Cove is crowded with three boats now, imagine it with the *Columbia*, the schooner *Adventure*, and the ship *Margaret*, of Boston, all in at the same time. A sometimes muddy trail across the small peninsula formed by Jackobson Point leads to a beautiful sandy ocean beach. Great beachcombing. Take the dinghy up the stream to the trailhead, but watch the tide. You can be stranded, with a long walk across tideflats.

Weather note: When strong winds from the northwest are forecast south of Brooks Peninsula, the Brooks provides a lee for Columbia Cove and adjacent waters. Winds may be strong but seas will be quiet. It's a good place to wait out a northwest gale. It's not a good place to wait out a southeast gale.

⑦ **Battle Bay.** Battle Bay, north of the Bunsby Islands, has acceptable anchorages roughly off the Indian reserve, and in the

nook that makes up the northeast shore. Approach the Longback Islands before making your turn into Battle Bay. One interesting anchorage is immediately west of Battle Bay, against the east shore of Acous Peninsula. To reach that anchorage, leave the Skirmish Islands to starboard as you approach. From there you'll look across a sea of islands and rocks to the Bunsbys.

The Indian reserve on the Acous Peninsula is the former home of the Checleset Band, now located in Walters Cove. You can find fallen totem poles serving as nurse logs, and the depressions of old longhouses.

⑧ **Bunsby Islands.** "Did you get to the Bunsbys?" That's what people ask when they learn you've been down the west coast of Vancouver Island. Don't disappoint them by saying no. The Bunsby Islands are rocky, rugged, and beautiful. They were named for a character in the Charles Dickens novel *Dombey and Son.* A number of other features in the area also bear names from that novel.

Study the chart and know your location at all times. Enter the Bunsby Islands only through Gay Passage. Two anchorages are off this passage: either the cove in the south-

Solander Island off Cape Cook, the Cape of Storms, on a rare calm summer afternoon.

The rock formations surrounding Columbia Cove are worth exploring by dinghy or kayak.

The Bunsby Islands are not to be missed. The rugged scenery and sandy beaches are a highlight of the west coast of Vancouver Island.

ern island or the slightly larger bay in the northern island. Enter the northern island's bay favoring the north shore, to avoid a shoal extending from the south side. In this larger bay, note the rock directly beneath the 6-fathom sounding. The lagoon adjacent to this bay may be fine for an adventuresome trailerable boat.

The cove on the west side of Gay Passage is guarded by two rocks that dry 4 feet. The rocks are easy to identify and avoid if you're paying attention, but you must pay attention. The cove has room for several boats.

Checleset Bay has a large population of sea otters, the successful result of a 1969 effort to re-establish these delightful creatures. From the Bunsbys, where they were first re-introduced, the sea otters have spread up and down the coast, as far south as Barkley Sound and as far north as the Cape Caution area on the mainland. You'll sometimes see them in "rafts," groups of otters hanging together, in kelp beds.

If weather allows, take the dinghy or kayak around the islands. The rugged, wind-swept rocks and islets are too stunning to try to describe. It's easy to get disoriented. Carry a chart, compass, handheld GPS and handheld VHF radio.

KYUQUOT SOUND

With the exception of the outer islands and Rugged Point, Kyuquot (pronounced "Ki-YU-kit") Sound is protected and pretty, surrounded by high mountains, with easy waters. On the inside, Dixie Cove and Don Douglass's "Petroglyph Cove" (known locally as Blue Lips Cove) are excellent anchorages, and several others are attractive. The settlement of Walters Cove is a favorite.

From the south, enter Kyuquot Sound

CHARTS	
3651	Scouler Entrance and Kyuquot Sound
3682	Kyuquot Sound (1:36,700)
3683	Checleset Bay (1:36,500)

past whistle Buoy *M38*. Leave the buoy to starboard, and proceed through Kyuquot Channel. Most visiting pleasure craft, however, will approach from the north and stop at Walters Cove before entering Kyuquot Sound proper.

⑨ **Walters Cove.** For communication, call on VHF channels 06 or 14. The little settlement of Walters Cove has almost everything you might need after a week or two of working your way along the coast: outpost hospital, ice, charts, a small general store, pay phone, a restaurant and coffee shop, relaxed and friendly people, happy kids and lazy dogs.

One thing Walters Cove does not have is liquor. Walters Cove is dry, by vote of the Kyuquot Native community, and there's not a drop to be bought. Nor is liquor in evidence, even on the dock.

Another thing you won't find is fuel. Be sure you have enough fuel in your tanks. The nearest fuel is in Fair Harbour.

From seaward, the safest approach to Walters Cove in all weather is from Whistle Buoy *MC*, at the entrance to Brown Channel. Use Chart 3683. Go through Brown Channel and turn to starboard on a course to leave Gayward Rock to starboard. At Gayward Rock go to large scale Chart 3651 to work your way past the east side of Walters Island and into Walters Cove.

Boats coming down from the Bunsby Islands probably will follow Chart 3683's rather obvious passage along the Vancouver Island shoreline, leaving Cole Rock to starboard, and McLean Island and Chief Rock Buoy *M29* to port. At Gayward Rock they would move to large-scale Chart 3651.

New rock: On Charts 3623 and 3683 the 41-foot sounding at 50°03'03.0"N/ 127°27'01.0"W should be replaced with a sounding of 10 feet. This rock is along your probable shoreline passage course. At a depth of 10 feet at zero tide the rock is not a concern for most boats, but you should know it's there.

Without Chart 3651, entry to Walters Cove would be a tricky matter. Although it is marked by buoys and a daybeacon, the chan-

nel past the east side of Walters Island is easy to misread, and the unwary skipper could find himself on a rock. With Chart 3651 the channel is apparent, and following the rule of Red, Right, Returning, entry is safe. The one daybeacon along the way marks the narrow passage that leads directly into Walters Cove. Remember that beacons are attached to the earth; rock extends well into the passage from the beacon. Don't cut it close. Use a mid-channel course favoring the north side between the beacon and the 51-meter island opposite. The chart makes the route clear.

Several locals insist, "Don't anchor in Walters Cove!" The bottom, they say, is foul with debris. Furthermore, the floor of the bay is crisscrossed by high voltage submarine electrical cables, a Telus phone line, and the water lines serving the community.

Instead of anchoring, tie up at the public wharf to port as you enter. Long mooring floats are on each side of the public wharf. The general store and post office, owned by Susan (Kayra) Bostrom, is at the head of the wharf. Stock arrives Thursday afternoons aboard the supply ship *Uchuck III*.

Java the Hutt Coffee Shop, which began its life as a "boat-through" rather than "drive-through" coffee shop on the Kyuquot Inn dock, is now located in the renovated school house at the inn. When we visited in June 2013, the coffee shop was just opening for the season. They often have hot lunches and dinners available, in addition to pastries and drinks. Free Wi-Fi is provided. Showers are available at the inn. Owner Eric Gorbman is among the friendliest people on the coast.

The best time to arrive at Walters Cove is Thursday afternoon. The *Uchuck III* arrives that day, sometime after 5:00 p.m., depending on the other stops they have scheduled. Walters Cove becomes a bustle of activity when the ship lands, with skiffs arriving from all over the cove and outlying areas. Watching the *Uchuck III* unload its cargo is a slice of West Coast life you won't want to miss. Everyone pitches in. Fuel barrels and boxes are loaded off the boat's starboard side into waiting skiffs. Pallets of groceries are loaded off the port side onto carts on the dock.

Because the ship overnights at Walters

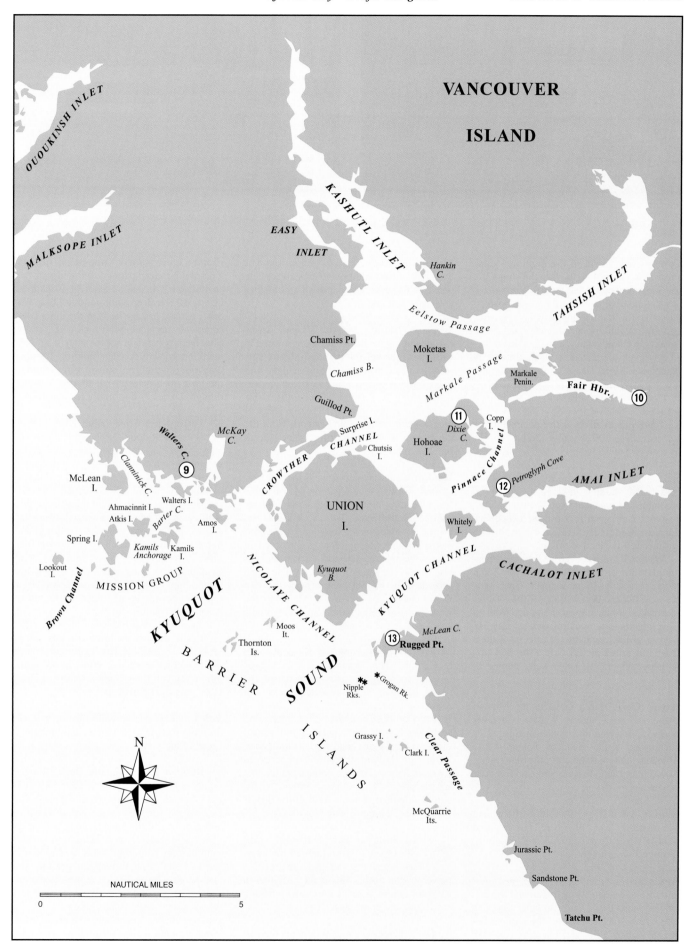

VANCOUVER

ISLAND

OUOUKINSH INLET

MALKSOPE INLET

KASHUTL INLET

EASY
INLET

Hankin
C.

TAHSISH INLET

Eelstow Passage

Chamiss Pt.

Moketas
I.

Chamiss B.

Markale
Penin.

Fair Hbr.

⑩

Markale Passage

Guillod Pt.

Surprise I.

⑪
*Dixie
C.*

Copp
I.

*McKay
C.*

Walters C.

Chutsis
I.

Hohoae
I.

Pinnace Channel

Petroglyph Cove

⑫

AMAI INLET

⑨

Clanninick C.

McLean
I.

Walters I.

Barter C.

UNION

I.

Whitely
I.

CACHALOT INLET

Ahmacinnit I.

Atkis I.

Amos
I.

Spring I.

*Kamils
Anchorage*

Kamils
I.

*Kyuquot
B.*

KYUQUOT CHANNEL

Lookout
I.

Brown Channel

MISSION GROUP

NICOLAYE CHANNEL

KYUQUOT

McLean C.

⑬
Rugged Pt.

Moos
It.

Thornton
Is.

✳✳   ✳*Grogan Rk.*
Nipple
Rks.

BARRIER

SOUND

ISLANDS

Grassy I.

Clark I.

Clear Passage

N

McQuarrie
Its.

Jurassic Pt.

Sandstone Pt.

NAUTICAL MILES

0   5

Tatchu Pt.

Walters Cove is a well-stocked village and a good stop for reprovisioning.

The Kyuquot Inn is home to Java the Hutt coffee shop.

Cove, passengers spend the night at lodges and B&Bs. For dinner, the Java the Hutt Coffee Shop becomes a restaurant. When there is space, the coffee shop also feeds boaters, guests at the lodges, and anyone else who asks by mid-afternoon. Dinner is delicious. Guests eat family-style at a long table.

For medical matters, contact the VIHA (Vancouver Island Health Authority) outpost hospital at Walters Cove, (250) 332-5289.

Good water is available at the store for a small fee.

The Kyuquot Band Native community of approximately 200 is across the bay, served by its own public dock.

All transport is by boat in Walters Cove, and from an early age the Kyuquot children (and Native children all along the coast) are accomplished boat handlers. Their outboard-powered craft seem to have but two directions: forward and reverse; and two throttle settings: full-power and off.

Walters Cove has been a popular gathering place for decades. Years ago it was home to five fish camps in the summer. When people were stuck in port waiting for the weather to break, the talk flowed. Long ago Walters Cove got its local name of Bull---t Bay, BS Bay in polite company. A cafe in Walters Cove was called the BS Cafe. (The BS Cafe, with its memorabilia-laden walls, burned in 1998.)

Barter Cove. Barter Cove in the Mission Group islands outside Walters Cove, is open, unprotected and not as interesting as anchorages inside Kyuquot Sound. Leave Ahmacinnit Island and the tiny islet east of Ahmacinnit Island to starboard, and feel your way in.

Kamils Anchorage. Kamils Anchorage in the Mission Group islands is more exposed than Barter Cove. Enter, very carefully, through Favourite Entrance.

Amos Island. From Walters Cove, the easiest entrance to Kyuquot Sound is around the east side of Amos Island into Crowther Channel. Use Chart 3651 to identify the channel between Walters Cove and Nicolaye Channel, then Chart 3682 to find the route past Amos

Island. The passage east of Amos Island is deep but narrow, and bounded by rocks. The first time through can be unsettling, but after you've done it once it's easy.

Surprise Island. Surprise Island, steep, round, and logged off to stumps, is located in Crowther Channel. On the south side of Surprise Island, Crowther Channel is deep and open, but on the north side a narrow passage is interesting. At zero tide least depths in this passage are approximately 18 feet. A ledge of rock, shown on the chart, extends from the north shore. Favor the Surprise Island side all the way through.

Hankin Cove. Hankin Cove is located near the mouth of Kashutl Inlet, on the east side. It is a beautiful little cove with good holding, completely protected, but the hillsides are marred by evidence of logging. Correspondents Gil and Karen Flanagan anchored in the southeast cove, and add, "Chart 3682 is way off on the shoal in this cove. The shoal extends only halfway across from the east shore. Depths are 12 to 18 feet along the west shore, almost to the south end of the cove."

⑩ Fair Harbour. Enter Fair Harbour south of Karouk Island, leaving the two lighted beacons to port. The passage north of the island has two newly-reported rocks, not shown on the chart.

Fair Harbour has a wide dirt launch ramp at the head, with ample parking and a small campground. A dirt road leads from Zeballos to Fair Harbour, the only road access to Kyuquot Sound. This is a popular trailer boat launch point. A good-sized public wharf, with a long float, is at the head. If the float is full, anchor in approximately 60 feet.

⑩ Swan Song at Fair Harbour. (250) 830-2230. Open all year. Limited moorage, gas, diesel, propane, water, garbage drop. No power on the docks. This is the only fuel in Kyuquot Sound. A small store carries fishing tackle, ice, and convenience food.

⑪ Dixie Cove. Dixie Cove indents the east side Hohoae Island, and is a wonderful an-

chorage. Enter south of Copp Island, through a narrow but deep passage to the first of two anchorages. The outer anchorage is approximately 30 feet deep, with good holding. Another narrow passage leads to the inner cove, completely secluded, with rock cliffs on one side. Depths here are approximately 18 feet, mud bottom with excellent holding. Landing on shore is a problem, so you're restricted to the boat. As a place to put the hook down, though, Dixie Cove is highly recommended.

⑫ Petroglyph Cove (Blue Lips Cove). In his excellent book, *Exploring Vancouver Island's West Coast,* Don Douglass describes this previously-unnamed anchorage and calls it "Petroglyph Cove." In the second edition of his book, Douglass acknowledged that others had not been able to find the petroglyphs. Hulsizer reported finding what looked like a faded pictograph (red ochre painting) and noted that the local name for the cove is Blue Lips Cove—because when residents went swimming the water was so cold their lips turned blue. Petroglyph, Pictograph or Blue Lips, the cove is located near the mouth of Amai Inlet, roughly due west of Amai Point. The narrow entry is hidden until you're right on it. The channel shallows to a least depth of 12 to 18 feet, but has no hazards. Once inside you are protected. While in our opinion Petroglyph Cove is not as pretty as Dixie Cove, it is an excellent spot.

Volcanic Cove. Exposed to the north, small, no room to swing. Temporary only for small boats, in our view.

⑬ Rugged Point Marine Park. Rugged Point marks the southern entrance to Kyuquot Sound. Our notes read, "Wow!" The beaches on the ocean side are spectacular, and deserve a visit. Anchor along the inside beaches in 18 feet on a kelp-covered hard sand bottom, and dinghy ashore. The Pacific swell, though diminished, can get into the anchorage. The anchorage is protected from southeasterlies and westerlies but is subject to occasional night-time outflow winds. Be sure you anchor far enough offshore to avoid swinging onto shallows if outflow winds develop.

THE LEARNING NEVER STOPS

Every boat owner goes through a learning curve that never stops. A person can, of course, start a little farther along the curve by spending time with others aboard their boats, or have the smarts to be born into a boating family, or, at the very least, take a Power Squadron or Coast Guard Auxiliary course. It may also be possible to take a few practical lessons from the person who sold you the boat.

But the curve remains, stretching endlessly into the future. After more than 60 years of boating, I'm still struggling to learn more, and seldom leave the harbor without some new problem presenting itself, calling on me to find a solution resulting in another little inch of travel along that curve.

Stretching out along the learning curve usually means doing something you haven't done before, whether it's adjusting the valves on your diesel engine or crossing the Strait of Juan de Fuca. Once you've done these things, they seem to be pretty simple. But until you try, they appear to be the product of some occult art.

Most people, when they first buy a boat, spend enough time close to the dock to get used to the "feel" of the boat: how quickly it turns, how it steers in reverse, how long it takes to stop, and where the sides of the boat are in relation to the dock. Before long, it will be time to head out for larger waters. If those first experiments were in Seattle's Lake Union, as many are, the skipper is going to have to deal with the Ballard Locks before those larger waters can be experienced. Approaching the locks for the very first time takes a leap of courage. You sure don't want to make a fool of yourself in front of all those "expert" skippers and the usual crowd of gawkers lining the lock walls.

But having screwed up the courage to try, you will soon find that running the locks doesn't take the skill of a brain surgeon. A little common sense and patience, and you're free of the confining lakes and out into the broad reaches of Puget Sound, where a boating family can easily spend a cruising lifetime.

On the other hand, you will have heard about the glorious San Juan Islands, invitingly situated only 20 miles or so across the Strait of Juan de Fuca. If you're like most of us, eventually you'll take a deep breath and brave the strait for a chance to vacation in our own world-famous islands. Once again, you'll discover that making that crossing is not beyond your ability, and that trip can become almost routine. Almost, I say, because the strait can kick up a fuss, and part of your learning curve will be discovering how to handle rough water, how to pick a time to avoid the rough water, or some combination of both.

In any event, you will have made another major step up the learning curve. You can handle yourself and your boat under another set of conditions. And the steps stretch out as far as you can imagine. There's the Strait of Georgia in order to reach Desolation Sound; a series of rapids and Johnstone Strait in order to reach the Broughtons cruising area; Queen Charlotte Strait, Dixon Entrance, the west coast of Vancouver Island.

All are milestones on the learning curve. All can be (and have been) negotiated by thousands of people in all sorts of boats.

And they aren't all brain surgeons or old salts either. Most are just ordinary folks, screwing up the courage to take that next step up the learning curve.

– Tom Kincaid

A trail, now upgraded with a boardwalk, leads through the park to the ocean beaches. Bear and cougar prints have been sighted, so be noisy. Once on the ocean beach, you will find a series of paths leading around headlands all the way to the Kapoose Creek. Some of the paths are steep and involve climbing ladders or using ropes for assistance.

Cachalot. Cachalot, the site of a former industrial whaling center, makes an interesting lunch stop or afternoon exploration. Locate it by finding the abandoned pilings between Cachalot Inlet to the east and Cachalot Creek to the west. Although pronounced locally as "catch a lot," the name means sperm whale in French (and in French would be pronounced "caa-shaa-low"). The whaling center operated between 1907 and 1926, then served as a pilchard reduction plant until the 1940s.

Anchor off the old pilings in 30 to 60 feet of water and take the dinghy ashore. You'll find old whale bones, crockery, and miscellaneous hardware on the beach, and rusty equipment in the forest. Next to the creek, a ferrocement statue of a sperm whale serves as a memorial to the whales that were processed at this site. The statue was placed there anonymously by a Vancouver Island artist in the 1970s. Hulsizer gives the history of the site in *Voyages to Windward*.

When anchoring, avoid the drying shoal on the north end of the site near the river and be sure to anchor in at least 30 feet of water to avoid your anchor being entangled in kelp.

Kyuquot Sound to Esperanza Inlet. Depending on the course chosen, it is approximately 13.5 miles between Rugged Point and the entrance to Gillam Channel, which leads into Esperanza Inlet. In good visibility the route through Clear Passage is smooth and interesting. In poor visibility, we would head seaward from Rugged Point to entrance Buoy *M38*, then turn southeastward toward Gillam Channel.

Clear Passage to Tatchu Point. Clear Passage takes you about 4 miles along the coast in waters protected by the Barrier Islands, past a steady display of rugged rocks and rock islets. The channel is free of hazards. To enter Clear Passage, leave Grogan Rock to starboard, watching carefully for the rock to port, marked by kelp, that dries 4 feet. Heading down-island, we got a little close to Grogan Rock, and the depths came up sharply. We moved off to port and they went back down. You will have no trouble identifying Grogan Rock. It is an awful 23-foot-high black pinnacle and it commands attention. Lay a course to take you north of McQuarrie Islets, and exit Clear Passage leaving Mc-

The beaches on the west coast of Vancouver Island, like this one at Rugged Point Marine Park, are often made up of fine sand.

Quarrie Islets to starboard. The rocks and islets along Clear Passage all look alike. It helps to plot a waypoint at the spot where you intend to turn to exit past McQuarrie Islets. Clear Passage is also a good route when heading north. Leave McQuarrie Islets and Grogan Rock to port.

The island just south of Grassy Isle is a good place to hunt fossils. "We anchored south of Clark Island and took the dinghy ashore to a shell beach on the southeast corner of the island. The fossils were just lying on the beach. We recommend doing this on a calm day only. With the new, more detailed, metric chart, it might be possible to find anchorage between Grassy Isle and Clark." [*Hulsizer*]

Local fishermen say the waters from Jurassic Point past Tatchu Point can be an "ugly patch of water." Use caution and careful judgment.

⑭ **Rolling Roadstead (Catala Island Provincial Park).** Rolling Roadstead offers acceptable anchorage in fair weather. From the west the approach can be tricky. Douglass and Watmough describe the approach in their books. Careful navigation is called for, including the finding and identifying of the various rocks and reefs in the entrance. The hazards are easily identified, either by the breaking surf or kelp growing in the shallows. With the hazards accounted for, the entry is reported to be safe. All agree that it should be run in fair weather only, with good visibility.

If you're coming down from Tatchu Point, especially in a fresh westerly, it's easier to enter via Gillam Channel, leaving Black Rock and Entrance Reef to port and approach Rolling Roadstead from the southwest. Anchor in the lee of the point of land that juts abruptly from Catala Island.

Catala Island, which protects Rolling Roadstead, is a provincial marine park. The beach on Catala Island is beautiful. Several sea caves are accessible.

Gillam Channel. Gillam Channel, more than one-half mile wide and well-buoyed, is the safe entrance to Esperanza Inlet. Approaching, leave buoys *M40*, the entrance buoy and *M42*, which marks the west end of Blind Reef, to starboard. Leave buoy *M41* to port, and continue into Esperanza Inlet.

ESPERANZA INLET

Esperanza Inlet is on the west side of Nootka Island, and ultimately connects with Nootka

CHARTS	
3677	Kyuquot Sound, 1:40,000
3675	Nootka Sound (1:40,000) Gold River (1:10,000) Princesa Channel (1:10,000)
3676	Esperanza Inlet (1:40,000) Tahsis (1:12,000)

Zeballos Inlet is bounded by impressive mountains.

Sound. The inlet is part of the "inside route" through this portion of the coast. This route is served by three communities—Zeballos, Tahsis, and Gold River—and by the Esperanza Mission, with its fuel dock and excellent water. The waterways are beautiful, and contain several good stopping places. Tahsis Narrows connects Esperanza Inlet with Tahsis Inlet on the Nootka Sound side, and is not difficult to run.

Nuchatlitz Inlet. Reader Don Thain reports that Mary Basin is a delightful and protected anchorage with good holding in mud. A pretty waterfall on Laurie Creek is reachable by dinghy on a 7-foot tide. The Inner Basin is a tidal lagoon.

⑮ **Nuchatlitz Provincial Park.** Nuchatlitz Provincial Park is a beautiful and interesting stop with a well-protected anchorage. It's a favorite among kayakers and campers. The area contains a number of archeological treasures, including burial canoes on land and burial caves on the outer islands.

The entry to Nuchatlitz is marked by rocks and wildness to seaward, rocks and rock islets to landward. Inside, a large bay has a uniform bottom with approximately 30- to 40-foot anchoring depths. In good weather, if you choose an anchoring spot where you can see over the islands towards the northwest, you may be rewarded with a magnificent sunset. The anchorage can be absolutely calm when the wind dies in the evening, but you can hear the surf breaking on the outer islands.

The abandoned Indian village of Nuchatlitz is on the shore of a 44-meter island marked Indian Reserve, above a marvelous beach. At low tide you can walk the drying sand bar from the reserve island to a second 44-meter island to the west. Although the village was moved from this site to Espinosa in the 1980s, the site is still visited by the band. Local kayak tours use it as a landing site.

A number of private homes dot the shores of a privately-owned unmarked island on the south side of the anchorage. Private

buoys mark the route past submerged rocks to homes on the island's back side and to a shallow lagoon. Use Chart 3676, which reflects hydrographic survey work performed between 1992 and 1996 at the cost of many survey launch propellers.

The easy but long entry to Nuchatlitz is from the northeast, passing east of Rosa Island. From there the chart makes the course clear: Follow the winding channel east of the 37-meter and 34-meter islands, and east of the two red spar buoys *M46* and *M48* (Red, Right, Returning). At Buoy *M48* the bay opens up. Both Douglass and Yeadon-Jones describe a second, more direct entrance, leaving the light on the 37-meter island (known locally as Entrance Island) to starboard as you enter.

⑯ **Queen Cove.** Queen Cove is a short distance inside the entrance to Port Eliza, the first inlet to port as you enter Esperanza Inlet. It is a safe and satisfying spot to put the hook down and go exploring, although not as beautiful as Nuchatlitz on the east side of Gillam Channel. Queen Cove is a popular anchorage among island circumnavigators. Anchor here and you'll soon have company. The cove is well protected, and has excellent holding in 20 to 40 feet. It is large enough for several boats to swing. A cabin with dock is at the north end of Queen Cove. The Park River enters at the north end, and makes a good dinghy exploration.

The most protected anchorage is the nook at the south end of Queen Cove, between the little island and the rock that dries 3.4 meters (11 feet). Swinging room is a little restricted, but the anchorage is workable. We overnighted in Queen Cove, anchored in the wider and much more exposed northern area. At 5:00 p.m. the wind came in, and built to about 25 knots before dying at sundown. We sailed back and forth on our anchor, but we didn't budge. [*Hale*].

Espinosa Inlet. Espinosa Inlet is deep and high-walled. No place to anchor. The Native village of Ocluje is located at its head.

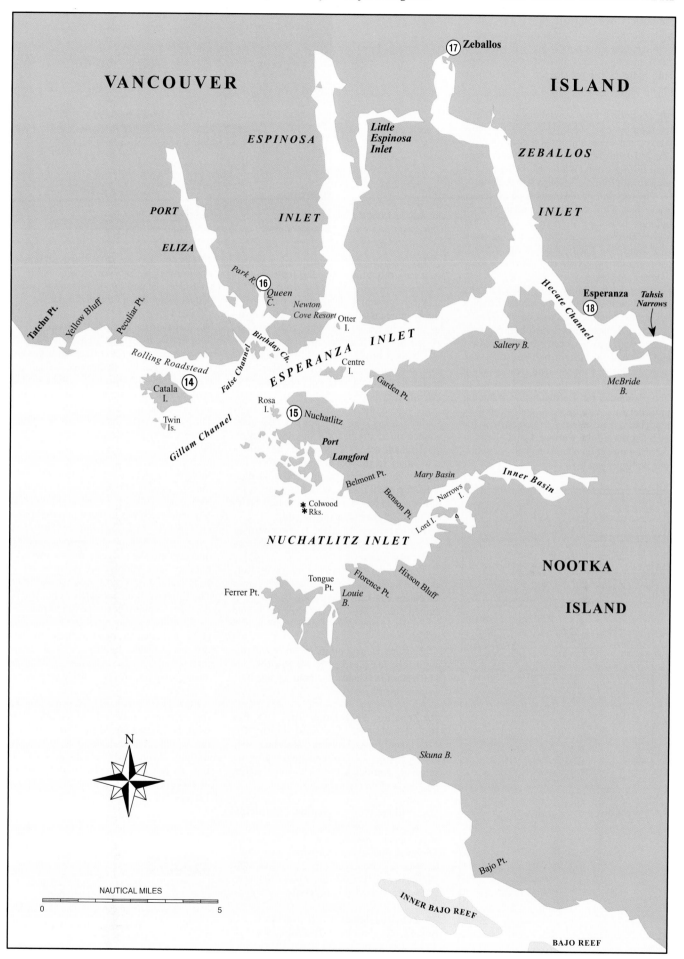

Newton Cove Resort. (877) 337-5465; info@nootkamarineadventures.com; www.nootkamarineadventures.com. Call ahead to check moorage availability. Moorage, restaurant, lodging, fishing charters. Located near the mouth of Espinosa Inlet.

⑰ **Zeballos.** www.zeballos.com. Zeballos (pronounced "Ze-BAH-los") is the most unexpected town on the west coast of Vancouver Island. While other settlements range from fishing camp (Winter Harbour) to bustling town (Tofino), Zeballos stands alone.

The trip up Zeballos Inlet is an especially scenic one, with odd-shaped mountains with bulbous tops and sheer rock faces rising above the shores. Zeballos is a mining town that looks like Cicily, Alaska, the fictional town made famous by the television show *Northern Exposure*, with wandering streets, false-fronted buildings, and a museum. The town is built at the mouth of the Zeballos River, next to mountains that go *straight up*.

The Zeballos Hotel, which burned down several years ago, has been rebuilt as the Post and Beam. It includes a pub and café. The museum, located on the main road heading out of town, is one of the town's main attractions. It's small but fascinating, with mining paraphernalia, photographs, and a full-scale model of a mine entrance. If you arrive at the museum during the workweek and no one is there, inquire at the municipal hall and someone will give you a tour.

The floats at Zeballos are well maintained, with power and water.

The town recently constructed a boardwalk trail through the Zeballos River estuary. It's a beautiful walk along the river.

Much gold has been taken out of the highly mineralized mountains around Zeballos. Over dinner at the hotel on our first visit, we talked with a wildcat prospector whose eyes burned bright as he told of pockets of gold still waiting to be taken. He insisted that he didn't have gold fever, *but he knew where the gold was.* [*Hale*]

Tie up at the public dock, to the right of the fuel dock as you approach. Pay telephones are at the head of the dock and on the seaplane dock. The village has built a new wharf to the left of the fuel dock, but it is for large vessels, loading and unloading only. The small float next to the wharf is for short-term (a few hours) tie-up. A bird-viewing platform overlooks the estuary.

A fish-processing plant is shoreward of the fuel dock and is one of the town's economic mainstays.

Provisioning: At present, no good store exists. The store near the fuel dock carries ice cream and convenience foods, as well as limited perishables. The Other Place, located at the Iris Lodge Motel, has a small general store.

Zeballos is a good place to spend the night. The inlet leading to the town is long and beautiful. There's no point going both ways in one day.

⑰ **Zeballos Fuel Dock Inc.** P.O. Box 100, Zeballos, BC V0P 2A0; (250) 761-4201; keithfraser@recn.ca. Monitors VHF 68. Open all year. Gasoline, diesel, propane, kerosene, petroleum products, some marine supplies. Keith Fraser is the owner.

⑰ **Village of Zeballos Municipal Wharf.** (250) 761-4229. Open all year. For large vessels, loading and unloading only. The small float next to the wharf is for short-term (a few hours) tie-up. Some overnight moorage with permission. Access to power and water if absolutely necessary.

⑰ **Zeballos Small Craft Harbour.** P.O. Box 42, Zeballos, BC V0P 2A0; (250) 761-4333. Monitors VHF 06. Open all year with

400 feet of moorage, 20 amp power, seasonal washrooms & shower, water, waste oil collection, launch ramp, long term parking (launch ramp is run by the village).

⑱ **Esperanza (Nootka Mission).** Box 368, Tahsis, BC V0P 1X0; (250) 483-4162; www.esperanza.ca. Fuel dock with gasoline, diesel, lube oil. Excellent water. A small store is on the fuel dock. Moorage may be available at the dock in front of the old boathouse, except during the month of July; call ahead. The mission runs camps for local children. When a camp is in session, facilities may not be available.

Esperanza is the home of the Nootka Mission. Its story goes back to 1937, when the Shantyman Mission began a hospital at Esperanza. This was in the tradition of the Mission, which was founded in northern Ontario in 1907 to serve shanty dwellers in outlying areas. The Esperanza hospital no longer operates and the property is now owned by the Esperanza Ministries Association, serving people of the west coast of Vancouver Island. The property is immaculately kept. The fuel dock is an important source of revenue.

Showers, washrooms, some 15 amp power, Wi-Fi, water, ice, pay telephone, and laundry are available. Inquire about availability for visiting boaters. Sometimes, fresh Esperanza-grown produce is available for purchase.

Tahsis Narrows. Tahsis Narrows connects the Esperanza Inlet side of Nootka Island with the Nootka Sound side. From the chart, one would think reversing tidal currents rage through the narrows four times a day, but they do not. The narrows are deep and free of hazards, with little tidal current activity. Passage can be made at any time.

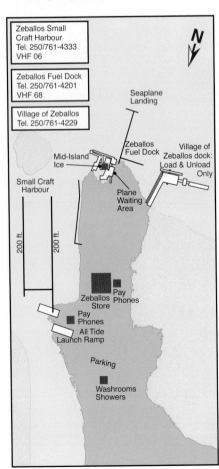

Zeballos Small Craft Harbour
Tel. 250/761-4333
VHF 06

Zeballos Fuel Dock
Tel. 250/761-4201
VHF 68

Village of Zeballos
Tel. 250/761-4229

N

Seaplane Landing

Mid-Island Ice

Zeballos Fuel Dock

Village of Zeballos dock: Load & Unload Only

Small Craft Harbour

Plane Waiting Area

200 ft.

200 ft.

Zeballos Store

Pay Phones

Pay Phones

All Tide Launch Ramp

Parking

Washrooms Showers

Zeballos

CHARTS	
3675	Nootka Sound (1:40,000) Gold River (1:10,000) Princesa Channel (1:10,000)
3676	Esperanza Inlet (1:40,000) Tahsis (1:12,000)

TAHSIS INLET

Tahsis Inlet (Tahsis is pronounced with a short-*a*, as in *cat*) is long and narrow, and bounded by mountains. The wind funnels and blows up-inlet or down, depending on conditions. The normal situation in prevailing westerly winds is for light or outflow winds in the morning and strong inflow winds in the afternoon, building stronger as you approach the town. But during extended periods of warm weather, strong outflow winds can also develop, especially at night and early morning. Gale-force easterlies rarely reach upper Tahsis Inlet, making it a good place to wait out a storm.

⑲ **Tahsis.** At the head of the inlet the sawmill town of Tahsis once had full facilities, but the mill closed and has been dismantled. The loss of the mill just about killed the town. Now, Tahsis is struggling but surviving. Outsiders bought the houses at bargain prices, which, at least initially, gave the economy a small boost. Through it all, the Westview Marina has remained an outstanding operation.

In town, the Tahsis Supermarket has consolidated many of the operations previously run by others. The Supermarket sells groceries, liquor and fuel. It also has a small cafe. This is a small town and grocery selection is limited. A hardware store, the Tahsis Building Centre, is just north of the Supermarket. A post office is located at the other end of town, near the seaplane dock.

The Tahsis library, in the municipal building, has free Wi-Fi and an excellent view. It's a wonderful place to while-away a stormy afternoon.

⑲ **Westview Marina & Lodge.** P.O. Box 248, Tahsis, BC V0P 1X0; (250) 934-7672; (800) 992-3252; info@westviewmarina. com; www.westviewmarina.com. Monitors VHF channel 06. The fuel dock has gasoline and diesel. Washrooms, showers, laundry, free Wi-Fi, a small store with ice and good gift selection, and licensed restaurant with

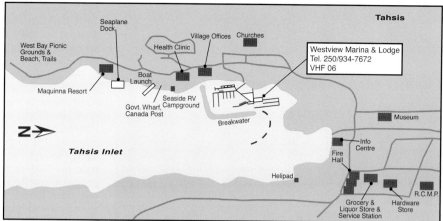

Tahsis Inlet

patio, and the Island Attitude Coffee Café. The Café opens at 5:00 a.m during the summer. Moorage has 15, 30 & 50 amp power. Courtesy car available. Email your provisioning list a week ahead and they'll have it ready for you.

This marina, at the head of Tahsis Inlet, is set up to serve the summer flotilla of small sportfishing boats. The docks have been expanded and the welcome mat is out for cruising boats. Reservations recommended May to September, but the marina will always try to fit you in. The restaurant has live music and steak dinners on Friday nights, June through September. Each year, we receive positive reviews from readers, praising the facilities and the treatment they receive. The marina is neat and attractive, the people helpful, and the fuel dock easy to approach.

Tsowwin Narrows. The major navigation danger in Tahsis Inlet is Tsowwin Narrows, created by the outfall from the Tsowwin River. A beacon marks the edge of the shoal. Pass between that beacon and another beacon on the west shore of the inlet. Remember that beacons are attached to the earth, and shoal water can extend into a channel from a beacon. Give each beacon a good offing. While we did not see much debris, Tahsis Inlet is

reported to have considerable drift and deadheads, depending on logging activity. Keep a close watch on the water ahead.

Princesa Channel. Princesa Channel runs between Bodega Island and Strange Island, and connects Tahsis and Kendrick inlets. A route through Princesa Channel gets a boat out of the Tahsis Inlet chop and cuts some distance off a passage for southbound boats heading to Friendly Cove, but the Tahsis Inlet entrance to Princesa Channel is narrow and partly guarded by underwater rocks.

From Tahsis Inlet to Kendrick Inlet (east to west) the problem is the flood tide. The flood current flows northward into Tahsis Inlet, and a boat entering Princesa Channel will find a definite northward set to its course. This northward set will tend to put the boat onto a submerged rock charted about 200 feet north of the Princesa Channel light, at the east entrance to Princesa Channel. Don Douglass, in his book *Exploring Vancouver Island's West Coast*, believes the rock is closer to 100 feet from the light. One hundred feet or 200 feet, the rock is not far away. The goal is to wrap around the Princesa Channel light but avoid yet another charted rock south of the light, while not being set onto the rock 100 to 200 feet north of the light. Chart

Sport fishing is excellent around Tahsis and is a major draw to the area.

The Island Attitude Coffee Café at Westview Marina.

Hisnit is a gorgeous anchorage. Mountains rise high above.

3675 shows the rocks clearly. Study the chart and you will understand not only the challenge but the decisions required to meet the challenge.

We ran Princesa Channel in a stout flood current and had no problems. In our case, we ran south in Tahsis Inlet until the Princesa Channel light bore 235° magnetic, then turned toward the light. We kept the light on our nose (we had to crab to make good our course) until the light was close aboard, then laid off to starboard to give the light 50 feet of clearance, and entered the channel. The key was to be aware of the rock 100 to 200 feet north of the light and keep our course south of that rock. Once past the light we held a mid-channel course and waltzed on through. [*Hale*]

Bodega Cove. Don Douglass calls this previously unnamed anchorage "Bodega Cove" and we see no reason to argue. Bodega Cove lies at the head of Kendrick Inlet, between Nootka Island and Bodega Island. The area has been logged, so the scenery is not that of primeval forest. Protection is excellent, however, and the shores are accessible. A reef extends from the Nootka Island side of the entrance. Favor the eastern, Bodega Island, side. The recommended approach is to divide the entry channel in half, then split the eastern, Bodega Island, portion in half again (in other words, three-quarters of the way toward the eastern shore), and run down that line.

A large log dump and booming ground is on Nootka Island near the head of Kendrick Inlet. When it's in operation, you can watch huge machines dumping piles of logs into the water.

NOOTKA SOUND

Nootka Sound is where European influence in the Northwest began. Although Captain Cook first landed at Resolution Cove in 1778, it was at Friendly Cove that Captain Meares built the *Northwest America*, 48 feet on deck, the first ship ever built on the west coast, and launched it in 1788.

The long arms (Muchalat Inlet and Tlupana Inlet) that reach out from Nootka Sound have few anchorages, and they tend to be deep. The Port of Gold River is at the head of Muchalat Inlet. The town of Gold River is 9 miles from the dock. Trailerable boats, most of them here for salmon fishing in Nootka Sound, are launched at Gold River.

⑳ **Critter Cove.** Critter Cove is the name given by Cameron Forbes to this previously unnamed spot about 1 mile south of Argonaut Point on Tlupana Inlet. Cameron has established a sportfishing resort in the cove and named it after his nickname of "Critter," when he played hockey. The inner cove is no longer suitable for anchoring.

⑳ **Critter Cove Marina.** P.O. Box 1118, Gold River, BC V0P 1G0; (250) 283-7364; info@ crittercove.com; www.crittercove.com. Open July and August only. Fuel dock takes VISA/MC/debit/cash and carries mid-grade gasoline, oil, ice, bait, coffee, convenience food, tackle. In-season hours are 8:00 a.m. to 9:00 p.m. Moorage, cabins, lodge rooms, suites, restaurant, showers, washrooms. No power or water on the docks. Showers are for overnight guests only.

Cameron Forbes, one of the nicest guys you'll meet, has quite a sportfishing camp here. Most of Critter Cove is on floats, including the restaurant and some of the accommodations. There are also self-contained beach cottages on the land adjacent to and behind the floating portion of the resort. Most of the boats at Critter Cove are trailered into Gold River, where they are launched. They do have room for a few visiting cruisers, though.

Nootka Sound Resort. (877) 337-5465; info@nootkamarineadventures.com; www.nootkamarineadventures.com. Call ahead to check moorage availability. Moorage, power, water, restaurant, lodging, fishing charters. Located in Galiano Bay.

Hisnit Inlet. Hisnit Inlet extends north from Tlupana Inlet. Hisnit is one of the few anchorages in Nootka Sound that is well-protected, shallow enough for convenient anchoring, and large enough for a number of boats. Two submerged rocks lie almost mid-channel a short distance into Hisnit Inlet. Do not be deceived by the open and safe appearance of the inlet as you arrive or depart. Favor the south shore.

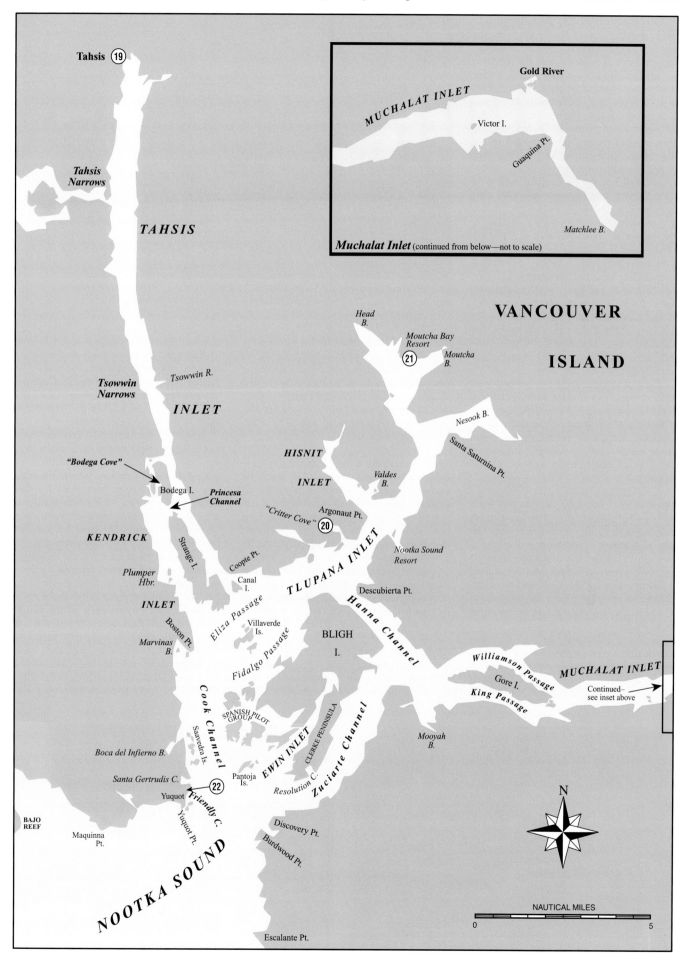

Tahsis (19)

Tahsis Narrows

TAHSIS

MUCHALAT INLET

Gold River

Victor I.

Guaquina Pt.

Matchlee B.

Muchalat Inlet (continued from below—not to scale)

Tsowwin R.

Tsowwin Narrows

INLET

Head B.

Moutcha Bay Resort

(21)

Moutcha B.

VANCOUVER

ISLAND

Nesook B.

Santa Saturnina Pt.

HISNIT

"Bodega Cove"

INLET

Valdes B.

Bodega I.   ***Princesa Channel***

"Critter Cove"   Argonaut Pt.

(20)

KENDRICK

Strange I.

Coopte Pt.

TLUPANA INLET

Nootka Sound Resort

Plumper Hbr.

Canal I.

Descubierta Pt.

INLET

Eliza Passage

Villaverde Is.

Hanna Channel

Boston Pt.

BLIGH

I.

Williamson Passage

MUCHALAT INLET

Marvinas B.

Fidalgo Passage

Gore I.

King Passage

Continued— see inset above

Cook Channel

SPANISH PILOT GROUP

Saavedra Is.

EWIN INLET

CLERKE PENINSULA

Zuciarte Channel

Mooyah B.

Boca del Infierno B.

Santa Gertrudis C.

Pantoja Is.

Resolution C.

(22)

Yuquot *Friendly C.*

N

BAJO REEF

Yuquot Pt.

Maquinna Pt.

Discovery Pt.

Burdwood Pt.

NOOTKA SOUND

NAUTICAL MILES

0   5

Escalante Pt.

Extensive clear cutting mars the hills. In 2013, logging was underway high on the hills and noise filtered into the anchorage. Still, the view of mountains up the stream at the head of the inlet is stunning. A marble quarry once operated on the east shore. Piles of white marble are visible on the beach and in the nearby forest. The quarry itself is buried under fallen trees and is difficult (and dangerous) to locate. Near the head of the inlet on the same east shore is a large rock shaped like a human head.

Anchorage at the head of the inlet is in 40 to 60 feet. It is open but protected. The shoreline is accessible.

㉑ **Moutcha Bay Resort.** (877) 337-5464; info@nootkamarineadventures.com; www.moutchabay.com. Newly constructed Moutcha Bay Resort has moorage to 150 feet, fuel dock with gasoline, diesel and propane, water, 15 & 30 amp power, pumpout, Wi-Fi, and a concrete launch ramp. Washrooms and showers are at the top of the docks. The docks are brand new, beautifully built, wide and stable. A small store carries limited groceries, gift items, ice, and tackle.

The restaurant is good and features local seafood, meat, and produce. Fishing charters, guided and unguided, are available on a fleet of rental boats. Fish processing and packing is offered. Yurts, hotel rooms, and campsites can be rented. The staff is helpful and courteous. This is a luxury resort with facilities to match.

Ewin Inlet. Ewin Inlet indents the south side of Bligh Island some 3 miles, with no anchorages until the head is reached. The cove to the west at the head of the inlet is quite protected and has depths of 30 to 40 feet. "We rounded the little islet in the cove at low tide, about 100 feet off, and the depth sounder abruptly but briefly showed a depth of 15 feet. We suspect it found an uncharted rock." [Hale]

Resolution Cove. Historic Resolution Cove is on Bligh Island, near the south end of Clerke Peninsula. In March, 1778 Captain Cook anchored his two ships there and found

Friendly Cove has space for several boats to anchor. The land ashore is owned by the Mowachaht Band. The red roofed buildings are the Nootka Lightstation.

and fitted a new foremast for the *Resolution*. A flagpole and plaques commemorating Cook's visit have been placed on a knoll above the cove. Anchor in 40 to 50 feet, either with a stern-tie to shore or enough room to swing. You'll probably make your visit a short one. Swells from the ocean wrap around the Clerke Peninsula into the cove.

Santa Gertrudis Cove. The western cove in Santa Gertrudis Cove is an excellent anchorage: cozy, good holding, protected. As you enter you will see an island in the northern cove. A submerged rock extends from that island a considerable distance toward the south shore, farther than we expected. Be sure to identify this rock and give it room as you favor the south shore. There is sufficient room to pass between this rock and the drying rock shown off the south shore on the chart. The north cove of Santa Gertrudis Cove, around the island, is foul and tight.

㉒ **Friendly Cove.** Friendly Cove is where Captains Vancouver and Quadra met in 1792 and attempted to negotiate the final details of the Nootka Convention of 1790,

in which Spain relinquished to England all its claims to Northwest lands. Hulsizer gives an interesting and succinct explanation of the complicated events in Friendly Cove that brought Spain and Great Britain to the brink of war before they worked out their differences in the Nootka Convention.

Friendly Cove is shallow and fairly protected from typical summertime winds, with good anchoring for four or five boats on a sand bottom. Outflow winds can make Friendly Cove bumpy. Nearly all the land ashore belongs to the Mowachaht Band, and a fee ($12 per person, no credit cards) must be paid for landing. The band has summertime staff on hand who collect the fee. The landing fee is the same, whether you dinghy in from an anchored-out boat or tie up at the wharf and floats on the west side of the bay. An additional fee will be levied to tie up at the float in the center of the bay. In some years this float sticks out into the cove a significant distance, restricting anchoring room.

When you anchor, be aware that the *Uchuck III* delivers tourists and freight to the dock regularly. To watch the *Uchuck* wind

The floats at Moutcha Bay Resort are outstanding.

Moutcha Bay Resort's lodge is first class.

Three Spectacular Resorts
in Nootka Sound & Esperanza Inlet

MOUTCHA BAY

Moorage to 150' • Gas, diesel, propane, water, power, pumpout and provisioning by request • Store, ice, bait, tackle • Luxury lodging • Campground • Gourmet dining • Superb Nootka Sound fishing • Guided and unguided fishing charters • Fish processing • Concrete launch ramp • Scheduled seaplane service from Seattle on NW Seaplanes

NEWTON COVE RESORT

Moorage (by reservation) • Lodging • Pacific NW cuisine • Guided fishing charters • Guided kayaking • Hiking • Diving

NOOTKA SOUND RESORT

Comfortable 22-bedroom floating fish resort located in Galiano Bay • Flagship & Officer's suites • Gourmet dining • Fire pit • Moorage to 150' (by reservation), power, water • Fishing charters

Crafting Your West Coast Wilderness Experience

NOOTKA MARINE
ADVENTURES

MOUTCHA BAY RESORT | NOOTKA SOUND RESORT | NEWTON COVE RESORT

www.nootkamarineadventures.com | info@nootkamarineadventures.com

1-877-337-KING (5464)

its way through anchored boats is awe-inspiring —and terrifying if you're on one of the boats.

A trail runs through campgrounds and above the ocean beach. It passes the Native graveyard and leads to a lake that's good for swimming. Six rental cabins, small and rustic, are just beyond the lake. The spired Catholic church is filled with Native carvings, and has two marvelous stained glass windows. They depict the transfer of authority over the area from Spain to England in 1792, and were a gift from the government of Spain.

㉒ **Nootka Light Station.** You can walk from the Friendly Cove beach to the Nootka Light Station on San Rafael Island. A well-maintained series of stairs leads up from the beach to the light station. Once at the station, be sure to sign the guest book.

Nootka is a repeater station for Tofino Coast Guard radio, and has considerable radio equipment. Every three hours from early morning until nightfall, the Nootka station reports weather conditions for the marine weather broadcast, including estimated wind strength and sea conditions offshore.

Thanks to the miracle of the Fresnel lens, the light uses only a 500-watt projector bulb to cast a beam that can be seen for 16 to 18 miles.

The Nootka Light Station and its light keepers are powerful arguments for retaining manned light stations along the coast. They are invaluable for timely and accurate weather information and communications in areas that may not have good cell phone coverage. We are told that many of the lightkeepers maintain an open Wi-Fi signal for visiting boaters.

Estevan Point. Estevan Point is the southwest corner of Hesquiat Peninsula, another of the headlands where winds and seas build and become confused. Estevan Point can be ugly in a storm, but in more settled conditions it does not present the challenge found at Cape Cook or Cape Scott. In fog, the problem with Estevan Point is its low, flat terrain, which makes its shoreline a poor target for radar. The rocks more than a mile offshore make Estevan Point unforgiving for the navigator who is off-course.

From Nootka Sound, a rounding of Estevan Point first must clear Escalante Rocks

This boardwalk stretches 1.2 miles from the dock at Hot Springs Cove to the hot springs.

and Perez Rocks, both of them on the west side of Hesquiat Peninsula. Unfortunately for the navigator, no single chart shows all of Estevan Point from Nootka Sound to Hesquiat Bay in large scale. You will be forced to plot your course on small scale Chart 3603, which doesn't give much close-in detail. Once at Estevan Point, you can use Chart 3674 to continue to Hot Springs Cove.

Especially with the lack of a single good large scale chart for the west side of Hesquiat Peninsula, the general advice is to give Estevan Point "lots of room." Give Escalante Rocks and Perez Rocks lots of room, too. This applies when heading north as well.

Weather information: The Estevan Point lighthouse provides updated wind, sea, and atmospheric conditions every three hours. Listen to the continuous marine broadcast for the latest weather information.

Hesquiat Harbour. Hesquiat Harbour is protected from westerly winds, and Hesquiat Bar, 24 feet deep, knocks down the Pacific swell. Beware the bar in a southeasterly; storm seas can break over it. Rae Basin is a

well-protected anchorage in the northeast corner of Hesquiat Harbour. From there you can take the dinghy to Cougar Annie's Garden for an interesting tour. Tours arranged through the Boat Basin Foundation; email daniel@ecotrust.ca a couple of days before your arrival. Admission is charged to pay for the restoration and ongoing research there. We're told the visit is well worth the cost.

Hot Springs Cove Area. Hot Springs Cove is adjacent to Sydney Inlet, the northern entrance to Clayoquot Sound. Depending on the points of departure and arrival and the exact course chosen, the distance from Nootka Sound around Estevan Point, past Hesquiat Peninsula, and east to Hot Springs Cove, is approximately 30 to 31 miles. When traveling south, once you are past Chief Matlahaw Point, you can duck into the lee of Hesquiat Peninsula to avoid the worst of the ocean swells.

㉓ **Hot Springs Cove.** www.env.gov.bc.ca/ bcparks/explore/parkpgs/maquinna/. Hot Springs Cove is one of the reasons cruising

CHARTS	
3603	Ucluelet Inlet to Nootka Sound (1:150,000)
3674	Clayoquot Sound, Millar Channel to Estevan Point (1:40,000) Hayden Passage (1:20,000) Hot Springs Cove (1:20,000) Marktosis (1:10,000)
3675	Nootka Sound (1:40,000) Gold River (1:10,000) Princesa Channel (1:10,000)

The hot springs at Hot Springs Cove are a popular and welcome stop.

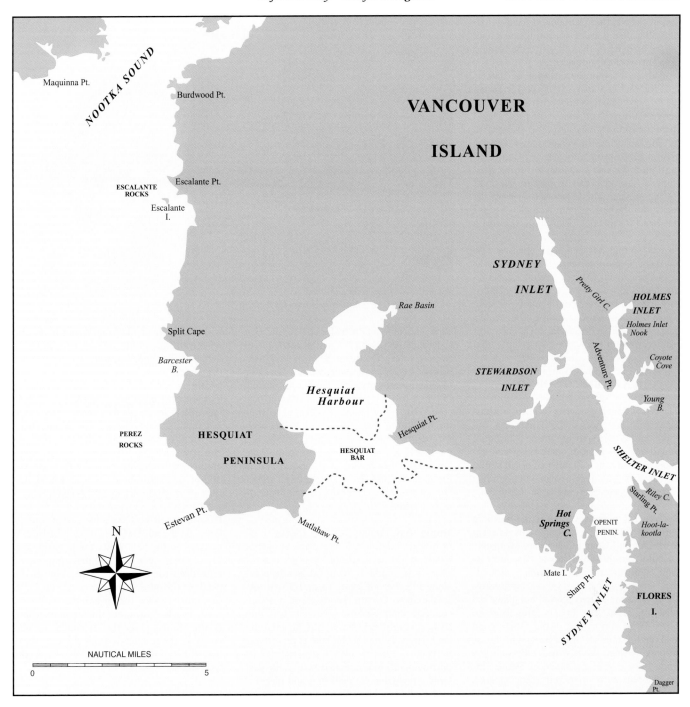

boats do the West Coast. The challenge of getting to Hot Springs is sufficient to make the reward—a soothing bath in comforting water (no soap, please)—worth the entire trip. In earlier times most visitors came the hard way, up from Barkley Sound or down from Cape Scott. Now the hot springs are visited many times a day by tour boats and even float planes, carrying visitors who have arrived without effort at Tofino, and up they go to Hot Springs Cove. An hour by high-speed boat and they are there.

The cove is easy to enter. Chart 3674 shows that the mouth is open and the channel free of dangers. The marine park public dock is approximately 1.7 miles farther into the cove from the hot springs themselves.

You can anchor out in 24 feet, or tie to the public dock. The B&B boat *Innchanter*, with attached dinghy floats, is anchored bow and stern beyond the public dock. When you anchor, take into account that they don't swing with the wind.

A 1.2-mile walk along a well-maintained boardwalk and path leads to the hot springs. A $3 per person parks fee is payable at a dropbox near the head of the dock. Moorage on the dock is $2.00/meter. In 2013 a park attendant was living in the cabin to the right of the public dock.

In the past, visiting craft had a tradition of bringing a 2" × 6" plank about 4 feet long to add to the boardwalk. On the plank would be carved the name of the boat and the year

of the visit, plus other information as deemed appropriate. Many of the planks showed remarkable artistic talent. Well, they rebuilt the boardwalk and replaced the old planks with pressure-treated rot-resistant wood. But the tradition lives on. Determined cruisers have brought woodcarving tools and carved their boats' names in the new planks. Recently, boaters have resumed the practice of bringing precarved planks. The park attendant will place them where needed, when needed. For those planning to bring a precarved plank, the dimensions are 42" × 8" × 2".

The hike through rain forest to the hot springs is easy and beautiful. Toilets are available at the end. The modest will find a pleasant changing room in which clothes may be doffed and a bathing suit put on. Traditionalists will lament that the hot springs no longer can be enjoyed in the old way, sans bathing suit. The place is popular.

Although a constant stream of bathers hike the trail and soak in the springs during the day, savvy boaters know that if they come before 9:00 a.m. or after 6:00 p.m., they'll share the springs only with other boaters.

The kids from the village across the cove play at Hot Springs, in part (as Contributing Editor Kincaid suggests) to further their study of anatomy, and in part to show off for the *touristas*. The braver lads dive off the rocks into the surf. It's not Acapulco, but it's not bad. Watch your belongings. We lost a towel.

Hot Springs has campsites, often used by kayakers. During an earlier visit, a kayak-borne fisherman brought several catches to the dock and gave them away. They included rock fish, sea bass and coho salmon. He went out to the rocks just outside the cove, made a pass, and came back with his catch. Each time his line went in the water it came up with a fish.

CLAYOQUOT SOUND

Clayoquot Sound is a series of inlets and passages with entrances at both its north and south ends. By traveling inside Clayoquot Sound you can explore many coves and anchorages, and avoid 20 miles of ocean swells. Tofino is the only major town, although fuel and some groceries are available at Ahousat.

Sydney Inlet. Sydney Inlet is the northern entrance to Clayoquot Sound. It is adjacent to Hot Springs Cove and leads approximately 11 miles into the mountains of Vancouver Island, with several good anchorages. Rounding Sharp Point after leaving Hot Springs Cove, be aware of two charted but unmarked off-lying rocks. The first is fairly close to Sharp Point and easy to avoid. The second is about 0.2 mile off. Most boats will choose to pass between the two rocks. Be sure you know where you are. Once in Sydney Inlet, the fairway is open and unencumbered. Reader Don Thain reports that sea otters are now well established in Sydney Inlet and that crabbing is poorer where the sea otters have colonized.

Sydney Inlet Unnamed Cove. This is the cove that lies behind the 65-meter island

CHARTS

3673	Clayoquot Sound, Tofino Inlet to Millar Channel (1:40,000)
3674	Clayoquot Sound, Millar Channel to Estevan Point (1:40,000) Hayden Passage (1:20,000) Hot Springs Cove (1:20,000) Marktosis (1:10,000)
3685	Tofino (1:20,000)

Mountains rise dramatically around Bacchante Bay.

about 0.5 mile south of Hootla-Kootla Bay, at latitude 49°21.85'N on the east shore of Sydney Inlet. (Don Douglass, in both editions of *Exploring Vancouver Island's West Coast*, mistakenly calls this cove Hootla-Kootla, but the chart leaves it unnamed and calls the next cove to the north Hootla-Kootla.) Enter from the south. You'll see a beautiful white beach. Although the water is a little shallow near the beach, it's the prettiest spot in the cove. You could also anchor at the north end of the cove, behind the 65-meter-high island. Do not attempt to enter the cove at the north end. It is foul.

Young Bay. Young Bay, on the east side of Sydney Inlet, is a lovely place to anchor, although a little deep until you get close to shore. The middle is 50 to 60 feet deep, but along the shore it's easy to find 35- to 40-foot depths. On the south shore a stream connects with Cecilia Lake, one-half mile away. A rough trail leads up the stream to the lake. Trout fishing at the lake is reported to be good. A copper mine and a pilchard reduction plant both operated here in the past. Only a few concrete platforms and pieces of machinery remain.

Enter Young Bay right down the middle, to avoid shoals that extend from either side. Once inside you will see a small islet with trees on it. Pass to the south of that islet.

Bottleneck Bay (Coyote Cove). This is an otherwise unnamed bay that cruising guide author Don Watmough fell in love with. Bottleneck Bay is located just north of Young Bay, east of Adventure Point. The entrance is narrow but deep. Inside, the high, treed hills make the feeling of seclusion complete. Easy anchoring in 30 feet.

Holmes Inlet Nook. Occupied now by aquaculture and a floathouse and dock with a very possessive dog. No longer an anchorage.

Hootla-Kootla Bay. Hootla-Kootla Bay

is located about 0.25 mile north of the 65-meter-high island on the east shore of Sydney Inlet, approximately 1.6 miles from the mouth of the inlet. This cove is known locally as Baseball Bay, but the chart shows it as Hootla-Kootla Bay. The entrance is shallow, and is partly blocked by a charted rock just south of mid-channel. Divide the channel north of the rock in half, and enter the northern half "mid-channel." "Least depth on the depth sounder was 12.5 feet near the bottom of a 3.6-foot low tide at Tofino. Anchorage is good once inside." [*Hale*]

Riley Cove. Riley Cove is just east of Starling Point, on the northwest tip of Flores Island. It may not be the best choice for an anchorage. The cove is open and uninteresting, and a little deep for anchoring until close to the head. At the head, Riley Cove is divided into two smaller coves; the cove to the west has a sandy beach. A rock, not shown on the chart, is just off the point that separates the two coves. A shoal extends from the east shore near the entrance of Riley Cove. Favor the west shore.

Steamer Cove. Steamer Cove is on the north side of Flores Island, behind George Island. The small cove at the southwest corner of Steamer Cove is well protected and has easy anchoring depths. Unfortunately, the hillsides around the anchorage have been logged clean, right down to the water, so the outlook is uninteresting. If you're looking for shelter in a storm, the outlook would be irrelevant. In that case Steamer Cove would serve excellently.

㉔ **Bacchante Bay.** Bacchante Bay, at the east end of Shelter Inlet, is a dramatic anchorage, with steep cliffs on both sides, an inviting grassy meadow at the head and a snow-capped mountain beyond. The narrow, shallow entrance is hidden until you are close. Bacchante Bay is part of Strathcona Provincial Park.

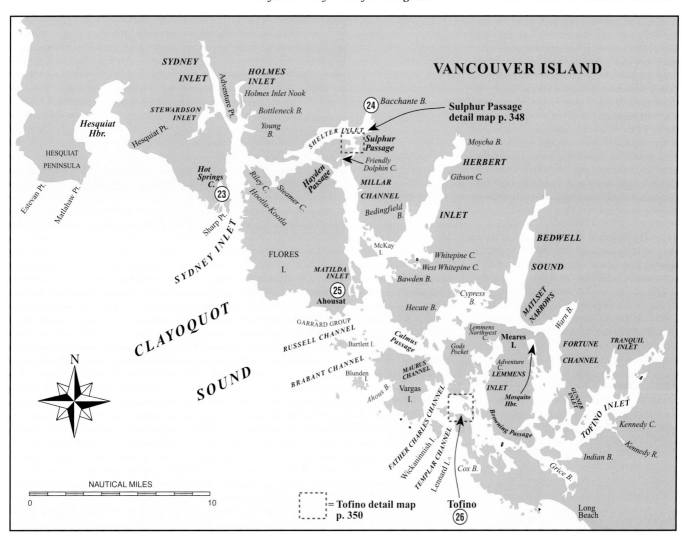

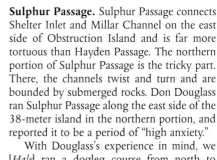

Sulphur Passage requires careful navigation for a safe transit.

Bacchante Bay has ample room to anchor in 40 to 50 feet. Holding is excellent. If you run to the head of the bay, watch for abrupt shoaling off the meadow. At high tide explore Watta Creek by dinghy.

Readers Mike and Sandy Cecka report fouling their anchor in Bacchante Bay. They anchored on the west side of the bay, below steep cliffs. We've had no problem anchoring in the middle of the bay.

Hayden Passage. Hayden Passage is on the west side of Obstruction Island, and connects Shelter Inlet with Millar Channel. Tidal current predictions are shown with Hayden Passage as a secondary station in the Tide and Current Tables, Vol. 6. The flood sets southeast; the ebb, northwest. Be sure to pass west of the red daymarker beacons (Red, Right, Returning).

Because the flood currents meet at Hayden Passage, you may find that the currents don't behave as predicted. The cautious passage would be at slack water. If transiting sometime other than slack water, maintain a constant watch for current set, and crab as needed to stay in the channel.

Sulphur Passage. Sulphur Passage connects Shelter Inlet and Millar Channel on the east side of Obstruction Island and is far more tortuous than Hayden Passage. The northern portion of Sulphur Passage is the tricky part. There, the channels twist and turn and are bounded by submerged rocks. Don Douglass ran Sulphur Passage along the east side of the 38-meter island in the northern portion, and reported it to be a period of "high anxiety."

With Douglass's experience in mind, we [*Hale*] ran a dogleg course from north to south on the west side of the 38-meter island. We found it to be straightforward—albeit with careful planning and cooperation between navigator and helmsman. For reference, the course is described here. (Following this course on Chart 3674 will be helpful. The directions North, South, East and West in this description are true, not magnetic.)

Our course leaves Belcher Point close to port and continues to the south corner of the charted fish farm. Cross to a point of land northeast of a 290-foot hill on the west shore. Turn south again and favor the west shore until past the 38-meter island and the tiny islet south of it. Then turn east, point the bow at the mouth of a creek that enters on the eastern shore. Once in the middle, and approximately due south of the 38-meter island's western tip, turn south once more and motor through. While other courses probably would be safe, this course has the advantage of using easily-identified landmarks (the fish farm, the point under the high hill, the stream outlet, the tip of an islet) either as turning points or as points to aim for.

Friendly Dolphin Cove. Friendly Dolphin is Douglass's name for the cove that indents Obstruction Island, just inside the south entrance to Sulphur Passage. The cove is pretty, private and appealing. Anchor near the head in 40 to 50 feet, probably with a stern-tie ashore to control swinging. Dave Letson, a former wharfinger at Hot Springs Cove, said he thought this cove was "too deep and too buggy."

Shark Creek. 49°23.95'N/126°04.00'W. "This is a kayakers' secret: a beautiful 70-foot-high waterfall in a chimney, accessible at high tide by dinghy only. It is located in Millar Channel, just north of Atleo River. Anchor north of the small island and dinghy in. Best in late afternoon when sunlight makes a rainbow on the rocks behind the falls." [*Hulsizer*]

Matilda Inlet indents the southeast corner of Flores Island and is bordered on the east by McNeil Peninsula. Anchorage is possible

Ahousat has a general store, café, fuel and haulout.

near the head of Matilda Inlet. From the anchorage, a warm springs in Gibson Marine Park can be visited (best at high tide; at low tide it's a muddy hike) or a trek made to the beach. Don Watmough describes the area in fond detail. The Native community of Marktosis is on McNeil Peninsula. Across the inlet and a short distance north are the store and fuel dock of Ahousat.

㉕ **Ahousat.** General Delivery, Ahousat, BC V0R 1A0; (250) 670-9575. Ahousat, with its general store, fuel dock, cafe and marine ways, is on the west shore of Matilda Inlet, at the southeast corner of Flores Island. Hugh Clarke is the owner. Gasoline, diesel and stove oil at the fuel dock, washrooms, 15 amp power, showers and laundry, haulout to 40 feet. Potable water, pay phone, post office, and motel rooms are available. The store is a rough-and-ready place, with a cougar head on the wall, but with luck, it may have what

you need: groceries, miscellaneous hardware and marine supplies. No charts or liquor. Hugh Clarke's father gave the Hot Springs Cove property (35 acres) to the province so it could be a park.

Marktosis. Marktosis is the Native village across Matilda Inlet from Ahousat. It is the starting point for the Wildside Heritage Trail, a beach and boardwalk trail along Flores Island's west coast to White Sand Cove and Flores Mountain. Tie up at Ahousat or anchor south of Ahousat in the bay near the "slightly warm" springs, and take the dinghy back to the village. Leave the dinghy at the first pier on the right as you enter. Permits for the Wild Side Trail must be purchased at the trail office ($25 per person in 2013). The location of the trail office and the route to the trailhead change frequently, so ask for directions or call the trail office at (250) 913-0022. They also monitor VHF 68; call Wildside Office. The trail was a cooperative effort among the Ahousat Nation, government agencies and private companies. When walking the trail, keep in mind that it runs through real wilderness and is home to cougars, bears and wolves.

You can visit the large red boathouse near the main public dock and see Native canoes in various stages of restoration. Marktosis village is full of friendly people eager to help and share their knowledge.

Gibson Marine Park. Gibson Marine Park is at the head of Matilda Inlet, past Ahousat. At one time, Hugh Clarke, at the Ahousat General Store, hacked out a trail from the head of the inlet to the hot springs. Boots are necessary on the trail, which transits some boggy areas. Clarke recommends going in at half tide on a rising tide, to avoid tramping across the mud flats. Correspondent Gil Flanagan tells us that you can hike for many miles on the ocean beach to the west. The only problem, Flanagan says, are bands of gravel that make barefoot walking uncomfortable. He adds that the beach is popular with kayakers and tourists from Tofino. The park requests that dogs are kept out of the park as there have been incidents of wolves killing the dogs.

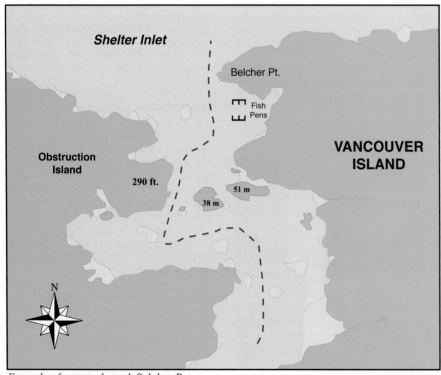

Example of a route through Sulphur Passage

Herbert Inlet. The run up Herbert Inlet is even more spectacular than many other inlets along the coast. High mountains and rock walls line the shores. Deep alpine river valleys lead away into the mountains. Snow-capped peaks can be seen in the distance.

West Whitepine Cove. Although unnamed, both Watmough and Douglass call this delightful anchorage West Whitepine Cove, and we shall do the same. West Whitepine Cove lies to the west of Whitepine Cove, near the mouth of Herbert Inlet. Entry to the inner bay is along the south side of the 67-meter island. We entered slowly, strongly favoring this island. Rocks were visible underwater and easily skirted. Once inside, the cove is lovely and protected. Bears are reported to frequent the south shore.

A charted rock is in the cove, off the tip of the little peninsula that extends southeast from the 94-meter island. When anchoring, stay away from it.

Gibson Cove. Gibson Cove indents the west side of Herbert Inlet, about 5 miles north of Whitepine Cove. Since Gibson Cove is not on the way to anyplace else, we suspect it sees few visitors. Those who do visit are in for a treat. Gibson Cove is beautiful, but a little deep for anchoring. Although it appears protected, strong afternoon westerlies can bring wind and waves.

Quait Bay. Quait Bay is located on the east shore of Cypress Bay. With its 35-foot depths, anchoring is good just about anywhere in this bay. The most popular spot, though, is in the little cove in the east corner, in about 10 feet.

A submerged concrete structure lies in the mouth of the two nooks at the back of this cove at 49°16.603'N/125°50.843'W. A reader reports the structure dries 2 feet. Enter Quait Bay on the northwest side of the 45-meter island, favoring the northwest shore. The chart makes the course clear. In 2013 the large floating lodge building just inside the entrance was closed but occupied by a caretaker. If you check with the caretaker, you may get permission to walk their boardwalk, which climbs alongside a roaring waterfall to the lake above.

Matlset Narrows. Matlset Narrows runs to a maximum of 4 knots on spring tides. The flood sets east. Sailing Directions warns of strong tide-rips in the vicinity of the Maltby Islets at the east end of the narrows. We ran the narrows against a west-flowing ebb. We saw definite current activity, but had no problem. We suspect any tide-rips would be on a flood.

Calmus Passage to Heynen Channel. The route from Millar Channel to Heynen Channel via Calmus Passage and Maurus Channel is the beginning of shallower water. The channels are well marked by buoys and beacons but the navigator must stay alert,

Tofino has a Coast Guard station.

keep an eye on the depth sounder, and know the vessel's position at all times. Large-scale Chart 3685 is extremely helpful.

Cell phones: In 2013, on our counter-clockwise circumnavigation of Vancouver Island, Calmus Passage was the first place with cell phone reception since leaving Quatsino Sound.

Lemmens Inlet. Lemmens Inlet indents Meares Island, just a few miles from the town of Tofino. Be sure to use large scale Chart 3685 while navigating around Tofino and into Lemmens Inlet. The entry channel to the inlet is amply deep, but bordered by drying flats. Once inside, you have your choice of three possible anchorages, although float homes now are moored in all of Lemmens Inlet's coves, so anchoring may be a challenge.

Adventure Cove. Adventure Cove, where Capt. Robert Gray built the small schooner *Adventure* in 1792, is filled with history. The beach is easy to land on. While walking in the woods we could almost feel the presence of Gray's Fort Defiance and the shipbuilding activity. Though the area is now overgrown with large trees, some say you can feel as though *something went on here.* Watmough and Douglass describe the history well. Hulsizer discusses it more thoroughly in *Voyages to Windward.* Unfortunately, a floathouse and a fish farm take up most of the cove, leaving little room for anchoring. Discarded fishfarming equipment on the beach makes beach access challenging. A reader tells us an uncharted rock lies SSW of the island in the mouth of Adventure Cove.

Lemmens Northwest Cove. Lemmens Northwest Cove is Douglass's name for this anchorage in the northwest corner of Lemmens Inlet. It is identified on the chart by the 38-meter island and the fish pens in the mouth. Drying rocks obstruct the entrance. Locate them and then run midway between the rocks and the 38-meter island. Once inside, you'll find good anchoring depths and adequate protection. We were not charmed by the cove, however.

Gods Pocket. Gods Pocket is the cove northwest of Lagoon Island, on the west side of Lemmens Inlet. Protection is good, with anchorage in 25 to 30 feet. Two very nice float homes occupy the cove, however. You'll be anchoring in their front yards.

Fortune Channel. Fortune Channel connects Tofino Channel with Matlset Narrows, which in turn connects with the waters of upper and western Clayoquot Sound. In Fortune Channel you can choose from three good anchorages: Windy Bay, Heelboom Bay and Mosquito Harbour. Chances are, you won't see much boat traffic in this area.

Mosquito Harbour. Although not as scenic and cozy as Heelboom Bay, Mosquito Harbour is big and open and easily entered. Anchor in 20 feet behind the Blackberry Islets. Approach on either side of the Wood Islets, but from Fortune Channel you'll probably approach by way of Plover Point or Dark Island. Kelp marks the rocks off the north end of Dark Island. Note the location of Hankin Rock. We would trend toward Plover Point before turning to enter Mosquito Harbour.

Heelboom Bay. Heelboom Bay, located near the south end of Fortune Channel, is a good anchorage, surrounded by lush evergreen forests. We found outstanding holding in 35 feet. This Bay was the site of a major protest against logging in Clayoquot Sound and is considered almost sacred by some residents. Approaching, favor the east shore and stay well clear of rocks off the western shore. One of these rocks is considerably detached from the shoreline. Chart 3685 helps understanding.

Windy Bay. Windy Bay is beautiful. The south shore is heavily forested, and the north shore is sheer rock wall. Westerly winds accelerate over the saddle at the head of the bay, but they have no fetch to build up seas. With 15-knots of wind outside Windy Bay, we had gusts to 30 knots inside. Anchor in 30 to 35 feet with excellent holding.

Browning Passage and Tsapee Narrows. Rocks abound and shoals threaten. The larger scale Chart 3685 will show you the way. If you are coming from Heynen Channel or Lemmens Inlet, the course will be clear: Pass west of Morpheus Island and east of Buoy *Y35*, and continue down Browning Passage and through Tsapee Narrows. Note that currents on springs can run to 5 knots near Morpheus Island and 4 knots at the narrows. Go slowly. Look ahead and identify all buoys, islands and visible rocks well in advance. Keep a close reference between your charts and your navigation electronics. Done this way, the passage should not be difficult.

If you are departing Tofino, leave Buoy *Y29*, opposite the 4th Street dock, to starboard, and run toward Arnet Island until you can safely turn to run south, along the west side of Riley Island. Favor Riley Island to pass clear of the rocks shown on the chart. Once south of Riley Island you are in Browning Passage.

TOFINO INLET

Not a lot of boat traffic here and only a few attractive anchorages.

Island Cove. Island Cove is easy to enter around either side of Ocayu Island. Study the chart to avoid the rocks that lie off the southwest shore of the approach. Unfortunately, the hillsides surrounding Island Cove have been logged down to the water's edge and the cove isn't very pretty. Anchor in 40 to 50 feet, close to the west shore.

Gunner Inlet. It's tricky to get into the inlet and not very scenic when you make it. Approach favoring the east shore and use a small low islet with a distinctive white top as your leading mark. Make an S-turn around the islet and follow the chart in.

Tranquilito Cove. Tranquilito Cove is the name Douglass gave this otherwise unnamed cove on the east side of Tranquil Inlet, near the head. This cove is secluded and beautiful. The rock wall on the north side has been

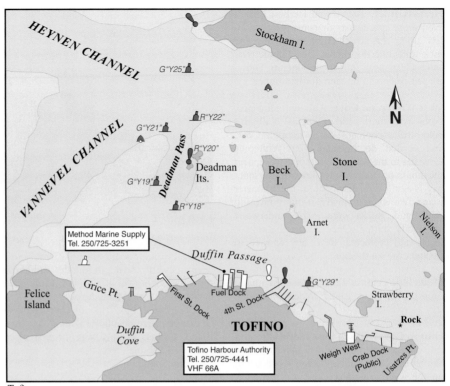

Tofino

strikingly sculpted by glaciers. Favor the northern side of the entry to avoid a shoal that extends from the point of land on the south side. Anchor in 20 feet.

Cannery Bay. Cannery Bay, at the mouth of the Kennedy River, is easy to get into and despite its flat terrain is rather pretty. Consider the nook just to port as you enter. Anchor in 15 to 20 feet.

Kennedy Cove. Kennedy Cove is easy to enter by favoring the 68-meter island. Anchor wherever you like in 15 to 30 feet. Kennedy Cove is a pretty spot.

㉖ **Tofino.** If you come from up-island, Tofino will be your first major town since Port McNeill or Port Hardy, and it's more vibrant than either of them. During the summer season Tofino's bustle and busy-ness may sur-

prise you. After growing accustomed to the slower life up-island, Tofino, with its commerce, fast traffic and loud engines, can cause culture shock. Welcome to the city.

As long as you're in the city you might as well spend some money. You can choose from several good restaurants, the kind that serve meals without french fries. Gift shops—at last!—are available for mementos and presents. The Co-op store, close to the waterfront, is a complete supermarket and will deliver if asked. The Co-op also carries clothes. Showers are available at the 4th Street Dock and at the laundromat at 4th & Campbell. The laundromat has enough machines to do all the crew's laundry in one cycle. Common Wolf and Sobo Bakery are all-organic and feature a local favorite: peasant bread. Correspondents Dick and Judy Juntunen strongly recommend a visit to the botanical gardens, approximately 1.5 miles out of town. They

Method Marine Supply is Tofino's fuel dock and marine supply source.

Tofino Harbour Authority's 4th Street launch ramp.

say the Gardens' excellent guidebook will explain everything you see. Lunch or snacks are available. "A nice change from the tourist activity on the waterfront." The "Beach Bus" will take visitors to all the local beaches and park for $2.

From seaward, enter Tofino via Templar Channel. While Chart 3673 gives a good overall view, for the close navigation needed we strongly recommend large scale Chart 3685. Note how the buoyed fairway twists and turns to avoid shallows. Identify each buoy as you proceed, and leave the buoys off the proper hand.

From the north, enter Tofino via Deadman Pass, narrow and bordered on both sides by drying flats. Be sure to use large scale Chart 3685. Note that while you may be returning to Tofino, the buoyage system in Deadman Pass is not. As you head south in Deadman Pass you will leave the red buoys to port.

The approach to Tofino, whether through Templar Channel or Deadman Pass, is one of the few places on this coast where you need to carefully watch the currents. Time your arrival for slack water to avoid the strong currents that swirl around the docks.

Stay close to the docks once at Tofino. A serious drying reef lies a short distance off.

Anchoring can be a challenge because of strong currents that sweep through the harbor. Although Tofino has several public docks, moorage for visiting boats is limited. The District of Tofino Dock (called the Whiskey Dock) near Grice Point is closest to the Co-op and the liquor store, but is busy day and night with water taxis and locals. Moorage may be available at the Method Marine Supply fuel dock. It tends to be full during the busy season, but you can check.

The most popular moorage is the Tofino Harbour Authority 4th Street Public Dock. Farther east, Weigh West may have space, but without advance reservations the docks often are taken by their sport fishing guests. The easternmost public dock is called the Crab Dock. The Crab Dock is a longer walk from the commercial district, however. Currents can make landing on a flood tide tricky. Do not proceed eastward past the Crab Dock. A major rock blocks the channel.

㉖ **Tofino Harbour Authority 4th Street Public Dock.** P.O. Box 826, Tofino, BC V0R 2Z0; (250) 725-4441; tofhar@island. net. Monitors VHF 66A. Vince Payette is the harbormaster. The docks have 20 & 30 amp power, water, pumpout, washrooms, showers, laundry, Wi-Fi. This is the best moorage prospect in Tofino, well-signed and convenient to the commercial district. Watch the current.

A shoal extends into the channel from a piling east of the easternmost dock, and leads across the ends of B, C and D docks. At low tides sailboats might ground.

Recreational moorage is on D and E docks only. Unfortunately, they are nearly full with permanent live aboard tenants. Rafting is common.

The dock water system operates by a "loony" timer, similar to pay showers. Make sure all the other faucets are closed, then feed a loony to the timer, which pressurizes the dock system for about 15 minutes. Water pressure is good and one dollar should get you about 100 U.S. gallons of water. Be all set up before you start the system.

㉖ **Method Marine Supply.** Box 219, 380 Main Street, Tofino, BC V0R 2Z0; (250) 725-3251; sbernard@methodmarine.ca; www.methodmarine.com. Open all year. Gasoline, diesel & biodiesel, lube oils, propane, water, ice, divers' air, vacuum waste oil disposal. Moorage has electrical hookup, but moorage often is fully reserved in the busy season. This is a modern, well-run facility, with a good chandlery that carries a wide range of equipment and supplies, including sport fishing gear, bait, snacks, foul weather wear, and charts. Storm Light Outfitters, a well-stocked outdoor gear store, is right behind, up on the street.

㉖ **Weigh West Marine Resort.** P.O. Box 69, 634 Campbell, Tofino, BC V0R 2Z0; (800) 665-8922; (250) 725-3277; marineandadventure@weighwest .com; www.weighwest.com. Docks have water and 15, 20 & 30 amp power, showers, laundry. Primarily a sport fishing resort with lodging, restaurant, fish-packing facilities. They tell us moorage usually is available, but only with advance reservations.

CLAYOQUOT SOUND TO UCLUELET

It is approximately 19 miles from Lennard Island, at the southern entrance to Clayoquot Sound, to Whistle Buoy *Y42* offshore from Ucluelet Inlet. This 19 miles crosses the ocean face of the Pacific Rim National Park, but since you'll probably be about 3 miles out you won't see much of the park. Sailing Directions says to stay 2 miles off the coast; Watmough likes 3 miles. So do we. Plot a waypoint for Whistle Buoy *Y42*, go 3 miles offshore from Lennard Island, turn left, and make for the buoy. In fog, radar is a big help in avoiding the many fish boats that work these waters. Absent a GPS and radar, in fog we would go out to at least 30 fathoms deep and follow the 30 to 40 fathom curve to Buoy *Y42*.

Weather information: The Lennard Island lighthouse, just outside of Clayoquot Sound, and the Amphitrite Point lighthouse, just outside of Barkley Sound, provide a picture of outside weather conditions. Listen to the continuous marine broadcast for the latest weather information.

Amphitrite Point. Amphitrite Point, at the end of the Ucluth Peninsula, can present a challenge. The essential navigation problem is to get around Amphitrite Point while staying well clear of Jenny Reef, shown on the chart, yet staying off the Amphitrite Point shoreline. The problem is made more difficult in fog, when the radar may lose Buoy *Y43* against the shoreline.

Carolina Channel is the entry suggested by Sailing Directions, except in thick weather, when Carolina Channel can be too rough for safe navigation. The outer entrance to Carolina Channel is marked by Whistle Buoy *Y42*, about 0.5 mile offshore. The channel leads past Bell Buoy *Y43*, which lies but 300 meters off the rocky shore. In reduced visibility, life can get interesting when you're trying to raise Buoy *Y43*. If you have trouble seeing the buoy against the rocky shoreline, the light structure on the east side of Francis Island could serve as a leading mark.

As you approach Carolina Channel, leave Whistle Buoy *Y42* close to starboard, and turn to a course of 037° magnetic to raise Buoy *Y43*. After passing close south of Buoy *Y43*, Sailing Directions suggests using the summit of the South Beg Island as a leading mark. It should bear approximately 075° magnetic. Run approximately 0.2 mile until the eastern extremity of Francis Island is abeam, then round Francis Island and enter Ucluelet Inlet.

BARKLEY SOUND

Depending on your direction, Barkley Sound is the first sound on the way north or the last sound on the way south. Barkley Sound is named after English Capt. Charles William Barkley, who in 1787 sailed into the sound on his ship *Loudoun*, which he had illegally renamed *Imperial Eagle* (Austrian registry) to avoid paying a license fee to the East India Company. With Capt. Barkley was his 17-year-old bride Frances Trevor Barkley. Capt. Barkley came to trade with the Indians for furs. You'll find reminders of the Barkley's in many names around Barkley Sound, including Imperial Eagle, Loudon and Trevor Channels.

Barkley Sound is roughly square in shape, measuring 15 miles across its mouth and approximately 12 miles deep, not counting the 20-mile-long canal to Port Alberni. The sound is dotted with rocks and islands, and the waters are famous for their excellent fishing. A cruising boat could spend weeks in Barkley Sound, fishing, exploring, and moving from one nook to another. In fact, many boats do just that, coming directly here from Puget Sound, Oregon, or the Strait of Georgia region.

During the summer months fog often forms just offshore. In minutes, it can sweep in, even with no wind. It is essential, there-

Gray whales are often sighted in Barkley Sound.

fore, that the navigator know the vessel's position at all times. A GPS and electronic navigation will prove useful in foggy conditions. Radar is a big help. Most boats cruising Barkley Sound, large and small, have radar. Even with electronic help, the navigator must remain alert and aware.

If approaching from up-island, you will probably enter Barkley Sound from Ucluelet. Note that a course across Sargison Bank from Ucluelet to the Broken Group takes you very close to a rock that lies approximately 0.7 miles east of Chrow Island. The rock is shown on the chart not with a rock symbol, but by a depth of 0.5 meters. It is easy to overlook while scanning the chart for hazards.

If approaching from the Strait of Juan de Fuca or Oregon, leave Cape Beale at least one-half mile to starboard, which will leave the offshore rocks a safe distance off. If the boat is coming from the United States, it must go directly to Ucluelet for Canadian Customs, although it may duck into Barkely Sound to get out of the ocean swells. A good option is to enter Imperial Eagle Channel, leave Effingham Island to port, and proceed west between Clarke and Benson Islands to Loudoun Channel and Ucluelet.

In Barkley Sound you will find superb exploring everywhere: Pipestem Inlet, the Pinkerton Islands, Julia Passage, the Chain Group, the Deer Group and the famous Broken Group. Settled summer weather makes it possible to anchor in any of hundreds of coves or nooks and explore by dinghy.

We do not cover all the areas mentioned above, an unfortunate consequence of limited exploration time. Other references—especially Douglass's *Exploring Vancouver Island's West Coast* 2nd Ed.—are excellent resources. In the end, your own inquisitiveness and derring-do will determine the range of your exploring.

Ucluelet. Ucluelet is pronounced "You-CLOO-let." With moorage, fuel, provisions, repairs and good dining, the village of Ucluelet (pop. approx. 1800) is the commercial center of Barkley Sound. The channel leading into Ucluelet is well buoyed. Following the rule of Red, Right, Returning, you will have no problems. Spring Cove, to port a short distance inside the channel, is where fish boats used to discharge their catches. The plant deep in the cove is closed and the docks are posted with No Trespassing signs. Spring Cove is a good anchorage.

Ucluelet has one fuel dock, located on the town side. Several fish processing plants and public docks used by large commercial boats are also on the town side of the inlet. Small public docks used by the Ucluelet Native Band are on the east side of the inlet, across from town.

West of the north tip of Lyche Island, the Ucluelet Small Craft Harbour is the principal marina, and the one we recommend. The Oak Bay Marine Group's Canadian Princess Resort, a former Canadian Hydrographic Service survey ship made into a floating hotel and restaurant, is moored in this marina permanently. The ship is part of a major sportfishing resort that has several charter boats. The boats depart early in the morning, filled with eager fishermen, and return in the afternoon. The restaurant on the quarterdeck is good, reasonably priced and offers good entertainment at night. Visit www.canadian-princess.com.

Another marina to consider is Island West Fishing Resort, on the west side of the inlet just before the turn to the small craft harbor. The docks are built almost entirely for trailerable boats. They have no designated guest dock, so call ahead by telephone or radio.

In town, halfway up Ucluelet Inlet, Pioneer Boat Works has a marine railway for haulout and repairs. Their chandlery, next to

CHARTS	
3602	Approaches to Juan de Fuca Strait (1:150,000)
3603	Ucluelet Inlet to Nootka Sound (1:150,000)
3646 Plans	Barkley Sound
3647	Port San Juan and Nitinat Narrows
3668	Alberni Inlet (1:40,000) Robbers Passage (1:10,000)
3670	Broken Group (1:20,000)
3671	Barkley Sound (1:40,000)
3673	Clayoquot Sound, Tofino Inlet to Millar Channel (1:40,000)
3674	Clayoquot Sound, Millar Channel to Estevan Point (1:40,000) Hayden Passage (1:20,000) Hot Springs Cove (1:20,000) Marktosis (1:10,000)

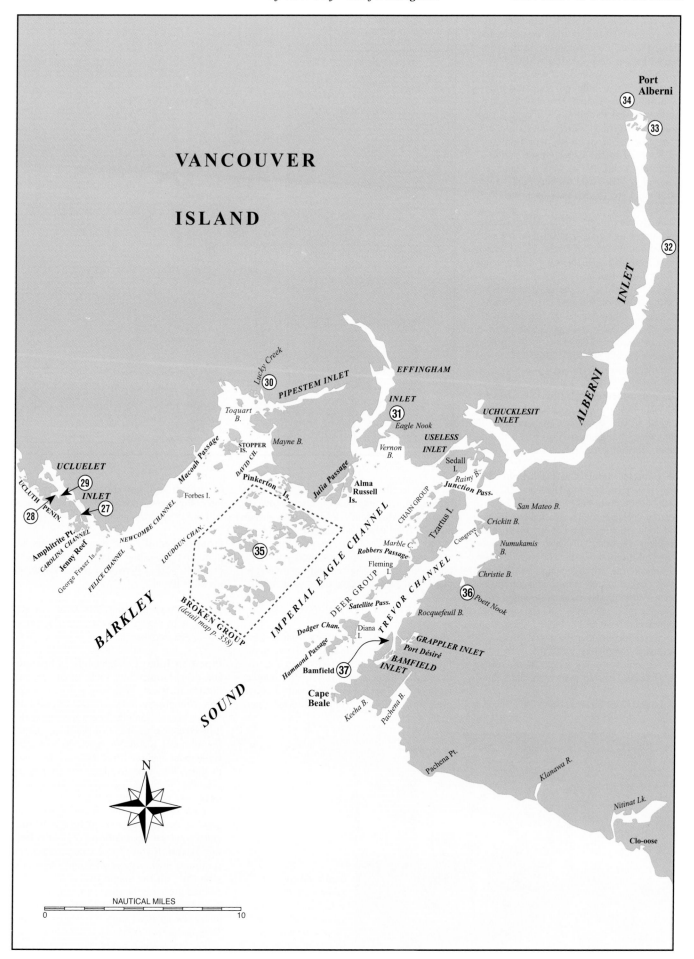

VANCOUVER

ISLAND

Port
Alberni
(34)
(33)
(32)

Lucky Creek
(30) PIPESTEM INLET
EFFINGHAM

Toquart
B.
INLET
(31)
Eagle Nook
UCHUCKLESIT
INLET

STOPPER
IS.
Mayne B.
Vernon
B.
USELESS
INLET

Macoah Passage
DAVID CH.
Pinkerton Is.
Julia Passage
Alma
Russell
Is.
Sedall
I.
Rainy B.
Junction Pass.

UCLUELET
(29)
INLET
(27)
Forbes I.
CHAIN GROUP
San Mateo B.

UCLUTH PENIN.
(28)
Amphitrite Pt.
CAROLINA CHANNEL
Jenny Reef
NEWCOMBE CHANNEL
LOUDOUN CHAN.
(35)
IMPERIAL EAGLE CHANNEL
Tzartus I.
Congreve I.
Crickitt B.
Numukamis
B.

George Fraser Is.
FELICE CHANNEL
Marble C.
Robbers Passage
Fleming I.
TREVOR CHANNEL
Christie B.

BARKLEY
BROKEN GROUP
(detail map p. 358)
DEER GROUP
Satellite Pass.
(36)
Poett Nook

Dodger Chan.
Diana
I.
Rocquefeuil B.

Hammond Passage
GRAPPLER INLET
Port Désiré
BAMFIELD
INLET

SOUND
Bamfield (37)
Cape
Beale
Keeha B.
Pachena B.

Pachena Pt.
Klanawa R.
Nitinat Lk.

Clo-oose

N

NAUTICAL MILES
0   10

the ways, has a good stock of marine supplies, commercial and sportfishing tackle, and charts. Pioneer Boat Works serves the commercial fishing fleet. Cruisers will find what they need there. Around the winding streets of Ucluelet you will find gift shops, art galleries including an excellent Native Gallery, dining from casual to quite nice, a large Co-op grocery and general merchandise store, and other essential services. It's a pleasant hike out the road to the Coast Guard station at Amphitrite Point. We've walked it and recommend it. The Wild Pacific Trail begins just beyond He-Tin-Kis Park, near the Coast Guard station.

In Ucluelet Inlet, Lyche Island can be passed on either side. If passing on the west side (the town side) of Lyche Island, check Chart 3646 and leave the buoys and beacons off the proper hands.

Customs: Ucluelet is the only customs reporting station on the west coast of Vancouver Island. Open June 1 to September 30. The 52 Step Dock in Ucluelet Inlet, a short distance beyond buoy *Y44*, is the official Customs dock. Call (888) 226-7277 by cell or at the on-dock payphone.

㉗ **Eagle Marine, Ltd.** Box 430, Ucluelet, BC V0R 3A0; (250) 726-4262. Open 7 days a week all year, summer 7:30 a.m. to 7:30 p.m.; winter 8:00 a.m. to 5:00 p.m. Gasoline, diesel, lubricants, ice, bait, convenience items.

㉘ **Ucluelet Small Craft Harbour.** P.O. Box 910, Hemlock St., Ucluelet, BC V0R 3A0; (250) 726-4241; (250) 725-8190; kcortes@ucluelet.ca. The marina has 30 amp and some 50 amp power, water, washrooms, excellent showers and laundry, pumpout, waste oil disposal, Wi-Fi. The outside basin, before entering the large main basin, has two floats marked for recreational and commercial boats. Although the floats are inviting, we'd continue inside. Docks B & C are marked for commercial boats only; docks D, E & F are for recreational and commercial boats. The facility is completely protected, well maintained, and quiet. It's where most cruising boats tie up. The staff is attentive and helpful.

㉙ **Island West Resort.** Box 879, 1990 Bay

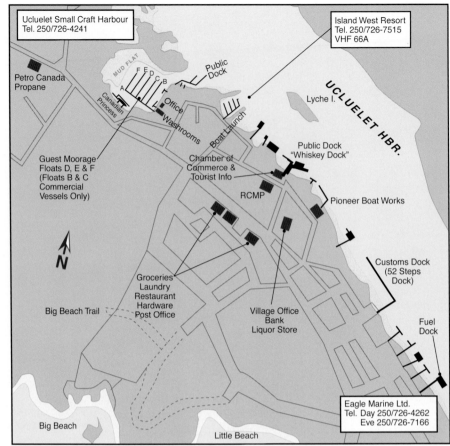

Ucluelet Harbour

St., Ucluelet, BC V0R 3A0; (250) 726-7515; fish@islandwestresort.com; www.islandwestresort.com. Monitors VHF 66A. Call ahead. A busy sportfishing resort, often fully reserved a year ahead for August. Limited 15 amp power, washrooms, showers, laundry, portapotty dump, launch ramp, marine supplies, charts, ice, deli take-out, excellent pub.

WESTERN BARKLEY SOUND

The western part of Barkley Sound, from Ucluelet to the Pipestem Inlet and over to the Pinkerton Islands, is relatively open and easily run. As long as you stay in the middle, Newcombe Channel and Macoah Passage present no problems. They lead to the Stop-

per Islands and, beyond them, to Pipestem Inlet. Pipestem Inlet is where the magical falls at Lucky Creek await.

Stopper Islands. The Stopper Islands are quite pretty and beg exploration by dinghy or kayak. Anchor between Larkins Island and the large island.

Toquaht Bay Marina. This small marina, protected by orange railroad tankers, is closed due to elevated arsenic levels.

Pipestem Inlet. Pipestem Inlet is beautiful and deep, bordered by high mountains and lined with forest. With one possible exception, though, the only anchoring possibilities are near the mouth. That exception is the little cove near the head of the inlet, behind the 32-meter island. We saw a 20-foot trailerable boat anchored in there and stern-tied to shore, but we didn't have the courage to take the 37-footer in. Maybe this cove is okay—we don't know. [*Hale*]

Near the mouth of Pipestem Inlet, the good anchorages are behind **Bazett Island**, either southwest or southeast, or behind **Refuge Island**. If you choose Bazett Island, the southwest anchorage is well into the southwest cove, off the mouth of the drying inlet colored green on the chart. The southeast anchorage is in the little thumb-shaped inlet, or along the adjacent shore, stern-tied. Reader Dick Drinkow reports that a number of large yellow buoys are in Bazett Island's southwest

Bonnie Gurney, at Pioneer Boatworks in Ucluelet, carries a large stock of just about everything a boater might need.

Ucluelet is a bustling commercial fishing port. In summer, there's ample room for visiting pleasure craft.

cove.

The Refuge Island anchorage is directly north of Refuge Island, a bit east of the 16-meter island. This anchorage and the Bazett Island anchorages are within easy dinghy commute to Lucky Creek. Aquaculture buoys occupy part of this cove but still leave room for boats to anchor.

(30) **Lucky Creek.** John Schlagel, fearless longtime explorer, did not suggest that we see Lucky Creek, he *instructed* us to see Lucky Creek, and he was right. This is a window-of-opportunity trip and the window corresponds with high tide.

We suggest taking the outboard-powered dinghy up to the falls an hour before high water and coming out an hour after. Managing Editor Sam Landsman took a shallow-draft, outboard powered 22' C-Dory in, and wouldn't want to go in anything much bigger.

The entrance is directly across Pipestem Inlet from Bazett Island. After crossing the shallow entry (bordered by meadow grass and wildflowers), the channel winds through marvelous mature forest, with overhanging cedars. The deeper part of the channel tends to follow the outside of the bends, river-style. The water is clear. We kept our eye on the bottom. Close to the falls the bottom shoals and we sought out the narrow, U-shaped channel to follow.

Suddenly, before our eyes was a storybook waterfall directly out of Walt Disney's imagination. Seeing that waterfall, we knew Tinker Bell was about; she was just too quick for us to see. When you go, tie the dinghy off to the side and climb up to a se-

ries of bathing pools. Be careful, the rocks can be slippery. And remember, just as Cinderella had to run when the clock tolled twelve, you cannot stay. If you tarry too long the falling tide will close you in.

You probably won't be alone at Lucky Creek. The lodges and resorts in the area are fully familiar with Lucky Creek and the boat drivers know the channel well. We got to Lucky Creek a half-hour after high tide, and the guests were all leaving—at top speed in the narrow waterway that was unfamiliar to us. They came right at us and swooped past, all smiles and happiness as we splashed through their wakes. No matter, the trip was worth it. [*Hale*]

Entrance Inlet. Entrance Inlet indents Vancouver Island at the northeast corner of Mayne Bay. Anchor in the outer basin in 40 feet. During the day you will have boat traffic from the fishing resort in Cigarette Cove.

Cigarette Cove. You can anchor in Cigarette Cove, but the resort takes up much of the space. The entry is narrow and bounded by rocks. If you pay attention, you will have no problems.

Southeast Cove. This cove is open to the west, but is good in settled weather. Anchor in 35 to 40 feet.

Pinkerton Islands. Far from the wildness of the outer islands, the Pinkerton Islands are north of the Broken Group, next to Vancouver Island. The Pinkertons are small and protected, with narrow channels, and are ideal for gunkholing.

Watch for rocks. The easiest anchorage is in the cove northwest of Williams Island. Unless several boats want to share the cove, no stern-tie is required. A study of the chart will suggest a number of other possibilities, most of which will require a stern-tie to shore.

UPPER BARKLEY SOUND

Effingham Inlet. Sailing Directions says Effingham Inlet is high, steep and deep, with few if any anchoring possibilities. Correspondents Bruce and Margaret Evertz explored Effingham Inlet and here is their report:

"We found anchorage in the bay on the west side of Effingham Inlet about one-quarter of the way in. The center of the bay is fairly flat and approximately 75 feet deep. Our anchor set well at 49°00.959'N / 125°10.659'W. Another secure spot would be at the south corner of the bay in 30 to 40 feet with a stern-tie. We were told that boats often anchor on the north side of the small peninsula near John Islet, at the entrance.

"While several oyster farms

are in the lower part of Effingham Inlet, we saw few signs of man farther in. It isn't Princess Louisa, but like Pipestem Inlet it's still pretty. The sides are high, steep and forested, with many interesting cliffs. We saw only two waterfalls. We didn't see many anchoring opportunities unless you want to stern-tie, and there were many small bights for that. We were told that afternoons can be windy, but the trees grow right to the high water line so we don't think the winds amount to much." [*Evertz*]

(31) **Jane Bay / Franks Bay.** This bay, known locally both as Jane Bay and Franks Bay, is not named on the chart. It is located at the back of Barkley Sound, connected by a narrow but safe passage with Vernon Bay at 48°59.80'N / 125°08.80'W. Anchor, carefully, near the head before the flats shoal too much. A water line is clearly marked with yellow buoys. Or tie up at Eagle Nook Lodge.

(31) **Eagle Nook Resort and Spa (Vernon Bay).** P.O. Box 289,

The Wild Pacific Trail leads to Amphitrite Point Lighthouse.

These are the pools at Lucky Creek. Recommended.

Ucluelet, BC V0R 3A0; (800) 760-2777; (604) 357-3361; info@eaglenook.com; www.eaglenookresort.com. Monitors VHF 73. Marina is immediately to starboard as you enter the bay. Moorage to 100 feet, 30 & 50 amp power, water, Wi-Fi, washrooms and showers. Reservations recommended, especially for larger boats. The lodge's exterior is Pacific Northwest style, interior is traditional lodge. Open May to mid-September. Restaurant, spa, and guided fishing are available to visiting boaters. Well-maintained walking trails lead through the forest.

Useless Inlet. Useless Inlet contains a number of aquaculture leases and recreational float homes. Entry to the inlet is made interesting by a series of large rocks that are covered except at lower stages of the tide. The rocks were covered when we were there and the wind rippled the water, making them hard to see. The obvious safe entry is along the north shore, to avoid the rocks in the middle. We attempted that route twice but didn't feel comfortable. We did see several trailerable sport fishing boats roar in and out of Useless Inlet, running between the rocks in the middle. They knew where the channel was; we didn't.

Correspondents Bruce and Margaret Evertz went into Useless Inlet. They report that "Useless Nook," described in Don Douglass's book, has an oyster farm in it, and a sign on shore that says, "No anchorage or trespassing in bay—oyster farm."

ALBERNI INLET

Alberni Inlet begins between Chup Point and Mutine Point, where it meets with Trevor Channel and Junction Passage. The inlet continues some 21 miles into the heart of Vancouver Island to the town of Port Alberni. Alberni Inlet is narrow and high-sided, with little to interest the cruiser along the way. A well-protected detached public float is in San Mateo Bay, near the mouth of the inlet. In Alberni Inlet itself, the only good stopovers are at the public float at Hook Bay or at China Creek, about 6 miles down-inlet from Port Alberni. Tidal current flows are less than 1

knot both directions, but the surface current can flow as fast as 3 knots when wind and current direction are the same. Except for trailer boats (see Port Alberni entry below) boats without a reason to go to Port Alberni seldom make the trip, preferring instead the many pleasures of Barkley Sound.

In the summer, an up-inlet thermal wind develops at 1:00 p.m. ("You can set your clock by it," says a friend in Port Alberni), and will increase to 25 to 30 knots by mid-afternoon. The wind produces a short, uncomfortable chop. We would run Alberni Inlet in the morning.

Port Alberni. *Port Alberni is the best single saltwater trailer boat destination in the Northwest.* We say this because Port Alberni gives the trailer boater safe and easy access to Barkley Sound, the most diverse and interesting cruising ground in the Northwest. (Note that by trailer boat, we still mean cruising boats with sleeping, cooking and toilet facilities, or at the very least, boats suitable for camping out. It's a 21-mile run down the Alberni Inlet to Barkley Sound; once in Barkley Sound you won't be coming back for a few days).

To get to Port Alberni, trailer the boat to the BC Ferries terminal at Tsawwassen, near the U.S. border, or to the Horseshoe Bay terminal, north of Vancouver. Large, comfortable ferries will take you to Nanaimo's Duke Point or Departure Bay terminals. (Or take the private ferry Coho from Port Angeles, Wash. to Victoria.) Our trailer boat friends tell us the fares for trailered boats are not inexpensive, so be prepared. From the Duke Point ferry terminal at Nanaimo, an easy and often beautiful 1½- to 2-hour drive on paved highway will take you to Port Alberni.

Along the way, be sure to stop at Cathedral Grove for a walk through a towering forest of 1000-year-old cedar, hemlock and Douglas fir. The trail is easy and well-maintained. If you hurry along, you can walk it in 20 minutes. If you linger to absorb more of the majesty, it could take about an hour. Interpretive signs explain everything.

To reach Port Alberni you do have to go over a 1230-foot-high mountain pass, with an 8 percent grade on the east side and a 6

percent grade on the west. Be sure your rig has enough power and brakes.

Once at Port Alberni, you'll find good launch ramps at Clutesi Haven Marina at the mouth of the Somass River and at China Creek, located 6 miles down the Alberni Inlet. Long-term parking is available at both locations. All the marinas are operated by the Port Alberni Port Authority; www.portalberniportauthority.ca.

In Port Alberni you'll find complete services of a small industrial city, including hospital, shopping, marine supplies and repairs, and dinner out.

A steam locomotive pulls a train that runs from downtown Port Alberni to the McLean Mill National Historic Site, the only working steam-operated sawmill in Canada. It takes about 35 minutes each way. The McLean Mill is a fascinating tour, with interpretive signing to explain what you are looking at. The cookhouse, blacksmith shop, workers' housing and other buildings have been restored. Mill demonstrations and a guided theatrical experience are offered daily. Logs are in the mill pond. A trip to the McLean Mill is a step back in time. The entire family will enjoy it. Call (250) 723-1376. Better yet, for latest information and schedules see www.alberni heritage.com.

For information on other attractions and events, contact the Alberni Valley Chamber of Commerce, (250) 724-6535.

Salmon festival: Port Alberni's Salmon Festival (www.pasalmonfest.com) is held Labour Day weekend each year. We are told that the Somass River is the third largest salmon stream in B.C. Only the Fraser River and the Skeena River have larger returns.

Haulout: Alberni Engineering and Shipyard has haulout and complete repairs for boats to 100 feet. Call (250) 723-0111.

Golf: The Alberni Golf Club is an 18-hole par 70 course, with deep rough and excellent greens. Call (250) 723-5422. Hollies Executive Golf Course is a 9-hole, par 30 track. Call (250) 724-5333.

Fuel: No marine diesel fuel is available in Port Alberni itself, although diesel and gasoline are available at China Creek. Gasoline is available at Clutesi Haven.

Harbour Quay Marina in Port Alberni is close to downtown. Showers and laundry are in the new building, top of ramp.

㉜ **China Creek Marina & Campground.** (250) 723-9812; chinacreek@portalberni.ca. Open April through September, 88 slips and 2300 feet of side-tie moorage, 4-lane launch ramp. Gasoline, diesel, propane, 15 amp power, washrooms, showers, laundry, garbage drop. Fuel dock is shallow on low tides. RV hookups are adjacent. This is primarily a trailer boat facility.

㉝ **Harbour Quay.** 2900 Harbour Rd., Port Alberni, BC V9Y 7X2; (250) 723-1413; harbourquay@portalberni.ca. Harbour Quay has 15 slips and 2000 lineal feet of side-tie moorage, 20 & 30 amp power, washrooms, showers, laundry, potable water on the floats, garbage drop. This is a breakwater-protected marina close to downtown. The docks have been reconfigured to create more side-tie moorage, making it attractive for larger boats. Check ahead for availability. Adjacent to the Maritime Heritage Discovery Centre, in a genuine west coast lighthouse.

㉝ **Fisherman's Harbour.** 3140 Harbour Rd., Port Alberni, BC V9Y 7X2; (250) 723-2533; fishermansharbour@portalberni.ca. Open all year, 7600 feet of moorage, 20, 30 and some 50 amp power, water, new washrooms & showers, garbage drop, pumpout, winch on the wharf. Fisherman's Harbour is adjacent to downtown Port Alberni, with all the services of downtown close by. They never turn anyone away, but be prepared to raft. June is the busiest month; August is the quietest.

㉞ **Clutesi Haven.** (250) 724-6837; clutesihaven@portalberni.ca. Open all year, gasoline at the fuel dock, 2460 feet of moorage including side-tie moorage, call for availability. Power, water, washrooms, garbage drop, 4-lane launch ramp. Clutesi Haven is located behind a breakwater near the mouth of the Somass River. Best suited to boats 25 feet or less. This is a popular launching spot for trailerable boats. Hotels, pubs, and liquor store are nearby. Groceries are 5 blocks away.

BROKEN GROUP

The Broken Group extends from the wind-and-wave-lashed outer islands to peaceful islands deep inside Barkley Sound. The Broken Group is part of the Pacific Rim National Park, to be preserved in its natural state in perpetuity. For many Northwest boaters, a holiday spent in the Broken Group is the fulfillment of a lifelong dream.

Boats visiting the Broken Group will find dozens of little nooks and bights to put the hook down, depending on weather and the mood on board. Don Watmough, Don Douglass, and the Yeadon-Joneses all describe a number of them in their guides. The major anchorages are Effingham Bay, Turtle Bay and Nettle Island.

Chart note: On Chart 3670, the water faucet symbols on Effingham Island, Benson Island, Clarke Island, Turret Island, Willis Island and Gibraltar Island should be deleted.

Pets: The Broken Group is part of Pacific Rim National Park. In order to protect native flora and fauna, pets are not permitted on shore anywhere in the Broken Group.

Effingham Bay. Effingham Bay is large, pretty, and protected. On the nights of our visits we have shared the bay with 10 to 20 other boats, yet everyone had room to swing and we didn't feel crowded. The chart shows the entrance. Anchor in 30 to 50 feet, good holding. Sunsets, seen out the mouth of the bay, can be dramatic. Because Effingham Bay is open to the west, westerly winds can make the anchorage a bit bumpy.

Take the time to dinghy ashore and hike to the ancient Indian village site on the east side of Effingham (Village) Island. The trail begins on the right side (as you face the land from the water) of the little thumb of water at the head of Effingham Bay and leads through lush and mature forest. In 2012, there was a sign on the left side of this thumb of water that misled some hikers to the wrong side. Don't be fooled; the wrong trail leads to mud, fallen trees and other obstacles. The sign warns of wolves on the island. Do pay attention to what it says:

"When in a group, act in unison to send a clear message to the wolves they are not welcome.

"Back away slowly, do not turn your back on the wolf.

"Make noise, throw sticks, rocks and sand at the wolf."

The trail across the island is generally easy, but a little primitive and challenging in places. The village site, on the eastern shore, is mystical. Widely-spaced trees suggest the location of the main village. The large midden, with shells poking out of it, indicates a long and populous habitation. Near the beach you can find an old longhouse beam that now serves as a nurse log. A sea cave is located there, but is inaccessible at high tide. Late in the day the view eastward from the beach—the sea, with the mountains of Vancouver Island painted in low reddish light—is inspiring.

Benson Island. In settled weather you can take anchorage off the east shore of Benson Island, in the cove opposite the water faucet icon on the chart. A trail leads across the island to a scenic rocky beach with a blowhole that sounds just like a whale blowing.

Sunset in Effingham Bay. Photo by James & Jennifer Hamilton, www.mvdirona.com

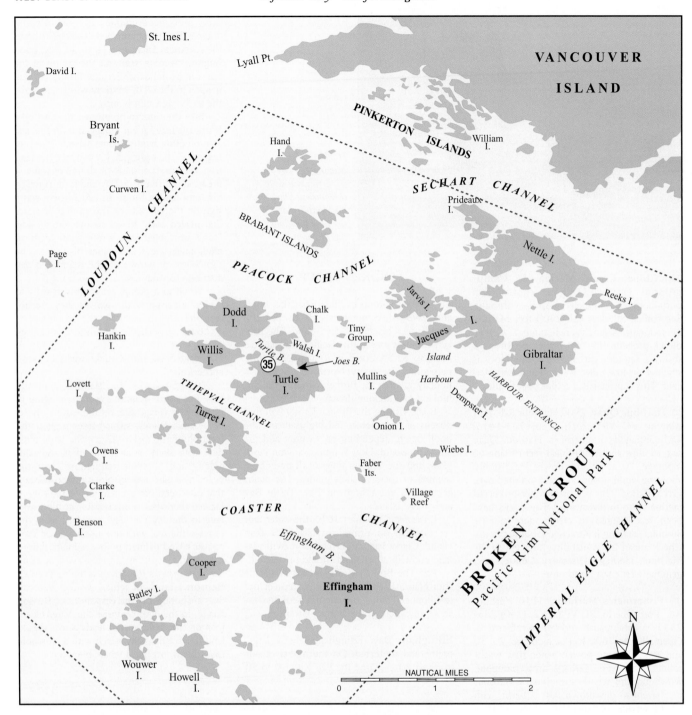

Clarke Island. Temporary or settled weather anchorage can be found on the east side of Clarke Island.

Turret Island. The cove formed by the 36-meter island on the southwest side of Turret Island is okay for anchoring, though the bottom is thick with kelp. The surrounding area has interesting rock formations and is good for exploring by dinghy or kayak.

㉟ **Turtle Bay.** Turtle Bay is a local name for the bay formed by Turtle Island, Willis Island, and Dodd Island. Joes Bay, an appendage of Turtle Bay, indents Turtle Island. It is the little nook where Salal Joe, the Hermit of Barkley Sound, made his home.

The best entrance to Turtle Bay is from the north, off Peacock Channel, between Dodd Island and Chalk Island. A study of the chart shows the entrance channel bounded by rocks and drying rock outcroppings along the way. A careful entry, proceeding slowly and identifying the hazards, will bring you in safely. Those who have been in a few times know where the rocks are and roar right in.

Anchor in 25 to 30 feet on a mud bottom, good holding.

Nettle Island. Nettle Island has three good anchorages—one in the large bay that indents the southern shore, and the other two in the channel between Nettle Island and Reeks Island to the east. In Nettle Island's

large bay we prefer the eastern portion, off the park ranger's float cabin. The center of the bay is a little deep (50 to 60 feet, depending on state of tide), but you can find depths of 20 to 30 feet near the shore north of the ranger's cabin. Reader Dick Drinkow reports that the park ranger warns that boats have grounded on the shelf, and recommends anchoring in the center of the bay.

Watmough describes two other anchorages along the east side of Nettle Island, opposite Reeks Island. These nooks will hold a couple of boats each, and Watmough says they are delightful. The charted rocks are easy to identify and avoid.

After a careful entry into Turtle Bay, it opens into a scenic anchorage.

Outer Islands. The outer islands of the Broken Group are marked by twisted trees, the result of relentless onshore winds, especially in the winter. If your needs include the desire to navigate "at the edge," the outer islands can satisfy that need. Here, you'll have your opportunity to run in wind and fog, with the Pacific Ocean swells beating against the rocks. Navigate carefully. The low islands are easy to get mixed up. Rocks and reefs are charted, but they're everywhere. This is beautiful, raw country. The kayakers have it best. The favored anchorage is at Wouwer Island.

Wouwer Island. Wouwer Island is breathtaking, both in its scenery and gunkholing. At half tide or higher, most boats can make it through the slit between Batley Island and Wouwer Island. A bow watch will only scare you.

We anchored temporarily in a nook south of two islets, west of the slit between Batley and Wouwer Islands. A trail leads across the island to a lovely beach with great beachcombing.

EASTERN BARKLEY SOUND

Limestone Bay, located at the mouth of Uchucklesit Inlet, has satisfactory anchorage in 12 feet with some protection. Use the southwest entrance only.

㊱ **Poett Nook.** Poett Nook is on the eastern shore, at lat 48°53'N. It doesn't look like a nook when you see it. It is a spacious, rather pretty bay, with good anchoring in 25 feet. The entry is narrow but deep. The Poett Nook Marina, a large sport fishing resort, is on the eastern side of the bay.

㊱ **Poett Nook Marina & Campground.** Mailing: P.O. Box 411, #1-5765 Turner Rd., Nanaimo, BC V9T 4M6; (250) 758-4440; (250) 720-9572; poettnookmarina@shaw.ca; www.poettnook.com. Gasoline at the fuel dock, washrooms, showers. No power, non-potable water. A small store carries convenience food, ice, and tackle. Fee based garbage drop. This is a busy small-boat sportfishing resort, with 160 RV/camping sites and berths for 177 boats. Maximum length 34 feet. Most boats launch at Port Alberni or China Creek.

Robbers Passage. Robbers Passage leads between Fleming Island and Tzartus Island in the Deer Group, and is a likely route for boats bound between points near the head of Barkely Sound and Bamfield. A rock that dries 1 meter is in the western approach to Robbers Passage. Although the rock is clearly charted, people at the Port Alberni Yacht Club swear this is one rock that moves. Give the rock a wide berth. The S-shaped channel leading into Robbers Passage requires close attention, but with attention it is safe. A study of large-scale chart 3668 will make the route clear. Inside the passage, the Port Alberni Yacht Club has its floating clubhouse and docks.

Port Alberni Yacht Club. Consider spending at least one night at the Port Alberni Yacht Club. The facility is clean and well-maintained and the folks are friendly and helpful. They have a wealth of local knowledge to share. Be sure to walk the beautiful trail around the peninsula behind the yacht club. The moorage charge is modest and goes back into the facility. All are welcome; no yacht club membership needed. Washrooms, showers, and non-potable water available.

Aquaculture ventures have left considerable debris on the seafloor. Anchoring not recommended, although Elsie and Steve Hulsizer report that on several occasions when the moorage was full they anchored off the docks without any problems. Several large buoys might be mistaken for mooring buoys. These buoys are not designed for mooring and have dragged when boats tied to them.

Fleming Island. The day was sunny with only a gentle breeze, so we left the boat at the yacht club and motored the dinghy around Fleming Island. The impossibly rugged shoreline is dotted with sea caves. We were told that some of the caves extend far into the rock. For thousands of years the First Nations people in Barkley Sound put at least some of their dead in bentwood boxes and hid them in sea caves. One man told of crawling on his belly, flashlight in hand, and coming on centuries-old boxes, secreted away. The floors of the sea caves are made of gravel or small round boulders. Kick aside some rock and uncover a skull. We were fascinated by the stories, but didn't follow them up.

We did, however, ease the dinghy through a narrow cleft in the rock and up to the mouth of one cave. The opening loomed above us, and we could see the floor of small boulders rise and disappear in darkness. The rock walls of the cleft were covered with orange and purple sea stars. Other neon-hued sea life waved in the surge. The word *impressed* does not begin to describe the effect on us. [*Hale*]

Tzartus Cove. Tzartus Cove (our preferred anchorage on Tzartus Island) is the name Don Douglass gives to this excellent anchorage about 0.5 mile north of Marble Cove. Rocks extend from both shores, so go right down the middle when you enter. Anchor near the head in 25 to 30 feet. Sea caves are nearby. Reader Dick Drinkow reports that a bit of northwest swell can get into the cove and that kelp fouled their anchor.

This wolf was spotted on Turtle Island.

The Port Alberni Yacht Club docks in Robbers Passage.

The Bamfield General Store is well stocked.

Marble Cove. Marble Cove is on the west side of Tzartus Island, and often is mentioned as a good anchorage (we would choose instead the cove one-half mile north). A rock stack between two islands and reddish rocks on the shore add to the scenic nature of the cove. A float house is on the north side of Marble Cove. Anchor in 25 to 30 feet off the gravel beach on the island opposite the float house. This is a good place to explore tidepools at low tide.

Grappler Inlet. Grappler Inlet joins near the mouth of Bamfield Inlet and leads to **Port Désiré**, a protected anchorage with a launch ramp and a public dock. Although Grappler Inlet is beautiful, it is surrounded by homes.

Bamfield Inlet. Bamfield Inlet is open and easy to enter. The village of Bamfield is along the shores of the inlet. Several public docks are located on each side. Commercial fish boats have priority, but space usually can be found for pleasure craft. At the head of the inlet, past Rance Island, is a quiet basin where boats can anchor although an overhead power cable limits mast height to 17 meters (55 feet). Larger boats anchor off the East Bamfield public dock. The mooring buoys shown on the chart have been removed. The West Bamfield public dock is largely reserved; even a dinghy may have trouble finding a spot.

③ **Bamfield.** They call the inlet "Main Street." The village of Bamfield covers both sides of the inlet, and the west side is not connected by road with the east side. You cross by boat or you don't cross. The Bamfield General Store, with liquor agency, is on the west side of the inlet. A boardwalk runs along the homes and businesses on the west side, and folks get around by walking. The Boardwalk Bistro located near the West Bamfield public dock serves espresso drinks and delicious salmon burgers.

The east side has roads that tie its businesses and homes together. They connect with the 60-mile-long dirt logging road that leads to Port Alberni. The east side has a hardware store and a marine store, pub, a small grocery store with deli counter and small cafe. In 2012 the pub was not open in June, except on weekends. The trail to Cape Beale begins on the east side of the inlet. A launch ramp is at Port Désiré.

A small Outpost Hospital is located on the east side. It is set up to treat illness or injury, deliver babies, and dispense medication. The hospital is operated by registered nurses, and a visiting physician calls on a regular schedule. They work closely with the Coast Guard for emergency helicopter transport when needed. A fee schedule accommodates non-Canadians who need medical attention.

Wi-Fi is available through Community

Wireless Networks, (250) 728-3647.

The large building on the east side of the inlet near the entrance houses the Bamfield Marine Research Station. The station is owned by five universities in British Columbia and Alberta, and began operation in 1971. Visitors are welcomed, and tours are offered Saturdays and Sundays during the summer, no charge. This facility once was the eastern terminus of the transpacific cable that connected North America with Australia. Its first message was sent on November 1, 1902; its last message was sent in 1959. See their website at www.bms.bc.ca.

Bamfield offers several events during the year, including the Music by the Sea Festival, with classical and jazz musicians from all over. Lodging is at a premium, but boaters can stay on board. See www.bamfieldchamber.com/events.html for events and dates.

③ **East Bamfield Public Dock.** Moorage, water, garbage drop, limited power. No washrooms. The docks have recently been resurfaced.

③ **Bamfield Fuel Barge.** (250) 728-3771. Located on the east side of the inlet, just past the government wharf. Gasoline, diesel, ice, convenience food. Open 8:00 a.m. to 8:00 p.m. in the summer.

③ **West Bamfield Public Dock.** (250) 728-3500; broken@island.net. Moorage, 20 & 30 amp power, water. No washrooms. Reservations recommended during July and August.

③ **Harbourside Lodge.** (250) 728-3330; requests@harboursidelodge.com; www.harboursidelodge.com. Moorage, power, washroom, showers, laundry. Store has ice, bait, tackle. Located on the west side of the inlet, just past the government dock.

③ **McKay Bay Lodge.** (250) 728-3323; mckaybay@island.net; www.mckaybaylodge.com. Located on the west side of the inlet. Gasoline, diesel, tackle, ice. Limited moorage, washroom, guest rooms.

This tunnel in Marble Cove can be explored by dinghy in settled conditions.

BARKLEY SOUND TO SOOKE

The final leg of a counter-clockwise circumnavigation of Vancouver Island is from Barkley Sound into the Strait of Juan de Fuca. On the Canadian side, Port Renfrew is the only protection between Barkley Sound and Sooke.

The typical summer weather pattern calls for calm conditions in the early morning, with a westerly sea breeze building by afternoon, often to 30+ knots.

Currents in the Strait of Juan de Fuca can be strong. This can speed up the passage, especially for sailboats. Or, it can substantially slow the trip. When the wind blows against the current, steep, sometimes-dangerous seas result. Pay attention to the current when planning to transit the Strait of Juan de Fuca.

Several weather resources make the trip through the Strait of Juan de Fuca less nerve-racking. Lighthouses at Cape Beale, Pachena Point, and Carmanah Point provide regular weather updates. Automated stations at Shearingham Point and Race Rocks report hourly wind speed and direction. The Neah Bay weather buoy (46087) provides regular wind speed updates, and the New Dungeness buoy (46088) provides wind speed, direction, and sea state. Put together, you can get picture of conditions on the Strait before venturing out.

Cape Beale. Cape Beale, surrounded by off-lying rocks, marks the eastern entrance to Barkley Sound. Trevor Channel exits at Cape Beale, and is the safest entry to, or exit from, Barkley Sound in thick weather or poor visibility. Seas can be difficult off Cape Beale when an outflowing current from Barkley Sound meets the longshore current outside. The collision of currents, combined with wind and shallow depths around the cape, can make for heavy going.

The usual advice is to round Cape Beale in early morning, before the summertime westerly wind gets up.

Nitinat Narrows. Nitinat Narrows connects Nitinat Lake with the Pacific Ocean. Entrance

The shoreline near Bamfield has sandy beaches that give way to dramatic rock formations.

to the narrows is obstructed by rocks and a shallow bar. An onshore wind can cause breaking seas over the bar. A crossing of this bar and negotiation of the narrows to Nitinat Lake is considered a supreme Northwest navigation challenge by a small number of adventurers. Each year a few boats do make it through.

Many years ago Don Douglass took his Nordic 32 tug across the bar, through the narrows, and into Nitinat Lake. His guidebook, *Exploring Vancouver Island's West Coast, 2nd Ed.* describes the experience, including the comment that his crew refused to ever try it again.

㉚ Port San Juan. For shelter off the Strait on the Canadian side consider Port San Juan, about halfway between Victoria and Barkley Sound. Port San Juan is a rectangular notch in Vancouver Island, with Port Renfrew on the eastern shore near the head of the bay. A public dock, with very limited moorage, is at Port Renfrew.

You can also anchor, with some protection, close to shore along the west side of Port San Juan, or tie to one of the log rafts

boomed in the mouth of the Gordon River, at the northwest corner of the bay.

Readers Mike and Sandy Cecka report good anchorage behind Woods Nose, close to shore. Woods Nose breaks up the swell, and trees ashore block much of the wind. A well-maintained trail leads from this anchorage to a paved road. Take a right at the road, walk another 15 minutes, and arrive at Botanical Beach Provincial Park.

The old hotel and pub at the head of the public dock has rooms, and just beyond is the Lighthouse Pub, modern and up-scale. Port Renfrew is the end of the road and the large Lighthouse Pub seems out of place until it's explained that in the summer some 2,000 people per day—hikers, kayakers and sightseers—pour through the town.

㉚ Port Renfrew Community Dock. 17280 Parkinson Rd., Port Renfrew, BC V0S 1K0. VHF 06 & 68 "Medd-O Base." Floats with room for 20 boats are installed from mid-May through mid-September. All are taken by charter boats. No electrical power; water is on the wharf but not on the floats. Best to call ahead for availability and reserva-

Sooke is one of the few stops for boats coming from or going to Barkley Sound.

Anchorage in Sooke can be found behind Whiffen Spit.

tions. Stan Medd is the harbormaster.

㊳ Pacific Gateway Marina. (250) 412-5509; contact@pacificgatewaymarina.ca; www.pacificgatewaymarina.ca. Open mid-May through mid-September. Gasoline, no diesel. No power or water. Moorage to 80 feet, but most slips are designed for small sport fishing boats. Large vessels should call ahead for availability.

SOOKE

㊴ Sooke Harbour is entered between Company Point and Parsons Point. The harbor is protected by Whiffen Spit, which nearly blocks the passage. Enter by keeping Whiffen Spit (with its small lighthouse) close to port, and follow the marked channel to town. An area just inside Whiffen Spit has good anchorage, although wakes from passing boats make it rolly. The Sooke Harbour Marina, with guest moorage and other facilities, is south of the Sooke Harbour Authority wharf. The city floats usually are taken by commercial fishboats, but pleasure craft will find room when the fleet is out.

Sooke has a wide variety of services close to the city floats, including a marine railway and machine shop, groceries, fuel, and restaurants. Currents run quite strongly along the city waterfront. Be careful when landing.

Sooke Basin, the innermost harbor, is seldom visited by pleasure craft. The shallow channel follows the curve of the shoreline east of Middle Ground, between Eliza Point and Trollope Point. Notices to Mariners advises that entry to Sooke Basin be made after low water during daylight hours, when the drying banks are visible. Contributing Editor Tom Kincaid has anchored in a little, almost landlocked, bay behind Pim Head.

Sooke is the only completely protected harbor between Victoria and Barkley Sound. It is 15 miles closer to Barkley Sound than downtown Victoria, and often used as a departure point for boats heading up the west coast of Vancouver Island.

No customs clearance is available in Sooke. The nearest Canadian Port of Entry is Victoria.

㊴ Sooke Harbour Resort & Marina. 6971 West Coast Road, Sooke, BC V9Z 0V1; (250) 642-3236; admin@sookeharbourmarina.ca; www.sookeharbourmarina.ca.

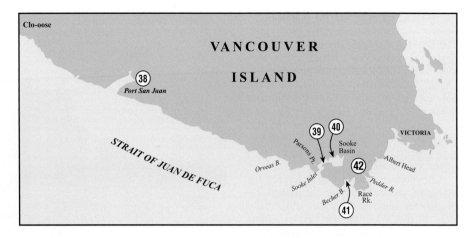

Open all year with guest moorage to 50 feet. Services include washrooms, showers, 20 & 30 amp power, Wi-Fi, and 2-lane concrete launch ramp. No long term parking. This is the first marina as you come into the harbor.

㊴ Sooke Harbour Authority. Open all year, guest moorage along 797 feet of dock, 30 amp power, no washrooms or showers.

㊵ Sunny Shores Resort & Marina. 5621 Sooke Rd., RR 1, Sooke, BC V9Z 0C6; (250) 642-5731; www.sunnyshoresresort.com. Open all year. Gasoline and diesel at fuel dock. Guest moorage for 6 to 10 average size boats, call ahead for availability. Washrooms, showers, laundry, 15 amp power, haulout. Motel accommodations and campground. Mini-golf, playground. Store carries ice, fishing tackle, local charts, limited groceries. Taxi to town 3 miles away; bus to Victoria, 28 miles away.

Becher Bay. Campbell Cove on the west side of Becher Bay is a pleasant anchorage, but be careful of a drying rock near the south end. It's a good jumping-off point for the run to Barkley Sound. Kelp is on the bottom; be sure of your set. Murder Bay, at the north end, is another recommended anchorage, also with kelp, though.

㊶ Becher Bay Marina & Campground. 241 Becher Bay Rd., Sooke, BC V9Z 1B7; (250) 642-3816. Open May 1 to September 30. Limited guest moorage by reservation only, maximum boat length 30 feet. Services include washrooms, no showers, 2-lane concrete launch ramp, no power. Smokin' Tuna Cafe on site. RV parking.

Pedder Bay. Pedder Bay is a mile-long inlet, shallow and narrow, just south of William Head. No anchoring in bay due to submerged utility pipes. A launch ramp with floats is at the head.

㊷ Pedder Bay Marina. 925 Pedder Bay Drive #12, Victoria, BC V9C 4H1; (250) 478-1771; pbm@obmg.com; www.pedderbay.com. Monitors VHF 66A. Open all year, gasoline only at fuel dock. Most guest moorage maximum 26-foot boat length. Call ahead for larger boats. Washrooms, showers, laundry, 30 amp power, free Wi-Fi, 4-lane concrete launch ramp, RV resort, camping. Approaching, use Chart 3410; watch the breeze. Located between Pearson College and Dept. of National Defence (you can't stop there; it's a prison).

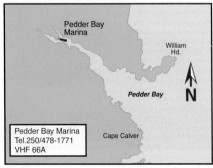

Pedder Bay Marina

The Pedder Bay Marina offers nice facilities but has few spots for boats larger than 26 feet.

ROUNDING CAPE CAUTION

PINE ISLAND ROUTE
Pine Island • Egg Island

WALKER GROUP ANCHORAGE
Kent Island • Staples Island

PULTENEY POINT–JEANETTE ISLAND ROUTE
Malcolm Island • Jeanette Islands • Harris Island •
Hot Spring Island • Richards Channel •
Allison Harbour

MAINLAND ROUTE
Blunden Harbour • Allison Harbour • Miles Inlet
• Nakwakto Rapids • Southgate Group

To get to the central and northern B.C. coast you first must round Cape Caution. Although the distance in open water is only about 40 miles, the seas can be high and steep. The bottom shoals from 100+ fathoms off the continental shelf to 20-70 fathoms in Queen Charlotte Sound itself, causing seas to heap up. The problem is made worse when these seas are met by the outflowing ebb currents from Queen Charlotte Strait, Smith Sound, Rivers Inlet and Fitz Hugh Sound.

After more than 30 crossings, we've refined our "go, no-go" decisions to six factors: weather forecast; time of day; lighthouse wind and sea reports; flood or ebb tide; size of tidal exchange (spring tide or neap tide); and the automated swell-height reports from the West Sea Otter Buoy.

Weather forecast. Regardless of other factors, we want a favorable forecast or we're not going.

Time of day. The typical summertime weather pattern calls for calm early mornings, followed in late morning or early afternoon by a rising westerly sea breeze, sometimes to gale force. "Typical," however, does not mean every day. We've seen windy mornings and flat-calm late afternoons.

Lighthouse wind and sea reports. From south to north, lighthouses at Scarlett Point, Pine Island, Egg Island and Addenbroke Island report conditions approximately every four hours, posted on the Continuous Marine Broadcast. Pine Island and Egg Island seem to be the most important. Addenbroke Island, inside the mouth of Fitz Hugh Sound, often reports quiet conditions when Pine Island and Egg Island are much rougher. Scarlett Point, just off the north part of Vancouver Island, usually is quieter than Pine Island and Egg Island. In our case, we can tolerate "3-foot moderate" seas, but we don't like them. "Two-foot chop, low westerly swell" is our preferred upper limit.

Flood or ebb tide. Flood tide is preferred. On a flood, the incoming swells and prevailing westerly wind are aligned and the seas are flattened. The ebb is the reverse: outflowing ebb currents meet the westerly swells, making them higher and steeper. One year we made the mistake of crossing the mouth

An early morning crossing could mean fog in light winds. This area is busy with commercial traffic and other boats. Keep a sharp lookout on radar.

of Rivers Inlet in a mounting sea breeze that was blowing against a strong outflowing ebb, and we took a beating. We *will not* do that again.

Size of tidal exchange. If possible, cross during a time of neap tides. If that can't be done, try to cross on a flood. If that can't be done, try to cross at the end of one tide, when currents are growing less, and the beginning of the next tide, while currents are still low. Avoid crossing the mouth of Rivers Inlet on an ebb.

West Sea Otter Buoy. Seas 1.3 meters or less at West Sea Otter Buoy often indicates a pleasant crossing. Combine this information with the weather forecast, lighthouse reports, and flood and ebb tides. We learned about West Sea Otter from a towboat skipper who had been waiting for days for the buoy to report 1 meter or less so he could tow a raft of precious cedar logs south.

Radio note. South of Cape Caution, Comox VTS, channel 71, controls large vessel traffic. North of Cape Caution, traffic is controlled by Prince Rupert VTS, channel 11. Especially in reduced visibility, one radio should be monitoring VHF 16 and a second radio should be scanning channels 11 and 71. If

large vessels or tugs with tows are around, you want to know about them.

Pine Island Route. This is the most popular route from Vancouver Island. It begins at Scarlett Point at the mouth of Christie Passage on Gordon Channel, and ends at Fury Cove, at the north end of Rivers Inlet. The distance is approximately 40 miles. Boats often provision and refuel in Port McNeill or Port Hardy, and move to a jumping-off point near Christie Passage for a crossing the next morning. God's Pocket in Christie Passage, Port Alexander in Browning Passage, or Clam Cove in Gordon Channel just west of Browning Passage, are often used. Another good spot is the cove between Staples Island and Kent Island in the Walker Group.

The Pine Island route leads westward in Gordon Channel to Pine Island, then northward past the tip of the Storm Islands, past Egg Island, and on to Smith Sound, Rivers Inlet or Cape Calvert. This route will give Cape Caution an offing of 1.5 to 2.5 miles.

Gordon Channel is a principal passage for commercial vessels. Display a radar reflector. In thick weather or fog, radar and GPS are extremely useful. Especially in low visibility or fog, most commercial traffic can be avoided by crossing Gordon Channel to the Redfern Island/Buckle Group side, and favoring that side to Pine Island.

Pulteney Point to Jeanette Islands Route. If Queen Charlotte Strait is behaving, this can be a good route from Port McNeill on Vancouver Island to the mainland side. From Pulteney Point at the west tip of Malcom Island, turn to a course of 309° magnetic. This will leave the charted kelp patch to port. Twenty miles later you will arrive at the Jeanette Islands on the mainland side of Queen Charlotte Strait. Turn to approximately 290° magnetic and proceed through Richards Channel until flashing green Whistle Buoy N31 is abeam to port. Alter course slightly

The Pine Island Lighthouse provides useful weather updates.

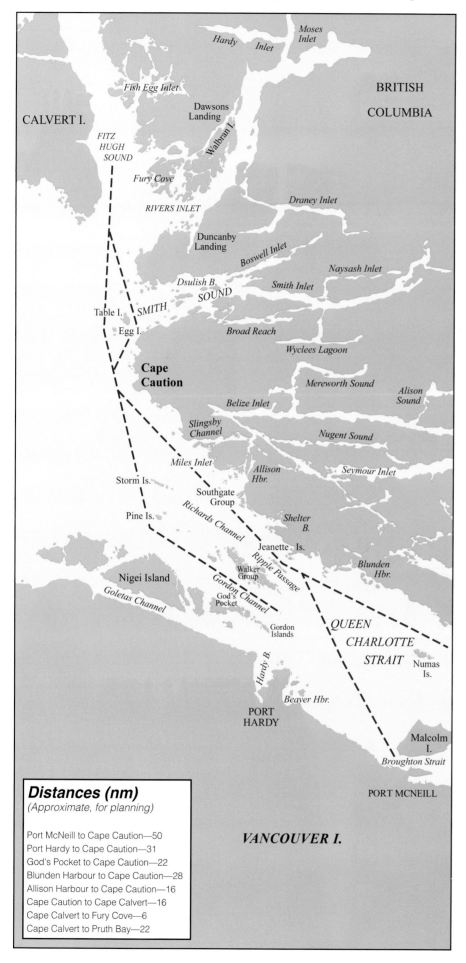

Distances (nm)
(Approximate, for planning)

Port McNeill to Cape Caution—50
Port Hardy to Cape Caution—31
God's Pocket to Cape Caution—22
Blunden Harbour to Cape Caution—28
Allison Harbour to Cape Caution—16
Cape Caution to Cape Calvert—16
Cape Calvert to Fury Cove—6
Cape Calvert to Pruth Bay—22

to leave Harris Island to starboard and Allen Rocks Lighted Whistle Buoy *N33* to port. From there a course of approximately 293° magnetic will take you to a common intersection point west of Cape Caution.

Caution in Richards Channel. On an ebb, especially a big ebb, Richards Channel can be difficult. One year, although the wind was calm, a big ebb set up a 2.5-knot outflowing current that opposed the incoming swells, creating larger and more threatening seas. We aborted our crossing and anchored instead in Allison Harbour. High winds kept us in Allison Harbour the following day and night.

Mainland Route. The mainland route offers more shelter in case of a blow and lets you visit Blunden Harbour, Allison Harbour and Miles Inlet. You could even take a major side trip through famed Nakwakto Rapids (at slack) and spend time in Seymour Inlet and Belize Inlet. Many boats prefer the mainland route for its greater interest and possibility of shelter. The major cautions are Richards Channel on an ebb (above) and the waters off Slingsby Channel on an ebb.

Slingsby Channel Caution. Slingsby Channel is the primary drain for the hundreds of miles of inlets behind Nakwakto Rapids. What Slingsby Channel does to Queen Charlotte Strait on a big ebb can be terrifying. Outer Narrows at the mouth of Slingsby Channel runs to 9 knots on an ebb. The water firehoses into Queen Charlotte Strait, where it collides with the Pacific Ocean's incoming swells. If a westerly is blowing against this vast outpouring, conditions can be as bad as the worst at Cape Mudge.

Outer Narrows currents turn 10 minutes before Nakwakto Rapids, both flood and ebb. In 2009 we departed our anchorage in Allison Harbour at 8:00 a.m., not realizing that two hours earlier the maximum ebb at Nakwakto Rapids was 11.4 knots. Shortly after 8:00 a.m. Slingsby Channel was still roaring. Although not a breath of wind was stirring, we found ourselves in large, steep seas that lifted the bow high, then crashed us down into the troughs. We pressed on, hoping not to meet a log in the bottom of a trough, and got through without injury or damage. The turbulence diminished but persisted all the way to Cape Caution, which we rounded at 10:10 a.m., a half-hour after the turn to flood in Slingsby Channel.

Summing up. We have rounded Cape Caution 30 times, and only twice have the crossings been unpleasant. The first was the beating we took when we were off Rivers Inlet. We knew we were pressing our luck and we paid dearly. The second was the frightening conditions off Slingsby Channel, even with the wind calm. In both cases it was the ebb that led to the trouble. [*Hale*]

NORTHERN B.C. COAST

Planning a Trip to the Northern B.C. Coast. Most cruisers limit their voyages to the waters south of a line that runs between Wells Passage on the mainland to Port Hardy on Vancouver Island. North of this line the northern part of Queen Charlotte Sound is a natural barrier. It takes time, a strong boat, and good navigation skills to proceed farther up the coast. To be fair, a lifetime of cruising could be spent south of that line with complete satisfaction.

But—to those with the time and inclination—the coast north of Wells Passage is a special experience. The scenery is magnificent, the population is small and self-sufficient, the fishing can be exceptional and you can even take a warm soak at one of several hot springs. You can anchor in bays with no other boats and take in the scenery all by yourself.

This is the part of the coast where you'll find the famous names: Nakwakto Rapids, Rivers Inlet, Fish Egg Inlet, Hakai, Bella Bella, Ocean Falls, Ivory Island, Fiordland, Butedale, Grenville Channel, Prince Rupert. It's a coast filled with history and possibilities. If it's wilderness you seek, you can find it here.

Be prepared to be self-reliant. Between Port Hardy and Prince Rupert, there are few marinas with services for pleasure boats. Be glad the facilities are there, and don't complain if they're a little rough. Don't expect marina help to come down to take your lines as you land.

Most facilities and businesses are set up to take credit cards, but not all. Forget about ATM services. Except for a machine at Shearwater, and sometimes in Klemtu, there aren't any. You'll still have telephones, but not as often. Expect cell phone coverage to be spotty. Land line pay phones are in Bella Coola, Shearwater, New Bella Bella, Ocean Falls, and Klemtu. Some boats rent or purchase satellite phones if the crew needs to keep in touch with family or for business when cruising this area.

Insurance. Most vessel insurance policies don't cover these waters without a special rider.

The boat. Not many small boats cruise the northern coast. You'll sometimes see jerry cans filled with extra fuel, or water lashed to the rails or in the cockpits. Radar and GPS should be considered standard equipment. This is remote country. The boat should be in top mechanical condition. Complete spares should be carried.

Many anchorages along this coast are 60 to 90 feet deep, with shallower water too close to shore to swing in comfort. You'll need ample anchor rode—300 feet should be considered the minimum.

Bottoms often are rocky. Because of its resistance to bending and its ability to set and hold in nearly any bottom, including rock, Bruce is a popular anchor. Manson Supreme, Rocna, CQR plow, and Delta anchors also

Humpback whales are a common sight north of Cape Caution. In the summer they come to the Pacific Northwest to feed.

are popular. You don't see as many Danforth style anchors. Danforth style anchors are good in sand and mud, but they have trouble setting in rock, and once wedged they are easily bent.

Be sure to carry at least two anchors. Whatever the style of anchors chosen, they should be big, strong, and ready to deploy.

Fuel and water. Fuel is plentiful, both gasoline and diesel, all the way up the coast. Rivers Inlet has gasoline and diesel at Duncanby Lodge & Marina and at Dawsons Landing. You can get gasoline and diesel at Bella Coola, Shearwater, New Bella Bella, Klemtu, Kitimat, Hartley Bay and Prince Rupert. The longest distance between fuel stops is roughly 70 miles.

Water is available all along the way. Some of it may be tinged brown from cedar bark tannin, but people have been drinking cedar water for decades with no ill effects. Ocean Falls has sparkling clear, purified water. New Bella Bella, Klemtu and Hartley Bay have multi-million-dollar water treatment plants that deliver ample amounts of clear, pure water.

Weather. Bring clothes for all conditions, from cold and rainy to hot and sunny. Expect wet weather at least part of the time. The residents of Ocean Falls call themselves "The Rainpeople" for good reason. Some years have been so wet that a few boats quit their cruise.

Plan for clouds down on the deck, for fog, for rain (both vertical and horizontal), and for storms. Leave enough flexibility in the schedule to anchor through serious foul weather. Be sure the boat is well-provisioned, and equipped with generator or battery power to spend several days at anchor in one location.

Plan on sunshine, too, maybe a lot of sunshine. It can get *hot*. Bring bug spray, and equip the boat with screens on doors, hatch-

es, opening ports, and windows.

Cabin heat is essential. Many boats use a Red Dot-style truck heater while under power, and a second heat source at anchor. Depending on the boat, secondary heat can be electric (generator required), diesel furnace, diesel heater, oil galley stove, wood stove, or propane catalytic heater.

Sailboaters will want some sort of cockpit protection, from a companionway dodger to full cockpit enclosure. Keep the cabin warm and dry, or you'll be miserable.

Marinas. There aren't many marinas on this coast. In Rivers Inlet, Duncanby Lodge & Marina has guest moorage, fuel and dining. Dawsons Landing has moorage, fuel and supplies. Depending on deliveries, the Native band stores at New Bella Bella and Klemtu have a good grocery selection. Shearwater, near New Bella Bella, has moorage, a restaurant, groceries, fuel, water, haulout and repairs. Ocean Falls has ample moorage, water and a restaurant. A small store, with intermittent hours, is in Martin Valley, about a mile from Ocean Falls. Farther north, Hartley Bay has fuel, water, and limited moorage.

If you're in a jam, you could seek help at one of the sportfishing lodges along the coast, but remember that their business is serving their fly-in fishing guests, not recreational boats.

Dogs and hiking. Shorelines often are steep and rocky along this part of the coast, with few good places to walk the dog or take a walk yourself. Although we have seen many pets on board, we've met a number of cruisers who feel it's just too difficult to get a dog ashore. People who enjoy regular walks and hikes will find their options limited. All agree that the coast is beautiful, but some would welcome more opportunity for exercise.

Repairs. While it's best to carry complete spares and know how to fix whatever goes wrong, nobody can be ready for everything. Parts and mechanics can be flown in anyplace along the coast between Port Hardy and Prince Rupert. The only full-service shipyard is at Shearwater. Kitimat also has facilities and a yard for repairs.

Charts and reference books. The Canadian Hydrographic Service has more than 65 charts that cover the coast from Wells Passage to Prince Rupert. Most boats will make the passage with fewer than 65 charts, but the number of charts on board a well-found boat likely will be closer to 65 than 35. Despite their cost ($20 Cdn.), consider buying every chart, both small scale and large scale, in the area you plan to cruise. Include a few extra charts for unplanned side trips, unless your schedule calls for a straight passage up the main route (Interstate 5, as it is sometimes called). It takes a capital investment to cruise this coast safely and enjoyably.

Tides and currents are shown in Canadian Tides and Currents, Vol. 7, (the purple book). North of Cape Caution you may want to consider getting the new 3-volume set of Sailing Directions for the North Coast, PAC 200, 205, and 206.

Many boats carry a copy of *Marine Atlas, Vol. 2*. The charts in the atlas are long out of date and many of the place names have changed, but the course lines are helpful. The book is a good quick reference.

The most complete guidebook is *Exploring the North Coast of British Columbia,* 2nd Ed., by Don Douglass and Réanne Hemingway-Douglass, published in 2002. *Cruising the Secret Coast,* by Jennifer and James Hamilton, opens up anchorages in some of the most scenic, out-of-the-way locations.

We also recommend a subscription to *Pacific Yachting* and *Canadian Yachting West,* both published in Canada. They are well-done monthly magazine with cruising articles and updates on boating on the B.C. coast.

CHARTS	
3547	Queen Charlotte Strait, Eastern Portion (1:40,000)
3548	Queen Charlotte Strait, Central Portion (1:40,000)
3549	Queen Charlotte Strait, Western Portion (1:40,000)
3550	Approaches to Seymour Inlet & Belize Inlet (1:40,000)
3552	Seymour Inlet & Belize Inlet (1:50,000)
3598	Cape Scott to Cape Calvert (1:74,500)
3921	Fish Egg Inlet & Allison Harbour (1:20,000)
3934	Approaches to Smith Sound & Rivers Inlet (1:40,000)

Blunden Harbour is a beautiful anchorage, with room for many boats. It's a good starting point for an early-morning rounding of Cape Caution.

BLUNDEN HARBOUR TO SLINGSBY CHANNEL

Wells Passage to Blunden Harbour. The entrance to Blunden Harbour is approximately 11 miles northwest from the mouth of Wells Passage.

Blunden Harbour. Blunden Harbour is a lovely, well-protected bay, with excellent holding ground. As you approach the entrance it is important to identify Siwiti Rock and leave it to starboard. Study the 1:15,000 Blunden Harbour inset on Chart 3548. Note the several rocks along both sides of the passage into Blunden Harbour. These rocks make a somewhat serpentine route necessary as you go in.

Anchor anywhere in the large basin, or between Moore Rock and Byrnes Island. We feel that Moore Rock is closer to Byrnes Island than the chart suggests. An abandoned Indian village is on the north shore, and the beach is littered with relics. A large "no trespassing" sign warns against exploring the uplands, however.

You can explore **Bradley Lagoon** in the northeast corner of Blunden Harbour. Those who have say it's interesting. Take the dinghy through the rapids at high water slack.

Southgate Group. The Southgate Group is a cluster of islands at the corner of the route between Blunden Harbour and Allison Harbour. A passage between Southgate Island and Knight Island makes for a scenic, sheltered shortcut. Basins on either side of the narrows appear to be just right for anchoring. Chart 3921 shows the passage in large detail.

Allison Harbour. Allison Harbour is large, long and nicely protected, with room for many boats. Log booms may be tied to the shore. Crabbing is said to be good. The best holding ground is toward the head, in 20 to 25 feet. *Favor the western shore as you enter and leave, to avoid a rock that lies almost mid-channel, about halfway in.*

Murray Labyrinth. This one is for the brave, who will be rewarded. Don Douglass has a good description of Murray Labyrinth in his guidebook to the north coast, and *Best Anchorages* authors Kelly and Vipond describe Murray Labyrinth in glowing terms. Waggoner Correspondents Lorraine and John Littlewood report:

"The inner cove is a special place to us and nearly a perfect anchorage. It's guarded by what looks to be an impossibly tortuous, kelp-choked entrance, so most boats pass on by (in 10 years, we've not seen another boat there). It's not that hard, though, and the reward is that extreme rarity on the coast: a landlocked, completely protected anchorage with access at any tide and endless exploration potential by kayak or dinghy."

"We took our 43-foot Ocean Alexander in twice, and other boats before. It was a piece of cake each time—just keep a bow watch and go dead slow, in and out of gear as necessary to give yourself plenty of time to react. All obstacles are plainly visible or charted (although Douglass's tree-covered rocks aren't tree-covered). Use the south entry only. Do not attempt to enter or leave through the northern passage in anything other than a kayak or dinghy. It's foul, and what appear to be two rocks are really one rock with the middle part awash at low tide." [*Littlewood*]

Skull Cove. Skull Cove is on Bramham Island, roughly opposite Murray Labyrinth. It is one of the prettier anchorages you will find. If approaching from the south, we would pass behind Southgate Island and follow the eastern mainland shore almost to City Point. Then we would turn northwest, leaving Town Rock to port, and go through the passage between the Deloraine Islands and Murray Labyrinth, thus avoiding all the rocks and reefs that lie offshore. If approaching from the north, follow the Bramham Island shore.

Enter Skull Cove on the east side of the unnamed island and take anchorage in the cove immediately to port, in 20 to 25 feet. The view on the west side of the island is superb.

Miles Inlet. Miles Inlet indents the west shore of Bramham Island and is beautiful. The narrow passage is lined with silver snags. The trees are not tall, suggesting wind from winter storms blows strongly in the inlet. The entrance is narrow, but using McEwan Rock as a reference the entrance is easy to locate. Offlying rocks are on each side of the entrance. Go directly down the middle. Once inside, anchor in a little nook on the north side of the entrance channel or at the T intersection. The two arms of the T shoal rapidly, but the north arm has more room.

Schooner Channel. Schooner Channel, along the east side of Bramham Island, is narrow and requires constant attention to avoid rocks and reefs. With constant attention, however, the channel need not be difficult to run. Watch tidal currents closely. The flood can run to 5 knots and the ebb to 6 knots. Schooner Channel currents are shown in Tide and Current Tables, Vol. 6, as a secondary station based on Nakwakto Rapids.

An unnamed bay opposite Goose Point at the north end of Schooner Channel is mentioned in Sailing Directions as a good anchorage for small craft.

LOCAL KNOWLEDGE

TIDE RIP: Mike Guns, a commercial fisherman with much experience in these waters, reports that when an ebb current opposes a westerly wind, the entrance to Outer Narrows and Slingsby Channel is on par with the worst conditions that Nahwitti Bar or Cape Mudge can produce. He has seen "noticeable turbulence" as long as 3 hours after maximum ebb at Nakwakto Rapids. Take this patch of water seriously.

Belize Inlet, behind Nakwakto Rapids, is beautiful and seldom visited.

Slingsby Channel. Slingsby Channel runs between the mainland and the north side of Bramham Island. Currents in Outer Narrows, between the Fox Islands and Vigilance Point, can run to 7 knots on the flood and 9 knots on the ebb. Outer Narrows is shown as a secondary station based on Nakwakto Rapids in Tide and Current Tables, Vol. 6 or Ports and Passes.

You can enter Slingsby Channel via a narrow, scenic channel that runs between the Fox Islands and Bramham Island, thus avoiding Outer Narrows entirely. Sailing Di-

rections mentions the channel but does not encourage it. We found the channel easy to run, and deeper than the chart shows. [*Hale*]

Treadwell Bay. Treadwell Bay is a good, protected anchorage at the east end of Slingsby Channel. It is often used by boats awaiting slack water at Nakwakto Rapids. Favor the east shore as you enter to avoid rocks off the Anchor Islands. The rocks are shown clearly on the charts. Inside, beware of rocks shown on the chart off the south shore of the bay.

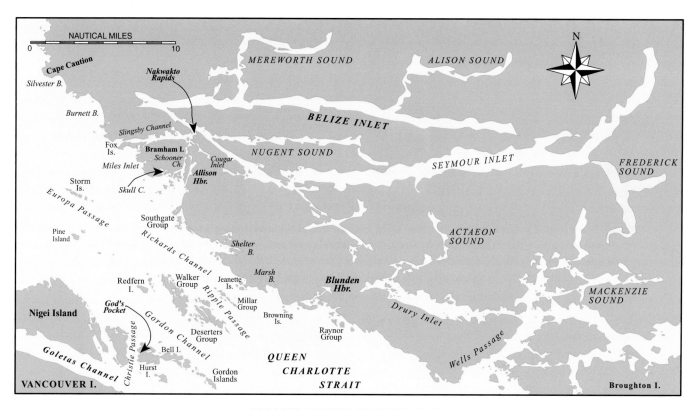

SEYMOUR AND BELIZE INLETS

We have not explored these inlets behind Nakwakto Rapids, but correspondents Gil and Karen Flanagan and Richard and Carol Larsen were good enough to send these brief and intriguing reports.

If you prize spectacular anchorages that you have all to yourself, this is the place. In four days and 192 nautical miles inside Nakwakto Rapids we saw just seven other pleasure boats. Three of the four nights no other boats were within sight or hearing.

The water at the head of Mereworth Sound was 69°F. There was much wildlife and the only fish farm was back near the entrance. The downsides were rain and logging. We went past five logging operations, one with a helicopter. The loggers were served by frequent seaplane flights.

This is a large area, though, with minimal clearcutting visible from the water. Most logging roads appear as thick bands of alder crossing green hillsides and allow for good walking.

The best anchorage we found was at the head of Alison Sound. What we call "The End of Alison" has it all: granite walls, snow-capped peaks, a large salt marsh, isolation and reasonable anchoring depths. We anchored in 75 feet between the remains of the log dump and the **Waamp Creek** delta. No stern-tie was needed. It was so calm we probably didn't need an anchor, either.

On an incoming tide at the end of the day we went about a half-mile up Waamp Creek in our tender. I said, "Look, there is a river otter." Karen said, "Look, there is a bear!" A big grizzly was standing on his hind legs about 100 feet away, looking at us intently. It was just like the Adventure Land ride at Disneyland.

Being as we had our dog and our tender won't plane with the three of us, we didn't stop. Unfortunately, we didn't have our camera and the bear was close enough that we didn't need our binoculars. This was on the way up the river. The sun had set early over the steep wall to the west. It felt very wild on the river.

When we came back down 20 minutes later we didn't see the bear. The next morning, our son Patrick went looking around the delta for the bear, but couldn't find it. When we hoisted the tender on deck we saw the bear ambling across the grass where Patrick had been. This time we did need the binoculars.

– Gil Flanagan

If you are looking for wilderness, wildlife, seclusion, seafood and awesome beauty, Seymour and Belize Inlets are the places to explore. We stayed eight days and had outstanding weather. There is substantial logging in Seymour Inlet, generally staged from turnkey barges. The loggers are friendly, and often have extremely useful information about the area. With our kayaks we explored many lagoons and lakes. Pack Lake, at the head of Strachan Bay (Belize Inlet), was of particular interest. Once on the lake we saw logging relicts, machinery and other equipment apparently still in working condition.

Strachan Bay is where Charlie lived year-round with Buck and their two dogs. It was a delightful and informative visit. During the summer Charlie always had a fresh rose for the ladies. Charlie was a third generation descendent of the area, and lived there full time for 22 years. [Charlie passed away in 2005—*Ed.*]

– Richard Larsen

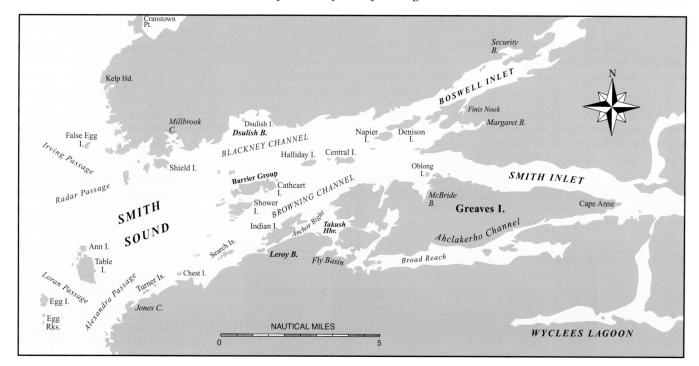

Nakwakto Rapids. Nakwakto Rapids is among the world's fastest. Especially at springs, they must be transited at slack water only. At neap tides the window of safety opens a little wider. We have been told that high water slack is much preferred over low water slack. On big tides in particular, take this advice very, very seriously.

Turret Rock, known locally as Tremble Island, sits in the middle of Nakwakto Rapids. The favored passage is on the west side. We are told Turret Rock actually shakes during the full rush of a maximum tidal current. Brave mariners have nailed boards with their boat names on Turret Rock's trees.

Behind Nakwakto Rapids lie the extensive waterways of Seymour Inlet, Belize Inlet, Nugent Sound, and Alison Sound.

Note: Our sister publication *Cruising the Secret Coast*, by Jennifer and James Hamilton, devotes three chapters to the approaches to Nakwakto Rapids and the extensive waters of Seymour Inlet and Belize Inlet. Highly recommended.

SMITH SOUND

Note: Cruising the Secret Coast, by Jennifer and James Hamilton, devotes an entire chapter to cruising Smith Inlet and Boswell Inlet, which extend from the east end of Smith Sound.

Smith Sound doesn't see many pleasure boats, but it's reputed to be full of fish. We

CHARTS	
3931	Smith Inlet, Boswell Inlet & Draney Inlet (1:40,000)
3932	Rivers Inlet (1:40,000)
3934	Approaches to Smith Sound & Rivers Inlet (1:40,000)

visited during an opening for gillnet commercial salmon fishing, and the boats turned out in force. Picking our way among the nets called for close attention, but all went well.

You're on your own in Smith Sound itself. There are no resorts or settlements. Several bays are good for anchoring, although only one, Millbrook Cove, really appeals to us.

From the south, enter Smith Sound through Alexandra Passage, between North Iron Rock and Egg Rocks. From the west, enter through Radar Passage. From the north, enter through Irving Passage. We suggest that you plot waypoints to keep clear of rocks. This is especially true in reduced visibility.

Table Island. Table Island is in the mouth of Smith Sound, and the casual visitor would not think of it as an anchorage. But fish boats anchor there and have no problems. A boat waiting to make a southerly dash around Cape Caution could find this anchorage useful, as could a boat seeking shelter from a westerly in Queen Charlotte Sound.

Jones Cove. Jones Cove is on the south shore of Smith Sound, near the mouth. The cove is cozy and well protected and often used by commercial fish boats. Anchor in 20 feet with limited swinging room. Depending on the rise and fall of the tide and the presence of other boats, you may choose to run a stern-tie to shore.

Fly Basin. Fly Basin is on the south side of Smith Sound at 51°16.35'N/127°36.20'W. "It is very private and protected, but entry requires care. Study of the chart will show that you should favor the western shore until opposite the point of land extending from the eastern shore. Then swing to the east side of the channel. The charted rocks can be difficult to see except at low water. Once in, an-

chor in 15 to 25 feet (zero tide) in the eastern section of the bay, excellent holding in mud." [*Hamilton*]

Correspondents John and Lorraine Littlewood report the western basin is also good. Work your way in past the rocks, and anchor in pristine surroundings on a good mud bottom. They begged us to not tell a soul about this anchorage, but since we are friends we feel safe letting you in on it.

McBride Bay. This bay is on the north side of Greaves Island, at the east end of Browning Channel. It is deep until near the head, which has 30 to 40 foot anchoring depths. Protection is excellent, but swinging room is a little limited.

Ahclakerho Channel. Ahclakerho Channel leads along the south side of Greaves Island. The current runs hard in the channel. Transit at slack water, especially on big tides. Slack appears to be around the time of high and low water at Bella Bella. Correspondent Gil Flanagan reports: "This is an overlooked gem. The narrow part of the channel is probably 200 feet wide. The anchorage on the east side of the 78-meter east Ahclakerho Island gives good protection from west winds in Smith Sound. We stern-tied among numerous rocks and small islands. It was beautiful."

Margaret Bay. Margaret Bay is at the head of Smith Sound, on the point of land that separates Boswell Inlet and Smith Inlet. Chambers Island, rather small, is in the middle of the bay, about halfway in. West of Chambers Island depths are too great for anchoring. East of the island they shallow to 50 to 55 feet. The head shoals sharply, and old pilings take up much of the room at the head. Protection is excellent.

Ethel Cove. Ethel Cove is just outside the mouth of Margaret Bay. It looks right out to sea, however, and we found a very low surge coming in. Get close to shore or anchor in 50 to 60 feet farther out.

Finis Nook. Finis Nook is located near the mouth of Boswell Inlet, on the south shore, sort of "around the corner" from Margaret Bay. It is nearly landlocked and completely protected; it seems a perfect anchorage. A log boom blocks the back bay, however, and a float house is on the east side, with the wreck of a fish boat. Anchoring depths in the area not already taken are approximately 35 feet. We were disappointed, and went back to

Milbrook Cove to overnight. (In *Cruising the Secret Coast*, the Hamiltons like Finis Nook).

Dsulish Bay. Dsulish Bay, with beautiful white sand beaches, is on the north shore of Smith Sound. A trail reportedly leads to Goose Bay to the north. The best anchorage is behind the 46-meter island, deep inside the bay. It is a little open but workable. We have seen fish boats anchored along the west side of Dsulish Bay. In the right conditions it would be a good lunch stop, though we're not so sure about overnight.

Millbrook Cove. This is the outermost anchorage on the north side of Smith Sound.

To us it is the favored anchorage. The cove is completely landlocked, with 25 to 35 foot depths, good holding ground, and ample room.

Getting in will hold your attention, at least the first time. Find the red spar buoy *E6* marking Millbrook Rocks. The buoy has a small radar reflector on top. Leave this buoy to starboard (Red, Right, Returning), and aim the boat toward the 30-meter island. Keep a sharp lookout for rocks on both sides, especially the west side, as shown on the chart. The 30-meter island can be passed on either side, although the east side is a little deeper.

Once in, watch for a drying rock a short distance off the northeast corner of the 30-meter island. Minding your depths, anchor anywhere.

RIVERS INLET

Note: Cruising the Secret Coast, by Jennifer and James Hamilton, contains an entire chapter devoted to cruising the parts of Rivers Inlet not covered here, with a little overlap.

Rivers Inlet is a famed salmon fishing area and, at one time, had 18 salmon canneries. All the canneries are closed now and most are sinking into ruin. Absent its commerce of former years, Rivers Inlet is prime cruising ground. The scenery is beautiful and the anchorages excellent. The area is served by two marinas: Duncanby Lodge & Marina and Dawsons Landing. In Goose Bay, a substantial concrete float provides access to the Goose Bay Cannery, but no amenities.

Open Bight. Open Bight, well named, is just inside Cranstown Point at the entrance to Rivers Inlet. Anchorage, with protection from westerlies but not northerlies or easterlies, is along the south and west shores. The west shore is preferred. We would put the hook down outside the kelp line in 25 to 30 feet, within view of a stunning white shell midden beach. Gentle swells will rock the boat.

Home Bay. Home Bay, on the south shore a short distance inside the mouth of Rivers Inlet, is a pretty spot.

Just west of Home Bay is another nook, which Douglass calls **West Home Bay** in *Exploring the North Coast of British Columbia,*

CHARTS	
3727	Cape Caution to Goose Island (1:73,584)
3784	Kwakshua Channel to Spider Island (1:36,800)
3785	Namu Harbour to Dryad Point (1:40,533)
3921	Fish Egg Inlet & Allison Harbour (1:20,000)
3932	Rivers Inlet (1:40,000)
3934	Approaches to Smith Sound & Rivers Inlet (1:40,000)

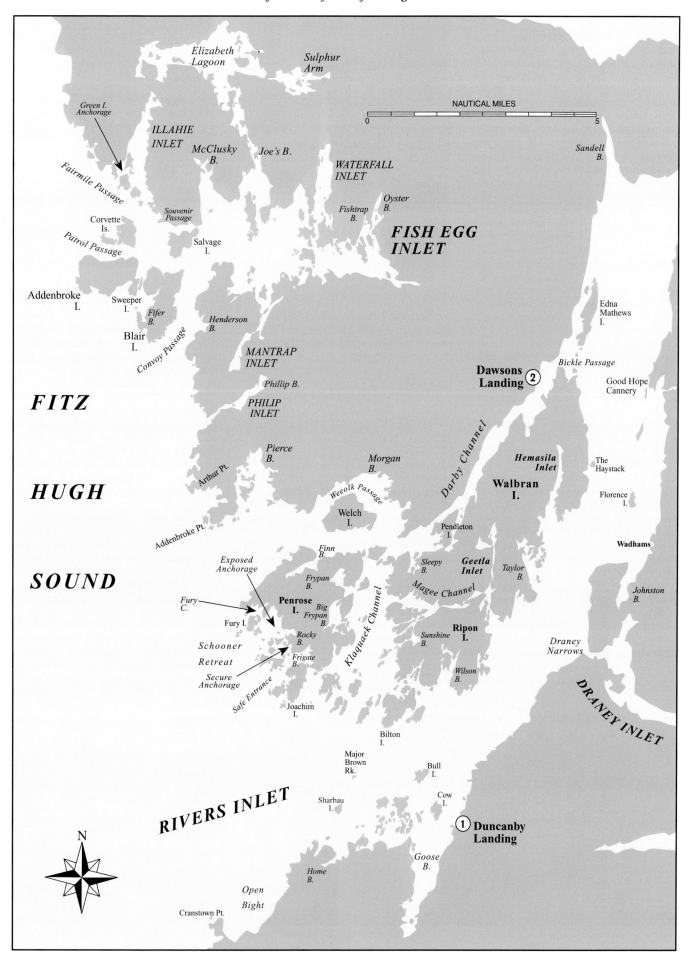

2nd Ed. The bay has anchorage behind the first of two islets inside. Contrary to Douglass's illustration, however, low tide reveals rocks that foul the western side of that first islet. We would pass the islet only to the east.

Other anchoring possibilities lie in the unnamed group of islands just west of Duncanby Lodge & Marina. Larger boats will find good anchoring in deep water in the unnamed cove marked with 29-meter and 35-meter soundings. The large island with the 105-meter hill is at the north end of this cove. Smaller boats can creep into the unnamed cove east of the deep water cove. This cove is marked with a 9-meter sounding in the mouth and a 16-meter sounding inside. A King Salmon fishing resort outpost is moored on the eastern shore. The little nook at the northeast end of the cove offers quiet anchorage in 60 to 120 feet, but be careful when you enter this nook. A reef extends northward nearly halfway across the entrance, much farther than the chart suggests. Favor the north side.

① **Duncanby Lodge & Marina.** 100 Golden Dr., Coquitlam, BC V3K 6T1; (604) 628-9822; (877) 846-6548; www. duncanbylodgemarina.com. Monitors VHF 06. Open 7 days a week, June through mid-September. Gasoline and diesel, water on the docks (filtered but still tinted brown). Power (30 & 50 amp) is available but pricey. Check before plugging in. Guest moorage, showers and laundry. The restaurant is open for breakfast, lunch and supper, and is very good.

Duncanby is a high quality destination fly-in fishing resort. Gone are the commercial boats. Gone are the boys from around the inlet who used to hang out in the bar. Meals at the restaurant are delicious and priced attractively.

The resort offers a quality experience, priced at the upper end of typical, but still affordable. Moorage reservations are strongly recommended, especially during high season.

Goose Bay. Goose Bay, beyond Duncanby Landing, is empty now. The Goose Bay cannery has been purchased by a group from

Duncanby Landing visitor moorage is to the right of the deck.

the Burnaby area and is being restored. A good concrete dock has been installed; visitors are welcome. If the work scheduled for that day permits and if you're polite about it, you might be able to finesse an invitation for a brief tour. It's quite a place. Anchorage is good in 15 to 20 feet on a sticky bottom behind the little island across the bay from the cannery buildings. Crabbing is reported to be good, too.

Hemasila Inlet. "Entry to the inner basin looks impossible on the chart, but isn't. The charted rock is central in a 200-foot-wide channel and is visible except at very high tides. Favor the east side—it has slightly more room and the shore is steep. We anchored in 35 feet just north of the 9.1-meter sounding with plenty of room to swing. Holding was excellent in thick mud. It was sheltered and pretty, with a small creek at one side and a small waterfall at the other side. Watch for a rock 2.5 meters deep at zero tide in the mouth of the inlet where the *R* symbol and 24 meter sounding are located." [*Hamilton*]

Taylor Bay. Taylor Bay indents the east shore of Walbran Island and has tranquil,

lovely anchorage in 35 to 50 feet, although swinging room is limited. Anchor all the way in or try the nook behind the north end of the inner island, between the inner island and Walbran Island. The net-drying float in the back bay has been removed.

Draney Narrows & Draney Inlet. The current runs hard in Draney Narrows. We looked in 1½ hours before the predicted turn and decided against it. Fifteen minutes before the turn the narrows were flat. Predictions are shown in Tide & Current Tables, Vol. 7 as a secondary station based on Prince Rupert Tides.

Draney Inlet, approximately 24 miles long, is surrounded by high, steep mountains. It's beautiful. Because it is not on the way to anyplace else, it sees little pleasure craft traffic. Good anchorage in 30 to 35 feet is available in Fish Hook Bay, a short distance inside the narrows. When we visited, a float home with two floating outbuildings was on the south shore of Fish Hook Bay, near the entrance. A large sign read, "Warning, Private Property, No Trespassing." A convincing watchdog greeted our boat with don't-mess-with-me barks and growls. We didn't argue.

Everything at Duncanby Landing is high-quality. These are the visitor moorage docks.

The Good Hope Cannery, now a fishing resort, is easy to spot but offers no services for visiting boaters.

Here's Nola at Dawsons Landing, ringing up orders from one of the Rivers Inlet fishing lodges.

Dawsons Landing has plenty of dock space.

Note: Our sister publication, *Cruising the Secret Coast,* by Jennifer and James Hamilton, devotes a chapter to Draney Inlet, with much information about anchorages and what to see.

Johnston Bay. Johnston Bay, on the east shore of Rivers Inlet just south of Wadhams, is a former cannery site. The bay is quiet and beautiful, but deep until very near the head. As the chart shows, a reef lies in the center of the outer part of Johnston Bay, and a rock is close to the eastern shore at the entrance. Favor the western shore all the way in and you'll have ample depths with no hazards.

Sandell Bay. "North shore of Rivers Inlet, where the inlet takes that east bend. Anchor well into the bay in 25 feet, zero tide. Excellent holding in mud/sand/rock/shell. Kind of like a cement mix, and held like it, too. Sandell Bay looks exposed on the chart, but is actually protected. It was blowing 30 knots in Rivers Inlet when we came in, and from the anchorage we could see a line of whitecaps out there. But hardly any wind or fetch reached us." [Hamilton]

Good Hope Cannery. Good Hope Cannery is the large, white building visible when cruising past Draney Inlet. The facility is a high-end fly-in sport fishing resort. No services for cruising boats.

② **Dawsons Landing (Dawsons Landing General Store).** (604) 629-9897; dawsonslanding@gmail.com; www.dawsons landing.ca. Monitors VHF 06. Phone service is spotty; it's often best to communicate by email. Open all year, gasoline and diesel fuel. Guest moorage, Wi-Fi, hardware, groceries, charts, ice, water, fishing and hunting gear, liquor, washroom, showers, laundry, post office, three rental cabins with kitchenettes. They take Interac, Visa and MasterCard. A heli-pad takes up part of the dock. They have scheduled air service from Pacific Coastal Airlines.

Dawsons Landing is owned by Rob and Nola Bachen, and has been in the family since 1954. This is a real general store, with an excellent stock of standard grocery items and an astonishing accumulation of tools and hardware. One year, for example, we needed an in-line fuse holder to replace a spare we had used. Dawsons had it. The facility goes back a long way. The docks, which were a little rough in past years, are pretty good now. Rob keeps working on them. Note that

instead of cleats, you'll tie to loops of rope set into the planks. Absent bull rails, it's easier and safer to clear the docks of snow in the winter. The one dock with bull rails is used by float planes.

Rob and Nola are friendly and helpful, two of the most genuine people we know. The more we are around them the better we like them. Both have an impish good humor. They're a treat.

Smoked salmon: It's almost worth a trip to

Dawsons Landing simply to stock up on the Bella Coola Valley Seafoods smoked wild Pacific salmon that Nola carries in the store when she can get it. Several flavored smokes to choose from. [*Hale*]

Darby Channel (Schooner Pass). Darby Channel, locally called Schooner Pass, borders the west side of Walbran Island, and is easily run. Southbound boats should favor the west shore of the channel to avoid being lured into foul ground behind Pendleton Island. The rock off the southwest corner of Pendleton Island is clearly marked by a beacon and easily avoided.

Pierce Bay. Pierce Bay is near the entrance to Fitz Hugh Sound, across the street, you might say, from Finn Bay on Penrose Island. Exercise caution, because Pierce Bay contains dangerous rocks not necessarily shown on the chart. One of the rocks is east of the south tip of the largest island, at 51°31.665'N/127°45.667'W. This rock is in relatively open water, and could surprise a person. Another is off the northwest point of the large island, where the anchorage opens up.

Pierce Bay has a couple nice anchorages, though. One is in the basin north of the 61-meter island on the west shore. We left the 61-meter island to starboard when entering, and departed leaving the 29-meter island to port. The other anchorage is in the bight created between the large island and the west shore. Run north in the narrow channel along the west shore. Watch for rocks.

Frypan Bay. Frypan Bay, spacious, scenic and well protected, is at the northeast corner of Penrose Island. Anchoring depths, along the south shore, are 25 to 40 feet and, in the middle, 50 to 85 feet with wonderful holding. This anchorage is a favorite of many cruisers.

Finn Bay. Finn Bay, on the north side of Penrose Island, is well protected. A sport fishing camp is in the bay. Logging activity is on one side and commercial fishing equipment is on the other.

Fury Cove. The cove behind Fury Island is a beautiful and a popular anchorage, with a perfect white shell beach. Fury Cove, as it is commonly called, is entered by leaving Cleve Island to port, then turning to port to raise the narrow entrance.

Fury Cove is a good place to spend the night before a southbound rounding of Cape Caution. While at anchor, you can look across the beach and see conditions on Fitz Hugh Sound. Inside, avoid the charted rock that dries 10 feet close to Fury Island.

Overboard discharge: No black water overboard discharge, please. Fury Cove does not flush well.

Cleve Island is mentioned in Sailing Directions, but shown on the chart only as a

Fury Cove is beautiful and well-protected with a white shell beach for walking and exploring.

61-meter island—no name.

Breaker Pass: Breaker Pass separates Fury Island from Cleve Island. We have run through the pass in calm weather, but we could tell it wouldn't take much of a southwesterly for Breaker Pass to live up to its name.

Philip Inlet. Philip Inlet indents the mainland side of Fitz Hugh Sound approximately 3 miles south of Addenbroke Island. On a sunny afternoon we found the entrance hard to identify. Use caution when entering: the chart does not show the ledges of rock that extend from each side of the inlet near the mouth.

About halfway in, a small island creates a rock-strewn, tight and tricky narrows. We would not want to go through the narrows without a bow watch or good visibility from a fly bridge helm.

Once past the narrows the inlet becomes rather open-feeling and uninteresting. Depths near the head are approximately 30 feet. We went in planning to anchor for the night, but decided instead to anchor in Green Island Anchorage at the mouth of Fish Egg Inlet. [*Hale*]

Fifer Bay. Fifer Bay indents the western side of Blair Island, with lovely 6- to 12-

foot anchorage for small craft at the head of the southernmost cove. There's room for one boat if it swings, more if all stern-tie to shore. When entering, favor Sweeper Island to avoid the rocks lying off the southern side of the entrance. When clear of the rocks, turn south and work your way into the anchorage.

FISH EGG INLET

Fish Egg Inlet indents the east side of Fitz Hugh Sound, behind Addenbroke Island. This is beautiful cruising country, and is becoming one of the popular spots on the coast. Those who say you'll be all alone are wrong. The gunkholing possibilities are many, but here are notes on some of the better-known anchorages.

Mantrap Inlet. Once you're inside, Mantrap Inlet offers good anchorage. The entrance, however, is narrow, made narrower by an uncharted ledge of rock that extends from the west shore. Consider going through at half tide or higher, dead slow, with a lookout.

Oyster Bay. Oyster Bay, next to Fish Trap Bay at the head of Fish Egg Inlet, is a nice anchorage with a remote feel to it. We had a late and relaxed lunch there, anchored in 20

Taking a day off at Fury Cove. The white shell beach is flat. At low tide it goes out quite a distance.

ELIZABETH LAGOON (FISH EGG INLET)

Elizabeth Lagoon is a large body of water connected to Joe's Bay by a narrow and fierce reversing tidal rapids. High tide was at 9:15 p.m. We went in at 7:30 p.m., well after low water slack and had a good ride down the rapids. We had four people and our dog, about 850 pounds total, in our 9-foot RIB. Loaded this way, top speed was only about 5 knots.

The tidal rapids were flowing against us when we came back about 8:30 p.m. We tried going uphill, but the current was considerably stronger than when we went in. To lighten the load, my son and I got out to walk the beach. The east bank is cliffy and looks close to impassable, so we chose the west side.

With two people and the dog, the RIB would not quite get up on a plane. The best it could do was about 8 knots, and they almost made it. We, on shore, thought they had. The RIB's bow was just into the flat water at the top of the rapids when the outboard motor hit a rock. Instinctively, the throttle was cut and the boat was swept back down the rapids. The motor, now turned off, clunked on another rock. There is a turn to the west at the bottom of the falls, and the RIB, with my wife, son, and dog aboard, disappeared from sight.

Luckily, people from the other boat anchored in Joe's Bay had come over to see the falls. They rescued the two of us from the west side and got us to our Polywog rowboat, which was tied to a small island. With the rising tide the island was quickly vanishing.

I was facing the likelihood that we were not going to get our tender out until near high water slack, which probably would be sometime between midnight and 2:00 a.m. It is hard to imagine hitting a rock solidly and having much prop left, especially at full throttle. My mind was racing, trying to come up with a reasonable course of action.

After what seemed like an hour but was only 15 minutes, we saw the tender running with just my son aboard. It circled, got up to about 20 knots, and whistled up the rapids in major leaps off the standing waves. Shortly afterward, my wife and the dog came out of the woods on the west side. It was only 9:00 p.m., and all of us were out of the lagoon.

While this excursion ended happily, we gained considerably more respect for the many reversing tidal falls in British Columbia.

— Gil Flanagan

feet near the head of the bay. Recommended. [Hale]

Fish Trap Bay. Awfully tight, but room for one boat, stern-tied. At lower water levels the Indian fish trap is clearly visible.

Waterfall Inlet. Pretty spot, but we couldn't find any comfortable anchorages. We felt that the west entry, leaving the 99-meter island to starboard, was safest. Go slowly and watch for rock ledges that extend from each side of the narrow pass.

Joe's Bay. Joe's Bay has become quite popular. When we visited in early July, five other boats were already anchored. Joe's Bay is worth the crowds, though. It's tranquil, tree-lined and snug. Anchoring is straightforward in the southern basin; rocks and reefs make the northern portion somewhat trickier. A stern-tie to shore might be called for, to keep the boat from swinging onto a rock. Once anchored, the tidal rapids leading to Elizabeth Lagoon and Sulphur Arm are a big attraction.

Souvenir Passage. Sailing Directions says that Souvenir Passage is very narrow at its eastern end and the chart shows a rock on the north shore. We have found good water all the way by favoring the south side of the passage.

Illahie Inlet. The head of Illahie Inlet would be a delightful anchorage in 30 to 40 feet, mud bottom, good protection, except that logging has scarred the surrounding hillsides. Favor one shore or the other as you go in

CLOSE ENCOUNTER IN FITZ HUGH SOUND

We were southbound in thick fog and calm seas in Fitz Hugh Sound, having left our anchorage in Kisameet Bay early and hoping the fog would lift and the seas would remain calm for an uneventful rounding of Cape Caution later in the day.

The fog did begin to lift as we motored along the eastern shore. A mile in front of us, in front of Fairmile Passage, the northern entrance to Fish Egg Inlet, we could see two humpback whales close together, spouting and apparently feeding.

We altered course, but it seemed the whales were moving in that direction as well, so we altered course again in the opposite direction. The whales moved in that direction, too, as if to intercept us.

Finally, the whales were very close. Each of them was easily the size of our boat, a 1982 43-foot Ocean Alexander. We had slowed to idle and then into neutral as one of the whales broke off and slid past us, about 25 feet off to port. We were looking frantically for the other one when, without warning, there was a spout directly under our bow with an accompany-ing loud whoosh. The mist drifted over the foredeck and onto the cabin windows, and we felt a gentle but very discernible bump as our new friend decided to have a close encounter of the third kind (apologies to Spielberg). The boat lifted slightly and slid off to starboard, while we, in no particular order, shouted to each other to: (a) Watch Out! (b) Get the Camera! (c) Hold On! We managed only (c). Suddenly our heavy old Ocean Alexander didn't feel so substantial.

We've been told that humpbacks sometimes like to do this and it doesn't appear to be accidental, but this was the first time for us. You simply cannot believe how big these animals are until you see/hear/smell/feel them at this range. "Immense" is the first word that comes to mind. Clearly, they knew we were there. With two engines running and two depth sounders pinging at two different frequencies, we weren't exactly stealthy. The whales just delivered a gentle reminder about who belongs where. We got the message.

— Lorraine & John Littlewood

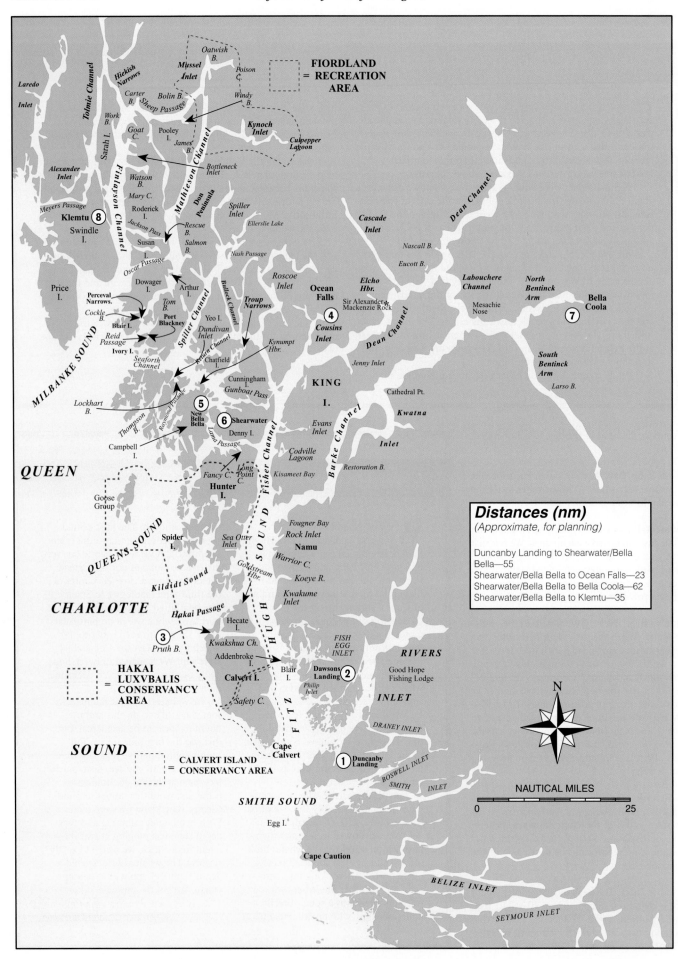

FIORDLAND
= RECREATION
AREA

Distances (nm)
(Approximate, for planning)

Duncanby Landing to Shearwater/Bella
Bella—55
Shearwater/Bella Bella to Ocean Falls—23
Shearwater/Bella Bella to Bella Coola—62
Shearwater/Bella Bella to Klemtu—35

HAKAI
LUXVBALIS
CONSERVANCY
AREA

CALVERT ISLAND
CONSERVANCY AREA

NAUTICAL MILES
0   25

Illahie Inlet. Rocks lie in the middle of the channel, partway in.

Green Island Anchorage. Green Island Anchorage, just off Fitz Hugh Sound at the mouth of Illahie Inlet, is about as cozy as an anchorage needs to be. Excellent holding in 35 to 40 feet. From seaward, wrap around the 70-meter island and follow the shoreline in. This is a good spot to rest after crossing Queen Charlotte Sound.

FITZ HUGH SOUND

Fitz Hugh Sound begins at Cape Calvert and continues north to Fisher Channel. Boats crossing Queen Charlotte Sound from the south will find the ocean swells quickly vanish once Cape Calvert is behind them. A southwesterly can still make things nasty, especially in a south flowing ebb current. Even in settled conditions, expect to find rougher water where Hakai Passage joins Fitz Hugh Sound.

Northbound boats that don't stop at Rivers Inlet probably will stop in Fifer Bay, Safety Cove, or Pruth Bay. Green Island Anchorage is another good choice for passing traffic.

Safety Cove. Safety Cove is a steep-walled, uninteresting bay that indents Calvert Island approximately 7 miles north of Cape Calvert. The bottom shoals sharply a fair distance from the head of the bay. Sailing Directions recommends anchoring immediately when the depth reaches 100 feet. If you press in to find shallower water, watch your swing or you could find yourself aground on the shelf at low tide. Despite its name and regular use, Safety Cove is not our first choice of anchorages in the area.

③ **Pruth Bay.** Pruth Bay is at the head of **Kwakshua Channel**, some 7 miles north of Safety Cove. Pruth Bay has long been a

A trail leads from Pruth Bay to beautiful West Beach.

favorite stopover point. It offers ample room, 40- to 50-foot anchoring depths, and a flat bottom with good holding. Storms coming off the ocean can make the bay quite windy.

This entire area is part of the **Hakai Luxvbalis Conservancy Area**, a huge provincial park that includes the northern half of Calvert Island, the southern two-thirds of Hunter Island, and Goose Island. A float house ranger station is moored on the north side of Pruth Bay.

Correspondents James and Jennifer Hamilton have anchored in about 50 feet with good holding in the unnamed cove west of Keith Anchorage, on the south shore of Kwakshua Channel, a short distance east of Pruth Bay. Anchor in this cove or one of the others that indent that shore, in Pruth Bay itself, or in the bay north of the thumb of land marked by Whittaker Point.

Note: Our sister publication, *Cruising the Secret Coast,* by Jennifer and James Hamilton, devotes a chapter to this area. It describes anchorages not included in the Waggoner, and includes coverage of anchorages at the mouth of Hakai Passage.

③ **Hakai Beach Institute.** In 2010 the luxury fly-in fishing resort at the head of Pruth Bay was purchased by the Tula Foun-

dation and became the Hakai Beach Institute. The facility is now used for research and as a conference center. Visitors are welcome.

No fuel or commercial services are available at Hakai Beach Institute. When arriving by dinghy, moor only at the clearly marked "dinghy dock" section of the float. The Institute requests that visitors sign the guest log at the Welcome Centre, at the head of the dock. A public washroom is adjacent.

The grounds are immaculate. Follow the signs for the trail to West Beach, one of the finest beaches on the coast. The trail used to be muddy in places, but is now covered with a boardwalk. Carry bug spray. After a pleasant and flat hike of almost a half-mile, you hear the ocean and break out of the forest on a beautiful beach. Fine white sand runs in both directions. On a sunny day it seems almost tropical. On an overcast day, with crashing waves, it carries the beauty and furor of the wild Pacific Ocean. A less-developed trail leads north to North Beach, a sandy beach facing Hakai Pass.

Visiting boats are welcome to anchor in Pruth Bay, as long as they stay 100 meters from the dock so seaplanes have room to maneuver. Free Wi-Fi covers the entire bay. The Hakai Beach Institute asks users to limit their bandwidth usage and refrain from uploading

The Hakai Beach Institute welcomes cruisers. Sign in at the top of the dock when visiting.

HAKAI BEACH INSTITUTE – PRUTH BAY

Pruth Bay has always been a good overnight stop along the Inside Passage. The bay, at the head of Kwakshua Channel, is well protected and scenic. But the real attractions are West Beach and North Beach, two of the most beautiful sand beaches in the Northwest.

Access to the beach areas, however, has not always been easy. As the owners of the property have changed, the state of the trail leading across Calvert Island has ranged from poor to acceptable.

A few years back the property, formerly a fishing lodge, was acquired by the Tula Foundation and rechristened as the Hakai Beach Institute. Eric Peterson and Christina Munck, the principals of the Tula Foundation, have since transformed the property into a world-class conference and research center.

The improvements are apparent as soon as you arrive. Beautiful new docks have been installed, welcoming signage posted, and top-notch facilities constructed. Signs direct visi-

tors to the West Beach trail, now a well-maintained gravel and boardwalk path devoid of mud.

Researchers and educators use the facilities to investigate and collaborate. Areas of research include local archaeology, ecology, and First Nations culture. The institute has a fleet of boats available to transport personnel and equipment throughout the area and scientific labs to support research activities.

Due to its location, the Hakai Beach Institute is totally off the grid. Electricity is generated by a 50 kW solar farm feeding into a nearly 10,000 amp hour battery bank. Water is collected on site. Sewage is heavily treated before being released. And perhaps most welcome for visiting boaters, internet is piped in through nine satellite links and distributed wirelessly throughout the property and anchorage (please, no streaming video or other bandwidth intensive tasks).

We are fortunate to have people like Eric and Christina, focused on understanding our environment and sharing the beauty of this area with visiting boaters.

You can learn more about the Hakai Beach Institute and the work of the Tula Foundation on their blog and website, erichakai.wordpress.com.

– Mark Bunzel

---

pictures or video, or downloading movies. The best reception is close to the head of the bay.

Meay Inlet. Meay Inlet leads north from Kwakshua Channel to Hakai Pass. Immediately after the turn past Whittaker Point is a small scenic cove with room for 4 or 5 boats. The Hamiltons, in *Cruising the Secret Coast*, named this cove Whitaker Point Cove and report anchorage in 40 to 60 feet, with good holding in mud mixed with shell.

The Hakai Lodge fly-in fishing resort is in a nearby cove. While the resort has no services for boaters, it is owned by the principals of NW Seaplanes, with almost daily floatplane service to the Renton/Seattle area. This can be a good place to drop off or pick up crew or parts.

Hakai Passage. Hakai Passage is one of the great fishing spots, yielding 50- to 60-pound salmon and large bottom fish. Since Hakai Passage opens to the Pacific Ocean, it can get rough. Treat it with respect. On an otherwise pleasant afternoon we overheard two well-managed boats discussing on the radio

whether the swells they were facing in Hakai Passage began in Japan or just Hawaii.

Goldstream Harbour. Goldstream Harbour is a lovely little anchorage at the north end of Hecate Island. Enter from the east favoring Hat Island, which extends from the south shore about 0.2 mile inside. Don't favor Hat Island too closely, though; rocks extend out from it. Hat Island is not named on the chart, but its height (39 meters) is shown. Once past Hat Island, pass Evening Rock, which dries 1.2 meters, leaving it to starboard. Evening Rock lies about 300 feet off the northwest corner of Hat Island (it helps to refer to the chart as you read these instructions). Inside, the middle of Goldstream Harbour is about 30 feet deep. Rocks extend out from the shore, so pick your anchoring spot carefully to swing safely. Nice protected spot with an opening in rocks to look out at the conditions in Hakai Pass.

Ward Channel. Ward Channel connects Hakai Passage with Nalau Passage. Running it is straightforward as long as you follow the chart to keep track of the rocks.

Edward Channel. Edward Channel, west of Ward Channel, also connects Hakai Passage with Nalau Passage, but the southern entry is much tighter than Ward Channel. Pass between the 27-meter and 31-meter islets, staying well clear of the detached rock that dries 1.6 meters off the south tip of the 27-meter islet. Chart 3935 (1:40,000) is quite clear. Don't try the south entry with the older Chart 3727 (1:73,584). It doesn't show enough detail where you need it. The primary reason to be in Edward Channel is the lovely anchorage of Lewall Inlet.

Readers Norm and Jane Lermer report an uncharted rock on the west side of Edward Channel, at approximately 51°46.171'N/128°06.264'W. The rock dries on a 3.7-foot tide in Namu.

Lewall Inlet. Lewall Inlet indents the east shore of Stirling Island and is a delightful anchorage. Run all the way to the bend and anchor in 10 to 20 feet, north of the north shore of the entry channel. Stay well off the little treed islet near the south shore. A ledge of drying rock reaches out from that islet.

Nalau Passage. Nalau Passage, scenic and open, separates Hunter Island and Stirling Island, and connects Fitz Hugh Sound with Kildidt Sound. A conservative, mid-channel course has no hazards. The western entrance, however, is made interesting by drying rocks offshore from the north side of the passage. Eastbound boats crossing Kildidt Sound may have anxious moments finding the exact entrance. We used the following waypoint for the western entrance successfully: 51°47.10'N/128°07.20'W.

SPIDER ISLAND AREA

Note: Our sister publication, *Cruising the Secret Coast*, by Jennifer and James Hamilton, contains extensive coverage of these cruising grounds, including Kildidt Sound, Kildidt Inlet, the Goose Group, the McNaughton Group, and other wild areas between Hakai Passage and Seaforth Channel.

Kildidt Sound. Except to cross between Nalau Passage and Brydon Channel, we have not explored Kildidt Sound. Our waypoint south of Lancaster Reef is 51°48.95'N/128°10.10'W.

Serpent Group. Correspondents James and Jennifer Hamilton have anchored successfully in the cove on the easternmost side of the 57-meter island, southwest of the 31-meter island. Their anchorage was tranquil, but when they dinghied ashore and climbed to the seaward side they found windblown trees barely holding to the shore.

Kildidt Narrows. Kildidt Narrows is the reversing tidal rapids at the entrance to Kildidt Inlet, which the Waggoner does not yet cover. We include it here only because observations by Waggoner Correspondents James and Jennifer Hamilton, and confirmed by Canadian Hydrographic Service, indicate that the Sailing Directions times are incorrect. High water slack occurs approximately 1.5 hours after high water at *Bella Bella*. The time difference for low water slack varies with the height of the tide. For a low water of 0.4 meter, slack occurs approximately 2 hours after low water at *Bella Bella*; for a low water of 2.5 meters, slack occurs approximately 1 hour after low water at *Bella Bella*. Bella Bella is italicized because Sailing Directions calls for Prince Rupert tides.

For complete coverage of Kildidt Narrows and Kildidt Inlet, see *Cruising the Secret Coast*.

Brydon Channel. Brydon Channel connects Kildidt Sound and Spider Anchorage. Westbound across Kildidt Sound, lay a course well south of Lancaster Reef, then turn north toward the Brydon Channel entrance. When studying the chart, you will see the easternmost dogleg in Brydon Channel is foul with rocks. Mike Guns, a commercial fisherman with much experience in these waters, told us the safe route through is to hug the northwest end of the 72-meter island at the eastern

James & Jennifer Hamilton found this perfect anchorage in Kildidt Sound's Serpent Group. Photo by James Hamilton.

end of the channel. This keeps you clear of the rocks farther out. See the reference map.

Brydon Anchorage. Brydon Anchorage extends northward into Hurricane Island at the west end of Brydon Channel at 51°50.25'N/128°12.25'W (NAD 83). Cor-

respondents James and Jennifer Hamilton anchored in 30 feet near the very head. They report, "An amazing view to the south, not a soul around. It was an astonishingly quiet and beautiful anchorage—like no other. Most places remind us of somewhere else. This one stands alone." [*Hamilton*]

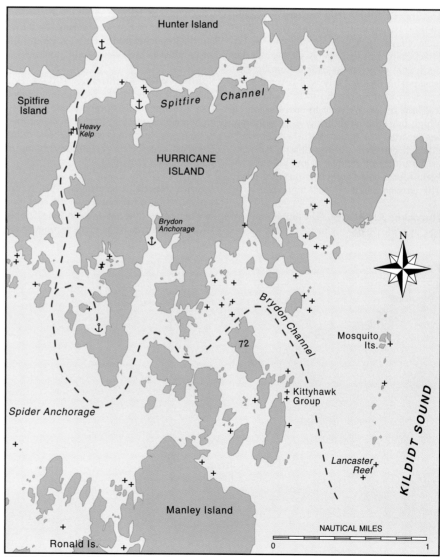

Kildidt Sound and Brydon Channel

Spider Island. This area is beautiful, raw, remote feeling, and little visited. The waters are also full of rocks. This is perfect gunkholing country, a paradise for kayakers.

You have a choice of two ways to get there, outside or inside. The outside route goes out the mouth of Hakai Passage into Queens Sound, then bends northwest toward the west side of Spider Island. Breadner Point, on the west side of Spider Island, is a famous hot spot for spring salmon. South of Spider Island, enter through Fulton Passage, or north of Spider Island through Spider Channel.

The inside route goes through Nalau Passage, across Kildidt Sound, and through rock-choked Brydon Channel into Spider Anchorage. An alternate to the Brydon Channel portion is Spitfire Channel, along the north side of Hurricane Island. Spitfire Channel has one spot so tight, however, we recommend you explore by dinghy before committing the mother ship.

The following information is an overview of the main places. It would take several days to poke around all the delights of this area.

Passage between Spider Anchorage and Spitfire Channel. This passage separates Spitfire Island and Hurricane Island. The route shown was recommended to us by Mike Guns. The passage is clear until the north end, where rocks extend from Spitfire Island. This area is fairly well covered with bull kelp floating on the surface and thick leaf kelp below. We went in near the top of a high tide without difficulty. Next morning we departed 1½ hours after a 3.3-foot low tide and gathered a heavy glop of leaf kelp on our props and rudders. A low-powered fin keel sailboat could have been stopped dead. This passage is best run near high water.

Hurricane Anchorage. "Hurricane Anchorage" is Don Douglass's name for the other-

Spitfire Passage is narrow, challenging and beautiful. Here three Grand Banks yachts from NW Explorations pass through carefully with a bow watch ready to call out the clearance to the rocks.

wise unnamed cove in the hook formed by the south end of Hurricane Island. As shown on the reference map, enter north of the group of islets that make up the hook.

Spitfire West Anchorage. This is Don Douglass's name for the otherwise unnamed cove that indents Hurricane Island, immediately west of the Spitfire Channel narrows. Several people have recommended it to us. Douglass says the bottom offers only fair to poor holding, however.

Spitfire North Anchorage. This is our name for the otherwise unnamed cove that indents Hunter Island, west of the Spitfire Channel narrows. Mike Guns recommended

it to us. We would anchor in the outer part only. At low water the mouth leading to the inner lagoon appeared to be impassable or nearly so. The east side of the outer cove had a bottom that felt like a thin layer of mud on top of rock, and we dragged easily. The west side of the cove yielded good holding in 50 to 55 feet.

Spitfire Channel. Spitfire Channel separates Hurricane Island and Hunter Island, and except for the narrows at the west end, is easily run. The narrows are another matter. A medium-size cruiser can go through these narrows without difficulty, but with great caution and a sharp lookout. Underwater rocks extend into the channel, especially from the north side. Plan your transit at high water slack—high water, to get the greatest width possible; slack because we wouldn't want current pushing us where we didn't want to go. Least depth is 1.9 meters (approximately 6 feet) at zero tide.

FITZ HUGH SOUND, CONTINUED

Kwakume Inlet. Kwakume Inlet is a beautiful and roomy anchorage, but study the chart closely before entering. A rock awash at zero tide is shown outside the entrance, and you'll want to steer a course to avoid it. Mike Guns, a commercial fisherman with 35 years' experience in these waters, says the preferred approach is from the north. He recommends favoring the mainland shore, to pass between the rock and the shore.

Once past the rock, pass between the larger islet in the entrance and the little dot islet south of the larger islet. Inside, two rocks are shown a short distance along the north shore, one of them drying 1.5 meters. Near the head of the main basin and south of its

Brian Pemberton of NW Explorations is shown here on bow watch through the narrow neck in Spitfire Passage. We did go through the pass carefully with a 49-foot Grand Banks.

islet, another rock is shown, this one drying 1.8 meters.

The south cove immediately inside the entrance has been recommended as an anchorage, but might be filled with aquaculture. Other aquaculture is located along the north side of Kwakume Inlet. Fortunately, it doesn't occupy any favored anchorages.

With the south cove taken, the best anchorage is in 25 to 30 feet (zero tide) at the head of the inlet, between the shore and a rock shown as drying 1.8 meters. Anchor either there or in the inner basin.

If you can get into it, the inner basin is unusually secluded and snug feeling. Be aware, however, that the short fairway leading to the inner basin is narrow, and that a substantial drying rock lies in the middle, with more rocks on each side. *High water only, this little pass, dead slow bell, with alert lookouts.* We favored the north side.

Having a high tide when we arrived in early evening, we felt our way into the inner basin for the night. We were treated to glass-smooth water and the most plaintive loon's call we've ever heard. As we slipped out at high water early the next morning we were stopped cold by a wolf's cry—a long lonesome troubled howl, repeated just once. [*Hale*]

Koeye River. A charted rock lies north of Koeye Point. Enter north of that rock and wrap around into the cove behind the point. A lodge is near the point.

A few years ago we talked with the lodge caretaker, who told us that an onshore wind blowing out of Hakai Passage creates large seas that roll into the bay. He also said this is grizzly bear country. Later, we talked with a boat that experienced the seas mentioned above. The skipper said the seas were awful. They had come back from the mine and had much trouble getting from the dinghy to the boat. Stay away in a westerly.

Although in our opinion Koeye (pronounced "Kway") River is not a good spot for overnight anchoring, several people have told us a dinghy trip up the river to the mine ruins is beautiful. At the mine you'll find two open pits connected by a tunnel. The remains of a shop are there, and a huge old 1-cylinder steam engine. The buildings on the point at the mouth of the river are a Bella Bella Native band summer camp. [*Hale*]

Sea Otter Inlet & Crab Cove. Sea Otter Inlet, on Hunter Island, has two arms that form a "T" at the entrance. Crab Cove, the northern arm, was recommended by a park ranger at Pruth Bay. Anchor near the head in 30 to 35 feet. The south arm is prettier than Crab Cove and more private feeling. Anchor near the head of the south cove in 35 to 40 feet.

Kiltik Cove. Mouth of cove 51°53.80'N /128°00.05'W. Kiltik Cove indents the east side of Hunter Island, approximately across from Namu. It is extremely well protected.

The bottom shoals abruptly just past the tiny rock islet on the east shore of the arm. We would anchor in 35 to 40 feet a short distance north of that rock.

Warrior Cove. Warrior Cove is on the mainland (east) side of Fitz Hugh Sound, approximately 1.5 miles south of Namu. With a typical westerly wind, a following sea will chase you into the cove, but the seas subside when you pass the 82-meter island (in a southeast gale a lump may get in). The inner cove is pretty and protected. Scout around for just the right spot, and put the hook down in 20 to 25 feet, good holding.

Namu. The falling-down cannery at Namu has gone through another transition. For many years caretakers Pete and Rene (pronounced "Reenie") Darwin, and Rene's longtime friend Theresa managed the facility. They created a unique marina destination on a collection of floats, complete with a covered common area, gift store, workshop, greenhouse, and docks. They transformed the uplands of the old cannery with art and and creative landscaping. Pete and Rene have moved on, physically moving their floats to Lizzie Cove on Lama Passage. They plan to be fully operational in the new location by summer 2014. Updates will be provided in Waggoner eNews and on www.WaggonerGuide.com.

Anchorage is still available at Namu, but the old cannery may be posted with no trespassing signs.

Navigation note: The beacon is gone from Loo Rock, between the Namu floats and the entrance to Rock Inlet, but Loo Rock still exists. It is marked now by a round float. The Namu Harbour inset on Chart 3936 shows the rock's location. In front of the cafe, another rock is marked with a ball.

Rock Inlet. Rock Inlet extends northeast from Whirlwind Bay (Namu), and it's a good, protected spot. Entering or departing, be sure to identify Verdant Island, near the mouth, and pass east of it. Keep a mid-channel course and watch for rocks. The chart shows the way. Inside, anchor in 25 to 40 feet. A float is in the south cove, with room to an-

chor nearby. The float is near drying rocks, shown on the chart. Favor the west shore.

FISHER CHANNEL

The north end of Fitz Hugh Sound divides into Burke Channel and Fisher Channel. Burke Channel leads eastward to Bella Coola, which is connected by road to Williams Lake and the highways inland. Bella Coola has facilities and is mentioned often by the few residents on this part of the coast, but is little visited by pleasure craft.

Fisher Channel is a continuation of the Inside Passage route, although the Inside Passage soon leads west and north, via Lama Passage or Gunboat Passage, to Bella Bella and Shearwater. If you remain in Fisher Channel you will reach Cousins Inlet. Ocean Falls, at the head of Cousins Inlet, is the most complete and interesting ghost town on the coast.

Humchitt Island. Humchitt Island is immediately off the south tip of King Island, at the intersection of Fitz Hugh Sound, Burke Channel and Fisher Channel. "With 15-knot southeasterlies blowing up Fitz Hugh Sound, we overnighted in the cove on the northeast shore of Humchitt Island. The seas were 2 to 3 feet outside, but our anchorage was tranquil and calm, with an amazing view up Fisher Channel. Anchor in 10 to 20 feet, moderate to good holding over rock, with a 150-foot swing radius." [*Hamilton*]

Kisameet Bay. Kisameet Bay is on King Island, about 3.5 miles north of the mouth of Burke Channel, roughly east of Fog Rocks. Correspondents John and Lorraine Littlewood report: "A splendid anchorage. The northernmost part of the bay, behind the island, is the place to be. It's quiet and fully protected from wind and sea, with a 'window' out into Fisher Channel to observe conditions." This is a very pleasant place to hide out. Anchor in 30 to 40 feet. We overnighted in this anchorage last season before heading south to cross Cape Caution. We found it to be just as the Littlewood's described it and recommend it.

The Kisameet Bay anchorage is somewhat smaller than this photo suggests. Work your way in around rocks, all of them charted.

A hiking trail leads from Codville Lagoon to Sagar Lake and its sandy beach.

Codville Lagoon. Codville Lagoon is a provincial park on the east side of Fisher Channel. It is a popular anchorage, protected and pretty, but with somewhat limited anchorage room. Readers John and Deb Marshall reported that strong winds will work their way to the back cove. The narrow entrance is hard to locate, but Codville Hill, its moonscape of three peaks and barren rock slopes, is a good landmark. Favor the south side of the entrance to avoid a rock off the north shore. Anchor in 40 to 50 feet along the east shore, opposite Codville Island. A trail runs from the head of the anchorage to sandy beaches at beautiful Sagar Lake. This is bear country. Make noise as you walk.

The Trap. The Trap is located behind Clayton Island on the west side of Fisher Channel, about 2 miles south of Lama Passage. North entrance 52°02.35'N/127°56.80'W. South entrance 52°01.05'N/127°56.80'W. We read about this spot in Iain Lawrence's *Far Away Places* (now out of print). Southbound on a windy, rainy afternoon we decided to tuck in for a look. The passage behind Clayton Island is as Lawrence describes it: deep, but protected from the wind. Lawrence says the bottom is rocky and requires a stern-tie to shore to prevent swinging. The Trap itself is the bay at the very south end of the passage.

Lawrence says this bay empties at low tide, revealing a labyrinth of ancient fish traps.

Long Point Cove. Long Point Cove is located on the west side of Fisher Channel, approximately 1 mile south of Lama Passage. Although Sailing Directions mentions Long Point Cove as a good anchorage for small craft, it isn't as scenic or interesting as other anchorages in the area. On entering, favor the west shore to avoid a rock that dries some 250 to 300 yards north of Long Point. The rock is shown on the chart.

④ **Ocean Falls (Cousins Inlet).** Although a ghost town, Ocean Falls is a busy ghost town. The winter population of 25 swells to 100 in the summer, but services are limited. Darke Waters Inn & Adventure Lodge has good breakfasts and dinners, showers, laundry, and ice. Nearby Martin Valley has Saggo's Saloon, and a small grocery store that also stocks souvenirs and fishing tackle.

From the top of the ramp at the docks, a right turn leads to Ocean Falls proper. Other than the small gift store in the corner of the marine ways building, Darke Waters is the only operating business.

The dam dominates the head of the inlet and supplies electrical power for Ocean Falls, Shearwater, and New Bella Bella. The dam also provides water and power for the town's controversial new industry: a multi-million dollar hatchery and rearing pen facility for Atlantic salmon smolt for fish farms. Some 30 large green fiberglass rearing pens have been installed beside the former Crown Zellerbach mill. Mixing ponds, where freshwater and saltwater are blended in exact proportions for the developing smolt, have been blasted out of the rocky mountainside leading to the dam.

You can walk up the road to the dam and back along Link Lake. Make noise—you might meet a bear. Trout fishing in Link Lake is said to be excellent.

A left turn at the top of the dock leads visitors on a 1.5-mile road to Martin Valley. It's an easy, scenic stroll. The first house you come to is Saggo's Saloon. Check the hours for the saloon; they may be different than you expect. A little farther along, a concrete launch ramp serves amphibious planes. Some visitors use the side of the ramp to land a dinghy to shop at the Rain Country Store. It's located at the head of the ramp and has a wide variety of goods, though stock is sometimes limited. When the orange light is flashing, the store is open. Notices at the head of the Ocean Falls Small Craft Harbour give the hours of operation for both the store and saloon.

The houses in Martin Valley were taken over by the province when Ocean Falls was abandoned. They have since been sold to people who enjoy the beauty and solitude of the area. With calls by the BC ferry from Shearwater and Port Hardy, and the tourists the ferries bring, a small crafts industry has begun.

Crabbing is excellent off the mill. Halibut and salmon can be caught in Cousins Inlet. Consider dropping a prawn trap in Watson Cove on your way up the inlet. We think Ocean Falls is a "don't miss" stop for its unique charm and beauty.

Air service to and from Ocean Falls is available through Pacific Coastal Airlines.

④ **Ocean Falls Small Craft Harbour.** General Delivery, Ocean Falls, BC V0T 1P0; (250) 289-3859; www.oceanfalls.org.

OCEAN FALLS

Ocean Falls, at the head of Cousins Inlet, is a ghost town, lost on the B.C. coast. When you round Coolidge Point in the inlet you see the "falls," the spillway from the dam. Below the dam are extensive docks, and on top of the docks is a huge mill. To the left of the mill are tall, modern buildings. It is only after you land and walk uptown that you realize most of the buildings are empty, and the north coast wind is whistling through their open windows.

Until it closed more than 35 years ago, the Crown Zellerbach mill was the second largest on the coast, and Ocean Falls was a busy community of more than 5,000. Championship swimmers came from its Olympic-size swimming pool. The pool is filled in now. When Crown Zellerbach gave up the mill in 1973, the province, unwilling to lose the jobs, tried to run it. On May 31,1980 it gave up too. The mill's machinery was removed, and in 1986 bulldozers came to level the town. The town's residents stood in front of the bulldozers and backed them down, though not until many of the houses and buildings had been destroyed.

The "museum" is an interesting collection of all kinds of items left behind when the mill was closed.

Downtown, fortunately, was largely spared. The Martin Inn hotel, tall and imposing, is empty. Its doors are chained shut and signs warn off trespassers. Inside are papers from 1976. The Lions Club room has literature illustrated with drawings of briefcase-carrying businessmen dressed in suits and snap-brim hats. In the lounge, veneer lifts off the mantel above the fireplace dedicated to Archie Martin, the legendary mill manager. The carpets are soaked and rotting. Paint peels off the walls.

A dormitory where mill workers lived looks almost ready to accept a new crop of college students. Its doors too are chained shut. A two-story garden-court apartment complex, 1970s style, is overgrown with weeds. The windows are broken, the plumbing fixtures are torn out, and the roof is falling in. We watched as a lonesome wind fluttered the few ragged and water-stained curtains that remained. We thought, a story longs to be written. A film waits to be made.

On our first visit to Ocean Falls we met bearded Norman Brown ("Nearly Normal Norman Brown, they call me"), who befriended us and showed us around. Norman was living in the basement of the imposing company guest house on the hill, and a step at a time, he was making the house into a museum.

Something happened, and for several years the histori-

The mermaid welcomes you to Ocean Falls. Herb Carpenter, a local resident, created the sculpture.

cal artifacts Norman collected were moved down to the old Hudson's Bay (then Co-op) building. A sagging corner of the building was jacked up, and Norman, who is a glazier by trade, reinstalled windows. Heavy snowfall in the 2007–08 winter collapsed the roof of the building, and now Norman's displays have been moved to an upper floor in the marine ways.

Nearly Normal Norman Brown in his museum in the second floor of the marine ways.

With its infrastructure and deepwater harbor, Ocean Falls has sought new industry. A number of years ago a company tried to sell bottled water from the pure offerings of Link Lake, behind the dam. Stock was sold and publicity went out. The venture failed. Now the hatchery is in place, which, unfortunately, has failed to provide new local jobs.

For the present, Ocean Falls remains essentially a ghost town with a big fish hatchery. A short distance from the company guest house, a failing boardwalk fronts on what once were pleasant homes with a view of the inlet. The boardwalk is

"The Shack" is a homey place to hang out on the docks.

rotting and sagging and most of the houses are empty. Nearly Normal Norman Brown greets visitors and sells or barters antiques he has collected. Around the edges, Nature reclaims the land.

— Robert Hale

Approaching Ocean Falls.

Open all year, public dock with potable water, washrooms, showers, laundry facility at Darke Waters Inn & Lodge, free seasonal Wi-Fi, 20 & 30 amp power, no fuel.

The docks have power and all the Link Lake water you need. The water is sweet and pure to begin with, and has gone through a further purification process. We fill our tanks at Ocean Falls. [*Hale*]

Pay moorage at The Shack, a float house next to the ramp to shore, or wait for the wharfinger to come down the docks in the morning or late afternoon. Visa and Master-Card accepted.

Harbor manager Herb Carpenter runs the marine ways. Herb built Melissa, the gold-colored mermaid who welcomes boats to the docks. In the downstairs corner of the marine ways building, Herb's wife Lena has set up a little gift shop called C' shores Gift Shop.

No garbage drop: Recycling bins are located at The Shack. Anything fish or crabs can eat can be put in the chuck for the fish and crabs to eat. Take everything else with you.

Weather radio channel WX 1: The signal is spotty. If necessary, walk along the dock with a handheld VHF until you find reception. The dock is now monitored by a security camera.

④ **Darke Waters Inn & Adventure Lodge.** (250) 289-3585; darkewaters@xplornet.ca; www.darkewaters.com. Monitors VHF 06. Open April 15th to October 31st. Rob & Corrina Darke took over the old hospital building across from the marine ways building, a right turn and a short walk from the top of the dock. Darke Waters brings a number of amenities to "downtown" Ocean Falls: hot showers, coin laundry, Wi-Fi, ice, and Tuna's Cafe for breakfast, lunch and dinner. The Inn has 22 rooms.

Dinner is available with advance reservations only. Remote locations like Ocean Falls cannot have meals on standby for the next group that may or may not stop in. The best way to make reservations is by email prior to 8 p.m. the day before you'd like to dine. Daily specials are listed on their website. Rob has 30 years' experience as a guide and of-fers wildlife, waterfall, kayak, and hot spring excursions.

Lama Passage. Lama Passage leads westward and northward from Fisher Channel to New Bella Bella and Shearwater. Cruise ships and BC Ferries vessels use this passage regularly. Keep a sharp lookout ahead and astern.

Fancy Cove. Fancy Cove is on the south shore of Lama Passage and is a delightful little anchorage. Don Douglass writes about the cove in his book on northern BC and he deserves thanks from the entire cruising community for telling about it. Anchor in 10 to 25 feet wherever it looks good.

Fannie Cove. Fannie Cove is in Cooper Inlet on the south shore of Lama Passage. It's a beautiful little spot, with an obvious anchoring nook on its eastern shore just inside the entrance. Unfortunately, the holding ground is only fair. We tried twice to get a good set in the little nook and once farther out, but each time we dragged without much effort. We would overnight in settled weather only. Study the chart before entering. Leave Gus Island and the little dot islet west of Gus Island to port as you approach.

Lizzie Cove. Pete and Rene Darwin moved their floats from Namu to Lizzie Cove in fall 2013. The barbecue shelter and gift shop have also been relocated there.

The facilities will be open for business by summer 2014. Call on VHF channel 10.

We'd enter Lizzie Cove leaving Gus Island to port. Then turn northwest and wrap around the 45-meter island. Shoals extend nearly 100 meters north from the 45-meter island, so don't cut too close. Unofficial navigation aids on the rocks help boaters in.

Jane Cove. Jane Cove, on the south shore of Lama Passage in Cooper Inlet, offers shelter but lacks scenic quality. Study the chart carefully before entering to avoid shoals and rocks. Fannie Cove, despite its marginal holding, or Fancy Cove, which is spectacular by comparison, are preferred.

Darke Waters Inn & Adventure Lodge in Ocean Falls

The Rain Country Store is easily accessed by dinghy.

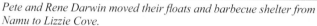
Pete and Rene Darwin moved their floats and barbecue shelter from Namu to Lizzie Cove.

The fuel dock at Shearwater has a helipad above.

⑤ **New Bella Bella.** New Bella Bella (Waglisla) is a major Native village, with gasoline and diesel fuel, good water, and garbage drop. In the summer of 2013, the grocery store, liquor store, post office, and café were destroyed in a terrible fire. An alternate store has been set up in the community center. Plans for a new store are in the works. It will be built across the street from the previous store and is scheduled to be operating by summer 2014. Check Waggoner eNews or www.WaggonerGuide.com for more details.

The village has a hospital. No laundromat. The closest laundromat is at Shearwater. The fuel dock attendants are courteous, but religious about their lunch hour. You may have to be patient. The fuel pumps and meters are on the wharf above the fuel float.

New Bella Bella's water treatment plant provides a steady stream of clear water at the fuel dock.

Guests at Shearwater can take the water taxi to New Bella Bella to shop at the band store or drop off or pick up passengers or parts from the airport. Scheduled service runs throughout the day.

The New Bella Bella airport is about 2 miles from the village. You can walk along the road or take a taxi. The taxi is often standing by before or after a flight. They know the schedules. Pacific Coastal Airlines serves New Bella Bella with multiple flights per day with service through Port Hardy to Vancouver.

Cell phones: Cell phone coverage is excellent in New Bella Bella.

Bella Bella. Bella Bella (Old Bella Bella) is on Denny Island on the northeastern shore of Lama Passage. The excellent docks and lovely buildings ("Whistler North") house the Coast Guard Search and Rescue vessel *Cape Farewell*, its crew and support staff, and Fisheries and Oceans personnel.

⑥ **Kliktsoatli Harbour.** Shearwater Resort & Marina is located in Kliktsoatli Harbour, 2 miles east of New Bella Bella on the north side of Denny Island. Good anchorage can be found on the eastern shore.

⑥ **Shearwater Resort & Marina.** (250) 957-2666 (ext. 2); moorage@shearwater. ca; hotel@shearwater.ca; www.shearwater.ca. Monitors VHF channels 06 & 66A, the fuel dock monitors VHF 08. Open all year, 1500 feet of guest moorage, 15, 30 & 50 amp power all the way out the main float. Wi-Fi codes can be purchased at the store during business hours. Potable water is now installed on the docks and at the fuel dock. This is a big improvement.

The fuel dock has diesel, gasoline, lubricants, propane, and Avgas and Jet A. On shore you'll find an ATM, propane, washrooms, showers, laundry, ice, restaurant, pub, haulout, launch ramp, garbage drop, waste oil dump, recycling, grocery store, liquor store, marine supply store with fishing supplies and charts, lodging, post office, cafe, and gift shop.

The showers and laundry room, in the building across from the store, are excellent.

Shearwater Resort has installed a cellphone booster system and antenna to reach the cell towers in New Bella Bella. Cell reception is said to be good throughout the resort.

Make moorage reservations or you may find the docks full. Phone (250) 957-2666 or call on VHF 66A. Old docks are set up as a breakwater in front of the resort. If the main docks are full, you can moor on the inside of the breakwater docks with no power.

Shearwater is the most complete marine facility between Port Hardy and Prince Rupert. For cruisers it's the narrow neck of the hourglass. Northbound or southbound, most boats pass through Shearwater.

The marina is the site of a WWII Royal Canadian Air Force seaplane base. The large hangar now serves as the shop. A long, floating breakwater protects the moorage and fuel dock.

The pub is popular and often has live en-

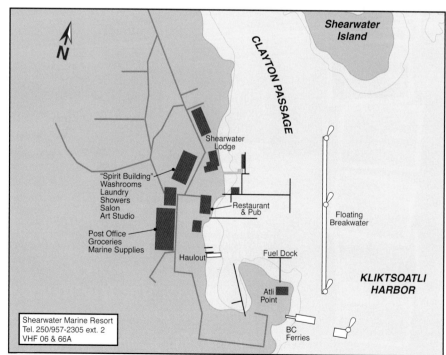
Shearwater Marine Resort

This new mural at Shearwater commemorates influential people from its past.

The bar and restaurant at Shearwater regularly has live music.

tertainment. The restaurant serves good food with a comprehensive menu. It's customary to share a table with people from other boats. In 2013, a new deck with excellent views of the marina was built to accomodate outdoor dining.

The store carries ice and a surprisingly broad range of grocery and liquor items.

Shearwater has its own airstrip for private aircraft a short distance away. Scheduled airline is available from New Bella Bella with service via Pacific Coastal Airlines through Port Hardy to Vancouver. Shearwater is also a stop for the BC Ferry system.

The Sea-Bus water taxi connects Shearwater and New Bella Bella (Waglisla) with a 10-minute ride. In calm weather you can scoot over in a dinghy.

Shearwater is the crossroads of the northern coast and gets a full range of visitors: crew boats, water taxis, pile drivers, towboats, government boats, commercial fishermen, sportfishermen, kayakers, yachts, Vietnamese prawners, Natives from New Bella Bella, fly-in fishing charter guests, and tourists off the BC ferries. Differing needs, preferences and cultures abound.

Service note: The shipyard can haul boats to 70 tons and handle almost anything, from toilet repairs to electronics to repowers.

The year 2013 was a big one for Shearwater. Craig Widsten, the principal owner of this family-owned resort, created two special tributes to the heritage of Shearwater and the surrounding area. When the end wall of the large shop needed replacement, Craig had it rebuilt. He then commissioned muralist Paul Gartua to paint the image of seventeen people who had an impact on the growth and development of Shearwater. This includes tribal leaders, medical professionals, the original manager of the Hudson's Bay Co. outpost,

and even Craig's father, Andrew. Measuring 120 feet wide and 22 feet tall, the new mural is quite striking.

Craig also installed a cenotaph to commemorate Shearwater and New Bella Bella residents' war service. He commissioned the casting of a scale replica of the Stranraer flying boat that was based at Bella Bella. The casting has a wingspan of 17 feet. It is mounted on a pylon and rotates like a weather vane. Nearby, a newly carved Eagle pole commemorates First Nations veterans. An obelisk commemorates other veterans from the area.

Kakushdish Harbour. Kakushdish Harbour, long and narrow, extends into Denny Island immediately east of Kliktsoatli Harbour (Shearwater). An overhead power cable with 23 meters (75 feet) vertical clearance crosses the entrance. "We favored the north shore through the entrance bar and saw a minimum depth of 11 feet, zero tide. Anchor in 20 to 25 feet, good holding in mud. The anchorage was surprisingly deserted and tranquil." [*Hamilton*]

LOCAL KNOWLEDGE

NAVIGATION NOTES: The trickiest spot in Gunboat Passage is the narrow fairway between Denny Point and Maria Island. Use caution to navigate away from the rocks. A second tricky spot is the reef that extends from the southern shore toward Dingle Island. Watch the currents in this area. A red nun buoy marks the outer end of this reef. Red, Right, Returning assumes you are returning eastbound, from the sea. The third tricky spot is the range at the west end of Gunboat Passage. Entering or departing, stay on the range.

Gunboat Passage. Gunboat Passage connects Seaforth Channel with Fisher Channel and is a scenic route between Ocean Falls and New Bella Bella/Shearwater. The passage is littered with reefs and rocks, but well marked with aids to navigation.

Dunn Point Bay. The entrance looks tricky on the chart, but if you leave the small islet to port as you enter you'll have good water. Anchor inside in 30 to 40 feet. Stay well clear of the mouth of Beales Lagoon. At least two detached drying rocks lie in the cove off the lagoon's mouth. Excellent protection.

Gosse Bay. Gosse Bay is west of Maria Island, a good anchorage on the west side of the westernmost cove.

Forit Bay. Forit Bay, on the eastern approach to Gunboat Passage, is an excellent, protected anchorage in 15 to 25 feet. The entrance, however, is encumbered by a large rock between Flirt Island and the point of land that marks the inner part of the bay. The rock

is not visible at high tide, but it is visible through the water at a little less than half tide.

Enter Forit Bay by wrapping around the north tip Flirt Island, leaving the island to port.

BURKE CHANNEL, DEAN CHANNEL, BELLA COOLA

Important chart note: In October, 2011, Canadian Hydrographic Service (CHS) released new Chart 3974 and cancelled Charts 3729 and 3730. All coverage of this area is now shown on 3900-series charts—Chart 3936 for the mouth and western portion of Burke Channel, and Chart 3939 for the mouth and western portion of Dean Channel.

Burke Channel and Dean Channel border the south and north sides of King Island and plunge deep into the Coast Range mountains. We had been told that this is some of the most beautiful and awe-inspiring country imaginable, but after seeing so much beautiful country all along the B.C. coast, we expected it to be just more of the same. We were wrong. A circumnavigation of King Island will astonish you. Gone is the raw coast with its low, wave-pounded islands. A short distance up either channel puts you inland, bounded on each side by high mountains. If you're going to spend some time on this coast, see these waters.

LOCAL KNOWLEDGE

EBB CURRENT: On warm summer days heating of inland air produces an up-channel sea breeze in Burke Channel that can begin as early as 10:00 a.m. and blow strongly until sundown. Make your runs early and find shelter before the wind starts blowing.

WEATHER TIP: The surface water in Burke Channel is often in an almost constant ebb, the result of fresh water flowing toward the sea. When this surface ebb meets a spring flood, tide-rips, whirlpools, and general confusion results.

Burke Channel. Burke Channel leads 38 miles inland, beginning at Edmund Point, just north of Namu. From Edmund Point to Restoration Bay the lower reaches of Burke Channel are subject to strong tidal currents and heavy tide-rips, but in the upper reaches the tidal streams are weak.

The north end of Burke Channel divides into South Bentinck Arm and North Bentinck Arm (Bella Coola is at the head of North Bentinck Arm), and Labouchere Passage, which leads to Dean Channel. When the ebb current is flowing and the up-channel sea breeze is blowing, expect rough seas at the confluence of these channels. Early morning, before the B.C. Interior heats up, is often the calmest time of day.

All these cautions make Burke Channel sound impenetrable, which isn't the case. The

prudent skipper simply will avoid being out there in the wrong conditions.

The best anchorage along Burke Channel is at the head of Kwatna Inlet, with a second-best choice being the small cove just north of Cathedral Point.

Approximately 8 miles up the channel from Edmund Point, a large logging camp is located near the outlet of Doc Creek. We have been told that while the logging camp definitely is not in the marina business, they will not shoo-away a boat that really needs a place to tie up for the night. We are not encouraging such visits, but it's good to know the option exists if it is needed.

Fougner Bay. Fougner Bay is near the mouth of Burke Channel on the south side, just east of Edmund Point. The outer part the bay is somewhat protected, with anchorage in 40 to 60 feet. To us it feels uninviting. An inner cove, however, is a perfect spot.

Find the 41-meter sounding back in the bay. That's the cove. To get in, the chart shows good water by leaving the + symbol (indicating a dangerous underwater rock 2 meters or less at zero tide) to starboard. Douglass, however, shows an approach leaving that rock to port, and that's how we went in. Correspondents Carol-Ann Giroday and Rick LeBlanc checked out the area by dinghy. They report that leaving the rock to starboard puts you in a wider, deeper channel. Once clear of the rock, loop into the cove. Study the chart carefully before entering Fougner Bay. The rocks off the entry are easy to avoid, but you want to know where they are and where you are.

Kwatna Inlet. Kwatna Inlet extends some 12 miles into the mainland and is too deep for anchoring until near the head. Watch carefully for the drying flats at the head. We are told by several people that it is an excellent place to put the hook down.

Cathedral Point. Cathedral Point, a weather reporting station, marks the north entrance to Kwatna Inlet, and is easily identified by its white building and tower. Just north of the point, a tiny cove with dramatic granite walls makes good anchorage in 25 feet. The cove has excellent protection from up-channel winds, but the mass of large logs on the south beach suggests that down-channel winds and seas blow right in. We patrolled the cove but did not stay. Early Correspondent Bill Hales, from Victoria, anchored for the night and reported a pleasant experience.

South Bentinck Arm. South Bentinck Arm, 25 miles long, lies between high mountains. The relatively few cruisers who have gone all the way up the arm say it is beautiful. We have gone as far as Larso Bay, which has good anchorage in 35 to 70 feet. The mountains across from Larso Bay are beautiful. Correspondent Gil Flanagan found one of the largest red cedars in B.C. by walking about 1 km up a logging road that begins in the north part of the bay. The tree is on the

TALLHEO HOT SPRINGS

Tallheo Hot Springs is picturesque and popular with the residents of Bella Coola. The main pool is about 3 feet deep and sits in a rock fissure about 5 feet above high tide. It holds about 15 people. The rock sides extend 5 feet straight up from the surface of the pool. You are in a forest with large trees and moss and have a great view onto South Bentinck Arm.

There is no beach by the pool, just a steep-to rocky shore. Fifty yards north is a spit with a beach and a large, well-maintained cabin. The anchorage off this beach is exposed, but your boat will be directly in front of you as you lounge. If the wind starts to blow it off, you should have plenty of time to get to it. The wind blows parallel to the shore. Even if you raised anchor and simply drifted, you probably wouldn't be on the rocks in less than 20 minutes.

When we were there, we met a very friendly local who had a 20-foot aluminum boat that he ran up on the beach. He offered to take us back to our boat. He may have thought our 7-foot Polywog wasn't up to the 1.5-foot waves.

– Gil Flanagan

right side of the road, marked with a plaque.

Tallheo Hot Springs. Tallheo Hot Springs is located about one-quarter mile north of the mouth of Hotsprings Creek on the west shore of South Bentinck Arm, a short distance south of Bensins Island. Anchorage is exposed.

North Bentinck Arm. The water in North Bentinck Arm is green and milky, the result of the Bella Coola River emptying into the head of the arm. We found no good anchorages, so you have to hope for room at the Bella Coola docks. Watch for drift. Log booming activity is going on, and we saw a large number of floating propeller-benders. Windy Bay is on the south side of North Bentinck Arm, near the junction with Burke Channel. When we crossed the mouth of Windy Bay in early afternoon we learned how it got its name. Whew!

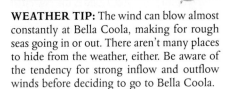

LOCAL KNOWLEDGE

WEATHER TIP: The wind can blow almost constantly at Bella Coola, making for rough seas going in or out. There aren't many places to hide from the weather, either. Be aware of the tendency for strong inflow and outflow winds before deciding to go to Bella Coola.

⑦ **Bella Coola.** Bella Coola is seldom visited by yachts but interesting nonetheless. The government floats are run by the Bella Coola Harbour Authority, and they are making improvements. Water is available all the way out the docks, with 20 & 30 amp power. Showers and washrooms are at the head of the ramp.

The Columbia Fuels fuel dock is adjacent to the public floats.

Correspondent Gil Flanagan says the best way to visit is to overnight in Larso Bay in South Bentinck Arm or Eucott Bay on Dean Channel, and come over in the morning. A visitor at the Seattle Boat Show recommended anchoring in Bryneldsen Bay, near the north end of Labouchere Channel, and going to Bella Coola early the next morning. Use Chart 3974 (formerly 3729). Bryneldsen Bay is behind the thumb of land that extends southeast, approximately 0.8 miles from Ram Bluff. The bay is not labeled, but Chart 3974 does show an anchor symbol beside it.

The town of Bella Coola is located 3 kilometers (about 2 miles) from the dock. Taxis may be available. When we visited in 2013, the taxi service was not operating. We walked instead, and the lush vegetation, waterfalls beside the road, and the Bella Coola River Estuary made for a beautiful stroll. Stay on the water side of the road, since it's wider and safer for walking.

We urge you to see the Bella Coola Museum, housed in buildings dating from 1892 and 1898. It is on the edge of town along the road from the marina. Bella Coola is where, in 1793, Alexander Mackenzie touched saltwater on his transcontinental crossing of Canada. Much of the museum's display is about Mackenzie. We bought a booklet of Mackenzie's journal entries (including comment about the unrelenting wind) in the Bella Coola and Dean Channel area.

The town has provincial and federal government offices, a post office, hospital, motel, liquor store, laundromat, showers, and a well-stocked Co-op grocery store and Moore's Organic Market. Take a tour of the area on the Bella Coola Valley Bus for $2.50; call (250) 799-0079 before 8:00 p.m. the day before you want to ride the bus.

Correspondents Bruce and Margaret Evertz add the following: "A worthwhile attraction in this area are the petroglyphs. The Native band wants them preserved, so they are not marked on any maps. Guides may be available. You can get information about them at the museum."

Correspondents Gil and Karen Flanagan report that rental cars are available (Bella Coola Vehicle Rentals 250-957-7072). "We put about 150 miles on a Dodge Caravan, all on good paved roads. The spectacular drive to Tweedsmuir Park is rated as one of the 10 most scenic drives in Canada."

Bella Coola is the B.C. Interior's window on the coast. Each year remarkable numbers of boats are trailered from the Interior to Bella Coola, where they stay the summer, either tied to the dock or on trailers.

⑦ **Bella Coola Harbour Authority.** P.O. Box 751, Bella Coola, BC V0T 1C0; (250) 799-5633; bcha@belco.bc.ca. They try to monitor VHF channels 06 & 16. Open all year with guest moorage. Facilities include 20 & 30 amp power (20 amp shore power breakers have 20 amp receptacles—bring adaptor), water, washrooms, laundry and showers (showers closed November through March), tidal grid, garbage drop, waste oil drop, pumpout, launch ramp, pay phones, Wi-Fi. Fuel dock adjacent. The harbor office

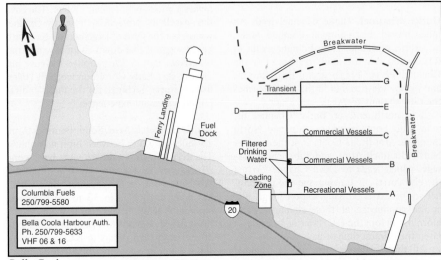

Bella Coola

The Bella Coola docks look more spacious in this photo than when we were trying to raft off in 20-knot winds.

This cairn marks Sir Alexander Mackenzie Rock, where Mackenzie ended his westward explorations in 1793.

is at the head of the pier. Office hours June through September 8:00 a.m. to 6:00 p.m. and off season Monday through Saturday 8:00 a.m. to 12:00 p.m.

Float "A" is dedicated for visiting pleasure craft 14 meters and longer. The float is exposed to westerly winds. Smaller boats can tie up there, but if a boat 14 meters or longer arrives, the smaller boats will have to move.

Bella Coola is a popular launch point for trailerable boats. The Harbour Authority has added additional boat launch floats to make launching and retrieving easier.

The marina is tight and the wind can blow almost constantly. Rafting is required. If necessary, take temporary moorage at one of the commercial floats while figuring out where to go. Put out lots of fenders, both sides. Of all the places we have landed, Bella Coola is one of the most challenging.

The floats are located south of a rock breakwater, behind a floating log breakwater. They are home port to a large number of commercial fish boats. All of A dock and the south side of B dock are reserved for pleasure craft, however. You may have to raft to a permanent boat. The channel on the land side of A dock is narrow, especially at low tide. Feel your way in and find a spot.

Now that the local Harbour Authority is running the facility more interest is devoted to visiting boaters. Even so, Bella Coola is not a "resort marina." Self-reliance is the key.

⑦ **Columbia Fuels Fuel Dock.** (250) 799-5580. Open Monday through Friday 9:00 a.m. to 4:00 p.m. all year, closed at lunch. Call for off-hours service. Gasoline, diesel, lubricants. Dwayne Saugstad is the manager. Dwayne's great-great-grandfather led the original band of Norwegian settlers to Bella Coola. Dwayne's great-grandfather remained, as did Dwayne's grandfather, Dwayne's father, and now Dwayne and his two children. All have called or presently call Bella Coola their home. Six generations.

Labouchere Channel. Labouchere Channel connects the north end of Burke Channel with Dean Channel. **Mesachie Nose**, at

the confluence of the two channels, is a magnificent glacier-smoothed rock prominence on the north shore. Tidal currents combined with winds and surface water runoff can create very difficult seas in this area. If the water is flat, see Mesachie Nose up close. In 2013, we noticed someone had painted a cartoon character and graffiti on a small section of the rocks near the waterline. This unfortunate act of vandalism has visually scarred the area.

The waters of Labouchere Channel itself are generally smooth and wind-free. The scenery, with waterfalls spilling from high mountains, is fabulous. Our notes say, "So many waterfalls!"

LOCAL KNOWLEDGE

WEATHER TIP: Strong up-channel sea breezes can develop when warm temperatures in the Interior heat the air and suck cold ocean air up the various inlets. This sea breeze can begin as early as 10:00 a.m. and last until sundown. Because summertime freshets often create a nearly permanent ebb surface current, an ugly chop can develop when the wind blows against the current.

Dean Channel. Dean Channel connects with Fisher Channel at the mouth of Cousins Inlet (Ocean Falls) and continues 53 miles northward and inland. It is bordered on both sides by high mountains, and, with Burke Channel, offers some of the finest scenery along the coast. In Dean Channel we felt as if we were high up in the mountains on a huge lake; like we should be chewing gum to clear our ears. The concept of being at sea level in these surroundings was hard to grasp.

The principal points of interest on Dean Channel are Elcho Harbour, Sir Alexander Mackenzie Rock and Eucott Bay and hot springs. Cascade Inlet is stunning, but not a good place to anchor.

Jenny Inlet. If Jenny Inlet were someplace else it might be interesting. But we found it ordinary, too deep for anchoring, with a log-

ging camp near the head. Elcho Harbour, 8 miles farther up Dean Channel, or Cousins Inlet (Ocean Falls), 5 miles down-channel, are better choices.

Elcho Harbour. If you are looking for a scenic spot, Elcho Harbour qualifies. It's stunning. The inlet reaches a little more than 2 miles back between steep high mountains, and appears perfectly protected from all winds. Waterfalls plummet from the sides. A lovely bowl is at the head of the inlet, with the obligatory stream that creates an estuary and mudflat. Anchor in 90 to 110 feet off a delightful waterfall on the west side, about one-third of the way in. Or anchor at the head in 90 feet before it shelves up to mudflat. Take the dinghy back out to Sir Alexander Mackenzie Rock for a little history.

Sir Alexander Mackenzie Rock. Sir Alexander Mackenzie Rock is marked by a cairn at the mouth to Elcho Harbour. On 22 July 1793 Mackenzie completed his overland journey across Canada to the Pacific Ocean, and marked his accomplishment with ochre paint on the rock. Later, the inscription was carved into the stone. You can bring the boat right up to the monument, watching for underwater rocks close to shore, and take your own picture of it. Or you can anchor out and dinghy ashore, leaving somebody aboard in case the wind kicks up.

Apparently, Mackenzie ended his westward trek here because the waters beyond were Bella Bella Indian country, and his Bella Coola Indian guides could not guarantee safety. A few miles west on the north side of Dean Channel, ochre pictographs on white cliffs are thought to be boundary markers. They are a short distance east of Frenchman Creek. We found the pictographs and took the lat/lon coordinates off the GPS: 52°20.44'N/127°29.07'W.

Eucott Bay. Eucott Bay is a gorgeous spot, about as pretty as any we have anchored in. The mountains along the eastern and northeastern sides remind us of Yosemite. Photographers, bring your camera—half-dome exists in Eucott Bay. Eucott Hot Springs is near the head of the bay, inshore of a line of pilings. The hot springs have been improved with concrete to make an excellent soaking basin. The water used to be too hot for soaking, but now the temperature can be adjusted.

Craig Widsten, principal owner of Shearwater Marine Resort, told us that in 1948 his father and he journeyed to Eucott Bay to pack mud and hot spring water for sale to health and beauty fanatics in Europe. We're sure it was elegant—hot spring water and mud from the remote Canadian coast, to smooth away the wrinkles and cure what ails you.

Enter Eucott Bay along the east (starboard) side. We are told the entrance has silted up, and is much shallower than charted. Once inside, a large basin unfolds. Find a good spot in the middle and put the hook down. Take the dinghy up to the hot springs. Insect repellant might be needed to protect against deer flies ("those man-eating winged demons," one reader wrote). At low tide wear boots. The beach is muddy.

Nascall Bay. Nascall Hot Springs is near the mouth of Nascall Bay. You'll recognize the buildings by their blue roofs. Previous owners had ambitious development plans, but they didn't work out. Last we heard, the present owner has posted No Trespassing signs.

SEAFORTH CHANNEL, MILBANKE SOUND, FINLAYSON CHANNEL

LOCAL KNOWLEDGE

NAVIGATION NOTE: Although Seaforth Channel is connected with the sea, west of Lama Passage the buoyage system defines "returning from the sea" as returning from south to north, not west to east. If you are outbound in Seaforth Channel, west of Lama Passage you will leave red aids to navigation (buoys, beacons, lights) to starboard (Red, Right, Returning from the south). If you are inbound in Seaforth Channel, west of Lama Passage, leave red aids to navigation to port.

"Returning from the sea" changes at Lama Passage. East of Lama Passage, inbound vessels will leave red buoys, beacons and lights to starboard.

Seaforth Channel. Seaforth Channel connects the New Bella Bella/Shearwater area with Milbanke Sound to the west and is part of the Inside Passage route. Ivory Island is at Seaforth Channel's western entrance.

Troup Passage. Troup Passage runs between Chatfield Island and Cunningham Island, and leads to Roscoe Inlet. Troup Narrows is at the northern end. Near the southern end of Troup Passage an unnamed bay sometimes called Discovery Cove is an excellent anchorage.

ANNIVERSARY ANCHORAGE

In early July 2000 Marilynn and I anchored in the westernmost of the two nooks in Discovery Cove, the only boat there. The day's cloudy skies cleared as supper was prepared, and the rays from the setting sun made the surrounding mountainsides glow. Piano music was playing on the stereo. We were relaxed and content.

Our 25th wedding anniversary would be in 20 days. By then we would be in the Gulf Islands or San Juan Islands, heading home. Traffic would be all around and we would be feeling the pressure of concluding a long cruise. On an impulse I went forward, and from its hiding place I retrieved a small wrapped box, which I presented to Marilynn. I told Marilynn thank you for 25 wonderful years. I thanked her for standing by me when

I decided to start and build a business, for standing by me when I wanted to create this guidebook, and for enjoying the many weeks we spend afloat each year, expanding the book and keeping it up to date.

Most of all, I thanked Marilynn for building a family of her two daughters and my son, a family that is, in the truest sense, a family.

Inside the box was a bracelet. Although Marilynn looks best in gold, this was our silver anniversary. The bracelet is silver and gold, with a blue stone that brings out her blue, and at that moment tear-filled, eyes.

We call this perfect spot on the British Columbia coast Anniversary Anchorage. Very good holding.

— *Robert Hale*

Discovery Cove. Discovery Cove (we're using Douglass's name, which other cruisers seem to be adopting) at lat 52°13.50'N is the only major indent of Cunningham Island from Troup Passage. It was first recommended to us by John and Evonne MacPherson, who spent many summers cruising the coast in their perfectly-maintained 45-foot Grenfell, *Malacandra*. The chart shows rocks on the southwest shore of the entry, but if you go in along the northeast shore you'll have no problems. This is one of the most beautiful coves on the coast. It is surrounded by mountains and seemingly immune to any storm winds that might be about. Anchor in either of the two nooks along the north shore.

Troup Narrows. Troup Narrows, with maximum tidal currents of only about 2 knots, is easily run. Assuming a passage from south to north, identify the reef that dries 15 feet near the south entrance to the narrows. The chart shows a beacon on this reef, but the beacon is gone. Leave the reef to port, and slide west to the beautiful rock cliffs of Chatfield Island. Stay on the Chatfield Island side until the point of land on Cunningham Island is abeam, then trend east to the far shore of Cunningham Island to avoid the reef that extends from the 65-meter island. Study the chart to find the rocks you must avoid.

Roscoe Inlet. Roscoe Inlet is drop-dead beautiful. Beginning where Johnson Channel meets Return Channel, Roscoe Inlet winds some 21 miles back through high mountains that plunge straight down into the sea. Exquisite bowls and valleys lead into the mountains. Sheer cliffs tower overhead. In some

places you can bring the boat alongside a vertical granite wall that rises to a mountain peak 3600 feet above and still have more than 450 feet of water below. Dramatic.

Good anchorages are scarce. For a day trip, we suggest motoring up in the morning, dropping the hook for lunch at the head of the inlet, and motoring back in the afternoon. You can overnight, of course.

CHARTS	
3910 Plans	Milbanke Sound and Beauchemin Channel, 1:20,000
3911 Plans	Vicinity of Princess Royal Island (1:25,000)
3728	Milbanke Sound and Approaches (1:76,600)
3936	Fitz Hugh Sound to Lama Passage (1:40,000)
3938	Queens Sound to Seaforth Channel (1:40,000)
3939	Fisher Channel to Seaforth Channel and Dean Channel (1:40,000); Troupe Narrows (1:6000)
3940	Spiller Channel & Roscoe Inlet (1:40,000)
3941	Channels Vicinity of Milbanke Sound (1:40,000)
3942	Mathieson Channel Northern Portion (1:40,000)
3945	Approaches to Douglas Channel (1:40,000)

Roscoe Inlet has some of the most awe-inspiring scenery on the coast.

Other than the head of the inlet, in our opinion **Boukind Bay** is the easiest anchorage along the way. A large, 25- to 30-foot-deep area allows plenty of room to swing. If an inflow wind is blowing, however, it might be a little bouncy. **Quartcha Bay** is a visually stunning anchorage, although deep until close to the sides or the mud flats at the head. Waterfalls tumble down the mountain sides. From near the head you can look back into two glacier-polished bowls of rock (called *cirques*) and extensive meadows. Correspondent Gil Flanagan reports that evidence of ancient fish traps can be found on the large tide flats. **Shack Bay** and **Ripley Bay** are exposed to inflow winds, and deep until very close to shore. We didn't like them. **Clatse Bay**, at the south end of Roscoe Inlet, is a good anchorage. Go all the way to the head and anchor in 40 to 50 feet.

Bugs: Several readers have warned about ravenous deer flies. Bring insect repellant.

Morehouse Bay. Morehouse Bay, indenting Chatfield Island off Return Channel, has a lovely one-boat anchorage (more, if all are stern-tied to shore) in a cove at the very back, or room for more boats in 60-foot depths outside the back cove. To enter the outer anchorage, leave the 53-meter island to port and the 44- and 59-meter islands to starboard. The more secluded back cove is in the south part of the bay, behind the 59-meter island. Leave a large rock, shown as a 1.2-meter depth, to starboard as you enter. The entry is easy—just be sure you know where that rock is. Anchor in 25 to 35 feet.

Wigham Cove. Wigham Cove, on the south shore of Yeo Island, is a popular anchorage and an excellent place to overnight before transiting Seaforth Channel. Favor the west shore as you enter, until abeam the islets in the middle of the bay. Then turn to pass north of the islets to the favored anchorage in the northeast nook of the cove. This nook has room for several boats. We have shared this anchorage with a 60-footer and a 43-footer with no crowding at all. An 80-footer was anchored in the southeast cove.

Dangerous rock: Be careful if you enter the southernmost nook of Wigham Cove. A dangerous underwater rock with a depth of 0.5 meters at zero tide is reported lying close to and just east of the northernmost of the 3 drying rocks that extend from the eastern shore of the entrance to Wigham Cove. When entering this nook, favor the islets to the east.

Spiller Channel. Spiller Channel and Bullock Channel run north and south on either side of Yeo Island and lead to famed Ellerslie Lagoon, whose entrance rocks have bumped many a boat. Neither run is particularly scenic. Compared with other areas, the hillsides are low. On Spiller Channel especially, clear-cut logging patches abound.

Neekas Cove, across the channel from the north tip of Yeo Island, is the only easy anchorage in the southern part of Spiller Channel. Yeo Cove, near the south entrance to Spiller Channel, has a rock-studded entry and only limited anchorage deep in the southeast corner. Tate Lagoon, which leads into Don Peninsula, has a treacherous entrance. This lagoon is shown as unnamed on Chart 3940. Douglass describes both places, but we're not brave or determined enough to do them ourselves.

The top of Spiller Channel is a little better. The hidden anchorage Douglass calls "Nash Narrows Cove" is lovely. Decent anchorage can be found in the bay immediately south of Ellerslie Lagoon. Spiller Inlet, extending northwest from Spiller Channel, is interesting, but having seen it once we're not inspired to see it again.

Neekas Cove. Neekas Cove is opposite the north tip of Yeo Island in Spiller Channel. The cove is narrow and pretty, but deep until close to the head where the bottom shelves rapidly. Anchor in 50 feet (zero tide) if cautious; 35 feet if braver; less, at your peril. Watch for bears on the shore here.

Nash Passage. Nash Passage (Douglass's name for this otherwise unnamed winding channel), separates Coldwell Peninsula from a good-sized unnamed island on the approach to Ellerslie Bay, just before Spiller Inlet. The chart shows rocks, but the ones to watch out for dry 4.3 meters, so they should be visible much of the time. **Nash Narrows Cove** (Douglass's name again), is the little cove at the turn of Nash Passage. It is beautiful, and would be a good spot to put the hook down.

A peninsula separates Ellerslie Lagoon from a substantial bay immediately to the south. Anchorage is in the inner bay, east of an islet in the middle of the fairway. Pass either side of the islet. Our preferred spot is in 60 feet (zero tide) on the south side, under a towering cliff. The north side of the bay might get down to 40-foot depths, but isn't as protected or cozy feeling.

Ellerslie Lagoon. We have not gone into Ellerslie Lagoon and probably never will. If we do go in, it will be by dinghy only. Because of dangerous rocks, a spring tide high water entry is called for. Two sets of narrows lead in. Ellerslie Lake pours a lot of water into the lagoon; expect the outflowing current through the narrows to last longer than usual. Courageous cruisers do take their boats in, however. We tip our hat to them.

Spiller Inlet. Spiller Inlet extends northward from the top of Spiller Channel. The sides are steep and the water is deep until near the head, where the depths shoal rapidly to a shelf. Near the head of the inlet, the granite cliff on the east side has fractured and fallen away to create Weeping Woman, a Picasso-like natural sculpture on the mountainside. It's quite dramatic.

Bullock Channel. Bullock Channel is a straight run between Return Channel and the top of Yeo Island. Study the chart and favor the Coldwell Peninsula side of the channel. The shoal areas on the Yeo Island side have a tendency to be right where you think you should be going.

The only good Bullock Channel anchorages are on the Coldwell Peninsula side— one at the south end, the other at the north end (where we overnighted). We checked the purported anchorages on the Yeo Island side, but they weren't satisfactory. We found poor holding in the northernmost anchorage, and rock, rock, rock in the bight a little south of the north anchorage.

The water is warm near the top of both channels. In colder waters we like our cabin heat in the morning, but we had no need for it there. [*Hale*]

This is the view from the excellent anchorage at the north end of Bullock Channel.

Bullock Channel North Cove. This is Douglass's name for the otherwise unnamed anchorage behind the 39-meter island at the north end of Bullock Channel, on the Coldwell Peninsula side. We found excellent overnight holding in 50 feet (zero tide) opposite the west opening to the cove. The chart shows a rock awash at zero tide in this west opening. Douglass says the rock dries 4 feet, but we couldn't see it at the bottom of a 2.6-foot tide. Four feet or zero feet, don't take chances. Except at the top of a high tide, enter and depart this cove from the north.

Bullock Spit Cove. Again, Douglass's name for this unnamed anchorage located inside the 70-meter island on the Coldwell Peninsula side, near the south entrance to Bullock Channel. As the chart shows, you don't want to go very far in or you'll run aground. We found good holding in 35 feet just south of the tip of the island.

Kynumpt Harbour. Kynumpt Harbour indents the north tip of Campbell Island, east of Raymond Passage. Sailing Directions says the local name is Strom Bay. The entrance is open and easy, but study the chart carefully to identify and avoid rocks on the western and southern shores. The northernmost indent on the eastern shore is reported to be a good anchorage, as is Strom Cove, the arm that extends to the southeast. We poked around Strom Cove to find a good lunch stop, but saw mostly 55 to 75 feet on the sounder. At those depths, even a 3:1 scope would swing us too close to rocks near shore, so we anchored in the outer bay, 40 feet, west of Spratt Point.

Dufferin Inlet. Dundivan Inlet indents Dufferin Island west of Raymond Passage. It's a pretty spot with several islets to break up the scenery, but the water is deep except near hazards. Two arms make up Lockhart Bay near the head. The western arm is the more attractive anchorage. For overnight we would run a stern-tie to a tree. The eastern arm is deep (60 feet) until very near the head and requires a stern-tie. Dundivan Inlet would not be our first choice unless weather was ugly and we were looking for a place to hole up.

Raymond Passage. Raymond Passage connects Seaforth Channel with Queens Sound and sees few pleasure craft. The passage is open, free of hazards, and connects with Codfish Passage at the south end. If you're looking for a raw and exposed wilderness experience and have the boat and navigation skills to manage it, Raymond Passage is a good choice.

Thompson Bay. Thompson Bay is on the west side of Potts Island. Examine the area on your chartplotter or study Chart 3938. At the northeast corner of Thompson Bay an excellent, protected cove indents Potts Island. Enter the cove from the north, at

52°09.75'N/128°20.75'W. This entire area is beautiful and seldom visited.

To get from Raymond Passage to Thompson Bay, run a course of approximately 239° magnetic from the southern tip of Alleyne Island to the 45-meter island, then turn to a course of approximately 292° magnetic to **Agnew Islet**. You will leave Seen Island approximately one-quarter mile to the south. Rocks will be all around you, but stay in the pass and you will have water.

Milbanke Sound. Milbanke Sound is the shortest route north or south for boats trying to make time along the Inside Passage. In quiet conditions Milbanke Sound is easy. But if the wind is blowing the crossing can be brutal.

From Seaforth Channel to Finlayson Channel, leave Ivory Island to starboard and lay a course that passes north of Susan Rock and west of Vancouver Rock Buoy *E54*. From there, lay a course to the mouth of Finlayson Channel. Our course took us fairly close to Jorkins Point and the east side of Swindle Island. Total distance was about 12 miles. We've seen boats pass east of Vancouver Rock and take Merilia Passage. This saves about a mile.

Tuno Creek Anchorage. "At the south end of Reid Passage, Blair Inlet extends nearly 2 miles eastward into the Don Peninsula. Tuno Creek empties into the head of Blair Inlet.

FULL MOON PARTY AND THE MESS AFTERWARDS

On June 23rd I was moored at Rescue Bay. As night fell, a particularly bright full moon rose from the horizon: the supermoon. When a full moon coincides with the moon's closest pass to Earth, the moon appears particularly large. Thus, the term *supermoon*.

During this celestial event, tides are at their absolute peak. This means currents are particularly strong, but more importantly, any buoyant material sitting below the highest high tide line will be washed into the water.

On June 24th the seas were calm.

Mathieson Channel, Perceval Narrows and Seaforth Channel were packed with logs and there was no wind to push the logs and other debris back to shore. All day I dodged log after

log. Some were rafted together, others floated independently. One thing was for sure: the supermoon party was over, but someone forgot to clean up the mess.

– Mark Bunzel

Anchor south of the creek in 25 to 30 feet, good holding over mud. Strong westerly winds probably will reach the anchorage, but wind protection is good from other directions." [*Hamilton*]

Reid Passage & Port Blackney. If there's much wind at all, most pleasure craft headed north or south will avoid Milbanke Sound and use the Reid Passage route east of Ivory Island. Chart 3710 makes navigation straightforward. At the south end, be sure to identify all the rocks and islets, and Buoy *E50*. In the middle of Reid Passage, pass to the east of Carne Rock. Port Blackney, at the north end of Reid Passage, has two anchorages, Boat Inlet and Oliver Cove, that can be used before crossing to Perceval Narrows.

Boat Inlet. Boat Inlet, at the southwest corner of Port Blackney, has a delightful basin for anchorage, with an untouched feeling. The passage that leads to the basin is shallow, however, and rocks encumber the south shore and middle of the channel. Favor the north shore all the way in, with an alert lookout for underwater rocks. The little bay on the north shore at the east end of the passage is shallow and rocky. Stay out. Depending on your vessel's draft, wait for half tide or higher before running Boat Inlet.

Oliver Cove. Oliver Cove Marine Provincial Park, on the east side of Port Blackney, is a safe and pretty anchorage. Enter carefully to avoid a charted rock in the middle of the fairway, and put the hook down in 35 feet.

Perceval Narrows. The Inside Passage route leads across Mathieson Channel between Port Blackney and Perceval Narrows. Tidal current predictions are found as a secondary station under Prince Rupert in Tide and Current Tables, Vol. 7 and Ports and Passes. From south to north, lay a course that gives Cod Reefs a good offing to port as you leave Port Blackney. Then turn to approximately 270° magnetic and cross Mathieson Channel toward Martha Island, leaving Lizzie Rocks to starboard. We found turbulence in Mathieson Channel off Lizzie Rocks on an ebb tide.

Cockle Bay/Lady Douglas Island. Cockle Bay, a short distance north of Perceval Narrows, has a beautiful beach and good protection from westerlies. You can find 30- to 35-foot depths along the south shore and 60 to 90 feet in the middle, as shown on the chart.

Tom Bay. Tom Bay is on the east side of Mathieson Channel at lat 52°24.20'N. It's a good anchorage, though scarred by recent logging. As with most bays on this coast, Tom Bay shoals at the head. Anchor in 60 to 70 feet.

Dowager Island & Arthur Island. The coves north of Arthur Island, approximately 1.5 miles south of Oscar Passage on the west side of Mathieson Channel, are mentioned in

As Jackson Narrows draw near, steer to avoid kelp on the right side of the channel. At right: This rock, surrounded by kelp, is in the squeaky part of the Narrows.

Sailing Directions as a small boat anchorage. Neither cove is very scenic and driftwood clogs the eastern cove. We would choose Rescue Bay on Susan Island, Salmon Bay to the north, or Tom Bay to the south.

Salmon Bay. Salmon Bay is on the east side of Mathieson Channel, opposite the mouth of Oscar Passage. It is deep until the very head, where the bottom comes up to 50 to 60 feet. The bay is cozy and we heard a loon—always a refreshing sound.

Oscar Passage. Oscar Passage is the wide-open Inside Passage route between Mathieson Channel and Finlayson Channel. On an ebb, however, the seas can heap up where Oscar Passage joins Finlayson Channel, the result of swells from Milbanke Sound meeting outflowing current. In relatively quiet conditions, with little wind, we found these seas uncomfortable, and don't plan to repeat the experience. Jackson Passage, a short distance north, is our choice now, even if we must wait for slack water at Jackson Narrows.

Rescue Bay. Rescue Bay is the most popular anchorage in this area. It is well protected with good holding, and has room for many boats. Study the chart carefully before entering, and steer a determined mid-channel course between the two islands and their reefs that mark the entrance. Once inside Rescue Bay, scout around with the depth sounder and pick your spot carefully. We saw one boat on the western side find the bottom at low tide, after being too eager to get the anchor down.

Note the drying rock in the southeast corner of the bay. Note also the drying reef that extends from the east side of the bay, south of the round islet. The reef covers at high water, and we anchored a little close to it. After checking things out by dinghy and seeing how near the reef was, we re-anchored

farther out. At low water the reef showed itself. We were glad we had moved.

Jackson Passage. Jackson Passage is the scenic route between Mathieson Channel and Finlayson Channel. The passage is easily navigated, except for a tight spot at Jackson Narrows at the eastern end, where the depth shows as low as 12 feet on the charts. The fairway through Jackson Narrows is quite narrow, and kelp marks the rocks. While neither the chart nor Sailing Directions shows the current directions, our observations from several transits indicate the flood current sets east and the ebb current sets west.

Jackson Narrows is blind. Before entering, either direction, it's a good idea to call ahead on VHF channel 16, low power, to announce your intentions (*Securité, securité, this is the 34-foot motor vessel Happy Days, about to enter Jackson Narrows eastbound. Any westbound traffic please advise, channel one-six*). One year, to our astonishment, a boat approaching the other end called back on channel 16. Since we were about to enter, the other boat waited until we got through. Strongly favor the *south shore* all the way through the narrows, and keep a sharp lookout. A transit near high water slack would be the least anxious, although we have gone through at low water slack with no difficulty.

James Bay. James Bay, on the west side of Mathieson Channel, is open to southerly winds, but gets you out of the chop in the channel. It is a pretty spot, but the bottom shoals abruptly in the northwest corner. Anchor in 75 feet, where the little anchor symbol is on the chart.

We aren't good enough photographers to capture the size, scale and impact of Fiordland.

Waterfalls abound in Kynoch Inlet.

FIORDLAND RECREATION AREA

The Fiordland Recreation Area was established in 1987 and is some of the most striking country on the coast. The mountains are sheer and beautiful and the wildlife abundant, but anchorages are just about nonexistent. Fortunately, good anchorage can be found in Windy Bay, only a short distance away.

Fiordland begins just east of Bolin Bay at the north end of Sheep Passage and includes Mussel Inlet and Kynoch Inlet. We include Bolin Bay in this section because it is so pretty and Windy Bay because it is the best anchorage near Fiordland.

Windy Bay. Windy Bay is on the south shore of Sheep Passage near the eastern end. The chart shows anchorage in the middle, but more protected anchorage is in 60 feet in what we call **Cookie Cove**, just east of the little island at the northeast corner of the bay. Excellent holding.

Bolin Bay. Bolin Bay is set in a bowl of sheer rock mountains with a beautiful drying flat at the head. We didn't anchor, but we did find a few spots with depths of 35 to 60 feet near the head of the bay. With care you might get a safe amount of scope out and stay off the flats. Windy Bay is a better choice.

Oatwish Bay. Oatwish Bay is at the north end of Mussel Inlet. Amazing Lizette Falls will have you reaching for the camera. The bay is too deep for anchoring. We enjoyed lunch there, drifting, engines off.

Poison Cove. The run to the east of Mussel Inlet to Poison Cove left us awestruck. Our notes say, "Poison Cove dwarfed us. I run out of superlatives."

Kynoch Inlet & Culpepper Lagoon. Kynoch Inlet is off Mathieson Channel. Mouth 52°45.55'N/ 128°08.00'W. On a coast filled with unspeakable beauty, no places we have seen surpass Kynoch Inlet. Most fall well short. Words such as *amazing, awesome, incomparable* and *magnificent* suggest but do not capture the grandeur of this inlet. It starts with the large Kynoch waterfalls and continues with black rock mountains that rise straight up and lead away into bowls of rock. Waterfalls spill down the faces of the mountains. One waterfall shoots out into the channel. The inlet is so narrow and the sides are so steep that our GPS lost its satellites. Unfortunately, the year-round snowfield that once extended almost to the water near the head of Kynoch Inlet has melted away com-

pletely. Anchor at the head of the inlet off the drying flats of Lard Creek or continue into Culpepper Lagoon.

Culpepper Lagoon. Enter or depart Culpepper Lagoon around slack water. Bill Hales, one of our early correspondents, says the current in the entrance turns 15 to 30 minutes before high or low water at Bella Bella, with a least depth of 10 to 15 feet. Gil Flanagan, another of our excellent correspondents, adds to those thoughts, along with personal experience in the narrows when they are running.

Flanagan went into Culpepper Lagoon around high slack without difficulty. Coming out the next morning was a different matter. They departed on a falling tide, an hour or two before low water slack. Flanagan reports: "We could hear the roar of the rapids well before we could see the narrows in the fog. I went for it, but it was quite a ride. We estimated the current in the narrows at 7.5 knots, and we are sure we dropped more than a foot. The depth sounder was unusable because of the turbulence. We didn't have time to look at it, anyway. There was no turning back. Just steer the sled to the bottom of the hill and hope we miss the Kainet Creek mudflats. Yahoo!"

After comparing Bella Bella tides with Hiekish Narrows current predictions, Flanagan thinks Hiekish Narrows might be a better predictor of slack water. At this point the Waggoner draws no conclusions, except to arrive early and—unlike our correspondent—wait for slack water before going through.

On our own visit to Culpepper Lagoon we went through the narrows an hour after low water at Bella Bella with no difficulty at all. We tried to anchor off Riot Creek, where an old cabin is shown on the chart. We didn't see the cabin (Douglass, in the 2nd Edition of his North Coast book, says the cabin has burned down), and couldn't find a place we liked to put the hook down. Flanagan anchored south of the Lard Creek mudflats at the head of Culpepper Lagoon, inshore from the 60-foot sounding. He saw a sailboat anchored southwest of the Lard Creek mouth.

CHARTS			
3736	Kitimat & Kemano Bay (1:12,000)	3945	Approaches to Douglas Channel (1:40,000)
3743	Douglas Channel (1:73,032)	3946	Grenville Channel (1:40,000) (Replaces Chart 3772)
3911 Plans	Vicinity of Princess Royal Island (1:25,000)	3947	Grenville Channel to Chatham Sound (1:40,000) (Replaces Chart 3773)
3927	Bonilla Island to Edye Passage (1:77,800)		
3938	Queens Sound to Seaforth Channel (1:40,000)	3955 Plans	Prince Rupert Harbor, Venn Passage
3941	Channels Vicinity of Milbanke Sound (1:40,000)	3957	Approaches to Prince Rupert Harbour (1:40,000)
3944	Princess Royal Channel (1:40,000) (Replaces Chart 3739)	3958	Prince Rupert Harbour (1:20,000)

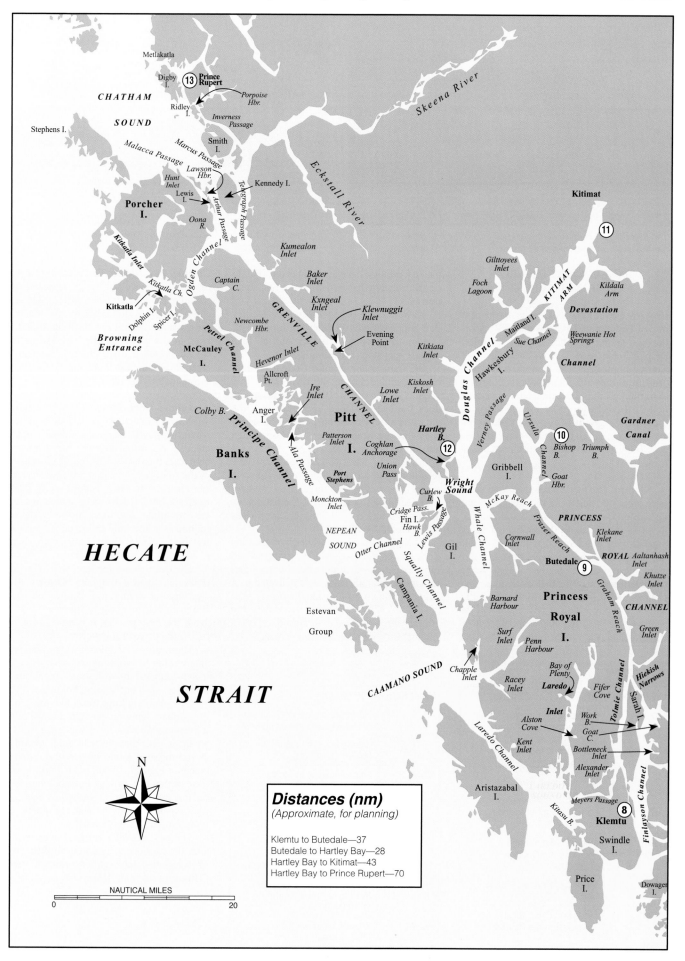

Metlakatla

Digby
I.

⑬ **Prince Rupert**

Porpoise Hbr.

Ridley I.

CHATHAM

SOUND

Stephens I.

Inverness Passage

Skeena River

Smith I.

Marcus Passage

Malacca Passage

Lawson Hbr.

Kennedy I.

Eckstall River

Kitimat

⑪

Hunt Inlet

Lewis I.

Telegraph Passage

Porcher I.

Oona R.

Arthur Passage

Kumealon Inlet

Gilttoyees Inlet

KITIMAT ARM

Kildala Arm

Kitkatla Inlet

Kitkatla Ch.

Kitkatla

Dolphin I.

Spicer I.

Ogden Channel

Captain C.

Baker Inlet

Kxngeal Inlet

Klewnuggit Inlet

Foch Lagoon

Devastation

Weewanie Hot Springs

Browning Entrance

Newcombe Hbr.

GRENVILLE

Evening Point

Kitkiata Inlet

Maitland I.

Sue Channel

Channel

McCauley I.

Petrel Channel

Hevenor Inlet

Allcroft Pt.

Ire Inlet

Lowe Inlet

Kiskosh Inlet

Douglas Channel

Hawkesbury I.

Verney Passage

Gardner Canal

Colby B.

Principe Channel

Anger I.

CHANNEL

Pitt I.

Patterson Inlet

Coghlan Anchorage

Hartley B.

⑫

Ursula Channel

⑩ Bishop B.

Triumph B.

Banks I.

Ala Passage

Port Stephens

Union Pass

Wright Sound

Gribbell I.

Goat Hbr.

Monckton Inlet

Curlew B.

Cridge Pass.

Fin I.

Hawk B.

Lewis Passage

McKay Reach

PRINCESS

Klekane Inlet

HECATE

NEPEAN SOUND

Otter Channel

Gil I.

Whale Channel

Cornwall Inlet

Fraser Reach

ROYAL

Aaltanhash Inlet

Butedale ⑨

Khutze Inlet

Squally Channel

Campania I.

Estevan Group

Barnard Harbour

CHANNEL

Green Inlet

STRAIT

Surf Inlet

Penn Harbour

Princess Royal I.

Graham Reach

CAAMANO SOUND

Chapple Inlet

Racey Inlet

Bay of Plenty

Laredo

Fifer Cove

Tolmie Channel

Hiekish Narrows

Inlet

Alston Cove

Work B.

Sarah I.

Kent Inlet

Goat C.

Laredo Channel

Bottleneck Inlet

Alexander Inlet

Aristazabal I.

Meyers Passage

Finlayson Channel

Kitasu B.

⑧ **Klemtu**

Swindle I.

Price I.

Dowager I.

Distances (nm)
(Approximate, for planning)

Klemtu to Butedale—37
Butedale to Hartley Bay—28
Hartley Bay to Kitimat—43
Hartley Bay to Prince Rupert—70

N

NAUTICAL MILES

0　　　　　　　20

The fuel dock at Klemtu is located just below the fish processing facility and can be very noisy.

The interior of the Big House across the bay from Klemtu.

FINLAYSON CHANNEL TO PRINCE RUPERT

Nowish Cove. Nowish Cove is on the east side of Finlayson Channel, south of Jackson Passage, at the entrance to Nowish Inlet. Despite being shown as an anchorage, we weren't impressed. The bottom is 85 feet deep and currents from Nowish Narrows swirl through the bay. If protection is needed from a southerly storm we would consider this cove. Otherwise, if we were looking for a place to hide and had the time, Bottleneck Inlet, 11 miles farther north, is a better choice.

⑧ Klemtu. The fuel dock and Kitasoo band store are at the north end of town. Both are open Monday through Saturday, closed for lunch 12:00 p.m. to 1:00 p.m., limited hours Sundays. The Band Store has an ATM. You'll find gasoline, diesel, propane, stove oil, and ample clear water from the village's water treatment system. The fuel dock faces the channel and wakes from passing boat traffic are apt to bounce you against the dock. Be sure you are well-tied and well-fendered. If the attendant is not in the office shack on the pier, try calling First Nations Fuel on VHF 06 or ask someone in town what the fuel situation is.

Klemtu is the last fuel stop until Hartley Bay, approximately 65 miles north. In 2012, Hartley Bay temporarily ran out of fuel. Choose fuel stops accordingly.

BC Ferries and Pacific Coastal Airlines have scheduled service into Klemtu.

An 11-foot-wide, 210-foot-long concrete dock has been installed in the bay near the village. The dock has no power. The washrooms at the head of the dock have fallen into disrepair.

The village has a K-12 school, land line telephones, good cell phone coverage, two nurses, a post office and three stores. We have shopped in two of the stores: the band store at the fuel dock, and Robinson-Mason General Store in the village.

The band store at the head of the fuel dock pier carries a selection of groceries and other essentials (no liquor), but the stock gets thin a few days after the ferry delivered it. A pay telephone is just outside the store.

If you'd like to see the extraordinary Big House, contact George Robinson on VHF channel 06. Tours are $10 per person.

Clothes Bay. Clothes Bay is south of Klemtu on the west side of the channel, between Swindle Island and Cone Island. The bay appears open to the southeast. We anchored for the night behind the north tip of Star Island, at the mouth of the bay. At low tide we discovered that the charted "something" extending from Base Point, north of us, was a substantial drying reef.

Alexander Inlet. Alexander Inlet extends 5 miles into Princess Royal Island, beginning where Meyers Passage and Tolmie Channel meet. If you're fed up with the throngs of boaters and crowded anchorages on this part of the coast (we're joking), here is where you can escape. The early sections of Alexander Inlet are bordered by steep mountains, and are beautiful. The head, however, is surrounded by low hills and is rather ordinary. But, being 5 miles off the beaten path, chances are you'll be the only boat.

The chart shows the inlet well. The only tricky part is near Bingham Narrows. After clearing the drying reef before you reach Bingham Narrows, sag to the west shore to avoid the drying rocks, marked by kelp, just before the narrows themselves.

The head of the inlet is wide open, with ample room to avoid the rock that dries 2.4 meters lying off the west shore. Anchor in 30 to 35 feet with outstanding holding.

One of the hilltops looks like the profile of a woman lying on her side, and we called it Sleeping Woman. See if you agree. We saw a pair of birds that our field guide identified as red-throated loons, not seen as often as common loons. A lagoon pours into the very head of the inlet, making fluffs of white foam on the water's surface. We rowed over and took pictures, but didn't take the time to explore further. It's very pretty.

The next morning our final note, written after the previous day's notes called the head of Alexander Inlet rather ordinary, reads, "This is a neat spot." [*Hale*]

CHARTS

West Side of Princess Royal Island

3721	Harbours on the West Coast of Pitt Island, Mink Trap Bay & Adjacent Inlets, Port Stephens & Monckton Inlet, Buchan Inlet (1:18,300)
3723 Plans	Hecate Strait, East Shore (Various scales)
3737	Laredo Channel Including Surf Inlet (1:77,400)
3910 Plans	Milbanke Sound and Beauchemin Channel (1:20,000)
3911 Plans	Vicinity of Princess Royal Island (1:25,000)
3943	Finlayson Channel and Tolmie Channel (1:40,000)

West Side of Pitt Island

3721	Harbours on the West Coast of Pitt Island (Various scales)
3741	Otter Passage to Bonilla Island (1:72,900)
3742	Otter Passage to McKay Reach (1:72,900)
3927	Bonilla Island to Edye Passage (1:77,800)
3945	Approaches to Douglas Channel (1:40,000)
3984	Principe Channel (1:40,000)
3985	Principe Channel Central Portion & Petrel Channel (1:40,000)
3987	Kitkatla Channel & Porcher Inlet (1:40,000)

OUTSIDE ROUTE – PRINCESS ROYAL ISLAND & PITT ISLAND

At this point we step away from the main Inside Passage route to describe the routes west of Princess Royal and Pitt Islands. Those continuing through Finlayson or Tolmie Channels, past Butedale, and through Grenville Channel will find that information resuming on page 402.

Without question, the preferred Inside Passage route to Prince Rupert and beyond is through Finlayson or Tolmie Channels (past Klemtu), past Butedale, and up through Grenville Channel. The waters are protected, the scenery is outstanding and there's enough boat traffic that if you have a problem, somebody will be along to help out.

An alternate route is on the outside of Princess Royal and Pitt Islands. This route is popular with sailors and adventuresome motorboaters. It's as beautiful as the traditional route, but wilder and much less traveled, with more islands and anchorages but fewer waterfalls. Sailors will find more consistent and stronger winds due to the wider channels and lower hills. There's even room for tacking. Because of their remoteness, we recommend these passages for more experienced cruisers only.

From south to north, the outside route first leads up the west side of Princess Royal Island. It begins by running west through Meyers Passage (near Klemtu), then through Laredo Channel and Whale Channel, and rejoins the Inside Passage at Wright Sound. To cruise the outside of Pitt Island, the route runs west from Wright Sound (south end of Grenville Channel), and north through Principe Channel and Petrel Channel, then east through Ogden Channel to rejoin the Inside Passage.

On the outside of either island you could travel all day and only see one or two other pleasure boats, although you're sure to see a few fishing boats and perhaps a tug and barge, or even a cruise ship. You'll find good anchorages on the outside. In many cases you'll be the only boat.

Weather permitting, you could travel the traditional Inside Passage going one way and all or part of the outside route going the other. The inside and outside routes are roughly the same distance. However, if you take only part of the outside route, going back and forth between the inside and the outside, your total trip will be longer. If you are considering the outside route, carry *Sailing Directions* PAC 206, and *Exploring the North Coast of B.C.,* 2nd Ed., by Don Douglass and Réanne Hemmingway-Douglass. The Waggoner describes only the most direct outside routes and focuses on good anchorages. The other books cover a wider area and describe places that require caution and may be more challenging than some skippers would like. If you have the desire for a coastal cruising challenge, with the boat and skills to meet that challenge, the west coast of Princess Royal

Island and Pitt Island are excellent cruising areas.

If winds are favorable, sailboats (or slower powerboats) can cut almost a day off their time on the outside route with an open water passage that avoids Klemtu and Meyers Passage. Northbound, go out Seaforth Channel, cross Milbanke Sound, and transit Catala Passage. Or, go around McInnes Island and its lighthouse, then north up Laredo Sound to Laredo Inlet. This open water route has no stops until you reach Laredo Inlet, so pick your weather carefully. Pay careful attention to your chartplotter or charts in Catala Passage. The islands and rocks are easily confused, especially in fog. Watch for cruise ships and freighters that occasionally use Laredo Sound.

WEST SIDE OF PRINCESS ROYAL ISLAND

LOCAL KNOWLEDGE

NAVIGATION NOTE: Red spar Buoy *E70* is in the middle of the tight spot in Meyers Passage. Pass north of the buoy, midway between the buoy and the north shore. Currents to 3 knots flood east and ebb west. Sailing Directions says least depth at zero tide is 4 feet. Kelp shows the places to avoid.

Meyers Passage. Meyers Passage separates Swindle Island and Princess Royal Island and is the low-anxiety way to travel between Finlayson Channel and Laredo Sound. The only tricky spot is kelp-choked Meyers Narrows. Although the narrows are not difficult to run, the kelp may cause concern the first time through.

We went through slowly, not liking the kelp but pressing on because others told us we should. When we got through we said, "Piece of cake."

Although we have not tried it, our fisherman friend Mike Guns says there's good anchorage in 45 feet in the bay on the south shore of the passage.

Laredo Channel. Laredo Channel separates Princess Royal Island and Aristazabal Island, connecting Laredo Sound at the south end with Caamaño Sound and Campania Sound at the north end. Aristazabal Island, on the west side of Laredo Channel, is incompletely charted and considered extremely challenging. We have not explored it.

While several inlets lead off Laredo Channel into Princess Royal Island, Laredo Inlet at the south end and Surf Inlet at the north end are the major indents.

LOCAL KNOWLEDGE

INACCURATE CHART: We've heard reports that Chart 3737 is based on an unknown datum, resulting in significant inaccu-

racies. Electronic charts based on Chart 3737 have similar inaccuracies.

Laredo Inlet. Laredo Inlet is about 10 miles long, and is well protected from westerly storms. If you're approaching from the south, such as from Meyers Passage, the closest entry is through **Thistle Passage.** Rocks extend first from the east side of the narrows, then from the west side. They aren't shown well on the chart. We went through at the top of a 12.8-foot tide. We didn't see any sign of the rocks and they were not marked by kelp. Caution advised. The chart shows 4½ fathoms least depth at the north end of the narrows. Douglass says the depth actually is more like 3 fathoms (18 feet). Our depth sounder suggested it was somewhat less than 18 feet. If you go through Thistle Passage at low water, watch your depths.

Palmer Anchorage. Fisherman Mike Guns suggests Palmer Anchorage at the south end of Thistle Passage as a good wait-and-see temporary anchorage in a northwest gale, but it's deep, and not what we'd select as the best overnight cruising anchorage.

While several overnight anchorages are available in Laredo Inlet, consider Alston Cove, Bay of Plenty, and Fifer Cove. We spent the night in Alston Cove and explored Fifer Cove and Bay of Plenty.

Quigley Creek Cove. From the top of Thistle Passage, turn east just beyond the first small island, leaving the remaining islands to port, then follow the shore into a landlocked basin at the mouth of Quigley Creek. The basin has a depth of about 60 feet at zero tide. A beautiful spot, protected by surrounding islands from wind and waves. This is one of the few outer channel anchorages that you might share with another boat.

Alston Cove. Mouth 52°45.10'N/128°45 .75'W. Lovely Alston Cove is easy to enter and is surrounded by mountain peaks. We put the hook down in sticky brown mud just onto the 6½-fathom area on the north side of the cove, near the flats. When we departed the next morning we were glad to have the anchor washdown system. It took a long time to hose the chain and anchor clean. Correspondents Laurie and Anita Dowsett told us they found Native fish traps with salmon in them.

Fifer Cove. Mouth 52°52.15'N/128°45 .15'W. Fifer Cove is surrounded by mountain peaks and is very scenic, but most of the cove is too deep for easy anchoring. To enter, wrap around Tuite Point, leaving it to starboard. We found 40- to 50-foot depths near the head of the cove, off the stream mouth. Correspondents James and Jennifer Hamilton report the creek shoals out much farther than the chart indicates or they expected, and holding was poor.

These extraordinary falls are at the head of Surf Inlet.

Kohl Island Anchorage. "Kohl Island is in Weld Cove, directly south of Bay of Plenty. The bight at the northwest tip of Kohl Island is a sheltered anchorage with mountain views. Approach between Kohl and Pocock Islands and turn west when clear of the rocks off the north tip of Kohl Island. The anchorage is at 52°49.00'N/128°46.09'W between two uncharted rocks. One rock rarely covers and the other is awash at 12 feet. We dropped the anchor between the rocks and pulled back 150 feet to stern-tie onto Kohl Island. Holding was good in 10 to 20 feet over mud and shell." [*Hamilton*]

Bay of Plenty. Mouth 52°49.90'N/128°45.15'W. Bay of Plenty was recommended to us by Correspondents Mike Guns and Laurie and Anita Dowsett. On our chart, Guns drew the entrance channel south of the 120-foot island, and north of the little islet in the middle of the Bay. Anchor in 30 feet, short of the flats. Those flats, by the way, come out a long way. We almost drove onto them. The bay is open to southwest storms. Not recommended if weather is approaching.

Our chart notes from the Dowsetts say Bay of Plenty is great for crabbing and fishing.

Buie Creek. "A spectacular two-level waterfall is a short distance up Buie Creek at the head of Laredo Inlet. To visit, anchor temporarily off the head of Laredo Inlet at 52°58.128'N/128°39.763'W in 90 feet with a 250-foot swing radius, moderate holding." [*Hamilton*]

Kent Inlet. Kent Inlet is on the east side of Laredo Channel. Mouth 52°41.40'N/129°00.85'W. Once inside, Kent Inlet is scenic and appears to be well protected. To get inside, however, you must go through Phillip Narrows, which is guarded by rocks. Sailing Directions says currents through Phillip Narrows run to 8 knots at

spring tides, and recommends a transit at slack water only.

We arrived at Kent Inlet near high water slack, so we went in. Kelp marked the rocks at the entrance, off Laredo Channel, and they were not a problem. Kelp did not mark the rocks a short distance east of Loap Point, however; we went into emergency reverse to stay clear. Those rocks are out in the middle, exactly where you think you want to be. Stay south of those rocks. Give them room.

At slack water Philip Narrows was easy. Correspondents Laurie and Anita Dowsett recommended anchoring either near the west shore immediately inside Phillip Narrows, or in the back basin off the tidal waterfall. Favor the north shore to get to the back basin. The water in Kent Inlet was dark with rain runoff when we visited; we couldn't see more than a foot or two into it. We had good depths all around the point that defines the back basin.

Surf Inlet. Surf Inlet stretches 13 miles into Princess Royal Island at the north end of Laredo Channel, ending at a stunning waterfall over a dam that separates Bear Lake from the inlet. The water in Surf Inlet was brown from rain runoff when we visited. Our wake was a creamy tan color.

An abandoned concrete power house is on a point below the dam at the head of Surf Inlet, and when we visited, logs (individual logs, not a raft) were moored offshore. A road leads to a point on the opposite side of the stream outlet below the falls. Perhaps the best way to get ashore would be to tie to the off-shore logs and take the dinghy in, although a tug could bring a log raft in and then you'd be in trouble. We've been told that if you can get a dinghy up to the dam (the road looks like the way to go), you can go up Bear Lake to an old mining camp that is surprisingly intact.

Chapple Inlet, at the mouth of Surf Inlet, has a few anchorage possibilities, but Surf Inlet itself has only one, Penn Harbour.

Penn Harbour. Mouth 52°57.95'N/128°58.35'W. Penn Harbour is beautiful and spacious, with a straightforward entry and ample anchoring room in 40 to 50 feet near the head. A stream cascades into the east end and makes little white icebergs of foam on the surface—except that on the night of our visit the icebergs weren't white, they were tan. The water was brown and the anchor turned brown as it penetrated the surface. It disappeared altogether within a foot or two.

Chapple Inlet. Chapple Inlet leads north from the mouth of Surf Inlet, and has anchorage possibilities. These include a little nook on the west shore at Doig Anchorage, another nook behind Chettleburgh Point, and in Kiln Bay. Entry to Chapple Inlet is easy at Mallandaine Point. Simply follow a midchannel course along the east shore.

At **Doig Anchorage**, try the area just north of the point at 52°55.10'N/129°07.80'W. We didn't verify the depths, but we saw three rafted powerboats anchored and stern-tied to shore.

Behind **Chettleburgh Point**, at approximately 52°56.60'N/129°08.60'W, we would anchor in 60 feet, with ample swinging room. This is where you will appreciate an all-chain anchor rode so you can swing in a smaller circle on shorter scope. If you move closer in for shallower water you'll probably want to run a stern-tie to shore.

In **Kiln Bay**, anchor in 60 feet, north of the little island at approximately 52°57.95'N/129°08.85'W.

Emily Carr Inlet. Emily Carr Inlet is on the north side of Surf Inlet, right at the mouth. The inlet is beautiful, but you'll need Plans Chart 3719 for the rock-lined inlet itself and Chart 3737 to see the approaches. We think you'll also need the dinghy to give the rocks and islets a thorough exploration.

The main body of the inlet is open. With close attention it should present no problems. A reef, however, extends from Webber Island nearly across Holgate Passage, making the entry from Chapple Inlet a little tricky. When we visited, a fly-in fishing camp was moored in Chapple Inlet, and they marked the safe channel with floating balls.

We went through Emily Carr Inlet from north to south, then turned northeast to complete our circumnavigation of Princess Royal Island. Although the winds were light, we got into a nasty tide-rip off the 207-foot island south of Duckers Island and wet the boat down pretty thoroughly. It wasn't fun. We crowded over close to Duckers Island and found calmer water. [*Hale*]

Barnard Harbour. Mouth, west side of Borde Island, 53°04.90'N/129°07.75'W; east side of Borde Island, 53°05.20'N/129°06.65'W. Barnard Harbour is shown on Charts 3737 and 3742. If you are approaching from McKay Reach on the Inside Passage you will use Chart 3742, which shows all of Whale Channel.

Barnard Harbour is big, open, and beautiful, and a center for fly-in sport fishing. When we visited, three impressive lodges on barges were moored along the east shore. There's plenty of anchoring room for pleasure craft, however, in the Cameron Cove section of Barnard Harbour. Anchor in Cameron Cove along the west shore in 30 to 35 feet or in 40 to 60 feet off the mouth of Barnard Creek.

Campania Island. Campania Island, with its bald, knobby mountaintops, is recognizable from miles away. Several inlets on Campania Island's west shore provide sheltered anchorages, interesting views, and opportunities for exploration by kayaks and dinghies. All are well charted; use Chart 3724 and Plans Chart 3719.

McMicking Inlet. McMicking Inlet, in Estevan Sound on the west side of Campania Island, is one of the few places in the outer channels where, at least in July and August, you might have competition for the best anchoring spots. The looming granite mass of Pender Mountain makes for a dramatic anchorage, and twisted cedars growing among the rocks add to the scenic character. Use Chart 3741 and plans Chart 3719. Although the entrance to McMicking Inlet is open to the south, islets, rocks and reefs diminish any swells. Enter south and east of a chain of islets and drying reefs extending from the south end of Jewsbury Peninsula. Anchor north of the narrows.

Dunn Passage. Use Chart 3742 and Plans Chart 3719. Dunn Passage, in Estevan Sound on the west side of Campania Island, provides good shelter from all weather. Anchor at the head of Dunn Passage and explore a labyrinth of rocks and islands by dinghy or kayak.

Weinburg Inlet. From Dunn Passage, turn south one mile from the entrance, just beyond a string of connected islands, then loop around this final island before turning east into a long narrow inlet. Granite domes and stacks make this an intriguing and picturesque anchorage, although not as dramatic as McMicking Inlet.

WEST SIDE OF PITT ISLAND

This route leads from the south end of Grenville Channel.

Otter Channel. Two possible anchorages appear to be available on the south tip of Pitt Island (the north side of Otter Channel). The first is Dillon Bay, where we saw a sailboat anchored. The second is Saycuritay Cove.

Saycuritay Cove. "Securitay Cove is the official name, not labeled on the chart, for the small cove east of Fleishman Point on the southwest corner of Pitt Island. Approach from 53°12.67'N/129°33.54'W, heading

north. Favor the Pitt Island shore beyond the islet at the entrance, and wrap around the north side of the first of the three small islets inside. Minimum depth on entry is 10 feet. Anchor in 25 feet with room to swing between the first and second of the three small islets. Holding is good over a soft bottom, with reasonable wind protection and views out between the islets. Good anchoring depths also are at the 6-fathom sounding on the chart. The ruins of an old settlement, now a kayaker camp, are on the east shore of the bight in the north side of the large islet that makes up the south shore of the cove." [*Hamilton*]

Monckton Inlet. Monckton Inlet indents Pitt Island at lat 53°18.65'N. The inlet is well protected, with three anchorage possibilities. The first is in 60 feet on the back side of Monckton Point, a short distance inside the inlet on the north side. Douglass says the 60-foot-deep spot's bottom is rocky and the holding poor. Douglass recommends the 4-fathom hole in the beautiful little cove farther in, but be careful. We tried to get into that cove near the bottom of a 3-foot tide. In absolutely calm conditions, with excellent visibility into the water, the rock ledges extending from both sides of the narrow pass got too close to the surface for our cautious tastes. We backed out. If you can get in and out near high water, this would be a marvelous, snug anchorage. With propellers and rudders hanging down, however, low water access is scary.

The second anchorage is about three-quarters of the way into the inlet in the bay that extends north almost a mile behind Roy Island. Go up near the head, past the two rocks marked with a + on the chart. Anchor with lots of room in 40 to 50 feet, mud bottom. We tried to find the two rocks mentioned above, but didn't see them. They were not marked by kelp. Be aware.

This is the "street sign" for Princess Diana Cove in Patterson Inlet.

The third anchorage is at the very head of Monckton Inlet in 50 to 60 feet, mud bottom. It's not very interesting.[*Hale*]

Kooryet Bay. Kooryet Bay, on Banks Island, roughly across Principe Channel from Monkton Inlet, can provide a convenient escape when fog sets in or winds kick up in Principe Channel. Inside the bay you'll have a good vantage point for watching changing conditions in the channel. In southerly winds, anchor in the south cove. In northerly winds, anchor off the creek bed or northwest of Kooryet Island.

Patterson Inlet/Princess Diana Cove. Patterson Inlet is narrow, beautiful, and appears well protected. The entry looks straightforward enough on the charts, but we found it a little difficult to identify. A waypoint of 53°26.10'N/126°51.00'W will put you just outside. The head of the inlet divides into a north arm and a south arm. The south arm is very pretty, with a stunning rock wall on the north side near the entry. The bottom is 90 feet deep, though, and a grown-over log booming ground is near the head. We see no need to anchor in the south arm.

A sign on a tree identified the north arm as Princess Diana Cove and that's where you want to be (we're told the sign was gone in 2009). We overnighted there. It was a perfect anchorage, 25 to 30 feet deep, thick mud bottom. Anchor in the middle. Rocks and reefs sneak up along the shores.

Note: A reader tells us this bay was not good in a southeast gale.

About the sign on the tree: Some of the best anchorages along this route (Princess Diana Cove, Colby Bay, Newcombe Harbour) have been marked with rustic signs attached to trees near the entrances.

Ire Inlet. Ire Inlet is entered from Ala Passage at latitude 53°30'N. The entry is narrow and quite dramatic, but the fairway is clear. The hillsides are covered with remarkable trees. They are tall and straight with very short limbs. They look like green pipe cleaners. The trees on top of the rock mountain on the north side of Ire Inlet are twisted and have few limbs. From our distance they looked like bonsai trees.

The little cove on the south shore has rocks as shown on Chart 3984 but not on 3741. Not a good spot. A much better anchorage is between the little islet and the head of the inlet in 20 to 25 feet. Pass north of the little islet. Rocks lie off the south side, and a large drying shoal extends from the south shore of the inlet.

If you visit Ire Inlet (recommended), study the chart carefully before entering Ala Passage. A number of islets and drying rocks must be identified and located. Everything is straightforward, but this is one of those places where you have to know exactly where you are and exactly where you are headed.

The view out the mouth of Bottleneck Inlet the morning after a storm. At high tide the entry looks wide, but a rock ledge extends from the south shore.

Azimuth Island. Mike Guns put us onto this one. A small unnamed island lies southwest of Azimuth Island and a convenient anchorage is behind that island at 53°31.45'N/129°59.50'W on the chart. Anchor in 60 to 65 feet. Be sure to enter this anchorage from the north. The southern entry is foul with rocks.

Tangent Island. Tangent Island lies in a cluster of islands located north of Anger Island near the intersection of Petrel and Principe Channels. The cove on the east side of Tangent Island provides good protection with a view to the mountains of Pitt Island to the east. Although the anchorage is deep (100 feet), it has good holding and is well protected. Tangent Island also provides an opportunity for a trigonometry lesson. Enter via Markle Passage, passing between Sine Point to the west, Tangent Point to the east and Logarithm Point to the south.

Colby Bay. Colby Bay is on Banks Island, the west side of Principe Channel, at latitude 53°32.10'N. Go down the middle and anchor in 30 feet where the bay opens up. You'll be surrounded by mountains and protected from northwest or southeast gale winds in Principe Channel. Mike Guns, who first recommended Colby Bay to us, called this spot "a joy."

Petrel Channel. Petrel Channel begins at the south tip of McCauley Island and winds along the west side of Pitt Island to Captain Cove. It has four anchorages, all on the Pitt Island side.

Allcroft Point. Just south of Allcroft Point, at lat 53°35.65'N, is an unnamed bay that gets you off Petrel Channel. Anchor in 75 to 90 feet when you get to the wide spot. The chart shows a rock awash at zero tide obstructing access to the back cove. You may prefer Hevenor Inlet.

Hevenor Inlet. Hevenor Inlet stretches 5 miles into Pitt Island's mountains and you have to go all the way to the head of the inlet for suitable anchorage. The hills on both sides have been clearcut, but already are green again. Anchor in 35 to 60 feet off the falls (you'll see them) or off the mouth of the lagoon.

Newcombe Harbour. Newcombe Harbour is marked with another of those signs attached to trees. It's a fine, well-protected anchorage. Motor straight in and anchor off the drying flats in 40 to 50 feet. We wouldn't bother with the little nook on the east shore, a short distance inside the entrance. It is rather tight and not that exciting. With such good, easy anchorage only a little farther in, it's not worth the effort. The log booms reported in the Douglass *Exploring the North Coast of British Columbia* were not there when we visited.

Captain Cove. Captain Cove is a cozy, protected anchorage at the northwest corner of Pitt Island, near the south entrance to Ogden Channel. Anchor in 60 to 80 feet in the large basin behind the 84-foot island, or in the 5-fathom basin along the south shore, behind the little dot islet. We have anchored twice in the 5-fathom basin and once behind the 84-foot island. If you don't mind 70 to 80 feet, the anchorage behind the island is excellent.

Kitkatla. Kitkatla is a Native village on the north end of Dolphin Island, west of Ogden Channel. It's a pleasant community. Fuel is available by jerry jug. Ann's B&B and gift shop has cedar weaving for sale—small baskets to conical hats.

Don't plan to stop at Kitkatla on a Saturday. Most of the village goes shopping in Prince Rupert on the weekend.

We left Bully Island to port and went up Kitkatla Channel, leaving the Kitkatla Islands to starboard. Sailing Directions says a church spire is a significant Kitkatla landmark from the water, but new construction makes the spire less significant. Green Buoy *E95* marks the end of a rocky shoal when you get close to the moorage area, and a little island lies beyond. Leave Buoy *E95* to port and turn toward shore. Head for the large loading dock, leaving the little island to starboard.

Go slowly. Kelp marks the shallow spots. Once past the island, run right along the public dock or as close as the rafted boats allow. Rocks lie along the island.

Deep draft boats beware: depth alongside the dock is approximately 6.5 feet at zero tide.

INSIDE PASSAGE ROUTE, CONTINUED

Mary Cove. Mary Cove is on the east side of Finlayson Channel across from Klemtu. It is a pleasant little cove, but it appears open to southwest winds. Anchor in 50 to 55 feet inside. A salmon stream empties into Mary Cove.

Bottleneck Inlet. Bottleneck Inlet, at latitude 52°42.8'N on the east side of Finlayson Channel, is an outstanding anchorage. It is protected and beautiful, and large enough for a number of boats. The north side of the inlet has superb rock walls. The chart shows a least depth of just over a fathom in the narrow entry, and a rock shelf extends from the south shore at the narrow part. Favor the north shore. Deeper draft vessels should enter cautiously at low tide. The chart fails to show a 13-15 fathom hole a short distance inside the entry sill. The bottom then comes up to 25-30 feet.

Although we have anchored in Bottleneck Inlet several times now, one night in particular was memorable. That was the night a forewarned on-shore gale struck the coast. Four people died in that storm. At 1:30 a.m. the winds hit. We could see clouds racing overhead and hear the wind roaring in the trees above us, but except for four tongues of strong wind that slammed into our boat between 1:30 a.m. and 4:00 a.m., the air around us was almost calm. [*Hale*]

Anchoring caution: A deadhead that covers and uncovers with the tide is near the head of Bottleneck Inlet along the south shore, at 52°42.588'N/128°24.104'W. A white buoy has been attached to it. At high water the buoy doesn't mark a crabpot, it marks the deadhead.

Goat Cove. Goat Cove indents the eastern shore near the north end of Finlayson Channel. An inner basin is reached by running through a narrow neck. Inside, Sailing Directions says good anchorage can be had in 17 fathoms, which is pretty deep. Don Douglass likes this inner basin, too, and would anchor near the head in 36 feet. We don't like it at all. We went in during a gathering storm, and wind gusts found their way to us with nothing to stop them. The bottom shoaled too quickly for us to anchor in 36 feet and pay out scope to stand up to the wind. "Oversold!" we decided, and left. We must add that since then, we have met other cruisers who like Goat Cove, so perhaps it comes down to what the weather is doing. [*Hale*]

Work Bay. Work Bay is on the west side of Finlayson Channel near the north end. The bay appears open to southerly winds, but we anchored there in the southerly storm that chased us out of Goat Cove and found no wind and only remnants of a few rollers from Finlayson Channel. In our opinion Work Bay has room for just one boat at anchor unless all boats stern-tie to trees. The bay is 40 to 50 feet deep. With only a 3:1 scope (150 feet) of anchor rode out, you must be in the center or you will swing onto shore or onto the drying shelf at the head of the bay. In 2010 we tried to anchor in Work Bay again. We found it so full of drift that we moved on. If it hadn't been for the drift we would have stayed. [*Hale*]

Lime Point Cove. Lime Point Cove, on Griffin Passage, is an indentation just south of the north end of Pooley Island. For years it has been passed by after the area above the cove was logged. New growth has filled in and once again it is a beautiful, quiet, and scenic anchorage. It is is exposed to southerlies passing up through Griffin Passage. Anchor in the shallow areas of the cove in 36 to 70 feet.

Carter Bay. Carter Bay is on the north side of Sheep Passage at the east entry to Hiekish Narrows. The bones of the steamship *Ohio*, which ran up on Ohio Rock in 1909, are there. Knowing he was sinking, the captain of the *Ohio* made it across the mouth of the narrows and into Carter Bay, where he grounded the ship. Of the 135 passengers and crew, only four were lost.

Hiekish Narrows. Hiekish Narrows connects with Sheep Passage and Finlayson Channel at the south end, and Graham Reach, the continuation of the Inside Passage, at the north end. Current predictions are given under Hiekish Narrows in the Tide and Current Tables, Vol. 7 and Ports and Passes. Maximum currents run to 4.5 knots

Graham Reach is scenic and easily navigated.

on the flood, 4 knots on the ebb. The flood sets north. The water behind Hewitt Island appears to be a possible anchorage, but the current runs strongly through it.

Graham Reach & Fraser Reach. Graham Reach and Fraser Reach are wide, straight, deep, and lined with beautiful waterfalls. Cruise ships make this their highway. The principal stopping point for pleasure craft is Butedale.

Horsefly Cove. Horsefly Cove is a short distance inside the mouth of Green Inlet on the east side of Graham Reach. The cove is cozy and protected, but 80 to 90 feet deep. You may have to stern-tie to shore to restrict your swing.

Swanson Bay. Swanson Bay is on the east side of Graham Reach. This bay is exposed, but interesting. Ruins of an old sawmill and pulp mill are on the beach and back in the trees. A 3-story concrete building is just inside the treeline. Farther back, a tall red brick chimney is hidden in the trees. Although the chart shows the chimney as a landmark, summer foliage has almost obscured it from view.

We had trouble finding a comfortable place to anchor at Swanson Bay, settling finally for the shallower water off the creek mouth. Current from the creek kept the boat from swinging. Ashore are the ruins of what once was a formidable shipping center. We have seen a photo of a long wharf at Swanson Bay, with a large square-rigger tied alongside. The wharf is gone, and only a few pilings remain. Unfortunately, the dense forest inhibited our exploration on land.

Our notes, written at Ocean Falls, say that Swanson Bay shipped its first load of pulp in 1909, and in the 1920s had a population of 500. Its last shipment was in 1934. For some reason the notes don't show the source of this information, so no guarantees as to accuracy.

A few years ago we saw a black-colored wolf on the south shore of Swanson Bay. It watched as our boat slowly approached. Then, with a dismissive air it ambled back into the forest. [*Hale*]

Khutze Inlet. Khutze Inlet stretches eastward from Graham Reach nearly 5 miles and rewards visitors with a stunning anchorage near the head. From there you can

This humpback was spotted in Fraser Reach just a few miles from Butedale.

Butedale continues falling into the sea.

Lou Simoneau, Butedale's caretaker, built these wooden flumes. They divert river water to a turbine, which spins an alternator.

Bishop Bay is a popular spot. The small dock cannot handle large boats, but several mooring buoys in the bay are available.

look across the drying flats of the Khutze River into a broad valley with mountains on both sides. Don't get too close to the flats. The bottom comes up sharply and the water can be murky. A long and beautiful waterfall tumbles down the mountain to your right. The outfall stream forms an alluvial fan off its mouth. We've seen boats anchored there, and earlier editions suggested that you could find a good spot on that fan to put the hook down. A few years ago, however, a 42-foot boat anchored in that location, but swung too close to shore and went aground.

We have anchored toward the river mouth in 90 to 100 feet,

and between the river mouth and the waterfall in 60 feet. Approach the drying flats slowly until you reach your depth, and put the anchor down. Note that a drying spit extends from the south shore of the Khutze River into the bay. You want to anchor on the south side of that spit.

You can also anchor behind Green Spit near the mouth of the inlet. One good spot is along the south shore, just west of the stream mouth. The chart shows the right spot.

⑨ **Butedale.** The historic Butedale cannery ruins are located on Princess Royal Island, at the south end of Fraser Reach. The site is in

an advanced state of disrepair and is not open for business. Anchorage is possible, though the bottom may be foul with cable.

New owners purchased the property in 2013. Some cleanup and stabilization efforts have taken place, but the future of the property is not known. Rudimentary floats are still in place, but no services are available. Longtime caretaker Lou Simoneau still lives on the property.

Check www.WaggonerGuide.com for updates.

⑩ **Bishop Bay Hot Springs.** Bishop Bay Hot Springs is located at the head of Bishop Bay on the east side of Ursula Channel. This is one of the don't-miss stops along the northern B.C. coast. Local residents have done an outstanding job building and maintaining the bathhouse and boardwalk. At the bathhouse, the hot spring water is an agreeable temperature and odor-free. The boardwalk parallels the shoreline through fabulous, moss-covered and moss-hung forest.

The dock is small; plan on rafting. Anchoring is only fair to poor, because the bottom slopes quickly to deep water. The two mooring buoys marked "Private" actually are for public use. A short distance south of the dock a shoal, not shown on the charts, extends into the bay from the shoreline. Be aware of that shoal and plan your swing to stay well off it.

Verney Passage. Verney Passage, along the west side of Gribbell Island, must be one of the more beautiful places on earth. It is lined, both sides, with raw, polished rock mountains, 3500 feet

high. Great glacier-carved bowls, called cirques, are hollowed into the mountains. From the water you can see their forested floors and sheer rock walls. Especially on a sunny day, a visit to Bishop Bay Hot Springs should include a circumnavigation of Gribbell Island, just to see Verney Passage.

Weewanie Hot Springs. Midway up Devastation Channel, Weewanie Hot Springs is a beautiful small bay, surrounded by sheer rock walls and forest. Two mooring buoys are available.

Though pretty, the hot springs on shore are the primary attraction. The Kitimat Aquanauts Scuba Club built a bath house and soaking tubs ashore. Land a dinghy and follow the trail past a campsite to the bath house. Or land the dinghy on the rocks just below the bath house and tie to a log ashore. We've found Weewanie Hot Springs less crowded than Bishop Bay, but no less enticing.

Proper hot spring etiquette is to pull the plug on the lower tub, drain, then replug. The tub will fill again from the hose to the underground hot springs.

Kitimat. Kitimat, pop. 10,000, is a small city located at the head of Douglas Channel. While it has shopping for nearly everything one might need, the town itself is located about 5 miles from the nearest marina, MK Bay Marina. Taxi service (Coastal Taxis, 250-632-7250), if available, is about $25 each way. We suspect a person needing to get to town for shopping could find a ride.

Kitimat was built in the 1950s to make aluminum. The Kitimat Museum and Archives is located

---

CHURCH OF URSULA

I am more spiritual than religious, but one morning last summer I went to the Church of Ursula for my Sunday services. Ursula Channel that is, one of the most beautiful waterways on the Inside Passage.

As I readied *Searaven*, Bishop Bay Cove was still in the shadow of the mountains. Across Ursula Channel, though, the rising sun brilliantly illuminated Gribbell Island. Lush green trees clung to craggy, gray rock faces. Snowcapped mountains reached for the deep blue sky. The water was glassy, with a gentle roll adding a constantly shifting element to Gribbell Island's reflection.

The view that morning, up and down Ursula Channel, was outstanding, even spiritual. I piloted *Searaven* from the flybridge, soaking in nature's majesty. Whoever created this world created special experiences like this. It had to be intentional and I was blessed to share it for a few hours.

– Mark Bunzel

Beautiful Devastation Channel connects Verney Passage to Kitimat Arm. Weewanie Hot Springs is on the east side.

A NIGHT TO REMEMBER

in the middle of the shopping area. This small museum has several exhibits that illustrate how the town was built, including the massive tunnels and dam for hydroelectric power and the smelting plant. The Alcan plant was one of the largest non-defense construction projects of the 1950s. Today, new owners continue updating and operating the plant.

⑪ **MK Bay Marina.** P.O. Box 220, Kitimat, BC V8C 2G7; (250) 632-6401; mkbay@ telus.net; www.mkbaymarina.com. Monitors VHF channel 68. Open all year, 30 & 50 amp power, 50 amp 220-volt power, water, gasoline and diesel fuel, launch ramp, haulout to 20 tons, guest moorage for everything from trailer boats to mega-yachts, new laundry and showers, store, coffee shop and deli, fishing and marine supplies, block and cube ice, Wi-Fi. Fresh baked goods in the deli. The marina is on the east side of Kitimat Arm.

Visitor boats usually will be on D dock, the dock facing the floating breakwater. Larger boats will side-tie on the seaward side of D dock. Boats to approximately 45 feet will use slips on the inside of the dock. Side-tied boats should consider extra fenders. Afternoon inflow winds produce waves that the floating log breakwater knocks down but doesn't eliminate. The winds usually die in the evening.

This is a complete facility. The wide concrete docks are in good condition, the washrooms and showers are very good, and the laundry room is beautiful. The new store and snack bar overlooking the marina is a welcome addition. *Call ahead for available space.* Moorage is charged even if you don't stay the night.

LOCAL KNOWLEDGE

WEATHER TIP: When crossing Wright Sound in an outflow wind in Douglas Channel, it is better to lay a course to Juan Point, at the north end of Gil Island. We tried this route in an outflow wind, and found it much smoother than our previous crossing, in

which we tried a direct (and wet) route between Point Cumming and Cape Farewell.

Wright Sound. Wright Sound is at the junction of Grenville Channel, Douglas Channel, Verney Passage and McKay Reach. All these passages pour their currents into Wright Sound, where the waters collide and mix. Especially on an ebb, not much wind is needed to make conditions ugly.

Coghlan Anchorage. Coghlan Anchorage is behind Promise Island, and is connected by Stewart Narrows with Hartley Bay. The anchorage is open to the south, but still decently protected. The mooring buoys shown on the chart no longer exist. One year we anchored briefly in 35 to 40 feet just north of Brodie Point. The protection and holding ground were excellent, if not scenic. Anchorage is also possible on the shore opposite Brodie Point, off Otter Shoal. [*Hale*]

⑫ **Hartley Bay.** Band Office, 320 Hayimiisaxaa Way, Hartley Bay, BC V0V 1A0; (250) 841-2675 (fuel station); (250) 841-2675 (marina); hbvc@gitgaat.net. Open all year. Gasoline and diesel, pure water (from the water treatment plant) at the fuel dock, 15 amp power on the floats. Garbage drop, but

Who says you need a big, fancy boat to go cruising?

Mark and Tanya, a young couple from Terrace, B.C., loaded Mark's 16 foot runabout with camping gear, towed it to Kitimat, and set off for a boating date at Weewanie Hot Springs.

The hot springs are in a small cove off Devastation Channel, about 18 miles south of Kitimat. Gorgeous cliffs rise above the cove. Mark and Tanya pitched their tent on a flat spot ashore and spent the afternoon lounging in the hot springs and soaking in the view.

Then an intrusive cruising guide publisher showed up with his camera and notepad. Mark and Tanya were sociable, kindly acting as models for my photos. Soon, I had to leave. When I changed in the bathhouse, I noticed candles throughout the building.

I imagined what the hot springs would look like later, bathed in candlelight beneath the starry sky, and I'm sure it was a night Mark and Tanya will remember forever.

– Mark Bunzel

The store, deli and cafe at MK Bay Marina.

KITIMAT PETROLEUM DEVELOPMENT

Kitimat and Douglas Channel are frequently in the news. Oil companies, buoyed by increased Canadian oil production, identified Kitimat as an ideal port to send petroleum products to energy-hungry markets in Asia. Kitimat has relatively easy access to the Interior, where pipelines can be built without crossing over or through the mountains, and it also has ready access to the ocean.

Liquid natural gas (LNG) pipeline construction is already underway. A large parcel of land is being cleared and a LNG gasification plant is under construction. Construction will continue for the next couple of years. Additional LNG plants have been proposed but will take years to come to fruition.

Early and controversial discussions are also taking place for Kitimat to be the terminus for a crude oil pipeline. The proposed pipeline would transport oil from inland tar sands to Kitimat, where the oil would be loaded onto ships bound for Asia. At this point, it is unclear where these discussions will conclude.

Many are concerned about the transport of crude oil through the pristine waters of Douglas Channel. The primary concern is that a single accident involving a large crude carrier could destroy the local ecosystem for decades. For the next several years, expect to hear controversy about this subject. You may see this battle played out in the towns and villages you visit.

For the boating community, the only short term changes are increased barge traffic for construction materials. Once the LNG facilities are operational, a growing volume of LNG tanker traffic will transit Douglas Channel.

— Mark Bunzel

The docks at Hartley Bay.

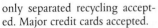

LOCAL KNOWLEDGE

STRONG CURRENTS: Sailing Directions says Grenville Channel currents run to a maximum of 2 knots, but the channel narrows between Lowe Inlet and Evening Point, creating stronger currents. We've seen 3 to 4 knots of current in this stretch, flood and ebb, with small whirlpools.

You can save time and fuel by riding an afternoon or early evening flood part way in, then overnighting in one of Grenville Channel's excellent anchorages. Then ride a morning ebb out.

Grenville Channel. Though sometimes called "The Ditch,"

Grenville Channel is a straight, beautiful, and unobstructed 45-mile-long channel running between Wright Sound in the south and Arthur Passage in the north. Tidal currents flow in and out of each end. Currents run more strongly in the narrower south half than in the wider north half. Flood currents meet in the area of Evening Point, about 25 miles from the south entrance. Ebb currents divide about 1.5 miles north of Evening Point.

The tide & current tables show no current predictions for Grenville Channel, but corrections for high and low tides are shown for Lowe Inlet as a secondary port under Bella Bella in the Tide and Current Tables, Vol. 7 (Index No. 9195).

---

only separated recycling accepted. Major credit cards accepted.

Hartley Bay, near the south end of Douglas Channel, is a friendly and modern-looking Native village, population 160-200, with a no-charge government dock behind a rock breakwater. The Cultural Centre is in a new building near the fuel dock. No liquor. No pay phone, but cell phones work. A medical clinic has two nurses and a visiting doctor.

Fuel dock hours are Monday through Thursday 8:00 a.m. to 12:00 p.m., and 1:00 p.m. to 5:00 p.m.; Friday through Sunday on call, VHF 06, Hartley Bay Fuel. In the summer of 2012, Hartley Bay ran out of fuel for several days between deliveries. Boats that must take on fuel at Hartley Bay may want to call ahead to ensure availability.

Fin Island. Fin Island lies between Lewis Passage and Cridge Passage, immediately west of Gil Island. Fin Island is fairly low

and not particularly interesting, but it has two workable anchorages, Curlew Bay and Hawk Bay. Hawk Bay is the better of the two.

Curlew Bay. Curlew Bay indents the northeast corner of Fin Island. It isn't a destination anchorage by any means, but it will do in settled weather or a southerly. The bay appears open to a northerly and to outflow winds from Douglas Channel. The chart shows shoaling a short distance west of the narrows. We anchored in 20 feet at the east end of the narrows. The anchor bumped twice on what felt like rock, then set solidly. [*Hale*]

Hawk Bay. Hawk Bay, on the west side of Fin Island, is more scenic and has more room than Curlew Bay. The anchorage is somewhat open to westerly winds and you'll swing around if it's blowing. Anchor in the middle in 60 feet.

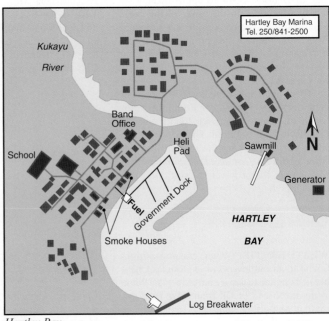

Hartley Bay

Commercial traffic regularly uses Grenville Channel.

Bears frequent Verney Falls and, on occasion, swim from one side to the other.

Be sure to give Morning Reef, north of Evening Point, a wide berth.

Grenville Channel is a major waterway on the Inside Passage. You may see tugs with tows, all types of fishing boats and commercial vessels, the BC Ferry, and cruise ships. In limited visibility, radar and AIS are helpful. We monitor Prince Rupert Vessel Traffic Service on VHF 71. Large vessels have report-in points shown on the charts. Their check-ins with VTS will help you develop a mental picture of the large vessels that may be a factor on your passage, especially those approaching and overtaking from astern.

Union Passage. Union Passage, on the west side of Grenville Channel, is served by Hawkins Narrows from Grenville Channel and Peters Narrows from the south. It is one of those places people talk about but not many visit. The problem is the two sets of narrows. The chart shows 8-knot currents in Hawkins Narrows and 7-knot currents in Peters Narrows. Hawkins Narrows slack is shown as 5 minutes in duration. Neither the chart nor Sailing Directions say much about Peters Narrows. Once inside, the scenery is not remarkable.

The currents often are much less than shown, and the window of least current much wider than 5 minutes. We entered Union Passage through Hawkins Narrows at low water slack, poked around for a few minutes, then departed the way we came. The day was windy, rainy and cold. Our spirit was with the great explorers, but our resolve that day was weak. [*Hale*].

The entrance to Hawkins Narrows is at latitude 53°22'N. The channel is open until the inner end is approached. There, a rock awash at zero tide lies off the eastern shore. Favor the western shore to avoid it.

Lowe Inlet (Verney Falls). Lowe Inlet, a provincial park 14.5 miles from the southern entrance to Grenville Channel, is an excellent spot to overnight. You can anchor either in the outer basin or in Nettle Basin, the co-

zier inner cove. Walt Woodward, in his book *How to Cruise to Alaska Without Rocking the Boat Too Much*, recommends anchoring directly in front of Verney Falls where they pour into Nettle Basin. Managing Editor Sam Landsman dropped his anchor in the white water at the base of the falls, but wouldn't recommend it in a boat larger than about 30 feet. Current holds the boat in place, and you are treated to a wonderful view of the falls. Depending on the time of year, you may see bears fishing in the falls. Holding ground is only fair, so be sure the anchor is well set and you have ample scope for high tide. An alternative is to anchor far enough from the falls that the current, while still enough to hold the boat steady, is not very strong.

Don and Reanne Douglass, in their books, like the Verney Falls anchorage, but also suggests an anchorage along the south shore of Nettle Basin, off the shelf formed by a creek

that empties into that area. We tried to put the hook down in 60 feet off that shore, but found that we would swing too close to the shelf. After two tries in wind squalls and heavy rain showers, we moved out to the middle and anchored in 100 feet with 300 feet of rode out. Shortly after we were settled another boat came in, tried to anchor as we earlier tried, then moved out to the middle as we had. Our holding ground was excellent. We had trouble tripping the anchor the next morning.

Lowe Inlet is beautiful. Our notes read, "If you're looking for a scenic spot, this is it." [*Hale*]

Klewnuggit Inlet. At approximately 120 feet, Klewnuggit Inlet is too deep for most boats to anchor. We talked with some folks, however, who found excellent crabbing near the head of the inlet.

Small boats can anchor just beneath Verney Falls where the current prevents you from swinging into the rocks. If the salmon are running the bear viewing is fantastic.

East Inlet. East Inlet is adjacent to Klewnuggit Inlet. The inner cove of East Inlet is a superb anchorage, surrounded by high mountains and protected from seas. In a storm, however, winds might swirl through. Anchor near the head of the inner basin in 50 to 55 feet. You can also find anchorage in the little cove on the south shore, just inside the entrance to the inner basin.

We anchored at the head of East Inlet, a perfect night in a perfect place. Mountains reflected in the calm water. A small stream drained from a lake into the head of the inlet, and waterfalls poured down from the sides. We found an inukshuk, a small, stonehenge-like marker, next to the stream mouth.

Back on the boat, a lively country music CD played while dinner was prepared. We invited Mrs. Hale to dance, and she accepted. There, in the lengthening shadows of the setting sun, two old folks danced and twirled and had a marvelous time. [*Hale*]

Kxngeal Inlet. Kxngeal Inlet, on the north side of Grenville Channel approximately 4 miles northwest of Klewnuggit Inlet, is a beautiful bowl in the mountains. Favor either shore as you enter to avoid a nasty rock that dries 16 feet in the entrance. The inlet is at least 130 feet deep until it shelves at the head, and when it shelves, it shelves *right now*. Trees are at the head of the inlet, with logged areas on each side. The shelf is on a line with the points where the trees begin. Anchor in 90 feet.

Watts Narrows. Watts Narrows is a short passage that connects Baker Inlet with Grenville Channel. A dogleg turn near the inner entrance makes the passage blind. Before entering, either direction, announce your intentions on VHF 16, low power. Sound the ship's horn as you approach the turn. The current runs swiftly through the narrows, but people tell us they have gone through in the presence of current without trouble. We have waited for slack water, which occurs about the times of high and low water at Prince Rupert. As the chart shows, the narrows are narrow, but they are deep. A mid-channel course will get you through safely.

Baker Inlet. Baker Inlet, entered through Watts Narrows, is wonderful. The best overnights are at the head of the inlet, 60 feet, good bottom, mountains all around. Beautiful.

Kumealon Island/Kumealon Inlet. The little cove behind Kumealon Island is a good anchorage for a small number of boats. The much larger Kumealon Inlet, immediately south, also is good. Behind Kumealon Island, anchor in 15 to 25 feet north of the island, near the head.

Kumealon Inlet is well protected and has beautiful scenery. Anchor in the inner basin, behind the little island. Find a good spot and put the hook down in 50 to 70 feet. A reader reported that two uncharted rocks lie close to shore near the southeast corner.

Oona River. The village of Oona River, a tiny Swedish fishing and boatbuilding community, indents Porcher Island at the east end of Ogden Channel. A public dock is behind a stone breakwater, and is served by a narrow channel through drying mudflats. From the white buoy, line up on the private range markers on the rock jetty and proceed along the markers set in the entrance. Use caution, but depths should be adequate for most pleasure vessels. Call "Oona River" on VHF channel 06 for additional information.

Cell phones work near Oona River.

Arthur Passage to Chatham Sound. Assuming a northbound route, begin your run from a waypoint west of Watson Rock (west of Gibson Island) at the northern entrance to Grenville Channel. Continue north to a waypoint off the flashing light on the southwest shore of Kennedy Island. Then turn westward slightly to run past the southwest corner of Hanmer Island and leave Bell Buoy *D9*, marking Cecil Patch, to port. Continue to a waypoint in the passage west of Genn Island, then to a waypoint east of Holland Rock.

From Holland Rock, run to a waypoint west of Barrett Rock at the entrance to Prince Rupert Harbour. The entire area is well-buoyed, but it is easy to get the buoys confused.

LOCAL KNOWLEDGE

WEATHER TIP: Chatham Sound can be downright ugly when the wind blows. Especially on an ebb, when the onshore wind meets the combined ebb current and Skeena River runoff, seas can get high, steep and close together. On the weather channel, listen to the hourly updates for Holland Rock.

If it's blowing at Holland Rock, conditions can be rough when you try to cross.

Lawson Harbour/Kelp Passage. Kelp Passage is on the west side of Lewis Island, across Arthur Passage from Kennedy Island.

Lawson Harbour indents the top of Lewis Island. Neither would be our first choice for scenery, but each serves as an anchorage if needed. A reef extends from the western shore inside Lawson Harbour. Anchor near the south end of the reef in 35 to 40 feet.

In Kelp Passage, anchor in the area marked 8.8 meters on Chart 3947, mud bottom. The small basin at the south end of Kelp Passage provides good protection in a northerly wind.

Porpoise Harbour. (250) 885-1986. Located at Port Edward, Porpoise Harbour gives priority to long-term year round customers. Transient moorage available on first-come, first-served basis, best to call ahead, 15 & 20 amp power, water, and garbage drop. Approach using the range south of Ridley Island marked with a buoy for Porpoise Channel.

The Port Edward Harbour Authority is improving their docks in Porpoise Harbour. New washrooms and showers are planned for the 2014 season. The harbor is close to the North Pacific Cannery, a museum showing what cannery life was all about. Bus service to Prince Rupert is available.

LOCAL KNOWLEDGE

SPEED LIMIT: A 5-knot speed zone in Prince Rupert Harbour is enforced within 600 yards of the Prince Rupert shore.

The green "Lightering Dock" is for Customs check-in and clearance.

The Prince Rupert Rowing and Yacht Club is the preferred moorage.

The Prince Rupert Rowing and Yacht Club docks often fill. Reservations recommended.

⑬ **Prince Rupert.** As you approach Prince Rupert, it's a good idea to monitor Prince Rupert Traffic (VTS) on VHF 11 in case a large ship decides to depart while you're coming in. The fairway gets narrow in places. This is especially important in poor visibility.

As you approach, the large coal and grain loading areas are part of the Port of Prince Rupert's Ridley Terminals. From Barrett Rock at the entrance to Prince Rupert Harbour, it is another 5.5 miles of slow speed travel to town. Three marinas serve Prince Rupert: Fairview at the south end, Prince Rupert Rowing and Yacht Club in the middle, and Rushbrooke at the north end.

Dock space may be available at Atlin Terminal. Rushbrooke Floats, Fairview Small Craft Docks, and Porpoise Harbour are all managed by the Port Edward Harbour Authority, (250)-628-9220.

Fairview is primarily a commercial boat moorage, although some pleasure boats do tie up there. It is fairly far from downtown, with limited bus service. Rushbrooke, at the north end, has better facilities for pleasure boats, but during the commercial fishing months many fish boats occupy the slips. The walk from Rushbrooke to town is long but manageable. Most pleasure boats go directly to the Prince Rupert Rowing and Yacht Club, located at Cow Bay, though it frequently fills up during the summer months. Reservations are recommended.

Prince Rupert ("Rainy Rupert"), population a little over 13,000, is a complete city. With a large fishing fleet to support, you can find anything you need for your boat. What isn't there can be flown in. Fuel and waste oil disposal are available at Cow Bay.

A shopping mall is a pleasant walk uptown, or you can take a cab. A Wal-Mart is now located in the mall. A large Safeway is located between the yacht club and the mall. The Overwaitea market, farther uptown, is another option for provisions and will deliver to the docks for a fee. The provincial liquor store is between the Safeway and the yacht club. A smaller, private liquor store is at Cow Bay.

The Museum of Northern British Colum-

bia is excellent, and sponsors a variety of informative day and evening programs during the summer. Highly recommended. Several restaurants are in town, some of them quite good. The Port Interpretive Centre, located on street level in Atlin Terminal, gives free tours about the past, present and future of the Port of Prince Rupert. Recommended.

In town, Trayling's Tackle Shop has an excellent selection, and they know fishing.

The King Coin laundromat in the center of town will do your laundry for a reasonable charge. It's a treat for us to leave all the ship's sheets, towels and dirty clothes at the laundromat and go for dinner at one of the local restaurants. A few hours later we pick up the laundry, clean, dry, and neatly folded. A bargain by any measure.

Up at 617 2nd Avenue, just beyond the mall, we found Gary's Lock and Security Shop Ltd., a lock shop with a twist. Gary Weick, the longtime owner, collects things. His shop is a museum. In the window were wonderful toys from the 1930s and 40s, Canadian Pacific Railroad conductors' caps, old photos–and a stuffed and mounted *fur-bearing trout*, very rare. It was caught in Lake Superior, from depths so great trout grow fur to keep warm. This trout's fur is white. Everything is explained on the sign next to the specimen. You have to see it.

If you have time, take the bus to Port Edward for a tour of the North Pacific Cannery, now a museum. You'll see how the workers lived and worked.

Prince Rupert was hurt by the decline of the commercial fishing and forest industries, and then the pulp mill closed. The town lost about one-third of its population. In the last eight years it has become a major deepwater seaport, in heavy competition with Vancouver, Puget Sound and California. Prince Rupert is closer to Asia than any other west coast port, and CN Rail owns tracks from Prince Rupert to Memphis, Tennessee. Transit time from Asia to heartland U.S. is cut by at least two days. Not only can Prince Rupert handle the largest container ships now afloat, it will be able to handle the largest on the drawing board. The major new docks and

cranes you see are for these ships.

Prince Rupert is the last major city in British Columbia before transiting Dixon Entrance on the way to Ketchikan and Southeast Alaska. While there is good shopping and a liquor store in Prince Rupert, vessels bound for Alaska may want to wait to provision until Ketchikan to avoid customs issues

Prince Rupert Harbour

Cow Bay has shops and restaurants.

with liquor, produce, and meat. A large fuel dock operates in Prince Rupert.

Moorage shortage: Moorage is tight in Prince Rupert. If possible, call ahead for reservations. If all marinas are full, Pillsbury Cove is a good nearby anchorage.

Customs clearance: Tie up at the 100-foot-long green-painted "Lightering Dock," where a dedicated toll-free phone for customs clearance is installed. The dock is located beneath the large shopping mall building at the top of the hill. The railroad museum building is near the shore, and a whale sculpture. Lat/Lon 54°18.827'N/130°19.930'W. Touch-and-go for customs clearance only. A locked gate prevents shore access.

You can also clear customs by telephone at Rushbrooke, the Prince Rupert Rowing and Yacht Club and Fairview Government Dock by calling 888-226-7277. Calls now go to a call center in Hamilton, Ontario. Agents on the phone have the option of calling out a local customs agent for an inspection.

Car rentals: Hertz, (250) 627-8444; National, (250) 624-5318.

Cruise Ships: Cruise ships call throughout the week during the summer. When one is in town, the streets and stores are apt to be crowded.

Golf: The Prince Rupert Centennial Golf Course is a good 18-hole course. Call (250) 624-2000. You'll probably take a cab. In early evening the no-see-ums can be thick and ravenous. Cover up.

⑬ **Fairview Small Craft Harbour.** (250) 624-3127, Open 7 days a week 5:00 a.m. to 8:00 p.m. during the summer; 8:30 a.m. to 5:00 p.m. Monday through Friday the rest of the year. This is the first set of docks as you approach Prince Rupert. Commercial vessels primarily, but sometimes room for a few pleasure boats. Water, 20 & 30 amp power, garbage. First come, first served.

⑬ **Prince Rupert Rowing and Yacht Club.** P.O. Box 981, 121 George Hills Way, Prince Rupert, BC V8J 1A3; (250) 624-4317; info@prryc.com. Monitors VHF 73. Open all year, 30 amp power, spacious washroom and shower, recycling, potable water, telephone, block ice, garbage drop, Wi-Fi, fish-cleaning station. Waste oil dump at the Northwest Fuels facility next door. Located at Cow Bay, a delightful area of shops, eateries and galleries.

This is the preferred pleasure craft moorage in Prince Rupert. Reservations strongly recommended. As you approach, call on VHF 73. The dock staff can be busy. Be patient.

Northbound boats could call for reservations by cell phone from Hartley Bay, at the south end of Grenville Channel, or in the small area of cell phone coverage (we think it's from Oona River) at the north end of Grenville Channel.

The yacht club docks are strong and safe, but well used. The main dock has been replaced, and more replacements are planned. New docks or old, be aware that you will be squeezed in more tightly than at most marinas. If the commercial salmon fishing fleet is in the midst of an opening the boats will come and go all night, and moorage at the outermost docks can be pretty bouncy. Put out lots of fenders.

A pay phone is at the head of the dock. The yacht club is close to good dining; you can walk or take a cab uptown. Moorage is open to all, no yacht club reciprocals needed.

⑬ **Northwest Fuels Ltd.** (250) 624-4106. Located in Cow Bay next to the Yacht Club. Monitors VHF 71. Open every day, extended hours in summer. Gasoline, diesel, lubricants, washrooms and showers. Block, cube and salt ice. Small convenience store on pier. Garbage drop, pumpout, waste oil disposal.

⑬ **Atlin Terminal.** Located next to the yacht club, it is almost entirely taken by commercial vessels. Larger pleasure vessels sometimes are allowed to moor there, but the policy seems to change from year to year.

⑬ **Rushbrooke Floats Small Craft Harbour.** (250) 624-9400. Open all year, seasonal water, 15 & 20 amp power. Commercial vessels have priority in the summer, but there can be room for pleasure craft too. Rafting required. Located about a mile north of town. Rushbrooke has the only launch ramp in Prince Rupert. First come, first served.

Pillsbury Cove. Pillsbury Cove, on the west side of Prince Rupert Harbour, is an excellent anchorage: level bottom, great holding, beaches and tide pools, and lots of crabs. If the marinas in Prince Rupert are all full, or you prefer anchoring, this is a good choice. Prince Rupert is a roughly 3-mile dinghy ride away.

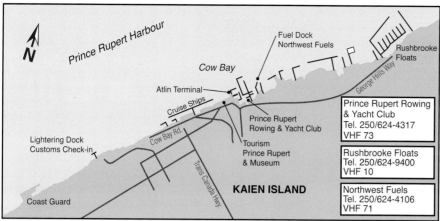

Prince Rupert Waterfront

THINGS TO DO

1. **Cow Bay**. Several good restaurants and shops. One casual favorite is Cowpuccino's for coffee and fresh baked goods.

2. **Khutzeymateen Sanctuary**. Also called "Valley of the Grizzly," this is the only park of its kind in Canada. It contains one of the largest populations of grizzly bears – about 50 – in British Columbia. Located 45 km NE of Prince Rupert.

3. **North Pacific Cannery**. The oldest, most completely preserved cannery remaining of 200-or-so that once dotted B.C.'s northwest coast.

4. **Museum of Northern British Columbia**. An impressive collection about the northwest coast. A First Nations longhouse describes the history of the people and area going back to the last ice age. It contains well-preserved, historical Tsimshian and other First Nations works of art, clothing, baskets and more.

5. **Firehall Museum**. Focused on the history of the local fire department since 1908. A rebuilt red fire truck from 1925 sits in the middle of the museum.

6. **Kwinitsa Railway Museum**. Authentic railway station with artifacts from the early 1900s, the heyday of the Grand Trunk Pacific Railway.

7. **Farmer's Market**. In town on Sunday afternoons during the summer season.

8. **Prince Rupert Centennial Golf Course**. Eighteen holes of golf.

9. **Seafest**. The town's biggest annual festival, held each June.

10. **Port Interpretive Centre**. Free guided tours about the Port of Prince Rupert. Informative and hands-on activities let visitors explore the growth of the Prince Rupert's commerce including, containers, coal and grain.

MORE THAN JUST A CROSSROADS

You meet the most interesting people on the Inside Passage…

While visiting the Rushbrooke Floats in Prince Rupert I noticed Bob's on the Rocks.

Turns out they serve the most incredible halibut & chips in the area. Fresh halibut comes right from the boats below. The owner is Heather Snow. She's a single mom with a 10-year-old and an engaging personality. She makes sure Bob's is open at 5:00 a.m. when the fishermen leave and at 8:00 p.m. when they return. The morning breakfast special is "Jig on a Muffin."

Heather works a full-time job during the day in an audiology clinic. By late afternoon, she's back at Bob's. She has been doing this every summer for almost 10 years and still loves it.

As I walked away, I realized I never asked the big question—who is Bob?

I phoned her and she told me that she and Bob went on the rocks about 5 years ago. She got the restaurant and debated changing the name to "Boobs on the Rocks." She thought it might be good for business.

Heather Snow, quite a character on the Inside Passage.

– Mark Bunzel

Atlin Terminal is one of the moorage options in Prince Rupert.

Rushbrooke Floats sometimes have space for visiting cruisers.

CHAPTER 17

HAIDA GWAII

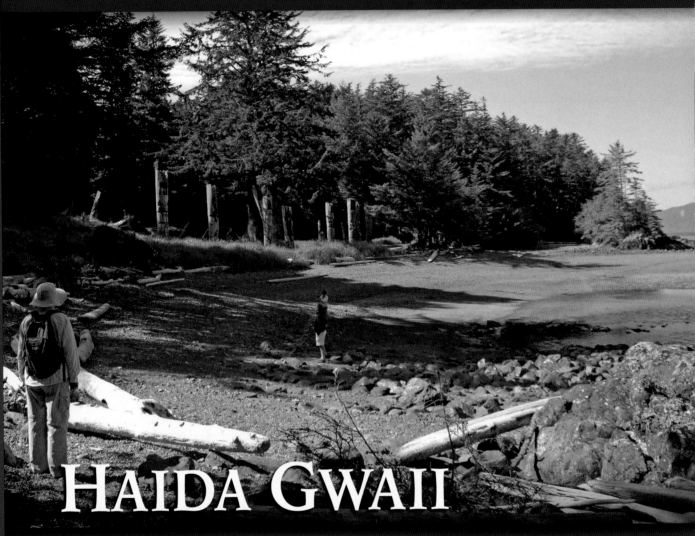

HAIDA GWAII

GRAHAM ISLAND
*Masset • Port Clements • Skidegate •
Queen Charlotte City*

MORESBY ISLAND, HEADING SOUTH
*Sandspit Harbour • Louise Narrows • Skedans Bay
• Dana Passage • Hoya Bay*

GWAII HAANAS NATIONAL PARK RESERVE
*Tanu Island • Louise Narrows • Hoya Bay
• Hotspring Island • Rose Inlet*

ANTHONY ISLAND (SGANG GWAAY)
Nan Sdins • Watchmans Cabin • Grays Cove

L ocated 130 miles north of Vancouver Island and 65 miles west of the B.C. coast's mainland islands, Haida Gwaii offers some of the Northwest's most spectacular cruising. Haida Gwaii, formerly called the Queen Charlotte Islands, is an archipelago of over 150 islands, best explored by boat. It is remote and pristine with a unique geological history. Glaciers once covered this area and receded 2,000 years before the rest of British Columbia, resulting in an ecosystem with some species of plants and animals not seen anywhere else. It has been referred to as the "Galapagos of the Northwest" with hundreds of species of birds, unique species of bears and many trees and plants growing in areas from the rain forests of the western coast to the dryer forests on the eastern coast.

Haida Gwaii means "Islands of the People" in the language of the first people to settle here. The Haida were revered and respected along the coast as ambassadors and warriors, with a unique culture. The islands had a population of more than 10,000 until the 1800s when many succumbed to small pox and other diseases from the western world. By 1900, only 350 remained. A visit to Haida Gwaii and the Gwaii Haanas National Park will take you to a place where you can see what remains of this once great culture. As you walk the trails through the rain forest and moss-covered rock canyons around the old villages you may even feel the presence of the people who once inhabited this rugged and beautiful area.

Haida Gwaii experienced the impact of an imbalance caused by western man. In the 1800s the sea otter was hunted almost to extinction. Sea otter pelts were highly valued around the world and greed took over. In time the sea urchin population grew out of control without the sea otters to keep them in check. Later, the health of the kelp beds was affected by the overabundance of sea urchins. Nature's balance was thrown off. Today the symbol of Haida Gwaii is the sea otter and the sea urchin, a reminder to keep the ecosystem in balance. The sea otter population is

Early morning departure for a smooth water crossing of Hecate Strait.

barely starting to come back and boaters are encouraged to report sea otter sightings.

Permits. The Gwaii Haanas National Park Reserve and the Protected Area was created in 1987 and encompasses the southern third of the archipelago. The Reserve is jointly managed by the Haida and the government of Canada. It is unique in Canada, covering both land and sea. A visit to Gwaii Haanas requires a reservation for the time you will be in protected areas, and payment of a daily fee if visiting between May 1 and September 30. The daily fee is $19.60 for adults, $16.60 for seniors, and $9.80 for youths. This daily fee is charged for a maximum of six days.

Only 100 people are permitted in Gwaii Haanas National Park Reserve at once. Advance reservations are recommended to ensure you'll get a permit.

All visitors are required to attend an informative 90-minute orientation in Skidegate, or during the pre-season the orientations may

be offered in Vancouver, Sidney, and Seattle. By taking the pre-season orientation, you can go directly to the protected areas on your reserved dates. This allows direct entrance to Anthony Island from the south, for example.

Call 1-877-559-8818 (M-F, 8:30 A.M. to 4:30 P.M.) for more information or to arrange for a permit.

Getting to Haida Gwaii. Separated from mainland British Columbia by Hecate Strait, and from Vancouver Island by Queen Charlotte Sound, getting to Haida Gwaii by boat requires crossing some of the Northwest's most feared bodies of water.

Hecate Strait is notoriously rough. With shallow depths, ranging from 50 to 115 feet, winds can quickly whip up uncomfortable seas. Early morning crossings are usually recommended when winds should be lighter. Tides move large volumes of water through Hecate Strait. When wind blows against current, dangerous conditions can result. Particularly during spring tides, be mindful of possible wind-against-current situations.

Many boats depart for Haida Gwaii from Prince Rupert. This route offers the shortest crossing (roughly 60 to 65 miles of open water), allowing boaters to minimize their exposure to potentially hazardous weather. Prince Rupert is a major city, and has anything a cruising boater might need before heading out to explore Haida Gwaii. It makes a logical jumping off point with the opportunity for fuel, provisions and internet access for weather information.

After leaving Prince Rupert, several anchorages provide a place to spend the night and wait for better weather before crossing Hecate Strait. Griffith Harbour, the Spicer Islands, and Welcome Harbour are all good choices.

Boats returning to British Columbia from Alaska may be tempted to cross Dixon Entrance to Masset instead of Prince Rupert.

CHARTS

3002	Queen Charlotte Stound to Dixon Entrance (1:525,000)
3800 Plans	Dixon Entrance
3807	Atli Inlet to Selwyn Inlet (1:37,500)
3808	Juan Perez Sound (1:37,500)
3809	Carpenter Bay to Burnaby Island (1:37,500)
3811	Harbours in Queen Charlotte Islands (1:18,315)
3825	Princess Royal Channel (1:40,000) (Replaces Chart 3739)
L/C3853	Cape St. James to Cumshewa Inlet and Tatsu Sound (1:150,000)

3855	Houston Stewart Channel (1:20,000)
3857	Louscoone Inlet (1:18,275)
3868	Port Louis to Langara Island (1:72,921)
3890	Approaches to Skidegate (1:40,000)
3891	Skidegate Channel (1:40,000)
3892	Masset Harbour and Naden Harbour (1:40,000)
3894	Selwyn Inlet to Lawn Point (1:73,026)
3895 Plans	Selwyn Inlet to Lawn Point (1:73,026)
L/C3902	Hecate Strait (1:250,000)

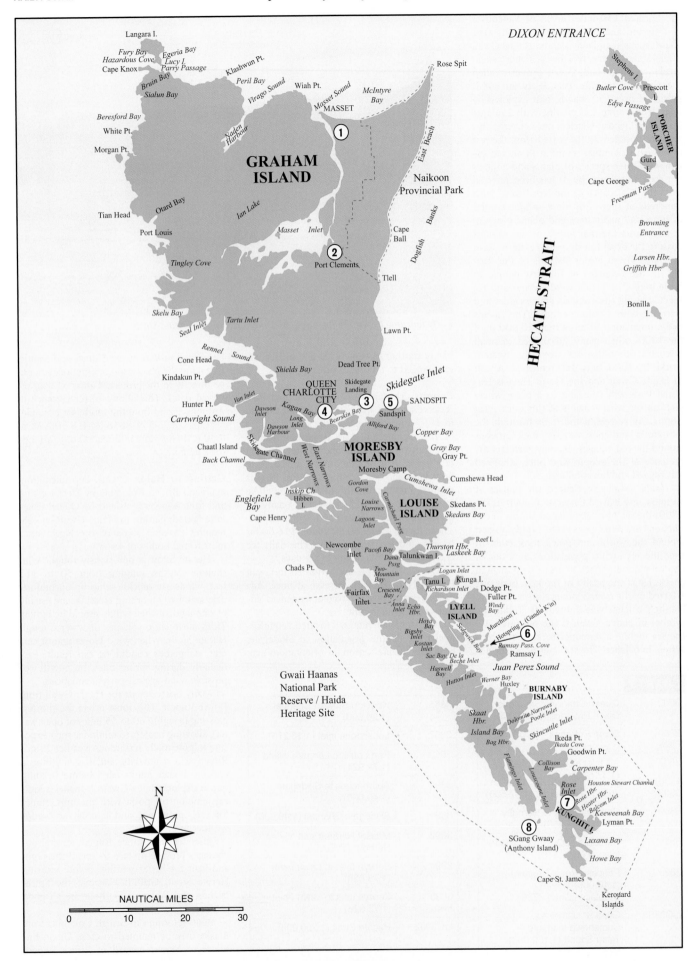

The docks at Queen Charlotte City with an area for anchorage beyond.

Briefings for entry into the Protected areas are held here at the Gwaii Haanas National Park Reserve offices in Skidegate.

Unfortunately, the Canadian Government no longer operates a customs office in Masset. Boats southbound from Alaska must first clear customs in Prince Rupert.

Haida Gwaii can also be accessed from Vancouver Island to the south. The trip is long—about 130 nautical miles—and exposed to the full brunt of the open Pacific Ocean. Sailboats and slow powerboats will have to make an overnight passage. For faster boats in settled weather, the trip can be completed in a very long day. Keep in mind, however, that sea conditions may not be conducive to high-speed operation. Also remember that fuel is not available anywhere south of Sandspit.

During our recent trip, we navigated a route from Prince Rupert to an anchorage between the Spicer Islands. For our early morning departure we listened for the wind and wave report from the North Hecate Strait weather buoy (Station 46183) and navigated directly across Hecate Strait, passing the buoy on the way, to Lawn Point. It is important to note the shoal area leading north from the entrance to Skidegate Inlet. If headed to Sandspit Harbour follow the deeper channel to the inlet or Shingle Bay. In settled conditions and higher tides, you can cross just above or below Bar Rocks near the green can buoy.

From the south, plot a route from the area north of Vancouver Island or from Hakai Pass. The open water crossing to the Houston Stewart Channel will be about 110 miles. Use the South Hecate Strait weather buoy (Station 46185) for wind and wave reports. This might also be your return route when leaving Haida Gwaii for points south.

Fuel. Fuel is available at Masset (on the north end of Graham Island), at Skidegate (Queen Charlotte City) and at Sandspit near the center of Haida Gwaii. Cruising in Haida Gwaii is quintessential wilderness cruising; be prepared.

Water. Masset, Port Clements, Sandspit, and Queen Charlotte City have potable water available. Parks Canada has placed water hoses throughout Gwaii Haanas, but this water is untreated.

Garbage Drops. In the remote and protected areas all trash must be carried back out with you.

Insurance. Not all vessel insurance policies cover Haida Gwaii. Before leaving on your trip, check with your insurance agent to ensure that you have coverage for this area.

Provisioning. Groceries are available in Masset, Skidegate, Sandspit, and Queen Charlotte City, however none has a true "supermarket." Selection may be limited as deliveries are sometimes once a week. Stock up in Prince Rupert for full provisions.

Trailering. BC Ferries serve Masset, Skidegate, Sandspit, and Alliford Bay. Check www.bcferries.com for schedules and prices. Boat launches are located at Alliford Bay, Sandspit, Masset, and Copper Bay. Trailering small boats to Haida Gwaii may save time and money and can minimize weather delays.

Resources. Don and Reanne Douglass's *Exploring the North Coast of British Columbia* is the most complete cruising guide for Haida Gwaii.

GRAHAM ISLAND

① **Masset.** During the summer months, Masset, the northernmost community on Haida Gwaii, is a hub of sport fishing operations. The local airport offers regular flights to Vancouver, and floatplanes run regularly from Prince Rupert. You'll find restaurants, a liquor store, two grocery stores, a hardware store, pubs, car rentals and an internet cafe.

Local businesses cater to tourists, with sightseeing trips and fishing charters. Hikes give boaters the opportunity to see a dif-

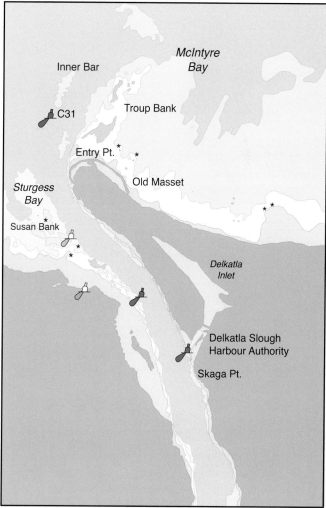

Masset Harbour

Delkatla Slough Harbour Authority provides transient moorage in Masset.

ferent side of Haida Gwaii and stretch their legs. The 9-hole Dixon Entrance Golf Club is 5 kilometers outside of town.

① **North Arm Transportation.** (250) 626-3328; www.northarm.bc.ca/masset. Located at the government dock. Gas, diesel, and lubricants available. Open from end of June through August 8:30 a.m. to 4:30 p.m. Monday through Saturday. September through May 8:30 a.m. to 4:30 p.m. Monday through Friday.

① **Delkatla Slough Harbour Authority.** Open all year, first-come, first-served. Power and water on the docks. Garbage drop.

Refuge Cove. Known locally as 7-mile Cove, Refuge Cove provides good protection from weather and has 600 feet of dock space. This is a good place to wait out a storm, or just wait for favorable currents to enter Masset. Use caution entering Refuge Cove. The fairway is narrow, about 100 feet wide, with 6-foot depths at zero tide. In stormy conditions, swells can break across the entrance channel, making it impassable. Fishing outside Refuge Cove is reportedly excellent.

Langara Island. Langara Island, the northernmost island in the archipelago, is known for it's exceptional salmon fishing. Sport fishing lodges on the island cater to fly-in guests. Several anchorages are available, although they are typically busy with sport fishing boats coming and going.

Masset Sound. Masset Sound connects Masset to Port Clements and Masset Inlet. Currents can run to 5.5 knots, although the Douglasses report there is little turbulence. Boats, particularly slow boats, should use caution when transiting the area. Vessels entering

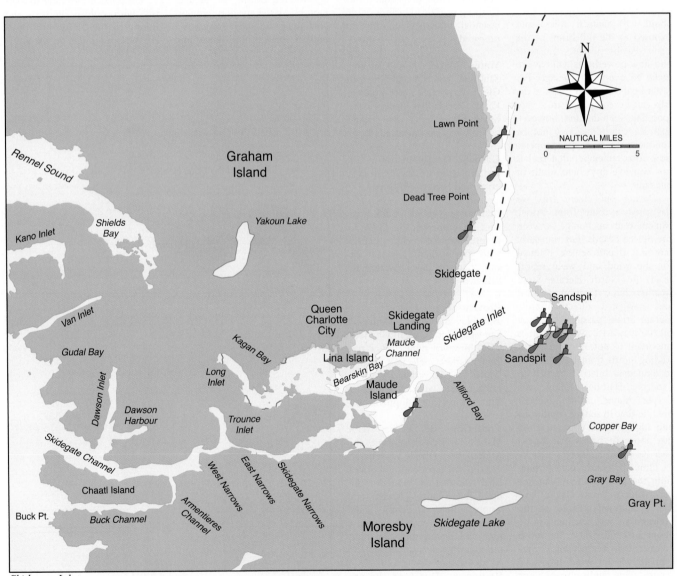

Skidegate Inlet

Regular community gatherings are hosted near the visitors center in Queen Charlotte City.

Masset Sound should do so on a flood, and exit on an ebb.

② **Port Clements.** Port Clements is a small town south of Masset. It has groceries, a laundromat, post office, health clinic, liquor store, restaurants, and a pub. A museum showcases the history of logging on Haida Gwaii. Local businesses offer sightseeing tours and fishing trips.

A hiking trail leads to the Golden Spruce heritage site, where a sacred, golden-colored Sitka Spruce tree stood until a logger-turned-conservationist famously cut it down to protest logging.

② **Port Clements Small Craft Harbour.** P.O. Box 198, Port Clements, BC V0T 1R0; (250) 557-4295; www.portclements.ca. Open all year. Transient moorage, 15 & 30 amp power, garbage drop, and boat launch. First-come, first-served, register at office three blocks away. Ice, a pay phone and groceries are available at the nearby Bayview Market.

SKIDEGATE, QUEEN CHARLOTTE CITY, AND SANDSPIT

③ **Skidegate.** Skidegate offers lodging, restaurants, groceries, and shops with local crafts. Temporary moorage may be found at the small public float next to the ferry dock, but be prepared for ferry wakes. Boats can also anchor offshore and dinghy in. The anchorage, however, is not well protected. Visiting cruisers may want to access Skidegate by road from Queen Charlotte City.

④ **Queen Charlotte City.**

Queen Charlotte City, on the south end of Moresby Island, has many services for passing boaters. Groceries, restaurants, pubs, a liquor store, ATM, marine supplies, a hardware store, rental cars, lodging, a post office, and an internet café are available. Local outfitters offer guided tours.

A visitors center is just east of the Harbour Authority floats. The staff is friendly and can answer most questions about the area. Many summer events are hosted at a "square" just below the visitors center.

The grocery store is located approximately ½ mile west of the Harbour Authority. It is restocked each Monday. The post office, laundromat, and liquor store are in the same complex. A farmers market is held each Saturday near the community center and library.

④ **Queen Charlotte City Harbour Authority.** P.O. Box 68, Queen Charlotte City, BC V0T 1S0; (250) 559-4650; harbor@qcislands.net. Open all year with moorage, 15 & 30 amp power, pay phones, and garbage drop. A tidal grid is available for haulouts, and a boat launch for trailerable boats. Water is available, but not on all docks. Transient moorage is on the south end of the first dock behind the breakwater.

④ **Haida Gwaii Fuel.** (250) 559-4527; fastfuel@qcislands.net. Located at the Island Air pier. Open all year for call outs. Gas and diesel. Call ahead for lubricants.

Skidegate Channel. Skidegate Channel is the narrow, shallow and winding channel between Graham and Moresby Islands,

EXPLORING GRAHAM ISLAND BY CAR

We wanted to visit the north end of Graham Island, but the 90-mile trip up the east coast and around Rose Spit didn't fit our schedule. Instead, we rented a car in Queen Charlotte City and drove north. National Car Rental and several local companies offer rentals, but availability is limited. It's best to reserve well in advance.

We only had the car for one day but managed to visit many sights. Our first stop was the remains of the golden spruce, a once sacred tree to the Haida. This tree was tragically cut down in an act of protest against the logging industry. John Valliant's compelling book, *The Golden Spruce,* tells what is known about the mysterious story.

Our next stop was a bit farther up the logging road. A short trail leads into the woods to the site of an abandoned, partially carved Haida canoe. A prominent sign at the trailhead marks the turn-off to the trailhead.

Continuing north to Port Clement, we stopped in a little museum with steam donkeys and local historical memorabilia, including a stuffed raven. From there we drove into Masset for a quick and delicious lunch at Pearl's Dining Room. The museum in Old Masset is now closed, but we drove through town to see the many carved poles sprinkled throughout the village. Sarah's Haida Arts in Old Masset has a beautiful selection of Haida jewelry, carvings and artwork. It is next door to a traditional dance house that the community is restoring after a fire.

We continued along the coast road to Agate Beach where we picked up dozens of luminous, pale honey-colored Queen Charlotte agates, each rounded and smoothed to a frosted polish. Tow Hill soared above the booming surf ahead of us. We wished we had enough time to hike the trail that leads to an observation deck that seems to touch the clouds. On a clear day Alaska is almost visible from here.

As the light faded we passed the wide, sandy beaches of Graham's east coast, then the fascinating shops and galleries of Tlell. Eventually we made it back to Queen Charlotte City. The short car rental opened up a vast amount of Haida Gwaii we couldn't have seen from the boat. Still, we'll be back to see the rest.

– Lydia McKenzie

connecting Hecate Strait with the Pacific Ocean. East and West Narrows are particularly challenging, though newly installed daybeacons make transiting easier than in the past. Because of the difference in tidal swings on the Pacific and Hecate Strait sides of Haida Gwaii, tides and currents in Skidegate Channel are complex and difficult to predict. It's best to plan on arriving at McLellan Point roughly three hours after low water in Queen Charlotte City.

⑤ **Sandspit.** Sandspit, on the northeast end of Moresby Island, is a settlement with a launch ramp and well-protected marina, groceries, restaurants, pubs, liquor

store, lodging, post office, car rentals and laundromat. Sandspit has hiking and biking trails, Willows Golf Course, Haida Gwaii's only 18-hole golf course, and an airport with scheduled commercial service to Vancouver. Taxi service is available to take you to the airport or the BC Ferry, which has frequent service to Skidegate/Queen Charlotte City. From Skidegate, a larger BC Ferry runs service to Prince Rupert several days a week.

⑤ **Sandspit Harbour.** P.O. Box 477, Sandspit, BC V0T 1T0; (250) 637-5700; sandspitharbour@qcislands.net; www.sandspitharbour.com. Monitors VHF 06, 08, 09, 73. Open all year with guest moorage to 100 feet, 15, 30, 50 & 100 amp power, seasonal water, pumpout, pay phone, showers, washroom, garbage drop, launch ramp. Reservations recommended in the summer for vessels over 45 feet. Bridgeview Marine is located across the road.

Ⓢ **Sandspit Harbour Fuel Dock.** Operated by and located at Sandspit Harbour. Open from June through August 7:00 a.m. to 9:00 a.m. and 6:00 p.m. to 9:00 p.m. September through May 9:00 a.m. to 12:00 p.m. Gas and diesel available.

Ⓢ **Bridgeview Marine.** 537 Beach Road, Sandspit, BC V0T 1T0; (250) 637-5432; www.bridgeviewmarine.com. Open all year 8:00 a.m. to 5:00 p.m., Monday to Friday. Haulout to 36 feet and marine supplies. Mechanics with extensive outboard and stern

Louise Narrows is best navigated at close to high tide when the depth is about 12- to 15-feet. The channel is wide enough for medium-sized cruising vessels.

drive experience, limited diesel and inboard experience.

Moresby Camp. Moresby Camp has road access to Sandspit, a public float, and a boat launch.

Louise Narrows. The small boat passage at Louise Narrows is scenic, shallow and narrow, only 30 feet across in some places. It is best to travel through the passage before high water and while the gravel banks are still visible. This way, you can see the channel, and if you inadvertently run aground, the rising tide will float you off.

When we transited we saw depths of less than five feet under the keel. It was manageable, but added a bit of excitement to the passage. Given the limited space for maneuvering within the narrows, boats transiting Louise Narrows should make a securite call on VHF 16 (low power) before entering.

Skedans Bay. Skedans (or K'uuna Llnagaay) is situated on the the eastern tip of Louise Island. It faces south onto Skedans Bay from

a crescent beach that forms the neck of a small peninsula. As the furthest north of all the Watchmen sites, its relative accessibility makes it one of the most often visited. Contact the Haida Watchmen on VHF 06 before coming ashore. K'uuna Llnagaay means Village at the Edge, but it was also known by the Haida as Grizzly-Bear-Town because of the large number of grizzly bear carvings found there. Visiting traders named it Skedans, a corruption of the name of its chief, Gida'nsta.

In the mid-1800s almost 450 Haida lived here in about 26 longhouses. Records show there were 56 monumental cedar sculptures, including frontal poles, single and double mortuary poles, memorial poles and mortuary figures.

K'uuna Llnagaay is one of the few remaining village sites with some standing poles and remnants of large longhouses. Crests featured on the poles, such as rainbow, frog, eagle, beaver, and two-finned killer whale, signify which families lived here. A path winding through the old village allows you to appreciate the artistry of the poles, now in varying stages of decay, and provide a glimpse of

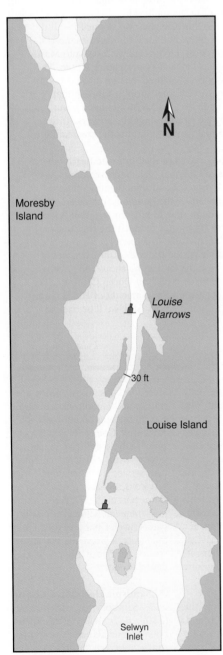

Louise Narrows

Crescent Inlet is a beautiful anchorage outside the protected area.

what life may have been like many years ago for the Haida.

This anchorage is considered temporary-only when visiting K'uuna Llnagaa.

Dana Passage. Dana Passage is a narrow and scenic route between Talunkwan and Moresby Islands. At the narrowest section, the passage is only about 100 feet wide, but depths are at least 30 feet throughout.

GWAII HAANAS NATIONAL PARK RESERVE

Tanu Island. The hauntingly beautiful village of T'aanuu Llnagaay is located on the east shore of Tanu Island, on Laskeek Bay. T'aanuu means eel grass, which commonly grows in shallow water around the village. T'aanuu Llnagaay follows the shoreline of two beaches divided by a rocky shoal. In the mid-1800s the village had about 550 inhabitants. More than 25 longhouses, 31 mortuary columns and 15 mortuary houses were recorded then. Present-day visitors notice the many logs on the ground and may mistake them for windfalls; these, however, are the posts and beams of old longhouses. The longhouses faced the shoreline, and were dug into the ground for protection from the weather. Large, rectangular pits mark their locations. Though there are no standing poles here, on close inspection you can see ancient carvings made smooth by time and furred by moss. Walking amidst the ruins, surrounded by the protective rainforest, one gets a strong sense of the people who lived there. Contact the Haida Watchmen on VHF 06 for permission before coming ashore.

Crescent Inlet. The head of secluded Crescent Inlet has sheltered anchorage with good holding. The inlet has beautiful views of mountains, old growth forest, and a meadow for wildlife viewing. It's an excellent stop. Moresby Explorers, a tour company, maintains a small floating lodge in Crescent Inlet.

Note: The inlet is just outside the protect-

Totem honoring the Eagle Clan.

Trail leading through the forest and rock to Nans Sdins.

ed area. An evening anchored here does not require a reservation or payment.

Hoya Bay. Hoya Bay, also known as Freshwater Cove, has a public float with untreated fresh water available. For overnight stays, anchor out or use one of the two public mooring buoys.

De la Beche Inlet. According to Douglass, De la Beche Inlet has two interesting anchorages, De la Beche Cove and Sac Bay. De la Beche Cove is a small nook on the south shore of De la Beche Inlet, landlocked by an island. Douglass reports adequate holding in the northwest corner.

Sac Bay. Sac Bay juts out to the south from De la Beche Inlet, good holding and spectacular mountain scenery.

⑥ **Hotspring Island.** *Due to an earthquake, the hot springs on Hotspring Island are no longer useable.* Hotspring Island has been one of the

most popular stops in Haida Gwaii. The hot springs, located on the south side of the island, were some of the finest on the coast. A magnitude 7.7 earthquake shook the area in October of 2012, and appeared to change mother nature's plumbing. Hot water no longer flows into the pools in the rocks. It is not clear whether this will change over time. A pool of hot water has been forming below the high water line, so perhaps, over time, the upper pools will again fill.

Haida Watchmen are still on site and require boaters to call on VHF channel 06 before coming ashore. They will direct you to an appropriate anchorage and the best place to land the dinghy. The anchorage directly off the hot springs should only be used temporarily, since it is exposed, with marginal holding. A better anchorage is between Hotspring and House islands.

Ramsay Passage Cove. Fairly well-protected alternative to Hotspring Island anchorages, but requires a 1.5-mile dinghy ride.

Dolomite Narrows. Dolomite Narrows is narrow, shallow, and poorly charted. One section dries completely on a 2-foot tide. The Douglasses recommend transiting Dolomite Narrows only after exploring the area thoroughly by dinghy first. We agree.

Bag Harbour. Bag Harbour is a secure anchorage at the south end of Dolomite Narrows. It's a good place to wait for appropriate conditions for a northbound transit of Dolomite Narrows, or relax after a southbound transit.

Ikeda Cove. Ikeda Cove is a lovely, protected anchorage with excellent holding. A grassy meadow is a haven for wildlife. We spotted deer, a bear and cub, and a pair of sand hill cranes. Remains of cabins, wharfs and machinery can be found on shore.

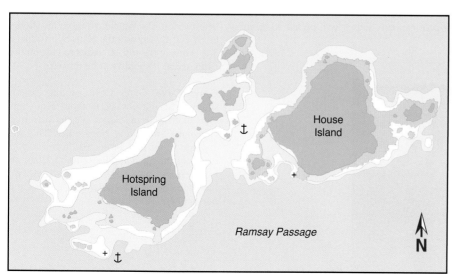
Hotspring Island

Collison Bay. Collison Bay offers good protection, easy anchoring depths, and good holding. The Douglasses report watching bears turn over rocks in search of food.

Windy Bay. Windy Bay, or Hlk'yah Gaaw-Ga, is a fair weather anchorage used to visit the historic fishing village called Hlk'yah Ll-nagaay (Falcon Town). Near here in 1985, the Haida blocked logging roads in their protest to put an end to logging on Lyell Island and protect the area that became Gwaii Haanas. The longhouse is named "Looking Around and Blinking House" to honor this victory. An old growth forest contains trees over 1000 years old and up over 200 feet tall. A trail leads through huge Sitka spruce and western red cedar trees, draped with mosses and lichens. The Haida Watchmen can point out culturally modified trees. Some of these trees show where test holes were cut in them to check their suitability for making a canoe or carving a pole.

In August of 2013, the first new monumental pole in 130 years was raised in Windy Bay, called The Legacy Pole. This pole was carved to celebrate the 20 years of co-management of the Reserve by the Haida Nation and the government of Canada. It is visible from the water.

Contact the Haida Watchmen on VHF 06 before coming ashore.

⑦ **Rose Harbour.** Once a bustling whaling station, Rose Harbour is now a small, quiet community and the only piece of privately owned land within Gwaii Haanas. Remnants of the old whale rendering facilities can still be found. Two public mooring buoys are available. Local residents provide bed and breakfast style lodging, tours, and meals.

Louscoone Inlet. Louscoone Inlet at the south end of Moresby Island has several possible anchorages. Small Cove, east of Crooked Point, is reportedly rocky and filled with kelp. Etches Point Cove, between two unnamed islands northwest of Etches Point, is the best anchorage and has one public mooring buoy. The Douglasses report another small and unnamed cove with limited swinging room 1

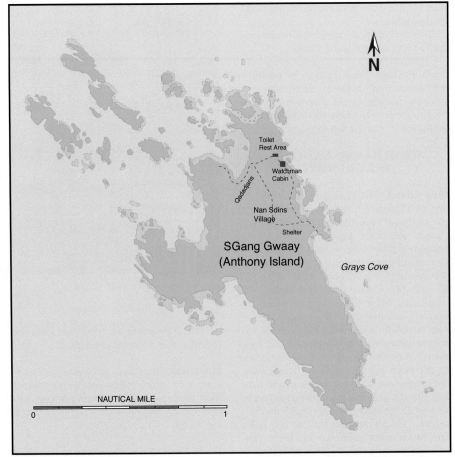

SGang Gwaay

mile northwest of Etches Point Cove and 0.4 mile north of Cadman Point.

⑧ **Anthony Island.** Anthony Island or SGang Gwaay, on the northwest side of Kunghit Island, is recognized worldwide as a historic UNESCO World Heritage Site. Nans Sdins (also known as Ninstints) is a former Haida village and the major attraction. Filled with the largest collection of original Haida heraldic and mortuary poles, Nans Sdins offers a remarkable look into the Haida culture. The poles at Nans Sdins have been reset upright for the last time. Going forward, when a pole naturally falls it will be left to decay,

following the tradition of the memory fading for the chief or family depicted by the pole, and for whom it was created.

Contact the Haida watchman on VHF 06 prior to going ashore. Anchorage is not available directly off of the totem park. Instead, anchor off the Watchman cabin (exposed), or in Grays Cove. Depending on the weather conditions, the Watchmen may tell you to anchor in the cove on the northwest corner of the island and dinghy to the beach where their boat is moored. You will most likely see other dinghies there. Look for the bright orange fishing float that marks the trail and boardwalk to the Watchman cabin for check-in. SGang Gwaay and the Nans Sdins Village Site is one of the top 10 places to visit on the entire coast. It should not be missed.

Grays Cove. Grays Cove, on the eastern shore of SGang Gwaay, is about a quarter-mile south of Nans Sdins. It's the preferred anchorage for visiting Nans Sdins. This anchorage is not well protected, however, and has only marginal holding. David Hoar, an experienced Haida Gwaii cruiser, writes, "We have NEVER (8 or 9 attempts) hooked the bottom here." Use caution.

Rose Harbour primitive log dock.

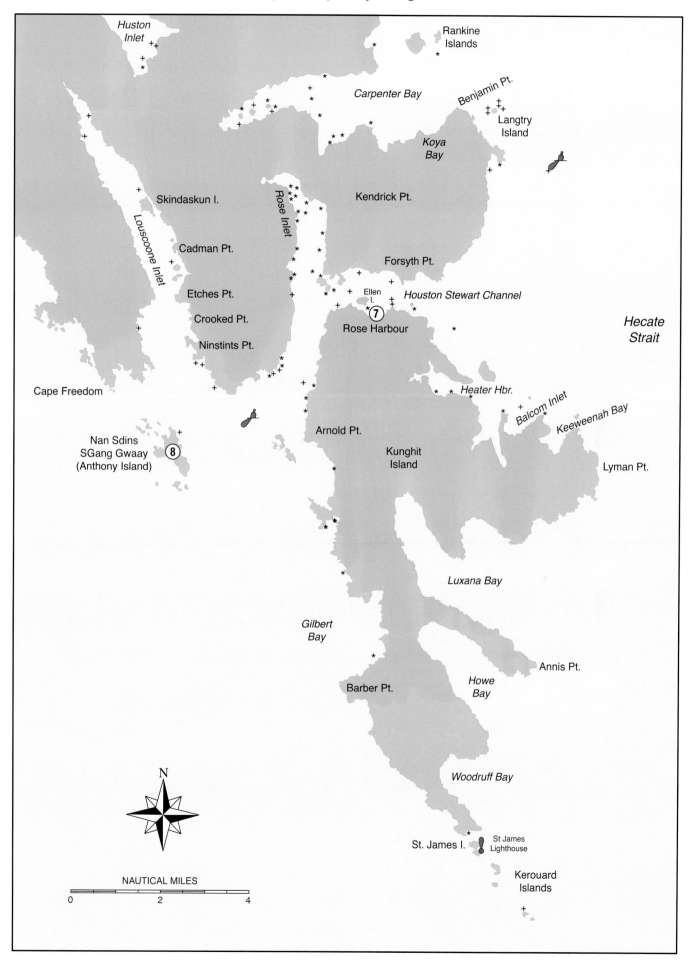

Huston
Inlet

Rankine
Islands

Carpenter Bay

Benjamin Pt.

Langtry
Island

Koya
Bay

Skindaskun I.

Rose Inlet

Kendrick Pt.

Cadman Pt.

Louscoone Inlet

Forsyth Pt.

Etches Pt.

Ellen
I.

Houston Stewart Channel

⑦

Crooked Pt.

Rose Harbour

Hecate
Strait

Ninstints Pt.

Cape Freedom

Heater Hbr.

Balcom Inlet

Keeweenah Bay

Nan Sdins
SGang Gwaay
(Anthony Island)

⑧

Arnold Pt.

Lyman Pt.

Kunghit
Island

Luxana Bay

Gilbert
Bay

Annis Pt.

Howe
Bay

Barber Pt.

Woodruff Bay

N

St. James I.

St James
Lighthouse

NAUTICAL MILES

Kerouard
Islands

0　　　　2　　　　4

CHAPTER 18

CROSSING DIXON ENTRANCE

VENN PASSAGE TO METLAKATLA BAY

PORTLAND INLET AND TONGASS PASSAGE ROUTE

NORTH DUNDAS ISLAND

FOGGY BAY OR MARY ISLAND TO KETCHIKAN

On to Southeast Alaska! This chapter covers departure routes from Prince Rupert and Chatham Sound, options for the open water crossing of Dixon Entrance, and the approach to Ketchikan.

The distance from Prince Rupert to Ketchikan (via Venn Passage) is 82 nautical miles. Depending on the speed of your vessel and the weather and sea conditions, a stop in Prince Rupert before crossing Dixon Entrance might be required. Foggy Bay is 50 miles from Prince Rupert. It's a pleasant and beautiful cove with good protection.

Ketchikan is a required stop for customs clearance into the U.S. Vessels that overnight in Foggy Bay before clearing customs in Ketchikan must first receive permission from U.S. Customs and Border Protection (907-228-5632).

Guidebook: For cruising in Alaska we recommend Don and Reanne Douglass' excellent guide, *Exploring Southeast Alaska,* 2nd Ed. Full disclosure: our sister company, Fine Edge, is the publisher. In 2007 the Southeast Alaska book was extensively updated by Waggoner correspondent Capt. Linda Lewis. It is the only comprehensive cruising guide for Southeast Alaska and includes additional tips for crossing Dixon Entrance and arriving in Ketchikan.

Before leaving British Columbia, however, consider some of the excellent cruising in Portland Inlet and Portland Canal, just north of Prince Rupert. Portland Canal is one of the longest fjords in North America and defines the border between the U.S. and Canada. It is beautiful and remote. Farther up the canal the water becomes increasingly opaque, almost milky, the result of glacial run-off. The outpost of Stewart, B.C., with Bear Glacier just above town, has a public dock, a "yacht club," and other services. Stewart, B.C. is so remote that there is no VHF weather radio reception.

Hyder, Alaska is on the other side of the canal, less than a mile from Stewart. Hyder does not have a U.S. Customs office for clearance. Ketchikan is the closest CBP office. The typical strategy is to explore British Columbia on the way north, then go to Ketchikan for customs clearance. When headed home from Southeast Alaska, explore the areas south of Ketchikan, such as Misty Fjord or

When anchored in Foggy Bay, outside conditions can be monitored by looking through the cut, shown above.

Hyder. Then go to Prince Rupert for customs clearance into Canada.

Both the United States and Canada require vessels to check in with customs authorities prior to anchoring, mooring, or going ashore.

In addition to Portland Canal, Observatory Inlet has a number of good anchorages. This area was the base camp for Captain George Vancouver when his expedition explored this area in 1793.

Cruising in Portland Canal is covered in detail by Don and Reanne Douglass in their cruising guide *Exploring the North Coast of British Columbia,* 2nd Ed.

Crossing Dixon Entrance: Heading North. Several options exist for transiting Chatham Sound and crossing the open water of Dixon Entrance.

Understanding how to read the weather, sea conditions, and currents is critical to planning a safe and comfortable passage. Good planning for the crossing starts with examining the weather forecast and course options.

A stop at Prince Rupert can be a welcome break after the long passage up Grenville Channel and through northern British Columbia. Prince Rupert is the last fuel stop in Canada, and some boats may need to take on fuel before proceeding to Ketchikan.

If conditions are favorable, many boats avoid Prince Rupert entirely on their way north. This saves approximately 3 to 4 hours of transit time. Anchorages are available in the Moffatt Islands and Brundige Inlet on Dundas Island, or in Foggy Bay after crossing Dixon Entrance (with a call to U.S. Customs and Border Protection in Ketchikan, (907) 225-2254).

The first route option is the shortest. From Venn Passage steer towards the northeast tip of Dundas Island. Then set a course past Cape Fox (leave plenty of sea room) to Mary Island and up Revillagigedo Channel. This is

the most exposed route.

A second route is a variation on the first: Cross Chatham Sound on a northwest heading and pass through the Moffatt Islands. They're beautiful and protected, but require good situational awareness to navigate among the many small islands, islets, and rocks. Several anchorages are tucked among the islands, pleasant enough for an overnight at anchor. At Dundas Island cross to Cape Fox and follow the coast line to Foggy Bay to overnight. The next morning continue up Revillagigedo Channel to Ketchikan.

The third choice is a longer route. First travel along the east side of Chatham Sound, then cross Portland Inlet. Sometimes referred to as the "mainland route," it offers some protection, and minimizes the open water crossing by harbor hopping along the shoreline. Attention needs to be focused on the effect of outflow wind and current from Portland Inlet.

The longer routes offer more shelter and duck-in points. The best choice depends on current conditions. It is critical to develop a good picture of the currents, wind speed and direction, and ocean swells from the Environment Canada and NOAA weather forecasts, buoy reports, and lightstation reports. Monitoring these resources for several days prior to crossing Dixon Entrance can give a skipper a good understanding of what to expect during a crossing. Once headed up Revillagigedo Channel, instructions for clearing U.S. Customs and arriving in Ketchikan are covered in the Ketchikan chapter, beginning on page 427.

Weather planning. For most, planning a Dixon Entrance crossing starts with NOAA and Environment Canada forecasts. Use NOAA's "Dixon Entrance to Cape Decision" forecast and Environment Canada's "Dixon Entrance East," forecast.

17434	Revillagigedo Channel, Ruys & Foggy Bays, Duke I. (1:80,000)
17435	Harbors in Clarence Strait Various
17428	Revillagigido Channel, Nichols Pass. & Tongass Narrows (1:40,000)
3955 Plans	Prince Rupert Harbour
3957	Approaches to Prince Rupert Harbour (1:40,000)

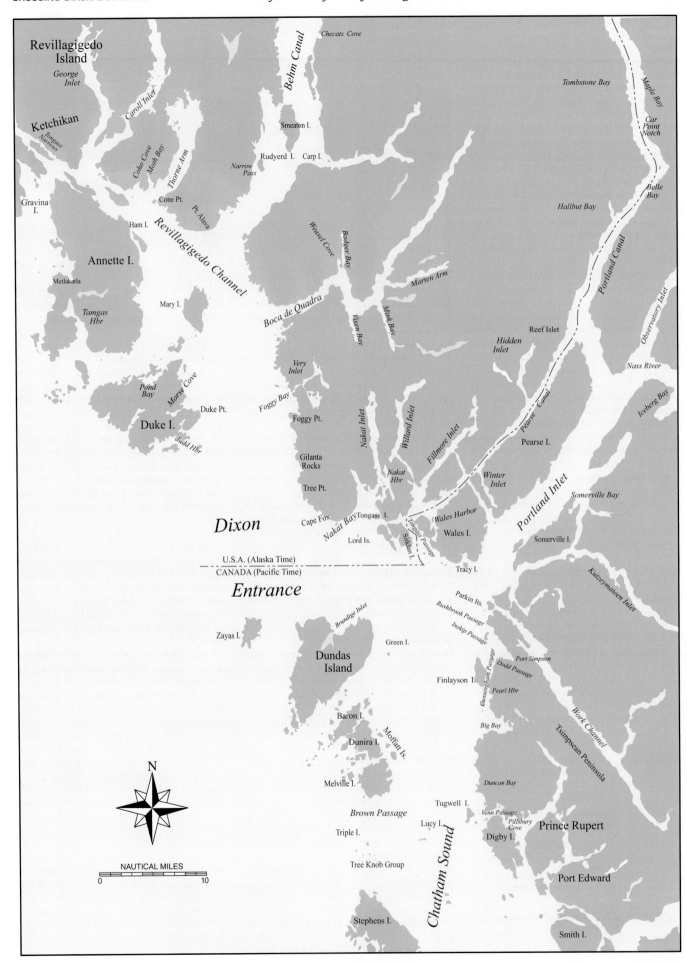

Revillagigedo
Island

*George
Inlet*

Ketchikan

*Tongass
Narrows*

Caroll Inlet

Coho Cove

Math Bay

Thorne Arm

Behm Canal

Checats Cove

Tombstone Bay

Maple Bay

*Car
Point
Notch*

Smeaton I.

Rudyerd I.   Carp I.

*Narrow
Pass*

Cone Pt.

Pt. Alava

*Belle
Bay*

Halibut Bay

Gravina
I.

Ham I.

Revillagigedo Channel

*Weasel
Cove*

Badger Bay

Marten Arm

Portland Canal

Annette I.

Metlakatla

Mary I.

Boca de Quadra

Vixen Bay

Mink Bay

Reef Islet

Observatory Inlet

*Tamgas
Hbr*

*Hidden
Inlet*

Nass River

*Pond
Bay*

Morse Cove

*Very
Inlet*

Iceberg Bay

Duke Pt.

Foggy Bay

Pearse Canal

Pearse I.

Duke I.

Judd Hbr

Foggy Pt.

Nakat Inlet

Willard Inlet

Fillmore Inlet

*Winter
Inlet*

Portland Inlet

Somerville Bay

Gilanta
Rocks

*Nakat
Hbr*

Tree Pt.

Kutzeymateen Inlet

Cape Fox

Nakat Bay Tongass I.

Wales Harbor

Somerville I.

Dixon

Nakat Bay

Lord Is.

Wales I.

Tongass Passage

Sitklan I.

Tracy I.

U.S.A. (Alaska Time)

CANADA (Pacific Time)

Entrance

Parkin Its.

Rushbrook Passage

Work Channel

Brundige Inlet

Inskip Passage

Zayas I.

Green I.

Cunningham Passage

Port Simpson

Dodd Passage

Dundas
Island

Finlayson I.

Pearl Hbr

Tsimpsean Peninsula

Baron I.

Moffatt Is.

Dunira I.

Big Bay

Melville I.

Duncan Bay

N

Tugwell I.

Venn Passage

Brown Passage

Lucy I.

*Pillsbury
Cove*

Prince Rupert

Triple I.

Digby I.

Chatham Sound

Tree Knob Group

Port Edward

NAUTICAL MILES

0   10

Stephens I.

Smith I.

Given a favorable forecast, several weather reporting stations are useful in determining if conditions are acceptable. The Central Dixon Entrance Buoy (*Buoy 44145*) provides regularly updated wind speed, direction and sea state information. This information can be accessed by listening to the continuous marine broadcast, using the dial-a-buoy service (888-701-8992), or online at www.ndbc.noaa.gov.

Automated, land-based weather stations at Lucy Island, Grey Islet, and Rose Spit provide wind speed and direction, updated hourly. The Green Island and Triple Island lightstations are staffed with lightkeepers year round. These lightkeepers provide weather observations every three hours. Their updates include wind and sea conditions. Listen for their reports on the continuous marine broadcast, or visit www.weather.gc.ca.

The NOAA Ocean Prediction Center, Pacific Marine section website has extensive forecast information (www.opc.ncep.noaa.gov/Pac_tab.shtml). The 24, 48, and 96 hour wind and wave forecast charts are a valuable resource for a graphical look at upcoming weather systems and conditions.

Consider reading a weather book or taking a weather course to help understand and interpret weather data. Much data is available, even if the only source is the continuous marine broadcast. The key is to understand the information as it streams by, and to use reports from multiple stations to paint a complete picture for the area you are interested in. An outflow wind from Portland Inlet blowing against a flood current, for example, will make for rough conditions as far away as Dundas Island. Even with the best preparations, conditions can change. Have a backup plan. Be sure your vessel and crew are ready for changing weather conditions.

Venn Passage to Metlakatla Bay. Venn Passage and the route through Metlakatla Bay is suitable for recreational boats of 65 feet or less. The route through Venn Passage is narrow and twisting, with shoals on each side. Buoys and ranges help navigation. Depths can be less than 10 feet, so some skippers time their passage for mid- or high-tide.

This route saves about 12 miles, compared with going south from Prince Rupert Harbour and rounding Digby Island. It's the channel favored by the fishing fleet, and it can be busy with fish boats. The route requires careful situational awareness and attention to the depth sounder. Even the buoys are suspect. In the past some have been dragged hundreds of yards out of position by log tows. Use caution when passing the landing for the ferry to the airport at Du Vernay Point. It is a no-wake zone. Spend time studying the charts to understand this route before attempting.

From Prince Rupert, head west to Grindstone Point and enter the channel. Follow the buoys and range markers. Note when heading west through Venn Passage, the range markers will be astern (back ranges). You will need either a clear view astern, or a stern watch with clear communication to the helm. At Tugwell Island, a turn to the north takes you into Chatham Sound toward Dundas Island, or along a route that follows the shoreline toward Port Simpson and Portland Inlet.

Dundas Island Route. The shortest route across Dixon Entrance is to depart Metlakatla Bay, take a direct course towards Green Island, then head up Holliday Passage. Round the top of Dundas Island and turn toward Mary Island and Danger Pass. Take Felice Strait to Revillagigedo Channel and proceed via Tongass Narrows to Ketchikan. If Dixon Entrance is too rough, you can anchor in protected Brundige Inlet on the north end of Dundas Island and remain in Canadian waters. If conditions allow a crossing of Dixon Entrance late in the day you can proceed to Foggy Bay for the night. The next day go from Foggy Bay to Ketchikan via Revillagigedo Channel and Tongass Narrows.

For planning purposes, it's about 26 miles from Metlakatla to Brundige Inlet. It's an additional 22 miles from Brundige Inlet to Foggy Bay. Foggy Bay to Ketchikan is 32 miles. The total distance from Prince Rupert to Ketchikan is just under 85 miles—a long day for a displacement speed cruising boat.

Moffatt Islands. For an interesting and scenic passage, depart Metlakatla Bay and head west to Melville Island. Carefully pick your way through the channel between Dunira Island and the Moffatt Islands. Cross to Dundas Island and Holliday Passage and proceed to the north end of Dundas Island. Several small anchorages are along the way in the Moffatt Islands. Canadian *Sailing Directions* cautions against this route without local knowledge.

Brundige Inlet. Brundige Inlet extends for about 2.5 miles. Enter at Prospector Point. The inlet is well protected, though windblown and barren in areas. Some have advised of vicious black flies on the island. Not the prettiest anchorage, but a good departure point to cross Dixon Entrance.

Foggy Bay. Foggy Bay is a well protected stopping place between Prince Rupert and Ketchikan. For those headed north, it can provide an escape from rough conditions in Dixon Entrance. Headed south, it is a good overnight anchorage to shorten the leg to Prince Rupert and allows for an early morning departure to cross Dixon Entrance. Most boats anchor in the "inner cove," which provides a view of the conditions in Foggy Bay and Dixon Entrance. If you want privacy in a remote environment, cruise deep into Very Inlet to the "north basin." Use the Douglass's *Exploring Southeast Alaska* for detailed information on the anchorage in Foggy Bay and other interesting anchorages in the area.

LOCAL KNOWLEDGE

FISHING NETS: From Cape Fox to Tree Point, you may encounter gillnet fishing boats. It is best to cross the bow of gillnetters and stay away from the up to 1800 foot long net strung out behind the boat. The end is noted by an orange float, which is often difficult to see in choppy seas.

Be on the lookout for commercial traffic in Venn Passage.

The Green Island Lightstation near the Dundas Islands is a useful weather site when planning a trip across Dixon Entrance.

Gillnetters, like this one, frequent Dixon Entrance. Be sure to steer clear of their nets.

Foggy Bay or Mary Island to Ketchikan.

This route appears to be a straight shot up Revillagigedo Channel to Ketchikan, although weather conditions can vary from one side of the channel to the other. You might also encounter changing conditions as you pass Behm Canal, Thorne Arm or other inlets, depending on the wind direction and speed. Expect to see more recreational vessels, fish boats, tugs with tows and even large cruise ships maneuvering in Tongass Narrows as you approach Ketchikan.

Note the location of Behm Canal as you pass. Later in the trip you might want to visit some of the majestic cruising areas in Misty Fjords. For now, continue to Ketchikan to clear customs.

Danger Pass.

At the south end of Mary Island and off Edge Point, this narrow passage will allow you to move out of the main channel and along the backside of Mary Island. Depending on the wind direction this route allows you to travel in the lee of Mary Island.

Portland Inlet & Tongass Passage Route.

This route is preferred when northern outflow winds from Portland Inlet create a sharp chop in Chatham Sound. It reduces the open water across Portland Inlet to less than 5 miles. The total distance from Metlakatla Bay to Foggy Bay is about 50 miles.

If planning to overnight in Foggy Bay, the skipper must call U.S. Customs and Border Protection (907-225-2254) in Ketchikan and inform them. You are now in the United States, which requires clearing with CBP before anchoring, mooring, or going ashore. Proceed to Ketchikan and clear customs as soon as possible.

Port Simpson.

North of Metlakatla Bay, Port Simpson can be used as a jumping-off point for crossing Portland Inlet. Port Simpson is a tribal village protected behind Rose Island. There are several floats, though they're often filled with commercial and fishing vessels, requiring rafting. A small store is in the village.

Lincoln Channel.

Lincoln Channel, between Tongass Island and Kanagunut Island on the west and Sitklan Island and the mainland on the east, provides an interesting stop with easy access for boats coming from either Ketchikan or Nichols Bay on Prince of Wales Island. The south end of Lincoln Channel is only two miles from the Canadian border and 38 miles from Prince Rupert, making it a good jumping-off point for vessels heading south.

This is a popular anchorage for fishing boats during the gillnet season. Several fishermen keep float houses here. Tongass Island was the site of Fort Tongass, the first U.S. Customs office in Alaska, and a major Tlingit village. The rocky shores of Kanagunut Island contain interesting rock formations. You may even find garnets near Garnet Point on the south tip of the island.

Enter at either the north or south ends of the channel, or between Tongass Island on the north and Kanagunut Island on the south. If entering between Tongass and Kanagunut, follow Chart 17437 carefully and watch for rocks. The best anchorage is north of a small unnamed island in 80-100 feet. Anchorage can also be found off Tongass Island or, in northerly winds, south of the unnamed island.

Crossing Dixon Entrance: Heading South.

Southbound vessels coming from Southeast Alaska must clear Canadian Customs if they intend to stop or anchor in British Columbia. If transiting non-stop between Ketchikan and the U.S., as delivery captains or fishing boats often do, customs clearance is not required. Most recreational boats will stop along the way and thus require clearance into Canada in Prince Rupert.

Approach Prince Rupert through Metlakatla Bay and Venn Passage, or continue down the west side of Digby Island and enter through Prince Rupert Harbour.

Once in the harbor, proceed to the designated customs dock (preferred) or one of the three marinas where customs reporting is allowed by telephone: Fairview Terminal, Prince Rupert Rowing & Yacht Club, or Rushbrooke Floats.

The customs dock, or "lightering dock," is painted green (for years it was painted blue). A dedicated phone on the dock can be used to call customs officials. The customs dock is located west of the Cow Bay area and below a shopping mall on shore. The gate to the street is locked.

If clearing customs at another facility, call by cell phone (1-888-226-7277 or 250-627-3003).

Until cleared, all crew must remain on the boat. Canadian Customs may send agents to your boat for an inspection. Once cleared, you will be given a clearance number to post on the dockside window of your vessel and record in the ship's log.

If the weather deteriorates and you must anchor in Canadian waters before clearing customs in Prince Rupert, call Canadian Customs by phone, or notify the Canadian Coast Guard on VHF 16.

Note: All calls to Canadian Customs are directed to a call center in Hamilton, Ontario. This was new in 2013, and some of the agents were not used to the geography of the Inside Passage. While the customs agents on the phone are not located in Prince Rupert, they can still call out local agents if a clearance requires an inspection.

With patience and a keen weather eye, Dixon Entrance can be crossed in calm conditions.

Welcome to Alaska's 1st City

KETCHIKAN

The Salmon Capital of the World

ARRIVING IN KETCHIKAN

KETCHIKAN
Thomas Basin • Casey Moran • Bar Harbor North & South

Ketchikan. Tongass Narrows is the transition from crossing Dixon Entrance to arrival in a bustling maritime city. The transition begins at Mountain Point, and the closer you get to the city, the more signs of humanity you will see. Overhead, float planes take summer tourists to Behm Canal and other sites. The shoreline changes from remote and pristine to a few homes, then a few more, and eventually a developed roadway. Soon cars are whizzing by. Off in the distance, up Tongass Narrows, the shapes of what seems to be a major city appear. In reality, they are the profiles of cruise ships lined up at the docks, towering 10 stories high, dwarfing the buildings below.

You will pass the red-roofed Coast Guard station, the fuel docks, the fish processing docks, and more.

The rip-rap entrance to Thomas Basin is straight ahead, but during the summer months the lineup of cruise ships can make it hard to identify. Three to six cruise ships could be standing by, their passengers off to tour the city, shop, or just hang out and absorb their first (or last) stop in Alaska. You may encounter one of the cruise ships headed towards you, an imposing sight.

Ketchikan calls itself "Alaska's First City"—the first city visitors see when they arrive in Southeast Alaska by boat. The cruise ships typically arrive early in the morning and depart by mid-afternoon or early evening. During the day the town can be bursting with 8,000 visitors if several cruise ships are docked. When the ships leave, usually in late afternoon or early evening, the tourist shops close and Ketchikan returns to a sleepy

Cruise ships are a common sight in Ketchikan. When arriving, the cruise ships can be seen before the town.

little Alaskan town.

Ketchikan has a good public bus system, the Ketchikan Gateway Borough Bus, that shuttles passengers to the main attractions, or from the airport ferry to downtown. Individual rides are $1 and a day pass can be purchased for $2. The bus also runs to several places you may want to visit, like Totem Bight State Park, and additional shopping farther from the waterfront.

Ketchikan has three marinas for transient moorage, each with its own advantages, disadvantages, and personality.

When approaching from the south, Thomas Basin is the first, located at the foot of Creek Street in the heart of the tourist district. It's an easy walk to groceries, local shops, and attractions.

Casey Moran Harbor, formerly known as (and still often called) "City Floats," is next. It's small and in the middle of downtown, right in the shadow of the cruise ships.

Bar Harbor North and South are about a mile north of the center of Ketchikan. A major grocery store, shopping mall, and chandlery are a short walk away.

A Walmart, north of town and Bar Harbor, runs a free shuttle between their superstore and the cruise ship docks. Ketchikan has several options for provisioning and picking up parts and marine hardware.

Ketchikan also has a number of local attractions and museums, including the Totem Heritage Center, the Southeast Alaska Discovery Center, and the Tongass Historical Museum. All are within walking distance of the marinas. Totem Bight State Park and Saxman Native Village are accessible by bus.

Time change. Ketchikan is in Alaska Time Zone, one hour earlier than Seattle and British Columbia. Set clocks back one hour when you arrive.

Weather. Ketchikan gets more than 150 inches of rain each year. Summer is drier than winter, but Ketchikan's driest month (July) is still wetter than Seattle's wettest month (November). Ketchikan gets more rain than most other parts of Southeast Alaska. Day-

CHARTS	
17428	Revillagigedo Channel, Nichols Passage & Tongass Narrows (1:40,000)
17430	Ketchikan Harbor (1:10,000)
17434	Revillagigedo Channel, Ruys & Foggy Bays, Duke I. (1:80,000)

This ferry is part of the Alaska Marine Highway system. Similar ferries operate throughout Southeast Alaska.

During the day, Ketchikan fills with cruise ship passengers. By evening, the cruise ships leave and the town empties.

time summer temperatures typically range from the high 40s to the mid 60s, but occasionally reach into the 80s. Rain boots, better known as "Alaska Sneakers," are readily available in local stores. Locals swear by the XtraTuf brand.

Moorage. The City of Ketchikan's Port & Harbors department manages the waterfront. All slips are permanently assigned with waiting lists for vacancies. Visiting boats are hotberthed. When a local boat goes out, the harbor notes the vacancy and rents the slip. It usually works well. Sometimes, though, a permanent tenant will return unannounced. If this happens the office will assign the visiting boat to a new slip. Harbor staffers are on the docks often, checking the status of slips. They work hard to accommodate everyone.

During a stay in Ketchikan, you may have to move between marinas, from Thomas Basin to, say, Bar Harbor. When your crew goes out touring or shopping, they could come back to find the boat has moved to a new

The Totem Heritage Center.

moorage a mile away. It helps to have a communication plan in case things change.

The Port & Harbors office does not take reservations. Things change by the hour; the

office will work with you to find moorage. Call on VHF 73 (preferred), VHF 16, or phone (907) 228-5632. Moorage is paid by calling the harbor office with credit card information, or in person at the harbor office in the middle of Bar Harbor marina. The office is open 8:00 a.m. to 5:00 p.m. seven days a week during the summer months, and 8:00 a.m. to 5:00 p.m. Monday through Friday during the winter. The Harbor Master is available from 6:00 a.m. to 10:00 p.m. during the summer months.

Airport. The Ketchikan Airport is convenient for visitors and crew flying to or from Ketchikan. Alaska Airlines has several daily flights to Seattle. The airport is located across Tongass Narrows on Gravina Island, and connects with Ketchikan by a ferry that departs and arrives just to the north of Bar Harbor Marina. The ferry leaves the airport terminal every 30 minutes. Crossing time is approximately 10 minutes. If flying out, allow time for the ferry schedule and ride to the airport.

Stairs and ramps connect the airport terminal with the ferry. If you have considerable luggage, it's best to take an airport shuttle van that will deliver you and your luggage door-to-door. A small dock is below the covered stairway, north of the ferry dock. A dinghy or small boat can be tied up to drop off or pickup guests and luggage. The modest moorage fee can be paid in an honor box on the dock if you elect to leave your boat go to the baggage claim or ticketing area.

Customs Clearance. Vessels entering Alaska from B.C. are required to clear customs in Ketchikan. When headed north to Southeast Alaska, it may be necessary to anchor for the night due to approaching darkness or worsening weather conditions. Technically, vessels are not allowed to drop anchor or land in Alaska until they have checked in at a U.S. Customs reporting station.

U.S. Customs and Border Protection (CBP) typically allows arriving vessels to stay one night in Foggy Bay before proceeding to Ketchikan. The procedure is to call (907-225-2254) and advise CBP of your plans.

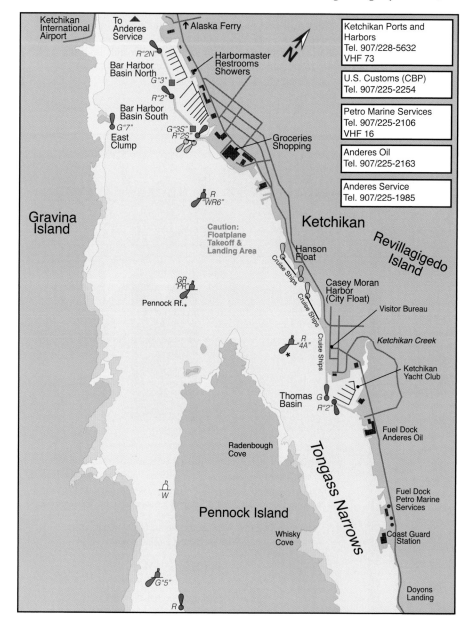

DON'T MISS MISTY FJORDS NATIONAL MONUMENT

Misty Fjords National Monument is among the most breathtaking places on the coast. Sheer granite walls plunge into the water from thousands of feet above and waterfalls gush from the snowcapped peaks. It's like Princess Louisa Inlet, only bigger and seldom visited by cruising boats.

Misty Fjords is on the west side of Behm Canal, which winds around Revillagigedo Island, and is entered either south or north of Ketchikan. Boats arriving from British Columbia typically pass the southern entrance, but because they have not yet cleared customs they are not allowed to visit. Thus, visiting Misty Fjords National Monument requires a bit of backtracking from Ketchikan.

Because of this, many save Misty Fjords for the end of their Southeast Alaska cruise. Upon exiting Behm Canal, they can overnight in Foggy Bay or proceed directly to Prince Rupert to clear Canadian Customs.

Some cruisers visit Misty Fjords by circumnavigating Revillagigedo Island. The downside is the relatively boring western section. An alternative is to head southeast from Ketchikan for about 20 miles. Then turn north into Behm Canal.

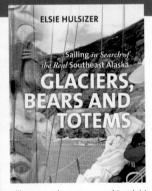

Smeaton Bay is the first bay and is not visited often. Rudyerd Bay is the next bay, just past New Eddystone Rock. New Eddystone has a sandy beach and a remarkable, tree covered spire of rock jutting 200 feet into the air.

Rudyerd Bay is probably the most visited area of Misty Fjords National Monument. Punchbowl Cove, the first anchorage, juts off to the south. It's deep and astoundingly beautiful. Think Yosemite, multiply by 3 or 4, and fill the valleys with water. A steep, muddy trail leads to a lake about 1000 feet above sea level.

Don't expect to be alone in Punchbowl Cove. Tour boats and floatplanes bring cruise ship passengers from Ketchikan to Misty Fjords. We were shocked at how many camera flashes we saw going off as they passed our boat!

— Mark Bunzel

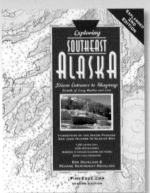

Many crews will call from Prince Rupert. For most U.S. cell phone carriers, coverage begins at Cape Fox, with fairly good coverage in Dixon Entrance. We haven't found cell phone coverage in Foggy Bay.

Assuming a good phone connection, a CBP agent will take all of the necessary information about your vessel and crew. Be ready with your information when you call. The next day when you arrive in Ketchikan, the agent will have this information when he or she comes to your boat.

The Nexus program is not used in Ketchikan. Ketchikan CBP has a 100% boarding policy.

On a recent trip, we knew we would arrive in Ketchikan after normal office hours. We called the CBP office from the water several hours ahead and the CBP agent took all of our information. When we arrived at our slip in Thomas Basin we called CBP again to inform them of our arrival and location. Although it was after office hours, an agent met us at our boat and we received our clearance number within five minutes. He had all the information on a computer printout and needed only to verify and inspect our passports. The friendly discussion took place on the boat. The clearance number was written into the ship's log, and on a slip of paper to be displayed from the cabin window on the dock side of the boat. CBP officers do check the marinas to confirm that all vessels have checked in.

When approaching Ketchikan through Tongass Narrows, you'll pass the fuel docks. Upon request, and if workload allows, CBP may meet you at the fuel dock for clearance, allowing you to refuel and clear customs at the same time. Call first to see if this is possible.

Note: Vessels that pass through B.C. without stopping or clearing customs do not need to clear customs in Ketchikan.

Petro Marine Services. 1100 Stedman St, P.O. Box 7398, Ketchikan, 99901; (800) 478-7277; (907) 225-2106; www.petromarineservices.com. Monitors VHF 16. Located

Thomas Basin, as seen from a cruise ship. Cruise ships moor just north (left in this photo) of the entrance to Thomas Basin.

on Tongass Narrows next to the U.S. Coast Guard station. Open 7 days a week, 7:00 a.m. to 7:00 p.m. in the summer and Monday through Saturday, 7:00 a.m. to 5:00 p.m. in the winter. Gasoline, diesel, propane, lubricants, restrooms, showers, garbage, and waste oil disposal.

Anderes Oil Inc. 900 Stedman St., P.O. Box 5858, Ketchikan, AK 99901; (907) 225-2163; www.anderesoil.com. Monitors VHF 16. Located on Tongass Narrows. Gasoline, diesel, propane, lubricants.

Doyon's Landing. 1716 South Tongass Highway, Ketchikan, AK 99901; (907) 225-5155; moorage@doyonslanding.com; www.doyonslanding.com. Power, water, 24-hour security, internet, telephone. Reservations encouraged. This is a full service marina that caters to large yachts. Located south of town near the Coast Guard station.

Thomas Basin. (907) 228-5632; www.city.

ketchikan.ak.us. Monitors VHF 73. Moorage for boats to 60 feet, call ahead as all stalls are reserved. Water, garbage and waste oil disposal, tidal grid to 100 tons (reservations required for grid). Power varies from slip to slip, check with the harbor office and inform them of power requirements when requesting a slip. Supermarket, restaurants and bars nearby. Located at the foot of Creek Street with many attractions within walking distance. Local bus and taxi available on nearby Steadman Street.

Ketchikan Yacht Club. (907) 225-3262; info@ketchikanyachtclub.org; www.ketchikanyachtclub.org. On Float 2 in Thomas Basin, with guest moorage when a member's slip is not being used. Pick an empty slip that fits your boat and check the whiteboard at the head of the slip for the return date of the slip holder. Long side: boats 36-45 feet. Short side: boats 24-39 feet. Slips cannot be reserved. Moorage is paid in the honor box at the yacht club. Power is 30 amp. A key to

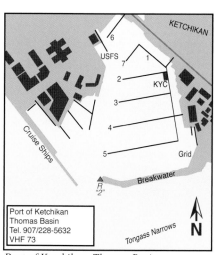
Port of Ketchikan, Thomas Basin

The charming Creek Street shops are located just above Thomas Basin.

the clubhouse is available for guest boats. The clubhouse has restrooms, showers, laundry, kitchen and social area. Guests are welcome to use the facility.

Casey Moran. (907) 228-5632; www.city. ketchikan.ak.us. Monitors VHF 73. Open moorage for boats to 90 feet, 30 & 50 amp power, water, garbage, pumpout, and waste oil disposal. Close to all downtown attractions and in the shadow of cruise ships during the day. Restaurants, bars, and marine supplies nearby. Bus and taxi service are on the busy street above the marina.

Bar Harbor North and South. (907) 228-5632; www.city.ketchikan.ak.us. Open moorage available on Floats 2 and 16 and on the ends of Floats 10 to 15 for boats to 80 feet. All slips reserved. Do not moor in a slip without authorization from harbormaster. Limited power (some of the docks are old). Pumpout, water, restrooms, showers (8 minutes for $2 in quarters, change available in harbor office), laundry, garbage and waste oil disposal at the head of the dock. Tidal grid available by reservation. Restaurants, groceries, chandlery and shopping mall nearby. Walking distance to the Alaska Marine Highway ferry terminal and the local ferry to the airport. Bus and taxi service available. The harbor office, with restrooms and showers, is in the green building between the north and south areas of the harbor.

Anderes Service. 4161 Tongass Avenue, Ketchikan, AK 99901; (907) 225-1985; www.anderesoil.com. Located on Tongass Narrows just south of the airport ferry. Gasoline, diesel, and lubricants. Open 7 days a week, 7:00 a.m. to 6:00 p.m. in the summer and Monday through Friday, 8:00 a.m. to 5:00 p.m. in the winter.

The Casey Moran floats are first come, first served. Cruise ships tie up just outside.

THINGS TO DO

1. **Totem Heritage Center.** Located south of Thomas Basin and within walking distance. Great display of historic old totems.

2. **Deer Mountain Tribal Hatchery and Eagle Center.** Located near the Totem Heritage Center. Offers an educational look at Alaska's salmon hatchery program. Showcases raptors and other birds that have been rescued and are being rehabilitated.

3. **Saxman Native Village and Totem Bight State Park.** A glimpse into the traditions of the Tlingit culture. Both can be reached by bus.

4. **Southeast Alaska Discovery Center.** Located just above Thomas Basin. National Park Service museum includes exhibits and interactive displays about the land, people, and culture of Southeast Alaska.

5. **Creek Street.** Just above Thomas Basin. Cute shops, though a little touristy. Still fun to stroll.

6. **Tongass Historical Museum.** Located at the top of Creek Street. This is the town museum; small and well done covering the history of Ketchikan.

7. **Float Plane to Misty Fjords.** A number of operators along the waterfront offer breathtaking tours of Behm Canal and Misty Fjords.

8. **Rent a Car or a Harley.** You can tour the area in a standard rental car, a classic 1950s rental car, or even a Harley. You won't be going far, though, since there aren't many roads around Ketchikan.

9. **Tongass Trading Company.** Above the Casey Moran Floats. A large store with souvenirs on the first floor and good stuff for cruising in Alaska on the second floor including boots, jackets, marine and fishing supplies.

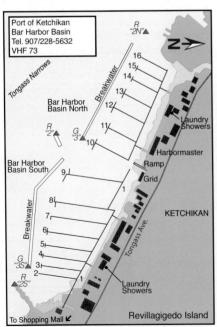

Port of Ketchikan, Bar Harbor Basin

Spectacular Punchbowl Cove in Misty Fjords is a popular stop on tours from Ketchikan.

TOWING, SERVICES & FISHERIES MANAGEMENT

U.S. TOWING AND EMERGENCY NUMBERS

CATeam Marine Assistance	(360) 378-9636
Fremont Tugboat Co.	(206) 632-0151
Vessel Assist all locations 24-hour dispatch	(800) 888-4869
Vessel Assist Anacortes	(360) 675-7900
Vessel Assist Everett	(425) 344-3056
Vessel Assist San Juan	(360) 378-1111
(Friday Harbor & Roche Harbor)	
Vessel Assist Lake Washington	(206) 793-7375
Vessel Assist Oak Harbor	(360) 675-7900
Vessel Assist Olympia	(360) 790-9008
Vessel Assist Port Townsend	(360) 301-9764
Vessel Assist Port Hadlock	(360) 301-9764
Vessel Assist Seattle	(206) 300-0486
Vessel Assist Tacoma	(253) 312-2927
Vessel Assist Whidbey (Deception Pass)	(360) 675-7900

U.S. Coast Guard Emergencies   **VHF Channel 16 or call 911**
(206) 217-6001 or (206) 220-7001

Cellular Phones Only   **911**
U.S. Coast Guard District Office: Seattle   (206) 220-7000

U.S. CUSTOMS CLEARANCE NUMBERS

For customs entry call: (800) 562-5943

The office numbers below are for weekdays only.

Anacortes	(360) 293-2331
Friday Harbor/Roche Harbor	(360) 378-2080
Point Roberts	(360) 945-2314
Port Angeles	(360) 457-4311
Aberdeen	(360) 532-2030
Bellingham	(360) 734-5463
Blaine	(360) 332-8511
Everett	(425) 259-0246
Port Townsend	(360) 385-3777
Seattle	(206) 553-0770
Tacoma/Olympia	(253) 593-6338

B.C. BORDER SERVICES CLEARANCE NUMBER

All locations & CANPASS
contact Canada Border Services Agency toll-free: (888) 226-7277

PARKS INFORMATION NUMBERS

Wash. State Parks Launch & Moorage Permit Program (360) 902-8500
B. C. Parks General Information   (250) 387-5002

PARALYTIC SHELLFISH POISON (PSP) NUMBERS

Washington State Paralytic Shellfish Poison closures   (800) 562-5632
B. C. Paralytic Shellfish Poison closures   (866) 431-3474

B.C. TOWING AND EMERGENCY NUMBERS

Vessel Assist Gulf Islands	(800) 413-8222
C-Tow VHF CH. 07A or	(888) 419-2869

Covers Victoria to the north end of Vancouver Island & the Tofino area

Vessel Assist Georgia Strait   (250) 247-8934

Canadian Coast Guard Emergency Numbers   **VHF CH. 16**
Search and Rescue: Vancouver   VHF CH 16 or (800) 567-5111
Search and Rescue: Victoria   (250) 413-8933 or (800) 567-5111
Search and Rescue: Other areas   (800) 567-5111

Canadian Coast Guard District Office: Victoria   (250) 480-2600

VESSEL TRAFFIC SERVICE PHONE NUMBERS

See page 31 for more information on Vessel Traffic Service.

Washington:
USCG Puget Sound Vessel Traffic Center   (206) 217-6040
B.C.:
Comox MCTS Centre	(250) 339-3613
Tofino MCTS Centre	(250) 726-7777
Prince Rupert MCTS Centre	(250) 627-3074 or (250) 627-3075
Vancouver MCTS Centre	(604) 666-6013
Victoria MCTS Centre	(250) 363-6333

CNG LOCATIONS

Washington:
Boater's Discount/LaConner Marina	(360) 466-3540
Boston Harbor Marina (Olympia)	(360) 357-5670
The Chandlery	
(Winslow Wharf Marina, Eagle Harbor)	(206) 842-7245
Harbor Marine Maintenance	
(North Harbor of Port of Everett)	(425) 259-3285
North Island Boat (Anacortes/Flounder Bay)	(360) 293-2565
Sure Marine Service (Seattle)	(206) 784-9903
Shilshole Bay Fuel Dock	
(Seattle/Shilshole Bay Marina)	(206) 783-7555

B.C.:
Vancouver Island:
All Bay Marine (Tsehum Harbour/Sidney)	(250) 656-0153
Anchorage Marine (Anchorage Marina/Nanaimo)	(250) 754-5585
Maple Bay Marina	(250) 746-8482
Quarterdeck Marina (Port Hardy)	(250) 949-6551

Mainland:
Gibsons Marina	(604) 886-8686
John Henry's Marina (Pender Harbour)	(604) 883-2253
River Marine Supplies (1023 Clark Dr., Vancouver)	(604) 324-9454

USEFUL FISHERIES & FISHERIES MANAGEMENT WEBSITES

Paralytic Shellfish Poisoning
PSP shellfish closures can be expected without warning at any time during the season.

For PSP closures in Washington, phone (800) 562-5632. Washington State Dept. of Health Paralytic Shellfish Poisoning page:
http://www.doh.wa.gov/ehp/sf/Pubs/PSPfactSheet.htm

For PSP closures in B.C., phone the Openings and Closures Toll Free Line: (866) 431-3474 or (604) 666-2828 in the Lower Mainland, or go to:
http://www.pac.dfo-mpo.gc.ca/fm-gp/contamination/biotox/index-eng.htm

(See sidebar p.244 about the effects of PSP. Thanks to correspondent Pat Shera for the initial information.)

Washington State Dept. Fish and Wildlife information on fish and wildlife action plans: http://wdfw.wa.gov/conservation/cwcs/

Washington State Dept. Fish and Wildlife information fishing and shellfishing: http://wdfw.wa.gov/fishing/

U.S. Fish and Wildlife Service Fisheries and Habitat Conservation: http://www.fws.gov/fisheries/

Fisheries Management Areas. Download map of Fisheries Management Areas to enable you to decipher closure areas at: http://www.pac.dfo-mpo.gc.ca/fm-gp/maps-cartes/areas-secteurs/index-eng.htm

Rockfish Conservation Areas booklet contains chartlets of all conservation areas. Many people do not realize that RCA's prohibit ALL hook and line fishing, not just fishing for rockfish. To view or download a copy of the booklet, go to: http://www.pac.dfo-mpo.gc.ca/fm-gp/maps-cartes/rca-acs/booklet-livret/RCA_booklet_2007.pdf

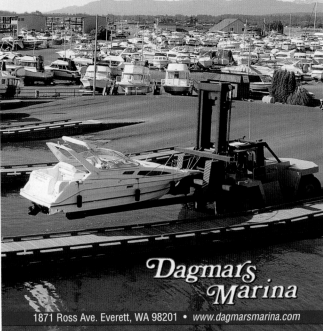

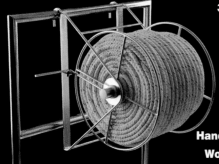

CONVERSION TABLES

TEMPERATURE (FORMULAS)

FAHRENHEIT TO CELSIUS
To convert temperature from Fahrenheit to Celsius:

$$(F° - 32) × .555 = C°$$

Example: Convert 40° F to C:
(40 - 32) = 8; 8 × .555 = 4;
thus 40° F = 4° C

CELSIUS TO FAHRENHEIT
To convert temperature from Celsius to Fahrenheit:

$$(C° × 1.8) + 32 = F°$$

Example: Convert 4° C to F:
(4 × 1.8) = 7.2; 7.2 + 32 = 39.2 (round to 40); thus 4° C = 40° F

QUICK REFERENCE

32° Fahrenheit = 0° Celsius
0° Fahrenheit = -17.8° Celsius

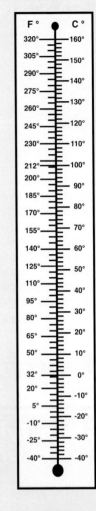

VOLUME

U.S. GALLONS TO LITERS
1 U.S gallon = 3.7854 liters

To convert U.S. gallons to liters, multiply U.S. gallons × 3.785.
Example: 40 U.S. gallons × 3.785 = 151 liters

To convert liters to U.S. gallons, divide by 3.785.
Example: 151 liters ÷ 3.785 = 39.89 U.S. gallons (round to 40)

IMPERIAL GALLONS TO LITERS
1 Imperial gallon = 4.546 liters

To convert Imperial gallons to liters, multiply Imperial gallons × 4.546.
Example: 40 Imperial gallons × 4.546 = 182 liters

To convert liters to Imperial gallons, divide by 4.546.
Example: 182 liters ÷ 4.546 = 40.035 (round to 40)

U.S. GALLONS TO IMPERIAL GALLONS
1 U.S. gallon = .833 Imperial gallons

To convert U.S. gallons to Imperial gallons, multiply U.S. gallons × .833.

Example: 40 U.S. gallons × .833 = 33.32 Imperial gallons

To convert Imperial gallons to U.S. gallons, multiply Imperial gallons × 1.20.

Example: 33 Imperial gallons × 1.20 = 39.6 U.S. gallons

LITERS AND QUARTS
1 liter = 1.0567 quarts, or 33.8 ounces
1 quart = .9467 liters, or 947 ml

SPEED

Convert knots to miles per hour: Knots × 1.15
Convert miles per hour to knots: MPH × .868

WEIGHT

1 kilogram (kg) = 2.2 pounds (lbs.)

1 pound = .4545 kilograms (454 grams)

1 U.S. gallon of fresh water weighs 8.333 lbs. or 3.787 kg

1 Imperial gallon of fresh water weighs 10 lbs. or 4.545 kg

1 liter of fresh water weighs 2.2 pounds or 1 kg

1 U. S. gallon of gasoline weighs 6.2 lbs. or 2.82 kg

1 Imperial gallon of gasoline weighs 7.44 lbs. or 3.38 kg

1 liter of gasoline weighs 1.64 lbs. or 0.744 kg

1 U.S. gallon of No. 2 diesel fuel weighs 6.7 pounds or 3.05 kg

1 Imperial gallon of No. 2 diesel fuel weighs 8.04 pounds or 3.66 kg

1 liter of No. 2 diesel fuel weighs 1.77 pounds or 0.8 kg

DISTANCE

1 inch = 2.54 centimeters

1 foot = .3048 meters

1 meter = 3.28 feet

1 fathom = 6 feet

1 fathom = 1.83 meters

1 cable = 120 fathoms

1 cable (British) = 0.1 nautical mile

1 statute mile = 5280 feet; 7.4 cables; 1.609 kilometers

1 nautical mile = 6076 feet; 8.5 cables; 1.852 kilometers

1 statute mile = 0.868 nautical mile

1 nautical mile = 1.15 statute mile

BAROMETRIC PRESSURE

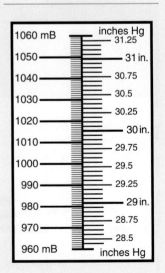

CONVERSION TABLES

CURRENCY

Generally, the most favorable exchange rates are on credit card transactions. Banks give slightly less favorable rates, and merchants tend to be the least favorable. Expect to pay more than the exchange rate when you buy currency, and receive less when you sell.

Examples:
Assume an exchange rate of $1.05 U.S./$.952 Cdn. (Exchange rates change constantly.)

To convert $100 Canadian to U.S. $,
multiply Canadian $ by 1.05 or divide by .952:
$100 Cdn × 1.05 = $105.00 U.S.
$100 Cdn ÷ .952 = $105.00 U.S.

To convert $105 U.S. to Canadian $,
multiply U.S. $ by .952 or divide by 1.05:
$105 U.S. × .952 = $100 Cdn.
$105 U.S. ÷ 1.05 = $100 Cdn.

INTERNATIONAL MORSE CODE & PHONETIC ALPHABET

A	ALPHA	•—	N	NOVEMBER	—•	1	ONE	•————
B	BRAVO	—•••	O	OSCAR	———	2	TWO	••———
C	CHARLIE	—•—•	P	PAPA	•——•	3	THREE	•••——
D	DELTA	—••	Q	QUEBEC	——•—	4	FOUR	••••—
E	ECHO	•	R	ROMEO	•—•	5	FIVE	•••••
F	FOXTROT	••—•	S	SIERRA	•••	6	SIX	—••••
G	GOLF	——•	T	TANGO	—	7	SEVEN	——•••
H	HOTEL	••••	U	UNIFORM	••—	8	EIGHT	———••
I	INDIA	••	V	VICTOR	•••—	9	NINE	————•
J	JULIET	•———	W	WHISKEY	•——	0	ZERO	—————
K	KILO	—•—	X	X-RAY	—••—			
L	LIMA	•—••	Y	YANKEE	—•——	DISTRESS/		•••———•••
M	MIKE	——	Z	ZULU	——••	SOS		

WEATHER WARNINGS

Light winds:	Less than 15 knots	Gale Warning:	34–47 knots
Moderate winds:	16–19 knots	Storm Warning:	48–63 knots
Small Craft/Strong Wind Warning:	20–33 knots		

BEAUFORT WIND SCALE

Scale Number	Wind Speed		Effects
	Knots	MPH	
0	under 1	under 1	Calm
1	1-3	1-3	Ripples
2	4-6	4-7	Small wavelets
3	7-10	8-12	Large wavelets; small crests
4	11-16	13-18	Small waves; some whitecaps
5	17-21	19-24	Moderate waves; some spray; many whitecaps
6	22-27	25-31	Larger waves; whitecaps everywhere
7	28-33	32-38	Sea heaps up; white foam from breaking waves
8	34-40	39-46	Moderately high; waves of greater length; foam blown in well-marked streaks
9	41-47	47-54	High waves; sea begins to roll; dense streaks of foam; spray reduces visibility
10	48-55	55-63	Very high waves with overhanging crests; sea takes on a white appearance; rolling is heavy
11	56-63	64-72	Exceptionally high waves; sea covered with white foam patches; visibility still more reduced
12	64 & over	73 & over	Air filled with foam; sea completely white with driving spray; visibility greatly reduced

VHF CHANNELS FOR PLEASURE CRAFT

WASHINGTON WATERS

05A VESSEL TRAFFIC SERVICE SEATTLE—Northern Puget Sound and Strait of Juan de Fuca. Vessels not required to participate are highly encouraged to maintain a listening watch. Contact with VTS is encouraged if essential to navigational safety.

06 INTERSHIP SAFETY. Only for ship-to-ship use for safety communications. For Search and Rescue (SAR) liaison with Coast Guard vessels and aircraft.

09 INTERSHIP AND SHIP-SHORE ALL VESSELS and CALLING & REPLY FOR PLEASURE VESSELS (optional, U.S. only). Working channel.

13 Vessel BRIDGE to Vessel BRIDGE, large vessels. Low power only. May also be used to contact locks and bridges BUT use sound signals in the Seattle area to avoid dangerous interference to collision avoidance communications between large vessels. Call on Channel 13 or by phone at 206/386-4251 for nighttime bridge openings (after 2300) in the Lake Washington Ship Canal, Seattle.

14 VESSEL TRAFFIC SERVICE SEATTLE—Southern Puget Sound. Vessels not required to participate are highly encouraged to maintain a listening watch. Contact with VTS is encouraged if essential to navigational safety.

16 INTERNATIONAL DISTRESS AND CALLING. Calling channel. Used only for distress and urgent traffic, for safety calls and contacting other stations. Listen first to make sure no distress traffic is in progress; do not transmit if a SEE-LONCE MAYDAY is declared. Keep all communications to a minimum. Do not repeat a call to the same station more than once every two minutes. After three attempts, wait 15 minutes before calling the same station. Pleasure vessels may also use Channel 09 for calling.

22A COAST GUARD LIAISON. A government channel used for Safety and Liason communications with the Coast Guard. Also known as Channel 22 US. The U.S. Coast Guard does not normally monitor 22A so you must first establish communications on Channel 16.

66A PORT OPERATIONS. Marinas in Puget Sound are being encouraged to use this common frequency for arranging moorage.

67 INTERSHIP ONLY FOR ALL VESSELS (U.S. only, Puget Sound.) Working channel.

68 INTERSHIP and SHIP-SHORE FOR PLEASURE VESSELS ONLY. Working channel.

69 INTERSHIP and SHIP-SHORE FOR PLEASURE VESSELS ONLY. Working channel.

70 DIGITAL SELECTIVE CALLING ONLY (No Voice) FOR DISTRESS AND CALLING.

72 INTERSHIP ONLY FOR ALL VESSELS (U.S. only, Puget Sound.) Working channel.

78A INTERSHIP and SHIP-SHORE FOR PLEASURE VESSELS ONLY (Not available in Canada). Working channel. Marinas in Puget Sound are being encouraged to use this as a secondary working channel.

BRITISH COLUMBIA WATERS

05A VESSEL TRAFFIC SERVICE SEATTLE—Strait of Juan de Fuca west of Victoria.

06 INTERSHIP SAFETY. Only for ship-to-ship use for safety communications.

09 INTERSHIP AND SHIP-SHORE. All vessels. Working channel.

11 VESSEL TRAFFIC SERVICE VICTORIA—Strait of Juan de Fuca east of Victoria; Haro Strait; Boundary Passage; Gulf Islands; Southern Strait of Georgia.

VESSEL TRAFFIC SERVICE PRINCE RUPERT—North of Cape Caution.

12 VESSEL TRAFFIC SERVICE VANCOUVER—Vancouver and Howe Sound.

16 INTERNATIONAL DISTRESS AND CALLING. Calling channel. Used only for distress and urgent traffic, for safety calls and contacting other stations. Listen first to make sure no distress traffic is in progress. Do not transmit if a SEE-LONCE MAYDAY is declared. Keep all communications to a minimum. Do not repeat a call to the same station more than once every two minutes. After three attempts, wait 15 minutes before calling the same station.

66A PORT OPERATIONS. Most marinas in southern B.C. will use this channel.

67 INTERSHIP AND SHIP-SHORE. All vessels. Working channel.

68 INTERSHIP AND SHIP-SHORE. Pleasure vessels. Working channel.

69 INTERSHIP AND SHIP-SHORE. Pleasure vessels. Working channel.

70 DIGITAL SELECTIVE CALLING ONLY (No Voice) FOR DISTRESS AND CALLING.

71 VESSEL TRAFFIC SERVICE COMOX—Northern Strait of Georgia to Cape Caution.

VESSEL TRAFFIC SERVICE—Prince Rupert, Dixon Entrance and Chatham Sound.

72 INTERSHIP. All vessels. Working channel.

73 INTERSHIP AND SHIP-SHORE. All vessels. Working channel.

74 VESSEL TRAFFIC SERVICE VICTORIA—Victoria-Fraser River.

VESSEL TRAFFIC SERVICE TOFINO—West of Vancouver Island.

83A COAST GUARD LIAISON. Primary Canadian Coast Guard Safety and Communications Channel. Also known as Channel 83 U.S. mode.

RADIO EMERGENCY SIGNALS

MAYDAY	Vessel threatened by grave and imminent danger and requests immediate assistance.
PAN PAN	Urgent message concerning safety of vessel or person on board or in sight.
SECURITÉ	Message concerning safety of navigation or meteorological warning.
SEELONCE MAYDAY	Mayday in progress, do not transmit normal communications.
SEELONCE FEENE	Resume normal communications.

**To contact the Canadian Coast Guard,
use Channel 16 to call the station nearest you:
Victoria, Vancouver, Comox, Prince Rupert or Tofino.**

Even though you may use alternate communication means such as cellular phone, MONITOR VHF 16. The safety of yourself, your family and your friends is enhanced by a watch on 16 by all vessels.

ADVERTISER INDEX

Discover Captn. Jack's books at coastwisepress.com

SIDEBAR INDEX